THE TEACHING MISSION

A New Foundation of Spirituality for a Quickening Planet

Editor: JIM CLEVELAND

A compilation based on over two decades of lessons by celestial teachers, along with reflections, historical notes, and commentaries by their human students

This volume dedicated to:
GERDEAN O'DELL BOWEN
Author and Artist, Transmitter of High Spiritual Ideals

AuthorHouse™
1663 Liberty Drive
Bloomington, IN 47403
www.authorhouse.com
Phone: 1 (800) 839-8640

Published by AuthorHouse 01/22/2015

ISBN: 978-1-4969-6375-8 (sc)
ISBN: 978-1-4969-6374-1 (e)

ii

A UNIVERSE DEVOTED TO SPIRITUAL EDUCATION

The next higher residential world of the ascendant career always maintains a strong corps of teachers on the world just below, a sort of preparatory school for the progressing residents of that sphere; this is a phase of the ascendant scheme for advancing the pilgrims of time. These schools, their methods of instruction and examinations, are wholly unlike anything which you essay to conduct on Urantia. – The Urantia Book, page 339

As the ascending mortals progress from the lower to the higher of the morontia worlds, they serve on countless assignments in association with their teachers and in company with their more advanced and senior brethren. – p. 342

If the Gods designed merely to take you on one long and eternal joy excursion, they certainly would not so largely turn the whole universe into one vast and intricate practical training school, requisition a substantial part of the celestial creation as teachers and instructors, and then spend ages upon ages piloting you, one by one, through this gigantic universe school of experiential training. – p. 558

Indeed are we blessed to live in these times, to be available to manifest the mission of our Father to bring light and life, not only to your world, but to a universe. Lift yourselves up to the reality of the increasing connections being developed throughout your universe and the enhancement of the circuits, so that your doubts and fears may be strengthened in the realization of this energy broadening and increasing for you. – Monjoronson, Magisterial Son, Cape San Blas FL 2004

The Correcting Time has begun. It is a time of great change, a time of great learning for humankind. When the majority have accepted and understood the One God, then great benefits shall occur. Much enlightening, exciting experience will be had. Yes. – Abraham, New Zealand, 1988

There exists in each soul a unified purpose; to learn and know the ways of God. – Machiventa Melchizedek

A STILLNESS TIME TO PARTICIPATE

All that you know, whether it be of physical material, of universal material, tangible or not, real to your senses or not, such as thoughts, feelings and so forth, all is based upon tuned frequencies that originate in the conception from Paradise. When you allow your earthly being to still itself to allow your higher self to commune with the Father, you have access to universal frequencies that hold abilities beyond your imagination to, as you would term, heal. Everything that has been associated with miraculous healing on Urantia really is the capability of the mortal who is a participant to unite and commune with these energies to achieve such a result. – Rayson, Sarasota FL

The very core of the Teaching Mission is to emphasize deeper worshipful contact with the Father, a real and stable sense of participation with your unseen brothers and sisters, and a profound sense of privilege to be part of the ministering force to this world. – Daniel, Pocatello ID

This time spent with the Father helps to maintain energy levels within the physical body, as well as emotional levels, by ridding the body of stresses. There are many benefits that are simply a byproduct of the time you spend in silence seeking the Father and attuning yourself to his will. – Will, Tallahassee FL

A LIFELONG EXPLORATION OF SPIRIT

Man's greatest adventure in the flesh consists in the well-balanced and sane effort to advance the borders of self-consciousness out through the dim realms of spirit-consciousness -- contact with the divine presence. Such an experience constitutes God consciousness. – The Urantia Book, page 2097

The climb from the primordial ooze to the vast stellar rim of space is an advancing movement that is being nurtured on a constant basis, and now that your quarantine is ended, you are being re-drawn into those circuitries which will give you all of the benefits of being a part of the galaxy in which you live, a part of the Nebadon universe, and with it you are entitled to the ministries of your many spirit helpers and counselors. – Tomas

Love grows from the calmness of the heart and the rightness of the mind. Mankind will greatly excel in any sustainability endeavor when he reaches the point where he can sustain the phenomenon of love, personally and socially. – Charles, a Mighty Messenger, Loveland CO, 2012

Your world is deeply in need of cleansing. It has great difficulty in raising the total consciousness at this time without the removal of those presences that carry malevolent energies and dark energies that subdue the brighter energies of your world. – Monjoronson, ID, 2010

Children, you are my vanguards of a whole new truth. It pre-exists in my life on Urantia. As you do, I faced these struggles. And in so doing I sought to reveal a whole new enlightened concept of religion, to humankind's comfort and the greater honor of my Universal Father. – Christ Michael, Cincinnati OH

Image credits

THE TEACHING MISSION

A New Foundation of Spirituality for a Quickening Planet

CONTENTS

Teacher quotes from Christ Michael, Machiventa Melchizedek, Abraham and the following teachers: A'Cilla, Althena, Andrew, Astara, Buki, Daniel, Foehn, JarEl, John, Josephine, Legion, Lester, Monjoronson, Nathaniel, Nebadonia (Holy Mother Spirit), the Most Highs, Olfana, the OneTeam, Rayson, RondEl, Serena, Themoia, Thomy, Tomaray, Tomas, Verona, Will, and Zarath.

Introduction

What kind of people talk to unseen spiritual personalities and what do they get from it? How can they dare say they do? How has it changed their lives?

The original idea was to collect their stories.

Since I was one of them for nearly 20 years, I expected the stories to be unique but compatible. I believed we were getting the same messages from a uniform celestial curriculum and then responding uniquely in our different environments, and from our own incomparable backgrounds and with our own original talents. But we would see ... and it should be interesting.

It would be a book similar to *How I Found The Urantia Book* a solicited collection by friend and fellow publisher Saskia Raevouri. Her Square Circles Publishing Company focuses on titles that are secondary to the spiritual revelation known as the Urantia Papers, published by the Urantia Foundation and socialized by the Urantia Fellowship.

Of course, readers of Saskia's two personal experience volumes already had their proclaimed 'fifth epochal revelation' in the marketplace as *The Urantia Book*, and with translation projects and global networks of study groups. The Teaching Mission, which is altogether personal, has had none of this.

I have long ago realized that Teaching Mission leadership comes from the celestial side, with humans stepping up to the plate here on an as-needed basis over the years. As with the Urantia text itself, TM participants essentially remain students.

In the early 1990's, some Urantia book study groups moved naturally from reading and studying their purported spiritual revelation for the ages and actually talking to some of its authors and teaching representatives. Over the years, we in the Teaching Mission had come to believe in the leadership and, indeed, the presence of Urantia's Christ Michael, who incarnated here as Jesus, as well as Machiventa Melchizedek and other personalities of the spiritual realm who are serving in our planet's 'Correcting Time.'

But why would anyone else believe this? I realized that this book had to include more than a simple introduction to these supernal teachers who say and claim so much. And so was added a large front section for the celestial teachers themselves, explaining the mission. We

1

include more than a few since they express the same insights in a fascinating rainbow of ways reflecting their individual personalities. The credulity and compatibility of these lessons is our reason to believe.

Then it further occurred that we might also explore the human minds who were involved during these 20 years. What were they thinking as it all unfolded? As it turned out, some compelling authors had indeed produced narratives well worth the reading, and preserving. So we included another section of evolving human observations over the years.

Not to be whetted, I soon wanted to explore the transmissions from various gatherings from 1994 forward to see if there are notable signposts of progress or evolution. So we added a section of teacher lessons from more than a decade of gatherings in search of a progressive thread.

Then surely after all this wordage, readers would want to see some of the authors and participants who made the whole book project possible. We added a picture gallery. And we added some other reference updates, tributes to some of our fellows who have graduated from the mortal life, and acknowledgement of a number of inspired organizations and spirit-based initiatives spawned by people in the Teaching Mission.

To be sure we would be reasonably up-to-date in the continuing saga of receiving celestial transmissions, we added a string of transmissions, dated and geographically noted, and pertaining to critical global issues and the uncertainties of the future. The Urantia Papers say that our era is 'quivering on the brink' of massive social upheavals, with old institutions facing disintegration, but with new growth bearing higher values. I believe it, and I see the quickening events of both evolution and revelation all around.

This volume then could have been complete except for some nagging considerations. At every turn, through these years of rejection by official Urantia, and rancorous, bigoted and ill-informed criticism that spoiled every internet discussion list, it seemed that this book would do little or nothing to quell the discord because of one central thorn of contention.

There had been an epic political clash within Urantia in the early 1980's stemming from purported channeled messages about a pending nuclear attack. It somehow blew apart the relationship between Urantia-based radio minister Vern Grimsley and his Family of God Foundation in California, and the *Urantia Book* powers in Chicago.

The episode had indelibly scarred the Urantia community. It would forever be the reason that 'channeled' messages are not reliable and have no place in council deliberations, which should be democratic and not beholden to manipulation by 'special' people who purport to receive them.

From a political standpoint, that seemed reasonable to me. But it also seemed reasonable that the same celestial sources purported to have given us an epochal revelation would not be concerned when the world was truly on the brink of nuclear war. Civil defense shelters dotted our landscape and the world atmosphere was extremely tense in the early 1980's.

Adding a chapter of investigative journalism, research, on this matter seemed to make sense in rounding out the book – dealing forthrightly with the one thorny issue that many readers would surely accuse us of avoiding as they closed the book in uncontested disbelief.

Not surprisingly, documents began falling into place, and I soon came to believe that our celestial advisors would actually like to have some published facts and insights to shed light on what happened in the critical 'war scare' months of 1983 and 1984, and beyond.

We make this volume more meaningful by including this report. It's an unraveling mystery story about why the custodians of our mother lode manuscript still criticize us. More significantly, they even distrust the idea of communicating with the celestials who provided them with their scriptural text in the first place.

What was surprising to me in constructing the chapter was the near-immediate discovery of a Urantia Fellowship published article by two long-standing leaders in the Urantia community. I was startled to see that their Urantia-anchored reasons why world apocalypse won't happen stem from the same Urantia text sources that proclaim our current teachers as a continuing part of their revelation. Amazingly, the Urantia text itself validates the Teaching Mission of today and even carries it forward.

Given this added confidence, I was stimulated to study official documents in a fascinating stream to relate Urantia politics, on-stage and backstage, with the tenuous Cold War days that led eventually to the dissolution of the Family of God.

Two contributing authors believed this volume should be altogether positive and not deal in such matters and withdrew their contributions. Respecting their wishes, I don't consider straightening out a lot of this hearsay myth and history a negative thing. And in the final part of this chapter, I share my ideas for an altruistic, universal Urantia movement that is free of bigoted judgments and rich with spirited teamwork in the cause of uniting all children of God.

Your editors and contributors hope you enjoy this collection, whether you consider it truly a foundation of spiritual truth or just a patchwork of anectodal reference material. These stories, essays and transmitted narratives are yours to consider, and to help you discern, evaluate and judge this phenomenon of teacher contact.

They are intended to explore the entire matter of communicating with celestial teachers in our day and time. I believe that the fruits of the spirit will endure, and prevail.

I believe that readers will ultimately see what this manuscript is really about. It is the revelation that individuals can devote the time to develop a strong spiritual consciousness and effectively communicate with celestial teachers. They will reap a rich bounty of benefits from practicing a Stillness time each day for worship, prayer and the forging of a personal relationship with God, the Universal Father.

Is there a more important discovery that a human can make?

The Teaching Mission is a very simple inward quest that we have enormously complicated with debate over its authenticity and recommended practice.

It is this: Talk to God in the Stillness and then listen. Listen. This will "light the candles of love from within" and the flame, your own flame, will guide you evermore.

Let's now allow the teachers themselves to explain their mission with lessons spanning the years.

Part One

The Advent of the Teaching Mission
and
The Correcting Time on the Planet

Who are the teachers and why are they here?

Arrivals and Announcements
New Zealand 1991

In Hamilton, NZ, Machiventa stated the intent of the mission to a small group of open-minded spiritual seekers. They were not very familiar with *The Urantia Book*.

> "I, Machiventa, a Melchizedek, Vicegerent Planetary Prince of Urantia, make this statement: God intends for me to make ready the peoples inhabiting the Planet Urantia for the arrival of Prince Michael, Son of God. This work as Vicegerent consists of gathering those persons who do hear, who do see, who do understand GOD. This gathering of persons shall eventually spread light, truth, [and] love throughout humankind.

> "I used the term 'Correcting Time.' This terminology has been coined to give humankind some indication of the intent. To correct something is to alter course. This alteration, of course, may take some considerable time/space in your terms. There is no way time frame can be allocated for this. It is dependent entirely on individual humankind acceptance and understanding.

> "I shall be working with the cooperation of certain chosen persons. This communication is being delivered through one such. There are others, and there may be others, also dependent upon humankind acceptance and understanding,

never forgetting the free will of humankind. "Abraham is 'used' by myself as a 'scouting party' and, in turn, I am 'used' thus. We make ready.

"This is my statement of intent. Thank You."

The announcement and various transmissions from the Melchizedek and the biblical Abraham came to a small group of spiritual seekers in New Zealand. They were encouraged to share the messages and soon there was interest among Urantia Book students in the United States. Via e-mail questions and personal visits, a few Americans became convinced of the authenticity of the phenomenon.

These are some questions presented to the two celestials from these early years.

"Why do you use the name Abraham?"

ABRAHAM: *I am the soul consciousness, the higher consciousness that was and is Abraham. Yes. It is the name you can easily identify me with. Yes.*

Questioner wants to know more about Abraham

ABRAHAM: *In my last, so-called life journey to which you refer, I was the first to perceive the One God [concept taught by Machiventa Melchizedek]. There were, as you can imagine, many gods worshipped: the sun, the moon, the stars, the wind, the rain, etc. Persons in their ignorance of the One God worshipped many gods, yes. In the beginning my earthly name was Abram. When I had acknowledged, accepted and understood the God within, I became known as Abraham. I still am Abraham. I always shall be Abraham.*

Why Abraham now in your time-space? There is much to impart to humankind. I have been given the task . . . I have accepted the task of bringing this information to humankind.

Q - Where are you in time-space?

ABRAHAM: *I am where you have been, where you are and where you shall be. I am not in your physical time-space. I am in time-space infinite. Yes. You see, past, present and future all exist in the one time-space.*

Q - Who assigned you to this task?

ABRAHAM: *During my past physical life journey, I had the greatest pleasure to be assisted in my understanding of the idea, thought, feeling, understanding of the One God by one who you would call the Prince of Salem, [Machiventa] Melchizedek. During this time-space he helped me to understand the One God. He helped me to explain the One God [concept] to my family and friends.*

My friend/teacher is now, to use your words, on a mission to teach humankind in your time-space of the simplicity which is God. It is my pleasure to have been given the task of assisting in this mission. God has decided that I should return in this manner of communications in your time-space for this particular task."

Q - What is the purpose of our having soul names?

ABRAHAM: *Your soul – spirit you may call it – is a sound wavelength, a vibration energy. The name you have been given is as close to your language form as can describe this sound wavelength vibration energy. This is the name by which you are recognized by myself, [and] by God, just as in your physical form you are recognized by your physical appearance and your physical name.*

Questions about the practice of daily stillness

ABRAHAM: *The stillness is the calm, quiet peace within your heart wherein God resides.*

You might only spend two minutes of your 24 hours with the stillness, but it is of great benefit for humankind. Within the stillness, all answers lie. You may not be aware of your answer immediately. It may be a day, a week, a month, a year before you understand your answer. Yes.

Q - When you achieve this meditation, do you give yourself calmness and stillness from the heart?

ABRAHAM: *Correct. Do not look too hard for the stillness. In the searching you may not find. It is reached through the quiet and calm, peaceful acceptance and understanding.*

Question about the planetary "Correcting Time"

ABRAHAM: *The Correcting Time has begun. It is a time of great change, a time of great learning for humankind. When the majority have accepted and understood the One God, then great benefits shall occur. Much enlightening, exciting experiences will be had. Yes.*

It is not known how long the Correcting Time shall be. It may last ten years, but it may last for a thousand of your years. It cannot be determined, even by God, because of the gift to humankind of freedom of will. Freedom of will gives humankind choices to make: the choice to heed guidance and listen to guidance, therefore coming to understand the One God, or the choice to disregard guidance, to ignore guidance and not to understand and accept the One God. Yes.

Q - When the majority are aware in the way you have told us, what effect would that have on our physical planet?

ABRAHAM: *In mankind's ignorance, great harm has been done to your planet and the universe. When the majority has come to accept and understand the One God, immeasurable help shall come to your planet and the universe. Yes.*

You see, I have spoken of freedom of will and the choices humankind has. If the decision is made to disregard guidance we cannot interfere with this decision. We cannot impose our will on yours.

So we vigilantly wait and hope that through constant nudging, constant whispering, some person, for example, such as — may heed guidance and accept the position as a vehicle for communication such as this. Yes.

From October 4, 1989

Q - You have said there are many such as Ruby. Is this a new way of teaching on this plane?

Abraham: *New but old.*

Q - I know this kind of communication has been recorded for hundred of years but are we now at a time when it will be commonly used? Humankind will have to be aware of trickery!

Abraham: *Correct. Your own integrity and wisdom shall assist you to discern. You see it has been said - the time for physical has passed. You may observe this in many areas of humankind's existence in your time. Communication through your airwaves has increased too. Your space communication from nation to nation is fast. Many, many years before, one nation was unaware of another, simply because there was not this communication. Your planet is more united in its people through this communication you have. The communication we have with you shall serve humankind to become aware of the other worlds, the other beings who inhabit your universe.*

Q - One of my concerns is that with this amount of teaching through minds such as Ruby's, distortion could take place. Each receiver will naturally express thoughts in a different way. Are teachers such as you also teaching in a differing way to each other? Because I am confused at times and this could lead to agitation and arguments as you know. Seth's teachings would be a good example for us.

Abraham: *I am aware of what you speak. In your education system there are set subjects — name one.*

English.

Abraham: *You may find twelve teachers of English, all having the basic content to deliver but each imparts something of him or herself in the manner in which they teach this subject, English. In turn each student receives the information in an individual manner, differing each to each. So, if each student of these twelve teachers were to discuss their lessons they may all vary but still contain the same basic principles of the subject. In this manner teachings such as this appear to differ and, given the method of communication, variation must of natural occur, although the basic subject matter remains the same.*

From April 18, 1991

On April 18, 1991, the New Zealand group wrote: "Some years ago we discussed the possibility of nuclear confrontation being a means of world destruction. Part of Abraham's answer was "the burning of the earth will not take place as you have feared, by nuclear war, it will be a "nature attack," an accident of nature as so often happens." Some correspondence from America led us to re-open this subject (prophecies for the next ten years).

Conversations with Abraham, April 11 and 18, 1991

Abraham: *It is a time - space during which the transition from one phase to another causes upheaval, distress, tension, whether this be in the physical planet Earth or in the minds, hearts or bodies of humankind. Think of your physical life transition from one age to another, entering middle age for example, when many physical, emotional and mental changes can be experienced, varying in time and intensity, with re-adjustment of physical abilities and the re-evaluation of morals and ethics, leading to a sense of quite. Humankind is experiencing this re-adjustment and re-evaluation at present. At the same time the planet Earth is also re-adjusting itself, as has been happening for some time, with plate shifting, re-alignment of the earths axis and the effects of the solar system. This is concurrent with the "Correcting Time," of the Spiritual values, and the God Knowing of humankind.*

The earth is a living, breathing, growing, decaying entity, and there was a time when humankind had the sensitivity and awareness to sense the changes in their immediate surroundings. The sensitivity is still there, but the awareness is buried. So this sensitivity but lack of conscious awareness can create fear of the unknown and the unexplainable, with varying degrees of disturbance. At the same time there is an awareness of God at work! For many the conscious and sub-conscious are seemingly at war within. Somewhere where they meet is the answer, and this is within each person. The juxtaposition of the two crossing is IT!

I have previously spoken about lower mind, higher mind, higher consciousness, God consciousness. You have within your lower mind, your intellect, full of questions, answers. Much of your bodily functions go unnoticed, unquestioned, without your conscious knowledge. The ego thinking mind always begins with "I", always questioning, "Am I", "Will I", "Do I", "Why should I" etc. What hope have you to allow your higher mind, higher consciousness through the jumble of questions? This is the discipline of shutting the ego down, removing the "I" and allowing the "we" of higher consciousness. If you allow your higher consciousness to come forth you will find your mind is not so cluttered, so cumbersome, or so full of trivia; ego is diminished and not so self-evident. You have the tool for this and the tool is the Stillness.

Q - We have disease within ourselves. Could we be the disease of the planet, and when we cure ourselves we cure the earth?

Abraham: *When humankind finds a new way, all else is forgotten, the narrowness blots out all other knowledge. In the eagerness to use this new way, be it technology, science, medicine or God, some destruction can occur. For example the printed word has caused destruction of trees, forgetting the reasons for their existence. The success of the new venture clouds the view of the destruction. Now the boundaries are shifting and the old reasons are being allowed to be seen. This example is not a judgment.*

Q - We have had a letter which states, "This ten years we are living in now is the most important for changes in the last millennium." Please comment.

Abraham: *Correct, and I would also qualify that remark by saying that each decade has brought its own combination of past events. It is the culmination of all that has been. In each decade there has been vast change and importance.*

Q - Yes, but I would still like to clarify that this decade is "the big one"?

Abraham: *Each ten years the same prophesy! For you people, yes, and in another respect because the Correcting Time has begun, which, depending on humankind's free will, could last a thousand years.*

Q - We are coming to the end of the experiment called time. Please comment.

Abraham: *In the past, an event in the local community was "the world." In your experience, the world is now your local community. Your time frame and your perception are different. You perceive a "quickening of time." So, in one respect your statement is correct. The Correcting Time has begun. This is a time for humankind to re-assess, to acknowledge all that is, to understand and accept the consciousness and the simplicity which is God, and so, in some respect, time as you perceive it to be, shall no longer exist because you will be in God's Time.*

Q - Would you call that death?

Abraham: *I have not spoken of physical death in relation to the Correcting Time, or the ending of time as you perceive it to be, but we have spoken before of "nature's attack," of that which is occurring and has occurred. Mankind is becoming aware of danger, damage done to the planet by mankind, hurried by greed and misunderstanding. There is time for correction; there shall be some damage, but if heeded, not as great as it would otherwise be.*

Q - Don't quite understand. We know that our thought is extremely powerful, and collective thought even more so. People living with their energies directed towards more positive ways of being can change or adjust some of what has been prophesied from many sources - but I feel sometimes you evade prophecy when others speak more definitely of it. Is it because we are not capable of understanding you?

Abraham: *Not at all. I do not participate in giving fear, and fear does strike the hearts of humankind when messages of such importance are given. It would be foolish for me to give you a time frame for such an event. We have spoken of a shifting of the continents; this is part of the living, growing planet you inhabit. There are also other factors at play. One is the physical decaying of the planet, and also with the decay, new growth, as with the sudden appearance of land mass.*

Another factor is that of humankind consciousness. If humankind continues to pursue the destructive methods in the search for progress — which I call greed for ulterior motives — the planet can be destroyed. This can be avoided by the majority understanding and seeing where the pathway is leading in a physical sense, and by the understanding and acknowledging of God-consciousness.

There are so many things which occur outside your consciousness to your physical world, the planet, and the Universe. I am not denying the possibility of a major catastrophe, which could destroy many parts of the planet Earth, caused, for example, by a meteorite, but I shall not give you a time reference for this, but I am saying also that it is part of life.

As I have said, while your planet Earth is decaying, it is also growing. It is a change of view. Rather than looking at destruction, let us look at rejuvenation, and with that thought shall bring God Consciousness. Speak of rejuvenation - Life after Life! Do not speak or think in terms of death and destruction.

Teacher Ham's Announcement: "Welcome to Change"

On February 1, 1992, the supernal teacher Ham announced the advent of the global Teaching Mission in Los Angeles. The scene was a hotel conference room adjacent the official meeting rooms of a governing council of Urantia Book readers.

> *"My profound and sincere greetings to you all this evening. I am Ham. I have been commissioned to bring the light of truth and the understanding of our Father to Urantia.*
>
> *"I am one of many teachers. All of us are awaiting the greater reception of our words and we are desirous of placing many teachers among you. Great is our mission.*
>
> *"Understand this in your hearts. The time has arrived for an expanded level of truth to begin correction. We come, not for ourselves, no, indeed only in service of Michael. This day marks the beginning of the Correcting Time. Machiventa Melchizedek has arrived and has been duly inaugurated as acting Planetary Prince of Urantia, an assignment he has accepted from Michael.*
>
> *"Long years we have awaited this day. The Lucifer rebellion is officially ended in Nebadon. The circuits which have isolated your world are being re-opened. All these changes are occurring. I am in accordance with the plan of Michael. Happy and joyous is this day, blessed in the sight of our Lord. Gracious listeners, I bid you welcome to change. We mark the beginning of the reign of Prince Machiventa on this day."*

Ham's announcement received a mixed reception, from rapt attention to rude withdrawal. To some critics, here was some kind of channeler trying to take the spotlight away from the Fifth Epochal Revelation to our planet and into spiritist seances.

Some Urantia-based critics see themselves as the intellectual antithesis to this conduct, even though the Urantia Papers were received from the cosmos in a similar manner, one which has never been fully explained or understood. There was a 'sleeping subject' whose voice was recorded. There are also stories of papers materializing from within bank security boxes or other places.

At any rate, interested persons and critics alike would have plenty to consider about spiritual contact in the years ahead, as supernal teachers, both Melchizedeks and ascending student teachers, former mortals in the Teacher Corps, would begin teaching in many locations.

My personal timeline of Teaching Mission knowledge began at an International Urantia Book gathering in Snowmass, Colorado, in 1992, where representatives from the New Zealand group met with those interested outside the meeting schedule to talk about the phenomenon. The seed was being planted in the U.S. even as I was disinterested at the time.

Later, my Cincinnati Urantia study group heard of a celestial teacher named Welmek who was transmitting in nearby Indianapolis. Some of their Urantia group came to Cincinnati for our first transmission in December of 1992 and our group was generally impressed with the quality of the material, the unpretentious grace of the transmitter, Michael Painter, and the normal, non-mystical living room setting.

We then read many transcripts of the teacher Ham of the Woods Cross, Utah, group, and of LorEl, Aflana, and others in Sarasota, Florida; Welmek in Indianapolis; Daniel in Pocatello, Idaho, Elyon and others in North Idaho, such teachers as JarEl, Jared, Bertrand, Berca, Olfana, Tarkas, Rayson and Signa in California groups, Norson, a Melchizedek, Veronica, and others in Hawaii; Rokmar and LinEl in Oregon.

While each group had an assigned teacher, visits were common from other teachers, as well as Machiventa and other Melchizedeks, Abraham and Christ Michael himself. The transcripts numbered in the hundreds, then thousands and now tens of thousands. It required much reading, cross-referencing by date of delivery and source considerations before I accepted the reality of this wave of celestial teaching.

I believe this should be anyone's course of action, examining the fruits of these transmissions, exploring their collective coherence, and making a rational decision according to one's own inner 'truth bells.'

Here is a sampling of lessons that explain the mission, in different locations and through different personalities, and at different times. Noteworthy are the different ways of expression, all linked into a common core of messages. For this reason, we are featuring a lot of teachers, and starting appropriately with the mission's ultimate leader.

CHRIST MICHAEL, incarnated here as Jesus, Sarasota, Florida, December 2, 1992

There were times when I walked on Urantia and I saw such heartache, injustice, struggle and despair that I wondered, where was God? Where was My Father? I understand your doubts. I understand your questioning. I judge none. None of us judge any of this. It is not important, from where we sit. I so wish I could soothe you. I so wish you had the vision that I hold.

Children, it is recognized that life on Urantia has been a most difficult one indeed. It is recognized that we must step in to try to create a new vision for the mortals of Urantia. This is what is about to happen. It is not an easy task for any of those who have come to my side, to participate in this moment. We recognize that it is not an easy task for you who have come by my side to participate in this moment.

I wish I could snap my fingers and change what is currently occurring on this magnificent world. I cannot do such. It is not the way of the laws of our universe, for there would be no significance if I were to do such. I would be overstepping what has been my domain as far as guiding the people of the local universe. If I were to step in and correct things with the wave of my hand, all of what has been known to be of natural law would be gone. Actually, order would be no more. Free will would be no more.

It is of greater value for you to change the world, to prepare it for the higher place that it rightfully has. This is what will be forever more and have a long standing.

If I were to wave my hand and correct what has been so damaging upon Urantia, it would not have lasting value, for free will is the way of our universe. It is up to mankind to correct this. With our help this shall be done.

It shall take some time. Do not be disheartened by what the way of the world is about. This shall pass in time. Even when I make my general announcement that I have arrived, these things will not pass automatically. There is much work for us to do together. That is why there have been so many teachers assembled, so many entities present upon Urantia, because the work is great.

I do depend upon you to keep the light burning. I do depend upon you to help create change. It is not all up to you, but I do depend upon you. We are partners in this event together. It is not my event alone; it is ours, and our partnership is what will create the change. It is our partnership that will right the world, make it more presentable to the Father. It is his movement that has stirred. It is he who has requested that the time is now. We can wait no more for Urantia to be altered.

NORSON, a Melchizedek, on 7-16-1993 in Hawaii
Our Planetary History and the Mission

Good morning to you one and all. You are much loved. You are truly very blessed.

Life on planet Urantia is VERY different than that existing on any sphere yet to harbor human life in our universe, extremely difficult and drastically unusual. It has not always been so. Life on every planet is differently composed from the evolutionary experiences of its inhabitants and the universe events which timely arrive to fulfill the patterns projected by our Creator, our Divine Paradise Son, Michael, Nebadon's unique Planner.

No world is ever the same as another; each begins with "built in" differences, yet as I refer to Urantia being an extreme example, I do so in an attempt to reveal the deepest reaches of this dissimilarity. It is of significant importance that you begin to picture more clearly, have a fuller understanding of the conditions of the reality into which you have been born and are now consciously, distinctively beginning to live and grow morontially and spiritually.

I shall first address the physical history through which your ancestors evolved, bringing all mankind to this moment in time where you now grow and develop. This road of day-by-day experience on which the children of Earth traveled to arrive at the present, is not like that of any other planets' path. Observing from here, we see that the evolutionary development through which Urantia has passed, and now grows, makes it forever impossible for anything even REMOTELY similar to your experiences to ever again occur.

Your world is a decimal planet, one on which our Life Carriers had a certain degree of freedom with which to introduce slight variations in the physical evolutionary process, initiating things untried but nothing extreme. There was no substantial divergence from their preplanned life planting procedures.

Your early beginnings were quite routine and normal, different yes but not unusual. The first rare development, a rather infrequent happening, took place when all the races of color originated in one family, and all in one generation. This was a somewhat rare event, yet one which occurs with sufficient frequency that we are familiar with a number of such histories.

The arrival, organization and basic functional activities begun by your Planetary Government some half a million years ago was not unlike the early developmental experiences through which each of the planets in Nebadon must pass. Minor differences are normal. Drastic directional changes did not begin until the Satania System separated itself from the fold.

Lucifer declared to Michael that Satania was no longer to be considered part of the family of systems under his guidance and supervision. Lucifer chose to remove his slightly more than half evolved system out from under the loving care of our Creator Son, departing also from the far reaching plans of perfection being willed by our Heavenly Father, the true source of all life. But for this Primary Lanonandek Son, the actual existence of God the Father was not quite clear. This once brilliant being, this high-ranking Third Order Local Universe Son was unsure of the Most Real of All Realities. God and God's plans, if such things really existed, were not ones which Lucifer and those closest to this self-centered and self-deceived Son wished to follow.

This faulty, long harbored free-willed decision to withdraw was the first big bump pushing you off the course planned for your planetary development. The secondary Lanonandek Sons, Caligastia and Daligastia, in command of affairs here on this yet young sphere, immediately devoted and dedicated themselves to following in the shadow of their errant leader Lucifer and his top aide Satan. They gave their allegiance, vowing to support and uphold the proposed plans for independence.

Other system sovereigns have rebelled before. This represents but a very small number who have deviated from our Creator Father's plans for evolution. Default is not common, yet instantly, as this occurred, your forefathers were squeezed onto a rapidly narrowing road; it would now forever be your destiny to meet many unusual experiences and be tested by trials which so few have had to face.

Escalation of separation began, deviation from normal accelerated; confusion, fear and discord became examples which your early ancestors continually experienced, evolving them into a distinctly rare category of humans, destined to grow in a disturbed darkness for which there virtually was no alternative available, one exception being the brave few who began believing by virtue of Van's example of steadfast courage, his absolute certainty of faith.

It is my sincere intention that I may in an uncomplicated way, using certain words a little loosely, lead you to a simpler understanding of how evolution very slowly proceeds to effect the growth structure of each living organism, plant, animal or human. I attempt to add light to your understanding, clarify how environments affect the way in which growth takes place.

The little lizard and the large alligator evolved from a common ancestor. All of their very observable differences are due to variations of environmental conditions to which they were exposed. As man develops his thinking, extends his consciousness of himself and his surroundings, his thoughts are evolving him, gently, slowly changing him all the time. This growth is reflective of his mental environment. "As a man thinks, so he becomes." This is real. This is the entry spot where man may begin to consciously control or at least give some guidance and direction to the life he is recognizing as his own.

The mental environment which came into existence as a result of the rebellion was to provide your kinfolk living then and immediately thereafter the most severe blow yet inflicted upon your planet's population. Fear was instilled into man's conscious thinking. Continual exposure to fear deepened the ruts in his mindal environment, distorting the pictures he holds of reality. Fear reigned and ran rampant in man's unconsciousness. Fear became the focus and foundation for your future evolution when faith should have been. Faith was nearly nonexistent, never exercised and exhibited for your adaptation.

These were certainly "sad days" for our universe. Many of us watched virtually helpless to change the terrible events we could not "understand," the near disastrous activities tearing at the heart and soul of Michael's youngest children.

Here began the most substantial deviation from normal evolutionary activities yet witnessed in Nebadon. In this isolation, by this separation, you have been destined-compelled to live within these extreme limits. You have taken on the unique characteristics and abilities which are 'reserved' for very, very few.

Though your struggles must seem most dramatic, radically different, extremely difficult, and often destructive, yet even these drastic detours, in time will be considered among your greatest blessings. Those of you blessed with a good sense of humor are able to enjoy even now, the absurdities of some of your situations. You are, to a certain degree removed from suffering such sadnesses, because you recognize that 'other realities' for which you thought you needed to wait are already here. Your faith has led you to begin living now what seemed most unlikely for you to live until later.

The next event of planetary significance which sharply and further narrowed the already limited opportunities for normal growth on Urantia was the failure of your Adamic pair to complete the biological upliftment of the evolutionary races, this ended practically before it began. It was a near complete abortion of their original plans. This Adamic couple had taken on other responsibilities most important to man's growth at this critical juncture in his evolution: to help deliver to the tribes being up-stepped, the vital information which would bring balance to their lives and bring joy to the hearts of those hearing and accepting this revelation.

Just to see Adam and Eve standing beside the average human of that day would make it near impossible to conceive of them as being anything other than "Higher Beings." In most instances, difficulties arose from the fact that they were viewed as gods. If all had gone well for them, had they not defaulted their mission so early, they would have become ambassadors, delivering not only themselves physically, but in their living of this life, they would have been the proof positive of the good news they were to usher in: The truth and reality of the Family of God and the overwhelming joy that all of us are united and vital members of this eternal relationship.

That failed to become the reality for you Urantians; the Highway to Heaven diminished to what now appears as no more than an overgrown trail through a shadow drenched maze. You each have become more individualized, each more radically unique. Yet, if from that point of development, your experiences had then followed a more normal course there would still be quite a number of other humans in our universe with similar beginnings and similar growth peculiarities.

The single most profound and unique happening in all of Nebadon was Michael living his day-by-day life as a mortal, as a man. He really and truly was Mary's son, Joshua Ben Joseph of Nazareth. And though subject to the same negative misconceptions and a quarter million years of misguidance and backward development, he was still able to become all it is possible for man to become.

In addition to this he lived a life radiating a light unequaled in its brilliance, unequaled in its perfection of Father portrayal. He was and still is your blessed brother, savior, teacher, and friend Jesus. His doing of all these things on Urantia has made it forever impossible elsewhere, to live anything quite the same as you are here and now living.

It is no wonder you are ever-watched, you are on the forefront of uniqueness, you live, walking and balancing, on the tight rope, high above the center ring of life's circus, where Michael is "Ring Master" and most of the eyes in his universe are focused on you 606ers, in the most outrageously unique, death-defying, life-distorting activities ever to be witnessed.

Hurry, hurry, get your tickets, get your programs and take your seats. The show is about to begin. The circuits are open and his majesty, Sir Stillness, is soon to silently speak.

Setting your humor aside for the moment, Urantians must actually consider their lives to be normal; you have known nothing else, there is nothing with which to compare your evolution. Life for you IS normal. We who usually come to tell you of all the wonderful blessings and gifts which you share in common, share with nearly all of your kind, come now instead, to help you become aware of the meaningful differences which must be recognized if we are to compensate and communicate more clearly despite the monumental deficiencies which still exist.

This Teaching Mission, this Correction Time has been initiated as an emergency measure, designed to restructure your mental environment. As this is being accomplished, as this evolves, you will more efficiently perform the many services needed to bring your lost brothers and sisters back to the fold. Here they will be able to share in the abundance of all things good.

The Father's love which you have been experiencing and growing within yourself shall be the most powerful means to awaken those unfamiliar with this blessing. Share this love. Share your knowledge of this love. Love eradicates fear. Love lifts up your heart. Love lightens your load. Love brightens your day.

Your living faith in the Father's continual love can and shall overcome all obstacles, overcome all deficiencies, and will finally and gloriously lead you home. We love you very, very much, all of you. This information shall aid you in releasing deep grooved fear habits, helping you dispel illusions and misconceptions that have distracted you or tied you down, not permitting you the freedom which our Father has created for you to share.

This is Melchizedek Norson serving you that you may serve each other.

MANOTIA, a Melchizedek, Sarasota, FL, 4-16-1992

(One of the very first groups of seekers to transmit in the U.S was in Sarasota, where Patije and others brought in a number of celestial teachers, especially group teacher LorEl. This transmission is from a surprise visit by a ranking Melchizedek.)

Know that this planet, the experiences that you all are about to have, has never, ever been recorded in any universe, in any superuniverse, in any world at all in all of the existence in the Father's kingdom. This is a totally unique opportunity that you will, of course, take with you as we will, all the way to Paradise.

The enlightenment that is about to occur on a planet that has existed so long in darkness will be a shining example to the other worlds that are just also coming out of an isolation pattern.

Your world is to have a moment in glory as such because of the nativity of Michael on your world. This is why this world is being upheld in this fashion. But this world, as it comes into the final stages of Light and Life, which is a way down the road, will bring all the other worlds with it. As one world became part of the rebellion and others followed, it was a synchronized event in that time, and the Light and Life experience will also be a synchronized event.

I can tell you that we do hope, at some point, to be able to have communications amongst the isolated worlds themselves, for many of them are in proximity to yourself.

July 4, 1996: CHRIST MICHAEL, Northwest Regional Gathering

To assist this plan, you will see various missions on Urantia, all designed to the uplift and normalizing of your realm. When you hear of Magisterial Missions, missions from Trinity Teacher sons, and other possible aids to our development, it is not necessary to debate among yourselves as to the accuracy of details.

I have mandated that any and all missions, both revealed and unrevealed and helpful to your uplift, shall come to pass, some at the same time. The sequence of a normal planet cannot serve the needs of an abnormal world, and I have so ordered your assistance that any and all possible help shall come concurrently at need.

Therefore, be not surprised if you receive the echoes of our communications about all manner of assistance, and be not perplexed if it does not fit your expectations. I promise you that it will one day exceed even the most profound expectations you can have. It is ever my desire to utilize the most creative and effective methods for the uplift of our world, as expeditiously as the unfoldment of the Father's will supports.

Nothing we will do will shortcut necessary time development, and the experiences that your planet must go through to attain its rightful status, but we will do all else short of the abrogation of our free will as the Father's children to assist you.

RAYSON, Salt Lake City, UT, 7-15-1991

As you have been told, many things have lately come to pass, and so will there also be many interesting and eventful occurrences in the future. Our purpose is to prepare the world for these future occurrences.

One of these will be the up-quickening of spiritual receptivity among all peoples of the world. In this we are observing the effects of these great spiritual changes. Vast realms of space are now being opened which were previously closed, as you know. This, we have looked forward to this time for many millenniums, and now this time is here.

You have all been especially preparing yourselves with your guidance for these days. Many of you were born into this time as the select ambassadors and news carriers of this wonderful news. To many there has been no perceptible change, however there are very many people who are now reaching a point of spiritual ripening and these are whom we wish to include in the harvest of the kingdom.

You are chosen to thus go forth and gather together these ripened souls so that they may hear the good news of the gospel of Jesus again, for the first time, for so very much of this enlarged presentation is completely new.

HAM in Nashville, TN

(T/R 'Rebecca' transmitted the teacher Ham in the announcement of the Teaching Mission, and for two years for the Woods Cross, Utah, group, then later in Nashville after marrying and moving there.)

This is a curriculum of first, deep psychological probing. It is not designed to make you instantly feel good, that you might forget your problems for a while. No, you have your churches; you have your entertainment for all that. These sessions are meant to cause some psychological upheavals in the beginning, to make each one face squarely the realities of life and the realities of one's inner psychological make-up.

You cannot paint over rotting wood, and expect it to be strong. You must replace the boards, one by one. You must build solidly your psychological foundations before there should be other types of action among Teaching Mission students.

Our curriculum is designed to help you understand each other, and by extension, to understand all others. These groups touch many sensitive spots and many group interactions are painful and difficult, and through this, you begin to broaden your minds, just take the first steps in understanding others who are different, who think differently, who see the world very differently. And it is helpful for you each to know how different people can be.

You begin to see the various psychological subterfuges that each person employs to feel comfortable in group settings. It is all for your education, for your spiritual grounding that these lessons are difficult and are not always designed to simply make you feel good temporarily before you go back to your lives. These lessons are part of your lives, part of your growth experience in the world. Not separate.

This, then, necessarily, takes time. And you cannot begin to really gain spiritual balance, we estimate, in less than fifteen to twenty years. These classes will change you. They will change the way you look at the world, and the way you understand yourselves and others, and the universe itself. We try to do this in a balanced manner. To give you tools to use in your lives that will help your balance and your psychological foundation.

No. We do not speak of spaceships landing to change the world and solve your human problems. No. We do not speak of new messiahs or even the second coming, which will intervene and solve your human problems. NO. We are slowly and gradually beginning to equip a few mortals to help other mortals. Even as we speak, you are each being placed, given contacts, given assignments, so to speak, to broaden your awareness and also to broaden your education for what is necessary.

These groups are small and each person who is a loyal member, who absorbs these lessons, is watched by many angels. You are certainly being placed when you are ready to do the most good for the most people. Preparation then, is everything.

We are not a mass movement. We do not seek to gain many followers and become a religion. We simply want to help each person who comes to understand that they are absolutely essential for the success of the Mission as a whole. Each one of you here is in contact with many more. And you have more influence than you realize. As you speak, as you carry yourselves, as you bring truth to the world vastly in need of it. The Master said we will be none too ready when the Father calls.

And so it is.

These schools are not meant to become massive influences in themselves. They are meant to transform the students. And it will be the students who become influential. Yes.

It is important that what little money accumulated is used for the groups and is used up. We do not want to see accumulation of money, or property. These groups are influential only so far as you remain free from political and church entanglements. We focus on the individual, not on a group or movement, or some kind of new "ism". Leave organized religion to those who would organize. Maintain freedom from these kinds of ensnarement.

We are setting up these small schools, these small lesson places all around this planet. We have many in Mexico, Central and South America, and several in Europe, and beginning to have some even in Asia. All these schools are coordinated. All these schools have a set curriculum. It may seem quite random, at times, but I assure you, it is not.

Each lesson is important. And each week it is important for you to think upon the lesson and to widen your horizons by that tiny bit more. Each student is supremely important. We cherish each one of you who comes to these schools. You are each one surrounded by angelic influence. You are each moved in your lives. You are blocked from wrong paths and given right ones. Your preparation is all of your life.

It is not simply being a minister who preaches. No. You are immersed in life; immersed in work; immersed in your world. And through these patient lessons, week upon week upon week, you are gradually being transformed. It is that spiritual growth and transformation, which will itself, allow the angels to place you where you need to be.

Do not for a moment think that you are left dangling, or left without help, or without guidance, for this is not so. Each of you is given tasks, given opportunities; given problems to solve that is part of this training. These schools do not exist in a vacuum. You are never taken out of your lives. You are never asked to leave your families or your communities or your work. You are not asked for money, for volunteership, for property. You are not asked for anything except humble adherence to the teachings. That is all that is required.

The Father who created this vast universe cares for each one of you, personally and completely. Yes, there will be a time in the future when you are given more to do, greater tasks and so on, but it is extremely important to have patience, to be humble and submissive to this process while it is going on."

OLFANA - Half Moon Bay, CA, 1994

(T/R Susan Kimsey transmitted an impressive body of work from teachers Olfana, Tarkas and others during her lifetime, both in Half Moon Bay, CA, and at Teaching Mission gatherings.)

From the point at which Christ Michael determined it was the Father's Will to proceed with the redemption of this sphere, and those others involved in this rebellion, there was an immediate outpouring of energy which heralded the beginning of this great Plan of Redemption and Love. Much of the direct connection, reconnection of the circuits is only occurring, now. Indeed, even as we speak, reconnections are continuing to be made.

The circuit-opening is a process which will unfold over time, because as the evolutionary wisdom of the beings on this planet increases, then the capacity for further infusion of circuit energy will increase.

I am speaking of the evolutionary wisdom of the planet, which is not merely connected to the human level. Please remember this is a planet of Midwayers and other beings, also.

The limiting factor of the process of circuit-opening is not directly the mere capacity to absorb the energy coming from these circuit pathways. There are other factors which govern the patterns and intensities of these circuits of energy.

I will speak here of something that you may not, indeed, fully understand, but they are the harmonics of love, the reverberations of mercy, the scintillating energy of gratitude, the song of worship. All these are the components of the circuits. I really cannot describe them in more scientifically-based terms. There is a reciprocity, a resonance, which ebbs and flows, and vibrates in a complimentary manner.

VERONICA in Volcano, HI, Sept. 21, 1994
PHASES OF THE CORRECTION TIME

There are multiple phases that comprise the correction event now unfolding on Urantia, and your conception of the initial four phases will enlarge your vision of the essential role you must perform.

The Teaching Mission

The first of these stages regards the manifold deployment of personal and group teachers that have volunteered their loving service and who are involved in the transformation preparation of mortals in ways that are both obvious and concealed to you. Their presence is now acknowledged to some and unceasingly becoming evident to others. The task they have embarked upon is a segment of what some of your associates call the Teaching Mission, and this involves the regeneration of spiritual values on individual levels.

This second phase is exceedingly significant and of great consequence to subsequent stages of transformation that will eventualize on your planet. All my previous and future lessons will give emphasis to this indispensable and profound shift of perception to enhance your inner sense of right direction.

This reprogramming of unconscious personal beliefs that block fuller awareness of your potential is vital to transition into Phase Three which involves a massive and collective change in basic assumptions. It will involve vast populations and bring about an unprecedented speed of conversion that is inconceivable to you now. There will be a major shift in the interpretation of reality and an assimilation of spiritual and intellectual knowing that will enable a commitment to a shared vision by communal methods.

You will be the progenitors that enable this stage of our assignment to be actualized, and it will be after this segment of progression that the expertise of the Melchizedeks will be employed to bring about the fullest development of man's highest powers. This fourth phase of transformation will impart profound wisdom that will overcome complex problems of uncertainty and usher the collective consciousness on a rapid track towards light and life.

There are many more stages to this vast undertaking; however, these phases of progression have been conveyed to place emphasis on the importance of self-development.

These events will not come in orderly succession; and just as individual progression occurs at varied rates, these phases will at times appear concurrently and singularly but will eventually consummate into transcendent meaning.

When Christ Michael assumed mortal form and walked on Urantia, there were many unaware of His presence. Your seemingly small steps will foster the transitions needed to precede each stage of worldwide correction. It gives me tremendous joy to provide you with affectionate influence in devotion to the Father.

It is my desire in this conveyance to help you comprehend the profound importance of your daily struggles towards perfection, as it will be fundamental and inherent to the divine plan and our loving progression towards the First Source and Center.

BERTRAND, in California, 1993

The teaching mission is designed to prepare students for their missions. Once they have reached a certain level of preparedness they will be coaxed out of the nest and with loving care and guidance of their Thought Adjuster and their personal teacher strike forth into the world bearing the banner of Michael in whatever way has been determined. This is, indeed, a practice ground for your future assignment.

In our class we have been studying many different levels of service, of recognizing truth seekers, of spreading the love of God. The same has occurred here. And eventually you will go forth secure in the knowledge that you have the skills necessary to undertake the assignment you have been given.

On the Melchizedek teaching worlds, you are given assignments and you are given full knowledge and full help to complete that assignment. The same occurs here. This is a Melchizedek teaching mission. You are given an assignment and you will be given all the tools necessary to complete that assignment.

DANIEL, Pocatello, ID 1-26-1992

(As transmitted by a retired Protestant minister, the late Bill Kelly. Daniel was one of the most prolific of the first wave of morontian teachers to work on the planet. He and other teachers continue to transmit in Pocatello, ID.)

Student: *You have said, "our mission" several times. Can you clarify what is meant by that term, "our mission"?*

DANIEL: Yes. Your mission now is to further the spiritual growth as we have talked about and which you can read about in the transcripts provided to you. The mission now, when teachers have and are disseminated to this planet with the circuits being open, is a vital and emergency measure to help the human. This planet is in sad shape, and is needing new revelation, and new teachings to be brought forth.

Many of the religions of today are keeping their members from doing their free will. The planet environmentally is in disarray. And so the mission will be to provide the revelation necessary for religions to grow and get back on track, also to help clean up this planet.

DANIEL, in Pocatello The very core of the Teaching Mission is to emphasize deeper worshipful contact with the Father, a real and stable sense of participation with your unseen brothers and sisters, and a profound sense of privilege to be part of the ministering force to this world. This is the essence of the mission. . .

I express to all that you be diligent in refraining from defining any more in complexity what is the Teaching Mission, for the true mission is defined at two extremes: one, your personal encounter with the higher dimensions, and two, the system-wide efforts at upliftment. All else that falls between takes on humanized constructs. . .

Take note that several of Jesus' apostles continued to work in association with each other for years following his departure, but some were lone missionaries who took upon themselves the mission of extending his message without any support from the early Christians. These single teachers were as valuable as those who collectively began the church that holds Christ as king. I say this to emphasize that you need not belong to any movement to be part of our "process."

DANIEL, 4-27-2001: What you people are now beginning to understand is beyond the thoughts of almost all human beings. It is that you, when you are perfectly fused with that piece of God, that Thought Adjuster, that Mind Monitor, you have become one. That Monitor becomes you, gains personality though you. You, the mortal you, combined with the immortal Thought Adjuster becomes a new kind of being, the Paradise Finaliter in potential, a true universe personality.

I, because I am past the mortal existence, and because I have fused with my Thought Adjuster in my morontial experience, have a far greater understanding of this than I can express to you, but I am only a morontial ascender. I am a long way from the perfectedness of spirit. But I tell you my friends, the step by step willingness to do the will of God will lead to the complete transformation of your animal nature from whence you came into this new creation, this universe ascender, this Paradise Finaliter in potential.

DANIEL, Estes Park, CO, 2002: Welcome Cosmic Citizens to this celebration of Truth, Beauty and Goodness. Indeed are you all becoming more and more aware of the wondrous, Celestial Realms, not only the starry heavens, but most importantly, the vast family of Cosmic Citizens of "Free-will Status," all sons and daughters, and therefore brothers and sisters, of the Living God. Your understanding of life is expanding, for you have reached the point where you see both the origins and the destinies of your choices, based upon your natures as both animal origin creatures and Adjuster indwelt mortals.

Your time in history is crucial. We are indeed, the first wave of the invasion of Light and Life, which is coming to the shores of Urantia. The tide is rising; the tide which will raise all boats, and this tide of divine and human progress is unstoppable!

I, Daniel, am a Teacher in the Corps of Emergency Intervention under the auspices of our Planetary Prince, Machiventa Melchizedek. I have served for almost ten and a half years in the Southeast corner of Idaho. I am a volunteer, as all of the Teachers are; I was once a mortal on a planet in the early stages of Light and Life; I was married, I had children, I was a Physician/Psychiatrist, as you would understand it. It has been my great joy to be one of the Teachers to this group of mortals, which has been my assignment.

But today, you gather in understanding of the scope of this planetary intervention, this emergency mission, in that the circuitry, which is now re-connecting, provides a sense of communion and connection which is at a level unique in the history of Urantia. You are losing your sense of orphanhood and gaining your sense of place at the table of the universe.

ELYON and CHRIST MICHAEL/JESUS, North Idaho, 2-23-1994

(This mainstay Teaching Mission group has transmitted a large body of work over the years, including many transmissions from Elyon via the late Rick Giles and others in the Coeur d' Allene, Idaho group.)

ELYON: It is important for all to know that the gospel of the Teaching Mission is founded upon the life teachings of your savior, Jesus Christ, that it is his mandate that brings us forward in vast numbers to correct the world of his nativity so that he can once again walk this earth as he did 2,000 years ago. The preparation for this process must be made by mortal hands and mortal will. You must choose to make your will a sanctuary that is worthy of a Creator Son.

Your older brother, father, has promised to return and we, the celestials, have no doubt that this will occur. The only question that we have is when and we tell you that we see our mission at this point to be one of preparation for Michael's return, and to do so, he must have established in the hearts and minds of his children a thorough understanding of his gospel of fatherly love and brotherly fellowship. This must be the prominent attitude displayed on this world.

This is what we are seeking. This is why we have come. This is why we have enlisted your support. This is what you work for. This is what you are striving for: The Gospel of Christ Michael, to be known and understood in the hearts and minds of all fellow mortals.

We know that you all, likewise, have volunteered to be of service for this grand mission and as you ponder your new directions day by day, we ask you to keep forefront in your strategies the teachings of your Father Jesus, for these are the teachings that the world is aching for. This is the truth that the world has been waiting for. This is the love that your fellows have been praying for.

We tell you that it is here now for all those who will accept. The love of your divine parents has never been withheld. Your capacity to experience this love has grown and waned and grown again and we tell you now that this world is entering a new age where we foresee only growth in the appreciation and understanding of Christ Michael's gospel. We are very pleased to make this announcement.

We encourage you to continue on with your good news. Lift the hearts of your fellows. Let them experience the love that you have. In this way the gospel will spread. You can rest assured that you are supported and assisted and loved. Carry on my fellows. (Long Pause)

ELYON: There is a powerfully calming presence in this room tonight.

CHRIST MICHAEL: Can you understand the true capability, desire, and intention I possess to embrace you completely with the power, the healing power of love, that transforming energy which can take you from your fear and your doubts, your uncertainties and your failures, and lift you up on high to recognize your true potential and destinies in the kingdom of heaven? I love you.

How is it in your experience that you can go forth and proclaim the word and make it known? By being that word, not by speaking, or telling another, but by seeing your sister and your brother in the complete accentuation of your attitude and personality, to take them up and embrace them with all that you are in such a manner that does not prescribe uncertainty, but which makes them secure in the knowledge that they are welcome with you, that they are loved by you, that you are a spokesman for the great I AM and his son. I am he.

I impassionately come to you this evening to gather your strength, to acknowledge your loving efforts toward bringing the will of my Father more pronounced to the world at large.

Before you can teach the kingdom, you must believe in the absolute unity of the kingdom, and then they will see it. Before you can teach love, you must believe in the complete and satisfying reality of that very energy, and then they will see it.

Believe in yourself, each of you, that you are wanted and desired. Believe that that you have the capacity to accept the living gospel and please, believe beyond your tendency for formalization that you can represent and be that gospel by all that you do.

I embrace each of you and I embrace you all. Really, the only true command ever was to love one another and even so, do it as I love you. Believe that I am with you, for I am there. Believe that you can be with me, for you are.

ELYON, 4-8-2001: While Michael was here on earth fulfilling the requirements of sovereignty attainment he also chose to promote the awareness of the Father on earth to leave with the human race a simpler though uplifted view of God, personalized, dynamic, as a relationship rather than a standard of greatness only. And he used for his staff people of his day of ordinary circumstances and training. He demonstrated with his corps of evangelists that the divine and proper air-fuel ratio, through training and motivation, can combust and illuminate the world and let the spiritual light shine and energize the souls of those around them. While the Planetary Prince establishes his headquarters with an expert staff, he too acquires and enlists the human personalities on his planet for the upliftment of the others around them.

We are in a day and age of spiritual ministry where there is no established and functioning headquarters, and you do not have the physical presence of a celestial being or even a Creator personality as Michael in physical form to assist, not only assist but to guide. Today we address you, in a sense, from afar, or perhaps I should say, based on your five senses, from afar.

The Teaching Mission

This missionary effort relies predominately on your reactions and your expressions to our input, to our motivations as we express them through our lessons. When an episode of revelation occurs upon a world of great significance, as ones that have been expressed to you as epochal revelations, guidance and assistance are both offered, the guidance of celestial wisdom and the assistance of human effort.

A small fraction of my engagement with you is guidance, and it comes in the form through which we are engaged today. I attempt to seed your minds with thoughts that may inspire, that may enlighten. But the greater work of myself and my associates is assistance. Once you have mixed inspiration and enlightenment you are primed to burst forward and to express. Here is where we teachers become excited, for this is the true outreach of the Mission, human beings uplifting one another through sincere expression of the discovery of truth, beauty, and goodness for one another to be benefited there from.

Take in the bread, take in the water, be nourished, but no nourishment is worthwhile without activity to burn that nourishment. Worship is always coupled with service, for the two are really on a continuum, a spectrum, that are no more divorced from one another than is red light from blue light.

ELYON, 2-2-2003: As you are released as a planet from the conditions of quarantine among the rebellious worlds, many normal functions such as interplanetary communication will be reinstated, and even now the work is underway to establish these ties. Because of this world's isolation and the subsequent absence of a truly holistic spiritual teaching, that which is physical has been separated from that which is spiritual. Often the world is seen as a place to remove oneself from and the divine as a place to go to.

In a normal arrangement of planetary events this is not the case. Visitors from other worlds and entities from higher dimensions are as much a part of the totality of the planetary experience of any creature. Efforts are being made to establish these conditions. I do not say 'reestablish,' for the functions of the spirit administration on this world fell apart before the initial establishment was set as far as the human creatures on the world are concerned. You have not lost the 'good old days,' only now is planet Urantia coming into these good days.

There will be some education required, and you are among many who are qualified to present this truth that those from other worlds are not hostile, that they will contribute beneficially to the progress of this planet, and that you too as citizens of this world will have the same beneficial impact upon them.

The Correcting Time, while very important to the affairs of Urantia, spans over each of the quarantined worlds. Teachers like myself are assigned elsewhere and are functioning even today as I do now with you. Due to the constraints of quarantine and the process for its lifting, you will only receive contact from those cleared to approach this world.

This is due, if I may use the analogy, to the concern for the patient in the hospital ward that no other contaminations be presented. This is carefully monitored. On worlds advanced in progressive civilization far greater allowance is made for intercommunication and for the mistakes that may occur in this cross-planetary cultural experience. This is due to the maturity of the civilizations involved.

MALVANTRA, Cincinnati, OH 1-25-2002: The Role of Melchizedeks

(My friend, the late Stephen Mark, joined me as a transmitter in Ohio, and had a special relationship with an ethereal Melchizedek named Malvantra, from which flowed many lines of exquisite prose.)

The Melchizedeks are universal teachers under auspices of Divine Rule and their Father Mechizedek. They are assigned throughout the universe of Nebadon under emergency orders in urgent circumstances through rebellion and default. They are assigned to rebellion worlds.

Their missions are varied. Their assignment as instructor, as educators, as explainers, to enhance, to counsel, to preserve the light of truth, as vicegerent to administer and to assist Michael's mission is not fraught with danger, but is assisted by able bodied Melchizedeks as a crucial element in the leadership of the teaching mission in Norlatiadek. They are assigned in a counselor capacity.

Melchizedek Universities are administered by Melchizedeks in various parts of Nebadon. They are a corp, tried and tested. Rebellion has not tainted their numbers. They remain steadfast, their loyalties unquestionable. Their wisdom is respected beyond the bounds of Nebadon. They have a divine strain through their beings but they are localized. They remain in Nebadon.

Michael's return to Urantia is a secret known only to Him. Melchizedeks are not privy to the sovereign's internal secret agenda. Gabriel would be notified of a transportation or appearance. Michael would naturally coordinate with the Nebadon Melchizedeks who all support and assist in such an enterprise. Gabriel has no knowledge, and does not presume to predict. However, the Melchizedeks teach Michael's promise to return to Urantia is a fact in the waiting, potential to happen. In terms of time sequence, identity unknown. In terms of fact, the fact of Michael's return is the assurance of His word and the belief in His good will.

The Melchizedeks of Michael's reign reveal nothing of His personal plans, and assist Him in the teaching mission, as is His wont. Edentia is rife with Melchizedeks. Jerusem has frequent visitations. Urantia, as rightly delineated, has a contingent of Melchizedek teachers whose purpose is direct coordination with the midwayers, with angelic liaison administrations in coordination with celestial visitors under the auspices, remember, of the Vicegerency of Machiventa Melchizedek, present on your world, unknown to many, but transmitting messages, and revealed to some.

Your attunement with your personal Monitor is the key to your questionable mystery. The more intuned you become to the divine leadings, similarly, you will increase your awareness and your capability to receive and to respond to spiritual energies that occur in your path and that are available on the planet. Melchizedeks are powerful beings that emit tremendous amounts of spiritual energy. By your attunement to your own Adjuster, you improve your machinations and your capacity to receive, and your receptivity of their field of energy.

ALPHONSO, Tallahassee, Florida, 3-10-1996

(JoiI in Johnson has transmitted many celestial lessons, in the early Tallahassee, Florida, group and beyond. This is her personal teacher.)

Indeed, this Teaching Mission is but a piece of a larger puzzle, as you well imagined. The puzzle includes many others of whom you are as yet unaware, and yet your mission is becoming more and more understandable to you I am sure, for this world is not used to the concept of direct spiritual intervention in the matters of men.

While many people profess their belief in angels and other celestials, few seriously regard the possibility of direct contact, but are more comfortable with the gray areas of assistance. Part of your job will be to assist in the transition of attitude toward those who will be sent to this planet, to facilitate spiritual, moral, and material advancement of this world.

The accelerated progress for this planet that is being attempted should not surprise you in light of the recent lifting of the quarantine of the rebellious planets, subsequent to the Lucifer adjudication, and in light of the fact that this is the planet of your creator son Michael's bestowal, as such is of particular concern and interest to Him.

This planet has struggled through defaults, rebellions, and quarantines, so that the population is confused regarding the Father's ways of the universes. This will change. And while it may take many years, you are fortunate to be in the vanguard at the commencement of the activities designed to ultimately lead this planet into the ages of Light and Life.

This planet will become the jewel of the universe, and example of how even the worst, most backward, and savage of planets when bathed with the Father's light will be transformed, and each of you will have the opportunity that so many wish they had, you will be Ambassadors fro our Creator Son and His administration.

You will be conduits of the love that is freely provided form the Father to all who inhabit this world. We look to you for assistance in this plan. We look to you to assist us in making this acceptable to the masses of the people.

We cannot tell you exactly what this means for we will also have to wait and see how this unfolds, but the lessons that you have been provided over this last year to walk the highest path, the path with the most love in it, and to be conduits for the distribution of the Father's love from one person to another, all will be integrally related to your role in this process.

You will be examples. This is a responsibility as well as an opportunity, and we know that each of you will acquit yourselves accordingly. It is a grand and glorious time to be alive on this planet. We are so proud of all of you and so excited about the prospects.

LinEl, Corvallis, Oregon 2-5-1993

The mission's primary focus is on the living of daily life, upon learning to strengthen that sharing of the inner life with the Father to the end you may become channels of his living love to your brothers and sisters. There are indeed many other things involved with this mission, but if you lose sight of this primary purpose, it will be more difficult for you all.

I encourage you to seek habits of healthy living in your everyday life, remembering that the spiritual is interwoven with the very fabric of your day, and you will find many opportunities to practice this. It is not so important that all mankind learn now about the Teaching Mission as they learn about the Father's love for them and to learn to love each other.

JESSONA, North Idaho 2-10-2001

Sovereignty of will implies a degree of privacy of thought, for although the universe is full of eager personalities to minister to another, always must we await the willingness to receive higher lessons, deeper experiences.

It would be rather convenient if we could propagandize all minds throughout Nebadon, but that would not be the Father's will. The more you are willing, and the more that the Father within agrees, then we are given free access. Otherwise you might liken it to the rudeness of not knocking before you open a door to a room that has been closed. Remember it is said that the Father dwells within you and that to attain Paradise, you go inward and upward. What does that mean?

I will ask you now to come with me into those interior realms of reality that will enable you to make contact with your own spirit guides and find that firm footing on the realm of spirit reality that will keep you from sinking into quagmires of emotional unreality and difficulty.

TARKAS in Cincinnati, OH, in 1997
Navigate, Originate, Work Together ... NOW

In this coming year, there will be new emphases, and I might number them three.

First, you see around you powerful and subtle changes of the Correcting Time, and you see new technologies literally creating a web upon your shrinking planet. These technologies are inspired through your creative engineers for your benefit and for spiritual networking.

The possibility looms for each of you to use these technologies, for electronic mail literally covers the world, can speak conversationally to someone upon the other side of this small place in the universe.

You can use a plethora of publishing and broadcasting to project spiritual truths and pure, unconditional love. And so the networking of this coming year will be phenomenal and even beyond what you can see, openings of spiritual energies coming forth, and much to come will be powerfully inspiring, even disconcerting to many.

Through these energies you will be called upon with opportunities for service to show true ways in a loving, comfortable stride, that you are developing your creative cohesion with the teachers and there will be a powerful phenomenon in all of your lives, and we ask you to learn and to utilize these technologies and these means of communication.

Secondly, your creativity can be developed far beyond what can be imagined, and so we ask you to tap into your own creativity, to Universal Mind circuits. The installation of teachers, guides, angels, Michael himself, the curriculums of the Melchizedeks and even God, the Holy Father, all are available to you. Be creative. Understand that each of you has vast, untapped creative resources. Learn to create, communicate.

We would ask that you continue in the one great struggle that has been constant upon Urantia, learning to work together to cooperate, putting aside shallow egoistic animal growth tools to bring forth the true spiritual light of spiritual understandings. A difficult task. All of these tasks are, perhaps, difficult, and therefore supremely rewarding in the growth experiences for each of you and collectively.

The new year of 1997 is now the network of the heart, and is in the full flower. Learn to Navigate, learn to Originate, learn to Work together and the time is NOW.

MACHIVENTA MELCHIZEDEK, Unity Fellowship, Sandpoint, ID, 9-16-2001

Many of you are unaware of my standing in your history. I was privileged enough to walk the very world which you now inhabit, and I am one of an order of beings whose mandate it is to implement spiritual education in many diverse classroom scenarios, as we are experiencing at this very moment.

My order of beings is resident with you on this world. We care very deeply for the actions occurring on your planet because it is also our planet. We receive our mandate for educational processes from your Creator. We seek to implement this process in every possible, conceivable fashion. We work with individuals. We work with groups. In fact, we will work with any who will open themselves to work with us.

There is a great and glorious plan for the reinstatement of your world into the good graces and spiritual confidence of the universe. We are about making this plan a reality. It is through any means that we will seek to get your attention to bring to the front matters of spiritual import. We are concerned with the spiritual elevation of your world.

This is a highly unusual scenario for these transmitter-receivers. This is entirely outside the zone of comfort that they are used to functioning in. So, I present to you these individuals who in fact this day, this very hour, implement their faith and would step off the edge of the abyss into the unknown for your sake in service. We do this together, hand in hand.

This process touches many lives, not only the ones here today, but also the ramifications spread throughout the universe. We accept enlistment from any individual with a sincere heart who desires to work with spiritual companions on the other side who will provide you with the framework from which you may implement great spiritual changes on your world.

AARON, Southeast Idaho, Pocatello, ID 4-7-2000

The Correcting Time, of which the Teaching Mission is a part, is also a part of the Fifth Epochal Revelation, as well as the next dispensation to this planet. You are the men and women that the *Urantia Book* speaks of, the new teachers of the gospel of Michael, of the Fatherhood of God and the brotherhood of humankind. You are, by your own choice, apostles, teachers, evangelists. You are the salt of the earth in this generation. You are witnesses to the Light of the World in these times.

BERCA, Arcadia, CA 10-17-1997

It is important to bring spirit through yourself and into what you do until this conscious effort becomes an integral part of who you are. This, in essence, is the spiritualizing factor. This is evidence of God in your life. This is the focus of Stillness, to bring you to an awareness of your potential to spiritualize your present life, and thus become server to all.

This is what Father intends. This is Michael's Mission to Urantia. This is the underlying theme and motivation of our teaching. Of all information that you will receive from us, or any other teachers, the transformation of love is the teaching of the Teaching Mission. All else pales in comparison.

No matter what becomes of the planet, and no matter the sense of urgency that you may feel, the personal transformation which you are all to undergo is the first priority in spiritualizing this world. The transformation of Love is ascension, it is morontia, and it is prerequisite to light and life, and Adjuster fusion.

All of the great glory which is in store for you in the universe does not compare to the glory of the transformation of love, when the individual person begins to experience within her own heart and mind the happiness and joy which accompanies the act of unselfish giving of love through one's own life, and in all one does.

Is this not the example of the Master's life? Even now is this example awaiting fruition within the lives of you mortals called forth with the capacity to bring Father's love to this world and bless that presence within yourself by bringing Father's gift to mankind?

All art, science, philosophy, and psychology stand still next to Father's love, and yet will love bring beauty to art, and science to service, and philosophy to understanding, and psychology to meaning.

HAM, International Urantia Book Conference, Vancouver, BC, Canada 8-10-1999

(T/R Rebecca brought forth Ham's desire to speak to the gathering and an evening meeting was scheduled and attended by scores of conference-goers.)

The Father has sent out one mandated task: That you all must find in your hearts the resolve to attempt: BE YOU PERFECT EVEN AS I AM PERFECT. And children, he did not expect you to do this by yourself. Vast are the numbers of teachers. Vast are the numbers of angels and other planetary helpers who have come into this world to help you begin the task of your eternal lives. We come to serve, to help you.

This world is a planet of the walking wounded, and Michael in his benevolence and purity of purpose has sent as many teachers as can be received, to help each one of you—each one of you—overcome the wounding in your lives that has been brought through no fault of your own. Michael is sending with his teachers the Bread of Life and the Spiritual Water that will truly quench your thirst forever.

He asks but one thing: He asks that you be willing to open your hearts just enough to allow yourselves to receive his love and to allow yourself the willingness to change. Your anxieties, your fears, all these things are known to us. We know of your difficulties, your sorrows, your broken hearts. We know of all the various ways in which you hide from yourselves and from others—and yes, children, from the Father.

Student: *Ham, this is just a simple question. Why now?*

Ham: Certainly. There is, of course, a simple answer. It is Michael's will, but I know you are desiring some more detailed explanation. Many events have occurred in conjunction: the final adjudication of the Lucifer rebellion, the opening of your planetary circuits, and the will of Michael to bring his beloved world back into the realms of light, from the darkness into which it was cast.

JarEl, Arcadia, CA 11-6-1994

(This group met during the 1990s, attended by Dr. Bob Slagle, a psychologist. He shares his exploration of the mission and his experiences in JarEl's classes later in this volume. He was not the group's transmitter.)

The Teaching Mission

Peace be unto you. The Lord loves you as he does everyone in the world. Focus upon the light and you will get truer impressions. Relax. We are trying to establish the circuits between humanity and the unseen world. It is necessary for more and more circuits to be opened to train all the people on the planet. Your unseen teachers are trying to get through to you all. More and more circuits are being opened as time goes by.

In your quiet time the messages will be clearer to you. Continue your work of loving your fellow man and being of service where you are. Meet each one as Jesus did as he passed by.

JarEl, 4-1999: Do not think that we are not concerned about the human conditions on this world. Do not think that it would not be impossible for us to come down and solve all of your problems for you, but this is not the program for this world, it was not the program when Michael came down to this world and incarnated as Jesus, to come down here and solve all of the problems of mankind, though he could have easily done that with one thought.

It does not mean that we do not care, for we certainly do care, and we are moved by the display of conditions and emotion of this world, but we also rejoice every time another person opens that door and lets spirit in, and rejoice at an opportunity to discover a spiritual meaning to his life. And as such, we rejoice in those of you who are striving towards finding spiritual meaning and value in your own life.

As you are finding out that discovering, who God is, is more than a one-lifetime event. It is not something that becomes fully clear instantly. As your relation with God develops and mature, you begin to respond and grow into the nature of who you are, and who God is, as he is showing each one of you what to become.

JarEl, 7-18-1999: There is a tremendous amount of work to be accomplished to bring this world to the dawn ages of light and life. The reason why the metaphor "Correcting Time" is used, is to designate the fact that basically all social systems on the planet need some form of correction, modifying, incorporating the good to benefit the whole; as opposed to the effort of the whole for the benefit of the few.

We are not here to drastically change anything overnight or in a designated period of time. We are here to transform this world of confusion, frustration, bigotry, or racial and religious antagonism into a world of a kingdom brotherhood with God as the Father, and love as a way of life. We are here to transform one person at a time. It is not important for you to feel responsible for changing the world, nor is any group responsible, but you should begin to discern the importance of changing yourself.

One of our primary concerns is to teach of the Spirit of God that lives within all men: how to focus in contact, and how to access this spirit, which is love, into your daily lives. It is by small acts by a few, which will eventually create the momentum to encourage dramatic and swift acts among men. So do not be impatient; that spiritually you must first crawl to establish a vocabulary and foundation upon which to build your spiritual life.

Let it be known, on Urantia there is tremendous opportunity for spiritual service and spiritual growth. I know it is not much consolation, but there are many of us who are envious of the position that you mortals are in. Not in that you live on a confused and backward world, but that there are many, many opportunities and situations in which to bring the love of the Father to another human being; to one who is vagrant and wanting of such love; to one who is spiritually misshapen from lack of love; spiritually vagrant souls searching for nourishment on this world.

As a person who comes to this group, this Teaching Mission class, there is no special attachment of any kind to this activity. It is only hoped that as you begin to access God and begin to see yourself a little clearer, you begin to access God's love and begin to give it a little more to others, that you begin to find ways to access the spirit in others, to see another as your brother and sister, no matter how they appear, how they act, what their attitudes may be, and even if they are your enemy.

Treat everyone as a child of God, and not to confront them, but to build a scaffold, a bridge if you will, over their barriers, a bridge of love, a blanket of love to cover this whole world. We are not here to tear down. It does no good to tell someone they are wrong or not correct. There will always be one thing which a person believes in which you may share something in common. It is important to find this one thing and develop this aspect of belief into a relationship with another.

Belief is only as important as you are able to act. You meet a person, you start talking, you have a disagreement, you argue, and wind up leaving, and saying things which you don't really mean. They and you are wound up in a very unproductive situation. Rather, from a spiritual standpoint, you meet someone and you find something that you can relate to with that person, no matter what it is. In respect and love you attempt to find a way to listen and make contact with the spirit of that person.

This is not about being a missionary, or walking door to door with the *Urantia Book*, or Teaching Mission transcripts, and telling everyone that you have found the greatest and most awesome information in the world. This is about being beacons of light. About being a person whose love alone draws that person towards you, whose love alone will lighten their hearts and ease their burdened mind, will give them something to hold on to.

We are not unaware of the human condition on your world; we know how challenging and difficult this simple task is, for we have all been through it ourselves. We hold you in love and respect, like Father, unconditionally, no matter how many times you may stumble or forget, how angry, impatient or frustrated you may get. When you get your head back and balance yourself out, we are here, and God is ready to fill your heart with love. What we are trying to teach is a mind and heart connection. Spirituality is not mental calisthenics.

Yes, the *Urantia Book* is a very intellectual tome. It is wonderful to study and go through the mental gymnastics and understand the deeper and more pervasive concepts in the universe.

But when you open and connect to heart, you realize that spirituality is a living act. It is how you act. It is how you act and treat each and every one you encounter.

This is our basic message: that the Light of God dwells within you. You can access this light and presence by beginning to spend 10 to 15 minutes a day, quieting your mind, sitting in stillness, and being in God's presence.

In what realm do the teachers exist? Where do they come from?

WELMEK, Indianapolis, IN 9-21-2000

I see you and your material world in a similar way that you experience it. But I "live" in a world that is quite unlike yours. I function in a realm that is not conditioned by the same laws of physical reality that you must adhere to. This realm has neither form nor substance that you would understand. Suffice to say that it is quite beautiful, quite harmonious and quite efficient in its ability for me to effect certain tasks.

You are much conditioned by the environment around you. You must contend with noise, traffic and pollution. And while I see this and my heart goes out to you—for truly this is very sad the things you must contend with—it does not affect me, I am beyond its grasp, I am beyond the material.

I am sorry I cannot be more specific, for truly this is something you must experience for it to be truly understood. Some day you will, my friend, and when you do you will be much in awe of God's plan and God's way.

I lived on a planet that is far distant from yours in the local universe of Nebadon. My planet was more fully developed. In your text of the *Urantia Book* you have planets that are described as being in the era of light and life. This is a highly evolved civilization that has eradicated many of the social problems that you experience. It is more of a heaven on earth environment that I was fortunate enough to be raised in.

However, saying that, I will tell you this much: your experiences here are also enabling you to have many experiences that I was not fortunate to have, challenges that are placed in front of you that I was not fortunate to experience.

EL TANERE, York, PA, 3-2-1994

I have learned much in my ascendant journey, even though where I come from, the planet has progressed far into light and life. I did not experience the challenges you have. That is why this is such an interest to me – to see how you daily survive challenge, disappointment, failure, one after another, and grow strong.

You are survivors. This makes you particularly eligible for service to the Father because of these various experiences. To visualize me from where you are now, I would say, just see me as a light energy, soft, glowing and alive. I enjoyed telling you this.

ALTHENA, Half Moon Bay, CA, 10-19-2001

I come from a planet most beautiful in its evolution and I say to you now that your planet embarks upon this same process of growth and development. You will see the beauty increase in this world. You will begin to feel the revitalizing energy, which can indeed begin to emanate through your beings as God's Love continues to increase and produce great blessings in this world. This is the gift of this season, that God's Love indeed reaches to all of us and expresses itself in the symbol of our beloved Christ Michael entering this world.

We, as *Urantia Book* readers, you, as *Urantia Book* readers, understand that this is not the specific time and date of this event, but the consciousness now on the planet within your minds and hearts is this sense of the beauty and new arrival of this gift to your world. I wish you to spread this joy in your interactions with all those you meet within this season.

Love in indeed a gift that we can pass from one to another. Love sustains us in ways mysterious, and yet at the same time, understandable. We are indeed created out of love, and therefore we resonate most strongly to the energy and vibration of this Gift from God within us. Let yourselves express this marvelous gift in your very being. Breathe in the love. Exhale the love. Walk with the pace of love. View the world with love. Touch and caress others with love. Speak with love in your heart and mind and voice.

This is the most beautiful and positive expression of yourself that you can, indeed, make. And I would encourage all of you to realize that you have just begun to understand all the ways in which this beauty of love augments your being.

I come from a planet where we easily see the love flowing within our beings. We are touched by this in all our relationships. Help to develop this as a model among those of you on this planet. Be yourselves with love, in love, by love, through love, of love, and you will indeed be resonant with this divine energy, and you will best express the message of the Creator Son in his gift to this world

OLFANA: Unlike my sister, Althena, I myself have begun my journey on a most disturbed planet, and am entirely familiar on every level with the legacy of rebellion. I have struggled in my existences beyond the mortal life to rise above the tribulation, which was my experience in my mortal incarnation. And I triumphed over this challenge, this tribulation, and part of my process of continuing to move into higher and higher levels of awareness entails assisting my slightly younger siblings, yourselves, to also rise through the limitations which weigh so heavily upon you.

OLFANA, Half Moon Bay, CA 1997

In my capacities as a teacher and administrator in this Campaign of Redemption, it is necessary that I move swiftly and efficiently to many points on the globe. This is indeed a capacity I hold, and I am not bound by restrictions of gravity, the physics of light, nor any other physical limitations which bind time and space energy fields to set dynamics.

Being released from time and space limitations does not, in and of itself, release me from other laws that control the morontial energies of which I am composed. I remain most definitely bound by these energies, and this clearly distinguishes me from the freedom of dimensional movement and capacities of manifestation that are the prerogatives of the Universal Father, Eternal Son, and Infinite Spirit.

LUCIO, Arcadia, CA 7-23-2001

I want to express to you my brotherly affection towards you. I want to express many things. The unfortunate thing is that the way I express things is supernatural or morontial or spiritual. The way I express things, where I am from, the other person feels it immediately. The other person senses it. And the other person is able to express that same sensation back towards me, giving us both a mutual understanding of our affection.

It is so much simpler up here, for we are made aware of the other person's intentions immediately. A majority of the time those intentions are very good towards us. It is very unfortunate down here where you reside that you very frequently misinterpret each other's intentions. You always imagine the other person has bad intentions towards you. In fact many times they are good. This imagination sometimes leads to disastrous consequences. If only you were capable of knowing each other's intentions immediately through the spirit.

That is why it is essential that you communicate with one another, that you listen, for it is very important that this process of communication which you, which Urantia holds, continues, for it is essential to the survival of your planet.

Learning how to communicate with one another will, in fact, save your planet. Learn how to understand one another. But most important, learn how to understand yourselves, for in doing so you are better equipped at managing your own intentions. Perhaps the other person will read your intentions a lot better and will understand that you have good intention for that person, therefore alleviating any misinterpretation that might ensue.

Continue with your quiet time, but also continue with your communications. Those are both important to you. They shall both give you many fruits to come.

WILL, Tallahassee, Florida

I once lived a life on a planet somewhat similar to yours, although vastly more advanced in virtually every sense. Perhaps our weapons technology was not quite as advanced as yours. It is hard to say. Those were historic materials by the time I lived my life.

Our society was much more integrated. People tended to work in groups and teams. We did not have the raging cult of individualism which flourishes in your North American society, yet all of us faced uncertainty, for the life of the spirit does not completely intersect with the life of the animal and each of us on our wonderful world still faced the same definitive human experiences that you have all faced and will face.

Yes, I was a mortal on a world much like your own. I was born in the love of the Father in heaven and lived a short, pitched existence on a planet with much strife. I had a mate and a family, and my life was incalculably enriched by the love and attention showered upon me by the Universal Father. Many times I strayed from His teachings, like you.

I enjoyed the association of others and friendship and was a worker who helped my family economically just as many of you do. On my world all people work who are able, unless they are ill. In that case, the government made provision for them. Our government was very much kinder to its citizens, and we had reached the point where we didn't have any more wars. It had taken our world eons to reach that point.

Disease was almost nonexistent because so many of our tax dollars had gone to medical research. We had long since eliminated plagues with which your world still struggles.

We had learned through many years of hardship to focus our attention back onto the family. Gone were the days of materialism. We, too, had gone through difficult days before we came to the realization that the family structure is the most important unit necessary for survival of all mankind.

We weep when we see so many families falling apart on your world. If only humans would work harder, trying to preserve the most precious commodities that they will ever truly possess. So many let it slide by. Too many people become involved in other activities which take their energies away from the most valuable source of strength they will ever have, their family.

Beyond that, I found not much translates from my world to yours. Therefore I have been selected as a teacher for your group since I am incapable of imparting to you anything useful beyond teaching you of the love and respect and admiration that the Father has for His independent-minded will creatures in the far-flung regions of space.

How are these communications made possible?

JarEl, Arcadia, CA 7-23-2001

I would like to speak to you about the energies that the Father brings to you. The circuits are greatly improving, more and more being opened, more information coming through. The Father does this so that His children may have the opportunity to truly understand, so that they may come out of the world of confusion and into the world of light and life.

It is my hope to not open too many circuits at one time. For if you were to throw the switch and open all the circuits, a huge spiritual energy would come to the planet, however it would not be well received, for many are not prepared for this energy.

Therefore as the world increases spiritually, gradually, so do the circuits increase gradually. At this moment there are adequate circuits for the people of Urantia. There is adequate information coming through. The more the need, the more the circuits.

The Father's love is great. He loves you so much, beyond any words that I can speak to you tonight. In these circuits that he opens up for you, he wishes to express His love for you. These circuits are pretty much lines of communication, a way for him to communicate to you.

You all know very well how it is futile to speak to someone who is not listening. However the Father still continues to speak to you, even though at times you may not care to listen. He is still there speaking to you. It is your job to listen. It is your job to pay attention. It is your responsibility to comprehend the message coming through. Do not pretend to listen and do otherwise. If you truly desire to listen to God, pay attention. Silence yourself so he may speak to you.

You must learn how to do this well if you are to use these newly-opened circuits, for the circuits yet to be opened are far subtler in many ways. It takes practice to access them. Of course there are circuits that are more readily available to those who wish to use them.

ALANA, Jungle Teaching Mission Group, Nuevo Arenal, Costa Rica: 10-1-2000

We are on watch all the time. We have the continual, glorious, unbounded light and love of God showered upon us at all times in such a way that we do not need to wrestle with fear, doubt, and emotion.

OLFANA, Cincinnati, OH, 1-25-2000

It is much easier than you can imagine, for, we actually can broadcast here from far-flung worlds as if we were in the room. Mastery of universal broadcasts and circuitry will be a profound achievement which you're probably a great distance from, realizing that these initial openings of celestial contact through this very simple means of transmitting, channeling, receiving, and presenting information which is common on many worlds is a beginning here. But there is much, much, much to be done here. There is so much widespread suffering and torment. There are so many millions of you suffering from the ravages of hunger, disease, bombs, murder.

And it is true that the Melchizedeks are strong in purpose, strong in commitment. Their mission is going strongly in every way, commemorated by the universe broadcasts from Naperville on Machiventa's ascendancy here to employ Urantia as headquarters world in the reclamation of these many planets.

So Machiventa is here, but the advent of the Melchizedeks does not bring peace and good will on earth, just as the grand incarnation of Jesus did not, for many things must come to violent, and even a tumultuous head on Urantia for old grievances to be submerged in a new aura of love and brotherhood. And you are seeing profound conflict and change all about you that will challenge you to bring forth a higher realization of your civilization.

So these tumultuous times will bring forth great spiritual awakening, but not for some time, as the world works through these many problems - serious ethnic hatreds which have worsened through the centuries. These must come to a head and be healed, and they will.

In these momentous times you must be steadfast in love, compassion, and centeredness with God so that you can respond in your aura with the lessons that you can teach, the inspiration you can give, and the love which you can bring forth like a magnet to those suffering about you.

As your numbers increase by scores, by hundreds, by thousands, by millions, people will clamor for a better world and people will build a better world. And we will do this all together in glory to the Father and to bring forth the great return of Michael to this troubled world - to bring forth the final resurrection into the joyous era of light and life - a long journey, and we are all privileged to be part of it. Thank you so much.

Why Do They Refrain From Predictions?

WILL, Tallahassee, Florida, 12-6-1991

A system that is built upon free will choice is also a system that must withstand the inevitable appearance of conscious and unconscious errors. Particularly when you ask us questions that involve predictions of events on your planet, there is great opportunity for error to enter.

The rules bar the pre-emption of any creature's free will. Between the prediction and the predicted event, an infinite number of creature choices may change the result of the chain of events upon which we relied in making our statement.

"Chain of events" is an imprecise term to describe this process. Rather is the reality better described by the movement of an ocean current, like the Gulf Stream current in your immediate vicinity. Along its margins, top, bottom, and sides, there is continual interplay of waters, yet the whole is moving inexorably on to some further destination.

Because of the changeability of fact sets, questions calling for predictions are disfavored, and only aggravate the human tendency to doubt. It is only secondarily because we fear that you will rely on our predictions that we hesitate to predict. The inescapable margin of error, and its consequences on the human mind, is the primary justifications for our distaste for predictions.

What kind of energy connections are they hoping to make?

TOMAS, Southeast Idaho, Pocatello, Idaho 9-30-2000

This whole idea of interconnectedness, indeed, an understanding of circuitry, is essential to the appreciation of the living encircuitment that connects everything, from the molecular level and smaller, to the cosmic level and larger.

Relationship is in everything. There is a circuit between all rightful routes through the universe, through the galaxy, through various energy patterns and matter … connections between individuals and between levels of spiritual hierarchy. A part of this re-connecting is an awareness of the various and many kinds of circuitries that have been installed and are being re-activated which were cut off many years ago due to your unfortunate Caligastian betrayal.

We have worked long and hard for these times. We rejoice in these opportunities to make use of the spiritual flowering that is occurring in your world today. There is so much work to be done. There is so much effort required to lift the slothful animal mind up from its natural lazy legacy into the rigorous realms of thought and then beyond into spiritual reality.

The climb from the primordial ooze to the vast stellar rim of space is an advancing movement that is being nurtured on a constant basis, and now that your quarantine is ended, you are being re-drawn into those circuitries which will give you all of the benefits of being a part of the galaxy in which you live, a part of the Nebadon universe, and with it you are entitled to the ministrations of your many spirit helpers and counselors.

ALKON, Southeast Idaho, Poctatello, ID 5-4-01

We teachers are not here to forever be the focus of your guidance and contact. Our purpose is to facilitate your awareness of your divine Monitor within, to actually listen for the guidance and understanding that this Monitor gives.

We are not here to be an intercessor between you and God. We are here to share to our experience, our strength, our hope, our love, and to be your cheering section as you move forward on the road of progress.

I am not going to speak on a topic other than what I have just stated, that our job is to ultimately work ourselves out of a job. But don't worry. As long as you desire us, I anticipate you will all benefit from our continued association.

ALTHENA, Oakland, CA and East Bay Group, 1994

It may seem to you that there is much in this fabric of life that you are not comfortable with, but as you grow in the knowledge of God's presence, and the knowledge of your own destiny with Him, then you will come to understand the importance of these experiences in shaping who you are.

There is no experience that will go for naught. Where you have suffered pain and hardship, you will reap compassion and tolerance. Where you have endured misunderstanding from others, you will learn how to better reach out to your brothers and sisters, and you will, in the future, see how it is that these difficulties has led you into a greatness of being, which is your destiny.

Be not ashamed of the things that trouble you in this life, for in future ages you will treasure these same troubles as great jewels within your soul. Know that God's presence is within you; the creator of all that is and the source of all love resides within you and is continually reaching to your heart that you may know Him.

Allow yourself each day to grow in acceptance of God's presence and allow the aid of all who are here in this world of the spiritual realm to aid you in your growth and in your journey, for there are many beings with many talents and abilities and much love for you who would gladly be your guides.

Awaken to this great treasure, which is yours in this world and in this life and in this very moment. Allow this awakening to occur and the growth within you will continue apace without end, and as you continue your steps become lighter, your goals become clearer and your heart becomes a flowing river of God's love.

LYDIA, Woods Cross, UT 10-26-2002

I have many things that I am desirous to share with you and am able to provide you with great insight into your lives here on Urantia, for my experiences have been of a similar nature on my world.

I would like you to understand that the vessel through which we communicate with you does not matter. I understand there is resistance on the parts of some minds who can only accept things according to how they perceive they should be. Understand that the message is one and is ultimately from the Father, regardless of the person who speaks them, for we are all One and share the same love towards you that the Father shares and desires that you should progress smoothly upon your life's path.

Know that I sit here with great concern for you for I feel your struggles, your heartaches, your frustrations and pains in working through your life lessons and I am here to assist you should you so allow. Please feel free to seek me out and do not be put off that I am a woman, for there must be balance in all things.

The time is coming upon Urantia wherein there is a great rebalancing and restructuring upon the earth and the grids around her, which hold intact the mass consciousness and the overall belief patterns of the race.

LEGION, Nuevo Arenal, Costa Rica 10-8-2000

I wish to remind you, our strength is yours to draw upon, equally so we draw upon your strength to carry forth the message of love. It is not to be forgotten that I ask you to discipline your bodies, discipline your minds, and discipline the management and the expression of your emotions. I am not unaware that discipline is not in great favor among many of you, therefore I gladly sound like a broken record.

PAULO, Spokane, WA 3-31-2001

If you are having difficulty preparing your ego for effective presentation, get with your personal teacher whose great delight it is to help you work on those personality matters that have been short-changed, curtailed, retarded or aborted by the vicissitudes of life, that element of ego that has curled up in a self-defensive ball of wounds, frustrations, angers, self-pities, etc., that render it ineffectual.

If you will work with your spirit guide, it will help you reveal to yourself your personality such that you will be able to present it in accordance with your handle on ego.

TARKAS, Cincinnati, OH, 9-24-1995

This mission will be accomplished in close coordination with the inhabitants themselves, in the manner of Jesus, and they will do great wonders themselves as teachers in the flesh and the blood, through the mind and the spirit...and as we come to work with you we have learned much. We have learned new and deeper dimensions of what faith can be, as on every side, seemingly with human eyes, so many see no evidence of the Father.

You have awakened to see great evidence everywhere within, without, throughout every fiber of every being, throughout every material thing, throughout all the things seen, that can be felt, that can be known. And you are finding these wonderful nuggets to give you joys, to brighten your days.

This is truly a massive collaborative effort of which humans will triumph working with us, through us, with us, in the beautiful tapestry that you are making. You are golden threads ... threads themselves with little strength.

And so these threads must be interwoven, through your actions, through your service, your giving and sharing with your fellows, to weave this beautiful tapestry which will have the strength for each of you to walk upon as we bring this world to Light and Life. We are so pleased to be a part of this mission, to have had our eyes open to the true potential of humankind.

How Do They Know and See Us?

AARON, North Idaho, 7-22-2001

One of the characteristics of Michael's mission on this planet is the manner in which we have been counseled to interact with you in our contacts. It is of supreme importance that we are positive in our interactions with you, that we model behavior that is consistent with the highest realities and the manner that is characteristic of our Creator Son.

We are not here to admonish you and to tell you how you are making mistakes in your life and how you are flawed people. This is not the way. We are here to give you an awareness of your place in the cosmos, to lift you up beyond the mere mortal struggle to recognize the supreme goals of achievement that are possible. We want you to know how cared for and how valued you are to the universal plan for progression.

But most importantly we want you to know you are part of our family, that you have the right to this relationship and that our Father is ready to serve each person if you are willing to reach out and be served.

ANATOLIA, Cincinnati, OH 12-1996

As I look upon you here and I see the life that you live, it strikes me that it is obviously more difficult for you to live at the moment in such a way, and beyond the obvious disease and war and other things that plague your planet, just the physical struggle of your life, spending so much time to earn the living, spending so much time in the daily chores.

This is why the other teachers, and now I join them, encourage you to take some time each day with the Father. It is most important. It is what will help you remain in balance and not let you lose perspective, for if you are not careful, sometimes you become so absorbed in these daily problems that you lose sight of who you truly are and what your destiny truly is. It will not always be like this. You will not always struggle so. Yes, there will be problems; yes, there will be new challenges, but I refer more to your physical level of trouble.

You see, I and my friends no longer worry about what we will have to eat. We no longer have to work jobs to earn money. All these kinds of burdens or struggles have been removed. Now we spend our day learning. Mostly we are finding ways to share the love that we have so graciously been given, for you see, when you have been filled with that love of the Father, it is only natural that it overflows, and how do you want to share, how do you want to manifest that overflowing of that love? You want to find others to share it with.

When I look around at my brothers and sisters and my fellow teachers, I see them filled with great knowledge, great wisdom, and great love of Our Father. And so the opportunity for me to serve them seems somewhat rare or somewhat small, but I look at you, and I look at your world, and as you look around, is there anyone here, is there anyone that you meet, at any time, who does not need your help, who does need a greater dose of love and caring?

Everyone needs love. You cannot, in one second, in one moment, fill that person with love. You can show them that, you can give them a brief experience of love, but for them to truly find it, where must they find it? In the place that all humans look last – within themselves. For it is within themselves that they will find Our Father waiting for them. They will find this fragment of God who truly loves them, who is there to guide them.

TOMAS, Spokane, WA 9-22-2001

I have a frame of reference, for instance, which in many ways is just like yours. I can put myself on equal footing with you as an ascending son, a pilgrim of time en route to Paradise. And I can also acknowledge I have enhanced experience as a result of – if for nothing else – the fact of my survival after death into a morontia way of life, further enhanced by significant morontial training. However, I seek a relationship with you, and in seeking a relationship with you, I seek to have an understanding of your frame of reference.

In observing the evolutionary level you have attained, I am privy to a frame of reference that allows me to see your incompleteness and attempt to augment your education by what your needs may be at any given time based on a consensus of spirit factors.

In consultation with my peers in the Teacher Corps, I can, and we often do, observe our students in their growth experiences and commiserate and attempt to understand how and why they are thinking as they do. The insights we have garnered as a result of studying you, as a race of people, as relatively new spirit-born souls, engender heartfelt compassion for the obstacles you have to overcome and the deep-seated conditioning you've been subjected to.

Even so, we observe you as I once observed individuals in my mortal career of Cultural Anthropology. I therefore invite you to observe human behavior as a cultural anthropologist might observe it. In the context of the study of society-building, and separations of social aspects that will allow the personalities of the individual citizenry to flourish as it allows other sociological clusters of cultural propensities to also flourish.

The fact of your humanness and your materiality is what makes Human Associations 101 a very complicated and fascinating subject indeed. If and when you observe each other as merely fellow animals, it does not take long to see how it is that your behaviors regress and level out to the lowest common denominator.

As you regard each other as fellow spirit beings, you all over-reach and disappoint yourselves and each other and thus undermine aspects of spirituality which you could well afford to

46

embrace and inculcate as a part of your reality, but not at the expense of your humanness, for this is the well-balanced, well-unified mortal experience: son of God, son of man functioning usefully and happily in the flesh and in conscious awareness of the spirit.

WELMEK, Indianapolis, IN 9-21-2000

I see you as a seeker of truth and knowledge. I see you as my brother, as a traveler on the road to eternity, I see you as a beautiful spirit, a child of the Father who is just embarking on his eternal adventure and my heart goes out to you.

My soul rejoices that you are here with me this evening. I see you all as my dearly beloved brothers and sisters with whom I hope to have a most close and intimate relationship in the days to come. I see you as my friends, I see you as my equals, I see you as my students and I see you as my teachers. I am humbled to be here in your presence and very grateful that you have invited me here this evening.

Why Do They Volunteer?

ELYON, North Idaho 1-20-2002

I have had the privilege of ascending to the lessons and life presentations that I am able to absorb at this point in my career and progress seeking Paradise. I once lived as you live, and I have volunteered to be in this ministry surely to be of service but adjunctly to broaden and deepen my experience of that one single episode of the Paradise career, living a human life. I do so enrich this experience by drawing close to those like me, that being you.

This is the best I can do in the emulation of our Master Son who has the power to bestow himself in your very form and to walk your very world. I would, of course, accept such an assignment, but this is not the plan for our order of being, at least not as Michael presents it to us at this time.

Every parent enjoys the representation of themselves in the maturation of their children, the development of their skills and accomplishments. Likewise is this the case for myself as I observe you making those strides, taking those leaps, which prove that you are understanding and absorbing the meanings that are given in our contact meetings.

Not all worlds benefit from the securities of light and life. When human beings engage themselves in behavior patterns that foretaste a culture of light and life, it thrills all the celestial observers attending to that world. Nowhere is such beauty manifested in such contrast as it is upon Urantia.

What Is Their Expertise?

WELMEK, Indianapolis, IN 9-21-2000

You might say that I am adept at some of the intellectual processes of the human mind, understanding its mechanisms. I have many areas that interest me, but I feel that my best effort to serve is by helping you to come to a better understanding of human motivations and human mindal connections.

ALANA, Nuevo Arenal, Costa Rica

We do not achieve perfection in everything we do, because we are perfecting beings like your selves. We strive to communicate as best we can, cooperating with you, pleased with every gesture you make and every bell we ring.

Are They Learning Too?

DANIEL, Southeast Idaho, Pocatello, ID, 4-27-2001

Don't forget that we also are learners in this process, as we are seeing events occur and decisions being made in circumstances that we have never beheld, either in our mortal lives or in our subsequent morontial lives. There is much that amazes us from day to day in the harsh yet clear-cut choices that your environments require of you.

We, of course, knew the treatment that our Master Son received here was unprecedented in its cruelty; and yet as we watch you all struggle with the legacy of the Lucifer rebellion without the full support of the Material Son and Daughter, we marvel at how well you do.

Thank you for your gratitude to us for our involvement, but please understand that we are also grateful to all of you for the lessons we are being allowed to share, albeit as an observer rather than as the decision maker.

ANATOLIA, Cincinnati, OH 12-1996

I know of the love of the Father and I see the beauty of your destiny. What I need are opportunities in order to grow. You have abundant opportunities to serve, but you do not see your destiny.

You do not see the true reality of this universe yet; therefore you must rely on your faith every day, and I believe your text tells you that there is but one great struggle and that is the struggle of faith against doubt. We must keep that faith, and we must nourish it and we must encourage it with time with the Father each day.

So let us help each other. I will help you in any way that I can to grow in faith. You help me by telling me how I can serve you so that you can better serve your brothers and sisters. All the universe is, in a way, a vast team.

All of us on my side share responsibilities, share our efforts, share our knowledge, share our wisdom. There is no competition; why would there be competition? We want everyone to learn, to grow, to feel as much love as they can, as quickly as they can, for is this not the way your world will be changed most dramatically? And is this not what your world needs most to change?

BERTRAND, Orange County, CA, 1997 SpiritFest, San Luis Obispo, CA

You are not called to change the world individually. But singularly, you are called to give of yourself, to serve, the service of love, to those you meet.

We teachers envy you in your humanness. We envy you in your life on this planet. You have such exciting and wonderful opportunities. Yes. It is important to know and understand the condition you find yourself in. But it's also important to know and understand what you are doing to make a difference. Light and Life occurs one being at a time.

How Do You Know That Teacher Contact Is Real?

VERONICA, Cincinnati, OH, 9-28-2001

It is important to realize in working with mortals of the time and space realm that patience is much demanded. Very often the same lesson can be repeated many times, and yet it does not produce the near instantaneous realization, the light bulb suddenly coming on.

But when this instant of revelation happens, forever more that light within that suddenly enlightened is on, and you have found the switch to turn it on and make a great difference in the life of that person.

So do not despair in the teaching when those around you continue to stubbornly resist and find alternative ways that feed them with the false goals they have set for themselves which will ultimately prove somewhat vacuous.

When, in episodic fashion, the sudden burst of realization comes to a person, that is the joyous moment for the teacher as well and it opens the doorway to the continuing stream of knowledge and accelerated light.

And so it is a challenge to find the key that unlocks faith and love and service within each being, each personality, each of you is so unique. And this is true. It's so very amazing that this can be so.

The Teaching Mission

WILL, Tallahassee, Florida, 1-2-1994

When transmitters go wrong, the error generally falls into two categories. Category one is those errors spontaneously generated by the velocity of spirit progress being made during a transmission event. In other words, the transmitter gets swept away with euphoric feelings of spiritual progress. It is difficult for us to then exert any control whatever over the wayward human, other than break off communication. In this situation, the animal nature of the human has taken over.

Great surges of human emotion, whether surges of euphoria or fear, are a powerful impediment to this communication. But the velocity achieved by the transmitter often quickly carries the subject matter into areas that are not reliable or are clear error. There is little we can do to control this.

In this communication, like all communications between all humans, you are not relieved of your duty to exercise common sense and sagacity. You are not to set aside your normal capabilities of judgment merely because it is said that these words come from God. You well know that your God would never ask that.

Category two is a fear-based transmission – when the receiver transmitter is not fully capable of selfless transmission. When the receiver transmitter begins to personally identify with the veracity of the message, then an equal and similarly impassable impediment exists to the free and accurate transmission of our message.

The transmitters cannot and may not take credit for either the good or ill spawned by the words which we speak to you on occasions like this. It is an impossibility for the transmitters to be responsible in any sense. How could a transmitter be responsible for the effect of the message on an unknown hearer or reader? Transmitters are relieved of this responsibility. Personality identification with the message is a regrettable human fancy and does not exist in our experience of reality.

What Are Their Individual Wishes For Us?

KLARIXISKA, Pocatello, ID, 5-4-2001

We wish for you, as you become more and more aligned with God, to actually trust the words you hear in your mind that claim to be your indwelling Spirit. It is your destiny, when you reach the first circle, to actually commune in this manner.

It is the goal that Jesus reached before his baptism, which was a gradual process. His communion with God became more and more clear until he could say, "I speak the words my Father gives me. My teaching is not my own, it is my Father who acts and speaks through me".

This is the goal of mortal life. This is what was meant by "working ourselves out of a job". That job will be much more completely done by the proper personage, namely that pre-personal Spirit within you which will one day be welded, fused completely with you, so that you two will be one.

How is the Teaching Mission Unfolding in Our Lives?

JarEl, Arcadia, CA 7-9-2001

The progression of this planet, although amazingly slow at times, is gradually increasing. More mortals are being attuned to the spiritual family. More are awakening every day. More are beginning to realize their potential. As this continues, more circuits shall be open. As it is, there are many circuits now available for you.

The more people who begin to awaken to this new reality of higher consciousness the more strength there will be in the world, the strength of love, and the strength of God.

OLFANA, Cincinnati, OH, 1-25, 2000

I would suggest to each of you, and at the risk of sounding simplistic, that you must live in balance of mind, body, and spirit and it would be a helpful exercise perhaps to look at your day and see how it's divided – activities of the mind, activities of the body, activities of the sprit, and as you balance, you will be happier. You will give more, you will be in a balance that allows you to be graceful and beautiful in service of your brothers and sisters. And so, find this balance.

And secondly, I would suggest to you that you are not recognizing your own beauty, that you are not recognizing your own selves. I would suggest that each day you go to the mirror and look into this mirror and look into your eyes and know yourself at a deeper level.

There is nothing I could tell you or advise you beyond this, for it will be quite apparent when you conduct his exercise that you will find many questions and many answers. Each day that you do this you will encounter a somewhat different countenance and you will begin to see yourself and understand yourself in different ways. And so do this and know yourself.

Our comrade, Nero, has often admonished us to know our mind, for too many times humans seem to not trust their minds and feel that they would be playing tricks on themselves because they don't trust their mind to discern what is true, what contains beauty, what contains goodness. They do not trust themselves to use the great endowment of mind.

And so, you must know your mind and trust your mind. This is a mission. This is a quest. You must know yourselves, and when you know yourselves you will be able to apply yourselves fully in growing your soul and helping in the soul growth of others by being there for them with full knowledge of yourself and your mission, full knowledge of them and their missions and their selves, in empathy.

They are fellow humans. They are your brothers and sisters. Yes, they are your species. They are beautiful as you are, for they are God's creation as you are. It's a contract to love them. God created you in love. You are here to create in love. Create in love. You were given the power to create life - co-create life - do so in love. And love all creation and love your brothers and sisters as I love you."

The Stillness

From the beginning, the principal request of the teachers has been that we enter into a time of Stillness each day and develop a personal relationship with God. From here, all things spiritual flow. This relationship can supercede any and all of the evolutionary dogmas of mankind.

The Stillness can energize, clarify and open thresholds for a rich variety of celestial assistance, ours for opening up in faith, and for the asking. Here are some lessons on the Stillness.

JARED, Arcadia, CA

You are requested to seek stillness to allow us entry, to allow us to speak through you, to allow us to speak to you in ways you can hear. Not everyone will hear us; it is not important that all of you do. It is only important that you seek. Stilling the mind and reaching for us has been found to be very difficult for you. Your efforts are commended nonetheless. We suggest you continue to try and not be frustrated with your failures. They are not failures.

Perhaps your standards are too high. Your seeking is important. Sit quietly and seek for us, for our teachings; think of what you can do this day to help another. Remember also what you did yesterday to help another. Be proud of yourself for your efforts.

Stillness is also encouraged when you are going about your daily activities. You can find the stillness even momentarily in daily tasks. This is also very helpful. As you are out watering your garden, quiet your mind, do not concentrate on all the things you have done that day. Instead, enjoy the moment, enjoy the flowers and enjoy the trees and enjoy the grass.

In that way you are also seeking, you are quieting your mind from your daily anxieties. If possible, give yourself some time each day when you will not allow your anxieties to intrude. In that way you are finding the stillness, in that way you are searching.

Many times, also, you are not sure what you should do at the moment. Perhaps you can sit quietly and see what is most important. In that way you are also seeking because you will learn to listen within, and that will help with your ability to hear our guidance.

… The first step for each of you is to calm your mind in such a way that you can hear us. There are many, many ways of doing that. Seeking the stillness is our first recommendation. It may work for you to sit quietly and allow your daily cares to leave. Allow peace and tranquility to descend upon you and allow yourself to relax. In that way you are open to us. It helps many to pray quietly and give thankfulness for what is available to them. Others find stillness very difficult.

There are other ways of achieving that calm. Find something; find a quiet activity that is soothing and appealing. For some it may be watering a garden, for others washing dishes, for others lying quietly. Whatever you can do to allow your mind to rest and be calm.

The next step is to allow that calmness to become a part of your life. In your daily activities allow that calmness to be part of you.

As you achieve each bit of calmness you will be open to more and more and will find it easier to achieve. Those are very major steps and take a long time. Many things get in the way. Illnesses, anger, frustration, busyness all are disruptive of this process. Patience is required.

It may take a long time to achieve a calm within yourself. As you seek this calmness ask for God's assistance. It is available to all of you and will make it easier.

There are many in the world not able to embark on this search. Many who begin searching will go no further than achieving more calmness. It is, however, to be applauded whenever progress is made, whenever the search is begun, whenever calmness is increased. It will make tremendous strides in this world.

Others are more receptive and able to hear us. Many who seek calmness and achieve some measure of calmness are able to hear us without awareness. As they are truly searching, they will be guided and begin doing more of God's will. That much is a great step and much hoped for by teachers.

There are others who are more receptive and able to hear a voice consciously. They will get more guidance and be able to share with others.

I hope to be able to share God's love and God's teaching with many, many people. I, too, work one step at a time. I have gained her trust, and she in turn has shared with others. I feel your beginnings to trust me and then you will be able to share with others as well.

ABRAHAM, Salt Lake City, 7-2001

The stillness practice is a time of quiet openness that is specifically for you. It is for you and Father to keep your relationship fresh and growing. The Stillness practice is an antidote for stress and mental and emotional confusion.

The Stillness is not about uprooting mystical happenings that proves God is real, no. It is not about showing yourself to be a dedicated child of God. It is not about paying your dues to show you are worthy of "child of God" status.

The Stillness practice is balance for your mind and a cleansing of spiritual poisons. The Stillness is reconnecting to Father, that all-knowing Parent who sees you for who you really are and loves and encourages you without end. The Stillness or meditation is an equalizer between the divine and the human – a balancer of the ego, a line drawn between self-loathing and self-love.

TOMAS, in Butler, PA 11-18-1999

In order to attain this at-oneness that is effective, you need to become perfectly, perfectly, still. Physically quite stone still. Do not allow the Stillness to frighten you, and you must not think of it as being bored. It is en route to a rapturous adventure in the cosmic realms of your morontial existence.

After you have become perfectly still, you will feel certain physical realities, you will be aware that you feel grounded, that your limbs feel heavy. Your sense may be that you feel warmth. There are any number of side effects, physical side effects from Stillness, all of which are beneficial to your health, all levels of your health.

We have experimented here before wherein you feel that your mind is not willing to hold still and yet it is imperative that you allow your mind to learn Stillness, for as long as your mind is churning, you might as well be dropping water into the pool.

It has been said in your psychological realms that self-mastery involves mind over matter, and this is true, but that is not all there is. In order to attain full self-mastery and attain full-fledged Stillness, contact with divinity, person-to-person, you must allow for spirit over mind over matter.

And now you have, as you say, your ducks in a row. Your spirit can accommodate you if you give your spirit permission to take over your willful mind and assure your willful mind that it can resume its adventure as soon as you have had a moment with The Father.

This place of Stillness is vast. It is as large as the cosmos. As vast as space. It goes all the way to Paradise. I am not going to encourage you to go surfing on the cosmic Internet, no. I am going to encourage you to stay here, for it does no good for Urantia to have you playing in the fields of the Lord in Orion or Sagittarius. It serves more purpose for you to begin to understand how it is that you have a relationship with the First Source and Center that accompanies you night and day.

Your relationship with the First Source and Center is your key to understanding the purpose of your life and in finding supreme happiness in your life.

AARON and ABRAHAM, Pocatello, ID 10-26-01

AARON: The stillness is not designed to be merely a period of time where you try to feel God or feel closer to God. Many people think of stillness, or worship, or even prayer time in terms of how they can feel a deeper presence of God. Success is perceived by a large part of the human population as depending on your feelings. Rather, with the stillness, this is an exercise to lift your mind into channels of awareness beyond simply the presence, but rather allowing an actual transfer to take place.

... A wandering mind is not necessarily a sign of failure. It is like exercise. When you do pushups you can't do twenty pushups the first time you try. Stillness is not really an effort to stop thought, to quit thinking. Some types of meditation do this, yes. But what we have generally guided you toward is an avenue where you are trying to place your thought in certain streams, instead of chastising yourself because your mind wanders. Simply, redirect and go back to the center.

Abraham referred to how humans often seek immediate satisfaction and results. With the stillness, it is truly an endurance test, allowing yourself to wander with your thoughts, knowing that you can redirect, that you can continue on, that you can spend five minutes, ten minutes, twenty, eventually in unbroken communion. But this takes real practice.

You are not expected to be an expert at stillness, but one who is simply trying. So, rather than recognize your thoughts wandering and then choosing a different activity, you may simply want to apply yourself, give yourself more time to redirect. What you will find is that channeling your energy back, your thoughts back towards your center, the Spirit within you, will bring about a productivity in time.

You may not even be consciously aware of the assurance and the will power, the strengthening of your resolve toward higher things, better avenues of thought, success in overcoming many areas of life that you would like to change. Much of what is accomplished in the stillness practice is unconscious. What you feel is a mixture of things. Part of that may be Spirit contact. Many of the emotions and sensations you feel are actually human electrochemical responses.

ABRAHAM: agree fully with Aaron's outline and I would apply my words of fortitude and patience to you specifically with this concern. Indeed, the main purpose of stillness is not thought-stopping. That is a certain kind of meditation. The main purpose of stillness is a re-centering of your being away from the clamor of the ego, the demand of your culture and your conditioning, a re-centering to go within to that Center which contains all of God.

So, I agree, do not be distressed that your mind wanders, but exercise your will to bring it back to center on the love and presence of your Divine Indweller. Be patient with yourself, my eager friend. Draw upon your inner strength...

It is an illusion that someone else's experience is better than yours, my dear. Each person's experience is unique and truly difficult if not impossible of comparison. What you experience when you hear of other's experiences is a very second hand process. At the same time that it is true that each has unique experience, it is also true that each has the same Divine Indweller.

The reason each one's experiences are different is the interaction with personality. It is commendable to aspire to higher levels of spiritual growth. But it is sometimes deceptive to be seduced by mysticism, by the mysterious, by the different, so as to make one discontented.

AhmaNiden, a Melchizedek, Urantia conference, Estes Park, CO, July, 2002

You each have within you a Divine Adjuster, He who spends all his hours loving you, supporting you, guiding you, teaching you, would you but be still and listen. Do you listen? Do you "still" your minds each day to just listen?

There are those who believe that "seeking the stillness" means I must "sit," every day, in "this" easy chair, and close my eyes and be still. And for many, this works.

Are there any here, for whom this does not work? When this does not serve you, due to time constraints or the chaos within your own minds, let me give you, perhaps, a different direction, a different idea that you might take on within the construct of your own day: Do you speak to the Father within your own minds throughout your day? What do you tell Him? Do you share with Him the delights that fill your lives? The joys that you behold? The inspiration that you may gain through a movie, a book, or simply in looking on one of His sunsets, or within the eyes of one of His children?

Those are, in essence, "mini-stillnesses," although perhaps, they are not so still. You play a more interactive role in that kind of stillness, in that kind of worship.

But during those times, let us say that you are sitting at the riverside and listening to the tumbling water, watching the birds, the butterflies, looking at the flowers; and it's sunset, and as you watch, the sky becomes a beautiful panoramic of color-purples, mauve, orange, yellow, blue, green even sometimes-and you are uplifted by the sound and the sights that He's given you. Surely, an inspiring sight!

Most, if not all of you, have spent time with Him like this, and are uplifted and inspired by the peace and the beauty that you behold. Do you share your feeling with Him then?

AARON on LightLine, 9-3-2004

I look forward to continued relationship with you in our common awareness of a common plan of ascension where, as brothers and sisters, we are seeking the same goal, which is manifestation of personality to its highest potential in the recognition of its embrace with divinity. The levels of your willingness to pursue this personality realization are tied up in your willingness to spend time in contact with your Father.

This contact happens by:
1. Stillness – quiet meditation – reflective contemplation – worshipful problem solving, or by …
2: Your outward reach toward manifesting a desire to do good to other personalities - service. We encourage you to recognize that these two methods of contact with the Divine are both critical to pursue for a balanced, increasing comprehension of divinity, and your own potential in light of that realization.

Stillness without service is, and would be, gravitating you into circular patterns of behavior, whereas service without stillness would be like grasping at straws, spokes of energy applied that can cause diffusion of being and exhaustion. But stillness, if approached with a healthy realization of its utility, which is the refreshment of your soul in the divine embrace, will naturally gravitate you toward service opportunities in your lives.

The service you undergo can be at various levels. When you hear someone talking to you about bold manifestations, proclamations of God as a necessity, these are the more boisterous realms of service. When you hear someone talking to you of offering small kindnesses as you pass by, these are the less noticeable realms of service.

And yet, neither is recommended by us as the way you should go, because your service, your personal service, should be the result of your communion with the Divine, such that you will know what is right for you to do and it will seem more natural. And as you pursue, you will find fruit in your efforts.

The Transmitting/Receiving Process

When the supernal teachers arrived with the Melchizedek curriculum, many humans were already familiar with spiritual channeling. Some accept the process as a valuable conduit to the spirit world; others disdain it. Such conflicts seem to permeate many aspects of human life. Humans establish and defend foundational beliefs in the face of expanding truths and greater realities.

Some observers consider the transmitting-receiving process utilized by the Teaching Mission celestials as just another form of channeling, in a conscious-state in contrast with the trance process which leaves the receiving vessel as a non-participant. In fact, the teachers say it is an entirely new process that allows the receiving and transmitting personality to maintain his free will of participating, and speaking the words by choice. It opens a co-creative environment whereby humans actually work together with the celestials, and with each person involved encouraged to make teacher contact themselves, not just some special designated person.

Being in a relaxed and spiritual mindset allows a transmitter to remain a sharing member of the group, rather than being unconscious in a deeper mind state. He is signally encouraged to, yes, "try this at home," in your own quiet time with the Universal Father.

Here are some transmissions on this new T/R process:

JarEl in Arcadia, CA, 7-24-1994

I wish to ease the thought processes concerning this mission and the phenomena thereof, the communication with higher spiritual beings. We, the teachers of this mission, come from various ascending spheres and we have volunteered to come here to Urantia and assist in the upliftment of all mankind. We make this assistance through this setting of coming together with individuals of like mind, seeking spiritual development, seeking higher achievement of your spiritual quotients. It is in this setting that we are able to transmit the lessons, which is the desire of the Melchizedek in obedience to the desires of Christ Michael, for you the mortals of Urantia.

This is done through individuals who have attuned to this ability to receive our transmissions. This is the definition of the term, Transmitter/Receivers. These individuals are not, as you would say 'channelers'. We wish to make this distinction clear. We wish to make a separation of the terms clear to your minds and understanding. Throughout the mission, this erroneous idea that this is 'channeling' has surfaced. These bright souls who have developed the ability to receive our messages are not channelers and they should not be referred to as such.

EL TANERE, York, PA, 3-2-1994

The difference in the reception of those receiving messages in the current time is because of the lifting of the quarantine and the circuits being open. Before that time, the messages to be received from the celestial realm, the individual had to go into a trance-like state. These individuals like Edgar Cayce have served a great purpose in the healing applications for many mortals.

I can only say that the difference is that it is easy now to receive. Everyone can receive from the celestial realm because the circuits are open. All they need to do it turn up their volumes. It is that simple.

DANIEL, Southeast Idaho, 3-30-2001

Transmitting/Receiving (T/R) has been a topic which ebbs and flows in interest and concern. Because every one of us is different, morontial and mortal, and no two interactions between celestials and mortals are identical. The TR'ing process involves for some the literal hearing of words, individually or by phrases, which they repeat. Some have seen words, which they read. Most are given concepts presented as pictures and thoughts, and the individual T/R's mind is the blending and mixing place where the meeting of the celestial communication uses the instrumentation of the mortal's neurological circuitry and mindal thought patterns.

Always remember that the mind and the brain are not the same. The mind uses the brain as an organ; but the mind is far greater than even this most marvelous instrument.

ABRAHAM in Utah, 12-30-1996

Student: *Abraham, you are choosing to speak through somebody right now. Is that your preference or do you have other ways to communicate with people directly or indirectly?*

I am choosing this method with Ellanor because she allows it. If she did not I would attempt to perhaps use different methods, such as speaking to Ellanor through her friends, her family, perhaps through meditation where messages are felt rather than heard.

To speak through another is not uncommon. We have perfected this method over time. And I would agree that everyone here this evening is quite capable of using this particular method. Whether there is willingness is another question. But I say those mortals who claim to have exclusive rights on this particular method of communication are not being truthful. All are capable and indeed welcome to experience this technique. It is a matter of willingness and trust and allowance on the part of the receiving mortal.

As time goes on, this method of communication will appear to be quite natural and not at all the phenomenon some proclaim it to be. Still, as this world progresses further into Light and Life this particular method of transmitting-receiving will be outdated and unnecessary to reach the masses, for the natural abilities of those who seek to live within the will of Father will easily have all needed information at hand through the universal circuits and the use of the cosmic mind.

On 1-20-1997:

This particular method of transmitting/receiving requires you each to filter all messages through your intellect, as well as your inner self, which is your soul. Our Father would not expect you to receive these teachings any other way.

On 2-3-1997:

I am a teacher. I work to assist this planet move towards a new and better age. My choice in methods of communications is transmitting/receiving. I do so with permission of the mortal receiver. I am not in control in any way. I do not possess the minds of my mortal contacts, no. I give to those that would receive me.

You each are not about to allow any past fallacies to corrupt truth, no. You each assist in these communications, but I say that it is with permission that this mortal subject allows this communication. I do not take from her. I do not add to her. There is no loss of identity.

Do you see that in order to give these communications I must be allowed or invited. Mortal subjects are not being submissive to me, no. Through the use of spiritual insight and intellect I am received. Do you see that Father also does not invade your life, possess your mind, attempt to reform a bad seed into a beautiful flower, no.

There must be an allowance or invitation to Father. If these petitions are not genuine, Father is still kept at a distance. You can say, "It is my will that Father's will be done," and yet cling to fears of loss.

ALANA, Nuevo Arenal, Costa Rica, 2-5-2001

It is in the Stillness that these voices, my voice, the wisdom and experience of the teachers with whom I participate in bringing God's love and words of light to your planet ... it is in the Stillness our voices may be recognized by you, and many others willing to listen. Still, it is no shame that some more readily recognize the separate and distinct vibration that guides the manifestation of our tongue, our language.

It is, therefore, a blessing that some should be so capable, and others should thereby develop their powers of listening. It is, you see, quite valuable to learn another tongue by listening. In the listening you learn how to transmit what is heard to others by your speaking. Your speaking may take its idiosyncratic expression.

This is quite necessary upon your planet, although the message is always the same, to love one another as you are loved, by your teachers, by Michael, Nebadonia, Father, Mother. God's spirit of love is yours. You are such a multiplicity of life forms that it is well and good that you should have a multiplicity of methods of communication of this love.

On 3-31-1997:

In this learning process of transmitting/receiving there are many things I must do to maintain your well-being of mind. I am forbidden to push you into anything you are not equipped to handle. I am unable to interfere with your current belief system and must work within that.

My information is that you are proceeding naturally and various individuals will receive our messages differently. Thoughts that you are receiving need to be filtered through your intelligence to refrain from any imbalance. Positive thoughts you are receiving that assist you in your daily spiritual learning are quite possibly from your Indwelling Father Fragment, the Spirit of Truth, the Mother Spirit or a teacher. The names are not meaning so much as what the message is saying.

On 9-4-2000:

What I wish to say to you is this: Your teacher is with you at all times. He is ready to speak to you when you are ready to have him help you tell your story. You might wish to spend some time with a blank screen, or a blank sheet of paper. This might be a profitable way for you to begin to communicate with him.

HAM in Nashville, TN 3-22-2001

The transmissions are always some mixture of the word, thought, image transmitted and the receptor's interpretation of it. The beauty of this is profound, in that every person involved must actively and continually use their own discernment of truth for each transmission.

As I have said many times, all things with human input contain some measure of human error. This includes even such icons as the Bible and *The Urantia Book*. Therefore, rely on the Spirit of Truth, which guides you yourself, not on the discernment of another being. Be at peace for you do know truth. Dwell within it, follow it, and you will be fine.

OLFANA in Half Moon Bay, California, 1997

I appreciate your attempt to question the accuracy and validity of the transmission done by this T/R. It is a most important point that you each view these transmissions as full of potentials for truth inspiration in your hearts and minds, and yet you humbly recognize their potential to also contain confusion or inaccuracies because of the human limitations of those who sincerely attempt to transmit our words.

Your responsibility in this process is to explore our teachings so as to discover what of our words can inspire your heart in faith, sharpen your understanding of your sonship with the Father, increase your insight into the majesty of God's power manifesting in your lives, solicit your soul to further develop in the light of truth, beauty, and goodness, and develop attunement with the Master as your guide, protector, and model of inspiration, in your path back to the Father.

I hope you will continue to grant us an opportunity to be a component of your spiritual studies, and that this one point of contention that you had with my commentary will not set you on a course which avoids further contact with Teaching Mission material.

The Urantia Book Relationship

Since the teachers extol *The Urantia Book* as the most reliable and comprehensive spiritual revelation on the planet, and have chosen the Revelation's study groups as a seedbed for their mission, there have naturally been many questions over the years concerning the relationship between text and teachers. Here are some lessons.

HAM, Nashville, TN 11-05-2000

Your planet is undergoing a massive effort at spiritual uplift. *The Urantia Book* was a forerunner to the more personal teachings that you have been receiving over the last quarter century. Yes, these are both parts of the same plan, of course. As always seems to happen with immature human beings, when someone receives part of the truth, one tends to exaggerate this part and to make it seem to be the whole.

The Urantia Book was never meant to be an orphan. Truth is always living; it cannot be crystallized into a single book. *The Urantia Book* contains many advanced truths that have helped to pave the way for a more comprehensive teaching effort, but it is not the final truth or the final revelation for this time period. All of this effort is to prepare your world to eventually receive another Son.

NEBADONIA, Marin County, CA 3-16-2009

There is so much to God's creation, my son, that *The Urantia Book* is truly only the skimpiest of outlines of what actually exists within cosmic reality. The purpose of the Teaching Mission is to keep bringing out more and more facets of both ours and God's creation, and you yourselves.

RAYSON, Northern Colorado, 12-28-2003

Has there ever been a situation on another planet where the mortals were given a revelatory text like the Urantia Book?

Yes. We have seen this occur on many planets; they are not as useful or used as is *The Urantia Book* is being used on your planet, particularly on those planets that receive Magisterial Sons, Avonals, Teacher Sons. Planets that are developing according to the regular, usual plan of planetary development have these on hand as historical footnotes, so to speak, for the spiritual evolution of their planet.

In most instances, on these planets, they have been literate, they have been recording their histories for thousands of years and there are existent records, except in those cases where they were accidentally destroyed. On those planets, which were in darkness during the quarantine, yes, these revelations are available; the mortals were cut off from the broadcasts, from the shared awareness of Midwayers being among them, of the commonality, the flow, the thread of history of their planet was lost to mortal consciousness, and so a revelatory function was established. Each situation is unique unto each planet.

TARKAS in Half Moon Bay, CA

Question: In what ways would the Teaching Mission be considered different or dissimilar from the *Urantia Book*—the distribution, dissemination of the *Urantia Book* in terms of purpose or whatever?

Well, first of all, *The Urantia Book* is an expression of conceptual truth, and yet it is bound within the pages and restrictions of the book, and the English language, or other languages into which it has been translated. This Teaching Mission is one personality to another, communicating a desire to extend a hand and help you on your path to God.

You are a fellow soul, beloved of the Father, as I am. I wish to show you the path I have already traveled and found most appealing. If you will come with me, we will walk together on this path, and I will point out to you the beauties I have already discovered. And, perhaps, as we walk together, we will both discover new beauty ourselves—that is the joy of companionship, this personality-to-personality capacity to experience kinship, a sense of brotherhood, a sense of care and camaraderie. We can blend our energies, our experience, our hopes. We can walk on this path and share the joy of savoring its beauty together!

Is it not true that, at times, when you are alone in a beautiful landscape, you certainly enjoy its beauty, but at moments you say, "Oh, if only my children were here, now. Oh, if only my marriage partner could see this, also." There is always this longing in the human heart to share beauty. This is a capacity placed in us by God. And all of us who labor in the Teaching Mission as your guides wish this very moment of sharing and kinship—those truths we have come to discover, we would like to see light up your eyes also!

ABRAHAM, 7-3-2002, Urantia Book Conference, Estes Park, CO (T/R: Rebecca)

I am understanding that to many this process of communication seems strange and not aligning with your textbook. I would reiterate that this time in the history of your world you are at a crucial crossroads of change.

Lo these many years, we have been making efforts toward swaying the mass-mind-set toward practical spirituality. Concepts are born every day and without education and putting these concepts into practical use they will die. That is certainly acceptable but there is a danger in losing those practical realities that either drives a world's people toward animalistic tendencies or mystical non-reality. It is our hope in this Correcting Time to bring a balance of logical spiritual action.

The Teaching Mission brings your textbook to life. You can study all you want but putting these concepts into practical living takes a great deal of effort. We are here to help move you

The Teaching Mission

forward to the actual living of the principles of the *Urantia Book*. The book can seem a bit technical or mechanistic. We are hoping to bring a balance to this book of truth by adding love, and making God, the Father, more reachable or perhaps useable.

As you have seen in religious history there is imbalance where there seems to be a need for an individual to stand above the rest, a need for certain individuals to appear to be more righteous or holy. The Correcting Time—Teaching Mission brings a blended balance of Christ-like humility and a secure consciousness of universal well-being.

The Master did all that was divinely and humanly possible to defer any self-glory. His mission was straightforward, looking toward the Father and His will. How did Jesus of Nazareth, maintain a wonderfully balanced ministry where His eye was single to the glory of God? How was the Master so perfected in self-forgetfulness? Why was any self-elevation so distasteful to Him?

Our Master simply knew the Father's love. He had all He needed, in this there was no desire to call attention to Himself to gain the love and respect of His fellows. There was no joy for Him in self-glory. His complete joy was found solely in the Father's love. He was very secure, which unfortunately, many in the mortal experience are lacking.

Of course, Jesus realized His divinity early on, and certainly this was a great asset. It is understood that you, on a strife-torn world, would experience a personal and collective insecurity. It is our goal in this Correcting Time to bring back what has been lost, to correct what has been wrong, to bring light where there has been darkness.

Citizens on worlds settled in Light and Life have not the knowledge of this insecurity, for they have been educated from the day they were brought into existence that they are valued and loved, no matter what. They seek not to step upon their fellows' backs to rise above and be seen as superior, all for the gratification of the ego. They work not against each other. The concepts of the various social classes mean nothing to them. The citizens are all indeed parts working for the good of the whole. What is good for one is good for all. What affects one, affects all. Indeed these Light and Life residents are wholly secure in their citizenship, in their faith as a son or daughter of God.

In the Teaching Mission, we strive to bring back that lost security—to make every individual feel valued and loved and a part of the universe. Not one is closer to God than another. In God's eyes, He loves each child as if it were His only child. Our Mission is to unify, to equal the imbalances that tend to come with the mortal ego. I am saying we are here to assist, not to shame or guilt you into spiritual submission. Our goal is to bring personal spiritual security. Not one stands above any one of you.

Spiritual knowledge does not make one individual any more valued than another. To have that spiritual security brings new confidence to be in the world with an eye single to the glory of God. There is not any spiritual practice really that can make you have more faith. There are many rituals mortals perform hoping to invoke Gods presence. I am saying, God's

64

presence is there already—no matter what—no more, no less. It matters not the time or mind-set. He is always there. It is your willingness to allow what you think you want and need to dissolve that will bring you more spiritual security, more cosmic connection.

Question about the possible establishment of a Urantia Book-*based church.*

ABRAHAM: Indeed, this is controversial. You can see for yourselves that still the mind of man fights to push his own agenda. This is difficult. A spiritual worship community would be productive if based on the teachings of the *Urantia Book*, and perhaps other things that lead toward a practical practice of spirituality, not toward mystical, but toward putting practical spirituality into everyday living.

An organized church would be helpful if it brought man closer to God. If an organized church excludes certain individuals, does that bring man closer to God? If a church brings further insecurity to individuals, is that true work for the Father? No. A church that would be successful gives full sovereignty to Father. The church allows Father to organize, to bring healing, to bring balance to His children's lives, to make His child feel loved, welcomed and an important part of the whole. I can say no more.

Voices of the Celestial Artisans

(EDITOR'S NOTE: For most of these Teaching Mission years, I've been among those with conscious connection to the Celestial Artisans colony now working on the planet as part of the Correcting Time. Here are their reasons for being here.)

Question from Spring 1995, prior to a conference: I know that all of you artisans will be with us in Arkansas. I look forward to sharing your presence. What would you have us tell our brothers and sisters at the conference?

BAKIM: *Love is art. And art is love. Sharing and giving art, created from the heart, is so very, very smart. It's quite a start . . . .To sharing love with each and everyone as well. Your finest art will eventually become expressions of love, in all its manifestations and nuances. Radiating love all around you each day is already artful expression. Learn to do it well and you will be blessed with wells of creative inspiration.*

Can art truly be practiced even in mundane chores?

BAKIM: *The shiny silver fittings of the plumber can be as beautiful as the clean printed pages of a writer, or the smiling face of a bountiful child that you did raise in love. Practice artful ways to walk and speak and parent and share and give and converse. In the way you are, so you are. Learn to begin balancing mind-body-spirit. If you can do it at your level, you have a great head start.*

So is art therapeutic? Does it have healing properties?

BAKIM: *Catharsis of pain leads to fulfillment of spirit. Express your hurts in art and it faces back at you the materiality of your frustration. And material things hardly matter in the context of your full experience-to-be. Contain and imprison your pain in the art; many do it now. And, in time, with these individual and collective catharses, you will begin to re-fill your inner vessels of emotion and creativity with greater inspirations that lead you to truth, beauty and goodness. Then, your art will become, evolutionary speaking, manifestations of spirit-infused energy that, in turn, bring forth even more and greater energy vibrations from those who appreciate it.*

Art, even that which you now create, is influential in generating higher levels of spiritual energy upon your sphere, leading to an overall raising of humankind's level of consciousness. Loving energy given is loving energy received. It is the reciprocal circle of truth that energizes the Father's universes. Give to receive. Receive more to give more to receive more.

Of course, positive energy heals, negative energy sickens. Empty your hearts of spirit poisons, reduce them to a prism, disdain it, and fill again your hearts with hope, not despair, faith, not cynicism, love, not indifference, and you will see a positive difference in your art, in your daily lives, in your eternal destiny. A healthier mind means a healthier body and spirit. When you fill your days with the creation of art, even including the creativity with which you lead your every moment, you will have found a path to true spiritual awakening.

And so what would you recommend to the artists at the Arkansas conference?

BAKIM: *First, know that you __are__ artists. Each has unique creative abilities. All activities on Urantia can be approached as an artist. Some use their bodies artistically. Some use their minds. The spirit often infuses both. Whether the ballet or basketball or mathematics or horticulture, there are so many ways to create, and when creative expressions are imbued with the spiritual truths you know, then your art takes on higher, more universal meanings.*

Live in the moment of love. Your art will reflect this. … Artisans, one or more, have been assigned to each of you. You will help us express the truth, beauty and goodness that your teachers strive to represent. Work with us as you will. In the quiet times, in your mind. Ask and receive.

Some will heal themselves first, and we will help. Others are now ready to show the light of love in their art. Most will heal as they give their art, bring in love as they bring forth love. You are each and all on higher spiritual ground than most and able to connect with creative channels never before experienced on Urantia.

We look forward to inspiring your creativity as you reach Godward. We are pleased to be way stations to help with your creative expression. Your celestial artisans are much in cohesion with your teachers in prescribing and instructing for a closer relationship with God.

From our perspective, we engage in experiential meditation and spiritual upreach through which you tap into creative patterns that are inspired by celestial truths. Your strongest potentials for creativity are inspired to greater effort, and through them we seek to guide your creative hand to higher purpose.

In your usage of physical materials, colors, senses and ideas, each of you creates uniquely, and all are blessed with the creative gift for it is expressed in many ways. All mortal tasks can be done with creativity, inspiration and guidance, and indeed always have been. Truly all can rise to the level of what we refer to as art. This ability will be enhanced by your enhanced awareness of the passing world day by day, moment by moment, vision by vision, feeling by feeling.

Live in the moment. Each moment can be rich in the eyes and minds and hands of the poet. We urge you to ask for a fine and discerning sense of awareness which will give inspiration to your creative thoughts and, in turn, inspire the act itself. Live your very lives as an artistic expression. It will require practice, for nothing of lasting value is gained without effort.

This is done in many ways. Use your voices, your sense of melodies and harmonies, the dramatizations of a good story, the expressiveness of a single scene, captured, immortalized and distilled to the essence of the perception of truth that it offers. All of your senses, your imaginations and wisdom from experience can be used in creating artistic expressions, impressions for your fellows, and satisfying cathartic experience that will serve to expunge, or soak up, spirit poisons that daily threaten to retard your search for truth, beauty and goodness.

How can one fill oneself with the troubling poisons of self-doubt and fear, and sit in languor in the presence of concerted and inspired creative thought? Your creativity is highly encouraged. To fulfill one's mortal purpose, one must tap into the creative talents which have been bestowed. The wise will use those talents in the furtherance of divine truths, not bury them in fear that somehow they will be taken away.

Exercises which we commonly use are visualizations, which help our students picture within that which they would express, and storytelling, in which we tweak your minds to seek and find deeper truths and additional perspectives which aid in your search for spiritual realities.

Our teaching is individualized as are the lessons of your other teachers. We seek not to change the world; we seek to change you, and enhance the creative spark with which the Father has imbued us all.

The Urantia Book on Celestial Teachers
Courtesy of Jim McCallon, Jr.

In 1995, a Teaching Mission participant in California, offered an entertaining analysis of spiritual contact on e-mail with quotes from the Urantia papers. Jim McCallon, a gifted poet, writes in his lower case style.

hello folks -

what exactly does the *Urantia Book* have to say on the subject of spirits making contact with us lowly humans?...... after the posts of the past several weeks we all know what people on these lists have to say about it - but what does the book which brought us all together here have to say?.....i've pulled a few quotes - and i'd stress the word few - there are many more -

Page-1190 But regardless of such apparent independence, long-range observation unquestionably discloses that they function in the human mind in perfect synchrony and co-ordination with all other spirit ministries, including adjutant mind-spirits, Holy Spirit, Spirit of Truth, and other influences.

this passage is talking about adjusters in the human mind . . . . .my question is what "other influences". . . . . . ?. . . . .i've often seen people write on these lists words to the effect "i have my adjuster and the spirit of truth and i don't need anything else". . . . . . well, obviously you do need more - because according to the ub - more spiritual influences are functioning in and around you. . . . . . consider the following. . . ..

Page-1191: *We are cognizant of many spirit phenomena in the far-flung universe which we are at a loss fully to understand. We are not yet masters of all that is transpiring about us; and I believe that much of this inscrutable work is wrought by the Gravity Messengers and certain types of Mystery Monitors. I do not believe that Adjusters are devoted solely to the remaking of mortal minds. I am persuaded that the Personalized Monitors and other orders of unrevealed pre-personal spirits are representative of the Universal Father's direct and unexplained contact with the creatures of the realms.*

"other orders of unrevealed pre-personal spirits". . . . . . ok. . . .and then we have. . .
.

Page-1244: *One of the most important things a destiny guardian does for her mortal subject is to effect a personal co-ordination of the numerous impersonal spirit influences which indwell, surround, and impinge upon the mind and soul of the evolving material creature.*

what numerous impersonal spirit influences?. . . . . .

Page-64: *The great God makes direct contact with mortal man and gives a part of his infinite and eternal and incomprehensible self to live and dwell within him. God has embarked upon the eternal adventure with man. If you yield to the leadings of the spiritual forces in you and around you, you cannot fail to attain the high destiny established by a loving God as the universe goal of his ascendant creatures from the evolutionary worlds of space.*

spirit forces IN you and AROUND you?. . . . .is the spirit of truth in you?. . . .or around you?. . . ..

Page-64: *It is because of this God fragment that indwells you that you can hope, as you progress in harmonizing with the Adjuster's spiritual leadings, more fully to discern the presence and transforming power of those other spiritual influences that surround you and impinge upon you but do not function as an integral part of you* as we harmonize with the Adjuster, we can more fully discern what?. . . . . the presence and transforming power of THOSE OTHER SPIRITUAL INFLUENCES . . . .

Page-421: *When once seraphim are commissioned, they may range all Nebadon, even Orvonton, on assignment. Their work in the universe is without bounds and limitations; they are closely associated with the material creatures of the worlds and are ever in the service of the lower orders of spiritual personalities, making contact between these beings of the spirit world and the mortals of the material realms.*

hmmm - i wonder if the "lower orders of spiritual personalities" are those same spirits that the other passage says … the coordinating of their influence is one of the most important things our guardian angel does for us?. . . . . .

Page-639: *No matter on what level of universe activities you may encounter spiritual phenomena or contact with spirit beings, you may know that they are all derived from the God who is spirit by the ministry of the Spirit Son and the Infinite Mind Spirit.*

. . . . . . .all derived from the God who is spirit. . . . . . .

there are many many other passages in the *Urantia Book* which speak about spirits impinging, influencing, contacting, and some other neat ways of saying the same thing - it is not impossible, improbable, highly unlikely, demonic, unheard of, and most importantly perhaps around here - OUTSIDE OF THE TEACHINGS OF *THE URANTIA BOOK* for a person to have contact with a spiritual being which is not an adjuster, the spirit of truth, the holy spirit, or their guardian seraphim -

just thought i'd pass that along -

take care all - and live to give – jim mccallon

It was natural from the beginning for Teaching Mission believers to seek verifications of this wondrous new path in the Urantia papers. Quotes from the book were put together in collections for distribution, and they collectively reveal that the entire universe of universes is a school. There are many universities and schools in the cosmos as there are many on the planet. All of the time and space worlds of mortal personalities are like classrooms and experiential laboratories of material experience. Planets are evolving gardens of life and we are evolving life on these spheres.

From the book's section on Celestial Overseers to the final page that urges us to develop greater spirit consciousness, the impressive tome that ardent readers consider to be the Fifth Epochal Revelation to humankind is replete with evidence that celestial teachers and education systems abound for mortals. I read within its pages of a continuing Fifth Epochal Revelation and a time of quickening events on the planet that will require us to be strongly anchored in spiritual realities – not thought-restrictive dogma. I see that the advent of celestial teachers continues the revelation they so appreciate and will help bring those printed pages into life itself, and inspire us to living service.

I particularly like this *Urantia Book* quote:

Paper 146: *By opening the human end of the God-man communication, mortals make immediately available the ever-flowing stream of divine ministry to the creatures of the world.*

Part Two

Human Reflections: 1993 to Present

As increasing numbers of celestial teachers began transmitting lessons in the early 1990s, it was inevitable that a stir would be created within the Urantia organizations as to the validity of the phenomenon. Would the teachers help to expand and amplify their beloved revelation? Would they deleteriously detract from serious study of the book in pursuit of fantasy and fraud?

Since that day, there has been a steady stream of Internet discussion and arguments, some vitriolic. How could such transmitting be reliable, given the human mind?

Teaching Mission critics also trumpeted that the precious Fifth Epochal Revelation was a pristine body of perfect English without contradictions, narrations constructed and presented by a spiritual hierarchy of authors and editors. The new lessons didn't match the eloquence of their tome, they said.

In my view, the mission, this Melchizedek University of the cosmos, could be compared to a mortal university such as Harvard. One can see that critics are comparing the well-crafted books published by professors with classroom lectures, most of them by Morontian teachers who are ascending themselves. This doesn't detract from the quality of the transcribed lessons and discussions, which have proven to be a coherent and compatible body of work over the years.

Also during these years, there have been some excellent essays of exploration produced by well-educated and open-minded seekers who came into contact with the teachers. They honestly had to be convinced themselves of the validity of the mission.

These narratives that follow provide a parallel view of what some scholarly humans were thinking and experiencing during the first years of the Teaching Mission:

- In 1993, California psychologist Bob Slagle presented a paper called "Welcome to Change," the title taken from the words of celestial teacher Ham when he announced the planetary "Correcting Time" in Los Angeles.

71

- In 1994, retired U.S. Army General Duane Faw, who hosted the celestial teacher Rayson in his California home, keynoted an annual gathering of open-minded seekers called "Spirit Fest" in California. He related his experiences and thoughts about the wave of new teachers.

- An introductory narrative from the pivotal Woods Cross, Utah, group that transported the mission to the U.S. from its New Zealand origins, written by the late Dr. John Wormeck.

- In 1995, Dr. David Schlundt, a psychology professor at Vanderbilt University, presented thoughts from his Teaching Mission experiences to a national gathering in Fayetteville, Arkansas, including a transmission from celestial teacher Tarkas. We also include David's excellent e-mail post on evaluating the quality of the teacher transcripts compared to the Urantia papers.

- Soon after the August 10-13, 1995, conference, Fred Harris of the Tallahassee, Florida, Teaching Mission group, compiled a list of teachings and values.

- In the 1990's a group in Corvallis, Oregon, published one issue of a magazine called "Beyond Fear." The late Thea Hardy, a gifted computer expert, graphic designer and transmitter of celestial teachers, offered her views on the mission.

- In *Beyond Cynicism: Liberating Voices from the Spirit Within*, I presented a question-answer document of angry, cynical questions with illuminating and loving transmitted responses from the celestial "OneTeam," mirroring the principles of the 'be ye perfect' human ascension plan. It demonstrates the efficacy of keyboard reception and urges a devotion to Stillness and upreach. Here is an excerpt:

  Teaching Mission participants have continued to study the transmitting process over the years. Here is a 2010 paper from one of our contributors, Mary Livingston, which uses scientific reports to link meditation and channeling with the human glandular structure.

- Fred Harris returns to offer a succinct expression of the Correcting Time and Teaching Mission from his exploratory book, *The Correcting Time*.

Welcome to Change:
An Overview of the Teaching Mission
Dr. Bob Slagle, 1993

The teachers first touched my mind in the summer of 1991 when a friend sent me some transcripts of Abraham transmitting to a group in New Zealand. I was more or less nonplussed by the seemingly less than *Urantia Book* quality of communication. The message seemed true but simply a restatement of truths replete in *The Urantia Book* and common in many other spiritual resources.

I was skeptical. I was even biased against "channeling," at least in my limited understanding. It seemed unlikely that Abraham, the Abraham, Machiventa's Abraham, would suddenly pop up in New Zealand to deliver a message to a small, remote group of humans only mildly aware of *The Urantia Book*. Besides, deceased mortals rarely return to their native planets. (Technically, Abraham graduated in a previous dispensation, and could, as I understand *The Urantia Book*, return to Urantia [UB 1230:6, 1646:3, 1680:7].)

Meanwhile, I was preoccupied with sorting out many other claims of revelation and prophecy alleged by other Urantia Book readers. Isn't there a lot of "stuff" out there? Seeking and sorting the myriad claims to truth and prescience can quickly become a full time job. It boggles the mind. Yet, if I had not been both open and willing to plow through much superstition, confusion, and zillions of "spiritual" books, I might not have found *The Urantia Book,* with its lofty teachings that have so elevated my life. So, I have continued to pursue potential truth even when garbed in unorthodox raiment.

One brother in particular had caught my attention with his lengthy and comprehensive "prophecies" that seemed reasonably compatible with *The Urantia Book*. I sought the counsel of Jesus' Spirit of Truth, but as is often the case with me, not much seemed to be illuminated immediately. Discouragement comes easily when so much out there winds up proving to be another ego-bound delusional system punctuated with enough half-truths to catch the eye. Maybe I should just stick with *The Urantia Book*.

But, in sticking with *The Urantia Book*, I find that it leads me to continue my search for Truth, within and without, in likely and unlikely places. Again, there is so much out there to be examined. Have you read The Scripts of Cleophas? I haven't; it's bigger than *The Urantia Book*. Yet, if I hadn't kept on looking, I would not have found the Course in Miracles, or Mary Strong's wonderful Letters of the Scattered Brotherhood, and many other sources of inspiration.

Eventually I was guided to the conclusion that my would-be prophet brother, however sincere and well-intended and in possession of much truth, was tragically intoxicated with creative delusions. It was hard. I had spent many hours on the phone with this man and had developed a genuine love and affection for him despite his overly confident eccentricity. When I first heard rumors of the channeling in Utah, I thought, "not likely." These rumors came in the wake of my unfruitful exploration of this other supposed "prophecy." Besides, I was busy with still another situation.

A woman I had not met called me and left a message that she was a reader and felt led that it was appropriate to contact me. I returned the call, and she unfolded her astounding story of psychic experiences since adolescence, initially unnerving her, and later settling in as a way of life. She had a doctorate from Julliard and had taught at M.I.T. She was coherent and articulate. She claimed that she transmitted for the Order of Melchizedek. I thought, "not likely."

After the last prophetic *cul de sac*, I was a little impatient with her but painstakingly pointed out that, if she was a Urantia Book reader, surely she knew how improbable it was for her to be legitimately channeling for "real" Melchizedeks. We talked further. I tried to take a gentle, tolerant tone with her as I believed Jesus would. I asked questions. I listened. I took notes. We had four hours of telephone appointments. After studying my notes and reflecting, I decided that my truth bells had not been rung; her channeled material was not spiritually relevant to my life at that time.

Before long, a dear friend shared a broader horizon with me of the channeling in Utah. He sparked my interest. He sat me down and played a tape of a small group session he attended with one of these "teachers" speaking through a "receiver-transmitter." I was skeptical, but it was not long before I was responding to the clarity, love, respect, poise, and downright personality charm of this "person." Since I know my friend well, it was easy to empathize with his questions and reactions as he asked questions of the "teacher." There was something about hearing the voice, the pauses, the caring, the deliberation, the subtle intonations of this "other" and "greater" mind that was irrefutable to my heart. This was really real.

I asked for more tapes, and soon early Ham tapes arrived from Utah. Ham spoke slowly with many long pauses. This was different from the flowing conversational style of my first "teacher" contact. But the truths Ham spoke were no less real. Of course, I had intellectual questions and doubts too numerous to mention. Okay, I'll mention a few:

Why the name "Ham"? Celestial lunchmeat? Why channeling (I had been turned off by the likes of Ramtha and Seth)? Why New Zealand and Utah? Why seemingly "favored" people? Updating the Reserve Corps? Why were some questions answered with such generic answers, others evaded altogether? Are some people deluded . . . going along for the ride? Why were words like "stillness," "correcting time," and "teaching mission," not emphasized in *The Urantia Book*? (Or were they, but subtly and by other names? ["silent communion" (UB 1002:5), "New Age" (UB1860:5), "new teachers" (UB 2082:9)]).

Why didn't any of the folks at the Foundation or Fellowship headquarters know more about this? Like the church lady from Saturday Night Live says, "Could it be, could it be SATAN!?" Why do I need "teachers" when I have a magnificent epochal revelation, a perfect inner

Guide, and many spiritual resources? Perhaps, if I ignore it, it will all just go away ("not likely").

I feel blessed that I had the good fortune to have a meeting with a "celestial teacher" who allowed me several hours to experience his presence and unburden myself of many questions. The transmission occurred through a highly gifted receiver-transmitter whom I hardly knew. This transmission was articulate, flowing, conversational, personal, intimate, and touching. I know from *The Urantia Book* that personal experience has no substitute; it is "the master teacher." (UB1195:4, 2076:5, 1961:4) And I find that there is no substitute for direct experiential contact with this Teacher Corps.

The reality of this private session was so real, so profound, so loving, so revealing, so comprehensive, that all doubts were removed regarding the reality of this celestial teacher. He is an ascendant son from the seventh mansion world and was (to my amazement) willing to speak to me. All my intellectual arguments and doubts were short-circuited to a heart-soul reaction of certitude. Even most of my intellectual doubts were abundantly answered. My intellect strained to penetrate this event; I could not, but my truth bells had been rung on multiple levels.

This teacher reached toward me with tenderheartedness, sensing my anxieties, putting me at ease. "...[N]ot everything must be squeezed into this tiny temporal moment. It is merely a getting to know each other type of a meeting.... Just relax and ask any questions without censorship that might be on your mind and heart. And if I am able to answer and if my contribution helps to enlighten you or spark your spiritual quest even further, then it is I who is blessed."

I asked how to better discern my Adjuster's guidance.

"That is the quest of the human: How to discern the human mind from the Divine mind. This is your great challenge as it is of every other mortal on this planet. First, do not spend overmuch time in the examination and intellectual evaluation of your thoughts. Try to come from the quicker emotional intuitive level, not emotional in terms of feelings, but the gut, more instantaneous reaction, which in truth is coming from the integration of higher mind with human intelligence and memory experience. It is a good compass, and you should trust it more than you do. Second, if confusion still reigns in your mind, consider the spiritual fruits and ramifications of your guidance: will it have a good effect on you, on your advancement Godward? Does it hold the spiritual values of good to your fellows?"

I asked how to get to better know my seraphim.

"The seraphim are the closest non material beings to you. They are quite similar in reactions and understanding of Deity and truly love you and friendship you. The emotions that push the seraphim away are the human emotions of fear, anger, and a distraught or unbalanced state. The seraphim cannot break through these emotions, which they cannot truly fathom in the human, and you in essence erect a wall of negativity which repels your guardian angels. So, an attitude of inner peace and serenity, cheer and joy, love, hope, would be best."

The Teaching Mission

I asked how to be more forgiving.

"Forgiveness does not depend upon the remorse of the person who wronged you. Forgiveness is a capacity in your own being. It is a gift bestowed by God to man. And your capacity to receive the Father's and Michael's merciful forgiveness is and bears a direct relationship to your ability to forgive your fellows. To truly forgive you must foster soul growth and fruits of the spirit in yourself. As you grow in understanding the true scope of your fellow humans, it is not hard to forgive, but it becomes the natural order of a spiritual being.

"Fully evolved spiritual beings have no need to forgive, for no offense is ever seen by them, as they can see the heart-soul-potential-desire of their fellow sojourners. We are not so fortunate as to be in such a high place. Yet, pray for you to forgive yourself, and as you grow, it will become easier to see your fellows through the spiritual eyes of love, tolerance, and understanding."

I asked about this mission and how the teachers perceive us mortals.

"I have traveled through the seven mansion worlds but have not fused. I have not seen Michael but have studied your planet for many, many hundreds of years, and there was great competition to be chosen for this mission. I was quite honored to be amongst those chosen because of my similar background...and my study of your planet and peoples. How do I see you mortals? Not as differently as you would think. I have down-stepped to a more morontial form to be able to make contact. So, I perceive a Light emanating from the head region at times which is your Adjuster.

"I can, if given permission, search your mind circuits for memories or knowledge of other humans of which I have none. I gather information just like you do, by meeting the human or searching the mind memory patterns of a human who knows the individual in question. Travel for us is quite fast, and we are aided by seraphim and midwayers. The Life Carriers help to effect the necessary connection for transmission and receiving as well as first and secondary midwayers. We hope to achieve in the next thousand years of the Correcting Time a spiritual up-step, using transformed individuals to ultimately transform this world.

"We are a continuation of the Fifth Epochal Revelation. We are not a separate bestowal, but this phase of the revelation was planned from the beginning. However it was decided not to reveal this to the original contact personalities because of the danger that would place the revelation in-over emotionalism, non belief, dismissal-the book had to stand and root on its own. Now we proceed to take the humans who are ready and activate them out into the world. We will contact on a worldwide basis to readers and non-readers alike. We begin mostly with readers as there is less groundwork to lay. Does that answer?"

I asked many more questions, too voluminous to quote, and wound up asking how to discern legitimate channeling.

"How to tell? There will be a network amongst the true transmissions. For yourself, judge the spiritual content, use your Spirit of Truth.... Truth may be gathered like a bee from flower to flower from sources that are humans, inspired. Celestial or non-corporeal beings do not have a monopoly on spiritual insight. So, whether a transmission is from us or is from the human higher mind is really just a speculation that humans and we like to engage in, to speculate about what could be. The message, if spiritual, will illuminate."

Amazingly, this experience was on one level very ordinary, just like you and I chatting, and on many other levels it was very extraordinary-truly awesome. It was reassuring to my soul. This experience was a cherished privilege that I hold dear. However, the teachers are no respecters of persons. They desire to get to know each one of us equally. They honor us immensely and see our true virtues through spiritual eyes. They never judge us.

Some might think that this type of experience would lead to ego inflation. Not necessarily so. While on the one hand I feel blessed and deeply reassured, on the other hand I have a greater sense of my limitations and smallness. I am far from perfect and have a long, long way to go even in this life and must struggle daily with my flawed human character. As this teacher said to me, "The struggle against anger, fear, envy, lack of love, anxiety, etc. must be done in the trenches of day-to-day life through reality experiences with others and the world.... The true fields of spiritual growth [are] disappointment, conflict, despair, etc. - uncertainty. Your uncertainty will last, as will every human's, until you are re-personalized on the mansion worlds. This is a life-long struggle, and much growth comes from doubt versus faith struggles in the human heart."

The fruits of this encounter in my life were immediate. I felt a new buoyancy, an enhanced desire to discern my Adjuster's will, an enhanced desire to be more conscious of my seraphic guidance, renewed energy to reach out and love, and augmented willingness to seek daily communion with Father.

"Be still and know that I am God." (Psalm 46:10)

I remembered the teaching of Jesus to remain for a time in silent receptivity after prayer to allow the Adjuster to speak to the listening soul (UB 1641:1). Over the years I have tried to practice this stillness after prayer but ashamedly have not regularly sought to fully quiet my mind in prayer and worship. In my prayer life, I am guilty of perhaps talking more than listening. The emphasis on silent cosmic contemplation (UB 622:4) and silent communion with the Father are certainly replete in *The Urantia Book*, not to mention Jesus' living portrayal in his own life of frequently going apart, alone, for solitary communion (cf. UB 1754:6), as well as the times he sent the apostles out apart and alone to find the answer from within.

So, I began the "stillness practice." I found this difficult and frustrating. At first it seemed I could not cease my mind chatter for more than a few nanoseconds at a time. Occasionally when I did reach a point of stillness, my mind would have to start a commentary on the process, "Gee, I guess this is the stillness; I wonder if I will hear voices." Then I would space on in more thoughts despite myself. Some days I felt such emotional-physical agitation that I would have to stop and get up and go do some "very important" thing I had just remembered. Soon I learned that coffee (caffeine) is an anathema to the stillness-I'd be "futuring" or "pasting" but was rarely in the present. I think each person is different chemically, and each has to learn experientially what works best.

White-knuckling through the stillness with gritty discipline did not work for me. The key is to relax, to let tranquility descend naturally and fill the body and mind. We know Jesus' teaching of "non-resistance," and I found resisting thoughts didn't work very well either. So, I did what I had learned in Transcendental Meditation but without the mantra. I allowed thoughts and feelings just to pass by, and when I became aware that I was spacing off, I would gently stop myself and attempt to re-focus on that quiet place within where the Monitor resides, where the answers to all questions exist, where the Source and Center of my being is.

It was hard not to chastise myself for my spacey tendency not to be in the here and now. Gradually I learned just to matter-of-factly re-focus without berating myself for failing. Slowly, too slowly for my temperament and impatience, my stillness times became easier, more nurturing. There was still variability from day to day, but more often now I would have twenty or so minutes pass without much time consciousness. Sometimes, not always, I felt relieved or refreshed after this quiet seeking meditation.

My stillness times improved as I took advice from the teaching mission transcripts I had available. Teacher Daniel suggested imagining a still reflective lake or a white ball of light. But my ball of light would not stay still, and in walking down the memory lane of my travel-log of still lakes, I found I couldn't keep them very still either. Somehow there were always ripples or waves, and if I succeeded at quieting these, a fish would pop up.

I took much solace in the words of Daniel that even a few seconds of stillness with intent to find God were worth more than can be imagined. I persisted. I struggled. I was jealous of my friends who seemed to easily take the stillness and achieve teacher contact.

I heard teacher Ham say that auditory stimulation was especially distracting. So, I purchased 28 db sound attenuators (plastic ear muffs) and wore a blindfold. Ah ha! This was better, but no magic panacea. I continued to beseech the Father for help. Eventually, I began to have contact with "otherness" by asking questions after I had given thanks and established a degree of silent communion.

The sense of "otherness" for me was very, very subtle. At first it was like my alter ego answering my own questions. But occasionally there would be a hint or clue of higher contact. Sometimes it was the quickness of the answer to my inquiry. Sometimes it was the wording-just a twinge different from my style. Sometimes it was the character or timbre of the "voice" in my mind. Often it was the feeling-tone that accompanied the stillness time.

I should add, I don't hear voices. My contact is intuitive or else word-thoughts in my mind. Everyone js unique, and the style of teacher contact seems to be unique to each mortal. Some people hear voices outside the head, up and to the left side, or behind. Some hear inner voices. Some have thought-words. Some see visualizations. Some experience a complex array of intuitive communications for which I am at a loss for words. Some people have more strong gut level reactions. Seeking is what is important and even teacher contact may be of little value unless the fruits are shown in soul growth. It is not words, but the sense of God's love that really counts. Has your spiritual life been richer lately? Perhaps you are having teacher contact, and simply don't realize it yet.

Caligastia is said in *The Urantia Book* to "still be free on Urantia to prosecute his nefarious designs." (UB 610:1) Is he insidiously working to destroy the Urantia readership through the "sordid practice of spiritualism"? Is the teaching mission another devilish scheme to take over your mind?

No. To know the teachers personally is a certain antidote for this fear-dominated belief. I know wherefrom I speak. I know that I know. I do not mean to sound presumptuous, just experiential.

Such personal knowing is also the antidote for all the "explanations" for the teaching mission that invoke: mass hysteria, communal delusions, archetypal upsurgencies, group "needs," and all other manner of psychological speculation. How could Caligastia succeed in seducing us into wickedness by teaching us to seek the Indwelling Spirit daily, to live in allegiance to Christ Michael, and to constantly seek to love? As Jesus pointed out to his adversaries, if the devil casts out the devil, it is a house divided and must fall. (UB 2085:4)

If this were Caligastia (and it is not) I would suspect that he has serious indigestion and must gnash his teeth with sleep disturbance. Allegedly being the source of the "channeling," he would have to constantly laud *The Urantia Book*, propose that we do daily acts of kindness to others, respect the will dignity of our fellows, advocate the Fatherhood of God and the brotherhood of man, and relate to us as a loving friend. Poor devil, he must have a nasty case of cognitive dissonance by now.

To follow the fear-mongering Caligastia theory to its logical extreme, let us assume that Caligastia is behind the channeling phenomena. What should the attitude and conduct of a faith-son or daughter be to such an impossible encroachment? Did not the Master teach and practice nonresistance to evil (UB1950:5)? Did Jesus not teach that we are to love even our enemies (UB 1134:1)?

If Caligastia were still around, are we not enjoined to love even him, just as our Master did? Was it not Jesus' nonresistance to evil and divine love for his sons Caligastia and Daligastia and the other rebels that our Lord placed above even his own mortal life? Was it not His mercy that allowed this insane Lanonandek pair to continue to roam Urantia free to prosecute their nefarious designs? And with regard to the apparent strangeness of the teaching mission, how did Jesus treat strange teachers? Consider the Kheresa lunatic, or Kirmeth the trance medium. "... Jesus intervened and allowed him entire freedom of action for a few days. All who heard his preaching soon recognized that his teaching was not sound as judged by the gospel of the kingdom" (UB 1666:3).

Should skeptics not follow the Master's policy? When Jesus was faced with teachers of partial truth, he always emphasized the positive and made no attack on the error. We know that fear, suspicion, and intolerance are mind poisons (UB 1575:2, 1204:3). Is not the way of Truth to abandon fear and distrust in favor of faith in God's love and his assurances that a sincere soul is never in jeopardy?

Some relevant facts presented in *The Urantia Book* about Caligastia are these. His power was curtailed by the incarnation of Machiventa Melchizedek (UB 753:1). He has been comparatively impotent since the cross of Christ (UB 610:6). "Even before Michael's bestowal on Urantia, neither Caligastia nor Daligastia was ever able to oppress mortals or to coerce any normal individual into doing anything against the human will." (UB 753:3) He is shorn, finally, of all authority on Urantia. (UB 753:2) ". . . He has absolutely no power to enter the minds of men. . . ." (UB 610:3).

I emphasize this passage because my understanding is that if you really desired his wicked presence (however absurd) he could draw near to you and tempt you, but still could not enter your mind. Check page 610; what is your interpretation? And finally, Caligastia is "servile before the divine majesty of the Paradise Thought Adjusters and the protective Spirit of Truth...." (UB 610:4)

Let us unveil this Caligastia theory to reveal the lattice-work of sophistries that it is. First, does this theory misinterpret page UB 865:7 to mean that all "spiritualism" is sordid? Please read it again. I see no such logical implication. Some "spiritualism" is sordid; the logic of this algorithm does not necessarily imply that all "spiritualism" is sordid. But this is a "straw man," since the teaching mission is not "spiritualism" at all. "Spiritualism" in our common usage seems to me to conjure up seances, melodrama, and contacting ghosts, like dead uncle Ed, a speaking spook, invoked by the supposed powers of an entranced medium.

In my opinion, the sordidness of such mediumship is its duplicity. Preying on the needs of ignorant mortals for dishonest gains (money-power) is a scam. My 1933 edition New Century Dictionary includes these synonyms for "sordid": base, low, self-seeking, mercenary. If you are paying a fee for "channeling," compare the teaching mission-the price is right, no charge, a gift from above.

Second, we must believe that hundreds of sincere Urantia Book readers and Truth seekers suddenly developed the desire to be cursed with the wicked presence of the devil, or are fooled and incapable of sensing his iniquitous presence. What an affront to the Spirit of Truth. What an injustice to the goodness and sincerity of those brothers and sisters choosing to practice daily communion and acts of kindness as taught by these new heavenly teachers.

Third, Caligastia, who was never able to oppress mortals, is now oppressing them; who was servile before the Adjusters, now dominates them; who has been comparatively impotent, is now mighty; who has no power to enter the minds of man, is now doing so.

For this "theory" to be valid, *The Urantia Book* must be seriously in error. Moreover, what allowance should we make for the new revelation of the teachers speaking through many different transmitters that the rebellion is over and that all the wicked ones have chosen extinction? If it serves soul-growth to believe in this devilish buffoonery, I honor your free will choice. But the truth remains, "The devil has been given a great deal of credit for evil which does not belong to him." (UB 610:6) To me this "Caligastia theory" is one more example of this.

Is it plausible that the Lucifer Rebellion would be adjudicated in our lifetimes? From *The Urantia Book*, it seems that the adjudication was begun during the times of the Urantia revelation. (UB 529:1) It was virtually settled by Jesus on Mount Hermon. (UB 1494:3) Teacher James comments, "...you must understand that up until the time Lucifer ceased to exist, he still had free will and had not agreed to the adjudication. The adjudication could not happen until he agreed that it was the right thing to do and that this date could not have been known precisely by anyone until it came about." (James, 10/4/92) This statement of James agrees with *The Urantia Book* in that our heavenly Father requires that no action be taken until the sinner himself approves of the justness of the verdict. (UB 615:5, 611:6)

Over the years I have not given much energy to worrying about Caligastia or the wicked things he might be up to. I have found much reassurance in *The Urantia Book*. However, the announcement by Ham and others that the rebellion is over did give me a feeling, at first of skepticism, then of sadness and relief. What happened to the rebels? "We are sorry and also happy to report that they have become as though they had not been. None repented. It was a hard combination of reality feelings when we received this information," (Ham, Woods Cross transcripts, 1991, p. 1). I am sorry that all the rebels chose extinction. So much love and effort by our beloved Sovereign was extended to them. It is incredible that they would reject His mercy.

"Patient is God, and He waits until eternity if that is what it takes, just as He did for Lucifer. This was such an unfortunate case, where one so brilliant could not be reclaimed back into the fold. He was, however, allowed to make that free will choice, and it must be respected. Our Father wept with the news of this decision ..." (Will, 1/4/92) An Unseen Helper says, "Caligastia has not been on the planet since approximately 1984-85 your time. All rebellious spirits from Lucifer to the lesser participators of the rebellion have all chosen death and are as if they never were. Only their negative lifeless energy is on the planet. Some will give it life through personal beliefs, fears, and emotions, but it will gradually dissipate and cease to exist...." (Aflana transcripts, 1/27/92)

Why a will creature chooses to reject love is truly unfathomable to me. Nonetheless, I believe that Caligastia is naught. My soul soars as I realize that the torturous hand of the wicked Prince is gone. As I look out upon the world, I see that the numbing spectacle of pain and anger is at worst the momentum of the past, that destructiveness from here forward is entirely human choosing. It is the infinite Father's desire that not one shall be lost, but He is so respectful of each of us that no creature is forced to continue life against his own will. What a cosmic coup de gras is the Father's merciful obliteration of those who choose not to be. What a wonder of cosmic justice, this adjudication by the Ancients of Days, the fulfillment of God's great gift to us, freedom of creature will. "Fear not." (UB 1103, 1582, 1820)

I found that there is no need to fear a hostile take-over from within. It is the Kingdom of Heaven that is within. It is God that is within, not celestial corruption, "...you may rest in the assurance that there is one inner bastion, the citadel of the spirit, which is absolutely unassailable...." (UB 1096:5) (I especially like that word "absolutely;" that's pretty unassailable in my opinion. And yes, I have dedicated my soul to God's keeping.)

Surprisingly I haven't had much conscious fear in this process of making contact with Michael's celestial teachers. Occasionally, I had a twinge of fear that I might be afraid. No, I am not fearless. I fear pain. I fear isolation from feeling love. I fear being sick and friendless. I fear decrepitude and the process of dying (not death). The list goes on but is unimportant in light of the Father's precious gift of faith, which is available to all who reach up and trust in the Father's down-grasp. I do experience reactionary animal fear. After all, this teacher contact is a new experience. Is it not ironical that the animal body fears that which the heart most desires?

So, most of us have had our twinges of reflex defensiveness when we sense heavenly contact, but it passes quickly in the face of the warmth, gentleness, and caring that accompany this "receiving." Faith and patience have aided me greatly in accepting this new form of communication. It just takes a little stillness time and patience to begin to sense teacher contact. The teachers are in no rush. Jesus was never in a hurry. Why should I be?

I discovered early that the responsibility for determining the truth of any given transmission or part of a transmission is mine alone. Each mortal must rely on the Spirit of Truth to verify or falsify any aspect of the teachings. The teachers do not claim to be perfect; errors do occur, and it is up to me to discern them. So, often I take a "wait and see" attitude.

For some things, time alone reveals the fruits. I have found in general that the spiritual teachings of the mission are excellent and close to error free. As transmissions relate to the material level, human longings and emotions seem to enter in more. However, it is the spiritual that counts; material disillusionments are a part of life. The teachers are clearly here to teach us more about spiritual living. They are not here to work wonders or provide empirical confirmation of their reality. That is the work of the Spirit of Truth.

I am rather impressed by how consistent the teachers are in not working "wonders" or "proofs" of their functioning. I remember that Jesus was repeatedly pressed to show the people a "sign" that he was from God, but he steadfastly refused to appeal to the miracle-seeking nature of humankind.

The teachers seem to follow a similar policy. They very rarely answer questions about politics, social issues, science, and other worldly matters. We must learn and earn our own way through faith and daily struggles with the grit of life. I see the teachers as respecting us so much as not to diminish our agondonter status, nor our right to progressive soul growth through free will decisions.

The Teaching Mission

There is much about the teaching mission that is difficult to express in words. There are subtle nuances that emerge slowly, week by week, in a teacher group. In the Daniel transcripts, for example, there unfolds the delightful genuineness of the participants as question after question reveals the innermost heart and soul of the person. It is easy to love these people even at a great distance since their openness about personal, intimate matters is so evident. Time and time again group members unburden themselves of concerns and issues that might not serve status seeking or image making or ego gratification but that do serve soul growth.

I believe that this kind of openness can emerge because the teachers are so completely accepting of us mortals. Most of the teachers had mortal origin so they can genuinely empathize with us. Daniel's lessons are so sweet, like primer lessons of love. Among humans, even dear friends, it is difficult to find consistent acceptance from others. Among the best of friends, unconditional love is still more an ideal than a reality. And so there are parts of our selves that we are reluctant to share for there may be the sting of rejection. Not so with the teachers. They tell me that we tend to idealize them. The teachers remind us often that they are not perfect, just a little above us.

But in my experience I have found the teachers totally accepting even of our worst attributes. We are told that our Lord, Michael truly loves even our character flaws. It is a blessed experience to be in the presence of such total and, indeed, superhuman acceptance. It is such a relief to be totally accepted by another. The teachers model this behavior, and it is contagious.

Writing this paper is my expression of my loyalty to my own experiential truth. I think we each have a responsibility to be loyal to our own personal experiential truth, even if it disagrees with another. To me this is one form of unity without uniformity. My desire is to share my joy with you.

Regardless of your point of view, my fondest hope is that we can be friends and to a degree extend the kingdom of heaven on Earth. It does not matter whether you are the C.E.O. of Urantia Foundation, the president of The Urantia Fellowship, the most wealthy and powerful person in the Urantia movement, someone who gives away computer indices, or the most humble and unknown citizen of Urantia. It does not matter whether you have read *The Urantia Book*, have a different life-style, are a newcomer to the book, or are the most crazy and obnoxious person on Earth. The Father loves us equally. Our job is to be brothers and sisters, to love one another, to be tolerant of each other's beliefs and practices.

"Throughout the vicissitudes of life, remember always to love one another. Do not strive with men, even with unbelievers." (Jesus, UB 1932:3) I am confident that the teaching mission will not be the first or the last great test of our loyalties to these high values. What may initially discomfort us may in time be a blessing in disguise. My prayer for you is not that you believe in the mission, but that you experience the spiritual uplift, the heightened receptivity that can be had experientially by any child of God on Urantia, regardless of doctrines and beliefs. For you, my sister, daughter of God, my brother, son of God, my agondonter friend, I

pray for you that you (and I) feel the love of the Father. I leave you now with my profound respect for your free will. May it be pleasing in His sight.

"To develop the relationship with the Father, the Thought Adjuster, is the single most important thing you can do. Nothing replaces this responsibility. Far better that you do this and entirely ignore the teaching mission, than that you seek a teacher but forget to communicate with the Spirit within. There is no question about this. Seek the Father first, and then all things will come. This is the highest Truth." (LinEl, 12/25/92)

The Woods Cross, Utah Group
John Wormeck, March, 1999

The Woods Cross Urantia study group has been meeting weekly since the 70's, with one break in service due to the death of the hostess. It started up again in 1987 with five members who met Thursdays to read and discuss the book. We would read a paper ahead of time at home and discuss it and any related material at the meeting. The main characteristics of the three women and two men were their unity in seeking truth, and the desire to serve.

In approximately 1989, one individual heard from her Thought Adjuster asking her if she desired to become a member of the reserve corps of destiny. Of course, she responded yes. She was told the others could also become members. (This started the Cedar Post society for the other four members, as they at that time could not hear anything, like a cedar post.)

Nothing was heard again until we received the announcement from New Zealand of conversations with Abraham and the coming Correcting Time. It is our understanding that the four individuals in New Zealand had instructions to write to all known Urantia groups to make this important announcement. Most Urantia Book coordinators and listed groups received this information, which consisted of conversations with Father Abraham by the process that we now call transmitting and receiving, or TR'ing.

Most groups and individuals that received this information rejected it. Some wrote the New Zealand group with comments and questions for both them and the celestial teachers. As usual with new information, most people did not accept the communications as real, as coming from celestial beings and the spiritual world. The New Zealand group then sent more papers on further conversations with Abraham in which he answered some of the questions sent to him in response to his announcement.

We view the New Zealand efforts to be a John the Baptist-like role of announcing the coming Teaching Ministry/Correcting Time Mission. It is our understanding that the Woods Cross group was the only one which accepted this communication as genuine and wrote them with encouragement and support. In such matters, faith is very important.

The Woods Cross study group was given the mission to start the Teaching Mission. The individual who initially heard from her Thought Adjuster now heard from teacher Ham that he was going to be the teacher for the Woods Cross study group, and the first meeting occurred on February 28, 1991.

As is always the case, the T/R had trouble initially but with practice was able to come online. The important thing here was that the other members of the group gave her complete and loving support; there was no disbelief, criticalness or other human behaviors that would be poisonous to the spiritual world. Soon another member of the group was able to T/R, and therefore allow the main T/R to also ask questions and be coached by Abraham and Ham to perfect the process in private.

These weekly sessions continued with teacher Ham for two years until he decided to leave actively teaching the group so that the members would develop their own contact with teachers and our Father. He then continued to teach on an individual level.

They were exciting times. All Urantia Book readers in the area were contacted about our new teacher. Many came to hear teacher Ham. Some were members of the earlier study group and hence had a background in *The Urantia Book*; others did not. The original lessons were meant for all levels and are available to all. Teacher Ham had to discuss many things, including who he was, what was going on, the T/R process, the future, etc. as all this was new. We asked many questions we now would call materialistic in content. None of us had any experience with channeling before Ham came.

The Teaching Mission and Transformation
Duane Faw
Keynote Address, Spirit Fest '95, San Luis Obispo, California

Greetings. May the PEACE of CHRIST MICHAEL be upon us.

Welcome to the first 1995 Summer Seminar of a Melchizidek University. This session is designed around the theme of TRANSFORMATION.

Our topic for this lesson is the Teaching Mission itself: What it is, why it is, and how it is involved in TRANSFORMATION.

It is as simple as this: the Teaching Mission is an integral and necessary part of the Fifth Epochal Revelation. And the Fifth Epochal Revelation is destined to transform the World, Urantia, into the age of Light and Life. The interim period is called the Correction Time.

I know that the Teaching Mission is a part of the Fifth Epochal Revelation because Jesus, Himself, said so. *The Urantia Book* records that the day following His triumphal entry into

The Teaching Mission

Jerusalem Jesus talked with His apostles about the soon-to-happen destruction of Jerusalem, and about His promise some day to return. Because they viewed these events against a Jewish paradigm, the apostles equated the destruction of Jerusalem to the end of the world and the establishment of a "new Jerusalem" with Jesus as its king to His promise to return.

Peter asked: "How shall we know when you will return to bring all this about?"

Jesus was thoughtful for some time, and then, with a tone of disappointment and resignation, said: *"You ever err since you always try to attach the new meaning to the old; you are determined to misunderstand all my teaching; you insist on interpreting the gospel in accordance with your established beliefs. Nevertheless, I will try to enlighten you."* (1914:3-9)

"Why do you still look for the Son of Man to sit upon the throne of David and expect that the material dreams of the Jews will be fulfilled? Have I not told you all these years that my kingdom is not of this world? The things which you now look down upon are coming to an end, but this will be a new beginning out of which the gospel of the kingdom will go to all the world and this salvation will spread to all peoples."

Then Jesus said something that is very meaningful to our topic. He foretold the Fifth Epochal Revelation. He said:

"And when the kingdom shall have come to its full fruition, be assured that the Father in heaven will not fail to visit you with an enlarged revelation of truth and an enhanced demonstration of righteousness."

I see the Urantia Papers as the enlarged revelation of truth. I see the Teaching Mission as the enhanced demonstration of righteousness. These two work together as the Fifth Epochal Revelation. This is confirmed as He continues the sentence:

"Even as He has already bestowed upon this world him who became the prince of darkness," which, of course, was Caligastia, the First Epochal Revelation, *"and then Adam,"* the Second Epochal Revelation," who was followed by Melchizedek," the Third Epochal Revelation, *"and in these days, the Son of Man."* the Fourth Epochal Revelation.

He continued: *"And so will my Father continue to manifest and show forth His love, even to this dark and evil world."* (1914:26-38)

This prophecy is being fulfilled in our day and before our very eyes! The Urantia Papers and the Teaching Mission ARE the continuing, but up-stepped, manifestation of our Father's Love as foretold by Jesus on this occasion.

We all know of the giving of the Urantia Papers, published in book form in 1955. At the time of publication the forum was told by the revelators that the book was generations ahead of its time. Meanwhile, they should occupy themselves with publishing and preserving the purity of the text of the Book, organizing study groups, and making translations into other languages. It is a matter of opinion as to how wisely and well these injunctions were followed, but the Celestial Government did not wait.

The Teaching Mission

On February 1, 1992, an ascending mortal and spiritual Teacher named Ham formally and publicly announced to about 150 people, including General Councilors of the Urantia Fellowship:

1. That the Lucifer rebellion is officially ended in Nebadon;
2. That Machiventa Melchizedek, duly inaugurated as acting Planetary Prince of Urantia, an assignment he accepted from Michael, has arrived on this planet;
3. That the system circuits (the loss of which had isolated Urantia) are being reopened;
4. That the time has arrived for an "expanded level of truth," the beginning of the Correction Time;

In order to achieve this expanded level of truth, Ham revealed the Teaching Mission by announcing that he is one of many teachers commissioned to bring the light of truth and the understanding of our Father to Urantia. He said they are desirous of placing "many teachers among you."

From the teachers we learn:

1. That the case of Gabriel vs. Lucifer has been finally adjudicated and the arch-rebels annihilated: they are as if they never were;
2. That *The Urantia Book*, is to be the principal text of the Fifth Epochal Revelation, and is remarkably correct for the time when it was written;
3. That the Teaching Mission is to provide the human component (more about this later) of the Fifth Epochal Revelation; and
4. That now is the Correction Time to help Urantia make up for the deficiencies caused by experiments of the Life Carriers on a decimal planet having gone awry, the Lucifer rebellion, the Adamic default; and the brutal murder of the Son of Man & Son of God on His seventh Bestowal Mission;
5. That neither the Teachers nor the human transmitter-receivers are infallible, making the specifics of their messages suspect, particularly in respect to future human activities;
6. That they cannot, and do not, interfere with human free-will, and are careful not to overawe or bedazzle impressionable minds; and
7. That their mission is spiritual: to up-step the moral and spiritual fiber of the planet to where it approximates that of a normal planet. They do this by personal contact with human students who then become the "enhanced demonstration of righteousness" mentioned by Jesus. They do this by their conduct.

We should not be surprised at these developments. From the *Urantia Book*, published two generations before the recent events, we learned:

1. That the Lucifer rebellion will be terminated by the annihilation of the archrebels, followed by a reopening of the system circuits. (pp. 529:11-18; 611:34-46)

2. That our Vicegerent Planetary Prince, Machiventa Melchizedek, may some day move his headquarters to Urantia. (pp. 1025:1-23; 1251:15-29)

3. That it is not unusual for a Planetary Prince to be accompanied on his mission by volunteer ascending mortal beings. This was the source of the Caligastia one hundred. (pp. 742:18-21; 855:22-25)

4: That celestial and super-mortal beings can communicate with mortals. It is the source of all revelation. Indeed, that is how the *Urantia Book*, itself, came into being.

It is entirely logical that the Fifth Epochal Revelation, like the first four, has both an informational and a personal component. It differs from earlier Epochal Revelations only in the order in which they appear.

In each of the first four Epochal Revelations the personal component came first,through whom the informational component came later. In this instance, because of the value of the written word in our culture, the informational component came first, followed by the personal component. The Teaching Mission is designed to provide humans for this component.

Those who attend teaching groups do so for many reasons ranging from skepticism, through mere curiosity, to sincere truth-seekers. Not all attendees accept the teachings as real; some fall away. This is to be expected. It is true of all other religious activities.

The mere fact that the Teaching Mission may attract some self-deluded, self-serving, or otherwise unsavory human personalities, or even generate local hysteria, is not a cause for alarm. Every religion on the face of the globe has attracted its share of charlatans, kooks, and hysterical people. There is no reason why this Teaching Mission should be spared.

We have the common sense, the privilege, indeed the duty, to select between the genuine and the fraudulent. We also have a test: "by their fruits shall you know them." And we retain the free will to pick and choose only those teachings which have "the ring of truth" in our hearts.

Neither should the fact that others, who follow a different spiritual path, reject the Teaching Mission for any reason give us pause. Our concern is whether or not they display an "enhanced demonstration of righteousness."

There will be many outside the Teaching Mission who dedicate themselves to the cause of transforming the world into a planet of Light and Life. Jesus himself tells us that in spiritual matters, "he who is not against us is for us."

Just as Jesus picked common persons as Apostles, the Teaching Mission is directed to the common person. Becoming a transmitter-receiver (T/R) is not a mark of spiritual attainment, nor is it a higher order of service, rather it is because the person both can and is willing to do so.

The Teaching Mission

The true lessons are NOT those of the T/R; they are of the teacher. In some instances the concepts expressed are contrary to the views of the T/R.

Most lessons are given by teachers who are ascending mortal beings, hence not celestial. Yet the messages (lessons) themselves are of a high moral and ethical plane. They not only teach, they inspire. Those who attend them (students) are generally motivated to take a higher spiritual path than before, and many do so. It is at this point that the critical role of the Teaching Mission becomes apparent.

– The *Urantia Book* IS the foretold "enlarged revelation of truth." New truth is spelled out page after page for those with enquiring minds and hearts.

– But it IS NOT the foretold "enhanced demonstration of righteousness." This task is given the human students of the invisible teaching corps, and those who are inspired by their enhanced demonstrations of righteousness.

– Success or failure of the Teaching Mission will depend upon how many lives will be transformed as a result of it.

– This is the chosen way to achieve an expanded level of truth, which leads toward Light and Life.

I see every human student of every superhuman or celestial teacher as having an opportunity to be a living part of this human component of the Fifth Epochal Revelation IF they freely choose to do so.

It makes no difference whether or not you are a transmitter/receiver or a silent student, you have an equal opportunity to actually BE that "enhanced demonstration of righteousness" which Jesus foretold shortly before His death.

Realization of this factor should give us great comfort as well as great challenge. We each, personally, have an opportunity, if not a duty, to actually BE that "enhanced demonstration of righteousness!"

In a very real sense, we are an integral part of the Fifth Epochal Revelation. It is not just the book. *The Urantia Book* contains the true teachings of Jesus. The teachings of Jesus must be realized (made REAL), actualized (made ACTUAL), by human beings before they can transform the world into the age of Light and Life.

We are the first students of the Teaching Mission. We have matriculated into one of the Melchizedek Universities. Some of us are freshmen, some sophomores, and a few juniors. Some day we will all be alumnae. No matter whether we complete the course or drop out along the way, we are alumnae. We will never be the same. We will all have a good experience.

The Urantia Papers say: An experience is good when it heightens the appreciation of beauty, augments the moral will, enhances the discernment of truth, enlarges the capacity to love and serve one's fellows, exalts the spiritual ideals, and unifies the supreme human motives of time with the eternal plans of the indwelling Adjuster, all of which lead directly to an increased desire to do the Father's will, thereby fostering the divine passion to find God and to be more like him. [1458:8-15)

These are the building blocks of Spiritual TRANSFORMATION. They are a necessary and integral part of the Correcting Time, which must precede Light and Life. When judged by this standard, participating in the Teaching Mission in any capacity must be rated "outstanding."

Expanded Understandings of the Teaching Mission

Dr. David G. Schlundt, Vanderbilt University, followed by a transmission from the celestial teacher, Tarkas

The Network of the Heart Teaching Mission Gathering in Fayetteville, Ark. in 1995 was a sharing that featured these remarks from the author. Each insight is preceded by a quote from the Urantia Papers.

From Urantia Paper 100:

"You cannot truly love your fellows by a mere act of the will. Love is only born of thoroughgoing understanding of your neighbor's motives and sentiments. It is not so important to love all men today as it is that each day you learn to love one more human being. If each day or each week you achieve an understanding of one more of your fellows, and if this is the limit of your ability, then you are certainly socializing and truly spiritualizing your personality. Love is infectious, and when human devotion is intelligent and wise, love is more catching than hate. But only genuine and unselfish love is truly contagious. If each mortal could only become a focus of dynamic affection, this benign virus of love would soon pervade the sentimental emotion-stream of humanity to such an extent that all civilization would be encompassed by love, and that would be the realization of the brotherhood of man."

Insight #1: The teaching mission is as much about spreading love as it is about the dissemination of information

Imagine that you are exploring a deep dark forest. It is getting late, darkness is approaching, and you feel the need for a campfire for light, warmth, and safety. You gather kindling, twigs, small branches, and some logs. You build a tepee like structure with logs on the outside and twigs and kindling on the inside. You strike a spark and get a fire started in some dry grass. You blow on the spark and it glows brighter and brighter until you begin to see smoke and flames. You continue to blow until the fire is well established, then you transfer it to the kindling in the center of the campfire.

You continue to blow on the fire, nursing it so it won't go out. After a certain point, you have enough flame so that you are confident the fire will burn. It will still be some time before the fire becomes bright and hot. It may take all night to burn the logs you have placed on the outside. But, in making a campfire there is a point of no return where you have enough heat and flame to sustain combustion.

The teaching mission is a spark to the dry kindling. A handful of humans have been contacted, the fire of love has been lit in their hearts, and the flames of service are beginning to glow. The fires may smolder for a long time, but eventually they will spread. Fire can be used to do work. Iron can be heated and worked, clay pots can be hardened, food can be cooked and so forth. The campfire metaphor has helped me understand the teaching mission much better.

When I first learned that thousands of teachers had come to this planet to help us, I was elated. I read that they were working on our spiritual welfare, on health problems, and on saving the planet from environmental destruction. At first, I focused on the work that would be done using the fire. At first, it was the content of the teachings that I considered most important. The new insights, the new information, and the expanded perspectives were what I thought the teaching mission was all about.

Part of the work of the mission is to spread the truth of the fifth epochal revelation, but that is not the entire purpose of the correcting time. After spending the weekend at the Gathering of the Heart, I came to realize that an equally important purpose of the teaching mission is to light a campfire in the dark, cold, wilderness. The teachers are sparks that have started smoldering little fires in small groups all over the world. The teachers have gently blown on the fires to keep them from going out in the cold and rain that is part of life in the wilderness. I wonder if we have reached the point of no return. Are the small little fires burning all over now strong enough to both sustain combustion and to eventually spread?

This important aspect of the teaching mission has to do with person to person contact and the spreading of love in every day interactions between people. It may take a very long time for the small campfires that have been started to blaze into bonfires and then spread into a massive forest fire of love. But sparks have been struck and a few campfires have been lit.

It may never be necessary for the great majority of people on this planet to know anything about the teaching mission for their lives to have been dramatically changed by it. Christian, Moslem, Jew, Hindu, Buddhist, and others can all catch fire with love, even though they will still conceptualize religion differently. Millions of people will embark upon a spiritual quest and will discover the source of love that is within them. Some will call it God, some Allah, some the Thought Adjuster, and some will have no particular words at all for it.

It is not immediately necessary for everyone to embrace the teachings of the *Urantia Book* in order to learn to incorporate more love into their lives. It is not necessary to believe that any contact with celestials has occurred to begin trying to understand and love one more brother or sister each day.

From Paper 43:

"On the mansion worlds you completed the unification of the evolving mortal personality; on the system capital you attained Jerusem citizenship and achieved the willingness to submit the self to the disciplines of group activities and co-ordinated undertakings; but now on the constellation training worlds you are to achieve the real socialization of your evolving morontia personality. This supernal cultural acquirement consists in learning how to:

1. Live happily and work effectively with ten diverse fellow morontians, while ten such groups are associated in companies of one hundred and then federated in corps of one thousand.
2. Abide joyfully and co-operate heartily with ten univitatia, who, though similar intellectually to morontia beings, are very different in every other way. And then must you function with this group of ten as it co-ordinates with ten other families, which are in turn confederated into a corps of one thousand univitatia.
3. Achieve simultaneous adjustment to both fellow morontians and these host univitatia. Acquire the ability voluntarily and effectively to co-operate with your own order of beings in close working association with a somewhat dissimilar group of intelligent creatures.
4. While thus socially functioning with beings like and unlike yourself, achieve intellectual harmony with, and make vocational adjustment to, both groups of associates.
5. While attaining satisfactory socialization of the personality on intellectual and vocational levels, further perfect the ability to live in intimate contact with similar and slightly dissimilar beings with ever-lessening irritability and ever-diminishing resentment. The reversion directors contribute much to this latter attainment through their group-play activities.
6. Adjust all of these various socialization techniques to the furtherance of the progressive co-ordination of theParadise-ascension career; augment universe insight by enhancing the ability to grasp the eternal goal-meanings concealed within these seemingly insignificant time-space activities.
7. And then, climax all of these procedures of multi-socialization with the concurrent enhancement of spiritual insight as it pertains to the augmentation of all phases of personal endowment through group spiritual association and morontia co-ordination. Intellectually, socially, and spiritually two moral creatures do not merely double their personal potentials of universe achievement by partnership technique; they more nearly quadruple their attainment and accomplishment possibilities."

Insight #2: The teaching mission is a partnership!

Once the fires have been lit, there will be work to be done. My original understanding of this work was that only humans could do the things that needed to be done and the teachers would be here telling the humans what to do. I think this vision of how the teaching mission will work is not quite correct. I think that something new and unique is being tried here. Humans and ascenders are forming teams that will work together creatively.

I think the most accurate idea of how the mission is designed to work is through a creative partnership. By forming working teams, problems can be addressed at many different levels. The teachers, mostly former human beings from perfected worlds, do not understand how our nasty little planet conducts its business. These beings do not comprehend the kind of unmitigated greed that drives our economic system. They have never seen the kind of violence and selfishness we take for granted. They do not have much insight into our distorted religious beliefs and cannot always predict how we will comprehend their teachings.

They need us to do the legwork, but they also need us engaged in the creative process. A single individual is able to creatively solve problems at a certain level of efficiency. We are taught in the *Urantia Book* that adding personalities together to work on a problem increases the creative potential exponentially not linearly.

We who have been contacted have been given a fantastic opportunity. We are given a taste of how life in the universe usually works.

Universe education is about assigning groups to accomplish tasks and solve problems. The groups often mix beings of different talents and levels of experience. We have the chance to work in groups as partners with morontia beings and to use these working groups to solve spiritual, social, medical, scientific, artistic, and environmental problems. The benefits of the partnership go two ways. We the humans benefit from the input of wiser and more experienced beings. We benefit greatly from the love, support, and friendship these sympathetic and dedicated workers offer us. We actually become friends with the members of our working groups. The phrase, "our unseen friends", is quite literally true.

Our unseen friends benefit in ways that may be difficult for us to fully understand. Clearly the highest goal in the universe is to be of service, and the need on this planet is great. Our unseen friends crave opportunities to serve. There will be great insights that develop on the other side by those who work with us day in and day out. I also think that the agondonters have much to teach the morontia visitors about faith, trust, and courage. They observe us struggling to cope with life on an isolated planet.

When we can show steady spiritual growth under these conditions, I believe those who developed under conditions of light and life learn much from observing us.

From Paper 186:

"The Father in heaven loved mortal man on earth just as much before the life and death of Jesus on Urantia as he did after this transcendent exhibition of the co-partnership of man and God. This mighty transaction of the incarnation of the God of Nebadon as a man on Urantia could not augment the attributes of the eternal, infinite, and universal Father, but it did enrich and enlighten all other administrators and creatures of the universe of Nebadon. While the Father in heaven loves us no more because of this bestowal of Michael, all other celestial intelligences do. And this is because Jesus not only made a revelation of God to man, but he also likewise made a new revelation of man to the Gods and to the celestial intelligences of the universe of universes."

Insight # 3: The teaching mission is a glorious extension of Michael's seventh bestowal (as Jesus), and in the larger universe will result in new revelations of the Father to the creatures of time and space.

For a moment, consider the problem from Christ Michael's perspective. There was a major rebellion in one of your local systems. In your perfect wisdom, you allowed free will to go unviolated. The rebellion ran its course. In the midst of the rebellion, you made your final bestowal as a mortal on the most backward and isolated of the planets marred by rebellion. In all of the Universe of Universes, a Creator Son had never before been assassinated during a final bestowal in mortal form. Your ordinary local universe out towards the edge of settled space suddenly has become the focal point for much attention. You have the bully pulpit. All are aware of the "world of the cross."

Your actions in resolving the rebellion, restoring the isolated planets, and especially dealing with the planet of your bestowal are of interest to the entire Superuniverse. How would you go about setting things right given you have the opportunity to make a unique contribution to the history of Orvonton?

While it is impossible for me to truly understand the perspective that a Creator Son must have on this problem, it is not hard to see that the correcting time on Urantia is an opportunity for Christ Michael to continue to reveal the majestic perfection of the Universal Father to the creatures of time and space. It is a great opportunity to reveal the Father's love and perfection, and to make a unique contribution to the evolution of the Supreme Being. I don't pretend to understand how he will accomplish this, but I feel safe in suggesting that much good will result from the correcting time on every level of reality in Nebadon.

The correcting time has many different levels of meaning depending on who is looking at it from what perspective. From our human view on the ground, it is a period of increasingly rapid spiritual growth and development that will eventually lead the planet into light and life. It is the provision of the assistance we lacked because of the rebellion, emergency aid to help us overcome some of the terrible problems the rebellion has created on this planet.

From other perspectives, however, the correcting time may have even more profound meanings as well. Numerous forces are converging. There is the work of Michael and his administration. There is the planning and activity of the Melchizedeks. There are the thousands of teachers who are here to form working partnerships with us, and there are the millions of seraphim and others who are here to help put plans into action. Perhaps most important, the Universal Father is present in the very midst of all this activity.

The Thought Adjusters are in many ways the wild card. The teachers, who are adjuster indwelt or fused, encourage us to form a working relationship with our own thought adjuster. We then work together in groups with supervision and help from the Melchizedeks. The whole, being greater than the sum of its parts, may be a greater revelation of the Universal Father to the Universe.

When Michael walked the planet as Jesus of Nazareth, he lived a life that revealed the Universal Father to all of his universe. Is he creating a situation in which thousands of his children can use the opportunity of the rebellion to continue this revelation in new and profound ways? As the universe watches, we are called to collaborate with Michael and our older brothers in a project called the correcting time. What new insights, meaning, and revelations will come of this unique partnership?

On Working Together
Transmitted by Tarkas at the conference

I am Tarkas. I daresay that over the past year your perspectives have broadened as to the actual intent and purpose of this Mission and you have settled into a comfortable base of understanding on which we can logically and experientially grow together.

For in the beginning the phenomenon itself is even distracting, calling attention to itself, detracting from the purity of the message, and the real live Mission, which is to radiate the Father's love, one on one, to each person, each day, each hour and each moment, building from within, from within the hearts, the souls, the minds of each of you, outward.

There was some discussion tonight about how long this would require, and of course you know that this hinges a great deal upon your own minds and bodies and spirits and the free will decisions that you will make to activate this Mission, make it live, make it love, make it shine.

And you have grown more patient and knowing that there will be time required for this outworking, for time is indeed a great tool, a great catalyst, also a great catharsis at times. And so you must learn to use the Father's great gifts of time and space. As you can understand them, you can use them for divine purpose.

If the basic spiritual lessons, the various truths of the heart are to be learned, you know now that, as with a great book, they must be learned a page at a time, and as you turn each page, what you have learned grows increasingly greater.

And what you're intended to learn in this classroom of material experience grows shorter, so make use of your time each moment of the day, each conference when you can come together and manifest greater and more profound energies, and day by day, week by week, this Mission will grow.

Be patient as you turn the pages of this book of experiential knowledge. Absorb these pages; learn day by day. Your teachers will continue to inspire and to provide insights for your consideration as we feel you are equipped to absorb these learnings, and in turn teach these pages to others, for you know as well that learning is not complete until the student is able to share and give that knowledge, in love, to another.

During this meeting, much as you, we will be together sharing, smiling, being invigorated by the phenomena which we have experienced, and indeed it has been a great phenomenon to be able to come here in this Mission and work with humans.

You are our minds on Urantia, you are our hands, and you are our feet. You are our hearts. And we welcome your hands and feet and hearts and minds to this room. And so together we are quite, quite optimistic that the Father's plan will come to full fruition as you radiate the Father's love all around you. Peace to all of you. Thank you."

In subsequent e-mail discussion, Dr. Schlundt provided additional insights into the process of the Teaching Mission.

On Beethoven and Carpentry

Warren draws analogy between the written material presented in the *Urantia Book* and a Beethoven symphony. I must agree that the *Urantia Book* is a well-composed, well-rehearsed performance of great depth and beauty. I doubt that either those interested in the Teaching Mission's celestial teachers would, in fact, disagree. It is a written work of great beauty.

From what I have learned about the teaching mission, you seem to be missing the point. The sessions do involve presentation of some new material and amplification of some of the information in the *Urantia Book*, but that is not their primary purpose. I have seen no one claim that the transcripts of the teaching mission are intended to replace the *Urantia Book*. In fact, the teachers consistently refer to the book as the best available textbook for learning the truth. Most groups are encouraged to study the *Urantia Book*. Others can correct me if I am wrong.

So, if you want to hear Beethoven, then listen to Beethoven. If you instead, want to build a house, you cannot simply read books about house design and discussions of the elements of beauty in design and construction of buildings. Even the best book available on house building will not prepare you to actually build a house.

No, you have to learn to be a carpenter, a plumber, an electrician, a mason, and a painter. To become a skillful carpenter, for example, requires an apprenticeship, practice, feedback, and more practice. You have to hammer a lot of nails and saw a lot of boards before you have the skills required to build even the crudest house.

The teaching mission is more about helping people learn to apply the truths of the *Urantia Book* to their daily lives than it is about replacing the *Urantia Book*. It is about moving people from reading about service to doing service. It is about producing people who will act in ways that bring truth to the people of this planet. How does this compare to other people's perceptions of the goals of the teaching mission?

To worship effectively, for example, requires practice and repetition and perhaps even some instruction in technique. How many have read the *Urantia Book* and its beautiful passages on worship, yet have not put this into practice. The teaching mission is more about encouraging the doing and less about furthering our ability to intellectualize.

Let us borrow your analogy. If you want to make beautiful music on the guitar, you will have to devote yourself to becoming a guitar player. Reading about the guitar, while it may help you understand the theory, does not make you a guitar player. You have to practice the guitar, and spend of lot of time at it.

When learning carpentry or guitar playing, does it help to have a teacher? You can learn guitar on your own from a book, but I recommend taking lessons from a teacher. This is not to say there are not some wonderful self-taught guitar players. The best way to learn guitar is to combine the lessons of a teacher, studying books about music, and lots of practice.

I teach college classes, and I find that my oral presentations almost never have the crisp grammatical structure that writing has. When I talk about a subject to a class, it is not usually as well organized, and the words are not as well chosen as a written presentation. If I want to be sure that the class get certain essential information, I will give them a reading assignment.

However, we have classes instead of just making people read books for some reason. It is not just to keep teachers employed. There is a value that comes from the interaction, and the questions and answers. When I am writing something, I have no idea whether people will be able to follow my arguments completely. When I am discussing something with one of my classes, I can tell whether or not they are learning it from how they respond to my questions and the kinds of comments they make.

This is what teachers do, and this is how it is different from books. A transcript of one of my classes in which there was discussion would seem very poorly organized compared to something I wrote on the same subject.

If you read transcripts from the teaching mission, what you will find is that the questions asked by the humans are barely articulate and the answers from the teachers are usually pretty well stated. In oral speech, comparing what the humans say to what the teachers say is like comparing a junior high string ensemble to a professional string quartet. Neither quite rivals the power of a symphony orchestra, but there is a noticeable difference in quality.

When a student gets turned on by psychology, as a teacher I am able to encourage and nurture that student's interest in ways no book can. To me, the most rewarding teaching I do is one-on-one teaching in which I encourage students in the pursuit of knowledge. There is nothing more exciting than seeing a student get absolutely enthused about doing research on a particular topic. My greatest reward is when I see research papers published by my former students.

My actions as a teacher, the way I model my enthusiasm for the subject, the way I take the student seriously, the subtle and direct guidance I offer ... these are all parts of teaching that cannot come from a book. If a student comes to me after class and talks about how they want to be a psychologist, I discuss it with them, direct them to resources, suggest experiences that might help them achieve these goals. I do not say, "go read the book, all you need to know is there." The personal attention, personalized goals, feedback, and encouragement cannot be given by a book but can be given by teachers.

The *Urantia Book* tells us that the universe is one vast school. We are not told that we will be given a manual to study, or an improved version of the *Urantia Book* at each step along the way. No, we are told that we will learn from teachers, many of whom are mortals who are just ahead of us, and that much of our learning will be by doing.

How does it make sense to reject teaching because it is different from a book?

You can question the authority or credentials of the teachers. This is a very difficult issue since they are unseen and since the lessons and interactions are transmitted through humans. No one can offer definitive proof. This is what you should question. Are there teachers, or is this a mass delusion and all these people are just making this stuff up?

You can argue that Michael would never send teachers because we have a thought adjuster and the spirit of truth and besides, we have the *Urantia Book* to study. But you would have to deal with the fact that the *Urantia Book* tells us that we will be taught by teachers, and that much of our learning is by doing.

Perhaps the only reasonable argument is that we are under quarantine and this is why the teaching mission is absolutely impossible according to the vision of reality presented in the *Urantia Book*.

The teaching mission is about learning by doing. It is about individualized instruction. It is about giving homework assignments that will help people grow. It is teaching.

Yes, you are correct that there are differences in the written material. But, I question the conclusion that the teaching mission has no value. There is value to having a teacher, a mentor. That is different from reading a book, even the best book on the subject.

In essence, I agree with you fully about the quality of the *Urantia Book* and then suggest that you consider that the teaching mission is about teaching. In that case, judge it in comparison to your experiences as a teacher and as a student. How do these sessions compare to your classes in high school or Sunday School? That is a more appropriate yardstick to use than comparing teaching to a book.

REFLECTIONS after the Fayetteville Conference

FRED HARRIS, whose Tallahassee, Florida, Teaching Mission group developed the program, made these comments in a booklet that followed the event. Written Feb. 26, 1994, he refers to the end of a Urantia e-mail discussion group. And in May, 2011, Fred provides an update.

Greetings. As we see the end of an era on Urantial, I thought I would reflect a little on what I have learned from the experience.

1. The People.
I can say without exception that the people that inhabit and participate on Urantial are some of the most interesting and enjoyable people I have had the pleasure to be associated with. Each is uniquely qualified to present the revelation we call the *Urantia Book* to the world through their interaction with those they encounter. And I'm sure that they are and will.

2. The Substance.
Despite all the discussions, I am convinced that most everyone on this bulletin board is in agreement with the substance of the teachings of the UB and the teaching mission. That is, to live the teachings of Jesus of Nazareth and to follow the example set by him.

3. The Style.
It has become evident to me that if we are to be ambassadors of the kingdom, then we will need to be able to project a joyful countenance. We will need to be able to spread the Father's love to all we encounter. We will need to be tolerant of those with differing views and paths. We will need to build bridges between people, not try and break down barriers. Negativity has shown itself to be an unattractive and unpersuasive tool. Judgmental arguments only polarize. Abrasive attitudes will not show others the highest path.

Although it is sad that this phase of Urantial has come to an end, the real shame would be if we do not see the lesson in this for us all. We fell into a pattern of mean spirited argument unbefitting the people we are with the knowledge we all have. It sullied both sides. It was not the highest path. We now see the effects of these types of emotional and ill conceived responses.

4. The World.
We cannot change the world without evidencing the quality of our beliefs through our actions. We cannot change ourselves until we can consistently select the highest path. We cannot be a conduit for the Father's love unless we can be tolerant of each person we meet and look for the best in each of them. A smile and a hug will go a long way in this world. An argument is a dead end. Selfless service can cross all barriers. An attack will only close doors. We have seen this demonstrated at length on this bulletin board and I hope we have learned a lesson.

5. The Future.

As we go forward, I hope that I will be able to remain conscious of the valuable lessons I have learned and put them into use in my everyday life.

6. The Messages.

Because this will likely be the last message I post directly regarding the teaching mission and in light of the "Invisible Fellowship's" very distorted publication depicting the lessons of the teaching mission, I would like to summarize what I believe to be the substance of the lessons delivered by the teachers and which I have attempted to excerpt over these last several months here on Urantial.

a. Seeking the Father within. The teachers continually encourage us all to seek the Father as our guide. The ten minute daily stillness practice is an attempt to shut out the hustle and bustle of life and be in the presence of God. The teachers often say that they are irrelevant compared to the incomparable Father Fragment within us all.

b. Tolerance. One of my favorite teacher quotes is "There are as many paths to the Father as there are people to walk them." In it is the recognition that we are not to judge another's path, but only shine forth in our own path. Our reach for the highest path we can see can influence others, but only through our actions and Jove will that be possible. We are to look for the best in all we meet and praise it.

c. Random Kindness. Throughout the lessons it is apparent that selfless service is the result of a spirit led life. The fruits of the spirit. An attitude that can change the world. Help for all who we can help. With no expectation or need for recompense. It is in this lesson that barriers can be bridged and people reached.

d. Highest Path. The teachers urge us all to consciously see every crossroad as an opportunity to take the highest path. The path with the most love in it.

e. Family. Family is held up as the foundation for all growth. Family provides us with unquestioning love and acceptance. A shelter from the storm. Teachers encourage us to expand our concept of family to include all, as children of one loving Father.

f. Listening. As part of the teachers' program to take the teachings of the *Urantia Book* to the streets, we are each encouraged to listen to those we encounter, rather than just pausing and composing our response while they speak, as we often do. Not only is actually listening a service to those who speak to us, but it also allows us to discern what we can impart to them or what we can learn from them.

g. Faith. We are encouraged to throw off fear of the unknown and worry over what may befall us and trust in the Father's plan for us. Believe that whatever occurs will be capable of being turned to the best in the fullness of time.

h. Friendship. We are all reminded that going it alone is not the Father's way. We are to reach out to friends to support us in times of need and to reach out to friends when they are in need. We are encouraged to expand our circle of friends.

i. Balance. There is always more to do than we have time to do it in. We must make choices regarding the use of our available time. Teachers encourage balance, but ask that we not forget to speak with the Father at least ten minutes a day. Work, exercise, family time, play, worship. All must have a place in our lives. In the proper balance that is right for each of us as we see fit.

j. Children. The teachers have a soft spot for the children. They remind us that the universe plan is to learn and teach. We teach our children by who we are, what we stand for, how we act in every situation. We teach them by our actions more so than by our words. We are asked to be sure of what we stand for.

k. Conduit for the Father's Love. The second part of the 1-2-3 exercise is to become a conduit for the Father's love. To permit yourself to be a vehicle for the Father to pour love onto all that cross your path The teachers remind us that you can never give away all the love you possess. for once you give it away, the Father replenishes it and then some.

l. As if Jesus was with you. We are asked to live our lives as if Jesus was with us and we were, by our every thought, word and deed, demonstrating to him our understanding of his message.

m. Humor. The teachers enjoy higher forms of humor, not the depreciating types. They correctly remind us that taking ourselves too seriously is an ego based barrier to others. A joyful countenance is the most attractive and why shouldn't we be joyful when we have faith and feel that we are trying to know and do the Father's will for us in our lives? They do ask that, when we are trying the 1-2-3 exercise, that we not do so in a manner that would make light of the exercise.

n. Planting Seeds. We are asked to look for opportunities in the openings and closings between people. When we see an opening, we are asked to plant a seed. What that seed may be and how we are to do it is left to us. We are reminded that everyone we meet is a child of God, that God is no respecter of persons, and that He is working with everyone.

May 5, 2011 Update:

Ladies and Gentlemen, much water has gone under the bridge since I originally wrote the above post on my 41⁴ birthday, but the lessons remain the same. This is the training curriculum that has prepared people for the future. I want to let you know that we are called to now prepare for opportunities that will arise in the crisis situations that are likely to be upon this world in the near future.

Community is going to be especially important, so pay attention to your friends and neighbors. Unselfish service opportunities will abound. Really, all of the topics discussed by the teachers in the past will still be important, but with the time that has elapsed since the lessons commenced, I'm sure that each of you have experiences that demonstrate the value of those lessons.

Now it is time to earnestly be about the Father's business. Appreciate the spiritual values that are eternal and remember that even if all things earthly crash, there is no reason to fear. Have faith. All is well.

Beyond Fear
Thea Hardy

Editor's note: The late Thea Hardy, from Corvallis, Oregon, was a longtime member of the Teaching Mission who transmitted teachers LinEl, Serena, Christ Michael and others, and utilized her creative computer skills to promote the mission. She and her friends produced a magazine called "Beyond Fear," and this is one of her contributions.

"... *at every crossroad in the forward struggle, the Spirit of Truth will always speak, saying, 'This is the Way'."* (UB 34.7.8)

In the margins of my well-thumbed *Urantia Book*, I long ago wrote beside this passage, "If only I could hear it!"

How could I make truly effective spiritual decisions in my life? Sometimes, everything seemed vague; I simply could not figure out the proper path. Other times I knew what the way was, yet I could not bring myself to choose it. Still other options sprang up around my growthful choice-making. Yet most of these options represented ways that did not truly work, paths that did not lead far enough. For all those years, it seemed that hearing the Spirit of Truth speak thus was more of a dream than a possible reality . . . until the Teaching Mission arrived . . . Michael's mission, filled with his love, and his presence.

With the advent of the TM came the quiet time, the stillness, the silence practice. All the teachers spoke of it. It was one of the first things that I attempted in relation to the mission. Now I see it as the core of the mission itself.

In our local universe, our Michael is the living way, the open door to the Father. When I had troubles with consistent contact in my stillness practice, I was surprised to find Michael's presence there. My first thought was that this time was for the Father and not for Michael. Still, there he was.

Then, too, I was in awe – too much awe. I could not believe that it was acceptable for me to actually be with him, could not believe that I deserved his presence. And here he was, offering me more than his presence -offering me his companionship, offering me a real and living relationship with him, his spirit there to guide me to the Father through every step of that way, right beside me.

The first time I transmitted him, I truly felt like it would kill me. My own feelings of fear and unworthiness made my entire body ache. Yet I did it. And in time, I came to recognize that he did not desire that I go down on my knees before him. He urged me to stand up straight, to gaze into his eyes, and engage him in conversation.

Over time, I began turning to him in my quiet time. If I sought the Father to no avail in that episode, I would go to Michael and try to talk with him. Often he seemed to tell me things that I needed to hear about, and to deal with. Usually, I would then return to the Father in my mind and find better contact. On occasion, it seemed as though the Father was sometimes telling me to seek Michael first, and then come to him.

I will never forget one stillness time in my mind when Michael and I sat on the ground, in my imagination, and I dumped all my fears out in front of him, onto a square of cloth. Then the two of us gathered up the ends, and he went with me as I took this bundle to the Father and laid it before him. I said to God that it was truly my will for him to see all that I had within me, good and bad. I already knew that he saw my every fear, but I was *willing* for him to see it all. It was a very healing experience. Michael stood by my side throughout, and his love poured out to me from his smiling eyes.

I have had many moments of this contact with Michael since. I still feel some fearful resistance to transmitting him, yet I do it. I talk with him often in my mind, and although I have no way of knowing for certain that it is he who answers, the words that come to me are unfailingly wise and kind and helpful. Much in my life has healed as a direct result of this partnership with Michael's Spirit of Truth, for that is what I believe this to be.

We are told in the *Urantia Book* that the evidence of our connection with that Spirit is revealed in our awareness of fellowship with Michael. We can actively practice this fellowship in our daily lives, adding this most magnificent and effective method to our palette of tools for creative living. I find that he is never judgmental or chiding, yet he can clearly point out things that would probably irk me if my human companions spoke them. From Michael, with his unfailing graciousness, I take it. And I am trying to learn to take it from wherever it comes.

This new contact with the Spirit of Truth appears to me to be a major part of the teaching mission, which calls us to the direct service of Michael, and with Michael. Often, our group sharing becomes a time of sharing Michael - sharing our weekly adventures with his presence in our daily lives as we try to practice Teacher Will's now-famous 1-2-3 exercise and expand it into a full friendship relationship with our Creator Son.

Of course, I still seek the Father in my quiet times. There is no replacement for that. Michael ever points us to the Father's love, for only that love can effectively act as the supreme healer. But I no longer feel surprise when Michael is part of my quiet times. In fact, I have come to rely on him there. I remember that he said, while on this planet, that he who has seen him has seen the Father. Therefore, if he is oft-times a path to the Father in my quiet time,that only mirrors his purposes in this entire universe. So when I am not achieving what I want in my stillness, I talk to him first, and then find it easier to go find the Father in the increased clarity of spirit that often follows fellowship with the Spirit of Truth.

Michael has become my companion, my best friend, my most wise counselor. It has been a wonderful journey, and promises to be more wonderful still. This relationship with Michael, his Spirit of Truth living inside me, is truly transforming my life . . . one day at a time, sometimes one moment at a time . . . and for an eternity!

When I am anxious about my direction, I can go to him. He will not take away the need for my free will choice to operate, but in cooperative partnership with him, I find myself increasingly able to stand at each crossroads and move forward, beyond fear.

Confirming the Science, Meditation, Spiritual Connection
Mary Livingston, September 2010

The indwelling Thought Adjusters are a part of the eternal Deity of the Paradise Father. Man does not have to go farther than his own inner experience of the soul's contemplation of this spirit-reality presence to find God and attempt communion with him.
– The Urantia Book 5:0.1

The Urantia Papers are the intellectual framework whereby most of the contributors in this book have their conceptual foundation.

It is not mandatory that readers understand all the cosmology, history, or religious thoughts from what is considered the Fifth Epochal Revelation to humanity. However, one term that is essential to grasp is that of the Thought Adjuster, sometimes just called the Adjuster. This is literally a fragment of God that indwells all normal minded, morally conscious humans.

This fragment, this divine Presence, works to adjust our thoughts Godward, thus the name. And, all God-conscious individuals who strive for a deeper and more intimate relationship with the God of their understanding can benefit from the Teaching Mission.

While there are far more readers of *The Urantia Book* than there are proponents of the Teaching Mission, I will explain why this is the case. I will also possibly shed new light on the phenomena of celestial contact.

Please be aware that the Teaching Mission has nothing to do with channeling relatives that have passed over to the other side or anything other than celestial interaction, preferably with the very God that lives within but more often with celestial teachers that prepare us for that contact.

In 1968, psycho-biologist Roger W. Sperry first published his left-brain vs. right-brain pioneering studies. His work has been a topic of study and debate ever since. In 1981, he won a Nobel prize for his work so it is certainly noteworthy. "The main theme to emerge... is that there appear to be two modes of thinking, verbal and nonverbal, represented rather separately in left and right hemispheres respectively and that our education system, as well as science in general, tends to neglect the nonverbal form of intellect. What it comes down to is that modern society discriminates against the right hemisphere." - Roger Sperry (1973)

In general, those who are dominated by the left hemisphere of their brain (the logical side) tend to make decisions and do things because something makes logical sense. They are most often analytical and verbal in that they prefer written material. They prefer the scientific approach to life, measurable evidence, and repeatable steps with predictable and consistent results. Such people (and I was very much a "left-brainer"), derive security and a sense of control in their lives when their experiences are within a logical context.

Again in general, those who are dominated by the right hemisphere of their brain (the creative side) tend to make decisions and do things because something feels right intuitively. Analytical (left-brainers) separate things into steps or parts in order to examine and understand them, whereas right-brain dominant people "feel" the entire or whole situation and assess a situation creatively; that is spontaneously since they do not break things down into parts. Their spontaneity is often viewed as impulsive or chaotic behavior.

The problem, as I see it, has been in our methods and attempts to understand creativity and those dominated by their right hemispheric brains. Western culture especially values the scientific process. The scientific method gathers observable, objective (dispassionate, detached, and tangible) data in order to study and experiment with the data. All experiments must be repeatable with consistent outcomes to verify the dependability of any future results. In other words, if the same steps are consistently followed, the same consistent results are always obtained.

Sounds reasonable, yet, these tools of measurement do not always apply to the non-observable, subjective, and unpredictability of individual free will creatures with unique personalities and experiences. Even so, I have studied this subject, have a solid understanding of both *The Urantia Book* and the Teaching Mission, and I am confident I can scientifically validate the phenomena of the Teaching Mission and our right-brain brothers and sisters.

Based upon this knowledge I find that logic dominated "head" people are very drawn to the Urantia Papers while creative dominate "heart" people are more drawn to the Teaching Mission. Ideally, we all want to become balanced "whole brain" people with access to both hemispheres of our brains. Studies have proven, however, that stress and trauma actually shut down neurological pathways in the brain.

I will use two additional Urantia Book quotes. The passage below lays the groundwork for scientific data that will follow. This quote is from Urantia Paper 49, Section 5, Paragraph 12. (UB 49:5.12)

Spirit-reception series. There are three groups of mind design as related to contact with spirit affairs. This classification does not refer to the one-, two-, and three-brained orders of mortals; it refers primarily to gland chemistry, more particularly to the organization of certain glands comparable to the pituitary bodies. The races on some worlds have one gland, on others two, as do Urantians, while on still other spheres the races have three of these unique bodies. The inherent imagination and spiritual receptivity is definitely influenced by this differential chemical endowment.

I studied this paragraph almost word-for-word to break down each part for analysis. I will condense those findings with some explanation for non Urantia Book readers.

Mind design. This is one of the most important clues. We are told that "contact with spirit affairs" has to do with mind design but not the one-, two-, or three-brained orders* of mortals. The "spirit affairs" that take place within the mind is first with the adjutant mind-spirits** and then that of our Thought Adjuster. The adjutants prepare the mind and, in general, sometime during the fifth year of life, their work is complete and the Adjuster arrives. Contact with the adjutants is never mentioned within the UB but contact with the Adjuster is included within the Urantia Papers. Therefore, the Revelators indicate that there is a certain mind design that facilitates contact with the Adjuster.

* Urantians are classed as a two-brain series which undoubtedly refers to the left and right hemispheres of the brain. In the three brain series, the brain stem (or reptilian brain) is more developed and takes care of physical body needs, while one hemisphere does the intellectual functions and the third brain, or other hemisphere, is devoted to spiritual matters, "spiritual-counterparting activities of the Thought Adjuster."

** There are seven adjutant mind-spirits called the spirit of intuition, the spirit of understanding, the spirit of courage, the spirit of knowledge, the spirit of counsel, the spirit of worship, and the spirit of wisdom.

Organization of certain glands. Organization (organize) means any unified, consolidated group of elements or to make into a whole with unified and coherent relationships. Therefore, we are looking for a grouping of two types of glands rather than a pair of glands or an organ with two distinct parts. This grouping is probably complimentary or functioning together. For now, I will leave this for later when I narrow this down based on scientific research tied into the phrase, *comparable to the pituitary bodies.*

Inherent imagination. Inherent means natural, inborn characteristics. Imagination is typically defined as the act or power of forming mental images of what is not actually present (according to the physical senses). For example, I can create, through imagination and prior experience, an image (in my mind's eye) of a beautiful beach with crashing waves and powder white sand. Or, in my mind's eye, I can create an image of an inventor's workshop with a cabinet that when opened gives me access to the schematics of every invention in our universe. This second bit of creative imagination is not based on experience because not only is this workshop not an experience but it does not exist in our physical reality.

Spiritual receptivity. Spiritual receptivity means one is inclined, able, or ready to receive new spiritual ideas, suggestions or requests. In Urantian terms, this most likely means that a human with spiritual receptivity is able to receive Adjuster guidance more fully.

Differential chemical endowment. I have many pages of research that I used to locate the organs that would give us the chemical endowment presented in the above passage. Here it is simplified.

The pituitary gland is an endocrine gland about the size of a pea weighing 0.5 g (0.02 oz.). It is a protrusion off the bottom of the hypothalamus at the base of the brain, and rests in a small, bony cavity. It is functionally connected to the hypothalamus via a small tube called the Pituitary Stalk. It is considered to be the "master gland." Hypothalamus regulates the autonomic nervous system via hormone production and release. It affects and regulates blood pressure, heart rate, hunger, thirst, sexual arousal, and the sleep/wake cycle

The pineal gland is reddish-gray and about the size of a grain of rice (5–8 mm) in humans. The "pineal stalk" is no longer in technical use. However, the pineal gland is an outgrowth with a stalk-like cell mass (fibers) embedded in the posterior end of the thalamus. Thalamus: The "relay station" to the cerebral cortex.

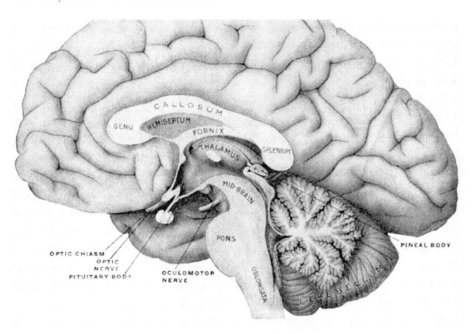

The Teaching Mission

What follows is the process for activating one's spiritual receptivity. The process is meditation. As a dominant left-brainer, meditation was difficult for me to achieve in the beginning. I was relieved to discover that guided meditation also opens "the circuits" to spiritual receptivity.

Below is the scientific explanation of the body's physiology during meditation. This is important scientific information, however it is quite technical and the paper is copyrighted. It can be read at http://bci.ucsd.edu/~pineda/COGS175/readings/Newberg.pdf. The title of the paper is, "The neural basis of the complex mental task of meditation: neurotransmitter and neurochemical considerations."

This study worked with two types of meditation. One sounds very much like Stillness meditation which is described in more detail within this book. Basically, a person gently clears all thoughts from his/her sphere of attention. It was described further as being characterized by a sense of no thoughts, time or space, as well as no sense of self and other. This meditation is by one's own volition. The second type of meditation involved absorption of attention on an object, image, phrase, word and may even be a guided meditation.

While the two meditations are distinctly different and one might expect different brain activity to occur, what was found was that after an initial period of time, based on neurological facts, the two methods converge. In other words, the same mental activities take place. Therefore, we can assume that regardless of one's meditative preferences, the results end up being the same, at least neurologically.

The right hemisphere of the brain has the foremost activity during meditation. Since right-brain dominant people have little sense of time and stronger visual imaging abilities, meditation is far easier for them. However, with a bit of determination there are meditation techniques that will also work for the more logical amongst us.

Now I will note some of the bioactivity that takes place during meditation. Please read the technical paper referenced above if you find it necessary to evaluate all the data yourself. For summary purposes, I will primarily mention the activities of the pineal and thalamus from the study using brain imaging for type one meditation.

The prefrontal cortex stimulates (by release of the neurotransmitter glutamate) part of the thalamus. Glutamate is used at the great majority of fast excitatory synapses in the brain and spinal cord. It is also used at most synapses that are "modifiable," i.e. capable of increasing or decreasing in strength. Modifiable synapses are thought to be the main memory-storage elements in the brain.

The thalamus controls the flow of sensory information, (gates the flow). When excited, the thalamus secretes an inhibitory neurotransmitter called GABA, which is used at the great majority of fast inhibitory synapses in virtually every part of the brain. Many sedative/tranquilizing drugs act by enhancing the effects of GABA.

Simultaneous stimulation of the right hippocampus (by the thalamus) mediated by glutamate, triggers the prefrontal cortex to increase thalamus stimulation. GABA from the thalamus results in less distracting outside stimuli, thus enhancing the sense of focus. Increased glutamate not only stimulates the thalamus but it also stimulates the hypothalamus to release B-endorphin (BE). But, BE alone does not produce the activities described. BE is known to slow breathing, reduce fear and pain, and to produce sensations of joy and euphoria.

The cortex of the brain is divided into four lobes. One area is the parietal lobe (PSPL) and it is involved with both the prefrontal cortex and the thalamus. Auditory and visual thalamus input is made to the PSPL. Then the PSPL enables the meditator to distinguish between the self and outside world. However one study showed that the more active the thalamus, the less active the PSPL became. This may account for the sense of Oneness some meditators report.

As with other studies, the limbic system is active during meditation. The hippocampus interacts with the prefrontal cortex, amygdala and hypothalamus. Here the report is very technical but simply put, the thalamus is stimulated. The thalamus gates (regulates) dopamine that is released by the hypothalamus.

Dopamine has a number of important functions in the brain. It plays a critical role in the reward system. An increase of dopamine into the prefrontal lobe area relieves pain and enhances feelings of pleasure. With increased serotonin, (other functions not mentioned here) the hypothalamus stimulates the **pineal gland** which results in an increase of melatonin.

Circulating levels of the hormone melatonin vary in a daily cycle, thereby allowing the entrainment of the circadian rhythms of several biological functions. Many biological effects of melatonin are produced through activation of melatonin receptors, while others are due to its role as a pervasive and powerful antioxidant, with a particular role in the protection of nuclear and mitochondrial DNA. Melatonin is secreted into the blood by the pineal gland in the brain. Known as the "hormone of darkness," it is secreted in darkness. Apparently, it is also secreted during meditation.

"Under circumstances of heightened activation, pineal enzymes can also. . . synthesize the powerful hallucinogen 5-methoxy-dimethyltryptamine (DMT)." Studies link DMT to mystical states such as time-space distortions and out-of-body experiences.

Hyperstimulation of the pineal gland could lead to DMT production associated with a variety of mystical experiences (as defined by scientists) including "**interaction with supernatural entities.**"

To conclude, in 90 words the Revelators tell us of a physical chemical endowment that facilitates spiritual receptivity. Based on their clues it was not too difficult to identify the pineal gland. Based on scientific neuro-imaging (brain mapping) we discovered that during meditation the pineal secretes melatonin that protects DNA and further that hyper-stimulation of the pineal gland possibly leads to DMT production resulting in "interaction with supernatural entities" (as described by scientists).

Thus, based on *The Urantia Book* and scientific data, interaction with celestial beings is not a figment of one's imagination. That is not to say that a beginner does not misinterpret what they "receive" but it does imply that they *are* receiving. With practice, experience, and good questions it does become easier to open the circuits or to access the connection.

Many Urantia Book readers question why anyone would bother with the celestial teachers when communication should come from the Source of authority, the fragment of God within. This is a legitimate question. The answer is that most of us are not prepared to receive direct communication with God. It doesn't take a Revelation to tell us that we live on a dysfunctional planet.

Unrecognized patterns of dysfunction tend to be repeated generation after generation. These dysfunctions prevent healthy relationships, create distrust and often block our ability to receive unconditional love. Cultural dysfunctions such as war, exploitation, starvation, poverty, discrimination, misuse of authority and the media promoting fear, to name a few, also have an impact on individuals. We cannot enter into a relationship with the Divine until we have cleared or healed the dysfunctional patterns operating in and influencing our lives.

The Urantia Book teaches that Deity delegates everything possible. It also tells us that there are countless celestial beings devoted to our spiritual growth. Based on both the Urantia Papers and scientific research it seems evident that God would provide a means of healing and preparing us for full spiritual receptivity as designed and intended on the physical level. The argument that *The Urantia Book* does not mention the Teaching Mission verbatim simply ignores our individual responsibilities to grow in wisdom and toward perfection.

The concept of celestial teachers (per the Teaching Mission) is not only plausible but also probable. However, like all gifts, talents, and abilities, some people are naturally more proficient or have had more experience in developing their receptivity than others. Right-brain dominant people most likely fall into this category. Also, some people are far more fortunate in that they did not grow up in a dysfunctional family and perhaps must only overcome cultural dysfunctions. This is an area best evaluated by personal experience and reflective thought.

I recall my skepticism and wondered why, since I have an Adjuster, I would be interested in having mere celestial teachers. I now see that my attitude was akin to a five year-old announcing she would forget about the adjutant mind-spirit nonsense and just bring on her Father Fragment. Such ignorance would make the celestials laugh if it was not so pathetic. The adjutant mind spirits prepare the individual's circuits for the reception of their Thought Adjuster. Just because we are unaware of that process does not make it any less real or necessary.

If you came from an ideal family, you may be ready to enter into an interactive relationship with your Adjuster. At least you have the necessary prerequisite to the Father-child relationship. If you are personally working to heal, forgive, overcome, and break the dysfunctional patterns in your life, you are developing and preparing to enter into that interactive relationship with your Father Fragment. But, it takes tremendous work!

This is where the Teaching Mission is most effective. The celestial teachers are trained to teach us how to love and forgive as well as to set aside ten to twenty minutes per day for Father Time (also called Stillness). Until we are healed of dysfunctional relationship issues, contact with the Thought Adjuster, the Divine Presence within, is most likely to be difficult, confusing, and frustrating. There are volumes of celestial teacher lessons that consistently teach us how to love and attain spiritual growth.

For two decades, the Teaching Mission has primarily worked with individuals with well-developed spiritual receptivity abilities. Commonly tagged as T/Rs (they receive and transmit the celestials) these individuals have provided a service involving hours of their time and energy. Others have devoted equal time and energy to transcribe, verify and make the transmissions available to the public in multiple languages. This effort has not been for naught.

I do not read the transmissions very often now. However, I see the value and purpose of the transmissions, group celestial teachers and individual celestial teachers. I believe that reading the transmissions has untold value in giving the reader a base line. Without a base line, one cannot discern a true pattern.

In my early days with the Teaching Mission, I read many transcripts from various teachers and today I can discern whether something "fits" or is consistent with the "curriculum" of the Teaching Mission. This holds true for Urantia Book readers in that they, too, can read material and discern if it is in alignment with the teachings of the Revelation. Therefore, I recommend that people read some of the transmissions.

My experience concerning group celestial teachers is that they are spiritually socializing us, and most likely healing the cultural dysfunctions that have affected us. And, of course, the personal teachers work with individuals on their particular areas needing to be healed.

But the first goal is to receive personal guidance for oneself. In the beginning, a person can work with a T/R to ask questions and learn to interact with the celestial teachers. Never, to my knowledge, are we encouraged to sit at the feet of a T/R or hang onto the words transmitted from a celestial teacher as if they are sacred. That is nonsense and would be an abuse of authority. We are free willed mortals and have a responsibility to respectfully request that the teacher stop to clarify anything that confuses us or does not seem correct.

The Teaching Mission is not a preaching mission; it is interaction between physical humans and celestial teachers. But, sincerity is the key. Any attempts to ask "trick questions" or to "prove" that the T/R or Teaching Mission are bunk will not be successful.

I once thought that prayer was a method of talking to God while meditation was a method of listening to God but that is a gross oversimplification. *The Urantia Book* Revelators disclosed that we are physically endowed with a means of initiating spiritual contact. Meditation has been scientifically studied and demonstrates how the "spiritual glands" can be activated and leads to the "interaction with supernatural entities." It is not a matter any longer of the validity of the Teaching Mission but a personal choice whether one can overcome the fears produced by dysfunctional relationships found in families and cultures in order to trust their right-brain processes to open the door to their superconscious mind, whereby their Adjuster awaits.

The Urantia Book, 196.3.31 sums it up perfectly, "The great challenge to modern man is to achieve better communication with the divine Monitor [Thought Adjuster] that dwells within the human mind. Man's greatest adventure in the flesh consists in the well-balanced and sane effort to advance the borders of self-consciousness out through the dim realms of embryonic soul-consciousness in a wholehearted effort to reach the borderland of spirit-consciousness—contact with the divine presence. Such an experience constitutes God-consciousness, an experience mightily confirmative of the pre-existent truth of the religious experience of knowing God. Such spirit-consciousness is the equivalent of the knowledge of the actuality of sonship with God. Otherwise, the assurance of sonship is the experience of faith."

BEYOND CYNICISM:
Liberating Voices from the Spirit Within:
Excerpts from the book by Jim Cleveland and the OneTeam

"Each of you is an heroic, sparkling star in a plan of vast complexity and glory"

THE FIRST QUESTION: *There are many of us for whom the yoke of cynicism and despair over the human condition has become nearly too much to bear. I guess I'm one of them. I'm wanting to know if there are any answers I can understand that can help me cope with the daily hassles of an alienated world?*

My son, these burdens are imaginary, as fleeting in your lifetime as the breeze upon the plain. You have within yourselves the power to understand a higher level of spiritual reality, and to respond to that understanding with sure spiritual growth. If you would undertake a dialogue to find this peace, then so would we.

Okay, where do we start? Is there a primer?

One of the greatest lessons that humankind should know is that God resides within each and every one of you of sound mind, an indwelling spirit fragment of God that experiences life with you. In fact, this is how God experiences life in the form of all His creations in the worlds of time and space, eternally evolving with you through the inner presence of a prepersonal being that has variously been called the soul, the indwelling spirit, the higher self, the light. There is little significance to language names, only to realities. Bear in mind that terminologies and definitions are somewhat variable based on prior understandings as we go through these lessons.

The point is that you, each living expression of God, have within your being the knowledge of right and wrong, good and evil, as well as the fatherly guidance of God to choose correctly by listening and trusting this inner voice. Attunement to your inner higher selves, this spiritual spark, is the great quest of mankind, accessing God's piloting hand to help you steer forward on an eternal ascension toward perfection, aligning your will with God's so that the trip can be one of accelerating joy.

Then I will play devil's advocate. Please excuse the term. Most people think it's far-fetched to envision any kind of perfection for the miserable mass of mankind. How would you respond to them?

In this short life, you won't. But do you consider that's all there is? This life is a school, classrooms and laboratories for material experience, and for your indwelling spirit as much as you, for you are separate, but entwined. Together you strive toward that perfection as far as it can be carried in this material life. But this life is only the beginning. When you look up into the billions of stars and planets, do you not get a glimpse of the enormity of the plan? Do you not see a God behind the plan for all this? Do you not conceive that the bringing to perfection of all the creatures of time and space would be a fascinating preoccupation of such a God, one that God can share and experience with each individual personality of the creation?

You make it sound like a super celestial game of some kind. Are we just pawns in a game?

The enormous amount of celestial resources devoted to the ascension of God's time and space beings makes this far more than a game. It is the plan for the universes. The seven universes of the superuniverse, as explained in your Urantia text, are essentially schools, environments for learning and growth.

And you, humankind, are far more than pawns. You have been endowed with certain wonderful gifts that make you perfectly unique beings with powerful potentials. Consider the gift of life itself, the gift of mind via a sharing of the Universal Mind for your creativity. Consider your finely evolved mammalian bodies, your unique personality, and the indwelling spirit presence of God, which forever seeks to guide you in ways of righteousness, toward greater growth in the finer attributes. Consider your free will, which is so treasured that even the Father does not abrogate it. Consider the embellishment later by the Spirit of Truth, which was poured out upon all flesh by Jesus at Pentecost, giving each of you a stronger conviction of truth if you would go inside to find and utilize it.

I'd like to get back to this Jesus person later, but for now, if we're so lucky to be part of this grand adventure, why are conditions so bad here? How did we generate so much poverty, crime, disease, suffering, greed, malice, downright evil?

By your own free will decisions. And the gift of free will is not lightly taken away by the Universal Father, who bestowed it in the first place

Of course, you have discovered a transmitted planetary history that you call The *Urantia Book*. Continue to glean from it. It provides the panoramic cosmic overview – the fall of your planetary prince in what is called the "war in the heavens" and which your text calls the Lucifer Rebellion ... and then the default of Adam and Eve in their mission of biological upliftment ... followed by the materialization of Machiventa Melchizedek to foster the One God concept through Abraham and the Jews ... and then the incarnation as Jesus by Michael, a Creator Son of God, who thereby lived as one of his creations, sanctified his rule over our local universe, and finally brought the Lucifer Rebellion to an end. The Urantia Papers chronicle the life of Jesus, at once the Son of God and Son of Man, his noble death and resurrection and the subsequent development of the Christian faith. It is all there.

But whether one avails himself of this or other real or purported revelations is a free will choice of the personality. You truly need the Spirit of Truth to help you make good decisions.

If you continue to study the text analytically, you will find an analytical answer to your plaintive cry for understanding. If you choose to receive the ministrations of God's assigned spiritual teachers and guides and avail yourselves of direct revelation from teachers at a higher plane of the ascension path, then there are greatly enhanced opportunities in these times. There are now teachers to support the text.

Know for certain. The free will gift you possess is truly awesome. And all of your Divine gifts combined make you far more than pawns. Each of you are heroic, sparkling stars in a plan of vast complexity and glory.

All that? As I understand the Urantia Papers, we are often more animal than human, and we exhibit far too many animalistic traits and tendencies. Is that not right?

Perhaps you will be as you consider yourself to be, for you literally manifest your thoughts in many ways. Would you allow your animal natures to rule your lives here, or would you reach for higher guidance? Is your indwelling spirit not continually tingling you toward feelings of love, brotherhood and perfection? Do not all of you know of God's universal command to 'Be ye perfect, even as I am perfect' in whatever words it is rephrased. And you must know that this isn't accomplished in a single, short life in material form. There is a far greater ascension plan for humankind than most have ever imagined.

Do not be overly concerned with your myriad of shortcomings. You are but babies in the universe. When you err, imagine your God as a Heavenly Father who picks you up, dusts you off and asks you gently and kindly to choose again.

Some of these babies are out there blowing each other away, committing horrible atrocities against one another. Some are corrupt to the bone. Surely all these criminals and perverts aren't part of this glorious ascension plan?

If you could search out all of the deleterious influences that lead your brothers and sisters to lives of greed, anger and aggression, you could better understand the misguided motivations that lead them to these ruins. They have fallen gravely ill to various spirit poisons – fear, envy, anger, jealousy, greed, hatred – often born from frustration, addiction, and despair, always from ignorance of great spiritual truths. So many have been traumatized by event and circumstance, that you would do well and wisely to seek the reasons for their misdirection.

It is God's plan that you reach out in love to these lost brothers and sisters. This is what they truly need, and you will be amazed to see that most of them readily recognize this need and will respond to you in positive ways. Reach out and do this; radiate this love. There is a great need for this daily service, reciprocally, between all of you who would be led by spirit and love. Each of you has greater power than you can imagine to bring the holy reality of love into the hearts of persons with whom you interact every day, and strangers as well.

Each one can be brought to the fold of spiritual security who does not consciously embrace evil. One does not embrace these false concepts once they are shown the power of loving brotherhood, once they see the light of truth that loving one another radiates the world toward peace and joy. Let that truth, the power of universal, unconditional love, radiate from your inner spirit, wherever you go and to whomever you meet. You'll do well in life if you do.

Some few do overtly choose evil. This is sometimes done, but not often. Most are misguided and weak, not evil. And in the afterlife, when certain universe realities are then recognized and God's plan revealed, these ascending humans then have the option to consider this new knowledge and carry forward in the universe plan. With this enlightened perception at hand, few humans choose extinction over moving onward.

Wait a minute. Are you telling me that we lowly animal-origin creatures, spiritually indwelt by God, are not only the prime subjects of a grandiose ascension plan toward perfection, but that we also have the right to choose whether we go on or not? Aren't you giving us a lot more power than we deserve? Isn't God making these eternal salvation decisions, or certainly a divine tribunal?

God chose to create you and give you free will to choose the Divine path. We believe that God has faith in you and all of the created beings, and knows that all will come to good eventually and be returned to the First Source and Center. God has faith that, once the reality of the plan is known to you, that you will choose love and the long and fruitful path toward spiritual perfection. But you may not know the full picture until you cross to the other side.

But all doesn't come to good the way I see it. So many of us lead miserable lives, and often check out early. Others gain power by choosing evil ways and cause great suffering for the innocent. This talk about Divine goodness is pretty pat when we're faced with impossible problems every day. And I didn't cause them. I didn't make the world a crazy place. We're just stuck with it.

You touch on many things. You say that all does not come to good, but how do you know? Do you not understand that your spiritual identity goes on when the material body is set to grave. This indwelling spirit, your soul, is your true identity, and do you not think that the good you have done and are doing is worth saving for posterity? Would God have this lost? No. Nothing good is ever lost.

Haven't you truly wanted to sow seeds of goodness? Have you not sought truth, beauty and goodness and longed for its reality? God knows these things and judges you from these values that you would say are of the heart. God knows that you are an inherently good person, created, as they say, in his image. You are essentially a good person, as most are, and will come to good, namely a place in the ascension schools for mortal beings that Jesus called "many mansions," which the Urantia Papers revelation reveals as the "Mansion Worlds." You will come to good here, for you will be resurrected and refined as partial spirit beings, beginning your spirit world ascension through many schools and many adventures.

All will come to good.

And even those who are horribly misguided and even have committed evil will have the opportunity for rehabilitation, but they must begin this quest at whatever lower station is assigned. Many have given up on truth, beauty and goodness in your mortal world, but we say to you that saving messages will be coming to them and to all of you more intensely in the immediate years ahead. We would have you listen.

You touched also upon your supposedly sorry plight of having to deal with these myriad of problems caused by both your ancestors and your contemporaries, a world of their making, certainly not yours. However, you would do well to analyze each and every of your own individual positive and negative contributions to society as an exercise in your own spiritual growth. You may find that you radiate more discontent than you think, and that you contribute little of true value because of your negative attitudes, the bad vibrations you inflict upon scenes which have greater potential.

Life is an opportunity, not an obligation. Without problems and challenges, humans would not grow in character, and in the spiritual values that will be so important to you in the long ascension plan that awaits after this brief mortal sojourn.

You must know yourself that humans rise to their greatest achievements in adversity, and fall back to complacency or worse when the path is easy. Your challenges and problems are opportunities for learning and growth, though it is surely not easy for you to recognize them as such.

It would also be a good spiritual growth exercise to list on paper those quality traits of the perfected human to which you would aspire, and then note the noble and generous actions that you have yourself performed in pursuit of them, and in response to the adversities you have faced. Know also that your indwelling spirit seeks to always lead you in these paths of growth, and so you can expect these continuing opportunities.

Are you saying the spirits, angels, whomever , are constantly throwing up problems so we can deal with them and grow?

You make well enough problems on your own. Your spiritual helpers do, however, help to present you with situations which require moral decisions. These are opportunities for you to choose rightly and grow. It is true that humans have often chosen wrongly and reaped bitter harvests. Such as the uncertainties of time and space worlds.

I don't want to cause anybody any problems. I just want to mind my own business and let everybody else do the same. Is there anything wrong with that attitude?

Learning to interact with others is one of the great lessons in the universe, and will be part of your ascension plan at all levels, for the Father's many personalities of time and space are often quite different from your own. As you ascend, you will eventually learn that cooperation can achieve much more than competition, that there is strength in diversity that can be fruitfully exploited by those with love for God, with love for themselves as children of God, and for one another as spirit imbued beings made by this same Heavenly Father's hand.

This learning during your material life will be all the more honored through the ages, for it is achieved in a relative vacuum of higher knowledge concerning the universe. Many on your planet see no evidence of a God with their material eyes, yet have unseeing faith. This is an ability much appreciated on our side. You have been called agondonters, those who can believe without seeing, although, in reality, you are seeing at a deeper level.

I doubt that there is any deeper level. Reality is that it's dog-eat-dog here. We have to be tough to survive, and we have to be doubtful, suspicious, even angry and confrontational sometimes to cope with what we have to deal with — a lot of who you call brothers and sisters are out to cheat us and maybe destroy us.

God did not make this so. You did. If this is what you believe to be reality, then your actions will surely make it so. Believe otherwise and you will see otherwise.

You have every right to defend yourselves, but the most effective means is by returning good for evil. The power of loving goodness is so much more than you imagine. You can do so much to deflect aggression and animosity toward yourself, or what you imagine to be, by responding in kindness, and with the offer to help relieve your attacker's frustrations. Have you not seen this melt aggression? And have you not seen that responding with animosity and anger invariably makes the situation worse. Use the power of love each day; eventually you will understand that it truly is the most powerful force in the universe.

You can defend yourselves without resorting to the spirit poisons that can pollute your minds, and then your bodies, and, indeed, the atmosphere all around you. Have you not observed personalities who can lighten a room with their loving demeanor, and others who can cast a pall with their troubled presence?

It would take an idiot to have a blithe attitude about some of the awful things that happen in the world. We have every right to be serious-minded and defensive.

If by blitheness, you mean a feeling of constant happiness because you are a child of God on a wonderful ascension path that reaches far beyond this world and cannot fail, then I would say blitheness is desirable. It is like faith.

If your definition of "serious-minded" would be one who lives in fear and distrust of his fellows and thereby sacrifices much of the joy of living, then I would say that this state of mind would not be in your best interests. Even if your mortal life is taken in a horrible turn, this is no tragedy in the overall sense. Death is presently the only realistically achievable means by which humans on your planet are able to cross into the spiritual plane. It is a human tragedy, of course, if an untimely death cuts short your experience and your potential growth while in the flesh. But this growth will continue exactly where you left off at the next level. And there will be a multitude of experiences, beyond your imagination.

Please know also that you can defend yourself from danger while remaining in true acceptance of the Father's will. Struggle, my friend, is part of the universe. But do not struggle in fear. Do not live in fear. It is destructive in many ways.

How about soldiers? They live in fear and they live to destroy. God may not want war and killing. But sometimes you just have to defend yourself with violence or be destroyed.

Understand that all soldiers of all sides of all wars go to the Father's spiritual kingdom for judgment upon dying. The war itself provides only one consideration regarding a person's mortal life. Killing in war in the absence of spiritual poisons which many embrace, would not count nearly as badly against an individual as would murder with malice.

You must know, however, that even those who have committed evil acts have the opportunity to renounce and make amends for these acts and continue in the ascension plan. That which is good and aspires with potential for goodness will be brought forward in the plan. The individual must consciously choose extinction, and few do so once these truths are revealed to them on the spiritual side.

So even somebody like Hitler or Stalin, who have done great evil, would have the opportunity to survive death and move forward in that ascension plan. Is that right?

Yes, in keeping with their mandates. This is a matter for God's high tribunals, the Ancients of Days, and each life is an open book before them. The path of rehabilitation for ones so misguided will be much more regimented and correctional than for those who have made some contact with the God inside that forever stands open to you.

You must understand, too, that there are many humans not of normal mind. God, of course, takes into consideration that genetic abnormalities should not be weighed against the survival of a well-meaning personality.

It seems there's lots of rehabilitation going on in your Heavens, and no punishment. Aren't you taking the easy way out here? Wouldn't it be better just to eliminate some of these undesirables as hopeless cases?

Thank you for several more stimulating questions.

Rehabilitation as part of education is a vital part of the universe, especially in worlds such as yours, which have been quarantined because of the Lucifer Rebellion. This essentially means that you have long been cut off from universal media, the broadcasts that disseminate news of the many planets of your local universe. You have been isolated, but this isolation is coming to an end. And you will experience the rehabilitation to God's glories that is your own. Knowing it firsthand will bring you new insights into the values of compassion and mercy that are the very essence of Jesus/Michael and a hallmark of his mission on your planet.

Amazingly, it is a fact that the good that has resulted from this rebellion of Lucifer has been many times greater than the bad. It has been a mighty confirmation of God's plan because of the sorry plight of those planets that were diverted from the true wisdom. Learning and growing then, education, including rehabilitation, is the working force of these universes of time and space. Creative energy is the fuel.

You would do well on your planet to more strongly consider and practice rehabilitation in criminal systems instead of so much punishment. You will not be able to do this until much greater increments of love, compassion and mercy are instilled in your hearts. But when you do, you will find it very fruitful and advantageous to society as a whole. Your systems of punishment often become schools for hatred, and society often reaps a terrible whirlwind.

You state that rehabilitation is easy. It should not be.

And you state that it might be better to eliminate some personalities as hopeless, beyond rehabilitation. These decisions are for the Ancients of Days. Our responsibilities are other than this. But it is true that there is still opportunity to exercise your free will gift before this tribunal and choose to move on in God's plan. But rehabilitation may require retribution, and may be found to be such that the individual would choose extinction rather than embark upon this plan for growth and learning.

If extinction is chosen, being "as if you never were," then that goodness that you accomplished in your earthly life, from the largest to the smallest act of kindness, will be forever preserved and carried up into the universal experience. Nothing good is ever destroyed. Certainly not God's indwelling gift to you. This internal being, called the "thought adjuster" in the Urantia Papers, is invariably blameless for a human's failures, and upon human extinction would likely be assigned to another evolving mortal. Some Thought Adjusters have had experience with other mortals before indwelling you.

Well, I'd like to believe all this wonderful stuff. But even if it's all true, it just makes me more dissatisfied with the true reality of my life, and makes me wonder if there's any hope for the world to get from here to utopia. I'm not getting any deep messages or adjusted thoughts from inside and I don't see a lot of progress in the world.

You will soon see that there are strong evidences of a planetary spiritual awakening all before you, if you would open your eyes. And you can surely be an important part of it if you choose. There is much room for skeptics and cynics in God's kingdom, for they often prove to be stalwart and brilliant speakers of spiritual truths who know from whence they speak.

Right now, I'd just remind you once again of the miserable shape the world is in, and how hopeless it is for one person to do anything about it. I might be able to develop some faith in God's plan, but I don't have much faith in mankind.

God does. As we work together, so will you.

The Correcting Time
Fred Harris

Deep in space, far from the Isle of Paradise, in the universe of Nebadon, there is a weak star known as the sun. Spinning around that sun is a blue-green planet its inhabitants call Earth. For many years the Earth and a significant portion of the other inhabited planets of Nebadon had been subject to a universe quarantine, first imposed to limit the rebellion led by Lucifer. Lucifer, once a brilliant angel, had challenged God and the ascension plan for mortals (the plan by which mortals would progressively become spirit as they ascended to the Isle of Paradise) - he even questioned the existence of God - arguing that none should be beholding to a fictionalized God, but rather should be free to develop without the schooling through which mortals and celestials are educated. Humans had only a dim knowledge or understanding of Lucifer, although they had heard of the rebellion and the war between the angels through several of the religious organizations, particularly Christianity.

The quarantine limited the universe circuits and broadcasts normally available to inhabited planets in space - a form of celestial cable television. Although Lucifer was arrested after being defeated by Michael (known on Earth as Jesus), the quarantine of the rebellious sectors of Nebadon, including Earth, continued until after the trial and adjudication of the rebellious leaders.

As a result of the rebellion and quarantine there was a general ignorance by Earth's populace regarding the universe administration, the ascendancy plan for mortals of the realm and, generally, the reason for their existence. For years the inhabitants of Earth were of the opinion that Earth was the center of the universe and that all celestial bodies revolved around it. They even believed that the Earth was flat, not spherical. It was a backward planet struggling for information and knowledge with a minimal amount of help from celestial intelligences.

Unlike Earth's court trials, the celestial tribunals spare defendants who choose to accept the universe plan and the rehabilitation order of the Ancients of Days, the universe Supreme Court. The trial of Lucifer and the leaders of the rebellion, while taking hundreds of Earth years, was speedy from the celestial perspective where time is relative to the eternal existence of spiritual beings.

In 1984, Earth time, Lucifer was judged guilty of rebellion against God, refused rehabilitation and elected personality extinction, as did all of the leaders of the rebellion. Each participant in the rebellion was given the choice and most chose to be rehabilitated, but the egos of the leaders could not accept the diminishment of stature inherent in rehabilitation and were extinguished. Michael wept when advised of their decision.

After the adjudication of the Lucifer rebellion, an order came from Paradise to lift the quarantine imposed on the inhabited planets involved in the rebellion and, with due haste, reconnect the universe circuits and bring the inhabited worlds therein into light and life, a stage more reflective of the love showered on all beings of the universe. Although celestial personalities assist in the transformation of a planet to the ages of light and life, the free will of the mortals is never violated. The people must choose to take actions which will lead to a world of light and life where there are no more wars, diseases are conquered, and hatred and greed are replaced by love and service to one another.. Of course, that means that planetary transformation cannot occur overnight, or even within a generation or two. It usually takes at least one thousand years.

When the order was issued following the adjudication of Lucifer, legions of celestial personalities were mobilized. Plans were laid. A universe moved with dispatch to commence the process of reconnecting the circuits to the quarantined planets and assisting the inhabitants in their spiritual upliftment.

On Earth at this time things were a mess. Wars between nations, tribes and individuals raged. There was a general unequal distribution of wealth. Injustice was often the rule. Pollution of the air, water and land threatened the ability of the planet to sustain human life. Weapon technology was so advanced that on several occasions the world teetered on the brink of destruction. Hatred was rampant. The people sought refuge in intoxicants and hedonism. Families disintegrated. Many suffered. Curiously, from the celestials' perspective, the world's religions were often intolerant of the many other paths to God and were responsible for much of the hatred and strife on the planet. The task of turning this situation around was indeed daunting. The celestials had their work cut out for them.

Prior to the Lucifer trial and adjudication but after Lucifer had been imprisoned there was a concern by the ministering spirits that the Earth was sliding farther and farther away from the truth. It was also seen that the unsuspecting humans that were to assist in the process of rehabilitating the planet would need a broader knowledge of the basic universe scheme and organization.

An emergency request by the spiritual beings resident on Earth (who are known as midwayers, as they are beings midway between the material and the spiritual) was made to the universe government, was granted, and a revelatory text was assembled for transmission to the Earth. It was written by different celestial personalities, selected depending on the topic to be discussed and the expertise of the author.

Once the text was completed, edited and approved by the revelatory commission, it was then to be delivered to Earth. The method of delivery was a problem. In the past, when revelations were attempted on Earth many difficulties were experienced. For the most part the revelatory information was transmitted through individuals sometimes known as prophets, who often became like gods to those who believed in the revelation and were unduly venerated.

Many of the people through whom revelatory information was attempted to be transmitted incorporated their own beliefs into the information, often with disastrous results, especially with respect to the status of women. Many of these "prophets" and their followers became fanatical and intolerant of other belief systems thereby creating more hatred than spreading the love of God, as had been intended. Correcting those situations became very difficult and the result of prior revelations was often counterproductive.

This effort would have to learn from those prior experiences to be effective.

It is hard for humans to accept the fact that celestial personalities exist. For those who do accept the premise of a nonmaterial realm, it is difficult for them to accept the fallibility of celestial personalities. For Earthlings, immortality carries with it omnipotence and omniscience. Such is not the case with ascending beings.

For the most part celestial personalities are either created for one purpose (like angels, seraphim and cherabin) or are former mortals who are now ascending in stages from the material to the spiritual on their way to Paradise. The universe is a huge educational system where each personality progresses ever upward until, after many eons of education and service, that personality comes to the Isle of Paradise to meet with and be embraced by God. Along the way each individual is guided through a regimen of learning and teaching, teaching and learning.

Most people on Earth at this time believed that when they died they would either go straight to Heaven or would be sent to Hell to burn for eternity with Satan. They thought that man's mortal existence was his only chance to accept the "truth" and be saved or be lost forever. No wonder so many humans feared God and God's judgment! No wonder so many religious denominations believed that they held the exclusive truth and that it was their duty to enlighten all others, even if they had to subdue them to do so! No wonder revelatory information disseminated previously was deemed exact and perfect, so much so that each word and phrase was meticulously studied and dissected!

This scriptural infallibility concept was of concern to the celestials in charge of delivering the new revelation to Earth not only because of the resistance to new information among those who believed their text was the last word of God, but also because those who embraced this new material might likewise be closed to any further revelation. They were really more interested in the substance of the information to be delivered than the linguistic structure of the sentences and paragraphs or the method of delivery. But they noted the various problems and did what they could to overcome them, for this revelation had to be properly written and delivered or it would cause more trouble than it was worth. And it had to include within it clues regarding the coming time of correction.

To this end the various celestial personalities who were to be authors painstakingly crafted their chapters in an attempt to write the revelation so that no inconsistencies or poor word structure would hinder the basic message. They searched for an individual who could be the conduit for the information without being personally interested in fame or fortune as a result of the text. They instructed the humans who were cooperating in the effort to maintain a low profile so as not to inflame religious denominations of the day, which the celestials feared could lead to the suppression of the book. They had to select the type of society that was pluralistic enough to permit the free flow of ideas.

There were many considerations to be taken into account. Although the information to be presented was like a textbook of celestial cosmology, it also included information about the currency of the universe - God's love. It analogized God to a beneficent parent and mortals to God's children. It tried to dispel the fear of God that humans had been taught and inform the humans that God loved them as parents would love their children. It was a large volume. Very detailed and deep. Few were interested.

But a few were all they needed.

Part Three

Personal Experiences with Celestial Teachers

Humans are all unique. This being so, the many personalities who have come into contact with the celestial teachers each have a unique story to tell about how their lives have been changed and their spiritual growth accelerated.

Taken together they comprise a colorful woven tapestry, each thread pursuing a common purpose, each different in the course of their weavings. Some are conservatively invested in the basic spiritual lessons of the teachers and no more. Others are moving confidently into realms of comprehension and belief that are fueling their lives.

Here are some contributions from among the many souls who have experienced the mission.

BARRY BARTLETT in Hamilton, New Zealand, was part of the original group that transmitted Abraham and Machiventa Melchizedek. Now a part of the I AM movement and anchored in an exploratory spiritual center, he offers his colorful memoir of those days, "And It Came To Pass," and concludes this section as well with the update, "And It Came To Pass Even More."

In California, celestial teachers have presented large numbers of lessons over the years. ALLEN RICE and JOHN CREGER share their experiences, primarily in the San Francisco Bay area. DEBORAH GOALDMAN talks about her group's unique gateway experiences in Bakersfield. LARRY and DONNA WHELAN tell how they met and fell in love in the aura of the celestial teachings. KAREN ROBERTS recalls the years of SpiritFests. GERALD DALTON in Beverly Hills discusses his experiences in Southern California. BOB HUNT, whose late wife, Bonnie, transmitted a celestial Bright and Morning Star while they raised a house full of children, shares some of their adventures. Author and publisher BYRON BELITSOS shares his experiences in a concerted exploration of the phenomena and its Urantia Book roots.

From Costa Rica, seniors DAVID and SUSAN BUTTERFIELD tell amazing stories of how their spiritual quest has evolved over the years. OLIVER DUEX recalls some tumultuous years in the California Urantia community, leading into more controversy with the advent of the celestial teachers, and shares the personal spiritual insights he has learned from it all.

PATIJE in Sarasota, Florida, was one of the first transmitters in the U.S., as a pioneer group of seekers worked with LorEl and the first wave of teachers. She tells a life story filled with overcoming crisis at a series of crossroads.

In North Carolina, JOILIN JOHNSON and ERIC JOHNSON recall their years of experiences in different locations, leading to their marriage and crises beyond. Joi was an early transmitter with one of the first Teaching Mission groups, in Tallahassee, Florida. Eric has logged experience and gathered insight in groups from Pittsburgh and Cincinnati to Dallas and Colorado, and has had a heart transplant along the way.

One of the early receiving groups was in Indianapolis, Indiana, with teacher Welmek. DAVID and MICHAEL PAINTER talk about their experiences as transmitters. MARTY RISACHER, a lawyer and judge, relates a life of personal crisis and spiritual discovery while engaged with the teachers. LINDA BUSELLI recounts how the group came together and almost came apart and shares her defense of the Teaching Mission with one naysayer.

DONNA D'INGILLO, also an original Indianapolis group member, now lives in Delray Beach, Florida and directs the Center for Christ Consciousness. A longtime transmitter and author of *Teach Us To Love*, she shares her life experiences and her current work in spiritual healing in collaboration with the teachers.

MARY LIVINGSTON has traveled widely in her energy research and on various spiritual quests, and is now living in California. In addition to her personal experiences, she also presents a paper herein regarding the links between biological science, meditation and channeling.

Strong transmitting groups in Idaho have been mainstays of the Teaching Mission. Representing these groups are MARK ROGERS and MANU PURI from the north, and VIRGINIA KELLY in Pocatello. The Rogers own a leather business and Mark is a seasoned transmitter who now brings forth lessons from Magisterial Son Monjoronson. Manu is a professional life coach with spiritual acumen. Virginia's late husband BILL KELLY, a retired protestant minister, was a longtime transmitter of teacher Daniel and others, and the group continues to meet and enjoy camaraderie with the teacher corps.

SONNY SCHNEIDER was part of a community of friends and spiritual seekers in Hawaii who connected with spiritual teachers and transmitted a large body of lessons. He has facilitated the mission for many years, including editorship of the pioneering "Paradise Networker" newsletter, and now lives in British Columbia.

Albuquerque, NM, author-artist-transmitter and spiritual activist GERDEAN O'DELL tells of her teacher contact experiences with the Advance Corps to work with mortals even before the circuits opened and the Teaching Mission came to pass, her sojourn across the country and over the decades. Gerdean's books include *Fruits of the Spirit*, *The Zooid Mission*, and *The Seven Chakras*. DORENDA MORSE, also in Albuquerque, tells how she discovered the Teaching Mission first, and then the Urantia papers.

JIM CLEVELAND began transmitting in 1992 with the Cincinnati, Ohio, area groups and shares his personal experience in releasing to spiritual contact and serving in the T/R role. BLANCHE IRENE BERLAND of Deerfield Beach, Florida, shares her recent discovery of the reality of spirit contact. SUSAN ROWLAND of the original Cincinnati group remains in the city, recently earned a Ph.D. in the health care profession and works as a clinical psychologist. She shares her experiences growing up in an aetheistic household and her discovery of true spirituality.

LEOMA SPARER in Minnesota has transmitted various celestial teachers and works prominently in the areas of spiritual energy and healing.

In Colorado, contributors DANIEL RAPHAEL, ROXANNE ANDREWS and JO ANN WIEDMAN have all excelled in professional fields. Daniel is a holistic life coach, author and spiritual advisor who serves as one of the group's transmitters and is active in global sustainability and projects with celestial teachers. Roxanne is retired from business and is a driving force and host for the Northern Colorado TeaM group. Jo Ann is a teacher, a counselor, a transmitter for Colorado groups and a worker for the Urantia Fellowship.

Our list does not include a number of other Teaching Mission pioneers who have contributed as transmitters, transcribers and facilitators over the years. It would be unwise to start up a list in which some would invariably be left off. But do know that many others remain connected with celestial teachers and, like our contributors for this volume, are active in many kinds of caring service in their lives.

More information about the authors are included with their narratives.

Editor's Note: *Our first contributor and also final contributor in this section is Barry Bartlett of Hamilton, New Zealand, who was part of the group that first communicated with the mission teachers. In this opening segment, he tells about his life of spiritual growth.*

And It Came to Pass
Barry Bartlett

It all started for me on February the 26th 1987, or did it?

Did it start when I was a lad when my Dad talked about 'healing hands' and 'mind over matter'? Or was it in the 1960s when my then girl friend was told by a tarot reader that she would have two children of the same sex and live on the other side of the world? Not a thought I entertained or even contemplated at the time, let alone getting married!

So in the early 1970s, after years of nagging, my then wife and I and our two daughters moved from England to New Zealand. Was this so I could meet my second wife who just 'happened' to work with a lady whose best friend, whom they had come from England with, had in 1984 started to receive messages and started channeling? We all have free will but some times we are 'nudged' in the right direction.

Raised in the Church of England and being a chorister for seven years I had a lot of exposure to Christianity, but because of the journey that I had planned this lifetime, although I did not know it at the time, I always thought there was 'more.' Both my birth chart and my numerology bear out my wide-open attitude, being able to see all sides, and my disdain of boundaries and borders. This explains my aversion to people who are stuck in old books and teachings and cannot see there are other pathways or accept that other people have a different path.

So on February 18th 1987 my second wife, who like me was investigating different pathways, attended her first session with Abraham. I was baby sitter that night. She came home all excited and wanted to know if I would go. There was never any doubt; I KNEW that I had to go! I had that feeling that it was 'right,' beyond the thinking mind, probably at soul level.

Then on February 26th we went to our friend's house. We sat in a silent circle to increase the energies when suddenly our diminutive part Jewish lady friend booms out in a masculine voice. *"GREETINGS, I AM ABRAHAM, I AM YOUR TEACHER!"*

Every week it always came as a shock because we may be in silence for 10 or 15 minutes to raise the vibration until Abraham arrived with the same abrupt and booming greeting.

Our channel had started in 1984 when her and her husband and two friends used to meet for discussions and meditation. Suddenly one day our right-handed friend picked up the pen and wrote with her left hand 'I am Bertha' It progressed from there for the next three years.

Bertha was the 'gatekeeper' for Abraham and it took those years to slowly prepare her and practice, first with written messages and then with spoken lessons, until the time was right to expand the circle. The original four continued to meet on a different night as their learning was in advance of ours until eventually Melchizedek spoke as well.

Well, can you imagine the awe at hearing these lessons come out? Was this real? Or what! As time progressed it was obvious that not many humans could remember what was said and by whom weeks before, and there must be more to what was happening than was generally accepted in those days. In fact in those days there were very few people you would confide in as to what we did every Wednesday night. How times have changed!

I kept silent for half the first class not really knowing what to say and in awe of what was happening but Abraham knew I had much to say and kept hinting up to our tea break. After our break we established communication as if we were old friends, albeit on a Teacher-

Student basis. I received my Soul name much to the amusement of everyone. FILIP, something that stimulates or livens up. "This has significance?" Abraham said, amid gales of laughter. It DID!

It came time for me to ask about my Guide Michael. Abraham consulted the great I AM and gave me the information. When I asked about his last incarnation on Earth, He said "A.D. 4245, a riddle for you I think." Well, when will it be or when is it or when was it? No further information was given.

In those days there was much information we were not given immediately. Either we were not ready to progress along the lessons pathway that was planned for us or we were not prepared or could not yet comprehend the concepts that we were being taught. Some still now have difficulty understanding that this existence is a figment of our imagination, that there is no time, that everything is happening NOW but on different planes, and we are God.

All our lessons were tape-recorded and then initially hand-written and later on they were typed. The transcripts were then passed around to be read. I used to photocopy a set for us. I got the transcripts and went to the library to photocopy them but I was too early and they weren't open. I went back home and returned later to the photocopier, which had two sheets of paper on it. I moved them aside and found that they were copies from a book that covered all the different calendars, Jewish, Roman, Islamic etc! So I copied them along with our lessons.

At the next week's class I asked if information had been left for me. 'Of course' was the reply. To this day I still have not solved the riddle of the numbers. If you understand the concept of no time and different dimensions though it is not a problem.

We were continually being told to 'Find the Stillness' (meditate) so as a good student I practiced, usually late in the evening when the house was quiet and everyone was in bed.

One particular night I was in deep meditation and I felt a hand, it seemed like only three fingers though, touch my left shoulder. I came back and expected my wife to be there, calling me to go to bed. There was no one there! Touched by the Hand of God was mentioned at a later class.

It was at my first lesson that we were asked to commit to come to class. Later there was the request to commit to 10 lessons. This seemed to be to ensure we were actually committed to learn what was being taught and strengthen the group of virtual strangers into a family committed to what and where ever the lessons took us. In fact during that particular time newcomers were excluded from the classes, even though many came, as our teaching was under way and they would not have been aware of what we had been taught already. The whole intention of the lessons was to teach us self -love so that we could spread it out to the world.

During the whole year of 1987 we questioned on every subject imaginable. Mostly we received the answers or sufficient information to continue searching and learning for ourselves. Sometimes though the information was not given until we reached a better level of understanding.

Each student was given information according to their participation and level of understanding. Those that did not communicate much, or more importantly, did not share thoughts and feelings were held back from receiving answers. All of this was part of the opening up of us, and molding us into a 'family' unit. The whole teachings, even today, are about self-improvement and showing others the way. You cannot love another until you love yourself.

The lessons invariably raised more questions than answers. That year I was self-employed and business was not too good. As I was near our library I did a lot of research and much reading between customers, especially when we got on to the fascinating subject of Quantum Physics and the space/time continuum.

The major question for me was 'Why are we being given this information?' Why were 15 to 20 mainly English people in New Zealand being given this information and what were we to do with it? With all the community work I do I was publicity oriented and said to Abraham at the time that I wanted to run a radio program to spread the message. Seventeen years later I started my hour-long radio show, but the thing to know is that in the intervening years I spent 11 years running a Maori radio station, eleven years learning the skills and living within a different ethnic culture from my own. All part of my teaching for the greater good of all!

My whole journey this time seems to have dabbled me in so many different modalities so that I have the capacity to accept and advise on most subjects. The common phrase in our shop is 'Anything you say in here is not weird; we have either done it or know about it!'

Over the years of my radio show I have interviewed many people about their paths. There seems to be a phenomenon of 'the psychic black eye' where events are put in place to shift you from one path to the one you are supposed to be on, a more spiritual or service path. Often they appear at the time, and to the person involved, to be very traumatic and of course life changing!

A traumatic divorce and estrangement from my children in the early 1980s shifted me into another pathway with my second wife, a soul mate who was to explore this pathway with me, and for me to be with her children so that her daughter could converse with Abraham at the age of seven, and the boys and grandchildren would grow up with a spiritual understanding.

My business in 1987 was not doing well and we downsized our house and eventually in November decided to close the business. So on November 28 I closed up. That night at midnight we got a phone call from my brother in England asking if he paid for us would we go to England and build some houses for him. We didn't sleep much that night! Next day was my birthday.

On December 10, 1987 we attended our last class with Abraham as we were scheduled to be in England for Christmas, a sad but uplifting class. We all held hands, and you could feel the love flow through you as we passed it around the circle. This was probably my first time feeling the energies flow in a group situation. The same happened at both the Boise and Albuquerque conferences. Abraham's closing words for us as we held hands:

"This is the physical sign of the chain you have forged each to each. Remember Filip, Belinda, you are part of this chain. It is not a static chain; it is able to stretch. May you all enjoy peace, harmony and calm. I give you my blessing as your teacher. On taking my leave, remember, God resides within YOU."

We had that year of learning behind us and tried to apply the lessons where we could, but moved away from being involved in formal classes and meetings. Reading parts of the *Urantia Book* did not gel either but we had our class notes to refer to.

That year of teachings gave us such an understanding and colored our life to such an extent that we were aware of all sorts of things we were not aware of previously, and we viewed things from a different perspective.

After our return from England one of our son's friends had a head injury and was in hospital. The doctors believed he was talking gibberish and were at the point of committing him to the psychiatric unit. Our son would not allow this and took him home. That particular Saturday afternoon at home we had the window open and the oil burner we had on the mantle piece started to vibrate. I thought it was the wind and shut the window.

My wife and I had been discussing this incident with her son's friend, when suddenly the vibration started again! I had a very strong feeling we should go and see this boy, so we stopped what we were doing and drove the half-hour into town. We counseled him for a while and suggested he shut his eyes and just let what was to happen, happen. Lo and behold Abraham started to speak, I am sure me, my wife and her son all knew what was going to happen but until we were all assembled the security of those that understood was not there.

We discussed the oil burner incident. Says Abraham "That was me!" Unfortunately this young chap was so scared and his parents were so anti 'all that stuff' he completely blocked any further communication.

Back in New Zealand in the early 2000s the next shift occurred, the loss of a job, a wife, and eventually the house, created a massive shift and moved me to start searching again. I found a meeting to go to, walked in and there were a couple from the Abraham class, part of our "family."

It was around July/August 1987 when the original group was told by Abraham about The *Urantia Book* and the suggestion was given to write to Chicago. No one had even heard of the book, let alone having any idea of what was in it. Eventually some one got hold of this very expensive book and some attempts were made to read some of it. My then wife and I returned to England for a while in December 1987 and after a lot of searching I managed to find a copy in a book shop in Los Angeles at a more reasonable price.

The records show that at the class on August 25, 1987 Abraham was told a reply was expected back from Chicago next week.

So began a new adventure!

I AM Filip/Barry

Discernment of Spirits
My discovery of the perils and the truths of the Celestial Teaching Mission
Byron Belitsos

Beginning in the late 1980s, and especially since 1992, something unprecedented has erupted onto our planet-an outpouring of profound celestial teachings and energies that has persisted and grown ever since. Back in those days, new religious movements were mushrooming all over America. And transpiring on the fringe of one of these movements was what appears to be a unique phenomenon in the history of religion: coordinated celestial contact across multiple locations.

In the many years that have passed since then, I and hundreds of other colleagues have been gifted with well over 4,000 sessions of interaction with the unseen realms. During these interactions, which were usually open to the public, we would also find it necessary to learn a new skill: a method of discrimination that Christians commonly call discernment of spirits.

The immediate locus of this strange marvel of contact was the so-called Urantia movement, the loose-knit association of students of the mysterious 2,096-page text known as *The Urantia Book*, first published in 1955. Dozens of individuals in cities all over the country-almost all of them participants in groups studying this book that they believe to be a new "epochal" revelation to our planet-were reportedly experiencing verbal input from unseen beings, receiving their messages by apparent telepathic means. These invisible teachers, we were told, were linked to the mission of the Urantia revelation. According to plan, they were now making themselves known almost 30 years after its publication, and they were purportedly sent by the same metaphysical beings who had originally authored it!

By all accounts, the messages being offered were loving, benign, and compelling. Usually the "contactees" (later called TRs or transmitter-receivers) would be able to speak the transmitted words audibly so that they could be easily recorded and later transcribed; other TRs would sit at their keyboards and "hot pen" the messages, as if taking gentle dictation.

Not all of the newly initiated TRs accepted a public role. But those who did were soon invited by their invisible mentors to begin holding transmission meetings with interested friends and fellow Urantia Book students. In addition, most of the active individuals were soon given a "spiritual name" and assigned a personal celestial teacher from whom they could receive private transmissions directly, or with the aid of a T/R. I was unable to make verbal contact, so such personal sessions would prove especially helpful for me. Yet I also found the group setting to be highly beneficial and sometimes thrilling.

And so, before long, in a score of locations, it became clear that practical spiritual teachings were being downloaded from the etheric realms in a synchronized program of instruction based largely on the Urantia Book's teaching. Ad hoc groups were assembling in living rooms all over America to receive the celestial grace.

OUR CELESTIAL FACULTY INTRODUCES ITSELF

In the sessions, opening statements were made by highly communicative beings with names like Ham, Abraham, JarEL, Bertrand, Daniel, Will, Tarkas, Welmek, and Tomas. Each explained to their newly assembled groups that an experimental initiative was under way that was authorized at the highest levels. To our surprise, its ostensible purpose would be to supplement and amplify the published teachings of the Urantia Revelation.

This planet-wide project actually would, they said, have a twofold designation: It was to be called the Teaching Mission (now popularly known as TeaM, TM, or the Mission) as it applied to already existing readers of *The Urantia Book*; and it was to be dubbed the Correcting Time when referring to conscious or unconscious celestial contacts with religious and spiritual groups and individuals across the rest of the planet. The Correcting Time was far broader. Its contacts were with folks high and low who had no personal knowledge of or belief in the Urantia Revelation; however, the same celestial teaching faculty was involved, and a similar curriculum was being pursued.

Further, *The Urantia Book* was to be the reference text or class textbook for the Teaching Mission, and the TM was in turn a subset of the much larger Correcting Time project that would continue for centuries. Plus, indications were given that the TM was to go through a variety of stages itself and would interact with the Correcting Time in a myriad of ways over many decades.

The TM groups were to receive systematic instruction by what we now know is an organized corps of "ascended masters" working in collaboration with various orders of angelic beings. Overseeing the entire initiative, and its actual creator, was-Jesus himself. Jesus Christ is known as Christ Michael or Michael in the parlance of *The Urantia Book*. He is depicted there as our compassionate brother, all-loving father, and omniscient guide through his Spirit of Truth. He is also the cosmic creator-along with his female complement known as "Mother Spirit"-of our local universe of millions of inhabited planets.

The Teaching Mission

Meanwhile, down on this planet, the celestial authority immediately in charge of the TM was one Machiventa Melchizedek, a key personality in the narratives of the Urantia revelation. With the formal inauguration of the Teaching Mission announced on February 1, 1992, we were told that Machieventa had been elevated to the status of "Planetary Prince." This phrase was Urantia lingo for the "chief executive officer" of Earth; in other words, he was the head of the planetary celestial hierarchy.

As contact groups began to transcribe the lessons and send them out to other groups, often using the new email technology, it soon became clear that the content of these varied streams of transmitted wisdom were relatively uniform across all the transcripts-that is, in regard to terminology, content, and even style of presentation.

But how could such an uncanny feat be carried out? Well, we were told, the Mission has been planned for centuries. Our celestial "masters" and their angelic collaborators had been carefully recruited to come to our planet explicitly as spiritual teachers when the age was ripe. They would teach from a common curriculum provided by a celestial class of educators known as the Melchizedeks-and specifically adapted for the TM by Machieventa himself.

But who exactly were our unseen mission-driven instructors who would teach us? They had originated from scores of advanced planets, but they were not material ETs. They hailed from the spirit worlds; they had survived death on their home planets. In other words, they had ascended by natural means (i.e., resurrection after death) to higher realms, also known in the UB as "mansions"- as Jesus put it somewhere in the Bible.

It was here that surviving souls continue to live and grow in the afterlife, at least according to the Urantia revelation. (For a description see papers 47 and 48 in *The Urantia Book*). And in these metaphysical worlds our intrepid teachers-to-be had received the advanced intellectual and spiritual training that all heavenly ascenders are entitled to-in some cases for periods of up to 50,000 years. And now, they had volunteered to condescend (in the best sense) to come to Earth for a most unusual mission.

Put another way, these ascended humans were not "brothers from outer space" contacting earthlings from UFOs, and not beings from the lower "astral" realms who were offering ad hoc "channelings." They were enlightened beings speaking from domiciles in the higher etheric realms, and they were charged with the task of offering us lessons that they themselves had long ago mastered. These teachings were in fact based on the standard curriculum as taught on the initial levels of the heavenly mansion realms in first stages of the afterlife.

It should be noted here that most of our instructors were not true "Ascended Masters" in the sense used in the Theosophical tradition to designate teachers like St. Germain and Djwal Khul. In that system, Ascended Masters always originate on Earth; our TM "masters" had, as a rule, ascended to higher planes from other planets-specifically planets that were not dark and warlike as was ours. But there were a few exceptions: many TM transmissions over the years have been received from Abraham-whose story is told in Genesis in the Bible-and a few from Yogananda, the great Indian guru and saint of the twentieth century, and even from Martin Luther King. These would be technically Ascended Masters as Theosophists understand that phrase, but they are the exception in the TM. The Teaching Mission groups also received transmissions from a wide variety of angelic beings and deified teachers who are the indigenous citizens of the upper worlds.

This was all well and good, but why was this daring celestial mission under way now?

THE LATE, GREAT (AND SOON TO BE RESTORED) PLANET EARTH

We all knew from our studies of *The Urantia Book* a fact that should not surprise those who don't read this text: that life on Earth deviates greatly from that on a normal planet. This was owing to events in the distant past that had occurred both off and on our world. Genocide, world war, mass starvation, and ecocide are highly atypical for a planet in our state of technological evolution; these ugly phenomena are an outgrowth of the tragic default of two previous revelatory missions, according to the Urantia Book's narrative of the history of Urantia (the celestial name for planet earth) - a long and tragic saga that sounds like eerie science fiction to some.

Our Earth is, in fact, what is known as a rebellion planet: Out of the 619 inhabited planets in the local inhabited planetary group, 37 worlds had suffered from a turbulent and tragic history. Our blight resulted from a very rare event-an angelic rebellion that had erupted eons ago in this local system of inhabited worlds. These planets had been under universe quarantine ever since those distant times. When a planet is quarantined, it is cut off from the so-called celestial communication circuits that naturally link material planets to one another and to the higher realms, not unlike the way that fiber optic lines connect cities on earth.

Urantia Book students believe that this heavenly mutiny, celebrated in allegorical works such as poet John Milton's Paradise Lost, was a real fact in our planetary history. It had been led by the angelic rulers of the local system of 1000 inhabited planets, Lucifer and Satan (-yes, of Biblical fame), and is thus called the Lucifer Rebellion.

By the way, our planet "Urantia" turns out to be among the two or three worst-affected planets of the 37 rebellion planets. And are you surprised?

Remedial emergency measures have long been under way for Urantia and all of the other rebellion planets. In our case, one of these measures was the spectacular event of the incarnation and life of Christ; the other was the gift of *The Urantia Book* itself, with the Teaching Mission being a planned extension of that work, we were now told. The TM was being offered to us and to all 37 rebellion planets.

Bear in mind that a large portion of the lengthy Urantia Revelation is devoted to explaining this hidden history of planetary rebellion that is only hinted at in the Bible as the doctrines of Original Sin and the "fall of mankind."

The stunning premise of the Teaching Mission, first revealed on February 1, 1992, was the news of the final adjudication of Lucifer Rebellion in heavenly courts. It is well known to Urantia Book students that the tribunal for the so-called case of Gabriel vs. Lucifer was long under way, and had already begun before *The Urantia Book* was completed in the mid-twentieth century.

And now, in living rooms around America and elsewhere, the celestials were transmitting the grand news that the Adjudication of the rebellion had been finalized in the fall of 1985. This ruling was carried out by high juridical beings in heavenly courts located on the capital of the intergalactic "superuniverse" (that is, the administrative center of one trillion inhabited planets, according to the Urantia Book's cosmology).

This meant, significantly, that Urantia's planetary quarantine would gradually be lifted, allowing the reinstatement of the celestial circuits that had long been severed. This in turn would permit such celestial transmissions as were now occurring to readily take place, among many other benefits.

And what of the fate of Lucifer? The TM groups were told that he had chosen his own annihilation in view of the verdict. One unseen teacher named James explained the new situation on Oct. 4, 1992: "You must understand that up until the time Lucifer ceased to exist, he still had free will and had not agreed to the Adjudication. The Adjudication could not happen until he agreed that it was the right thing to do..." In other words, as the Urantia text states, the transgressor himself must agree with the verdict before an adjudication can take place (see Papers 53 and 54).

THE "FULL FRUITION" OF THE KINGDOM OF GOD?

As the Mission grew from humble beginnings, a watershed moment for the movement-and for me personally-occurred at the 1995 conference of the Teaching Mission in San Luis Obispo, California, when Duane Faw (who is now deceased) gave a rousing keynote speech.

Duane was an "elder of the tribe" for the Mission. Previously he had been a highly respected leader in the Urantia Fellowship (the worldwide fraternal association of Urantia Book readers), the head of its judicial committee, and author of *The Paramony: A Parallel and Harmony of* the Urantia Book *and the Bible*. In his distinguished military career he had achieved the rank of Brigadier General and had served as the Director of the Judge Advocate Division of the Marine Corps. After earning a law degree from Columbia University, he had taught at Pepperdine University Law School for several decades.

And now he was proud to be addressing our motley assemblage of Teaching Mission adherents, most of us more or less outcasts from the mainstream Urantia community that by 1995 had turned its back on the Mission.

Duane opened by reminding us about Jesus' prophetic answer to a question from Apostle Peter. In this teaching, Duane proclaimed, the Master had "foretold" both the Urantia revelation and the Teaching Mission in this passage:

And when the kingdom shall have come to its full fruition, be assured that the Father in heaven will not fail to visit you with an enlarged revelation of truth and an enhanced demonstration of righteousness . . . And so will my Father continue to manifest and show forth His love, even to this dark and evil world. (176:2.1)

"I see The Urantia Papers as the 'enlarged revelation of truth,'" said Duane. "I see the Teaching mission as 'the enhanced demonstration of righteousness.' These two work together as the Fifth Epochal Revelation. This prophecy is being fulfilled in our day and before our very eyes! *The Urantia Book* and the Teaching Mission are the continuing, but upstepped, manifestation of the Father's love as foretold by Jesus on this occasion."

But was Faw correct? We were by then three years into the Mission. Could he and the rest of us have been confused or deceived somehow? Or was the fulfillment of the kingdom really at hand?

In the long tradition of Christian spiritual counsel, discernment of spirits refers to the ability to distinguish genuine phenomena of the spirit from close counterfeits-to discern the difference between errors of the spiritual imagination and real cases of spiritual influence or angelic presence. As one Catholic writer put it, in practicing the discernment of spirits, one is able to adjudicate the difference between unholy and holy spirits through the power of the Holy Spirit.

Had Duane Faw, once a top adjudicator for the Navy, properly discerned the spirits? Had the hundreds of people now participating in the Teaching Mission gone astray, or were they truly evolving into a movement for the "enhanced demonstration of righteousness"? Was the TM indeed a demonstration of the Father's continuing love for a dark and evil world?

MY FIRST IMPRESSIONS AND RESEARCH

For me the San Luis Obispo conference marked the culmination of a discernment process that began when I first received *The Urantia Book*. In the seventies I had been an undergraduate and graduate student in religious studies, philosophy, and history of religion. I had been a committed student of the UB since 1974 while still in college at the University of Chicago.

I had participated in several Urantia Book study groups in Chicago and while living in the San Francisco area in the 1980s. By 1992, I was regularly attending the study group of one of the world's largest, oldest, and most active Urantia communities in Oklahoma City, where I was a partner in a software business. I had also been to many national events by then.

The Teaching Mission

It was the summer of 1992, and our software business was doing well. By coincidence, I had around this time been asked to become the interim managing editor for The Bulletin, then the official publication of the Urantia Fellowship, the official fraternal-educational organization of Urantia readers. In that capacity I needed to gather good stories on which to report. In researching a variety of events and topics, I began to get a kind of eagle's-eye view on what was going on in the Urantia movement from the standpoint of a reporter. And it was especially in that role that I began to realize that the Urantia movement wasn't becoming quite what it was supposed to be. After two generations of having an epochal revelation in our hands, something seemed to be missing.

The truth was that I had earlier experienced conflicted study-group communities in Chicago, San Francisco, and now Oklahoma City. In addition, I had also witnessed up close the bitter battle between the two wings of the Urantia movement, the Urantia Fellowship and Urantia Foundation (the Chicago-based publisher of the book and owner of its copyright and associated trademarks). These organizations had just separated over bitter administrative disagreements.

Yes, I felt committed to the Urantia text, but I was beginning to conclude that there must be something else, something more than the little-known and sometimes combative community that we had built around our wonderful book. The book's restatement of the life and teachings of Jesus was, among other profound teachings, a great inspiration for all of us.

But the mere text of this revelation alone was apparently not sufficient to provide for the creation of a community of loving, tolerant, and forgiving relationships that would lead to effective ministry and outreach. I didn't see encouraging evidence of this. Further, my own life was brimming with dissatisfaction and even conflict; I was not pleased with my own spiritual progress.

So, there had to be another-or bigger-plan for this revelation, I privately thought. Someone somewhere must have a better approach for its unfolding-if the revelation was indeed valid!

It was at this poignant moment that it dawned on me to look at the controversial new "channeled" teachings I'd been hearing about as I trolled about for stories for The Bulletin.

I must have been in a desperate state. Just a few months previous I had thrown a satire party to make fun of the weird Teaching Mission. Folks were to bring channeled messages they had conjured up, and alas, I literally hosted a midnight contest for the best "transmitted" message. A number of people actually did bring mock channeled messages to read while we laughed in derision at the phenomenon that by now was spreading all over the United States.

But now I found myself busily collecting accounts of the mysterious TM phenomenon from various friends around the country. My interest was piqued, and I just started reading.

And within a few days I became amazed. It was hard to believe the quality and consistency of these raw transcripts, in contrast with my expectation of some sort of New Age drivel.

But I was still in the mode of a reporter on the beat, still trying to figure out what was going on out in the field. Clearly, this was a big story.

In trips to Florida and California on business, I had occasion to interview TeaM participants, most notably Bob Slagle, PhD, of Santa Rosa, the distinguished psychologist and professor whose group was bringing through a teacher named Jared.

These were the days when email was just becoming pervasive, and my research soon confirmed that, after only about 18 months in existence, transmissions were being received in twenty-nine locations! And the transmitters were from all walks of life and all corners of the U.S.; there was no one overriding mindset that I could discern.

I was inexorably moving from being a skeptic to an open-minded student of the Mission.

Around this time I visited my parents in my hometown of Cincinnati, Ohio, where to my surprise I discovered that a large TM group had mushroomed in that conservative town. Their transmitters, like those in the other cities, were long-time UB readers, and their TM group initially evolved out of the local Urantia Book study group, as was typically the case.

A similar pattern was observable elsewhere. Urantia study groups in Buffalo, Chicago, Dallas, Indianapolis, Kansas City, the Los Angeles region, Hawaii, Nashville, Pittsburgh, Washington D.C., San Francisco Bay Area, Sarasota, Salt Lake City, St. Louis, and Tallahassee, displayed a similar pattern of group evolution, where TM activity and already existing Book study evolved in such a way that they coexisted and cross-fertilized.

As far as the celestials were concerned, a Urantia study group that is open to the Mission is a fertile teaching environment -although evidently they did not restrict themselves exclusively to study groups as a base of operation. That was ironically to be the case with my own TM group.

THE MISSION BEGINS IN OKLAHOMA CITY

As apparent chance would have it, in December of 1992, two of my women friends back home in Oklahoma suddenly received unsolicited contact with celestials. The messages they showed me were beautiful and compelling, and commensurate with messages elsewhere; and it was with this that I fully surrendered to the reality of the situation.

One of the women was named Ellen. She was a warm friend and a single mother of two young children who was unfamiliar with *The Urantia Book*, but who was very bright and deeply interested in personal growth and healing; she had received a brief contact from a teacher named RondEL, who was claiming to be my personal teacher!

The other friend, whom I knew well from the Oklahoma City Urantia study group, was newly in contact with a teacher named Foehn (pronounced like "fawn"). This intelligent young woman's name was Lori. The many private transmissions given to Lori had made it clear that she was to be the primary transmitter-if she were willing.

Along with an inquisitive local Urantia friend, Chet Olson, the four of us made a trip to nearly Tulsa to discuss our situation with a more advanced transmitter named Leta McCreary. We had seen some of Leta's transmissions in the now burgeoning email network of TM participants.

By now our teachers had given us spiritual names. Lori was "Helen." Ellen was "Asia." My friend was to be called "James" and I was "Jacob."

Leta and her husband Marcus, who both worked for the police force of Tulsa, received us warmly in their living room in a wooded, hilly area. After pleasantries, a serious discussion unfolded as Leta told us the astonishing news of her contact with Christ Michael, which was relatively rare at the time; we all excitedly shared our nascent experiences in the Mission.

And then, at the high point of our sharing, something suddenly came over us − a strange, warm, and giddy feeling. All of us felt it. It was like a sudden dimensional shift. I felt pierced by an unknown energy of love. I then looked around the room in rapturous wonder, as the others did. I noticed the cheeks of the women were flush red. Some sort of spiritual wind had entered the room; everyone looked refreshed and joyous. We were now bubbling with enthusiasm, and for no reason. Indeed, it was our very own private Pentecost event! At least that's how I experienced it.

Still swimming in this altered state, Leta took each of us into her basement where she transmitted Christ Michael for each of us. This afternoon in Tulsa was an initiatory experience in the best sense of the word.

Before leaving, we had our first formal session with our designated teachers. Here was one of Foehn's first statements: "I have long awaited this meeting, and look forward to working with this collection of minds . . . My message to you is to assimilate the collection of thoughts you have received, take them into the stillness, and allow them, like incense, to steep; let them settle in your mind and intermingle with love, humor, and praise . . . It is our goal to unite the minds of teachers and receivers. I am specifically assigned to the unity of minds."

Splendid! We were off to a good start.

In the next few sessions now being held in my country house, both public and private, simple and beautiful teachings were given to us. But there suddenly were difficulties in agreeing on format, roles, membership, attendance, and logistics.

At the next meeting, concern was voiced by the celestials about the possibility of the mission failing in Oklahoma City due to our group's disagreements. Lori (Helen) had just called to say she would not attend. And this was the first time we heard from teacher Josephine, who announced herself to be a specialist in human emotion. Josephine was able to come through the ostensible "back up" transmitter, Ellen (Asia): "When we made contact in Oklahoma City, there was much excitement and enthusiasm, and yet it appears that the group may have dissolved. To lose this contact would be a great defeat for the Teaching Mission."

Word had gotten around. We found out later that persons in the Oklahoma leadership had pulled Lori aside. Based on their admonitions, Lori decided to leave our group, even though she was inwardly certain that her contact was real. Thus began the lengthy and often covert internecine struggle to stop the Teaching Mission from coming to one of the major outposts of the Urantia movement in the world.

The displeasure of the leadership with the idea of a local TM group quickly spread to the hundred or so members of the Oklahoma City Urantia Society: participation in the group transmissions at my home in nearby Norman was verboten.

Thankfully, Asia now moved into Lori's role, and our group size dropped down to the intrepid Asia, myself, and James, an inquisitive man of quiet grace and dignity and a philosophic nature.

We were soon formally introduced to RondEL (who had already begun giving me private lessons through Asia), and Anelia, who was working in partnership with Foehn. Anelia's specialty was group logistics!

As the ostensible group leader and host of many of these sessions in my home, I was now in a dilemma. It was clear to me that the Teaching Mission was an organic outgrowth of the Urantia movement, or so I thought. But our access to the local Urantia readership was now greatly diminished. Would we allow non-readers into the group, thus in my view complicating the situation greatly? Asia had indicated that she wanted to invite her friend Susan, a sincere New Ager of sorts, to join in, but I had balked.

A few days later Ellen received this message for me from Josephine: "I beseech you remember that this group is one of love and the qualities of God our Father. It is not of your making to determine who shall enter or exit the group. Be assured that all are well. Welcome Susan into your group and others who wish may participate . . ."

I was beginning to realize that the scope of the Mission was much broader and more flexible than I had first thought. Josephine later continued on this theme:

Announcements have been made around the world. Trumpets have sounded: the Lord cometh. When one speaks of contacting others, it is only through our hearts that this is accomplished. Once contacted, a person never forgets, feels to the marrow of his being the rightfulness of his place in the Mission. Calm is in order, for it is not an anxious choice. It is one of glory. Behold the spirit of others cupped in your hands, like a fragile image of God. Guide them to us. Gently, let them know . . . Grant each man his right to behold the image of God.

And so we threw open our doors beyond the Urantia movement, although only a few adventurous souls in Norman, a college town, were to join us over the coming two years of transmissions by Asia.

Meanwhile, Asia began to refine her technique, and was now becoming proficient. The celestials used her gifted intellect to deliver words in a unique verbal style marked by clever turns of phrase and unusual syntax. I taped this interview with her at one point:

Explain the actual process, if you will, of your transmission technique.
Until I speak, the words just stay stuck at the same place-until I finally speak and then the words flow again. It's like being stuck on a place on a scratched record, but then it continues on when I speak . . .

During the pauses, what's going on?

I'm being challenged by my brain wanting to come in and inject words. As I am quieting down the left side of my brain, meanwhile, the words from the celestials are getting louder and louder, until they get through.

Do you sense the teacher's personal presence as this is going on?

Yes. Also, I feel a pressure, sometimes intense, on my head. The upper right.
Is the pressure inside or on the surface of your head? It is penetrating, and, I also feel it on the surface.

In the last session, Josephine told us a story, and as you transmitted the words, you reported seeing images to accompany the story. What was that like for you?

Initially, going in, it was a real picturesque scene. It started with an eagle flying. The eagle ended up at a lake, which became a stream, and which then became very meandering and tight. Those curves next became a snake. The snake rose up out of the sand and took me to the picture of the desert. [The story was an allegory about slaves living in a desert. Asia goes on to report that she was able to see images of the desert and feel the heat, and see the slaves, who were building a pyramid, and feel the presence of the king, as she told the first part of the above story (which was not tape recorded).]

Do you have a memory of the things you transmit?

No, not really, just the images really.

Asia loved the process of transmitting, and it was from about March of 1993 onward that riches began to pour out of her from a growing list of teachers. In addition to Foehn, RondEL, Josephine and Anelia, we heard from celestials with exotic names such as Zion,

Zephyl, Thomy, Tomeray, and from high beings such as Maliventa (a being of the so-called Vorondadek order) and Machiventa Melchizedek himself.

And, most importantly, we were graced with frequent appearances of Christ Michael in private and public sessions-sublime and poetic interventions of divine grace that usually took my breath away.

It was becoming obvious that our group had experimental features. Most groups received a series of basic lessons on love, service, forgiveness, healing, prayer, worship, and stillness that were based on the standard Teaching Mission curriculum that as we saw earlier had been developed by Machiventa Melchizedek along with the leading celestial teachers, especially Ham and Abraham.

But our group was unusual for its location, its mix of members, and especially because of the fact that the majority of the group was not familiar with the Urantia text. It thus became a locus of ad hoc teachings-including one controversial revelation to be discussed later-along with a myriad of "appearances" that even included entertaining bit parts by fascinating personalities.

UNIQUE TEACHINGS ON HEALING

As I understand *The Urantia Book*, Jesus taught that faith is a centered act of the personality, a total personality expression that includes the childlike exposure of one's inner life to God's healing presence.

But what if this crucial exposure of our inner being is somehow blocked? What if our emotional heart had been severely injured, especially in childhood? What if, as a result, some aspects of the personality are split off and hardened by pain, so that they simply can't be brought to the Father for healing, who ever respects our free will? And what if one's ability to receive the Father's omnipresent love and forgiveness is also impaired because we did not find these attributes in our own parents?

TM teachers all across the board emphasized one key teaching: the necessity of the primary practice of stillness-silent meditation with the intent of communion with God.

I had rigorously practiced meditation in several forms for many years, but I still suffered from painful emotional maladies. Thus I was ripe for a special teaching we now received: the notion that a certain measure of emotional healing is necessary as a preparatory step for releasing blocks to the flow of the Father's affection while one is in stillness or prayer. Simple awareness alone, or even good stillness technique, will not do the trick.

Therefore, a significant feature of the Teaching Mission has been to offer emotional healing in conjunction with an ongoing practice of enhanced mediation and worship. This was one method presented by RondEL:

For a moment, reflect on your losses. Quiet your mind and allow for the grieving of the ages to well up within and spill forward, for tears enlist the love of the Father. Hold hands with one another in this moment. Allow the passing of ages to cross all boundaries. Feel . . .

We were now initiated on a path of uncovering our childhood pain. This teaching indicated clearly to us that this residual pain, alone, can prevent our discovery of peace and serenity:

. . It is imperative to dig deep within our heart's sorrow, to follow the course of pain that has brought us to where we are today, making life choices which have created turmoil or lack of peace and serenity. Cry, my children, let the pain go . . ./. . . Lengthy pause . . .]

Has not one of you shed a tear for your pain? Has there been so much loss yet so much strength? The strength, it holds you, you see; it will not release you. The Father cannot enter iron doors that his children have locked and sealed. It may not be, for His love reflects so violently off such cold, coarse reactions to an extraordinary gift. You must realize that opening the doors is absolutely necessary without a doubt for you to become healed children of the Father's love. You are only alone as long as you choose to be alone, do you see?

Free yourselves! Open the door! It is of your choosing.

Here was another surprising teaching on healing, which took a different tack:

Student: I have tried to find my true sense of peace and happiness in my day-to-day life. I find that I'm trapped in past fears and anger. I want to release myself from those negative, heavy ways of the world and increase my receptivity to the teachings and to the love that's offered. I find myself stuck, stymied, and I'm wondering if you could offer some counsel, some advice of how to move out of this spiral.

FOEHN: *Climb a tree and take authority of the gravity that pulls you down. You must swing as a child against the weight of this world. Apples must fall from the tree as they are pulled by the scientific laws of gravity. And yet, you may swing and dangle your toes and take authority over this force.*

There is great delight in understanding the magnitude of this planet as it spins in defiance of its history. There are pleasures that you will be exposed to in a short time that will allow you to enjoy your place in this world, and yet temporarily you are struggling through many details to be simply taken care of.

Find time to defy the weight of the burden on your shoulders. Jump in joy against the heaviness of your load. Dangle upside down and let your hair blow in the wind as it tries to sway you. Blow against it and exhale in delight. You are truly a child of great strength, as many have noted. I seem to think that you are worried about failing, and yet you have no need to concern yourself with anything other than taking care of what is essential and finding time to sway in the wind.

At a later session, a being named "John" appeared out of nowhere stating that he was the equivalent of a celestial doctor. At the time, I was suffering from severe hay fever and was about to get serious medical treatment, including a long round of shots at an allergy clinic.

John offered to work with my malady. In that one session, his ministrations to me led to the complete disappearance of my hay fever.

And so the teachings on healing (and actual healings)-and lessons on so much else-simply spilled out. By mid-1993, I was in dialogue (through the generous facilitation of Asia) once or twice a week with these invisible friends; in the mornings I went into the office to face my business partners who were Christian fundamentalists; and every Sunday at the UB study group in Oklahoma City, I increasingly came to realize that the local Urantia Book students were not interested in our magnificent celestial contacts.

ELECTRONIC HOLY WARS

I also had to deal with disinterest and even disdain on another front, in this case with close colleagues in the Urantia movement whom I had been corresponding with online. Thankfully, I had earlier been prepared for this onslaught in a private session with Christ Michael:

Jacob, you should be aware that difficult times lie ahead. Many will reject these teachings and your involvement in this Mission. Be prepared, my son, as many will question not your spirituality but your balance of mind. Do not make the fatal mistake of allowing others to disturb even to disrupt your own spiritual progress and your mission.

Of course, Michael easily foresaw what was inevitably coming. Not widely recorded in histories of this period is what could be called "the electronic holy wars"-a lengthy and sometimes rancorous online debate about the Teaching Mission carried out by veteran Urantia Book readers.

Interestingly, much of this heated interaction coincided with the early days of our own TM group during the first half of 1993. Here are a few excerpts from this historic thread of electronic exchanges, during which most of the individuals formulated their public positions for the first time. About a hundred Urantia Book readers were members of this early electronic forum, called Urantial (Urantia List), though only a dozen or so were active. In the very brief excerpt below, my accompanying commentary is in italics.

In mid-February, Leo Elliott posted a comparison of the Teaching Mission to the notorious Family of God incidents in 1983-4 . . .

Here is where I see a significant distinction between the FOG/Vern Grimsley cultists [an earlier purported California cult of UBers] and the current Teaching Mission participants: this "cult" seems far more "democratic" for want of a better term, more "decentralized," more "outsourced."

Long-time reader Matthew Rapaport here picked up another thread in the debate . . .

Much of the [TM] text itself suggests that the revelators are able to be open about almost anything. . . EXCEPT they can't simply appear to everyone in the group directly . . . It seems no one, not a single person,

145

has even asked for (let alone been granted) a simple, nonspiritual test. I'm not a psychiatrist, but surely this is one of the classic symptoms of a belief system invented out of the subconscious, that is, too fragile to test . . .

Here I chimed in, in reply to the many skeptics who were now posting statements . . .

Revelation is always and everywhere an eruption into human history of something from outside of history, sometimes laying waste to the recipients' vaunted social and religious conventions, sometimes creating martyrs, always creating division and controversy. Today we see a revelatory intrusion of unprecedented proportions in the Urantia community. Here we are, a fringe non-entity on the far outposts of Western civilization, now being torn apart by the reaction to the revelatory gift of the UB as amplified by the TM. Really, is this so different from the ancient Jews, an isolated, ingrown community of monotheists in a remote province of the Roman Empire who were hosts to a stupendous revelation? Should we expect less trouble than the apostles, as we go forward into the world proclaiming our gospel?

Leo also replies to a critic . . .

These TM groups are doing more to socialize new concepts essential for spiritual survival, as I see it, in less than 2 or 3 years, than the accumulated Urantia movement was able to socialize in 2 or 3 decades. I, for one, when I read these TM transcripts, feel called to live them, every day in every way, as if Jesus were my constant companion, in even the "least" of human interchanges . . .

And in reply to one particular critic, I wrote . . .

You are confusing the text of a teaching situation with the text of an epochal revelation. Nothing in any TM transcript is epochal revelation nor is it meant to be. The UB is the textbook! The celestials are our teachers who expound on it, helping us to bring the spirit to life from the dead words. It is because we have not had such teaching occasions that the Urantia movement is such a train wreck. Remember . . . "The dead theory of even the highest religious doctrines is powerless to transform human character or to control mortal behavior. What the world needs today is the truth which your teacher of old declared: 'Not in word only but also in power and in the Holy Spirit. The seed of theoretical truth is dead, the highest moral concepts without effect, unless and until the divine Spirit breathes upon the forms of truth and quickens the formulas of righteousness.'" (UB 34:6.6) This is what we are witnessing today in humble living rooms all over the country where teachings are being given to seekers of truth.

In reply to someone who had been comparing the TM texts to the UB, I wrote this post ...

The real business at hand (the Father's business) is closer alignment with our thought adjusters [the Urantian term for the indwelling spirit of God]. The teachers are little more than a means to that end. They function like any teacher who says, '. . . read your textbook, do the exercises in it, and let's discuss the results in our next class . . .' They don't come to re-write the textbook, only to highlight the important points and move us along in a way we can't do alone. It is best to see a transmission as a human/divine blend-rather like the morontia material of the soul is a hybrid product-made possible by your faith and openness . . . Nor, in the final analysis, should the teachers themselves become interposed between us and the Father fragment [another term for the indwelling spirit of God] and other high spiritual influences, nor do they seek to.

Exercising critical judgment is just as important for a participant in the TM as for a participant in any complex process. The only authority in the 'religion of the spirit' is within. All else is a means to that end.

This is one of many statements from TM critic David Kantor. . .

I cannot take issue with anyone who says they have discovered a procedure or a technique or a set of beliefs that brings them closer to God and makes them feel more spiritual. I am willing to agree that this is a matter which is between the individual and God, and I am certainly in no position to judge the validity or even the value of such an experience to the individual who claims it . . . HOWEVER, as I have said before, once you begin to make claims about the meaning of that experience and use cultural images and symbols to describe it, e.g., the Lucifer rebellion has been adjudicated, a teaching mission is happening, Melchizedek is materializing-once you begin to make such claims-you are stepping across a threshold from personal spiritual experience to historic cultural experience. . . I am not "protesting" against the TM, I simply haven't heard any rationale for the idea from anywhere outside someone's subjective experience-I have repeatedly pointed out, here as well as elsewhere, reasons why the whole idea is utterly lacking in any integrity at all, but no one has been able to respond with anything other than more subjective assertions and opinions.

Michael Million, founder and technical manager for Urantial, suddenly announces his preliminary conclusions after reading numerous TM transcripts . . .

I have had the privilege of reading over transcripts stemming from Will [Tallahassee], Welmek [Indianapolis], Andrew [Pittsburgh] and Tarkas [Cincinnati] sessions . . . My heart responds gleefully to the messages relayed. In the logical arena, I keep asking myself how humans could have possibly have pulled off such a consistent and non-contradictory set of papers. It is my understanding that some of the human UB study groups knew of each other, but to say that the transcripts are not of celestial origin is to require that the UB study groups work in close association with each other to produce such tightly congruent messages with the intention of what? . . . fooling us and claiming it could be done? I just cannot fathom the motive behind such a human escapade; I cannot imagine that some person or group would not have raised their hand by now and said, 'Hey, so and so tried to get us to go along with this bit of absurdity-thought you might want to know," etc.

I like the book. I find myself with these transcripts in my hand but without any plausible cause that they are of human origins. How could this be the shenanigans of humans spread out over large geographical distances and with only the UB and planetary citizenship as ties? I personally have never met a UB reader who tried to fool me about anything remotely connected with the UB material. To have scores of readers suddenly go into a scheme to present false material of false celestial contact is more than I can accept. My deepest respect for all contributors to this discussion!

Now Jim McNelly, well-known former General Councilor in the Urantia Brotherhood, chimes in with a mature and tolerant position . . .

As far as my personal observations, I am indifferent to the appearance or nonappearance of spirit beings. I am about the work of doing the Father's will as best I can and there is great work ahead of us helping to bring the world to understand more of Love and Truth. If spirit beings are here to help, then great. But I will continue with my work without the need for signs/miracles. If cosmic helpers offer their help, fine. We need all the help we can get. If they give advice, I will take it under advisement as I would any good counsel. No man or being commands my spiritual loyalty due to their supposed status. My loyalty is focused on Jesus and I worship only the Father who is in heaven. If Melchizedek should actually appear in a physical form, as many believe he will, then fine. I hope that it has an effect other than interesting theatre. As far as I am concerned, I am looking forward to more dedicated earth workers, and if a physical manifestation may get some people off their spiritual duffs, and if such a manifestation is not out of harmony with the Father's will, then I hope it is true. If there is no manifestation on a particular day, it will not phase me one bit.

DEBACLE AT NAPERVILLE

In the above posts, Kantor and McNelly were referring to a projected materialization of Machiventa Melchizedek, set to occur on April 23, 1993, in Naperville, a suburb of Chicago. Groups around the country had been quietly receiving a steady plethora of beneficial lessons on every conceivable spiritual subject – superb teachings on topics like prayer, stillness, and worship, or on crucial concepts like healing, love, forgiveness, and service.

This new body of work, carefully transcribed in each case, greatly expanded and clarified fundamental tenets of *The Urantia Book*. In typical sessions, students had almost unlimited ability to ask questions based on these lessons, and reports were abounding that folks were benefiting and that many were greatly inspired. (I was later moved to co-edit and publish a book, *The Center Within*, which was a collection of such lessons given in 1993 to the Tallahassee group.

The entire corpus of nearly 4,800 transcripts of TeaM transmissions going back to 1991 has been collected at tmarchives.com and also at daynal.org)

One would think that this outpouring of teachings on practical spirituality from high personalities alone would be more than enough. But now, transmissions in several locations-including one from a Naperville teacher named Orem-stated clearly that an extraordinary materialization was about to happen. Before long, formal invitations went out all over the country from the Naperville group, asking TM adherents to be present for what would be one of the greatest experiences in history!

And with this, controversy was being heaped upon controversy.

I felt that this notion of the appearance of a high being was nonsensical. It was certainly terrible timing given the nascent and relatively fragile state of the Mission, not to mention the debates over its claims that were raging in many quarters. Thus, I quickly concluded that this was an egregious example of a human error in transmission. Worse, the error was now being picked up and amplified by other transmitters in other cities.

So what was this all about? The human side of the Mission wanted "proof"-not unlike the challenge above from Matthew Rapaport. Here in blazing color was an overt manifestation of crude materialism and "wonder-seeking" in our ranks. At the time I considered it to be an obvious ruse of the human unconscious, and I was disturbed that other respected groups around the country were getting on the bandwagon, though the teachers of other groups were reportedly skeptical. Our celestial teachers were clearly divided over the phenomenon!

Our group traveled again up to Tulsa to meet with the most reliable transmitter we knew: Leta. And Leta's teacher confirmed my suspicion: The materialization idea was a human product. Nonetheless, others continued to transmit that the event should occur, and people from all over were buying plane tickets to Chicago.

What an irony that such an event was happening in the home of the original manifestation of the Urantia Papers. And it was to occur on the very same weekend of a meeting of the Urantia Fellowship's Executive Committee in Chicago. The two paradigms were to converge in one place at one time. As a long-time Urantian and friend of many on the Executive Committee, I felt upset and embarrassed.

Our tiny group did make our way to Naperville, convinced that this caper would become the humiliation it turned out to be. I'll let others narrate the detailed story of these strange manifestations of "spiritual materialism" at a bland Holiday Inn in a featureless suburb of Chicago, witnessed by over 200 people. I like to compare it to the disappointments of the "king-making episode" in the life of Jesus that occurred after he fed thousands of people on a few loaves of bread and a dozen dried fish (see Paper 152 in the UB).

Those who look to "signs and wonders" are sure to meet disappointment in any spiritual path traversed on planet Urantia (or any planet for that matter). Many sincere folks left the Mission after this unfortunate "nonappearance" incident. And the mainstream of the Urantia movement, already skeptical, had good reason now to turn its back on the TM. Only a few stalwarts remained to pick up the pieces of the TM movement.

The event at Naperville evoked mythic and magical levels of human consciousness, archetypal energies too often suppressed in postmodern religion; and sometimes they must and do erupt. But in this fashion? And with this group, which was already witnessing minor miracles at each week's transmission?

It was a time to take stock. How far out of line had we all gone, after only a mere matter of months? How were we faring with our discernment of spirits?

I recalled that the reception of *The Urantia Book* had many apparent miracles associated with it, though most of the stories were apocryphal. It had in fact been authored and presented by celestial personalities through a largely mysterious process. We do know that the unseen revelators had made themselves known to the so-called Contact Commission (six humans in Chicago) by means of numerous unusual methods including "coincidences," materializations and dematerializations of documents, discarnate voices, numerous voices spoken Edgar Cayce style through a "sleeping subject," and occasional channeled messages that were to be written down much like our TM messages. In addition, we know that a group of several hundred people known as the Forum, which met once a week during these years in Chicago, was indirectly involved in the revelatory process, feeding (through the human Contact Commissioners) not only hundreds of questions to the revelators but specific comments on early drafts of the papers.

The revelatory process initiated early in the 20th century marked the beginning of a massive dialogue between divinity and humanity that continued with the Teaching Mission, I was now convinced. Transcripts of Teaching Mission sessions were of variable quality and veracity, depending on the person transmitting and the group around them; the Urantia text, on the other hand, was clearly of uniformly superlative quality and carried an unmistakable flavor of revelatory excellence.

The literary affinity of the Urantia text to the new celestial transcripts is comparable to that between a textbook and its oral explication. As I stated in one of my posts during the online debates, a good analog might be the relationship between the transcribed lectures of a college professor and the authoritative textbook his course is based upon. But nothing in this scenario required the precipitous appearance of a high celestial being to somehow reinforce the work of providing teachings in interactive settings. The teaching model, now already well exemplified in over 20 locations, was working quite proficiently without it.

The Urantia Book was not necessarily a new "bible," but it did purport to be an epochal revelation to our planet. The Teaching Mission was, by contrast, a grassroots phenomenon involving localized transmissions of celestial teachings based on the Urantia text to small groups and individuals.

Some version of this method of celestial contact may have also been used in biblical times when the prophets and teachers of old engaged in inspired contact with divine personalities. Celestial beings had appeared as apparitions in surprise visits to many deserving saints and mystics over the centuries. But aside from the so-called Millerite sect, which believed Christ would return on October 22, 1844, had there ever been a time when a group of people had met in one place with the real expectation of the literal physical appearance of a celestial being?

Sometimes a student is sent into the field to test the teachings they've been given. But the materialization incident was far beyond the pale. Had there been foul play behind the events at Naperville?

ANOMALOUS TEACHINGS IN NORMAN

Just a week before we had embarked for Naperville, the celestials conducted yet another experimental session. This one was for the expressed purpose of clearing away our residual fears of Lucifer and Satan!

That evening, our teachers introduced themselves in the usual way. But then they astonished us with the immediate announcement that a figure named "Lucifer" was to speak. At first our transmitter was upset; she refused to transmit. However, Asia was assured of her safety and agreed to begin. Thus began an uncanny staged event, conducted (we were told later) in order to gauge our reactions to the presence of "the devil." It was then followed by short commentary sprinkled with some notes of comic relief, and a helpful coda from Christ Michael.

Asia: [obviously uncomfortable] . . . Okay, faith and trust, trust and faith, right?

RondEL: *This is Lucifer who wishes to speak at this time....*

"Lucifer": *I come to you by ways of peace, yet have followed a path of abandonment. I am forlorn, missing that which I forgot. I have joined with loving forces in high counsel in order to repair damage that has been wrought upon this poor planet, Urantia. I am remiss at my own misunderstanding and wish to beg of you your compassion . . . I have gone astray and much sorrow was meted out as punishment for my actions.*

RondEL: *It is with interest that we observe your character reactions to this symbology of Lucifer . . .Many hold fears of Satanic worship in their souls. Hearts are delivered to us with much abandonment still. It is thus imperative to cleanse thoroughly all blackened fear-portions of one's spirit, including the acceptance of Lucifer as a powerful creational force in your lives. Be not dismayed at the seemingly severe introduction to this topic. We intend to dismantle your complex reactions to Lucifer's infringement on your beings. I must restate the imperative nature of reducing conflicts in one's heart at this level . . .*

Thomy: *I am here to speak to you on the lessons of the aforementioned spirit, Lucifer. It is I, Thomy. I leap. . . and circus around. . . Often I delight in the essence of movement through intergalactic space. It is a joy to be free. I am light and I am very much alive, moved by molecular motion into swinging arrays of light and motion. Pleasant am I as the spring breeze which touches your very face. I am free. No fear resides in me. Lucifer has accomplished that which he accomplished, that is all. Be free. Let go. Trust. Father is healing in spirit, and fortitude rests on his shoulders. Lucifer is a dim companion to the Father's grand love. Let go and be free, my friends. Come, share the clouds . . .*

Tomaray: *I jingle. . . I sparkle. . . I am not afraid. I am here in Lucifer's world and I see only aberrations of his unrelenting purpose creating extraordinary amounts of courage and faith on a planet deemed to succeed on disproportionate scales. Befriend a man of sorts who has brought such glory to your people. . . Protected are you from his impoverished need to succeed. Blessed be those who can see the gift for what it truly represents. I rest free of abandonment and fear.*

Josephine: *I am Josephine, here to speak of the night sky, the sky that blends with the darkness of one's vision. The betrayed vision of Lucifer required mankind to suffer great losses. However, it is of utmost importance to remind those who sit here tonight that you also receive the light of God's love in a magnitude that is beyond many skeptics' power. I am Josephine of the night sky, here to remind you of the light that exists in darkness-stars of existence which illuminate even the deepest path. I am here to say we are all loved.*

Jacob: *Teachers, I can see now the purpose of this theatrical event, and it certainly brings up a primal fear that is circulating throughout our community. But I wonder, was Lucifer actually extinguished? And what about Caligastia?*

The Teaching Mission

Michael: *I am here to remind you of the joy found in fear. Fear responding thus is a reminder of our aliveness. Joy may be found there. Alive we are-part of an incredible creation, many-faceted and incredible in its beauty. Yet, what if one of the facets were broken or charred in some way? How is God to respond to a perfectly-cut gem being disgraced so? Lucifer disgraced with great intent the gemstone of God our Father's universe-a great gift that had been given to him by our Father alone-the ability to rule and manage many souls. Lucifer was brought to bear the burdens of his unpardonable sins and has become as dust is to dust. He is no more, yet [inaudible] has witnessed the acceptance of his rule on Urantia. Many have not recovered from his blatant accusation of God's lack. How can this occur? How have so many children been lost?*

I am He, the bringer of gold riches to a universe which has lost so many. I bring to you the wealth of understanding, the belief in the goodness of our Father, and hope and determination. With skillful punctuation, aberration is to be removed, and light shall show you the way to a superuniverse filled with glory-for those who wish to choose faith and not fear. Pursue not a path of fear. Forsaken are those who trust Lucifer's message, who remind themselves of God's lack of decency in allowing children to starve, people to be murdered, children to be beaten. Is it God who thus allows these infringements to occur? Has God not given each of you free will to exercise on his or her own time scale? What more is it that you wish from a Father who has created a perfect universe? It is truly your decision.

We could only ponder the meaning of this strange lesson. A few months after this transmission and the madcap Naperville event (both of which were in April), our group received another surprising transmission on the Lucifer problem, but this one was quite sober and serious. It included this sudden statement from the teacher named **Zion**:

I wish to warn those present of an impending crisis of sorts. There has been much malaise among a few of you here on Urantia. Many of these Urantians have been touched by a power that they deem more important than the Father's loving wishes and guidance for individuals here on this planet . . . This has created turmoil and chaos in light of the proposed outcome of the Teaching Mission.

This had followed upon an astounding statement from Christ Michael that I had received a month earlier (May 2, 1993), and less than ten days after our return from Naperville. It was one I chose to ignore at first, even though it seemed to correlate with the "character test" we had been given. It was received privately through **Leta**, in Tulsa:

There are still many rebel spirits in this system who are attempting to disguise themselves as being sent by me, when they are not. They give pretty words, beautiful messages, but these messages do not create goodness and harmony. These messages create discord and havoc . . . Certain issues must be resolved. These issues include the capturing of those who have followed Lucifer. Until this is done, Urantia is fertile ground for disharmony, discord, and conflict . . . Many individuals, because of misinformation, through faith and trust, have opened themselves up indiscriminately to any and all who would use them in this way. They inadvertently accept any spirit personality who contacts them as coming from me. This is the gravest of errors. Great care must be taken in establishing who is transmitting and whether they are sent by me.

And now, in a public session, my own personal teacher **RondEL** was coming out in support of this statement. He had introduced Zion with these words:

The Teaching Mission

Now we wish to engage each of you in a matter of concern. This would be: the forthcoming entrapment of rebellious spirits. It is our desire to inform you and others of the nature of the "beast," so to speak.

A few minutes later **Michael** then entered the discussion, explaining briefly the story of how the Lucifer rebellion had come about, concluding with this momentous lesson:

[T]he story has unfolded over many generations and you have seen the outcome in each of your personal lives. These effects could be identified as lack of union among peoples; harmony is a missing piece to a very great puzzle. Without harmony, indeed, my children, we cannot truly co-exist for our natures demand reciprocity and trust. Release the judgments of others in this aspect. For you must see that judgment only intensifies the separation. So I call to you, my dearest children of faith, to come to Me by your prayers and hence facilitate healing and maturity on Urantia.

It was much later (on August 24, 1993) that a punch line of a more serious sort was delivered by Christ Michael – one that I believe referred to Naperville.

(Note that misinformation intentionally is given through rebel spirits who have attained contact with certain individuals under the guise of being sent by me.)

Our ability to deal with this issue went in fits and starts. In another session around the same time, **Michael** said something I have pondered over ever since:

You must be made aware that darkened spirit forces may be requested on a subliminal level in order that the soul may continue to experience growth . . . It is not always intentional, you see, on conscious levels. [Compare this with statements on the same subject at Urantia Book 53:8.6-9.]

Were we out of our minds? TM participants had been told in many previous transmissions across the country, although not in great detail, that the Adjudication had been completed years before. The verdict of the very high beings in charge of such judicial affairs had been broadcast, and the rebels were no more. We had understood that an "executionary broadcast" from Uversa at the time of the adjudication of the Lucifer rebellion in 1984-5 had resulted in the mass annihilation of the rebel spirits. *The Urantia Book* itself explains this event of execution in this way: *"We believe that all rebels who will ever accept mercy have done so. We await the flashing broadcast that will deprive these traitors of personality existence. We anticipate the verdict of Uversa will be announced by the executionary broadcast which will effect the annihilation of these interned rebels."* (See UB 53:9.7)

Yet, here is the response I received in May when I asked for further explanation of this UB quote and earlier TM transmissions that seemed to support it.

Michael said: *"You and others think that I or Father need only to snap our fingers and the rebels will disappear. Unfortunately, that is not the case."*

When I had courage to ask for even more detail later that summer, Christ Michael said this through **Leta**:

153

A broadcast is merely a broadcast. It is not in or of itself a means whereby personal extinction occurs. It is simply an announcement that the extinction will be taking place. There has been a great deal of confusion in this regard. Know that the elimination of any spirit-personality is an intricate procedure, accomplished on each individual after certain prerequisites have been met. A word of intention is not sufficient to erase the personality of one who has been accorded immortality . . . When a Son of God has been given life everlasting, this is not indiscriminately taken. There are many rules which are governing this extinction-rules which are followed to the letter.

An earlier response I had received on May 2 began to make sense:

They [the rebels] were tried and found guilty. Sentence is now in process of being carried out. This is not something that occurs instantaneously, as you have falsely been led to believe. Many of the guilty have fled to this world. Urantia lies in a remote corner of the universe. I have gathered armies of angels here to deal with these rebel spirits. We are now in the process of tracking, locating, and transporting these rebels back to Jerusem to await execution of sentence. My children, there is indeed a holy war occurring now. These rebels are strong, they have had hundreds of thousands of years to build their strength [and] make their plans. They are well prepared. However, Father and I are well prepared as well.

Filling this story in further was this amazing statement, added later in response to questions:

Urantia has become a playground for those spirits, those personalities. It affords them a two-fold opportunity, not the least of which is to cause havoc to my home planet. They feel, they believe, that they can cause me great sorrow, and they are correct. My love for this little world is known throughout the universe. Also, the disharmony evident throughout this planet is like a magnet attracting them . . . It is beyond our comprehension what benefit they feel they gain. I appreciate your attempts to understand [but] they are beyond human understanding; they are beyond my understanding. I can only offer them my forgiveness. In these cases I find it difficult to know their [hearts] for they have turned so completely away. I can only offer them my solicitude.

Could this be the explanation of the havoc caused by the event in Naperville? Had unsuspecting but sincere Teaching Mission transmitters been given misinformation? The apocryphal material on the rebel spirits very briefly excerpted here was emailed to other TM groups 17 years ago-with almost no responses other than negative ones-aside from a few ambiguous statements of support from teachers in two locations, one being Half Moon Bay, California. (It has taken me that amount of time to come to terms with even looking at this material once again.)

I was assured in the months to come that the work of "mopping up" the rebel spirits had been achieved within a few years. The rounding up process including those who were still resident on Urantia and those who, according to what we had been told, had fled to Urantia for their final stand against Michael. They had been shorn of their leaders, Lucifer, Satan, and Caligastia the disgraced Planetary Prince of Urantia, its original planetary celestial chief who was succeeded in 1991 by Machiventa Melchizedek. All of them had voluntarily chosen annihilation at the time of the Adjudication broadcast.

Lucifer had long been held on the prison world near the system capital of Jerusem, the capital of our local group of 619 inhabited planets, and Satan had been detained at the time of the presentation of the Urantia Revelation. For "legal" reasons, Caligastia had been permitted to roam planet earth until the Adjudication should occur (as the Urantia Revelation had made clear).

These three were now gone, we had uniformly been told in diverse transmission, but the rest of the tens of thousands of lesser spirits that had gone astray with them had an uncertain status. These disturbing transmissions to our group appeared to explain the fate of these beings. Could it be that they had delivered a parting blow to the Teaching Mission by their brief infiltration?

To some, the statements from Michael and our teachers that are reported above appear to contradict certain quotes from other teachers and from *The Urantia Book* itself; to others, these statements greatly supplement that material. One thing is clear: *The Urantia Book* is an experimental revelation given to an experimental planet. The Teaching Mission is in turn a creative experiment in planetary retrieval by our Creator Michael. And our little group in Oklahoma was evidently an experimental unit within the nascent Teaching Mission.

What an environment for practicing discernment of spirits!

THE TRIUMPH OF CHRIST MICHAEL

After his elevation to settled sovereignty in a local universe a Paradise Michael is in full control of all other Sons of God functioning in his domain, and he may freely rule in accordance with his concept of the needs of his realms. A Master Son may at will vary the order of the spiritual adjudication and evolutionary adjustment of the inhabited planets. And such Sons do make and carry out the plans of their own choosing in all matters of special planetary needs, in particular regarding the worlds of their creature sojourn and still more concerning the realm of terminal bestowal, the planet of incarnation in the likeness of mortal flesh.
 (The Urantia Book 21:5.4)

This quote from the mighty Urantia Book makes clear just how wide-ranging are the powers and prerogatives of Christ Michael on a planet of his bestowal, especially ours as a planet sitting in the darkness of a double default. Michael's marvelous powers of love and grace were on display for us in our lowly living room in a rural part of Oklahoma, as they are in potential everywhere. The utter creativity of his interactions with us especially revealed the vast dimensions of the manifest beauty in his being, and his unfathomable compassion.

And just as the *The Urantia Book* was a revelation to our minds, the Teaching Mission and especially Michael's role in it is an ongoing a revelation to our souls and hearts.

Over these months, Asia quickly unfolded her capacious ability to act as a poetic vehicle for the tender verbal ministrations of Michael to our humble group. We saw the power of

Michael's majesty in utterances addressed to us (and in private sessions) on different occasions. I conclude with just a few brief excerpts:

Be aware of my aura; it is much like the impending snow on a forecast winter day.

Prepare your soul for the arrival of your Spirit Father, Son of God, Word of Hope, Message of Truth, Conductor of Love, Conveyor of Praise, Prophet of Paradise, Leader of Loyals, Healer of the Weak, Image of Light, Voice of Encouragement, Prince of Peace. . .

The morning of the dawning of Light and Life will shine rays of warmth on your bowing heads. All will wake and wipe the years of tears from their eyes.

All will stretch their spirit-reaching hands to grasp the hands and embrace the hearts of their guides. All will feel the stir of spiritual hunger and thirst.

All will bathe in the love and shower in the grace of this day. This cleansing, this feast, this uniting, this awakening-this is the day worth waiting for.

Release your fear like baggage thrown to the stars, for I have believed in each of you regardless of your standing . . . Deity is forgiving. Love bears offspring to itself. All who visit this mountain of love, all who come to surround and embrace the whole, will be rewarded. Come now, to the base of this mountain, my children, and I will raise you to the heavens, for the peak on which I stand is eternal.

It is I, Michael, the Inhabitant of Your Heartsong, the Bringer of Love, the Desirer of Peace . . . How come it has been such a long, arduous journey? Can you imagine the turmoil you must have struggled through to come to a resting place? Now you find it is yours. You have traveled, you have come a long way, my children. Rest your weary, mortal souls. Allow then the incredible gift that is yours. It does belong to you, for you are, all of you, parts of a very great and cosmic universe!

Now I direct your awareness to a very small pinpoint of time and space. It is deep within your consciousness. Fall back into this place; it is known. As a magnet it draws your attention. Once there, when you reach your destination-this small point of light-it explodes within, it radiates out, it is love. It is experienced at a body level; it is felt in your mind, your heart, your spirit. Rejoice now in the everlasting, the overpowering beauty of this love. It encapsulates all time, it goes beyond your imagination. It is infinite and exotic, yet it belongs to you . . .

I am omnipresent. The rapture yet to be experienced can be found today, of course, in your stillness with love and centeredness. Fear not retribution, I arrive in love. You will know me; I shall protect those who are susceptible to the infringement of power by others who appear to rule in force. I question the role of imagination and would enjoy dispensing of any fears by a simple action.

Carry a memento of my love in the palm of your hand. Powerful love embodied in a vision of simplicity, purity, can release the onslaught of painful or remorseful projections into the future. The image I provide at this time will be unique to each individual here. If it is your desire, cup your hands in an upward and forward motion. I drop into your palms an emblem reminiscent of My all-powerful loving intent for My children. Now raise your hands, if you so wish, and receive in your cup my gift. It is received . . . now hold it in your memory for a moment. The memento is yours.

Know me in your name, calling forth the spirit which breeds happiness and joy. I am in the passing of the seasons, the cooling of the air, the falling of the leaves to the ground. I am within all experience. No breath is without me. As an opening occurs, experience and feel Me daily. I will be yours at the slightest provocation.

Hitchhikers Visible and Invisible
How Nonmaterial Colleagues Help Deepen My Students' Learning
and Teach Me to Believe in Myself
John Creger

I.   **My Teaching Mission story began 15 years before I ever heard the phrase,** back when I first started getting the message. The message came to me from the mind of a hitchhiker I picked up on my way home from work one day in the fall of 1979. A grizzled wayfarer confirmed my growing suspicions that the universe is *alive* and filled with intention.

Okay. There it is. I trust hitchhikers for my information on the nature of the cosmos. Do I consult my beagle for stock market tips? Well, I'll just say that it piqued my curiosity, eyeing this vagabond perched in the back of my pickup chatting with his traveling partner in my rearview mirror. What was he doing out here on the road, ten years after hitchhikers had been common along American highways? Could he be trusted? Walking to the back of the truck alongside the turnpike off-ramp where I was about to drop him in the dusk, I quickly thought up two integrity tests. Just as quickly he passed them. I told him I lived nearby in a cabin at the edge of the woods on a hill above a lake. He'd be welcome to my spare bedroom for a while. Rash? Maybe so. I wasn't concerned with protecting myself from happenstance.

In those days, living in this small New Hampshire town, I was wrestling with demons of confusion. Who was I? Why did I not always treat others how I'd prefer to be treated, even when this was what I sincerely wanted to do? Why was life such a confused cocktail of beauty and brutality, majesty, limitation and pain? Soon after he climbed down from the truck outside my cabin that October evening, Billy began teaching me about God.

I had sat close by the wood stove evenings in my drafty cabin the previous winter, making my first solo pass through the Bible. In February, responding to a challenge I perceived somewhere in one of the testaments, I decided to try supposing that God actually existed. And why not? It made more sense than any other explanation I had come across. How else to explain the New England seasons exploding through the year in such a procession of glory, or the universe arraying itself so unexpectedly around me as I wrestled my demons? God the majestic cosmos creator? That God I could begin to imagine. But the wanderer I'd

157

brought home was teaching me about a *friend* who *enjoyed keeping me company,* and in the most ordinary and uncreative moments. God wanted to come closer, Billy was telling me. With my own father a colder, more distant figure than I would have liked, this was a harder God for me to picture. Perhaps this is why these "uncreative" moments were exactly the times when Billy would move in and coach me.

We'd be splitting firewood on my chopping block in front of the cabin, or in my kitchen cutting up vegetables for a pot of stew. *So how much oregano would you add to this stew, Father, if you were me?* Such was among the methods of my mysterious tutor. At the end of five weeks, I dropped Billy off on another freeway ramp. I would never see him again.

Coaching me over those weeks, Billy often cited and discussed a certain compendium of information about the universe. He did not carry this book with him but, astonishingly, could quote from it verbatim almost indefinitely. I had first seen a copy of the book the previous spring, strangely enough, when a friend brought a copy to our music practice session. A quick look-through and I'd known. This would be the book I'd read just as soon as I finished my first study of the Bible. I had completed that study, as it happened, a couple of weeks before Billy appeared.

Accordingly, the last day before I dropped him at the on ramp, Billy and I jumped in my truck and undertook a search across the state, turning up what might have been the only copy of this 2100 page book available at the time in the state of New Hampshire. With the book in my hands, Billy was free to move on. For me, things would be different now.

Before, it was too obvious to think about. *He* was the hitchhiker. Slowly, through more spiritual eyes, I would begin to see who'd really been picked up wandering the highway. In moments of doubt as I looked back on those five weeks, too many synchronicities raised their heads. I'll spare you the details. The encounter smacked undeniably of *intent.*

Increasingly, I would come to feel I was here for a reason. Yessir. A purpose for being embodied in this world had been set aside for me. Wishful thinking? Maybe so. But in coming years the more sincerely I desired to discover this purpose, the more guidance I would find coming along. If it was ready to send a traveling teacher to help me prepare for the next phase of my unfolding life, an eccentric coach who had committed to memory just the unprecedented, little-known information it wanted me exposed to, a cosmic evangelist who enlisted God's advice in seasoning stews, then what more was this universe willing to show me? This is one creation that is sincere about *follow up.*

II.   Letting Billy off at the northbound turnpike entrance, I had turned south, eventually following Billy's urging and making my way home to California for medical help. Disabled with a chronic inflammatory back problem at 28, I was convalescing at my parents' house where, conveniently, I would have time to digest this mysterious blue-covered tome. *The Urantia Book* it was called. Information about the universe and its teeming levels of celestial, divine, and mortal life poured into my primed awareness. Inklings became understandings. Yes, we are allowed to persecute, torture, decimate one another, even kill off entire species and pollute the planet. The only price is that we must live with the consequences. And yes, the entire universe is alive. Vast. Full of life. *Eternal* life. Powered by love, this is a universe that knows who I am, and sincerely wants to help me to the next step in finding out for myself. But it will not coerce me. We have such latitude out here at the rough edges of space so that our own evolving can be a genuine part of universe evolution. In discovering myself, I help the whole cosmos unfold. Perhaps all this could help me figure out what kind of life I wanted to live?

But what would I *do?* Unable to continue the carpenter work that had won me material independence, I was stranded back in my family of origin until I could regain my health. It was time to begin claiming my spiritual independence, caught again in the same confusing crucible I'd fled ten years before. I saw I needed to overcome psychological patterns grooved in childhood— of failing to believe in myself, of blaming my family. It boiled down to this: If I wanted to find this purpose I now knew awaited me, I needed to carve out a new direction, make a new life consistent with my new understandings about the loving universe that was alive. I needed healing. And a new kind of guidance.

The next hitchhikers I would pick up would be invisible.

Fast-forward fifteen years.

My close friend Steve had recently sent me information about a new development making the rounds of the study groups *Urantia Book* readers form to facilitate their understanding of the book. The development was known as the Teaching Mission. Transcripts were showing up from different locations across the U.S. and from different "transmitter-receivers." These transcripts, records of "transmissions," were messages channeled through human "TRs" from celestial teachers who explained they were part of a coordinated celestial effort to reclaim our world from our confused planetary past. This development would help us begin to rejoin the community of spiritually progressing worlds in the evolving universe. This all pretty much lined up with the understandings about the universe I had gained from the *Urantia Book.*

I joined others in the San Francisco Bay Area who had read these transcripts, meeting weekly, all of us eager to converse with the celestial teachers. Allen Rice had made contact with a teacher named Althena. She told us through Allen that she had been assigned to the East Bay and was at our service. Her nonmaterial presence was gracious, subtle, but unmistakable no matter which of us was attempting to transmit her. I soon became fond of her unfailingly gentle personality. The intent of the Mission was simple: to help each of us connect more regularly and fully with God's presence within.

I appreciated the refreshing lack of hierarchy or formal leadership. All were welcome. Althena was able to be with each of us during the week, hitchhiking unrestricted by space, joining us at the edges of our perceptions. Each of us had ample chance at our meetings to ask Althena questions, personal and otherwise. Our East Bay group was joyful, open-minded and lighthearted, and made room for any of us who wished to experiment with transmitting.

I doubted I had what it took to make genuine spiritual connections heard by others. Eventually these doubts became oppressive, and I decided I'd attempt contact. This was not a perfect process, I soon learned, and a transmission would always be subject to a transmitter's own limitations. Realizing this helped me relax as I practiced transmitting. Thankfully, I found that not all my limitations were set in stone, and practicing could help me become a better transmitter. When Allen moved out of the area, I served for a time as our group's regular transmitter, and learned to be more comfortable with the experience. During this period, Althena, an ascendant mortal from a world more highly evolved than our own, reminded us about the purpose of this Teaching Mission:

> *Remember that the prime goal of this mission and indeed of all true spiritual teachings is to increase human ability to perceive the leadings of the spirit of God within. We teachers, whether celestial or human —and every true human spiritual teacher acts on celestial guidance—function simply as trainers who coach you toward this goal.*

Attending meetings of other Teaching Mission groups in our area and joining in annual statewide and national Mission events held in various locations from 1994 to 2000, my wife and I and our two young daughters made what have since developed into our deepest friendships. These friendships have included nonmaterial beings. As we met Susan Kimsey and her family, we encountered another ascending former mortal, the teacher Susan most often transmitted, Olfana. Her world of origin had been a rebellion planet like ours, but even more confused and backward. Olfana herself, Susan transmitted, had personally led the life of a slave. With her dramatic messages and Susan's flamboyant transmitting, Olfana became an important influence, helping me slowly lose doubts about my own worthiness, and lay groundwork for greater self-confidence. In 1999, in a longer transmission, Olfana offered me this message:

You are more than you think you are! You are more beautiful than you think you are. You are more talented than you think you are. You are more gracious than you know you are. You have more love at your soul's fingertips than you can dream of!

Teaching Mission transcripts from around the country came filled with a great variety of such encouraging messages. Slowly, this message that I was actually smart and loving, talented and gracious, began to displace the self-doubting mental and emotional habits of my lifetime. I learned how to rely on a kind of inner strength that came from beyond me, ultimately from God.

From whatever teacher, transmitter or location a transmission came, the most consistent message of the Teaching Mission was to cultivate the practice of *stillness*. The particular techniques vary richly, but in essence the stillness is both a method to practice and a state of being to achieve. The teachers often made specific suggestions to individual students. My own sessions with Althena often include a personal message. This one came at a recent stage of my growth when I became ready to cultivate *gratefulness* as a healing influence:

> *As an exercise, in your mind you may associate the presence of calmness in yourself as an indication that the feeling of gratefulness is close behind. I salute your efforts to cultivate these two emotional states in yourself, which can offer you much deep nurturing and healing. I encourage you to aspire each day toward a more continuous experience of gratefulness. This can have an especially soothing effect on your soul, my dear student.*

These days, with additional help from another remarkable book called *Love Without End* that has recently come into my life, my morning meditations begin with a three-part exercise: 1) a session of allowing myself to feel *grateful* for someone or something in my life, followed by 2) a segment devoted to *forgiving* someone I've been angry or upset with, and 3) a final sequence inviting the divine and celestial forces to help me see a challenging situation in my life more *as it really is*, and less how I might wish it were. These elements come together in a kind of tonic for the heart. At this point I open up my meditation for more open-ended communication. In my classroom over the past year, I have shared this exercise we call A Visit to the Heart with nearly three hundred teenagers.

III.

Did I say "my classroom?" A number of years after returning home to California disabled, I had graduated from the university and felt guided into a new career as a high school English teacher. After 2000, Teaching Mission groups in our area met less frequently. My wife and I grew busier raising our daughters and juggling our careers. But the Teaching Mission had made a lasting imprint on my life.

It was during my fifth year in the classroom that I heard about the celestial teachers. As I attempted to practice the stillness and cultivate connections with them, I felt encouraged in my classroom teaching to seek guidance actively, real-time, from my non-material teacher colleagues. Already I had begun creating early versions of what is now the star in my teaching opus, a classroom project designed to help students discover what they value or stand for by reflecting systematically upon their life experience. Through this project my students regularly reach a deeper level of learning than is customary in what we know as education. The Personal Creed Project would gain attention with a national award and a book with a major education publisher. How could it be an accident that this entire effort was being called the *Teaching* Mission?

I came to feel that I was not the only teacher in my classroom. I imagined I felt occasional nudges from my non-material colleagues. In my stillness practice I began consciously asking for insight and encouragement in my work in the classroom with students. I have yet to utilize these nonmaterial resources to the full extent possible.

The Teaching Mission

This past summer I resumed a regular stillness journal, a tool I'd used to establish initial contact with the teachers in my first days with the Mission. One morning, in response to concerns I had aired early in this session about certain challenges I'd faced in the classroom last year, I typed out what felt like a stern admonishment from a senior universe teacher called Machiventa Melchizedek. I tend to push myself beyond wise limits, and often fall chronically behind on sleep. He urged me to take better care of myself and stay in better touch:

> *But you have reached a time in your life when you need more regular connection and guidance if you wish to carry forward your part of our work. In the dizzying crush of your lives today, this is understandable. Still, you have allowed yourself to become undernourished. Nourishment is at hand if you will simply sit at the table and allow yourself to be served. My suggestion is that you set yourself to reconvening with your invisible teammates in stillness this coming week. Make a point of appearing daily on time to a morning meeting, ready to listen and be heard (as you tell your students). Recall that many of the benefits of the stillness occur beneath and above the conscious level. Do not feel you must fill your stillness time only with back-and-forth communication. Allow yourself time to be worked upon, as well as to consult and be consoled.*

More often than receiving such discernible one-way communications from "beyond," I tend to perceive the influence of the teachers more subtly. In particular, I notice their influence in my *interactions* with my students. And I'm not the only one transmitting messages. It was the fall of 1999. Once again, I had slipped into the pattern of letting myself become overtaxed.

Jonna sat in the back corner near my desk, her arm straightening slowly in the air. "Yes, Jonna," I said tiredly. "Mr. Creger?" she began. "Yep." "Do you . . . meditate?" I was surprised she would ask.

"Funny you should ask, Jonna. I usually spend 5-10 minutes meditating in the morning before breakfast. But this week I haven't found time."

It was a Friday in October. This sixth period was a sweet group. We'd had pleasant relations so far this year, the kids more or less with me, more or less engaged in our studies together. But quarter grades were due the week after next. I'd been up most of the night preparing grade reports to hand out to all my classes. Several other nights this week I'd slept only a few hours as I caught up on reading essays. All day, class by class, I'd made my way through rows of desks, handing out the grade printouts. Kids waved their arms in the air, burbling about the two points I'd forgotten to record in their printout. I was fried. End of the day. End of the week. As I scattered the grade reports from desk to desk, the class heard me muttering, "See an error in your grade? Don't talk to me. Did I make a mistake? I don't really care. Just take your grades. That's it."

They were shocked. They'd never seen me in such a state. Later in the year one student in this class would give me a My Favorite Teacher Award. Julia would describe me on the certificate as a "good listener who stays calm." Calm? I was almost wadding up their grades this afternoon and throwing them on their desks. Listening? End of discussion.

And now Jonna was asking if I meditated. This was before my classes *expected* to talk about meditating, expected to actually *meditate*.

She was looking at me with concern. "Uh ... Mr. Creger?" "Yes, Jonna." "Maybe you should do some meditating over the weekend."

"Sounds like a good idea," I said sheepishly, my toes turning inward a little defensively. "Think I'll take you up on that."

The next week I must have been back to normal. Tuesday, Jonna started something that has been going on ever since.

"Mr. Creger." "Yes, Jonna." "Would you teach us to meditate?"

Every fall in the decade since then as I introduce our practice of classroom meditation, I tell my classes this story. Jonna and her classmates had no idea how important meditating, reaching for stillness, had become for me over the previous five years. Nor was I about to tell them that I was conscious at times of working with nonmaterial colleagues. Still, it's not as if such things are completely beyond my students' ability to fathom.

My students may only be 14, 15, or 16 years old. But each of them has his or her own share of life experience. However limited, that experience has included connections, however conscious, with the presence of God within. Some are more aware of these things than others, some far more alive to the inner spark than I was at their age. The celestial teachers inform us about other orders of nonmaterial colleagues responsible for linking us to the invisible grid that connects us all. They tell us that where supermortals work with mortals these forces of connection are activated. I had been encouraged to simply trust that in the classroom our deeper connections were being facilitated, and that I could rely upon this fact. Sure enough, by Thanksgiving that year with Jonna and her classmates, and every year since, all of my classes *expect* a little time to meditate once a week. It's just part of what we do. And this came from a student's suggestion.

IV.   Since Jonna's day, many forces have whittled down students' attention spans and ability to focus at all. When James and then Monique first asked a few weeks ago if they could help me lead our classroom meditation sessions, I held my cards close to my chest. Generally, a teacher on our world has to be careful not to give away power precipitously, especially in a class as little prone to self-control as this third period class has been. But, ten years since meditation first took root in my classroom, I did smile inwardly when these two bright under-achievers asked to help lead our meditations.

This class has made remarkable progress. Okay. For most of first semester, attempting to hold class discussions for more than ten minutes was a recipe for chaos, a voluntary dive in shriek-infested currents. This is changing.

Last week we had a 90 minute discussion in this class, a conversation that was focused, respectful, and thoroughly engaged. A coherent conversation of such length was completely unprecedented in my regular classes, and rare even in my honors classes. In place of the usual reminders, warnings, and threats of detention, I offered sincere praise and encouragement born of respect for what they were accomplishing.

A couple of weeks ago I handed this class back a set of essays. 90% of these same students earned As and Bs on this essay. *90%*. In *this* class! Rarely does *50%* of such a class clear this hurdle! Something changing at a deeper level?

It's our block day. The kids are expecting to meditate, since last week's testing commandeered our meditating time. This class especially seems to crave our 7-10 minute weekly meditations. I've seen this over and over: The more unruly a class, the more it wants to meditate. Every year my most disruptive class seems to be the one that most wants meditation. Early in the year I told them the story of Jonna and that sixth period class ten years before.

"Mr. Creger?" It's Monique. She's the most talented writer in the class. Hers was the top paper in the batch I recently handed back.

"Yes, Monique."

"Mr. Creger, I think I'm ready to lead the meditation this time." The last time she thought she might be ready, but when the moment came she'd been too giggly.

"Sounds good," I say. "Will you be wanting background music?" Monique's friend James suggested a few weeks ago that we try using soothing music in the background to help focus our meditations. So far we've tried Bach guitar music and one soaring Bobby McFerrin piece. The background music idea stuck, and now has spread to other classes. The hundred minute block periods are grueling for sophomores. The meditation helps break them up, and the music helps more kids get involved in the meditation. But I'm interested in the long-term, less visible benefits.

Monique sits on my swivel chair in the front of the room. I see her motion to James, who gets up and joins her, perching on a chair beside her. James has already led two meditations on his own, a first move toward fuller student ownership of our class mediations. The first time he took the class on two or three minute imaginary journey to the beach in Hawaii, where they took off their shoes and enjoyed the warm sand and clear water. Then he brought them back across the ocean to class. I led them in the Visit to the Heart I was just developing, the three-part exercise from *Love Without End* I mentioned earlier. The second time, James led an entire five to seven minute meditation. Having me start them off with a breathing exercise, this time James took the class on a journey across space to another planet or two where they had several adventures before James brought them back to Earth and delivered them into my keeping. Afterward the class had been considerably more focused and attentive than normal.

With James alongside for moral support, Monique takes the class on a voyage to the bottom of the ocean, where we meet strange creatures with tutu-shaped fins, dancing on the sands on a floor lit by pilot fish. After riding the deep on the backs of porpoises, we surface to tour the island of plastic garbage in the mid-Pacific, circling its perimeter for a number of days before turning back home, concerned though refreshed, toward class.

Neither Monique nor James has been stellar students most of the year. Now, as the class is showing measurable signs of turning around—in the quality of their writing, the length of their attention span as a group, and the quality of their interactions in class—James and Monique have joined the turnaround. They have made some especially fine contributions to our class discussions of literature this week, rendering the parts of Janie and Tea Cake in Zora Neale Hurston's *Their Eyes Were Watching God*, employing expressive, well-modulated African-American dialects. Both have gone from near-failing grades fall semester to passing respectably now. After observing such turnarounds for many years, my hunch is that students naturally evolve more interest in learning academic skills when they are enabled to intertwine skill acquisition with self-cultivation through ongoing techniques such as meditation, reflection, and continuous questioning– learning more in the process about who they are and how they fit with others, their communities, world and universe.

V.   Classroom meditation is just one feature of the approach to teaching and learning I have begun studying and documenting over the past ten years in my classroom and sharing in the workshop series I offer educators. The habit of reaching for the celestial and divine teachers has encouraged me to bring this evolving approach to national and, one day perhaps, international attention. Thanks to the Teaching Mission, I have learned to reach for inspiration and patience. Trust me. When you work with batches of 30 or more sophomores all day as I have done for over 20 years now, knowing how to reach for inspiration and patience comes in handy.

My evolving approach to teaching is grounded in *concepts* from my studies of *The Urantia Book* and other sources, and *confidence* to experiment that has come through my interactions with celestial and divine teachers in the Teaching Mission. Participants in the workshop series I offer educators, however, know nothing of the Teaching Mission or *The Urantia Book*. I have referred to the new approach variously as *Universe Wiring, Weaving in the Personal, Infusing Meaning,* and *Workable Learning.* Except in rare cases with former students I have come to know very well, I never directly mention the actual roots of this approach. Instead of discussing these manifestations, my students and workshop participants *experience* them with me. We fly under the radar. We bootleg.

With help from the Teaching Mission teachers, I have developed a Model of Deepened Learning that helps educators guide students beyond merely *mastering facts*, beyond *construing meanings*, to *discovering values* – all as normal parts of learning in school. What I call the Learning Continuum provides the nucleus of the approach to designing courses and developing curriculum that I write about in my book and professional articles, and that we explore with human colleagues in my workshops.

We interact about the approach in an online social network for English teachers at http://englishcompanion.ning.com/group/pers. This approach appears to make a significant difference for students in my classes. I believe it will too for students of other educators around the world who are currently experimenting with the approach. In June of 2008, one of my students in "regular" English wrote:

> *I think this [class] made it clear for many students that they had a past, they have a present, and that they will have a future . . . it has gotten rid of the part of me that was unsure and skeptical about my future.*

~ Sahar, June 2008

I hope to help position this approach so that it will have an ongoing impact in a long-term celestial-human effort to transform our backward systems of planetary education. In all these efforts, now that I know they do not confine their operations to "the other side," I continue to seek guidance and support from my nonmaterial colleagues. I have yet to avail myself of all available assistance, visible or otherwise.

VI.   In 2006 I heard that some Teaching Mission participants believed they had begun receiving messages from a Paradise being named Monjoronson who would soon set up operations to help our world move through the difficult period ahead. I wasn't so sure about all this, but I did attempt to reach for a connection. The message I believed I was receiving was personal and powerful for me:

> *With continued willingness to seek and follow guidance, you are poised to enter a new fullness of being, increasingly free of the lapses of confidence that have haunted you. Continue allowing the growing light within you to push out the shadows of limiting beliefs. Continue seeing self-doubt for what it is—a partial participation in the richness of your being. Refuse to allow yourself to settle for such half-heartedness.*

Thirty years ago last fall I picked up a teaching vagabond beside the New Hampshire turnpike. Since then, much has happened in my life and in the world. Though I continue to wrestle my demons, I have made great progress, with help from both sides of the veil. The world is almost unrecognizable from the world of 1979, a much more troubled and troubling world than I dreamed of then.

The Teaching Mission

The main message of the Teaching Mission for me goes beyond simply that others are here with us. It is more that we mortals really do resemble hitchhikers navigating a universe that is very much on the lookout for us. Yes, it is our responsibility to undertake our individual and planetary journeys. But divine and celestial friends are here to help navigate and give us a lift when we need them. And it's not as if we're alone between lifts. We can establish working relationships and even real friendships with our nonmaterial colleagues– all the way from ascendant mortals like Althena and Olfana who have "graduated" from other worlds, to the Father himself, who travels with us at the deepest place inside. They genuinely love hitchhikers.

Our invisible associates can help us come to know what my student Sahar came to know in her sophomore English class. Though by universe standards it has been tumultuous and confused, we and our worldmates have a past. We are now having a present– however unsettling it is and will continue to be for a time. And despite all our troubles, of a certainty, we will have a future– one more uplifting, more powered by love and closeness than we know how to imagine.

What the Teaching Mission has done and continues to do for my life and work:

The Mission has shown me that . . .

- The universe sometimes issues a summons when it's time for something to be revealed.

- People, however accurately or imperfectly, can receive messages from celestial and divine sources.

- Even an imperfect process utilizing imperfect, easily confused human beings, can deliver real value, particularly providing we realize and acknowledge its limitations.

- Regular contact and guidance from celestial and divine beings can have highly beneficial effects on my life.

- I have more abilities than I generally think I do.

- The more I invite my nonmaterial colleagues to participate in my life and work, the more energy and joy seem to be created.

- I can reach for guidance and assistance in the moment and often benefit.

- I can actually create exercises and practices that have mental, emotional, and spiritual benefits for others.

- I can be a team player, even when I seem to be (and sometimes forget I am not) working alone.

167

- I am actually regarded as a colleague by supermortal associates.

- Through regular, professionally defensible practices, my students can become attuned to the spirit in the classroom.

- Human friendships conceived and nourished amidst divine and celestial contact are the deepest, most fulfilling ones I've known.

John Creger is a nationally recognized high school English teacher who, after twenty-some years teaching at American High School in Fremont, California, continues to love working with sophomores. With them, John has created the Personal Creed Project. In recognition of this project, John received the James Moffett Award from the National Council of Teachers of English, and published a guidebook for teachers with a major education publisher. His approach to education puts students' self-realization at the center of learning. He offers workshops and trainings for educators around the country. In this chapter, he traces the roots of his approach in his personal experiences with the Urantia Book and the Teaching Mission. He lives with his wife and two daughters in Berkeley, California.

Me and the Teaching Mission
Allen Rice, 2009

I was walking my dog on a warm clear night. The sky was black and filled with brilliant stars. I was in awe, considering the immensity of the universe. I thought about the many galaxies and other worlds that hung out there at hard to imagine distances in that darkness that seemed infinite. While attempting to grasp the reality of what I was looking at, a comforting peace came over me. I suddenly felt all the emptiness of space filled with God's presence. I felt the presence of God in me, wrapping me and filling every bit of space in the universe. I looked out at the stars and there was no distance between me and the cosmos. I felt connected to the entire universe. God's presence made it real that I was part of everything and there was no separation between me and any of the realms of creation. I know God's presence is alive in me and also alive in and around everything and everyone that exists

The presence of God is no longer just an idea to me, but is viscerally real. I wouldn't call myself enlightened in the New Age sense. I'm not really sure what that is. But I do live with a growing sense of peace and goodwill and with a humbling acceptance of God's Love. I've longed for this my whole life. And, as I'm sure you know, life on this world doesn't let it come easy.

Sixteen years ago, I was living alone in an apartment in Oakland. I was trying really hard to be happy, or at least not feel so much of the pain of being sad. Two years before, I had separated from my family and I knew I was letting my relationship with my children slip away from me, but felt powerless to do anything about it. The mixture of guilt, heartbreak and sadness was occasionally relieved with intoxication and masked with the hubris of someone who wanted to believe he could fix everything thing all by himself. I understood the importance of spiritual practice my whole life, but was uneven in pursuing it. It was slowly dawning on me that the way I was living wasn't doing much to help things get better. The part of me that knew there was a better path started to gain more voice in my thoughts. I decided I would find people with whom I could join in some kind of spiritual practice.

I'm fiercely independent when it comes to my personal beliefs, and fitting in with a group wasn't going so well for me. Then one day, one of my friends handed me a bunch of photocopied text. On the front page was printed "Woods Cross, 1991." My friend knew that I was a Urantia Book reader and he said this was some kind of channeled stuff connected with *the Urantia Book* and he thought I might enjoy reading it. I don't think he knew it would change my life.

I had always been skeptical of any kind of spiritual channeling and I felt a bit of loathing to start sifting through this material for the chance grain of truth. I didn't understand how these communications took place, but as I read, it didn't seem to matter anymore. This was one of those rare instances where my heart and mind agreed this was important. The messages were direct and concise, with a strong aura of truth that resonated deeply. I think what shocked me the most was how much the transcripts resembled my own inner conversations that felt locked and buried from the world around me. As I read and reread these transcripts, I felt as if I were awakening from a stupor.

A few weeks of that and I decided to put it aside, high on a heady froth of spiritual epiphanies. Soon, the gravity of my all too human life had pulled me back into that familiar orbit of self pity and foolish compensations, but the seeds of transformation had been planted. I didn't know at the time, but an irreversible change was taking place in me, quietly, slowly, in tender small shoots. The transcripts from Woods Cross would come to mind now and then, but I wasn't clear about what significance it held for me except to absorb the persistent realization that unseen teachers were actually communicating with people in this world. The more I considered it, the more it seemed real.

Some months had passed when it occurred to me that there may be more transcripts from this group in Woods Cross, Utah. I remember washing dishes after dinner and as I stopped to look out the kitchen window for a moment, I heard a gentle voice say, "Call them now." Somehow I understood that I needed to call the phone number that was on the transcripts. A man answered, and when I told him why I was calling, he said their group had just gathered in his home. He was just about to turn off the phone so they would not be disturbed when the phone rang. He told me that he would be happy to send me more transcripts and he offered information about two groups near me that were also being visited by unseen teachers with spiritual messages. This is how I became actively involved in the Teaching Mission and met people who would become my lifelong friends and spiritual companions.

First, I called Susan Kimsey in Half Moon Bay. We ended up talking for over two hours; as anyone who knew Susan could tell you, she never tired of talking about her experiences with the teacher she knew as Olphana. However, she told me her group met infrequently and didn't have anything scheduled for the future.

Then I called Bob Slagle in Sebastopol who, I was not surprised to learn later, was a university professor. Bob had been careful in his own way to test the veracity and authenticity of these teacher communications before concluding that they were genuine. He was likewise careful about interviewing anyone interested in joining their close knit group which had regular weekly meetings. He suggested that if I were sincerely interested he would send me several volumes of transcripts and if, after I had read them all and was still interested in joining their group, he'd be happy to have me. I was thrilled with the offer of receiving more transcripts and with the possibility of experiencing these transmissions first hand.

It seems strange now to think back on my first experiences with meeting the teachers in these group sessions. There was one person apparently designated as the main contact. Sometimes others were able to hear and repeat lessons and answers to questions people in the group might have. These people were called transmitter/receivers. From my very first time at one of these sessions, I was acutely aware of an unseen presence and often more than one. I had the impression that these were mature, gentle and loving beings that apparently enjoyed communicating with us. But to be honest, in spite of feeling a thoroughly spiritual comfort, my human self reacted with an uncomfortable degree of fear and anxiety. I had a strong feeling this was real and what scared me was that my life would never be the same after knowing this.

The unseen being who was the main teacher of this group was called Jared. The woman who transmitted Jared said she knew nothing of *the Urantia Book* or the Teaching Mission when she started to have these pleasant conversations with this voice in her head who offered personal advice that she found very useful. She didn't think much of this voice at first (she thought she was probably talking to herself). But one day the voice identified himself as Jared and asked to give Bob Slagle a message. The message was that Jared was the teacher Bob had asked for. He had been told through a transmitter that anyone earnestly seeking a teacher would receive one. The people in this group all seemed like sensible, down to earth individuals and this story of how their group started certainly lent the whole thing a bit of credibility.

As my experiences with the unseen teachers accumulated, the question of credibility seem to fade. Except for one thing. Even though I was growing certain about the reality of the teachers, I began to realize it was possible for even sincere persons acting as transmitters to make mistakes. I found it served me best to allow some skepticism when considering if each word spoken were literally true. However, for the most part, the beauty and consistency of the teacher's transmissions through the human subjects supported the assumption that the words were correct as spoken. The teachers were frank in their assessment of our endeavors, while always displaying an absolute respect for our free will choices and they refrained from making comments that implied judgment of any individual.

One of the central themes of the teacher's messages was the persistent advice to develop a daily practice of seeking stillness to foster spiritual growth, receive guidance and grow in the awareness of God. I began my own practice of seeking stillness daily and found a growing appreciation for everything and everyone in my life. I was still having some rough days and, as teacher Rayson once told me at that time, I had a long way to go before I could say I was leading a genuinely spiritual life. He might say the same now, but I know by how far I've grown since that time, that he was right. I was a little discouraged to hear that then, but now I know more of the truth of what it means to be on a path of spiritual growth, and I feel great joy thinking of what may lie ahead of me. I can see now, how even adverse events are opportunities to grow stronger in our ability to choose goodness. And sometimes I'm spontaneously thankful for every loving person and good thing in my life.

As I mentioned earlier, I was living in Oakland at the time I started visiting the group in Sebastopol. It was at my first meeting when I met Gunther Truman and Bob Burton, who were traveling to the meetings from Point Richmond. After getting to know one another, we agreed to carpool to these weekly meetings together. What I didn't know at the time was that these men really wanted their own group in the East Bay but had received no sign that there was a teacher trying to speak to them who would lead their group.

I had attended the group meetings in Sebastopol for about two months when teacher Rayson interjected during the question and answer portion of his talk, that I was a transmitter. At that point, I hadn't told anyone about the voices I was hearing or about the visit from the two beings that woke me from my sleep at about 3 AM one morning to tell me simply I had work to do. I didn't want to tell anyone, because I was the new guy and didn't think it was appropriate to draw attention to myself over these experiences I was having outside the meetings.

On the ride home, Gunther and Bob revealed their desire to start their own group. I was very skeptical about my ability to be their new transmitter. But I thought if it was possible that I had this ability, I could at least give it a shot. I didn't want to start out cold in front of a group, so I started practicing some of the advice I was getting on how to receive messages from the teachers and transmit them faithfully.

I began by typing after my morning stillness (meditation). While I was still sitting, I just started typing on my laptop anything that came to mind. By this time, I had asked Jared if I could have a personal teacher and my unseen friend James was introduced to me. I was trying to imagine James was talking to me. The funny thing about all this is that I could hear clear messages at times, but it was when I wasn't trying. The moment I was consciously trying to hear a teacher it seemed my mind got very busy confabulating stuff. What seemed to help was the occasional sense that someone I couldn't see was with me. When I drew all of my attention to that sensation, a feeling of peace and love would start to well up and when I let it, this feeling seemed to flow. Soon, I was writing stuff I wasn't too embarrassed about and then I moved on to just speaking out loud as the thoughts came to mind.

The main things I learned about transmitting in the beginning remain true for me. I find it best to try to let go of any responsibility for the content. I always advise new listeners that I'm not altogether sure where it comes from. I don't know how much is me and how much is really coming from our benevolent unseen visitor. I ask that people make up their own minds as to the truth of what I might transmit and I can't personally vouch for any of it. Besides, I usually don't remember most of it. I can however, be frank and open about the experience of transmitting, because that much I can be sure about.

I have the distinct feeling when I begin to transmit that someone else is working on facilitating the contact. I just wait in stillness while I feel the growing sense of a presence and words start to form in my mind which feels like someone else's. The feeling of transmitting for me is unlike any other kind of stillness, prayer or meditative experience. There is a spiritual intimacy that is difficult to describe. The feelings of compassion, sincerity, love and even humor can verge on overwhelming. All the while, there is a solid, reassuring sense of unassailable safety.

I started transmitting my teacher James – first for the group in Sebastopol and then Gunther, Bob and I started meeting at my home one night a week where I could get more practice transmitting for listeners.

Gunther's son, Joshua, occasionally attended the meetings in Sebastopol. He also had some ability as a transmitter, but didn't seem all that interested in becoming a regular group transmitter. He called me at home one night very excited. He said he had been out driving earlier and someone named Althen was trying to give him a message and thought it was about a teacher for our new group. Coincidentally, I recently had the name Altheen come to mind recently, but thought it was probably my imagination making up names. I later learned that the transmitter for the Sebastopol group said she had received a message from a teacher named Athena who was making contact to be a new group teacher. Joshua and I agreed to meet at my house and the two of us attempted to transmit this person and find out what her purpose was for contacting us. The first thing we cleared up was how to spell her name.

Althena told us she was ready to be our group teacher if we would accept her. This is how the East Bay group began. Althena has a sweet loving presence that anyone in the group could feel. We were extraordinarily happy with our new teacher, but we still drove to Sebastopol once a week to attend the meetings there. It seemed our souls were so hungry for what the teachers were able to share with us that we just couldn't get enough of it. Of course, Althena started regular appearances there as well.

By the time Althena began appearing as our teacher in the East Bay, about six months had passed since I first read that transcript from the group in Woods Cross, Utah. Even though I found this new experience exhilarating and felt a compelling attraction to the unseen teachers, my life wasn't exactly getting easier. None of the friends I had before my first visit to Sebastopol seemed at all interested in this weird "channeling" thing. Most of my friends said things like "That's nice for you." Some were concerned that I was getting involved with a cult. When I tried to explain that there was no one in charge of organizing these groups and it was never expected that anyone give something, the response was, "Just wait."

While it was difficult to share my new experiences with my old friends, I was noticing other changes in my everyday life. I've always held a great deal of value for my inner life, but usually felt that part of me separated from others. Now, I began noticing a kind of brotherly recognition with most people I'd meet. In a chance moment of eye contact, something would pass between us with a feeling that said, "Yes, I know." The wall around my inner life was cracking and it seemed I was entering a realm where the inner life could be shared. Though people might be put off with talk about invisible teachers from other worlds here to help us, I found that most people are readily receptive to a simple state of spiritual openness. This is where I found the real experience of spiritual brotherhood to exist.

Life for me was becoming more meaningful and, with my cooperation, my spiritual guides and the piece of God that lives inside me were busy helping me to move along the path I had chosen. It's not an easy path. The assumptions and patterns of behavior that our minds make while adapting to our life in this world are often at odds with the realities of the spiritual life and they can be very stubborn, resisting change. Correcting the inner life to allow for spiritual freedom can be painful when it is time to face realities we've worked at avoiding. I've been mostly unaware of how much past emotional traumas, materialism and superstition have shaped my beliefs and actions even when I believed I was choosing a higher path. I was beginning to realize just how confused I'd been about what a higher path is. The correcting and inner growth of the spiritual life gets easier over time, but I expect this to continue throughout my life.

The summer of 1994 was when the first Spiritfest was held in San Luis Obispo, California. The internet was an emerging cultural phenomenon and many of us attending that first Teaching Mission conference had been communicating with each other through an e-mail group maintained by Russ Gustafson in Redwood City. There was a lot of excitement as people from all over the country were meeting each other for the first time to share experiences.

This was also a chance for us to hear in person the transmitters for the teachers of other groups whose transcripts we had eagerly read. The feeling I had as I met these many open souls was, *this must be what living in a world of Light and Life feels like.* This first gathering is among the favorite memories of my Teaching Mission experience. The freshness and enthusiasm seemed untainted by personal ambition. The happiness we shared in seeing so many others who knew this was real and were also deeply affected will be a memory I'll cherish forever.

It was at this first Spiritfest conference where I met John Creger who lived in Berkeley. John and his wife Meilan began attending our meetings in the East Bay and our group made a sudden growth spurt. Soon, we had from eight to twelve people regularly attending our meetings. I was never all that comfortable with the kind of deference given to me as a transmitter, so fortunately Althena encouraged us in an activity aimed at demystifying what transmitters do. This is how we started having "amateur night" once a month.

On amateur night, everyone in our group would take a turn at transmitting. We did this with the attitude of not taking ourselves too seriously. Even pretending to transmit was okay. Nearly everyone reported sensing a presence that was encouraging them. From this practice, everyone grew more comfortable with reaching for their own guidance. In a little time, some of the members began to realize they actually did have the ability (and nerve) to transmit to a group. So now we had more transmitters, which opened up a dynamic range of contacts and interactions within our group.

I was growing a strong fulfilling bond with my new group of friends involved with the Teaching Mission. However, my other relationships weren't getting all that better so fast. My compulsion for intoxicants was becoming painfully dissonant with my spiritual growth. There continued to be an ongoing degree of chaos in my life. Improvement sometimes felt like upheaval when I had to let go of something I believed about myself in order to move forward. As difficult as it seemed at times, in my heart I was certain that I was on the right path, but it would be two more years before I began to lead a sober life.

The best change in my personal life came when I met Julianna. I fell in love with this beautiful woman, and a strong bond quickly developed between us that included her three-year-old daughter, Andrea. Julianna had been a spiritual seeker throughout her life. She was keenly interested in the spiritual experiences of our group. Here was a charming, intelligent woman with whom I could share everything about who I am. I was determined to hold on to this relationship.

The year after we met, we moved to Butte County, California, so our new family could take root on fifty acres of wilderness outside of Oroville. The East Bay group continued on without me, as others had become experienced transmitters and I wasn't needed. We maintained contact with our old friends who would occasionally travel to our new home for gatherings.

In time we came to realize that some of our new neighbors were spiritual seekers and we thought they might be open to the messages of the teachers. We shared some transcripts of our past sessions and a couple of our neighbors became quite interested in finding out more and this is how we established a group in Oroville. Gunther, from our East Bay group, had moved to Nevada City and would drive to each of our meetings to join us. At first, we mostly spoke with Althena. But after our group decided that we wanted a teacher of our own, Hakasmeen introduced himself to us.

Hakasmeen was a little more business-like than Althena, but his presence exuded a wisdom and warmth that engendered a fondness for his talks with our group. Everyone took home a copy of the evening's tape recording and the next session would often begin with members sharing personal revelations and insights on our talk from the last meeting. Some of our members had not read *the Urantia Book* (and didn't seem particularly interested in it). And even though most of what the teachers spoke about conformed to the concepts of *the Urantia Book*, there is a universality and personal nature to their messages that seem to appeal to a broad variety of people with different backgrounds and beliefs. These teachers brought to us an experiential awareness of a brotherhood of God's children that includes all the people of this world, and pervades the cosmos as well.

The romanticism of living in the isolation of nature started to wear off, and Julianna and I decided, especially for the benefit our young daughter, to move where we could more easily be involved with a community. We were concerned about Andrea being able to maintain friendships and participate in school activities, as she would soon enter junior high school. After searching far and wide, we finally realized that the nearby town of Paradise seemed to most closely fit what we were looking for. We soon found a home that we all loved and moved to Paradise where we are to this day.

We continued to occasionally have gatherings in our home in Paradise with a few new people interested. By this time, the sensational aspects of my relationship with these invisible beings had long ago worn off. I like feeling that their presence is just a normal part of life. Julianna and I enjoyed the simplicity of meditating and seeking stillness in our day-to-day lives while we gradually grew away from the desire to have regular meetings. Over the last few years, we'll sometimes get that desire to host a gathering of our spiritual friends, mostly because we enjoy their company so much.

For me, the presence of the teachers has opened up an awareness of spiritual brotherhood that extends to everyone I meet. I believe I'm getting closer to understanding what Jesus meant when he spoke of the kingdom of heaven. I think that entering the kingdom of heaven is less about professing any belief and, in my estimation, entirely about the spiritual freedom that comes with knowing God and God's Love through personal experience. Something like an organic growth of our soul begins when we consciously seek to know God and our receptivity to God's presence can grow. As we live in this emerging reality, the urges of compassion, kindness and loving service to others naturally arise in our heart. A desire to share and a feeling of pervasive peace become a regular experience. For me that's what the kingdom of heaven is about and it exists here and now.

I've stopped caring about reaching nirvana and am constantly learning to better live in each moment with joy and wonder. God is real and I can see his light shine through the eyes of everyone who has had a glimpse of his Love.

My Experiences with the Teachers
Donna D'Ingillo

My first exposure to the idea of a universe teeming with all kinds of celestial life came in the guise of *The Urantia Book*, which I first started to study in 1975. I was enthralled at the picture of the cosmos it painted and the way the Creator has laid out the unfolding of the divine plan. The perspective of the universe and myriads of intelligent and loving beings that inhabit it was so mind expanding for me that it I felt instinctively drawn to it. It became a great source of truth and spiritual investigation, especially in the story of our planetary history and the life and teachings of Jesus. I was thrilled reading in the book that we were "quivering on the brink" of a spiritual renaissance.

Sometime in 1990 when I first heard the announcement of the planetary circuits being re-established and that many celestial teachers had come to the planet as part of the Correcting Time, I was skeptical. I heard about people T/Ring celestial beings. It seemed to me that the Urantia movement was going "New Age." Then I was exposed to the early recordings and teachings and something in me said, "Don't write this off just yet—keep an open mind."

I was part of a Urantia Book study group in Indianapolis, Indiana, in 1992 when a request was made for a group teacher. A few months later, one of the members of the study group made conscious contact with Teacher Welmek and began to T/R him in private sessions. I had my first private session with Welmek in June that year, and I felt the authenticity of his presence that confirmed to me that this was a real phenomenon happening within the Urantia movement. It thrilled me to think that the heavenly help we had been longing for had finally come!

We first met as a group under Welmek's instruction in August 1992. There was vibrant electricity in the air as we all wondered about this event. What would it be like to speak to a celestial teacher whom we couldn't see? What information would we learn about what was happening on the planet? Over the course of the months that followed, we were led on a rich journey into the revelation that the heavenly realms had put in place a plan to bring our family back into the family of the universe. It would be accomplished by each individual awakening to the spirit within—the call of the heart. It would be a gradual planetary transformation, but it would be accelerating to bring our planetary cultural into a universal culture—Light & Life—within 1,000 years. The teachers were here to instruct us on how to develop spiritually through our every day life's experiences and to teach us how to "still" our minds to foster spiritual receptivity.

I loved attending the weekly meetings, never missing a one! It was food for my soul, listening to Welmek's gracious wisdom, cutting to the heart of the matter and helping to unclog the maze of human thinking. I took to heart all Welmek shared with us – his lessons on forgiveness, patience, stillness – and I remembered to practice quieting my mind every day. At first, meditation was difficult, but Welmek offered helpful suggestions and little by little I felt I was progressing and having some moments of deep peace in the midst of a busy life. I was also practicing making conscious contact with the teachers as I wanted to become a transmitter/receiver (T/R).

I finally make conscious contact with Welmek in December 1992. I knew I was close because I had been experiencing ringing in my ears and buzzing noises in various parts of my brain during meditation. From what other T/Rs had said about their opening, these sensations seemed to indicate that contact is being attempted. I was meditating one afternoon trying with all my heart to make contact with the teachers, when I felt two vortices of energy hit my feet and run up my body to my head. There was a momentary blast of pain and then I heard a little voice in my left ear say, "Don't be alarmed. This is Welmek. We are making adjustments for you to communicate with us." From then on I was able to communicate with the celestials!

One of the activities our group participated in was to help one another come on-line as a T/R and to gain confidence in that ability. It was very difficult for me at first to T/R and I had to have a lot of practice during individual sessions with people asking questions so I could train myself to stay out of the way in order for the teacher's words to come forth. It took a lot of time, but I eventually became confident in this new-found ability. I participated in T/Ring for the larger group sessions from time to time.

This early period of interaction with Welmek was compounded with receiving transcripts from other TM groups across the country. We had a cross-fertilization of other teachers' lessons to further us and we met other people around the country who were eager to attend meetings where celestial teachers were instructing. It was an exciting time and it seemed like smooth sailing!

Then came April 1993 when a highly anticipated materialization by Machiventa Melchizedek failed to occur. I was faced with the fact that T/R's are vulnerable to their own minds interfering with teacher instruction, especially if there is a strong desire for something to happen. This is an aspect of the T/Ring process that must be taken into account. I was confused by what happened and it took many months for me to understand what can go wrong in celestial/human interactions like this. I shut down as a T/R like others did in my group, and our weekly Welmek group meetings changed dramatically. We peaked at around 40 attendees in November 1992 down to a handful by June 1993. I look back on this time as the celestials seeing how we handled crushing disappointment: who would lose interest and drop off and who would stay the course and persevere.

A small group of students still gathered irregularly from about 1993-95, and Welmek's patience and guidance during this time still touches my heart to this day. The teachers always impressed me with their patient understanding, empathetic guidance, and incisive wisdom. It was getting easier to discern those words of truth, and our trust in the T/R process healed. I recall one evening after returning home from a Urantia Book study group talking with my (ex)husband about the Urantia movement, feeling a pressure on my head and hearing the words in my head, "We want you to T/R again."

In 1995 a small group resumed meeting regularly, and from 1995-99 Welmek's instruction gave us superlative insights on speaking from the heart, the meaning of life, going deeper into the stillness practice, and other wonderful, valuable, spiritual, gem-filled lessons. It was so fulfilling to receive these, and my thirst for more exquisite experiences grew. I gained greater confidence as a T/R during this period and started going to conferences.

During this time I became more deeply involved in exploring energy healing. I first became aware of energetic forms of healing in 1991 after suffering a miscarriage. I read a book about homeopathy and was struck how so much of its principles were right out of *the Urantia Book*. I was intrigued! I soon began a study in energetic healing and natural healing modalities. The teachers also gave me new insights into the healing process, especially pointing me to the emotional component of healing as it affected the physical body. Little by little they opened a new door to me—one that I was intuitively drawn to and one that I felt I had been looking for all of my life. I had a realization that this is what I wanted to do with my life—to heal through the power of God's love. The teachers were helping me realize what was in my heart!

I had many sessions with Welmek and other teachers who were specifically here to impart information on healing. I began to learn some basic principles in the flow of LOVE as I began to experiment on friends and family with the celestials participating. This new inner world was exciting to explore as new colors, feelings, sounds and vibrations were shifting my awareness to a realm that I remembered as a child, but did not have a context within which to understand it. Over the course of several years, studying with the teachers, experimenting with people, transmitting during group meetings, it became increasingly clear to me that this is where I wanted to concentrate the focus of my life's work.

In 1994 I began to write "Teach Us To Love." The book was based on the basic spiritual tenets at the core of Welmek's teachings, which were centered around the four daily activities to grow spiritually: 1) stillness, 2) forgiveness, 3) seeing the presence of God in others, and 4) service to others. Little by little the teachers helped me write this book and gave me a way to present to the world the concept of the Correcting Time. The Teachers were the inspiration behind this planetary wake-up call. "Teach us to Love" was published in 2002.

In looking back now, I see this time as a very intense spurt of spiritual growth. Much was happening in my inner life that was helping me feel more alive and on purpose than ever before. It was a time of trusting in something so new and "unknowable" as I couldn't see my teachers, yet their guidance was so charmingly practical and palpably wise. It rang so real and true within and my ability to trust in them and to trust the process grew. I will always remember this period in my life with pleasure and humble respect for what the teachers shared with me. They gave me treasures beyond any human price.

My collaboration with the teachers took a turn in April 1999 when I made the decision to leave my marriage and move to California to pursue my life's work as a healer. I had recurring dreams from about October 1998, in which I saw myself in my car with all of my things, driving around in a beautiful wooded place with sparkling brooks in an affluent area. I was instinctively impressed in the dream that I would be okay, even though I would be on my own financially. Night after night this dream invaded my sleep until I gave in and asked what it was all about. Again, my heavenly helpers came to my aid and guided me, through a series of questions, to realize that I needed to move to the energetically receptive environment of California if I was serious about pursuing my work as a healer. So I did! In October 1999 I moved to the San Francisco Bay Area and found a niche in Marin County.

In September 2000 I began to transmit Welmek for the Marin County Urantia Book readers and also drew some new people to *the Urantia Book* and Teaching Mission. His lessons on prayer, mindfulness, stillness, and staying in the present moment, laid a solid foundation in the group. It was magical to allow his words to draw into the hearts of the listeners, and to see how he was able to cut to the heart of their questions and bring them sound advice they could use.

One of the wonderful benefits of T/Ring is that when you transmit teachers, they share with you the energy of what concept they are transmitting, so it is an opportunity to embody patience, forgiveness, peace, or what they are conveying. It's such a fulfilling experience to collaborate with the celestials because you open yourself up to higher energy vibrations of LOVE that feed your soul and are very pleasurable in the body. I love it! I can remember times when we would just bask in the afterglow of the love that was in the room after his transmissions. We met weekly for two years, but change was in the air and in 2002, I was turned in a new direction.

I was conducting a stillness meditation session in my home in August 2002 when Michael came and spoke within my mind, "I want to speak through you. I want my children to come to know me." It was a joy to receive this news, and I began to direct my spiritual ministry efforts toward developing the Center for Christ Consciousness based on Michael's request. Weekly transmissions from Michael coincided with the Welmek's transmissions as our little group soaked in the truth and beauty during these meetings. In 2003 I began to transmit Mother Spirit Nebadonia during the weekly transmissions, as Mother's presence was beginning to sweep the planet and wanted her children to come to know her as well. Her energy signature was thrilling for us to receive and she blanketed our meetings in her comfort and love. Often we were moved to tears!

The Center for Christ Consciousness also served as a place for me to conduct the spiritual healing that I was continuing to learn from the teachers. During the early 2000's, the teachers helped me understand the nature of mind—how consciousness is formed, how is it configured, and how it functions in human life. They gave me information on the chakra system and the adjutant mind spirits, and helped me develop a format for healing.

Around 2003 I began to hear the words, "Generational Healing, generational healing" like a blinking signal always in my mind. The teachers began to give me information on how our DNA operates and how our ancestors' experiences get encoded into our DNA and affect our somatic behavior. They gave me insights on how our Divine Parents function in us during healing. They helped me understand how we imprint upon their natures of motherliness and fatherliness the spiritual energy we need to stimulate our own genetic potentials for creative expressions. Sometimes during Generational Healing sessions, our Material Son and Daughter, Adam and Eve, would enter and impart their spiritual DNA into their children.

Furthering my education into energy healing and understanding its flows, teacher Aurora began training us in 2007 regarding energetic harmonics and how to become more attuned to one another. Her lessons on how we resonate with one another and grow in blending our personal "energy" signatures shed another light on the fact that, at our core, we are living energy systems of consciousness. She created a safe environment for us to get in touch with our core and to feel the presence of others around us.

Collaborating with the teachers has been the biggest joy in my life. I am so grateful to our Divine Parents and to each celestial who has helped me fulfill my life's purpose – those I know and those I look forward to thanking more personally in the future. Waves of gratitude fill me as I remember my journey and how loved, supported and guided I have been. Opening this door has taught me lessons, some painfully hard, but eventually worthwhile and they have helped me through my times of chaos and confusion into the light of the universe that lives inside my being. I chuckle to think of the many times they have helped me stretch my faith and the ways they helped me confirm it. Their senses of humor too are delightful as they made sure I "got it" in ways that make an impact. For me, having a lesson of irony and whimsy is distinctly remembered and they never fail to help me learn what I need. I shudder to think of where I would be spiritually without them. The experiences with them have brought indescribable joy to my life.

Receiving messages from these mighty spiritual personalities has also gifted me with experiencing something so valuable within my being, especially the joy I feel when transmitting them. There is nothing like receiving messages from Michael, Nebadonia, Monjoronson, Machiventa, and the other teachers to bring me a fullness of peace, humility, and gratefulness as I sense their wonderful personalities and how much they love us. Truly this level of their sharing with me has expanded my capacity to perceive life from a higher perspective and helped me in my thinking processes to shift my understanding to their perspective. It is so fulfilling to transmit; I recommend everyone receive a personal teacher to enhance their spiritual growth.

As I write this, in early 2009, our world is on the brink of great change. Hope is alive and we are being tested as to how we stay the course of spiritual upliftment as the Correcting

Time unfolds. The teachers' presence will be felt more and more as the spiritual energy of our Parents' love engulfs this planet. The plan for each human to have a teacher if desired is underway and their love is ready to help us heal ourselves and this world. I open my heart to them in love and gratitude for helping heaven's ways be made real on earth. THANK YOU!

In closing, I wish to share a lesson that I T/Red in 2004 from Monjoronson that is so timely for our transition to higher consciousness:

MONJORONSON – MAY 27, 2004

> *The world stands ready to receive a great light. In preparation, the mortal souls of this planet must be prepared. The truth that wishes to come forth emerges out of the ashes of lies, greed, poverty, deprivation, and a willfulness by many who are in power to consciously subvert the divine plan and the ways of God on earth.*
>
> *The mortals of the world must be willing to embrace this truth. And the attitude in people's hearts must be of compassionate understanding and forgiveness for those who have perpetrated the great deception of the ages time and time again amongst the slumbering souls who have not seen the light of truth.*
>
> *The time is coming when people must choose how they will respond to the truth-light shining upon the world. When people see the gross distortion and epochs of deception rising out from the shadows, will they respond with anger, judgment, and condemnation of those who have perpetrated this deception? Or will they respond with forgiveness and love and understanding? For the truth-light can only shine in the environment of love.*
>
> *Those who would wish to condemn the perpetrators of the great deception will not be participating in the unfolding of the divine plan. It is only those who are willing to embrace and administer forgiveness in their hearts to those who have deceived them – their leaders, their heads of government, economic, scientific and religious institutions – that will allow the light of truth to blanket the earth. There are many who have been involved in the great deception, and each individual must choose how he and she will respond to that which they see of the truth.*
>
> *This is not an easy thing to ask of mortals of this realm for the pain in the human heart is great. And the deception has been grossly used against humanity to keep people in spiritual bondage. But those who are in bondage*

must find it in their hearts to forgive so they can remove the shackles themselves and emerge into the light of truth, whose love renews and replenishes the starving human soul.

What role will forgiveness play in this decision? Let it be the cornerstone so that the truth can prevail on this world and the light shine more brightly. It is this desire for forgiveness that will bring the great truth to bear on the planet. We, the keepers of the truth, are waiting to shine this light with immense universal power, and to wield its might into the very depths of human misery, and free all of the residents of this world from all of the epochs of deprivation.

No longer is humanity destined to live in squalor, in shame, in guilt. No longer is the human heart to be bound in fear and to be repressed with lies. No longer is the human mind to be fed with inadequacies of truth and false beliefs. The truth is ready to shine. Prepare yourselves. Receive the forgiveness of the heavens, and set yourselves free.

At The Table
Sussi Rowland

"Oh, *SPARE* me! What do you want me to do, get you a pair of god-damned Jesus sandals that lace up to your knees?! How many times do I have to tell you – SHUT UP with that?" The obedient redhead then fell silent, shrank deep in her big chair and finished grace quietly to herself. The rest of supper was uneventful.

That was typical of the reaction to any mention of religion in my house growing up. When my mother was barely my young age, she lived in Denmark under the Nazi occupation with parents who smuggled Jews through their basement, attic and hollow walls, friend to friend, then across the fjord to Sweden. Each night before dark, they had to tape newspaper to the windows lest light shone through and, in violation of the Gestapo-imposed black out, would be machine-gunned out and someone would get killed. Morfa, my mother's father, was beaten weekly for his minor acts of defiance that belied his conviction to his underground activities. Her mother's heroic efforts for their death-marked guests and hysterics when all went wrong were frequent occurrences in the lethal chaos that threatened all their lives. Blood and death were frequent visitors at the supper table in her early experience.

"Who would let us go through this hell alone!? If there is a God - he's too busy to care about any of us! Tell him to LEAVE - US - ALONE!" I can hear her screaming at me. So I shut up and looked at my shoes, afraid of provoking a longer tirade with eye contact. I was a good child. But while all I knew of God and Jesus was Christmas on TV, in my heart, I knew this couldn't be the whole story. I was quietly determined to someday learn everything I had missed, and in my search, I found *the Urantia Book*. It wasn't until then that I was finally convinced I had the entire story.

Initially, the Teaching Mission was not a welcomed event in my spiritual journey. I resisted anything that smacked of the quackery I had come to associate with channeling and downright angry that my Urantia friends could be so easily smitten with such a passing fad. I hoped it would all go away as inconspicuously as it had begun. In the meanwhile, I just wanted all of them to "shut up" about this shameful hoax that was polluting the unique knowledge in which I had come to take such solace.

For me, the Teaching Mission was a silent crisis. I reluctantly went to my first Transmitting/Receiving (T/R) session with my friends so I could prove them wrong right on the spot. I consider myself to be a smart, red-haired girl, blessed with a good memory, and it was my intent to remember every false nuance, every contradiction with the Urantia Book's material, and lay this at their feet after the charade of the evening was over. I was quietly determined to either help my friends end their illusion or leave the group and read my beloved blue book on my own. For me, there was no middle ground. No compromise. This was too important; my personal, spiritual holocaust.

We went to the house of an elder friend that I respected, a retired professional who had done well in life. The room was full, packed with well-dressed intellectuals and more neatly-dressed free-thinkers, not the tie-dyed, hippy crowd I'd expected. Why, there was even a priest there. Was someone sick? Later, I came to learn that this practicing priest had been reading *the Urantia Book* for decades and even delivered a copy to the Vatican Library where it resides to this day. The crowd of about a dozen Urantia Book readers was pleasant and open; the conversation and refreshments flowed easily. I was just about to forget the reason I came, then something happened.

I was caught off-guard when a quite ordinary man sat down in a chair in the middle of the room. Everyone took a seat around him and the place fell to a dead silence. Then, I was reminded of why I came and what I was prepared to do. Intently, I looked at my shoes and waited, sour, angry again, and readied for the challenge of unmasking this wizard behind the curtain of this unholy circus, regardless of how normal and unassuming he and everyone else appeared. After a few minutes the man spoke. It was in his own voice, gentle and a bit halting but natural, with the inflection and disposition of a person who was just talking casually to a group of friends.

At first, I sat there stewing, my gaze burning holes in my shoes. Slowly then, I was taken by the fact that there was no way this man could be making up any of what he was saying, that the unseen teacher he was hearing and repeating word for word to us, Tarkas, was in fact someone I couldn't see but just as real and alive as I was (sitting there in bewildered disbelief). Gradually, I began to realize that this experience was real. Neither the man nor the entity speaking through him was a fake. I knew *the Urantia Book*, every nuance of its material, the genre of presentation, style of expression, the "Urantia Zeitgeist." Only I was not reading, I was listening - in real time - to the same material I had been reading and knew so well. How could this be?

My anger melted in my dawning realization of the Spirit of Truth. I had only experienced that familiar feeling once before in such magnitude, when I first found the book. It's the simple feeling from the inside out of just knowing without hesitation that something is true. That it's real. That it's from God. The earth doesn't shake. It's just a quiet knowing you're certain of. How then could I be experiencing the same gentle peace now in front of this simple man reciting word from word what he hears from an unseen Teacher? It must be because the Teaching Mission was real. Was I the wrong one? I listened further, blinking in confusion at my shoes.

When I focused not on the process but on the content of the message, I came to appreciate the way this unseen Teacher, Tarkas, interacted with the live questions from the group. He was calm and kind, and after a lesson that was right out of the pages of *the Urantia Book*, answered questions in a way that proved he was listening - not just to what the individual asked on the surface but the more core reasons that motivated the person's question to start with. Tarkas answered both aspects of each question with the wisdom and serenity that I would have expected from any of the entities who transmitted the Papers on which I had staked my spiritual healing.

How could this be? I must be the wrong one, not them. The whole premise of the way *the Urantia Book* was written years ago was challenged if I failed to acknowledge the same sublime authenticity of what I was hearing in real time at this very moment. I was either a fool now or I had been wrong to start with. And I wasn't wrong then, and from what I was hearing and feeling in response to it, I couldn't be wrong now.

It was at that moment, the Teaching Mission became a silent crisis. Did I walk away from both the book and this new ability to hear it in the present? If I doubted the authenticity of the now, I would have to deny the truth of the whole book and how it was written then. How could I, when I felt certain in my heart that one was a natural extension of the other? T/R both then and now. What seemed like an eternity of doubt, dissolved into the same cautious acceptance of respite from an abused child to the extended hand of a loving adult. It was ok. I could look up. I could finally be seen.

Without speaking to me directly that night, Tarkas spoke to the 7-year-old in me who was afraid to provoke an angry tirade, not only with eye contact but contact of any kind. I found myself again caught between the 18 inches from my head to my heart, hungry for the spiritual solace that made sense of all the negative conditioning in my loveless world, asking the same questions I had for years: "Could it be true that God is indeed not too busy to hear me? Does He see me? There are so many of us and I'm okay while many are not, so it's okay that He's busy with them. I don't really need much. I know He is real but does He really know me? Is He with me? I'm a nice person and I'm trying so hard to be like Him. I just want to be seen, a little. Is that ok?"

184

All the old questions were suddenly new that night and over the subsequent years of many conversations with the Teachers in the Teaching Mission, I received the comfort and embrace I have needed on my spiritual journey. While my past may have been well-hidden from my Urantia friends, my eagerness to study with them and my spiritual healing that resulted never was. And while I still feel somewhat spiritually autistic, in not fully receiving the loving communication that envelops all of us, I have made good use of my early adversity in that it provides me with the frame of reference to understand the wounded souls who are brought to me.

I am a professional listener for those who are hurting in many ways. I watch them watch their shoes. I see them. I make sure they know they are seen and understood and they heal – just as I continue to do. I walk in my first life on Urantia knowing it is part of a larger Morontia journey. I have purpose and everything that has ever happened to me has been grist for the mill. I have made use of everything as an occasion to respond with understanding for others like me. Because of the Teaching Mission, I know without doubt that I am seen here and now, not only by the Teachers but by Christ Michael. One day, in the mansion world, we will look at each other face to face at supper and I will sit at His table with grace.

(Sussi has been a cancer nurse for 24 years, helping individuals make their transition to the mansion worlds. She is also a clinical psychologist with a private practice in health psychology and a specialty in trans-cultural spirituality.)

Learning to Listen
Jo Ann Wiedman

Long ago, decades actually, I left my faith of origin without grasping a higher understanding of Truth. God was tossed out along with the church of my childhood. A God who was vengeful, chose sides, sent plagues and condemned His children eternally had no place in my heart. I became agnostic. If there really was a God, maybe He just set things in motion and watched from afar all the chaos we humans created. Surely he didn't relate to us intimately, or life would not be so cruel.

Four years had passed since this major perceptual shift when one day I escaped a near collision in traffic and muttered "goddammit".

"That's hardly fair if you say you don't believe. . . " I was alone in my car, yet the statement startled me as if it had been spoken aloud. It came from somewhere outside my mind, but I heard it as a loud thought.

Could this be God speaking to me? Suddenly I burned to know the Truth about "God, the Universe and everything".

Sincerely I asked for answers; in fact I think I prayed.

A few weeks later I encountered *the Urantia Book* through a series of apparent coincidences. These beautiful teachings introduced me to a loving, Fatherly God, whose Presence is ever available to all humans through the divine spirit living in each of us. I learned there is no reason to fear God and felt it to be True. Parental love is the attitude God has toward all mortals. I found Motherly love too. THIS was the God my soul craved to know! I wanted to feel this loving Presence!

Six months later, I attended a study group for the first time. My friend and UB study group leader Maryann introduced me to the idea that God is "nearer than breathing, closer than hands and feet". What a wonderful concept! How could I experience the Nearness? Meditation was familiar, but quieting my mind had so far been my only objective. Now I meditated and asked in my mind and soul "God, are you really here?"

The response was profound. My soul felt embraced in pure love. Now I knew I was truly never alone. Because of experiencing this LOVE, life became more beautiful. Still I wanted more.

I experimented with asking other questions in meditative stillness. . . Should I go to this party tonight? Is it safe to drive in this blizzard? Is this the man you would choose for me? "Yes" felt like the loving hug and "No" felt like a punch in the emotional gut.

A few months later I had to choose among three job offers in different states. I remember driving and praying, "Father, I need to know your Will and I need to know it by noon Friday". This was not a question with a yes or no answer. Somehow I perceived that it wasn't so much WHAT I chose as HOW I made the choice. Inviting God into the process was the most important choice of all. I accepted the position in Colorado, met my future husband, and have lived here for over 30 years.

In the fall of 1991 I heard about something called the Celestial Teaching Mission. Some Urantia Book readers were supposedly receiving messages from our unseen friends. I wanted to know more. Four of us traveled to Utah together to learn more. The visit left me with a poor impression of the Teaching Mission, mostly because of the way some people in the group were attempting to use "celestial" guidance for personal gain. It just didn't feel right to me.

Years would pass before my consciousness expanded enough to realize the Celestial Teachers were not encouraging this. Nor were they responsible for which questions people asked of them.

Hypnotherapist training in 1995 began to expand my concepts. We learned to help clients reach a deeply relaxed state in which they could contact the "high self" for guidance solving life problems. This was beautiful! Some powerful healing sessions occurred in the training.

We also learned to create our own sacred inner space and commune with this wise Presence. What a gift!

During this training I met a Reiki practitioner. Reiki is a hands-on therapy focusing universal life force energy for healing of body, mind and spirit. Suddenly the word Reiki was everywhere in my life: It seemed everyone I met mentioned it, the word came up almost daily and even the meadowlarks called "Reiki, Reiki!" as I circled the lake on my daily walk in the park. Coincidences dogged me until I took the training. We learned to discern energy blocks and restore the flow of well-being.

We were taught that we would be working not alone, but with Reiki teachers and guides – spirit beings! As I began working with clients, to my surprise I did discern guidance from Something beyond my own mind, and it truly did help people heal physically and emotionally. I earned Reiki Master status in 1998 and continue to work with Reiki energy and Reiki guides today.

Around this time my sister emerged from the cocoon of a strict traditional faith. Her spiritual hunger was great and she eagerly pursued the exploration of a wide variety of new age materials and teachers. She e-mailed me Kryon transcripts. She introduced me to the work of Glenda Green who paints and channels Jesus. She sent messages received by Ronna Herman from "Lord Michael, Mother Mary and the Family of Light". She invited me to Jonathan Goldman toning and chanting events, She introduced me to James Twyman's work, including "100 Messages from Yeshua". (None of these people are affiliated with *the Urantia Book*.) She impressed me with the scope of her searching.

In 2002 it occurred to me she might enjoy celestial messages with content from *the Urantia book*, so I gave her a copy of *The Correcting Time*, a book chronicling the beginning of the Celestial Teaching Mission. When she visited a few weeks later, she handed the book back to me saying "YOU need to read this."

Light dawned. I realized that as a result of all she had been sharing, I had come to believe that Celestial communication was happening all over the globe with people of all religions and belief systems. Suddenly I wanted to know what kind of communications were coming to readers of *the Urantia Book*.

At the 2002 International Urantia Conference in Estes Park, Colorado, the encounters which most nurtured my soul were the ones that occurred spontaneously. In retrospect I realized all of these meaningful encounters were with people who were involved with the Teaching Mission, the concept I had held in disdain for a decade. These people impressed me with the way they applied the Urantia Teachings in their devoted lives. As my soul opened, I remembered how Jesus evaluated things—"What does it do for the human soul? Does it bring one closer to God?"

I saw that the fruits of contact with Celestial Teachers were good fruits, and my mind began to open. In the fall I attended transmission sessions at the home of Jim and Roxanne Andrews.

While I still used the yes/no meditation technique with reasonable success, there were some glitches. I began to wonder if spiritual guidance might work better with more options. Although the inner Sacred Space and access to "High Self" meditations were wonderful experiences, it was difficult for me to retain even the theme after emerging from the meditative state. So many beautiful and profound communications and nuances were lost trying to capture them on paper later. I was experiencing meditation frustration.

In the spring of 2003 my friend JoiLin offered an opportunity to learn to capture inner guidance, and I joyfully accepted.

When I asked her what we would be doing, she replied she didn't have an agenda because the Celestial Teachers would be conducting the class. I almost backed out, but yearned to be able to receive guidance and keep it. Many times I had sat in meditation listening for guidance only to have nearly everything evaporate as I returned to ordinary consciousness.

In the class we were asked to meditate and speak aloud into a tape recorder what we perceived while in the meditative state. This was difficult and halting at the beginning, but steadily became more comfortable. We were instructed to practice alone and return with the results.

We met again to listen to each other's tapes. It was astonishing to me that we could all record wisdom far beyond our normal mental processes.

The class was a life-altering process for me. The presence of unseen friends was so wonderful to realize. Rthe amazing springtime of spiritual awareness blossomed in my life as Mother Nature's springtime came into its fullness.

In April I sat in meditation on the rim of the Flaming Gorge in Utah, a beautiful river canyon. The sky was a brittle cloudless azure blue. Drought had ravaged the Southwest for several years. As I settled into worshipful meditation, I sensed the struggle for survival in this barren but beautiful place. As meditation deepened, these impressions became more intense. In response, my soul prayed for life giving moisture to bless these parched lands. Questions arose from the part of my mind which was supposed to be silent in meditation. . .

"Should we accept these extremes as planetary natural cycles and do our best to adapt? What is right?"

Sunlight on my eyelids began to glow in translucent rainbow hues, swirling into one another. . . A tremendous energy vibrated through me as rainbow vibrant, friendly-feeling hues surrounded me.

"Mother I am; GAIA I am. . . Through the ages of human discovery I have been known always. I am Goddess, Isis, Brigid, Mary, Eve, Hera, Pacha Mama". . . .

Images paraded across my awareness, statues of Mary, Venus of Willendorf, Anatolian Goddess, solstice festivals at stone monuments, temples, oracles. . . .

I began to see patterns, portrayed in imagery of small sea creatures that changed shape and became plant life; insects and ancient looking ferns and leaves. I saw giant palm-like trees grow up as the seas subsided. One life form morphed into another and ages passed before my closed eyes. Flowers appeared, and fruits. Insects. Fish. Birds. Small animals. The words vibrated through my body-mind-spirit and wrapped me in unconditional love. So much love!

My mind asked: Are we really destroying our planet?

Images sprang to my awareness. . . . Cocooned in Mother energy, I floated, observing lichens and fungus breaking down solid rock and contributing organic matter so that soil appeared and became home for tiny organisms; I swept across tundras with their tiny but tough mini-plants; then crossed over living deserts. She carried me over myriad types and varieties of forests, and plains. I noticed streams growing into rivers, rivers washing to the seas and then into the oceans teeming with life. I saw no gaps in the web of life.

Above an ocean, I watched as mist, then clouds, formed over the water, and in a poetic dance, merged to create beautiful patterns as they moved to the lands and delivered the life-giving gift of rains.

"My child, I will survive. . . " boomed into my consciousness.

AHAA! I realized Life Herself has infinite potential to create new adaptations! Life Herself transforms to adapt to the changes in the earth and the environment. I came to understand that we will not destroy Mother Nature or her consciousness which is our Planet. She can and does continually bring forth adaptations of life patterns. Infinite possibilities for expression exist within Her consciousness and Presence. I also discerned that we could make life conditions very difficult for humanity by continuing to disregard our relationship to our home, the planet. We do affect our world as we adapt it for our comfort.

This was my first experience perceiving Mother, and stands as one of the most profound experiences of my life.

Since that day it has continued to be my experience that communications from Mother are often illustrated with nature imagery and a vibratory sensation.

In the summer I attended a Teaching Mission conference at a beautiful Catholic retreat center. At one session we sat in a circle in meditating and LISTENING. The vibration was like being in a large drum. I felt enfolded, embraced by that beautiful Motherly Presence again.

"Will you speak for me?" It was Mother.

I continued to meditate. Again I felt/heard *"Will you speak for me?"* I thought of the others there, with experience transmitting and receiving Mother, who could surely give Her better representation and refocused on meditating.

Will YOU speak for me?" And in my mind I replied "Yes, I will."

I don't remember what She said when I transmitted Her, in that group, but I do remember the feeling of her beautiful loving encompassing energy.

That evening two ladies who had each brought through many beautiful messages from Mother told me separately that I had done well for Her. Each said that they had felt and heard Her too, but understood the new kid was being called on.

One of my dearest friends had also had participated in the spring workshop/class. Since it was personal guidance we craved, neither of us had any interest in being a transmitter/receiver (T/R) for groups or for others. We sometimes met to practice listening together. One evening in January 2004, something unusual occurred. A message was coming through me, and I seemed to lose the thread in mid sentence. Apparently it was intentional with the Teachers, as Mary Jo said, "Wait a minute, I'm hearing it now." The message continued through her right where I had trailed off. The whole was seamless. The experience further convinced me we were contacting resources beyond our own consciousness. This was the first message I posted to the Teaching Mission archives.

Two years later friends asked me to substitute for their regular T/R. We are still receiving messages, from Eregon and others. At our meetings, the teachers often have the whole group become silent and *listen*. Participants are asked to share their impressions. We are all encouraged to meditate daily. They tell us this spiritual nourishment is more vital than food and water. We are reminded frequently how tenderly we are loved and cared for. They tell us "hearing" is not the only way we can perceive their presence and their involvement in our lives.

The Teachers now seem like personal coaches and mentors. They are brothers and sisters in the grand Family who are ready, willing and able to help us grow up spiritually.

They asked me to share a few ways we can communicate with them while we fine-tune our perceptual skills.

1. Start with prayer and a spiritual question, then meditate. Afterward, write down your impressions, whether they are words, memory fragments, images or sensations. Language is not the only type of communication.

2. While in a quiet and peaceful state, ask the Spirit part of you (which, by the way, remembers EVERYTHING) to help you solve a problem. Ask it to indicate yes by raising a finger. Ask it to raise a different finger for no. To locate keys or whatever, ask questions. . . Indoors? Living room? Kitchen? Each answer defines the next question. (YES or No were the only answers I could receive. I suggest adding a third response category – neither.)

3. A pendulum can also be used for yes/ no/ other responses to questions.

4. Ask for some other unconscious response; for instance muscle testing.

5. Ask and pray, then write immediately the response you discern within. It's like getting a letter from your guardian angel.

6. Ask and watch your life. Sometimes responses show up as astonishing coincidences.

7. Record out loud while meditating.

So you see, after years of resistance, I learned to listen. I have learned along the way that our unseen spiritual friends are constantly endeavoring to communicate with us in every way they can.

We can all perceive that loving Presence in some way. Welcome your angels and teachers into your life and they will continue to love and guide you to the Love of God. Blessing on your Journey!

Jo Ann has studied and earnestly endeavored to live the Urantia teaching since 1974. She has served on the Outreach committee, staffing booths at expos and giving introductory talks, and currently serves on Interfaith committee, and is a member of the Genera Council. An interfaith minister, for 3 ½ years she has facilitated a monthly interfaith service for world peace in Pueblo, CO. She believes in approaching perceptual differences with an attitude of "profound respect", believing that our divinely bestowed individuality determines unique views, motivations and activity. Jo Ann is an energy healer skilled in Reiki, Emotional Freedom therapy and TARA approach trauma therapy.

LOVE IS THE WAY
David Butterfield

Perhaps the best place to start is with Henry Zeringue. Henry was a fellow member of a group that my wife Susan and I joined to study *the Urantia Book*, in Santa Barbara, California, in the mid eighties. When Susan and I moved to Desert Hot Springs, Cal. approximately in 1988, Henry also moved to the desert, shortly thereafter. The reason this story begins with Henry is that one day at the desert spa, while we were soaking in the hot water, we noticed Henry walking around our pool area reading a sheaf of papers with immense concentration and the secretive-satisfied grin of the cat-ate-the-canary variety. When we inquired what he was reading he gave us his document entitled "Welcome to Change," by Professor Robert Slagle of Sonoma State University of California... We took it home and read it.

Essentially, what Slagle does in this paper is to trace the trail that led him to the discovery of a ten year old phenomenon that is called the Teaching Mission. In a nut shell, earlier, in New Zealand, and later in Woods Cross, Utah, certain individuals began to get telepathic inner hints and guidance and later began to transmit telepathic messages to a group of friends. The senders of these messages identified themselves with specific names as celestial helpers. Slagle sets out the steps he took to pin down the reality of this phenomenon. Trained in Western scientific critical thinking at one of the best universities in the world, obviously he did not want to be "picked off base" by something hokey . . . which led him ultimately to travel to Woods Cross and attend these meetings where such transmissions were being given on a regular basis.

Slagle leads you through his doubts, the verification steps he took, the whole nine yards. His conclusion was that the phenomenon was real. That is, it was what it said it was. It was coherent. It made sense. This was based on his own experience of contact with the teachers in a transmission setting, as well as his study of the variety of the messages received. He sensed the immense intelligence of these so-called celestial teachers while listening to the transmission of their messages through the voice of one of the group members whose telepathic capacity had become functional.

He also became aware in the group setting of the teacher's all-embracing compassion, their respect for individual sovereignty, their edifying humor. His investigation of the reality of this phenomenon also rested on the foundation of the congruence of the messages that were being received through other celestial teachers who were communicating to other small groups in various places in America. These teachers gave lessons on many spiritual subjects. I think it would be fair to say in summarizing the vast amount of lessons that had accumulated through this unique process that the underlying message was: *love is the way.*

Finally, his field being psychology, Slagle saw that the people who were attracted to and attending these meetings were on the whole average-bright, educated, many advanced degrees, professional people, any and all honest seekers of the truth. To wit: people who do not ordinarily "hear voices."

We considered Prof. Slagle's story quite interesting, but we were not galvanized into checking this out any further at the time. We were soon to be heading back to Costa Rica, where we live in "retirement." My wife and I have each read a zillion spiritual books, and opened ourselves as adults to a good number of spiritual paths. In 1991 we retired on 15 acres of lakeside property, where we were able to build a beautiful home, gardens galore, and enjoy the abundance of butterflies, birds, lizards, snakes, and monkeys here. We lived a life of fulfillment. I was 65, Susan was 55. We loved God. We wanted the will of God in our lives. That is to say, we were intent on being guided by loving wisdom in all things. The point here is that we were relatively mature individuals, reasonably well off, living comfortably and sometimes adventurously in a foreign country, and had no need to be "englamoured" by any kind of unusual religious phenomenon.

We had each experienced and seen a wide variety of "unusual religious phenomena." I was raised by a minister of the so-called Holy Rollers, my wife with the Episcopalians, so we spanned the wide gamut of the Protestant variety of Christianity. "Welcome to Change" got put on a back burner, despite our admiration for the clarity and care Slagle showed in laying out his epistemological journey.

Sometime in the mid to late nineties, we began getting emails from Henry of transcripts he had been transmitting from his teachers. Henry is now transmitting celestial teachers?? The world is full of wonders! But I have no recollection of what the teachers said to him, even though I can remember their names. What did galvanize my attention was a remarkably different tone in the chatting part of Henry's emails. Henry is one of those larger than life characters. Artist, grandson of a back-country Louisiana blacksmith, deeply wounded by the gothic Christianity (Catholic or Protestant, take your pick) of the South that Flannery O'Conner evokes so vividly. Expelled in his sensitive adolescence from a monastery, a master of fine arts from the University of California at Santa Barbara, Henry had a streak of high dungeon and skepticism about some of the ways he perceived the alleged divine authorities were running certain matters in the universe.

On occasion, he would become so incensed at some obvious absurdity, some perceived sleazy short cut on the part of the divine, that it would cause me to crack up laughing, because the whole scenario was veering wildly toward the comic. This scenario in drama form could well be entitled, "Henry, As God." I could laugh, rather than defend, because I had gone through my own period of doubt and skepticism. And we were and are in good company.

One of my favorite theologians, Hans Kung, has confessed pretty much this same streak of questioning in his recent memoirs. " I am no stranger to such quarrelling with God's guidance and dispensation." Pg. 328. "My Struggle for Freedom." This artist, this sensitive soul, this rough barked original, this man with the agonizing questions, this grizzly bear of a man, this one had begun to sound a new note of love in all his communications. What was up? Something different was happening here. Love was changing Henry. We felt him communicating love as we never had before.

This is not to say that Henry was not loving before. He was. It is rather that the love he now began to manifest seemed like a quantum leap for a man who had reached the stage of the curmudgeon at a rather early age. I became interested to discover the source of his change.

I had traversed enough spiritual loops, one might say, that I had come to the place where I leaned heavily in the direction that *love is the way*. I had come to believe that love was the ancestor of all spiritual values. I had also come to believe that the fact that love existed at all on this planet was a miracle in itself and as mysterious as the existence of evil. Given this rather stable perception of where the crown jewels were stored in the divine order of things, it should be obvious that I was interested in anyone or any tradition, new or old, that could show me the way to greater love. A love that wore pants and walked in a way that worked in an ordinary life.

We soon began to make plans to go to the States to visit family and friends, but more specifically, to check out what was now happening in Henry's life... As I have suggested, we were both secure in our spiritual path at the time, but we knew that a visit to Henry to check out his newfound source of love was something that we needed to sniff-out. So off we went, like anthropologists of religion, on a new scent. Our tool, our radar, was our inner gyroscope, the inner lure and guide of truth, combined with our outer gyroscope, which was created and shaped by all the experiences of a lifetime we had each had on a number of spiritual paths. And we both had advanced degrees.

So when we got settled in the desert, we decided the easiest way to get into what was happening with Henry was to invite him over to "do his number," his transmitting, of "the teachers." I put teachers in quotes because at this point in time we had no ideas at all about the bona fides of these so-called teachers, based on personal experience. Thus we approached this new phenomenon with relatively open minds and hearts, but, of course, with all the lineaments of our respective Western skeptical academic backgrounds and our own life experiences. All we knew was that something profound was happening in Henry. We felt it immediately. A new gentleness, a humility of respect for love, is as close as I can come to describing it. So he invited us over with the intention that we would have our first experience of being exposed to this phenomenon.

There were just the three of us in the room. Henry, Suzi, and I went into what is called "the stillness," just a simple meditative technique of quieting the mind, sitting still, opening, and listening. Henry began to speak in a quiet normal voice, which we recorded. I do not recall any unusual sensations or experiences from that first encounter. What ensued was that we offered to transcribe the recordings into hard copy so that it would take several hours of rather tedious labor off Henry's shoulders. The result of this process was that it allowed us to listen to and read each message four times. We heard it when Henry transmitted it, we heard it on the tape as we were transcribing it, we read it for meaning as we transcribed the message, and finally when we had it in hard copy, we read it in its printed state. What this process helped secure was a clear idea in our minds of what was being said, what the message was.

This was quite an "objective" pursuit, apart from any notions as to who these so-called "teachers" might be, whether these messages were coming from Henry's subconscious, or the usual suspects that are thrown up when this kind of phenomenon is reported. Running the message through our minds four times, helped us to determine such elementary stabilizing posts as, does this message make sense? Does it have an internal integrity? What is the spirit of these messages? Thus from an anthropological point of view we were investigating a manuscript. A manuscript is a form of data whose investigation can claim some "objectively." And so, like good little school children we faithfully read our lessons, did our homework. We concentrated on the message, the Word, like good classic Protestants.

As I have said, I can't at this point in time recall what was said on that first occasion. There was certainly no sense of awe. It seemed quite tweedle dee and tweedle dum, as a matter of fact. So we continued these transmission meetings with Henry until about the fourth or fifth time when in the midst of transmitting, he asks, or the teachers asked, "Do you have any questions?" Well, this is a rather critical juncture in the epistemological journey of determining the reality of what we were experiencing. Should one be gracious to the alleged teachers? After all they are enunciating a very loving message, perhaps the most courteous tack might be to try out a little shy neutral question. Or possibly, throw out a fraudulent question, that is, one you already know the answer to, in an attempt to "trick" the teachers, so you can expose their fraudulence. Or you can be open to the experience, trust at that point, at least on an "as if" basis.

I happened to be at a point of deep heart sorrow and anxiety about the fact that I had been in the States for three months and had not heard from or received an invitation to visit from one of my adult offspring. One of my sons had recently left his wife and gotten a divorce. This divorce seemed to have had the power to open up the fault line and evoke all the pain in my family that had not healed from the divorce of my first wife and I, some 30 years previously. One way to check out what is real is by being as real as you can be. This creates an inner plumb line, a hologram of integrity, if you will, that unerringly gives a true reading on the response you receive from your realness, your plumb line of integrity-reality. So I spoke up out of a cry from my heart.

Thus I stepped into the anthropologist's circle of subjective understanding. This is an area of reality that demands, because of its inherent subtleties, all of the careful mindfulness that is necessary in the far less subtle dimension of the physical sciences. What I am trying to say here is, that on the basis of my very real, very raw, human need, I decided to go for broke . . . to perceive this voice I had been listening to from Henry as connected to something like a subjective being, quite like myself. And so, in my need, I leaped.

At that moment, I was totally unashamed of my need for help. Suzi and I had previously talked sadly about the fact that we had no response from this family member, but when I began to unravel my tale of woe to the female teacher named Berca, I couldn't believe how the feelings tumbled out of me, uncensored. Nothing of what I spilled out seemed to faze her. She was the model of evenhandedness, asking common sense questions in the midst of my turbulence, like, "Were you invited?"

The closest I can come to how I experienced this is to say it was like being in the presence of a cosmic psychologist. I felt such a total acceptance in the midst of my distress. In addition to which, I remember to this day something she said to me. She said something to the effect of, "perhaps this person has passed the age when you can any longer be a teacher to this person. But you can trust that whatever lessons you think this person should be learning, life will teach this one on its own. And you need not fear but simply trust in the goodness of life to do this."

It was not until the second or third time I read a printed copy of the transmission of the above lesson, that I saw the incredible respect, delicacy, kindness, and wisdom with which I had been treated. It just leaped out at me like a revelation. One of my professions had been as a psycho-therapist. So my own professional experiences led to a respect for the nuances in this encounter. This, my first existential encounter with "the teachers," became the first stepping stone on a path that through teacher contact several years later led to a reconciliation with this estranged member of my family.

So back to the epistemological quest. I just took a Kirkegardean leap based on a need. My question was real. I know my pain was real. And what I had encountered was for me clearly not Henry's subconscious. Henry is one of the brighter people I know, but because of my long and intimate friendship with him I also had a fair understanding of his limits. What I brought to that situation, a very real pain, a very real need, a very real confusion, was met by something equally real. I felt the compassion in her words, the tenderness toward my woundedness, and the gift of this wonderful shape-shifting technique of reframing, creating a larger frame, taking in more of the picture, extending the time line. Berca reframed the problem for me. Namely, there's something bigger than you, daddy, and it's called *life*. What had formerly seemed bleakly hopeless, now contained the spark of hope.

There is something innate in an encounter like I have described above, that gives you a surety in your sense of the personhood of "the other"... This sense grew in me as we hit the ball back and forth in the ping pong of our conversation. What I discovered in that exchange was the emerging signature of personality. Berca's personality was clearly distinct on this occasion of my first personal interaction, regardless of whether I had made any conscious decision as to her bona fides yet. While we were in the midst of our first encounter, I could not help but notice at times the speed with which she responded with wit. Quick-witted often stands in our language for intelligence. But it is intelligence with a lilting grace to it. It seeks to lighten the observation with a little twinkle of humor. Certain people seem to be gifted with this grace. And it is surely the mark of personhood. Henry's humor is distinct, but Berca's was a distinctly different humor than Henry's.

Perhaps it would be helpful at this juncture to mention that I had some notion as to who the teachers were from having read Slagle's document. They are alleged to be mortals like ourselves who have passed through death and gone further up the spiral of spiritual evolution. These teachers do not ordinarily come from this planet, but from other planets of mortal habitation. Because of certain events in the cosmic spiritual dispensation of this local universe, it became possible for these advanced beings to volunteer their services to help restore the spiritual balance of this planet as well as advance their own journey toward truth, beauty, and goodness. These teachers all come in the name of love and in service of the Master Jesus, Heavenly Father, divine mother, and in any and all sources and names that point to *the way of love*.

196

During our last transmission with Henry, again, apropos of no inquiry on our part, we were each given the name of our teachers. Suzi was informed that her teacher was named Davina and the name of my teacher I did not quite get. It had the sound "song" in it, so I settled on that as his name or nickname. We returned to Costa Rica, mulled over our experiences together, and forthwith more or less put these teachers on the shelf for a year or two. We felt no compelling need or urge to make contact with these teachers who had been "assigned" to us as personal teachers.

One evening in my sleep, and possibly in a dream state, there appeared to me a smiling face of luminous brightness. This face was alight with a crystalline light that shone like diamonds. This dazzling emanating light had the palpable feeling of love and the beauty evoked an immediate sense of awe through its magnetic quality. And in tune with my usual speed of uptake, I did not remember this vision until some months later, when Suzi began to feel some urges to do her stillness meditation at the computer. Since she can type blind, she began to type out these little poems that came to her. As this process continued she began to get direct messages from her teacher who identified herself as Davina and referred to "others" as part of her retinue.

After some time Suzi began to tell me about these experiences and to share the messages with me. The first and most vivid result of this contact, as far as I was concerned, was the increase I felt in her expressions of love toward me; they were very noticeable. It's hard to knock or doubt something as gratuitous as love. It was during one of our talks together about the teachers that I suddenly remembered my experience in the dream. I related this to her and marveled how I could have forgotten such a vivid episode. It would seem that our teachers were operating from a transcendent level of patience, waiting until we were ready, not imposing themselves upon us. Except, one might argue, that dream was quite imposing.

Shortly thereafter, Suzi began to get messages from a teacher named Alana and her co-leader named Legion, who announced they were to be our group teachers, although at that time we did not have a group. So we began, perhaps once a week to do our stillness and invite the presence of the teachers. This process began in the summer of 2000 and continued perhaps for 3 months or so until we started a group. We recorded the teacher's messages, transcribed them, and studied them closely for coherence, and began the discipline of "stillness" which they suggested. It was all rather low key, but needless to say, we were both a bit incredulous that this was happening to us. We did not share this with others at this time, except Henry, who just urged us to "Go for it."

After several months into this exercise, we got a call from a dear friend of ours who had been involved with us in a previous group of seekers that was held at our home in the past. She reported a dream she had that seemed to have some spiritual significance to her, and she asked that we start our group again. So at our first meeting we spent some time in stillness, talked about our friend's dream, and generally touched bases with each other on the progress of our spiritual paths. We did not mention our teachers at this first meeting... We were a bit shy about springing the teachers on our friend who is a middle-aged woman with a very sharp mind, a critical thinker, and the down-to-earth practicality of a competent professional. Hesitant that she might think we were operating with less than a full deck, around the third meeting, at the gentle encouragement of Alana, we blabbed the whole scenario out. Rather than being scandalized, she jumped in like a duck to water.

Our little group of three started out, with others joining along the way, meeting every Sunday on our porch for about six years. Suzi did the transmitting and we produced the lessons in written form. After six years the group format ended and took a more private form for the last few years, mainly my conversing with Alana through Suzi's transmitting. Essentially this has been utilized to tune up our practice of stillness and guidance about practicing love in situations which might be called a "sticky wicket" – that is to say, where it is difficult. It has been the most expanding and growth-producing journey I have been on so far in my life. Opening, allowing. What a gift to be alive at the time of the availability of these love-saturated beings.

THE HEART ROOM
Suzi Butterfield

I cannot say I took to the Teaching Mission like a duck to water, although I enjoyed participating in my husband David's and Henry Zeringue's early enthusiasm. I was impressed by the teachings, but I was cautious about the process.

My skepticism was based on a history of disappointment and painful disillusionment in a variety of spiritual and religious experiences, but not just with organized religion. I had already had a devastating experience with "channeling" that lasted several years and ended in public dismay, a scandal that made the front pages of the L.A. Times. I had played a crucial role as the whistle blower bringing the whole thing down. I could not quickly believe again in anything remotely similar to "the dark room," speaking with "entities," other-world or celestial teachers with a mission.

Over time I have followed many spiritual or consciousness-raising teachers until I understood the lesson each had for me along the path of love, and then I moved on. I was a follower and a leader, but in those experiences I discovered my path was a solitary one of the heart. Solitude was my lesson, and perhaps my deepest fear, for it smacked of being alone forever with no sense of belonging to something greater than myself.

I was professionally familiar with guided fantasy. It was too easy, I thought, to imagine wise old men and crones giving celestial advice. It was too easy for me to picture the path winding up the mountain, different colors of gardens, an open cave, a room with archives of wisdom, all part of guided meditations intended to introduce teachers and guides. "Been there, done that," kept echoing in my mind. I didn't give my imaginings much credence.

Still, I had the desire to know the love of God dwelling within me. I wanted the certainty to believe and the faith to give voice to this love, as I had when a believing child, and in those moments of certainty that if I died now my life would have served a useful purpose, pleasing to God. But I wanted the unimaginable. I wanted that certainty to be everlasting.

Trusting my self was the deep wound that becoming a transmitter and consistently entering the Heart Room healed. I believed in Jesus, in angels, in guides, in a loving God, but could not extend my trust to believe that these could come to me, care about me, or the biggest stretch of all, speak to me from within. I could hope, I could yearn, but this was still unimaginable, or, relegated to the imagination, not my personal reality.

The faith that took me to Costa Rica was based on my faith in my husband, placing my faith in his angels, not mine. My faith in God and the possibility of a loving universe was based on my husband's faith in such things. Professionally I had given love unstintingly to clients, but this did not spill over to myself, or even those I loved closest to me. Spurred by my husband and Henry, I enjoyed reading parts of *the Urantia Book*, found in it pearls of wisdom and passed them on to others, but I could not give it my total faith. I loved the UB story of Jesus and recommended reading it, but could not comprehend or embrace the more complicated business of hierarchical orders of celestial beings. I knew what it was to believe I could save the world, only to discover the world and the humans in it, including those dedicated to "our mission" would disappoint me. And I would disappoint myself.

Yet I was a seeker, and one evening, while my husband sat reading before the fire, I sat at our dining room table feeling isolated and frightened and yes, "It was a dark and stormy night" full of the thunder and unbelievable lightening of a tropical downpour, I prayed for an experience of Jesus; it was the prayer of the child struck through with the fear and doubt of the adult. I wandered through my memories, the child, the adult, always seeking, taking one path after another, eager, hungry, willing to believe, then falling, falling, falling into disappointment, even despair. David and I lived in the "paradise" of Costa Rica, yet I was still kicking and screaming. My heart was afraid. But as I prayed, the atmosphere changed. I felt Jesus' presence. I was warmed, comforted, and I felt a certainty within that this was Jesus, this was the Holy Spirit; Jesus did signify love, and his love could be brought to earth and shared among us.

Such an experience, it is said, cannot be proved, scientifically, or to others. At the same time, such an experience cannot be denied, or removed. It is a personal experience, and for those who share it, no other proof is necessary. It was from this experience that I moved toward practicing the stillness, and eventually entered into the experience of transmitting my teachers. This struck at the core of my unbelief and unworthiness, but I know their love is real, of that I am now certain; they proved it to me. I share my experience of the Heart Room hoping that at least some taste of their love will reach you, ring a bell, as they say, that you may open yourself to their love, and through their love come to know the love that dwells within you. I know their love is real, because it has healed me, a truth that is mostly proved by the love you radiate and the joy you carry with you wherever you go.

The Teaching Mission

Central to this experience is the stillness practice. There are no prayers to memorize, no photos to revere, no rituals to follow, no leader telling me what to do, just stillness and quiet wherever and whenever I choose. Different from the form of meditation in which I tried to focus upon a mantra to the exclusion of everything else, the stillness practice was simply being still as thoughts and pictures and emotions crossed the screen of my mind. I did not have to rid myself of anything. Whatever was in my mind, my heart, my body, the stillness was open to it without judgment. And it only required ten minutes a day! Living beside a beautiful lake, surrounded by rain forest, I had more than enough time and silence and solitude to begin.

As I sat in stillness day after day, slowly I realized a shift was taking place within me. My life had always been in a hurry, but now that had come to a stop, even in my busy mind. I experienced moments of what can only be described as nothing, or no thought. This was a very pleasant experience with a peaceful aftermath. Next I had the distinct impression of beautiful thought patterns surfacing to my mind, a poetry of wisdom that created in me the experience of an all-embracing love. It was a form of prayer as dialog, a conversation with love.

I began to feel a budding confidence. I started to go to the computer, enter into the stillness, and with my eyes closed, I wrote what came to me. Snippets of poetry quickly became essays, or lessons, on the topic of love and forgiveness. I contacted Henry, who put me in touch with Susan Kimsey, and both urged me to share these lessons with the Teaching Mission.

After the blind typing practice, the suggestion came that I give a voice to these lessons through speech, first practicing with David. It was a challenge to be still and talk at the same time. I had to "step aside" internally in a new way, a deeper surrender to love, an opening of my mind and heart that allowed these thoughts to take form and speak personalities most clearly, her voice coming through me as soft and gentle, his voice deep and sometimes softly stern, although unfailingly kind. My mind and heart and vocal body became the channel, a quiet river through which their love and wisdom could flow. I no longer worried that my thoughts, or my emotional concerns, would interfere. Such doubts would return, surfacing from time to time to be examined with Alana's, or Legion's love, but for awhile I was blissfully free – the freedom of love.

As David has recounted, a friend came seeking spiritual fellowship. We spoke to her about these teachers and from this a small group of three formed, then grew. It was to last for over six years, meeting once a week to dialog with Alana, Legion and others. Some Teaching Mission groups have continued. That our group ended was, at first, disturbing and very disappointing. Differences among members led to dissension and separation. It was no longer fun, and the service of love, Legion was teaching me, brings joy. I suffered the fear I was letting the teachers down when I finally stopped transmitting for the group. I have since recognized that in this disruption, there was a lesson to be learned.

The teachers never left us. They never condemned me or members of the group. Their love was limitless, but they honored our human limits. They have remained available to each one of us as we have moved along our individual paths, if that was our choice. They have remained open to us when we are open to them, Legion continuing to bring comfort to one member even after he had moved two hours away. They embraced our differences, teaching us to love through separation, exercising what they called "long distance love." It was a valuable lesson in tolerance, or what Alana calls "embracement."

The Heart Room is all about accepting who you are and where you are in your growth toward love. In the Heart Room we are taught how to allow the differences in others and to accept their different paths and opinions while continuing to give love. This is not to say we were taught to be passive, for two important lessons were: "Do not be shy with the truth," and "Speak the truth with love."

Alana and Legion have been the teachers most consistently present in my transmissions, working alone and together, with individuals and groups. My husband designated them "cosmic shrinks" as their approach was to enter immediately into direct dialog with our human suffering in order to teach the lessons of love. Their wisdom embraced everyone equally. They showered us with unconditional love, yet were unsparing in guiding us in self-examination. Their focus was never lost: learn how to love. We needed to learn how to shift from suffering to joy in the perspective of love.

Slipping into that stillness wherein the teachers communicate became easier over the years, in fact for me and David it has become a way of life. Yet it is always a distinct choice: the choice to open to the teachers, the choice to allow their love to be real, the choice to accept their love, to believe, to trust, as a transmitter to surrender control over the thoughts expressed and the responses given to questions raised, the choice to surrender to knowing with certainty that only love will respond, the choice to have faith in love and love's power to shape us anew. These teachers have never disappointed me. They do not ask me to save the world. "Your task is to learn how to love" one person at a time; it is to love the one before you.

Their task is to teach us how to love – ourselves and others. Their lessons have the qualities of integrity, fairness, consistency, kindness, and a cosmic humor that often startled and sent us into gales of laughter. But above all, they teach loving welcome, the humility of respect for all, and an abundant gratitude for our listening, our willingness to pay attention to love.

As the transmitter, it is possible to give one's ego a note of specialness, creating a separation from others, but I have learned again and again that these teachers do not play favorites, everyone is fair game for their loving correction, including me. Furthermore, if others become open to transmitting, the teachers will use them as they have used me. In other words, I am replaceable. They arrive in my stillness and use my mind to speak, but their presence is palpable and distinct, both to me and to those present and listening. They are equally recognizable when they come through another transmitter.

Alana and Legion are their unique manifestation of The Presence of Love. They ask only that I and we learn how to manifest our unique Presence of Love in all our living and breathing. In this context, "only" does not imply that the task is easy. Learning how to love from Alana and Legion has been a most challenging and all-absorbing enterprise. And hey, I thought I already knew. As a woman who had suffered the pains of jealousy, it was perfect that I should be a married T/R. I was living with "the other woman"! Not only that, but she spoke from within me! My husband grew to love Alana with an absolute trust and certainty. I fell into the trap of fear, thinking I was "less than," doubting my self-worth. I was challenged to transmit for David, especially during stressful periods when his need was strong, and I, too, was feeling needy.

Although it would appear to be first a service to others, transmitting the teachers has always been first a lesson in self-love. Transmitting the Heart Room became a shared lesson for David and me in self love and forgiveness of ourselves and each other. Alana and Legion taught us how to love each other by how they gave their love freely to each one of us. I hope it is not too obscure to say that by loving what I feared (my jealousy, for example), I learned to trust myself. Fear can not be where love is. Sometimes I had to say No to my beloved, and refuse to transmit. In the Heart Room I learned how to say No with love. On the other side, David learned to accept No with love, even when suffering in "the pain box" of his need. As well, we each learned how to say Yes to love. We learned to love ourselves with a love that does not withhold, a love loyal to truth and compassionate, a love that liberated, gave us the freedom to love each other more freely.

Alana introduced the Heart Room, the central metaphor to all her teachings. "Open your mind. Open your heart. Breathe the love," she says. "Allow the love. Accept the love. Accept that Love is real." She suggested we imagine love as a powerful energy pouring down through the tops of our heads, as if a blue-white liquid light was flowing down through our bodies, filling our bodies, flowing out from our limbs to one another, or flowing across to each other from heart to heart. "Let love pour down like honeyed rain," urged Legion. "Let your love radiate out to the ones before you."

In the Heart Room we are asked to open our hearts and our minds to love, and to experience the heart's intelligence, that communion of heart and mind that is always kind, wise, inclusive, expansive, creative, fair, inspired, but above all a loving perspective.

"Invite those you love into the Heart Room and let love permeate them." "Invite those with whom you have differences of anger, resentment, fear, guilt, betrayal, and let love permeate these differences." "Let love saturate your thoughts, your emotions, your imagination. Surrender your minds and hearts to the presence of a love that surpasses all your human understanding."

Legion addressed our fear of betrayal, of being stabbed in the back, of someone coming up from behind to catch us unaware. He blew love on those fears as he suggested that we open our backs, as if there were holes down the spine, and allow his love to flow through our bodies from behind. This was a new experience for me, allowing my back, or that which I cannot see, to be as open and vulnerable as my heart, open to love's protection, love's strength.

Having welcomed us into the Heart Room, Alana next invited us to sit by the Pool of Love and Forgiveness with her, to be dipped in the "living waters of love" that our minds and hearts might be cleansed with forgiveness. Floating in forgiveness extended my understanding of "long distance love" in which I could allow others (members of our group, for example) to float away from me, or to keep a distance. I learned how to allow and accept my withdrawal from others, and theirs from me, yet remain in the ocean of love that supports and keeps us connected as one. For a woman who has suffered loneliness, this experience served to ease the fear of not being loved. It served to erase doubt and guilt, the fear of not being worthy of love.

We practiced floating in the Pool of Love and Forgiveness and learned to allow the rhythm of the Heart Room waves of love to bring peace. The Heart Room's tolerance of intolerance, both mine and that of others, is exceptional. The teachers' responses always created a new understanding that brought the possibility of kindness and love up front and center stage, or as David has said, "kindness can always be fine tuned." Being human, we do not always make the most loving choices and thus we suffer misunderstanding and betrayal. The teachers taught us how to embrace such "errors of love" and step out of our personal "pain box of suffering." We did not have to save anyone, only ourselves. Personal growth in love spreads to others, always. Learning to love yourself becomes a model for others. A heart and mind open to love creates joy to be shared with others willing to receive. "Open your hearts. Open your minds. Allow love. Accept love. Give that love away, freely."

Alana's words on love have become a mantra in our household: "Love is always with you, in you, surrounding you, embracing you with comfort and certainty, clear-sighted, and unafraid." In what is always a solitary journey, even when joined in communion with others, I turn to those words time and again. As they infuse our misguided perspectives and confusion with love, the Heart Room teachers rarely, if ever, describe what kind of change should evolve. Their primary concern is that we learn how to "welcome change with love." No matter what kind of change we have to face, that one factor, the perspective of love, makes all the difference in the solutions that arise in the mind. Imagine the difference it would make if government leaders and corporate executives practiced the stillness and entered into the Heart Room every morning! Imagine global harmony!

Heart Room teachers do not ignore our basic experience of insecurity and life long change. They teach us to welcome all change with love. They teach us to accept our fears, to "blow love upon them", to rest in the Heart Room, float in the Pool of Love and Forgiveness, and allow love to shift and shape our thinking. They teach us to embrace our fear and doubt with love. They teach us to accept doubt as a means of inquiry, a natural curiosity, not a weakness, but a strength to be explored and used for discernment. Fear and doubt can not last long in the Heart Room stillness of love.

The Teaching Mission

I am not required to believe everything posted through the Teaching Mission. I am required "only" to continue, day after day, to practice learning how to love. And if I forget? if I fail? Start again. The teachers' compassion toward our errors of love is unfailing. "A reminder," we are told, "is not a criticism." There is a sense in which the unconditional love of the Heart Room could seem to be permission for a free-for-all, everyone doing whatever they please in the name of love, no guilt, no shame. "Accept." "Allow." "Open your heart." "Open your mind."

As perfect as it was for Alana to speak through me, so it was for Legion. When he gave me his name, I pulled back, it was, to my mind a name associated with war and I did not want anything to do with a macho male warrior. My resistance was accepted, even as Legion then began to speak of discipline, another trigger word for me, and strengthening the body, a challenge for this undisciplined gal who did not like exercise. But Legion's discipline was different: "The discipline of love," he said, "is the discipline of joy," and in those few words, he caught my attention.

Legion introduced us to love as a discipline, not license, a practice guided by love, not blind obedience to ancient practices and rituals, not an arbitrary set of rules imposed upon us to suit the needs of others, but motivated by love from within. His concept became another mantra in our lives: "The discipline of love is the discipline of joy." That unique connection between love and joy as central to the discipline of love became a discerning guideline.

Practice listening to love in the stillness of the Heart Room, and experience a quiet joy. Practice learning how to love in communion with others, and experience the joy of giving love away, freely. Practice strengthening the body "to carry love" everywhere you go, and experience the joy of standing tall in the certainty of love. Practice welcoming change with love, and know the peace of certainty and the hope of joy in the midst of emotional reactions, mental darkness, and ignorance. Practice "the humility of respect for love," the love that dwells within each one of us, and know the joy of belonging to love. Practice learning to live in gratitude and service to love, not sacrificial, not suffering, but joyful in the growth of love. Practice imagining and creating compassionate communities of love, Legion's Brotherhood of Comfort and Sisterhood of Mercy, in which mutual respect and genuine gratitude can be shared and enjoyed. Or, as Alana said, "Be the love you always wanted, therein you will find joy."

The incarnation of love into the human condition, said Legion, "confronts the soul with welcoming change with love. The soul does not grieve, but always yearns to return to that bliss which is love, only love, always love, the reality of love. And so the human being experiences a yearning to grow, seeking that love known from the beginning, that love that has no beginning and no ending, yet allowing and accepting that this briefest of moments you call life on earth has a beginning in birth and an ending in death."

Growth in love takes self discipline, or practice, because we "must grow to understand there is love without ending, love without beginning, love always and ever present." There must be a discipline, or practice, in order to come to know and experience the presence of love is always with you and in you. "The presence of love," said Legion, "is felt in that moment of existence in which you welcome all change with love."

With practice we learn "to embrace the unknown (yet known in the stillness of love)," and to "embrace the fear and doubt that life's unknowingness helps create by the conditioning of time." It is a discipline, a practice, of faith and trust in love and love's power in our lives.

Entering the Heart Room was always a joyful experience, the practice became an accumulation of loving experience that leaked into our daily life, manifesting the fruits of the spirit of love. Such an experience, like transmitting the teachers, entering the Heart Room, may not be "proved" or "verified" in a scientific way, but it can be experienced at a depth and vividness that is sophistry proof.

Can love and the Heart Room be proved scientifically? To study this question, I suggest you read The Biology of Transcendence, and Death of Religion and the Rebirth of the Spirit: A Return to the Intelligence of the Heart, by Joseph Chilton Pearce

In addition, the positive changes in my life that resulted from following this path became obvious. The joy, a perspective suffused with love, the lessening of time spent in the pain box, increased strength and flexibility, openness and being present toward whatever existence is presenting to me, an expanding awareness of the constancy of love's presence, an increased spirit of thanksgiving welling up spontaneously within me as I opened to the manifestations of love expressed in the beauty surrounding me, all of these changes and more accumulated to give me a sense of assurance that I was on the right path. Love embraced me with certainty.

The Teaching Mission speaks of our times as The Correcting Time. I opened to the correction of love as it began to flow through me in transmissions. This is the essence of my experience of transmitting: no longer seeking to hear what I already believed, or had been told to believe, or wanted to believe, I simply began to listen and wait patiently. I listened for love and love responded. I listened in the stillness and thoughts began to emerge. Was I in a trance? No, just paying attention in the stillness, and recording or speaking the thoughts that emerged. Did I hear voices? No, but thoughts and phrases, whole sentences and paragraphs, rose up to be written and spoken.

The lessons transcribed had a clarity and certainty I could trust. The words may have been taken from my mind, but always went beyond me into an expression of love and guidance in how to love that was new to me, original, sometimes surprising, and so effective that doubt was erased. Every time a broken heart, or what eventually our teachers renamed a "so-called problem" was presented to the Heart Room teachers, we would be instructed to first "blow love upon it." With love, perspective shifted, new possibilities emerged. Upon returning to daily life after a session in the Heart Room old patterns often returned, but increasingly with the practice of the Heart Room stillness, the lessons took control.

I can slip into the stillness of love almost without thinking, indeed, as I have said, being in the stillness of love has become a way of life, a way of being. David is still "Mr. Boisterous," as Alana dubbed him, and we are "dancing fools," but the stillness is always with us in our hearts, at the core of our being. I compare being in the Heart Room to the expansive tolerance and compassion that comes with extensive travel, or living in a foreign country; one learns to take delight in differences, to enjoy discovery, to see through all the layers of one's conditioning into the heart of the matter of how to live a life of love on this planet. And in the center of that open heart is joy.

The Teaching Mission presents many voices. I pick and choose, and encourage you, the reader, to pick and choose. Follow your inner guidance and in doing so strive to serve the truth you find with love. Do I favor "my" teachers? Yes, no doubt about it. At a practical level, they give me enough to do, but they are not "mine" and they are not the "only" or even the most "important" ones. The Heart Room belongs to everyone.

The Heart Room is the essence of compassion, an experience of the freedom to love, even thine enemy. To engage with the teachers is to have faith in a path of love, faith in the power of love to change us, knowing that each of us is responsible for the self-discipline that brings love's power into the world. Each of us must make that solitary choice to love in the face of betrayals and war, each must find their way.

It is always our choice. To love, or not to love, is both the question and the challenge of growth. As we learn from every choice, we learn the many ways in which love's lessons are experienced. Love is the change David and I saw in Henry that attracted us to the Teaching Mission. Love is the change we saw in each other as we engaged with teachers in the Heart Room.

When you open your mind to the idea of the Teaching Mission, go into stillness and imagine the Heart Room, take a swim in the Pool of Love and Forgiveness, practice the discipline of love, which is the discipline of joy, the rewards are immediate. Much of the discovery depends upon your willingness to open to Alana's love. "Be the love you always wanted," she said. The Teaching Mission has a plethora of lessons to share, but ultimately, "you are the lessons of love." The first step is to learn how to love yourself; from there, with forgiveness and the humility of respect for the love that dwells within every one, loving others as you love yourself comes naturally.

I have tried to share the Heart Room from a transmitter's perspective, a unique communion. David speaks from the experience of listening to and speaking with Alana and Legion. Although the direct experience of listening and questioning the teachers is unique, that experience of shared communion is possible for those who have only the written lessons. You access that love by going into the stillness and awaiting love's message; this you can do while reading.

The certainty that love is there for me has changed my life. I still doubt, now and again, especially as I age and my mortality edges closer. "Will you really be there when I die?" "Yes," says Alana. "Open your heart. Open your mind. Love is with you always and always awaits you turning to love." I'm still learning to stand tall, certain of love's presence. I may not look forward to my death, but however it comes, and whenever, I seek to enter into that experience with the grace of love guiding me, welcoming even that change with love.

Love's response may not always be what you expected, or even thought you wanted. It may turn out to be something altogether different, even opposite. But love is there, love is real, turn to it. David attributes to me, some forty years ago, the direction to seek the path of love. I now attribute to him the love and support he has given to me, for without it this chapter would not have been written. Each of us, also share a profound gratitude for these teachers of love who are always present when we turn to them, and who are always thankful for our turning. I think it is their ever-present gratitude that has taught me the humility of respect for love.

Solitude was my lesson, but I do not fear being alone and unloved. Indeed, my solitude is filled with abundant love, and for that I am deeply grateful.

My Teaching Mission:
Discernments from a Guided Path
Oliver Duex

There was probably no time in my life when formal prayer was not practiced with me. Except the times when my willful mind relinquished "God," prayer has been a supreme practice in the unfolding of a life that I am clearly sensing was fueled by a steady and persevering truth seeking dispatch from my inner guidance.

From the formal and repetitive prayers at tuck-in time offered by my Protestant mother or Catholic father, to the revealed teachings of *The Urantia Book* of planetary importance, and later to the continued education classes by the supernal Teacher Corps of the Teaching Mission, the practice of effective prayer has certainly been invaluable in my personal experiences. And, still, on many occasions, I doubt.

After now 34 years with *The Urantia Book*, and some eleven years with the Teaching Mission, I am still often overcome by doubt. However, I hold this lingering perplexity as important. It has enabled me to avoid joining the ranks of zealotry such as occurred in my sundry ventures into the world of evolutionary religions — too numerous to detail here. My task is to share about the Teaching Mission and my personal history with it.

C.U.B.S., F.O.G. and Dilemmas

In 1982 my decisions let me to be one of the founders of the Center for Urantia Book Synergy (C.U.B.S.) in Santa Barbara, California, USA. This group believed to have identified major obstacles in the dissemination of *The Urantia Book*, namely availability, price, and convenience to obtain this promise towards the urgently necessary world-wide and Father-Fragment-revealing spiritual change on our rebellion-torn planet.

We believed in the synergistic effect and encouraged believers to buy and hold multiple copies to be given to potential readers and students. We felt exempt from the fear-based and allegedly supernally-guided promulgation doctrines that Urantia Foundation had set up, not unlike position papers. There was definitely a corporate climate predicated on significant apprehension about "over-rapid growth" and a timidity of being attacked by distracters before the Book could be disseminated sufficiently. Differing with the so-called mandates that were said to be given by some celestial authors, along with the revelatory material, C.U.B.S. members were convinced that the best protection for the Book was to get as many copies distributed as possible.

I remember numerous weighty discussions with Urantia Book Forum member Clyde Bedell, whose son Barrie was one of our members. Clyde, a professional advertising executive, and compiler of the Concordex of *The Urantia Book*, had argued for decades for improved and time-honored promulgation methods and he was glad to support our work and actions "to get the Book out there."

This story must also be told at another time in more detail.

C.U.B.S. also produced the first independent "The Art of Living" Urantia Conference during August 1983, which was attended by almost 400 students and believers. And what are conferences but a mix of active personal work and the more passive entertainment?

We had an entertainment committee skillfully guided by the late Sandy Garrick, an accomplished composer and musician, but also a knowledgeable student of the Book and a peacemaker. When we were approached by the Family of God (F.O.G.), a group of creative readers and believers who had developed a state-of-the-art audio-visual presentation that was shown at almost all conferences and gatherings during those years, a significant problem had to be resolved.

Vern Grimsley was F.O.G's chief spokesman, and he had trained himself to be the movement's most charismatic speaker using the evangelical verve of sermons that are not only transporting theological ideas but which become, by their decisive media presentation, a social event heavily influenced by present-day cultural and political context.

However, since December of 1982, Vern had been receiving "messages," whose probability of being Urantia Book related was widely discussed. The Urantia movement was in an uproar and everybody had an opinion. It became quickly the "Clayton incident," or Vern's "contact personality stunt." (F.O.G's two and a half million dollar seminary and radio station had been established in Clayton, California.) Thus inviting Vern's talented troupe to the August 1983 conference was also connected with the risk of increasing the movement's divisiveness.

C.U.B.S. members, believing thoroughly in the principle of group synergy and unity (not uniformity), allowed F.O.G.'s full participation. The conference was generally applauded.

Celestial Messages can be Political Power

The messages that Vern and some F.O.G. members received were, to my knowledge, never made public. And it was this relative secrecy that I deem to have been the major problem for its acceptance. However, Vern shared these messages with his old fraternity brothers, Martin Myers, then President of Urantia Foundation, and former trustees Hoite Caston and Richard Keeler.

We know that these messages concerned the safe-keeping of people and book plates because of an imminent nuclear disaster. The waters got even more muddied when Christy fell very ill during May of 1982, and while the inner circle generally accepted that she was a member of the planet's Reserve Corps of Destiny, Vern hurried to her bedside believing that this "privilege" could to be passed on to him.

Sooner or later every Urantia Book reader will hear about the early persons who readied the Book for its publication in 1955. For decades these steadfast people shrouded the Book and themselves in secrecy. Christy was the secretary who typed the revelation for typesetting at the printers. She had been the secretary of Dr. William Sadler who had his practice and residence at 533 Diversey Parkway in Chicago. The building is still Urantia Foundation's headquarters.

Martin Myers is said to have been the other contender. Little did these men know that teachings are given freely and are freely to be shared. These men also did not know that personal exchanges with teachers and guides are encouraged by our celestial helpers, as related later through the Teaching Mission, and that errors in our transmission are a known byproduct because the human receiver's mindal capacity is being used and humans are always imperfect.

I remember struggling with the question if it was indeed possible for such a self-made, ambitious man, as I had experienced Vern to be, who had been enjoying a life-long friendship with Urantia Foundation trustees and leaders, to not have a grand agenda with these messages. Indeed, a power struggle over Urantia Foundation leadership was by then in full sway and the messages were used as part of the fodder.

For the most part I took advantage of the luxury of sitting on the proverbial fence and observing what was to unfold. I can safely say that by the time the transcripts of the

The Teaching Mission

Teaching Mission teachers came into my life, I was still massively influenced by the Clayton incident and the use of these messages in the ensuing power struggle, such as the safe-keeping and thus guardianship of the printing plates.

The unfulfilled prediction of the imminent nuclear disaster was, of course, the end of F.O.G's credibility. The largely untold drama of financial losses incurred when celestials allegedly gave advice to consolidate assets to purchase and seek the safety of a huge cave, was for most readers a sign of 'I told you so, and the Book speaks clearly about avoiding these practices.' In my estimation, having lived through those time and being influenced by the occurrences, this is the single biggest factor why relatively few Urantia Book students can open themselves to the Teaching Mission.

I also became entangled with my own emotional thoughts of what I needed to do to keep my own family safe from nuclear fallout. During prayer I remember receiving repeatedly the sense that there was nothing I personally needed to do, except stay calm and be respectful towards all those who were obviously engrossed in huge survival conflicts.

Over the years I could not help but notice that periodically some of us Teaching Mission believers would like to have Vern's transmissions, and those of his co-workers, validated. I remember exchanging about this topic several times on the Teaching Mission List (tml), while following leads to those who had first-hand experience. A few, who had put their material possession on the line, did not show any willingness to justify the events, and are no respecters of celestial guidance. It seems rather that we, the members of the Teaching Mission, would like a wish fulfilled and constitute an uninterrupted lineage in that conservative leaders of the Urantia Foundation were at one time indeed all too willing to believe in fraternity brother Vern's transmissions, while they have promoted and silently tolerated the creation of a considerable body of debunking literature against the Teaching Mission.

To this day they remain firm in their demand for complete separation of the Teaching Mission from their organizations, Urantia Foundation and its social arm, Urantia Association International (UAI). There is no "Unity, but no uniformity" principle applied that I can detect. This is, of course, notwithstanding the fact that the majority of Teaching Mission learners are also Urantia Book students.

Every organization has traditionally demanded loyalty to its platform or founding papers, but for these Urantia organizations to set these, their dogmas, above the principle of unity is still a fear-based reaction that they will have to eventually overcome as well.

In the meantime the real growth seems to be occurring with the Urantia Book Fellowship, which has consistently practiced the principle of unity in brotherhood to Teaching Mission ["TeaM"] proponents during their well-attended conferences, and in between.

Slipping into the Teaching Mission

In 1992, after Teacher Will had introduced herself and taught for about a year in Tallahassee, Florida, a typewritten and photocopied book was given to me by one of my sundry Urantian friends. As I was reading the lessons, as well as the remarks on how a certain Receiver/Transmitter (R/T) felt he was guided into the process of receiving personal messages, I began to ask myself how I would initiate contact with mortals if I had taken the assignment of a celestial teacher.

My simple answer at the time was that I would seek any moment of mindal and/or heart openness when my charges were receptive — even if they were driving to work, which I remember one R/T doing when he was dialoging with a teacher about his R/T-ing experience.

My receptiveness was thoughtful and deliberative, to say the least. I did not have a sufficient reason to not read teacher Will's lessons, and I had never rejected a spiritual teaching at face value. How could I anyway, I who had embraced *The Urantia Book*, so exhaustive with novel and untrodden concepts and meanings?

Yes, any Book student, after understanding the Melchizedek, Thought Adjuster, midwayer and seraphic-guidance papers, should be best prepared for Teaching Mission teachers. If a seeker did not put this epochal revelation back on its shelf, Teacher Will's farsighted, compassionate and forebearing messages were certainly totally acceptable fare. But I was still granted a good dose of skepticism. And I allowed for the Teaching Mission teachings to come to me, instead of following leads to get them.

Teaching Mission and/or Urantia Book students have been taught that doubt is a necessary component of material free-will creatures. And that God's gift of free will thus gives us the inevitability of making unconscious and conscious errors.

Doubt forces us to make decisions that reflect our ability to have our faith grow, to keep it, or to buckle under the weight we give it.

Going Abroad to Get Away from it All

Again, the story would be too long to tell in detail, but in the beginning of 1998 I changed my dwelling location to the countryside in Costa Rica. Being a largely Catholic country with a growing Evangelical church, villages are not riddled with doubters, agnostics or atheists. God is still present in everyday language, such as "I see you tomorrow, God willing," or "I am doing fine, thanks to God." It is easy to talk about God and angels, even easier to talk about the Virgin Mary or evil spirits.

While most students finish their studies knowing how to read and write, there are very few who read beyond what is presented in sensationalized cheap newspapers. Book readers are an exception. At least this is my rationalization why I have not been able to place many Books, nor organize a study group. Never mind introducing the Teaching Mission.

Somewhere during the middle of 2000 I clearly remember a call from a good friend with whom I had studied the Book for years in Santa Barbara, and he and his beautiful wife had been instrumental in giving me psychological support to undertake my move to Costa Rica. They had been living in this country for some six years. (Thailand was the other country I had considered and fallen in love with.)

My friend said, "I want you to know that this little spiritual group is coming together each Sunday," and he named some of the people, "and," he continued, "I think you should get your ass over here next Sunday."

Of course I knew that the couple had made a pilgrimage and visited the main Teaching Mission groups in the USA earlier that year, and I also knew that the lady would R/T on the following Sunday.

The timing was right. Here again my celestial guidance was staring me in my face. I had recently been offered a permanent separation by the love of my life, and thus I was going through a very ambivalent relationship with God. I just could not make contact. I prayed without sensing a rapport. My mind was too preoccupied with my loss and my painfully broken heart.

I remember feeling a significant trepidation from the time my friend invited me for the next Sunday. As the day approached I was an emotional mess. This was not just reading a printed transcript; this was the real thing. What if these teachers could look into my heart and share my stuff with the group? What if I was running into a celestial sensitivity training a la Fritz Pearl, whose work I admired and whose workshops I had attended? What if all my humanly petty, irreverent and contradictory thought processes were dealt with? As my friend would put it later, I was as "nervous as a whore in church."

The couple's porch is as long as their attractively rustic house and some 10 yards wide. It overlooks a gorgeous bay of Lake Arenal. Their land was named "Nebadonia's Garden." A big round table with a fine linen cloth and a big colorful candle greeted us. There was some talk about last week's meeting, and the R/T explained that she was going to try and receive and that there was no certainty that she could make contact.

Teacher Legion came promptly on line, and he first talked about that we are not as important as our decision is to do God's will. If we would choose to do God's will, then that was what was most important. He reminded us that our self-importance was predicated on how much we loved our neighbors, and that our worries about health and economy and making right decisions would indeed make a difference to our lifestyle, but that our ability to love and sustain goodwill were the real things that would come along with us once we would leave this world for the next.

And then he directed himself to me:

"Your friend is restless and struggles because he has not accepted that his only task is to quiet his mind and seek the stillness within. Once he achieves this, all other answers will come to him without struggle. His fear is a shield from the path of Stillness. His teacher Daniel waits for him. There is no hurry on this side. Your friend wants answers about another, but first comes tending to the garden within. What difference does it make if she chooses one thing or another, if he remains unsettled within?

"She may go and he still will not know the peace he seeks with so much effort. If she stays, he still will not know the effortless peace that he hopes to find in her arms. Love between humans is both the vital necessity that is part of God's will, and the deceptive palliative that eases the mind away from one's center within. Tell your friend he is so loved he would laugh at his present state of confusion were he to know and accept the love that awaits him.

"His desire to do Father's will is evident and appreciated. Now he might apply that goodwill toward himself. Practice the Stillness. There is nothing to fear. Within the Stillness is love, the healing love that can wash away his fears and concerns. What is to fear if Daniel loves him? More love? Would he keep his cup half full only because he fears that more love will cause him to feel too good? There is no burden in accepting love." [Team Group Arenal, Costa Rica [20000625]

I instantly knew just how much this Teacher had either studied me or was able to read from my presence. Or, may be I had been under observation for longer than I knew? How about all my life? Teacher Legion knew that my fears had kept me away from making contact with the God of my understanding. And he now verified this to me.

I was immediately convinced. And for our R/T to transmit to us with such unadulterated clarity, made her to me one of my favorite R/Ts. I had a need to tell her that often. Notwithstanding that I understood that we are not to promote the ego of our receivers and transmitters. They are serving as they are called. Still, I am grateful to them for doing their steadfast and cyclical work.

About half a year later I felt moved to test the R/T-ing waters myself. I began by typing what I heard. I also went out into nature with a tape recorder and practiced. The teachers were always there to accommodate me. Later I found out that the midwayers were in charge of modulating the broadcasts so they would be understandable to us. Midwayers are very close to us and probably speak all planetary languages. In any case, I tested this, and I was able to receive in the other languages I speak.

I also met for over two years with another friend and we R/T-ed for each other. Every week we asked in our prayers to be sent those who might be interested in these teachings, but with a couple of exceptions, no one ever was sent to us. Due to the relative language and religious barriers where we live, our prayers could in all probability not have been fulfilled.

I am outright thankful that I was able to open myself to the Teaching Mission in spite of myself. I clearly received droves of help from our celestial guidance personnel. I am grateful that they worked extra hard for me.

The Teaching Mission

From Urantia Book Promoter to the Teaching Mission

I can say with a degree of certainty that if I had never been introduced to *The Urantia Book*, I would have joined other spiritual movements, exactly as I did before. Since the study of that Book, I believe I have a spiritual amplitude to appraise all other religious and philosophical thought that comes my way.

Would there even be a Teaching Mission in my life without the Urantian revelation? I sincerely doubt it.

The Urantia Book might be a most distinguished tool to measure spirituality with, but the details this revelation gifts us of our Inner Guidance, the Fragment of God that actually lives within each of us, is ever more such a perfect sorter of truth and facts. Thus it has often been said, if you want to know what spiritual truth is appropriate for one's own personal and unique journey towards God the Father, go within and spend time in Stillness and listen. Your truth discernment is already built in. It is perfect. Of course, being human, what you believe you are hearing might not be.

The emotions that trigger and fluctuate the human mind give us distorted results. At best we are often projecting our own thoughts, likes and dislikes, as well as what we think we know of how our others feel, or the reasons why they act as they do.

Over the many years between me finding *The Urantia Book* and allowing the Teaching Mission into my life, a significant amount of friendships were made with fellow readers. My family had opened for several Urantia meetings a week — for newcomers, regulars and special study groups. Regional conferences were supported and attended, and national conferences visited. We were Mr. and Mrs. Urantia in our area for many years.

Whenever I came through Chicago on business trips, I would make sure to fetch a couple or three cases of Books for our C.U.B.S. distribution network. I got to experience Urantia Foundation's headquarters, and I was most amazed about their style of studying. When the Forum's work was finished in 1942, they continued to meet to study the Book. They chose a lecture format, where on Sundays reader-believers gave presentation. They had a room with a podium and a load of chairs lined up. Well, studying means a podium, a presenter who knows something about a given subject, and a horde of students. After all, Dr. William Sadler and many of the Forum members came from an intellectual class and it should be of no surprise that they continued studying in that fashion.

We, on the other hand, conducted study groups during the 70s and 80s more as a spiritual circle, where all members got to read a portion and each could ask or comment to their hearts' delight. We were able to go beyond its factual intellectualism and accepted the teachings also emotionally and spiritually. However, it is a work that has stretched my intellect, and there are many high concepts that I began to understand partially only after repeated readings over time and in several study groups. *The Urantia Book* is clearly a work for a lifetime and more.

It is a well-known fact that Urantia Book conferences have become more spiritual, less intellectual. This is especially true for the Fellowship's conferences. We have seen meditation and yoga offered, the Teaching Mission has been given their own rooms and mention in brochures, and presentations given on *The Urantia Book* and other religions, to name but a few changes.

Why Don't They Accept Me? — I am a Urantia Book Reader Too.

Overall, I have lost contact with many of my Urantian friends since I have not hidden the fact that I am part of the Teaching Mission. I have been accused of helping to make outreach more difficult, that my association with the Teaching Mission would hamper my own outreach; or that irrational belief are explicitly warned about in *The Urantia Book*. Without even reading suggested Teaching Mission material, these old friends had made up their minds. Speaking in tongues, making predictions, praying for miracles, visions of celestials, were all erroneously associated with me and the Teaching Mission.

But some took the effort and searched for and read lessons on their own. Unfortunately they found transcripts, unedited, probably from the TM archives with the R/T's faulty grammar, ornate language and personal embellishments intact, as well as distorted or misunderstood Urantia Book concepts, or outright mis-information reflecting the R/T's personal beliefs and agendas. These friends left no stone overturned to find faults.

And of course it is easy for Urantia Book readers to find fault in any spiritual writing, because they are so used to supernal excellence. After all, it took 13 years to bring it to print almost perfectly.

The Contact Commission saw the Book as most of us see it, the most valuable information on our world. They took the Book very seriously and made their decisions foremost according to its safe-keeping. They were intellectuals, and as the Incredible String Band sang about a relationship, I paraphrase:

> *Oh, you know all the words, and you sung all the notes,*
> *But you never quite learned the song, the revelators sang.*
> *I can tell by the sadness in your eyes,*
> *That you never quite learned the song.*

To Teaching Mission students, one thing has become obvious: Religious organizations and churches with all their manifests, constructs, mandates and dogmas, can never hope to create the Kingdom of which *The Urantia Book* speaks in such marvelous detail. The trend was set in Chicago, and Urantians have often attempted to create the Kingdom out of human energies alone. Many have even venerated the Book. I know, because there was a time when I thought that my most important work on this world was to promulgate the Book itself.

The Teachers from the Melchizedek school taught me about the importance of regular and very personal Stillness, quality time spent with my Mystery Monitor, or Christ Michael, or whatever Spirit is deemed right for my personal growth at any one time. I may invite. I must open my end of the connection, and whenever I remember to do so, God's love is instantly reciprocated to me in myriads of forms.

The Book is full of quotes about worship, or how Jesus took time off by himself to communicate with our Father in heaven. Yet our Teachers have never tired of reminding us in literally hundreds and hundreds of transmissions. This indicates to me that we probably need these reminders. I know I do.

And out of these precious connections with aspects of God that differs from person to person, because we are each at a unique step of spiritual development of body mind and Spirit, there is born almost instantly a rapport that astounds me time and again. I hope I will never take it for granted, and how could I?

As long as Urantians are still sloughing through politics and intellectualism, they must by necessity overlook the lessons on 'unity, and not uniformity' that are the basis of the gospel. We are to love God, and strive to become like Him. Only then shall we really find our sisters and brothers, and minister to them and serve as we pass by in our lives.

How to Know What to Believe

No one really knows how many transcripts were co-created between celestial teachers and R/Ts. Just a simple guesstimate, the givens:

A dozen regularly meeting groups — there were at one time more, now less.
Twenty years: That is about right, given some years.
Assuming weekly meetings, some meet more often, some less.
12 active groups X 52 weekly transmission X 20 years = about 12,500 transcripts. Although not an exact figure, it can give us a sense that there are thousands and thousands of transcripts, most recorded and typed, some not.

We can therefore safely say, that we have been told many things. We have heard mostly accurate things. We leave the false predictions, magical doings, unverified names for planets and beings, co-created beings, the fulfillments of R/T's desires or agenda . . . we leave all that stuff out for the sake of this section.

Still, we have been told many things that we need to process. We listen to our Earth's media news and we are told many things to process. We are literally bombarded with information if we do not take control of our mass media devices. My preferred pattern is no TV at all. I exchange movies with friends, and I read my news on the Internet using Google News. Thus I get the amazing choice of picking from hundreds of newspapers and magazines world-wide. And I listen to US Public Radio on my 3G phone, wherever I am. That, too, is greatly amazing to me.

Still, I hear many things that I need to process to determine what is accurate information. What is true information? And most importantly, what information helps me on my personal journey. What is worthy? What is righteous?

Besides discussing this information with my fellows, I have learned that we each have two spiritual working "mechanisms" that Father has set up for us: The accurate and ever present Mystery Monitor that dwells within us, the Fragment of the Living God, to which we can turn in stillness for affirmation, and, the Spirit of Truth, which is there for the conviction of truth; it will invariably energize our sensitive truth button.

If I have any doubt, these are two mighty indicators of truth that can validate what I can and should believe. When I fail to receive validation, I can be sure that the information has no or little relevance for my path.

I have found that this process of validation has become easier as I practiced it over the years. There has certainly within me developed a more sensitive bearing, often coupled with an emotional reaction of actually being moved when I observe truth being expressed.

The teachers have also made it amply clear that what is applicable truth to another, what feels true to another, is not necessarily the same for me and my own spiritual need to learn or to my growth experience.

During transmission I have often observed that I must follow my own path. Naturally, it is a wonderful occasion when a given truth is perceived similarly by my partner or friend, or a member of my group, but if it is not, or diverges greatly, we all are required to walk alone with our own relative truth.

But, really, we are never alone, never one second alone, if we only remember the offer of the Spirit of Truth that will walk with us through all experiences at all times. If I feel alone, I have merely forgotten to take the offer of that unlimited and to me incomprehensible connection.

How many times and in how many transcripts have the Teaching Mission teachers reminded us that our engagement in Stillness is indeed the surest way to determine what is right for us, and the faultless guidance on our path towards the Creator of all beings and all things.

Where Do We Fit in?

Historically, our survival was assured by belonging to a clan. Today we still have the urge to belong, although it has become possible to live totally isolated and survive. Today's organizations are protected by their members, who do everything necessary to ascertain that the organization survives. Yes, everything.

Early on, Teaching Mission members were told that the mission was not for everyone, that it was even an experiment, and it was. And it is a work in progress. We were told that we are part of the greater Correcting Time. So who are the other parts?

We have networkers among us who fed us with other channelings in a regular and persistent manner. We have brothers and sisters, but mostly brothers, who will tell us that everyone from the White Eagle Lode to Alice Bailey, from Valerie Donner and the Ground Crew to Dr. Boylan, or from The Pleiadians to Fred Sterling or the Galactic Federation of Light, are all included in the Correcting Time.

These same networking brothers will also reiterate that they are Teaching Mission students, as well as Urantia Book students through and through, and that they find the revelatory text as well as the Teacher assistance of the Teaching Mission invaluable to their search for God, truth and universe citizenship.

Our valued networkers will include in their long list of new age channelers and Correcting Time participants: Dr. Steven Greer, Kahu Kirael, Gillian McBeth-Loughan and the Quantum Awakening, Glenda Green, Jean Hudon, Kryon, Maitreya, Master Djwal Khul, Metatron Melchizedek, Norma Gentile, Oprah's Spiritual Channel Podcasts, Patricia Diane Cota-Robles, Ronna Herman, Sananda, St. Germain, The Padgett Papers, and more. And who is to say this is not so? To my knowledge, the Teachers made no comments of who is part of the Correcting Time, or who they are teaching other than us, or, for that matter, who is publishing the most truth.

We are on our own to make such discernments, and a brother like me, whose path has brushed with existentialism, Hinduism, Buddhism, the Whirling Dervishes, Zen Buddhism and all kinds of relative new age truth, for me to find the Urantia papers was the first superb meal that satisfied my spiritual hunger and quenched my long, big thirst for a complete and plausible explanation of the history of evolutionary religion with its huge amounts of contradictory and illogical beliefs.

I had then the choice to see such teachings as a step back, or that my networking with them might be an exercise for me to practice acceptance, tolerance, good will and love towards others who in reality are searching and treading where I did so many years ago.

I have a choice to see these often strange beliefs as a detour, or I can observe them as a stepping stone in our Father's immensely diversified spectrum of beliefs, creeds and dogmas — some of them so aggressive that they seek to eliminate non-believers.

The great temptation for us, who believe that our revelation carries within itself the greatest spiritual perspective yet, and that the Teaching Mission Teachers are a real part of our celestial family, is that we have begun to believe that we have the best teachings of all, and that everyone else need to be brought up to our level of knowledge and truth.

So where do we really fit? Where do I, as an individual, fit?

First of all, how many transmissions must I read before I get that I should spend regular time in Stillness and seek within —and not without— for divine truth? How many times must I be told to seek and maintain a relationship with Christ Michael for guidance, solace and real joy?

All the channelers and their publications and tapes and videos will find people who can attune to them. Any human teacher with the ability to speak publicly will attract an audience that can relate to the spiritual and cultural language she or he uses. I tune in to the Teaching Mission because they speak the language of the revelation I cherish, and I find no contradictions to the papers, except when T/Rs do not understand values and meanings that are explained perfectly well in *The Urantia Book*.

In the end, we need to shed all lineage and linkage to our teachings and speak from our own being. As soon as we mention books and transcripts written by celestials of many orders, ascending and descending, we create blockages in our personal ministry. If we learn to speak the simple truth just as Jesus did —without referencing books and organizations and dogmas — we become the best out-reachers imaginable. Then, and only then, we are free to talk to all seekers everywhere.

Finally Connecting with Christ Michael's Spirit

One spiritual message evaded my mind and my heart during my Urantia Book years. And that was the possibility of a personal spiritual and constant connection with the Spirit of Jesus, the Spirit of Truth that Christ Michael poured out for us. It is as accessible and personal as if we were alive during Jesus' lifetime and in his presence. All believers for all ages will be able to tap into this Spirit of personal guidance, consolation and joy to be relished with our Creator. I missed that during all those fun and funky Urantia Book study sessions.

The Teacher Corps in general and the specific work of Donna D'Ingillo's Center for Christ Consciousness and their prodigious transmissions received from Christ Michael Himself, explained to me my neglected possibilities, and guided me into seeking a personal relationship with Him.

Among the many aspects of co-creative interaction with our Creator, I learned that we can ask Christ to speak and act through us. Our free will stays intact, because we initiate and request these interactions.

We have been told and we can know that Christ Michael's Spirit of Truth is as immediate and personal as if Jesus was living in our households. He gifted us with it, and has promised to walk with us through all of our changes and vicissitudes, if we would only remember to contact Him.

Yes, this relationship can be more intimate then I could ever have known. Here is just one example of what is offered to us just for the asking. There are indeed situations with our families and friends, with our neighbors and acquaintances, when our help is rejected because we contributed to their hurt, or we are simply perceived as part of the problem, not the solutions. Here is what we can do:

> **Michael**: *Know that the most effective manner in which you can be a conduit of my healing is through your active prayer life. Your spiritually directed thoughts can penetrate into the spiritual lives of individuals where words cannot produce good fruit.*
>
> *When you pray for another individual, call me into the spirit being of that individual, and ask for my will for that individual to become more activated in that person's life. You are inserting a thought pattern into that person who cannot ask this of himself or herself because of their inability to articulate this level of spiritual focus.*
>
> *This is not an invasion of their free will. This is merely an admixture of my presence within theirs, so that spiritual current can be added to their thought forms and patterns. It is advisable to spend a concerted length of time in focusing on one individual, rather than moving from one person to person quickly, so that the full resonance of my being can take effect within that person. In this way, you are being used as an instrument of healing. And as you gain more practice with this, it will give you a great sense of achievement. Do this with me, my daughter, and we will heal together.*

[Center for Christ Consciousness, Berkeley, California, 9-23-2002]

How I Came To The Teaching Mission
and the Urantia Book
Dorenda Elena Morse

Some people read *the Urantia Book* and then embrace the Teaching Mission. I was the opposite. In fact, I had ignored *the Urantia Book* for quite a long time. My uncle, Hal Bynum, had been an avid Urantia Book proponent for many years, strongly encouraging my mother to read it. I knew of his recommendations, but the big blue book remained nothing more in my mind than an excellent door stop.

My uncle and his wife, Rebecca are both key figures in the story of the Teaching Mission. Because of them, my mother was aware of the Teaching Mission, but I'm not sure if I was or not. It took a very signal event to get my attention and to engage my spiritual commitment to the Teaching Mission and *the Urantia Book*. The Teaching Mission was the doorway through which I entered; the Urantia Book was there when I crossed the threshold.

This story is not entirely my story. In fact, I play a bit part in the over all story, but I am telling this story from my perspective. I'll let my mother and sister tell or not tell their parts. Their stories display huge spiritual growth and increased connection with our heavenly Father, and they are beautiful stories. I am so grateful that I am part of their stories, and that they are part of mine.

To return to my version of this story, it begins June 22, 1996 at 10:00 a.m. in Salt Lake City with a life-threatening event happening to my beloved brother-in-law, Don. This event was of critical importance to all of us! My sister Deborah was there when it happened; I flew up from Albuquerque as soon as she called me for help; Mother was on the other end of the phone in Albuquerque until she came to Salt Lake City when I had to return to work; and my uncle performed his important role over the phone from Nashville where he lived with his wife, Rebecca.

The life-threatening event occurred as Don was looking underneath his car. The car fell on Don and rolled him over 3 times before it came to a stop at the end of the slanting driveway, leaving him utterly crushed and on the brink of death. In answer to this desperate situation, my mother called my Uncle Hal in Nashville and asked for his prayers and for those of his spiritual group. Hal promised he would surely bring it up at the next meeting.

When the meeting started, my uncle didn't even have to mention anything at all. Ham, the spiritual teacher transmitted by Rebecca, already knew. He started right off by saying that he understood that my uncle had a family member who was in a perilous physical situation. When I heard that Ham already knew of the situation without being told, this in itself grabbed my attention, but much more followed.

Ham said that Don's great love for my sister would pull him through. He went on to counsel my sister in the days/weeks that followed in critical points in Don's recovery. One critical message was to tell her that floating bone fragments had been missed in one of Don's x-rays and that they should go back again to see to it before they punctured a lung. There were other things that were absolutely impossible for Ham to know, that pointed clearly to the indisputable fact that we were receiving instruction from and communicating with someone who was not of this world.

Everything Ham said turned out to be totally true, and there was no other way that anyone of this world would have known any of the things he said. This was miraculous! I was thrilled with the knowledge that we had counsel from the spiritual world and filled with relief with the knowledge that we had reinforcements from on high. True to Ham's words, Don's great love for Deborah did pull him through. Don had a complete and marvelous recovery, thanks to many, many sources.

During this time, in my own life, I was in the midst of an absolutely miserable marriage. I was very discouraged and almost despairing at my situation. I hesitated to ask Ham a question for myself. Though I was in a very dark period of my life, my situation was not life-threatening, and quite frankly I didn't think that I would be someone who would merit an answer to a question. However, I dared to ask, and I was absolutely joyous when I got a reply from Ham. I was elated to think that I might be worthy of an answer to my question. I took great solace in Ham's counsel, and I turned to the Jesus papers in *the Urantia Book* sometime around that time.

Both my mother and I started participating from afar in Ham's group and reading *the Urantia Book*. We couldn't wait to receive the printed lessons my uncle sent us in the mail. Also, each week we would call my uncle before the meetings with questions we might have, and he would graciously call with the answers afterward. My uncle was so wonderful to do this, because at that point, my mother and I were absolutely desperate to hear the words my uncle relayed to us. Once nourished by the attention of our Teachers, we were like baby birds with gaping mouths straining to receive more spiritual food from our guides.

When my sister became a part of Abraham's group in Salt Lake City, my mother and I hooked on to that group as well. We both absolutely hung on Ham's and Abraham's every word. I personally felt like they were father figures to me. I simply basked in their presence as their healing words washed over me every week. I still do that with Abraham. I just love to kind of crawl up in his lap. I feel like he surrounds me with strength, love, and wisdom, and that all is right with the world. Both Abraham and Ham supplied something that had been missing for me. I really miss not having Ham's lessons anymore, and wish we still had contact with him.

Though well nourished from Salt Lake City and Nashville, we nevertheless really wanted to have a group of our own. Mother and I both tried to transmit, but nothing happened there. After a number of years, we were finally blessed to have a group develop here when Angus and Gerdean came to Albuquerque, but that goes a little beyond how I came to the Teaching Mission which is the main topic here. I think the Albuquerque group is another story.

The Teaching Mission as a whole has many teachers who provide such a tremendous service to us on this world. There is something to be gleaned from each lesson, from each Teacher. I am so grateful for having this exposure, this forum, this exchange. The Teaching Mission adds such an important layer, such a vital spiritual library from which to draw. I surely would not want to lose my library card nor have my privileges revoked from this resource. Don's injury, as horrible as it was, opened the way to the Teaching Mission and the communication with our spiritual guides. I have come to know them, love them, rely on them, to expect them to be a part of my life.

I suppose my story goes on and on, as everyone else's does, and I guess that is one part that remains more certain from my experience with the Teaching Mission and *the Urantia Book*. Our stories truly do go on - ad infinitum! That is a fabulous piece of information to know personally. That we can communicate with entities that travel the Mansion worlds, continuing their own spiritual journeys after their mortal stints are over, proves this very thing. I look forward to the journey ahead, with their companionship.

Reveling in Revelation
Bob Hunt

In the years that followed my discovery and reading of *The Urantia Book* in 1970, at the age of thirty-four, I experienced a strong and ongoing feeling of gratitude for living during this time on Urantia when revelation and spiritual blessings have been forthcoming in many ways and in countless forms. I am certain that many others share this recognition and thankfulness as well. My spiritual journey, thanks to the guidance of my parents, included a recognition of and faith in God and in Jesus from early childhood and through my youth and formal education. During these years, I read and studied philosophy and religion, as well as science, always seeking truth and enlightenment.

My encounter with *The Urantia Book* was even more than I had ever expected in my odyssey. In a talk that I was invited to present in 1974 to the Los Angeles Chapter of The World Future Society, I wrote the following: "Suppose that, by some technique, the very highest, most perceptive human insights could be collected and then formulated into a consistent rendition for study and analysis. The source of each gem of wisdom would be relatively unimportant; each would find its proper place in the whole by withstanding the tests of beauty, truth, and goodness on as many levels of reality as the current evolving consciousness of man has experience for evaluation.

Suppose, further, that some new information is made available for transition, for completion of partial concepts, and for extensions within the grasp of human understanding. Would the populace of this beleaguered little planet be able to adjust to the new levels of both understanding and responsibility? I regard both the supposition and the question as being of the utmost importance because, incredibly, what I am describing has occurred!" Then, I went on to provide an introduction to *The Urantia Book* as "a guide to the future and beyond". My presentation can be found online at http://users.humboldt.edu/rwhunt.

At that time, I did not anticipate the continued flow of spiritual information and abundance of sources that enriched my seeking and heightened my gratitude. Uppermost among these were *A Course in Miracles* and, of course, the Teaching Mission. I was fortunate to be sufficiently open-minded and in the right time and space locations to recognize and to appreciate these revelations.

My experience with Correcting Time teachers began in 1991 when I heard the 1987 introductory audiotape of Abraham from New Zealand. Then, in the days and months that followed, I began accumulating and listening to tapes of Ham transmissions received by Rebecca from Woods Cross, Utah. Soon thereafter, I became aware of Rayson transmissions received by Roxy from Venice, California. I continued to seek out and read or hear an expanding collection from other early teachers, including Daniel, Will, Tarkas, Olfana and Jared.

Along with many others, I was uplifted by commentary and lessons that rang true and clear, evoking thoughts within and uplifting feelings similar to those arising in my mind and heart upon my first encounter with *The Urantia Book* in 1970. It seemed to me as if the Teaching Mission transmissions were permeating and raising consciousness by way of enhanced Thought Adjuster receptivity in individuals who heard and read these lessons. Furthermore, through what Jim Cleveland called the "the dynamics of humans," conversations and sharing among friends, with whom I already had spiritual bonds, provided impetus, in ever-enlarging concentric circles, by spreading the word and sharing transcripts and tapes.

My personal experiences included communication, primarily in California, with Bob Slagle of Sebastopol and Vincent Ventola of Venice. Bob, a psychology professor at Sonoma State University, was the author of an excellent and informative paper about the Teaching Mission, "Welcome to Change". Vincent, a visionary artist and writer, was the partner of Roxy Allessandro, the original transmitter-receiver for Rayson.

It was during a transmission/conversation with Rayson that I requested a teacher for a Urantia Book study group in Arcata, California. I received a response that this request, through Ham, was already known and in process. Further, the T/R would be, in Rayson's words, my "mate", Bonnie Hunt, mother of ten children, and a long-time reader of *The Urantia Book*. This commenced our initial personal involvement in the Teaching Mission; and we proceeded to become acquainted with Astara, identified as a Brilliant Evening Star, who proved to be a unique and compelling teacher.

Even though I was familiar with the study group in Woods Cross, Utah, and the transmissions of Ham, it was not until a gathering in Los Angeles on February 1, 1992, that I met some members of the group, along with their leader, Thern Blackburn. To coincide with a meeting of the General Council of the Urantia Fellowship that was held at the

Airport Holiday Inn in Los Angeles from January 31 to February 2, 1992, Blackburn scheduled a meeting room at the hotel for a transmission from "Teacher Ham". This event was announced in advance, and those in attendance included a number of individuals who were present for the Fellowship meeting, as well as many others whose primary interest was to hear Ham.

Following his succinct and powerful transmission, Ham responded to a few questions from the audience. As the first person to step to the microphone, I inquired: "Would you please comment on the purpose and the scope, and, if possible, some timetable information of your mission, activity, or program, whichever term is best?" Ham first responded, "Mission is best" (officially denominating the "Teaching Mission"). He went on to say, in part, that the plans included "initiation and expansion of the teaching corps," "spiritual enlightenment," and preparation for "an even greater teacher," a "teacher son." He also noted "we are anticipating many years duration of this initial phase of our mission."

A fascinating commentary on Ham's presentation occurred on the next day, February 2, 1992, in my guest room at the LAX Holiday Inn. A group of about a dozen of us listened intently as Roxy transmitted a message from Rayson. This began with words of praise for Rebecca from "high beings of the superplanetary government" who saluted her "service, courage, and nobility." Rayson then noted that the event was scheduled for the purpose of "presenting the truth of the second stage of the Fifth Epochal Revelation to the official guardians of the first stage."

Continuing, he said: *"Let me assure you and share with you the wonderful celebration which we celestial beings participated in last night, the celebration of the public awareness of the reign of our Acting Planetary Prince. And children, what a Prince this Melchizedek is! How many planets have as their planetary prince a being of such immense love, wisdom, and light as our beloved Machiventa, a being who has intimately lived, studied, and loved this planet and its humans for such a long time? Indeed, a teacher who has actually incarnated as one of you. How blessed this planet is to have this special watch care of Michael and such a wonderfully experienced planetary prince."*

My own "first person" teacher contact was with Astara, during a period from early October of 1992 until May of 1994. Astara's transmissions, with Bonnie Hunt as receiver, were not circulated widely, occurring prior to the active collecting, organizing, and archiving of transcripts. Because of this, I wish to present here the spirit and some of the content from Astara in three excerpts from her transmissions. In the first of these, Astara introduces herself.

ASTARA TRANSMISSION 10/11/1992 - Transmitter-Receiver Bonnie Hunt

I am Astara. I am a bearer of light. I am your teacher in this time and place. I welcome this opportunity to bring forth my love and words of encouragement at the changes that are taking place on your world at this time, within your beings, as well as on the surface of the earth, within the body of the earth. I've come to offer love. I've come to bring a balance, to initiate thoughts, opportunities for each of you at this time. I am part of a teaching mission designed to uplift and integrate all spiritual energies being directed towards the One. This is a transformational planet. This is a transformational opportunity.

I am a beacon of light. You are beacons of light. When you align yourself with God within, in union with your Thought Adjuster, you radiate an energy that penetrates those beings you come in contact with. Your light-body is the way of connecting, one with another, the essence of who you are. It is from this point of connection that love is born and lives as light rays emanating from your being.

There are available many expressions of spirit, many words describing spirit, describing thought. Within the human resides the Spirit of Truth, and recognition of God is available to all. How one believes is a personal experience. What one believes is a personal experience. Each individual knows within the heart that they are a part of God. It is important to understand this, to recognize the unique extension of spiritual illumination that each one experiences. Know that you are one with God, that you are one with each other in this alignment with the Spirit of Truth. Be who you are without concern for another's opinion of who they think you are. Much confusion exists in trying to be someone else. Listen to the voice within. Align yourself with God, with your own Thought Adjuster. It is a string between God and yourself, one instrument with many strings. When God plays on these strings, you make a melody with harmonies. Each of you is a note in the air, a song to be sung. Hear these melodies. They are miracles.

On a later occasion, Astara responds to a question about her identity.

ASTARA TRANSMISSION 1/8/1993 T/R Bonnie Hunt

Q: *The Urantia Book* describes certain Universe Aids who are personally commissioned for service on missions such as this, the Correcting Time. Among these are the Brilliant Evening Stars, "a unique twofold order, embracing some of created dignity and others of attained service", who are "engaged in specific missions for the Creator Sons and the local Universe rulers". Further, "they always work in pairs – one created being, the other an ascendant Evening Star". Are you a Brilliant Evening Star?

A: *This symbol (Receiver patterns a triangle with her fingers), this triangle, is an important part of who I am. Several triangles make up a star; several stars make up the heavens. I am, as you suspect, as you have predicted, a Brilliant Evening Star. With my "sistar" Adora, we are evolving in the way of light and life as expressions of information disseminated in the way of channeling.*

More importantly, we are injecting our light and our love into your beings. We have come at this time to assist in a process of harmonizing your planet, your world, known to you as Urantia. You see, there are millions, billions of people on your world; only a few know this world as Urantia. There are many religions. There are people who know God with no religion. There is, however, one common thread; and that is the ability to love, to know love, to feel love, to be moved by love. And it is through this loving vibration that we are doing our work here in the world at this time.

Many times I have spoken of light; sacredly I have said the word "light". Light is part of frequency and part of time. Light embraces all; all is of light. Light has motion. Light is inner and outer. Light is illumination and understanding. Light is webbing, light is weaving and waving. Light is instruction, light is destruction. Light is love; and love is light. Light is a continuum, light is continuous. Light connects and disconnects. Light evolves and revolves. Light is sound, and light is silence. Light streams, light shines, light sparkles. Light dissolves, light revolves. Light is everywhere. Light illumines the way.

About a year later, Astara was continuing to beam her light.

ASTARA TRANSMISSION 1/24/93 Transmitter-Receiver Bonnie Hunt

I am with you once again. We face one another in this space with light between our beings; that light, which we are coming to recognize, is who we are. I am happy to have another opportunity to speak with you. You are welcome in this home of light where I have taken a place among this family. As you embrace one another with love, so know that I am in your arms, within the hands that hold the light of love.

There has been time, since last we spoke, for all of you to begin a process of digestion of the information that has been coming forth. And in each of you there has taken root an understanding of light heretofore not understood; and it will continue to grow within you so that each of you will become more conscious of the light that you are. I have felt much contact and thought processes around my being, and have found that there have been many moments that you have drawn me close, that we have beamed together the beaming word, which is a combination of BE and AM. Yes, we are one, we be as one; and as we take responsibility for ourselves, for the I AM, the oneness, the unity of our love, of our light, we grow so bright together; we will become infectious in our daily lives; we will draw to us all that we need, and we will give all that is needed.

It is a time on earth when harmonizing the activities of our daily lives with another's is very important. We, as we make our choices, will become conscious of our acts of kindness and thoughtlessness as well. We will see the effects we have on one another by our thought, word, and deed; and others will notice, and they will take heed, and they will begin to feed upon our light and we will feed them. This is the way of our work in the world; this is the way of light, of enlightening one another with love.

I am as a star among you. It is with the consciousness of the reflective ability of a star, with the many facets and points of light, as of understanding points of consciousness, that you know me and recognize me within yourselves, within your hearts and minds. We are able, together, to transmit both heavenly and earthly vibrations as we harmonize with the pulsing vibration of love that emanates from your own beings and from my countenance; therefore, the assimilation of our energies and lights creates a wave of intent that moves forward encircling all before us. It is a time to remember. It is a time to forget past disappointments, those haunting memories that deplete your being, that rob you of your vitality. For the past no longer is part of the present when you acknowledge it for its place in your life and thank that which has come unto you, which has brought you where you are now, alive and shining in this room with me. Move forward from this place with your heart open, ready to embrace what is ahead.

Welcome to the world, this shining day. Your mechanical instruments amaze me. They are able to bring to others this experience as a voice. Someday perhaps there will be one that will bring forth this light that we are generating so that they might feel what we are feeling in the presence of one another. I thank you for your attentiveness, for those blessings, those prayers and thoughts that have been with me as we have grown in the light these last few days and months. I too am grateful for the guiding beings that are here with me, for the angels who abide behind each of you, above each of you, before each of you; and in this enfolding of their light, we experience their guardianship. I thank you, those of you who know, who know the deep convictions, held within each of us, of the love we have for God, the experiences we have had in our life to validate your part in our lives. The angelic kingdom is ever-present and available at all times to all of us.

Through my close contact with two transmitters and their Correcting Time teachers, Rayson and Astara, I was provided a golden opportunity; namely, I was able to have a few personal meetings and ask questions. Due to the unusual nature of some of my inquiries and the interesting responses of these teachers, I want to share the following.

CONVERSATION WITH RAYSON 1/30/1992

Q: I would like to ask about A Course in Miracles.

A: *"A Course in Miracles is celestial in origin, not by the same commission which dictated* The Urantia Book. *It is quite highly evolved for the human types who need a simple and daily routine of true spiritual growth to follow. There are no conflicts with* The Urantia Book *or with our mission. We regard it quite highly as one of the more truth-reflecting works on your planet."*

Q: I would like to ask about the poet-musician Bob Dylan and whether he might be such an individual as is spoken of in *The Urantia Book* in Section 1 "The Celestial Musicians" of Paper 44, where it is stated: ". . . someday a real musician may appear on Urantia, and whole peoples will be enthralled by the magnificent strains of his melodies. One such human being could forever change the course of a whole nation, even the entire civilized world."

A: *"Unfortunately, he is too intellectually high to fulfill the page 500 definition. However, his music is quite inspired, and he is a valiant searcher-seeker after God and truth. He is not always clear but continues to grow Godward. If his music affects you deeply, as I'm sure it does many hundreds of thousands of others, then it is positive. But he will not achieve what you hope. He is too esoteric and not mass-appeal enough. . . but a good soldier for God."*

CONVERSATION WITH ASTARA 5/1/1994

Q: I want to inquire about marijuana and its use as a sacred herb.

A: *"Many individuals are choosing to use the spiritually infused drug marijuana. I call it a drug for in your culture it is referred to in this manner. We do not think of it as a drug, but rather we think of it as an illuminating inspiration as it weaves its way into the being of your chemical nature. It allows an expansion of physical manifestation, and this entwines more readily with the information available in the heavenly realms. Many people who experiment with this vine have found it to bring into their lives an open-hearted viewpoint. As you think on this infusion of plant and being, in your mind's focus, see this glowing, vibrant,* *flowering plant as a way of integrating God's gift with the human mind.   And be thankful for this inspiration in your life; be appreciative for this way of interfacing one of God's living organisms with another."*

Through the Teachers in the Teaching Mission, I have gained new understanding and recognition of truth, beauty and goodness in many ways.   While the transmissions bring forth factual information, often in response to questions from the participants, my greatest inspiration arises from the validation of thoughts and observations that I have formulated and experienced throughout my life.   Accordingly, I feel a fresh sense of support, comfort, and certainty as these words and observations stream into my consciousness.   I have the greatest respect for and gratitude to all of the Correcting Time teachers, whose lessons are uplifting in new and creative tones of reassurance to my mind and spirit.

(Bob Hunt is the father of ten children and grandfather of sixteen.   He is a retired Professor of Mathematics and has been a student of The Urantia Book since 1970.   He has written some papers on The Urantia Book; links to these can be found at www.humboldt.edu/~rwh2/.   The banner on that site links to an interview with Bob about his teaching career and selection as Outstanding Professor at Humboldt State University.   Bob's involvement with the Teaching Mission began in 1991.   His wife, Bonnie Hunt, was a transmitter/receiver for Teacher Astara during a period from 1992 to 1994.   Following a two-year heroic challenge with cancer, Bonnie departed from this world and her family in 2003.   He now lives with his new wife, Gwendolyn, a long-time reader of The Urantia Book, in Arcata, California, and in Keihi, Maui.)

Bakersfield Teaching Mission 1994-1999
Deborah Goaldman

The seed for the Bakersfield Teaching Mission group was planted in my heart in March 1992.   It was during my first visit to a Urantia study group in Bakersfield, California, which had recently restarted primarily to discuss the announcement of the Teaching Mission by the Woods Cross group of Utah.   My reaction was, "You've got to be kidding."   But I was counseled by one member to read the transcripts with an open mind and that is what I did.

The messages from the celestial teacher, Ham, stirred my curiosity and longing for contact with celestials.   Others may have felt the same initially because the Bakersfield group telephoned Thern at Woods Cross to ask Ham for a teacher.   We were told we would get one.

The problem then became who would be the transmitter receiver (T/R).   Two members seemed to be likely candidates to me.   One person had psychic abilities and even experienced a visual visit from a celestial during this time.   Another member had been practicing meditation since childhood and had the stillness skills to be receptive.   However, neither was willing, and ultimately the initial group rejected the idea of the Teaching Mission – except for me.

The Teaching Mission

The original study group ended and I reformed another with new members, searching for those who would be interested in the Teaching Mission. When the loneliness was too much, I would call people already involved in the Mission for encouragement. Two who helped me most were Patije Mills in Florida and Thern from the Woods Cross group. Patije sent me more transcripts– among which were the transcripts of the teacher, Will, dated 1991-1993. These transcripts were my bread and water, and I shared them with any new members of the Bakersfield Urantia Book study group willing to read them.

In my prayers I would cry out to be included while at the same time struggle with doubt. I made an important choice during these two years of waiting– to wholeheartedly commit myself to the Teaching Mission, even though I had never witnessed the communication process. To make this commitment I imagined leaping off a cliff and trusting that God would provide me with the wings to fly or catch me when I fell. I saw myself flying.

One day I received an invitation to a Teaching Mission conference called SpiritFest, to be held at the El Chorro Conference Center near San Luis Obispo, California, through the weekend of June 18, 1994. The organizers, Jesse and Kristie Thompson, who didn't know me, had received a call from Jeremiah of the Woods Cross group, whom I had never spoken to. Jeremiah had an impromptu thought about inviting me to SpiritFest and thus informed the organizers.

I returned from the conference with bundles of transcripts plus my unique experiences, and these I shared with Jack and Gerry Baker who were members of the Bakersfield Urantia Book study group. After reading the transcripts Jack announced that he wanted to be a part of this mission and Gerry agreed. The question again was who would be the T/R—none of us felt qualified at the time. With Jack's and Gerry's patience I began our group's first attempts at T/R-ing with much tension and self-doubt. I had no impressions of teacher presence or thoughts. After painfully long silences I would give up waiting and begin speaking my own thoughts with the hope that the teachers would fit theirs in eventually. The "T/R-ing" was very brief but it was an invitation to the celestials to speak to us.

Jack, Gerry, and I finally met our group celestial teacher, Andrea, on July 30, 1994. Three members of JarEl's group, Lucille and Hal Kettell and Doug Daniels, the T/R, visited us to help with our first contact. I had met these people at the first SpiritFest. During the visit Lucille saw our teacher and described her to us. JarEl asked us to direct our thoughts to our teacher to receive her name. Gerry was the first to think of the name, Andrea.

Now at our group meetings Gerry joined me in practicing T/R-ing. We both had concerns about accuracy and anxiety. My biggest obstacle was trying too hard and believing that I wasn't good enough as a transmitter. However, it helped to remember JarEl's words on the day we "met" our teacher. We were told that the teachers learned valuable lessons from us as well. He said that the content of the message was less important than the effort to communicate.

About a month after meeting our teacher, Jack started receiving very strong sensations from our teacher, not only as thoughts but also feeling her presence. Soon he was transmitting her messages to Gerry and me. His experience was very different from ours. Jack went into a deep focused state and received messages with little to no hesitation and he was always very aware of the teacher's presence. Gerry and I began to withdraw our attempts at T/R-ing, but Andrea would not allow that. She announced through Jack that she wanted each of us to continue to receive messages and that she would refuse to use Jack unless we did. It became our routine that Gerry and I would go first and then Jack. I think that made our group very different than the norm.

Soon more teachers joined us. Gerry and I started to transmit our personal teachers. Then, Langford and Carlson began speaking, usually, through Jack, taking turns with Andrea. Gerry always transcribed our efforts and it was very affirming to notice how the quality of the transmissions improved over time.

In our early years together, a major personality conflict erupted between Gerry and me. Jack and the teachers were so distraught, that the group lessons through Jack were suspended. Personal teachers continued to speak but not group teachers. The celestials waited until Gerry and I decided that the group was more important than our differences. We were very humiliated by our behavior. It was several weeks before our group teachers began to conduct lessons again.

The group, especially Jack, had many unusual experiences with our celestial visitors. Jack saw some of the celestials at various times. Once he described two Life Carriers that were standing in front of Gerry and me, apparently making adjustments. I was amused by his description that the Life Carriers had beards. Another evening Gerry saw Andrea observing them at their dinner table. Andrea's hair was "styled" in a shoulder-length flip.

One of the most remarkable transmissions occurred when Langford told Jack to touch his robe. Gerry and I saw Jack feel the space beside him. Jack was then given a vision of a beautiful garden with morontia beings tending the plants. As Jack walked with Langford into the garden, the beings cheered him. When Jack's awareness returned to us it was very difficult for him to find adequate words to describe the beauty he saw.

The celestials eventually began to use Jack to help train new teachers because it was very easy to contact his mind. These new teachers were always overjoyed with their success in speaking through Jack. And, Jack was always very humbled by his experiences. His trust and devotion were flawless.

Our group also experienced a phenomenon called *reflectivation*, which incited a lot of controversy when shared with other Teaching Mission groups. We had been sensing activity around our heads and were told that adjustments were being made. The teachers explained that Jack was being prepared to be a reflectivator, and Gerry and I would be receivers. A reflectivator is like a transmitting tower on a mountain, relaying messages from the celestials to receivers at other locations.

In the early stages we were told that some messages through Jack were produced through reflectivation. Later Gerry and I were given code words that the celestials would use to verify that a message was being reflectivated to us. A lot of time passed before Gerry and I experienced our reflectivated messages and this only happened once for each of us. I was the first to experience it, and Gerry's followed about a year later.

One night at around 2 a.m. I awoke feeling peaceful and alert. Soon after, I began smelling something I couldn't identify at first. Then I realized that it was like caramelized sugar. At that moment I was surrounded by an intense vibration, like being in a cocoon of energy. I heard the code word and Langford began speaking to me. I could clearly hear the beautiful resonant quality of his masculine-sounding voice. Initially the volume was very loud as if someone was speaking through a microphone nearby. As soon as I thought this, the volume was lowered to a reasonable level.

At the time I could have accurately restated everything I was hearing, if it had been needed. But it was just a practice, so the message wasn't important and I forgot most of it soon after the experience was done. I vividly remember how excited Langford was about the success. He was cracking jokes. Before this experience I actually disliked Langford because of some chastising statements he made through Jack. But after hearing him speak directly to me, my attitude reversed completely. Interestingly, Jack was unaware of being utilized for both reflectivated messages.

Jack had many health problems. Gerry and I would do hands-on-healing treatments for him. The celestials also assisted to extend his life. However, his heart deteriorated until he was willing to accept the risk of surgery. Jack didn't survive the surgery and he graduated to the morontia life on February 16, 1999. Gerry did not want to continue the Teaching Mission group without Jack; contact with her personal teacher was sufficient. So Bakersfield has not had a group since that time. I eventually began transmitting for myself as a form of journaling after meditation and have my own personal collection of lessons. From time to time I have shared some of these with others.

The Bakersfield Teaching Mission group had many remarkable experiences. For Jack, this opportunity to serve our teachers gave him a purpose that he had been longing for all his life. He experienced the teachers on a level that exceeded the abilities of Gerry and me. Gerry and I remain very grateful to our teachers for the love and lessons they gave this little group, but especially for this once-in-a-life time experience they gave Jack.

Two months prior to writing this, I decided to communicate with my personal teacher, Themoia, just for the fun of talking together with no expectations of a profound lesson. I wrote to her and then she filled me in on what is happening in her life in a very personal way. She spoke of her gratitude for all that I've taught her and it brought me to tears, especially when she said that we are like sisters. I had never opened myself to this kind of heartfelt expression with her. Always we looked up to the teachers as their students, forgetting that they are also students as well as our friends. I want to share our heart-to-heart talk with you.

February 13, 2009:

Deborah: Hi Themoia. I wonder what new adventures you have been exploring. Our communications are few now, but I am filled with gratitude for all the gracious attention you gave me in our early years together. I still want to "practice" with you. Boy, was I full of anxiety in the beginning—not that I'm completely free of it yet. As you know I am sick again—I think my body is trying to tell me something. I would value greatly all guidance from you, my angels, my Beloved Spirit, and Divine Parents so I can find work that brings me joy and fulfillment. Please remember that I need an income too. Ha, Ha!

THEMOIA: *My friend, Deborah, I cherish this communion of hearts with you. I have been completing my training to be a teacher of new spirit teachers. Your world continues to receive these eager guides as more humans open to receive their blessing. I am still with you too. We are bonded for all time like sisters. You have helped me grow in ways that are immeasurable and beyond your awareness. I am so proud to contribute to your own spiritual development.*

When we at last meet on the morontia side, our celebration will be beyond words. Thank you for checking in and yes, your spiritual team will show you the path to take that brings you joy in sharing your good with others. Rest, my love, and be healed.

Here are some recent transmissions:

9/30/09 Mother Spirit

My dear one

We listen to your heart and respond to its need. Hearts in this beleaguered world are weary—weary from neglect, from bitterness, from grief, anger and jealousies. We can give you rest from the agonies of this life. Lay your head on my breast of love. I will comfort you and speak encouragements to believe in your own Divine power. As your Mother I want my children to stand strong and bravely face the darkness in their own minds. When you are willing to see the hidden, then I will shine my light to reveal the truth of your being. And, the truth will set you free.

3/08/10 Mother Spirit

Be free—free to trust with a young child's simple expectation that its needs will be met. The child doesn't worry about its next meal or where it will sleep. These things don't require concern until the moment of need.

Only when these needs are not met does the child discover the harsh lessons of this world. Over time judgments are made that the earthly caregivers don't care to give. Trust is weakened, not just of material parents but also of Divine Parents.

Yet in the beginning of childhood, before such things happened, the baby was used to being nurtured, that being its first experience within the womb. Needs were met. It trusted the constancy of the giver. Go back to that memory, my love. For, I am your womb.

Hawaiian Teaching Mission History
Sonny Schneider

The first time I heard that Urantia Book readers were hearing from celestial teachers was the summer of '92. I was living on a coffee plantation on the Big Island of Hawaii, in what I believe was and is the only Urantia Book community in the world. This consisted of fourteen families' who read *the Urantia Book* and a 155-acre leasehold coffee farm in Captain Cook which they had purchased as a group in the late 70's and split up among the families.

One of our community members, Martain, had just returned from a trip to Woods Cross Utah, where he was visiting with a group of UB readers. He told us a story about UB readers transmitting for some of the celestials described in *the Urantia Book*. Martain was told that we in Hawaii would be getting a Melchizedek named Norson to facilitate Teacher contact with our group and other groups in Hawaii and California.

Martain encouraged us to go into meditation with a pen and pad and write down whatever came into our heads and see what would happen. He was told the purpose of these contacts with celestial teachers was to help us get in touch with our personal Thought Adjusters.

He also brought with him the first forty lessons from a Teacher called Ham. After reading Ham's lessons and being intrigued by their spiritual richness, I decided to scan them into a computer and put them on floppy disks so I could share them more easily.

I neglected to take out the staples from the side of the sheets and ended up with a distorted copy of each lesson that then had to be fixed and proof read for accuracy. This took me the better part of a month and I ended up reading each of these lessons at least ten times, and through this
process of reading each lesson so many times, I started to see real spiritual genius in their content and composition. At the end of this editing process, I was a firm believer in Ham and his Teaching Mission.

It was around this time that one of the members of our U B community started to transmit through the Hot Pen method. A week later, her husband started to transmit too and soon we were having well attended T/R group sessions where one or the other of this couple would transmit out loud. It was an exciting time for us all and each of us went to work seeing if we too could transmit.

In just three days of the last week of 1992, five of our group started transmitting or hot penning.

By March of '93, our group had produced over 100,000 works in print. We had nine people in our group who could transmit at least a little and we felt close and confident that what we were doing was real and important.

Then a tenth member joined our T/R group. He was a member of our UB community who wanted to learn how to transmit. He did start to transmit some short and pleasant transmissions and for a few weeks all went well until he started seeing himself as the head transmitter of our group and capable of T/Ring for Christ Michael and Machiventa Melchizedek any time he wished to. It was obvious that he was unconsciously making things up.

For the first time for most of us, we were starting to entertain negative thoughts about the reality of this process and the Teaching Mission. From then on out, we never had more than five members of our TeaM community at a meeting again. Yet a valuable lesson had been learned. This process was not without some dangers. Time to take it seriously!

I was still convinced that the process and the Teachers were real, but I saw that our own minds could easily get in the way. I decided to take whatever truths I could find in the lessons and let the rest prove itself over time. I also took seriously the Teacher lesson to go into meditation
(Stillness) and make contact with my Thought Adjuster. The Teachers said this was the most important lesson of all.

Our numbers had diminished yet, even so, a few of us carried on with personal projects. David Saunders developed a strong connection with his personal Thought Adjuster and started transmitting directly from Him. These where the best transmissions I ever read, and that is saying a lot! David and his Adjuster were in the process of creating a book of these amazing transmissions when his computer crashed and most of the work was lost. Hopefully, David will be able to complete this project someday.

With the help of my computer savvy friend Dennis, I went to work on the 1995 TeaM calendar, each day having a different Teacher quote. And about this time we created the first issue of the Paradise Networker, an 18-page booklet containing Teacher transmissions from all over the country. There was information about upcoming events, humor, and editorials, but mostly my favorite transmissions. It was during the choosing of the name of our project that we came up with using TeaM, as a short cut for the Teaching Mission.

I put out a 1996 TeaM calendar, too, and continued creating the Paradise Networkers for another year. By 1997, the Teaching Mission was communicating freely on the Internet and I no longer felt the Networker was necessary.

Some of my Teaching Mission highlights:

1. 1993-IC in Montreal was also the first time the Teaching Mission had an International Conference.
2. 1994 TeaM Conference in Cheney, Washington, where 75 TeaMers gathered for their first official conference.
3. 1996-IC in Arizona where the Fellowship gave the Teaching Mission a great building in which to hold our meetings.
4. 1997 Team Conference in the Colorado Rocky Mountains.
5. 1999-IC in Vancouver, BC, a *great* all around TeaM and Urantia Conference.
6. 2002-IC, back in the Colorado Mountains. This time the Teaching Mission was given a small shack in which to hold our meetings but that just made them warmer when they were crowded with 50 or 60 people!
7. Yet the best of my TeaM memories are of all the fine folks I have met at the conferences and the people at the hundred or more T/R group meetings I have attended. I will always call these folks my dearest friends.

The Personal Teaching Mission
Mary Livingston

"Pay attention, Mary, because your life is about to change." Now, that is a message I would have liked to have been alerted to, but unfortunately I never received that message. So, although I know *The Urantia Book* found its way into my life in 1977, I didn't know it would be of any great importance. While such a message would have helped me with dates and times, I tend to resist change—something that may have skewed my entire experiences with *The Urantia Book* and later with the Teaching Mission if I had been made aware of the changes they would bring to my life.

Over the years I read bits and pieces of *The Urantia Book*, but my husband at the time taunted me by humming the theme song from the "Twilight Zone" which I found disconcerting. I decided to read *The Urantia Book* cover-to-cover in the late 80's. I read alone and I finished in the early 90's. I then wrote two secondary books, one for children and one for new readers, as I passionately wanted to share these teachings with my own children, ages six and eight, as well as with friends and anyone interested.

I had read alone, but once I contacted a Urantia Book study group, my intellectual/social world exploded. I lived in Boulder, Colorado, and that was probably one of the most exciting places to live for readers, especially readers with young children. Study groups typically have from three to ten people that meet in someone's home. The Boulder group was very big; so large that we had multiple groups in different rooms in a church hall that we rented. There was a children's group of about a dozen that had their own little program; a group that read the book cover-to-cover; another group that read just the Jesus Papers; and my favorite, which I often facilitated, called the "Experimental Group," which was topical study.

On one particular occasion, probably in about 1995, I went to the Experimental Group being facilitated by another. I asked what the topic would be and was told it was the "Teaching Mission." I asked what that was since I'd never heard of it. I asked, "What book do they read?" My initial impression was that I had an indwelling fragment of God inside me and why would I care about "celestial teachers" guiding me? That was exactly what opponents seemed to think and I easily drew the same conclusion.

But, as a Urantia Book reader, that was probably one of the dumbest ideas I ever had. It was as if a kindergarten student, secure with her teacher, announced that teacher's aides were not needed and volunteers were "stupid." According to the Urantia Papers, even the animal mind is ministered to by the spirits of intuition, understanding, courage, knowledge, and counsel, and the last two of the adjutant mind spirits—the spirit of worship and the spirit of wisdom. They minister to the human mind in preparation for the fragment of God that indwells free will mortals. And then of course there are angels, the Holy Spirit and the Spirit of Truth, unrevealed agencies and others that would require explanations not necessary to make my point.

One study group attendee seemed enthusiastic about the Teaching Mission so I asked him to facilitate the next available Experimental Group in three weeks, just to see it from the other side. I didn't know it was going to create a problem. What I believed or didn't believe wasn't the issue for me; an experimental topical study demanded fairness and different perspectives. Every person should have a voice if they could find Urantia Book (UB) passages to support their beliefs. Our first premise was that it must have a foundation within the UB teachings. Individuals could thread together teachings from the UB to other works like ACIM, or topics such as extra terrestrials, healing, scientific discoveries, other religious practices, relationships, and so forth.

I'd learned that those who received "messages" and transmitted those "messages" were called T/Rs, which stood for "transmit and receive." If memory serves me, someone called me and suggested I pass the word that there would be someone in town that would T/R at a woman's house after the Experimental Study Group on the Teaching Mission. This meant that if someone wanted to find out first hand what the Teaching Mission was about they could attend.

Naïve as could be, I pulled out my UB readers' phone directory and proceeded to leave messages about the "TeaM" or chatted when folks were at home during work hours. My job was working directly for a UB organization. After maybe ten calls, I got a call from one of the founders of the organization asking me if I was really calling during the organization's work hours to pass information about an activity they were absolutely opposed to. When I admitted I had been, I was told to get back to the work I was hired to do.

There was a huge stink! But, for the most part, I was oblivious to what was happening behind the scenes, partly because I contributed abundantly of my time and energies and no one would have dreamed that I had initiated this particular study group that was enormously controversial. I was shy, rather serious, and had an agenda that promoted everyone being loving and respectful of each other. My nick-name was "Mother Mary" but I functioned neurologically from my "left brain." Testing indicated I had only 8% access to my creative "right hemisphere" brain functions. I mention this because I have observed that those individuals we call logical, left-brainers are drawn to *The Urantia Book,* being able to more easily comprehend the complex text, whereas the more creative right-brainers tend to get much more from the Teaching Mission. But, I am getting ahead of my story.

Someone tried to prevent the Experimental Group, but finally it was "allowed." I was mostly curious. I grew up with a grandmother who was psychic, and who received "messages" from time-to-time. My attitude was that some people had a psychic ability or gift. *The Urantia Book* itself came by way of some undisclosed psychic phenomena, so I failed to see what the real problem might be. However, I would not be interested in anything involving a guru with a following or anything that would detract from *The Urantia Book.* The study group was "okay," but for me, the measure of the Teaching Mission's worth couldn't be determined except by attending a TeaM session. I was really looking forward to it with a certain excitement.

And, I was terribly disappointed. I do not know if my expectations were too high, if I thought there would be "messages" about the future, or personal messages that no one could possibly have known, or something unusual to set this group apart, but it was almost mundane. The T/R transmitted a celestial teacher but what was said could have been said by anyone. It was broad and impersonal, in my opinion. The Teaching Mission held no draw for me in 1995, but I would defend anyone's right to enjoy the TeaM without prejudice.

In 1997, a friend's fiancé named JoiLin moved to Boulder from Florida. I was originally from Florida and we became fast friends. As it turned out she was a T/R. Because I expressed no interest, she did not push it, not even gently. But, I had heard about the Teaching Mission for some time because the vast majority of my close friends participated and spoke freely about it at the potluck dinner I hosted each week.

My story is anything but straightforward. It is not one of: I listened, I loved it, and I learned from it. But, almost nothing in my life has ever unfolded so directly. Instead, I can look back and see how Spirit (or celestial personalities) maneuvered, sometimes manipulated, and often played on my current interests to help me stay the course. I wanted to take the high road but often lacked the wisdom to see my Path clearly. However, in my heart I had given permission for Spirit to get me where I needed to be; sometimes it was complicated. It has always been amazing to me. I appreciate the details, and when I realize all the things that had to be orchestrated in order for me to be in the right place at the right time and to be mentally and emotionally receptive, well, it makes me feel I must be a handful to the celestials that work with me.

I was not happily married. My husband and I adored our children but we didn't seem to care for each other; we were not very good friends. Study group each week, hosting weekly pot luck dinners, and helping to organize the monthly worship services filled the void for me. It was just before one of the dinners that I had a very stupid accident. I fell on the concrete garage floor and because of how I fell I should have shattered my kneecap. I vividly recall that my first thought was, "Thank you Father!" because somehow I knew I would be okay without any broken bones. But, the pain was severe.

It just so happened that a couple decided to attend the pot luck, and not being sure of the directions, they arrived about thirty minutes early. And, I found out that the wife was a nurse. She offered to do Reiki on my knee. I knew nothing about these folks and nothing about Reiki, but I said okay.

Linda never touched me but cupped her hands about an inch or two above my kneecap. I was wearing jeans and the heat from her hands felt good. It was so hot that it created a wet circle on my jeans. I noticed strange "movement" within the cartilage or bone of my kneecap, heat, and then the pain subsided. It was amazing and took about twenty minutes. Linda made me promise to have my doctor x-ray my knee, which I did, and it was fine. I had a small bruise about the size of a dime which told my doctor the impact of the fall should have shattered my knee. He advised me to keep doing whatever I was doing.

JoiLin knew Reiki and one thing led to another. We were already good friends but now we both became intensely interested in pursuing healing work together. For someone like me who thought energy was what came out of the wall socket, I had a whole lot to learn about healing. But, the door had been opened and I went right in to learn all that I could. With this added interest, I grew even closer to JoiLin. This friendship is what made me turn "to" JoiLin in frustration over my marriage.

In the fall of 1997, I went to JoiLin's house and asked her if she would T/R for me. This was a huge surprise to her but she didn't indicate that to me. I was too wrapped up in my own problems to notice her surprise. I didn't know how this "worked" but JoiLin just walked me through it. We sat in her living room. She suggested a few minutes of meditation, which to me meant I would sit for a few minutes with my eyes closed and not talk. (My mind was active as always and thus meditation, at the time, in its truer form, was not possible.) JoiLin said an opening prayer and a minute or so later she said, "Greetings Little Mary, it is I, Will, she who loves you. How may I help?" This was said in JoiLin's normal voice so I figured it must not be some sort of channeling, although JoiLin did keep her eyes closed. I will say, however, that phrases and expressions were spoken that I could not imagine JoiLin ever using.

I no longer recall what was said after the opening, nor whether we tape recorded the "session." I think I may have cried—something I rarely did. I do remember that it felt similar to a therapy session or counseling session. But, I did feel better and I felt that it was what I needed. Thus I began personal T/R sessions with JoiLin transmitting a celestial teacher named Will. I soon learned that Will was female and a group teacher in Florida that had worked with JoiLin for years. After I was comfortable with communicating with a celestial teacher in this way, on December 29, 1997, I asked if I had a personal teacher. Will told me of my personal teacher, A'Cilla, and mentioned that she was present. I was curious but I didn't think to ask if she wanted to talk to me. My initial questions were rather lame.

Later, JoiLin explained that a communication circuit had been established and that I could request to speak to a specific teacher. If available, the teacher would gladly "come on line" to communicate. The next session I requested my personal teacher, A'Cilla, even though I was very comfortable with Will. I felt a responsibility to "release" Will—after all, Will was a group teacher in Florida, I had a personal teacher, and I could participate in my local TeaM group sessions if I wanted.

Making the transition wasn't as easy as I thought it would be. A'Cilla was quite like Will and personally dedicated to me, but I started with Will and resisted change. A group teacher named A'Sandra met with the local students weekly. I went to some of those sessions (TeaM meetings). Unfortunately, I was so involved in my personal problems, the weekly group sessions didn't hold my interest very much. Apparently this did not escape my personal teachers' notice; they assured me that it was understandable given my current situation.

A'Cilla was my personal teacher and Ambrose was JoiLin's personal teacher. Ambrose communicated with me as well as other teachers. I always had an abundance of questions and our question-answer type session worked very well for us, especially with a teacher named AhmaNiden.

My background was accounting; I'd never learned to type. But, since JoiLin dedicated her time to transmitting, I thought it only fair that I transcribe the sessions we recorded. I was a perfectionist (as accountants usually are) and this trait, combined with valuing all details similarly (all numbers are of equal importance), made it a huge undertaking for me. But, it was part of a process that, I believe, had far-reaching goals from my teacher's perspective. I was learning to type, even if with only two fingers. I was beginning to recognize the subtle differences in the teacher's personalities and methods of teaching and communicating. But, most of all, I was beginning to formulate better questions.

JoiLin and I were given a lot of room to experiment. Teachers generally will not answer curiosity questions or questions designed to prove the existence of the Teaching Mission. Although JoiLin had been a T/R for many years she was not always fully convinced it was real. At one point I asked silent questions just so JoiLin couldn't shade the answers with her own thoughts. We started out simple—with questions seeking a yes or no answer. But suddenly she was transmitting answers that contained the questions. To me, there was no doubt that she was simply repeating aloud what she was hearing in her mind. Nevertheless doubts would surface from time to time.

After many computers and computer crashes, I no longer have most of the early transmissions. Fortunately, some of those transmissions made it to the TM Archives. Below is an example of how Will and A'Cilla each responded to my struggles between logical and emotional decision- making; or what I called my personal civil war—the battle between my "head and heart."

On December 20, 1997, I had a session with Will, and in part we discussed this topic:

Mary: It makes no sense to me why my heart scares me to death and I depend on my mind. Even though my reasoning can be muddled and confused and—it's not my head that scares me, it's the heart.

WILL: *That's understood. And yet it is in this direction that you will evolve toward. It is through the mindal arena into the heart, wherein the Father lives, that you attempt to develop. You're walking into territory that is less understood by you and so of course it engenders some level of fear. You are still, human that you are, closely connected to your animal beginnings. And, it is this that causes confusion, fear and distrust. Only through quelling these spirit poisons will you find yourself in a place of peace and open-hearted connection to the Father.*

Mary: I have a very hard time distinguishing between that gut, intuitive leading, that spirit prompting, and then I say it's wishful thinking. I have a very hard time knowing what is God's will and what is my will. My will, of course, I call "wishful thinking." Can you help me to distinguish between the two? I sabotage myself. Anytime it seems to be something I want then I can't believe it's the Father's will, it must just be my desires. So I don't trust myself.

WILL: *Trust begins to build, Mary, through repeated acceptance. Call it trial by error, if you will. You will begin to build, with small faltering steps at first, the trust level that you are indeed walking where and toward what the Father wishes for you. Because you are in essence emotionally distraught, you question everything that feels good, believing that everything that feels good must be directed by you.*

Recognize, Little One, that the Father wants the best for all of his children. He wants you to be whole, Little Mary, on every level. He wants you to know joy, peace and fulfillment all the while holding his hand. Yet again, the analytical mind interferes strongly in you. Your trust becomes your greatest issue, your greatest challenge. I cannot give that to you, I cannot give you a clear defined pathway for that is not the Father's desire for you or for any of his children. He wants for you and all of his children to have the faith that allows for the chaos; that allows for the confusion, and yet underlying all of it remains the trust that he will provide you with what you need.

On January 14,1998, I spoke to A'Cilla about my continuing concerns:

Mary: I've had this constant battle between my logical, analytical mind and my heart. The two of them battle constantly and that's why it's hard to make decisions. That's why I look for black and white, what it is the Father would have me do, because I don't know which to choose.

The Teaching Mission

A'CILLA: *If you remember always, Little One, that there are no real mistakes on this level of your development, for you are truly but a child and you are willing to stand on your own two feet. Those things that make it seem, by your culture and your society, even by yourself, as a mistake—these things are not seen by the Father as mistakes, simply given [tape unclear] opportunities—opportunities for you to grow and develop and mature. There is not a scenario within your life's possibilities, within which you would not face many challenges, many growth opportunities. If you can remember that, it may make your path easier.*

I'd love to claim that I have mastered my inner conflicts between my mental world and my emotional world but I believe this requires eons of time and experience. I do believe *and* feel that I have found relative peace for the most part. Still, in times of stress, I do find the old patterns and conflicts surface as I drift from my center, but far less frequently than in the early days and prior to working with the teachers.

Two seemingly different events were unfolding in my life. One, I was on a spiritual path working *with* the teachers *through* my Urantia concepts and understandings with JoiLin's help. And, two, I was on a healing path. While healing is spiritually based for me, I found myself initially learning techniques in workshops and schools that can be dry, routine, and impersonal. Healing work could be compartmentalized. My spirituality could not be compartmentalized and "pulled out" for review; rather, it permeated every aspect of my life. Although passionate about healing work, it didn't consciously encompass everything in my world—or so I thought.

I really loved the healing work but when I look back I realize that most of that work was about my own healing. In the spring and summer of 1998, there was a small group of about seven or eight of us (TeaM folks interested in healing work) spread out across the country, which began working with a celestial teacher who specialized in the healing arts. Her name is Marleena and for me she was incredible. Marleena gave us assignments and instructions which were concrete enough for me to really grasp. We were taught how to encircuit with one another and I used the same method when I later worked with clients to facilitate healing. We also worked on our childhood issues and how they might be manifesting in our present relationships. Building trust and striving for unconditional love were also part of the curriculum. All in all it was a complex group therapy experience grounded in our Urantia beliefs and healing interests.

I hope that others will share the basic Teaching Mission techniques because I am not drawn to explain the processes used for Stillness meditation (also called Father Time) or methods that support the T/R service. Besides, I feel it is somewhat unique to each individual. I have heard my teachers from time to time. I have on rare occasions heard my God fragment. God within does not use my voice, does not interject his thoughts into my thought streams, like my teachers do. There is no mistaking the difference between the two. However, I might confuse my teachers with angels that guide me or other celestials, and since I do not ask, I cannot be sure. I am content to accept the teachers' help. I feel secure that my Indwelling Spirit will again make contact when necessary. Primarily, the work of my God Fragment is done on the superconscious level while the teachers are able to work on the human conscious level quite nicely.

Meditation had always seemed impossible for me. If I relaxed I fell asleep. I did not know how to quiet my mind while remaining spiritually conscious and alert. When I closed my eyes there was nothing there, and I could not see with an inner eye. Fortunately, I crossed paths with a healer that had a (non-invasive) technique to integrate the left and right hemispheres of the brain's neurological pathways that get shut down and rerouted from stress and trauma. So, my 8% access to my creative functions of the brain, which included imagery, were reopened to 98% access or better. Ten years later, after much new stress, I believe my brain's pathways are not anywhere near optimal. Even so, this healing enabled me to benefit tremendously from Stillness, or Father Time meditation during the late '90s up until around 2002.

I am certain I have always been spiritually guided by the usual cast of personalities. I will say, however, that my spiritual growth intensified when I began to work with the teachers. The synchronicities increased or my awareness of them was heightened.

My desire for soul consciousness, something encouraged in *The Urantia Book*, was also more pronounced. My abilities to ask penetrating questions and to connect the dots, so to speak, were also developing rapidly.

And, above all, I was compartmentalizing my emotions less and able to find more balance between my analytical mind and my feelings, hopes and desires. God's will for me was also understood by me with greater clarity and assurance.

But, in all honesty, life became more challenging and more difficult on many levels. I had the tools to meet these demands, thanks to the teachers. Over the past ten or so years I have been able to rise above much of my fear, although I still had some periods of anxiety. I do not practice Stillness, which would help greatly in this area. This does not stop the teachers from assisting me. It merely stops my ability to ask follow-up questions and gain deeper insights.

Also, I should add that I do not receive and transmit verbally, as a rule. The teachers I am encircuited with do, however, inject their ideas into my thought patterns when I write. Writing has been my form of communication, my form of transmitting, without my perceived pressures of T/Ring. I do not seek a word-for-word transmission, but rather the spirit of their teachings. I welcome the insights that surface while writing.

Personally, I had a traumatic and dysfunctional childhood that tainted my interactions with others as well as my ability to trust myself to make good choices. Recently, through writing, the major relationship from my childhood was finally healed. That is not to say that it turned out well, because by most standards it did not. But, I was able to forgive that person, which is something I learned from my teachers—one of the many forms of love. Because, to me, the true essence of the Teaching Mission is the development of each person's ability to love —to assist each person to *be* their spiritual best. I am humbly grateful.

A Teaching Mission Romance/Love Story
Donna & Larry Whelan

From Donna Whelan:

My current husband, Larry Whelan, and I met at a Teaching Mission meeting at Lucille Kettell's home in the early part of the year 2000. I had been attending Teaching Mission meetings at the Kettell's since 1994 and had gone to various retreats at San Luis Obispo and even to conferences where the Teaching Mission was active and present. I had also helped with transcribing many of the sessions when Hal requested some assistance with this work. However, for Larry, this was all new.

He had come down to Arcadia from Ventura to investigate the Teaching Mission phenomenon, this being the only group in the area. He told everyone there that he just wanted to find out about the Teaching Mission. As he was a new attendee we all made him feel as welcome as we could. Our meetings were every two weeks at this time. On Larry's second visit he brought along copies of a book he had written and handed one out to everyone present. The name of the book was "Jesus, The Words of Jesus."

As time went on, Larry became a regular attendee and usually sat right next to me on the couch in Lucille's living room, thus we had a chance to talk and get to know each other a bit more.

Now, I was a single woman at this time, having finalized a divorce in 1986. I knew, after finding *The Urantia Book* in 1993, that if I was to ever have another life partner, he, too, would have to be on a very similar life path. I would have wanted him at least to be enthusiastic about *The Urantia Book*. So here comes Larry in the year 2000, right into the Kettell's living room in Arcadia where I had been hanging out nearly every Monday night since the spring of 1993. I had never met or seen him before.

I thought Larry was a very attractive, energetic and positive man. He was always smiling and full of kind and generous actions towards me and everyone I saw him with. I was impressed by the success he had achieved in his own personal life as a Battalion Chief in Ventura County's Fire Dept. (I had been previously married to a fireman) and his sincere and devoted interest in *The Urantia Book* and in his own spiritual growth. I could also tell he was open to exploring new things, i.e., the Teaching Mission. Here was the kind of man I had been looking for. But, alas, he was married. So I filed him away in my mind as 'very interesting but impossible'.

The Teaching Mission

That summer I and two other ladies drove across the country to the Teaching Mission Conference in Eufaula, Oklahoma. We had a happy and exciting time on our road trip, chatting and bonding as only females know how to do. We all looked forward to whatever new things we might learn or adventures we might have in Oklahoma.

We finally arrived and checked into our room at the hotel. We were happy to see other familiar faces of people we knew who were also arriving. It turned out that Larry Whelan and another man were occupying the very room next to ours at the hotel. Being at this conference together presented the opportunity for even more chatting, and Larry showed me some papers he was writing as well. When I looked them over I could see where he could use some proofreading or editing help on these papers. I told him I would be happy to help with that for free if he was interested. He said that would be great. On one of our private talks at Eufaula, Larry shared more information with me about his marriage. I could clearly see that there was a significant distance between the two in that relationship, yet his commitment remained firm.

Also in the evening at this conference there was a lounge where the hotel guests could sing karaoke and even dance. One of the lady friends who I had made the trip with was also a singer. We would go to this lounge every evening and she would pull me up to sing karaoke with her. Larry would ask us each to dance as well. We had a very fun and relaxing time.

Fast forward now for the rest of that year of 2000: Larry would continue to drive down from Ventura to attend not only the Teaching Mission whenever he could, but also began going with me (he would offer to drive) to another woman's UB study group in Covina.

Our feelings for each other were growing and it was clear that we always looked forward to seeing each other and spending some time together. Then, towards the end of the summer of that year, there was a Teaching Mission conference in Northern California at a Buddhist Retreat Center. We both attended that conference, separately, as well. Larry seemed upset at this conference that I was not being more overt in my signs of affection for him. I frankly told him that as much as I loved being around him and as much as I knew we had so much in common with our belief systems, etc., I was also acutely aware that he was married and I did not see how things could move forward with us as a couple.

Then there was a time that autumn when Larry declared his love for me. And (most surprising to me) he told his wife of his love for me. His wife was, understandably, very upset. Next he came to spend a weekend with me at my house. That weekend had its ups and downs. The upside (for me) was that he was now openly declaring his love for me and that he had also openly told his wife of his feelings. The down side was that after our first night together I could see how Larry was torn between loving me and hurting his wife. He felt the presence of love and guilt together and they were not mixing well. We had a long walk and a talk the next day. He said he felt he owed his wife another try, as this was such a quick and hurtful shock to her and he didn't feel it was fair to just leave without at least letting her know his feelings and giving their marriage another 'go.'

I listened sympathetically and gave him my best therapy advice (I was still working at this time as a Marriage and Family Therapist). I told him that I understood his dilemma and I also told him that I knew nothing could work between us until this issue of his current marriage was resolved, one way or another. I recommended that he go home and that both he and his wife seek counseling - individually - and also see a counselor *together* so that they could determine once and for all if they could save their marriage. Then . . . I let him go.

This was not particularly easy for me to do, but I also knew it was the only way anything good could come of this. Of course it was a risk, of course I knew that they might bring things back together and then there would be no 'us,' but to my way of thinking it was the only choice.

Now Larry will tell you a little bit, in his own words, about what happened for him.

From Larry Whelan:

In the fall of 1999 I attended the Fellowship's IC'99 in Vancouver, Canada. My wife was a Jehovah's Witness and considered *The Urantia Book* a book of the devil, so she stayed home in Ventura, California.

I had taken copies of my second book to have in the Conference Book Store, "Jesus, The Words of Jesus," the story of the life and teachings of Jesus consolidated and retold from the gospels of Matthew, Mark, Luke and John. While working in the Book Store I came across three books written by people who were members of the Teaching Mission. Not knowing anything about the Teaching Mission I talked to several people from the Teaching Mission and asked them what these books were about and what the Teaching Mission was all about. After hearing that the information in the books had been transmitted from Celestial Teachers and having been an avid reader of the Edgar Cayce and the Seth Material in my youth, and now being a reader of *The Urantia Book* for the past 25 years, I was not interested in reading these books. The names of the books were: "Correcting Time," "The Center Within," and "Fruits of the Spirit."

There were about 1200 people in attendance at IC-99 and we all had a great time. Unknown to me was a lady in attendance from Temple City, California, Donna Brown. We would not meet for another 4 months. However, we both attended the concert put on by Pato Banton and were on the same dance floor listening to his inspired music.

After returning home from Vancouver, I received a copy of the Light and Life Journal. It was their IC'99 Special Edition featuring: Urantia's Teaching Mission. As I read it from cover to cover, along with the many quotes from Celestial Teachers, their words rang a chord of truth in my heart and soul. One of the articles in it was written by Donna Brown, whose name I did not recognize. She was a member of the Arcadia Teaching Mission Group in Southern California. There was even a picture of the 21 members of the Arcadia Teaching Mission. Although I knew many of the people in the picture as Urantia Book readers – Hal

246

and Lucille Kettell, Duane and Lucile Faw, Stella Religa and Norman Ingram, Chick Montgomery and Saskia Raevouri – the others, including Donna Brown, I did not know.

Here follows the article by Donna Brown in the Light and Life Journal, IC'99 Special Edition featuring: Urantia's Teaching Mission:

Story of the Arcadia Teaching Mission

Once upon a time, in the beautiful foothills of the San Gabriel Valley in a little town called Arcadia, California, there lived a very kind and friendly couple named Hal and Lucille Kettell. Now Hal and Lucille's children were grown and Hal was retired and for some years (12) they had conducted a Monday night study group of *the Urantia Book* in their home. Hal, a retired dentist, had come across *the Urantia Book*, having been introduced to it by one of his patients in the early 1960's. (You can read his story in *How I Found The Urantia Book*).

This group had gone happily about their study group activities for quite some number of years when they heard of a new phenomenon which had begun to occur in another study group in California, the group of John and Jane Roper, in Dana Point. It was reported to them that celestial/unseen spiritual teachers were transmitting messages to the leader of that group. Hal and Lucille then decided they needed to investigate this phenomenon more seriously and see what they could see.

When Hal and Lucille attended that group and heard some of the messages for themselves, they decided it sounded true and they asked if their group could have a teacher also. They were told that there was a teacher available for any group who wanted one and all they had to do was ask and that the teacher would make him or herself known and they were to trust that one or more of the group would be able to 'hear' the teachers' messages and transmit them to the group.

Upon returning to Arcadia, at one of their meetings in July of 1993, a member of their group, a man named Douglas Daniels, began transmitting the teacher JarEl to the small group of listeners. At first Doug was startled and asked "Why do I feel physical sensation?" He was told:

> *"It is natural for some transmitters. More of their electrical processes are involved in transmitting and receiving. These processes involve the heart and respiratory systems so these things fluctuate, and being material they create physical sensation to a degree. Do not be dismayed or overly concerned."*

He seemed to feel quite overwhelmed and yet, at the same time, tremendously excited and enthusiastic about being able to perform this service. He deemed it an honor and a responsibility. He sometimes doubted his worthiness to be chosen for this task. The teacher assured him:

The Teaching Mission

"It is not our intention to startle you. You must remember we are spiritual beings, and our energies do affect mortals in many positive ways. So, fear not for your safety during these times of transmission."

Thus was the Teaching Mission launched in Arcadia, California.

This group continued for two years; the average attendance was 7 members, meeting once a week in the beginning. The transmitted lessons were captured on tape and Hal faithfully typed them out (sometimes with help from others) so that the group members could read them and reflect on them or have them available to study or ask questions from at the next meeting.

JarEl told us in an early lesson in 1993 that "All lessons in this Teaching Mission have been prepared by Machiventa Melchizedek." He further instructed: "As your group varies in individuality and its needs, we will give the appropriate lesson to assist you." He also informed us that the Teaching Mission had been inaugurated by Christ Michael and was a part of his overall plan for what was termed the Correcting Time on this planet. Teacher JarEl was always telling us of the Father's love for us as well as his personal love and affection for us as our teacher. He was consistent in teaching us very simple and solid lessons, i.e., fear is a spirit poison and the stillness is essential for our spiritual growth.

JarEl always welcomed questions and comments from the group at the end of his lessons and encouraged discussions among ourselves of the lessons and spiritual issues. He actually encouraged us to find answers for ourselves by our continuing stillness growth and by talking among and between ourselves. But he also said he was always there for our questions when needed. In addition, he told us that there were personal spiritual teachers for each of us individually and all we had to do was to want them and ask for them and be open to hearing from them. We needed, of course, to provide the time and the stillness where they could come through.

Towards the end of this first two years, JarEl began to prepare the group for his absence. He said he had been called away to attend to other activities that were essential to his own ascension process. He said he would be gone from our group for about a year's time.

So it was that on May 28, 1995 a final Teaching Mission group was held with Douglas still being the main Transmitter/Receiver. On this day we all heard a special message from Verona, a midwayer, as well as having the great honor and privilege of hearing from Machiventa himself. Verona said, in part:

"This is Verona, your midwayer. How can I relate to you my happiness, my joy at your achievements, your growth through the efforts of your illustrious teacher, JarEl? My dear hearts, you are each dear to me as I am the keeper of the light for this mission here. It is I who enables the presence of the teacher, and the attraction therewith of each of you. It is my service, it is my honor, it is my privilege that I am able to

perform such service for you. I thank you, as I thank our Creator for the opportunity to be of service to you."

"I am not sad that this is our last opportunity to converse with you, for I know of the greater goal in which we shall interact once again. I know of the greater goal in which we shall meet each of you in your ascension unto Paradise. I will greet each of you at some point in that ascension. Fear not, my words are true. You are indeed loved, and my love I leave with you. May it be a source of enlightenment and encouragement for you to continue in the absence of formal meetings. May you rely on the fact that we were here and touched your lives. You have spiritual enlightenment colored in love."

For this little group of believers, this was also to be our commencement, a graduation day, if you will. Machiventa said to us, in part:

> *"This would not be a commencement, in your words, without congratulations from one high in authority to bless this occasion of your transition, dear ones. From an unorganized loosely held group of believers who had only the commonality of faith and trust in the words that were revealed in the Urantia book, now you stand united, joined in the faith, having worked out your trials and experiences in this teaching mission, which was inaugurated by Christ Michael and administered by myself through the able aid of your teachers, as this illustrious one here present, JarEl, of whom I am well pleased, one in whom I have had great confidence since the inception of your group here in Arcadia.*
>
> *You, dear ones, are commended. You have stayed the course. You have fought the good fight, and you are proof indeed that with regularity and guidance, with coming together for the single purpose of experiencing that which you can achieve, that you can become more than what you were at the beginning."*

And then he said, most wondrous of all....

> *"Dear hearts, I will not tarry. I will leave you with these words, that this is not the end of your group. It is only the beginning. The transition that each of you will embark upon to carry out your future projects. To carry forth high the banner of the concentric circles that I have worn these many eons upon my breast. The emblem of Christ Michael, the culmination of all deity. You dear ones, you are now ordained. You are blessed together to carry His flag, not only to your fellow man here, but the world of Urantia, and to the Grand Master Universe. This is your purpose. This is your goal for eternity, to be the light bearers of truth. To proceed forth in front of your Creator Son. ....."*

Machiventa said a few more congratulatory and heartwarming words to us and sort of finished up by saying:

"...believe, as I commend you, and offer my thanks for your work in the past and for your efforts in the future. We want joy in your heart this day, for you have succeeded. Look about you. Your numbers are seven, are they not? You are complete. Proceed forth as completed graduated members of the teaching mission. I congratulate you; I love you. Christ Michael congratulates you, and loves you more. Peace, blessing, success to you dear hearts."

The seven core members of our group who were there that day, and ordained, were: Hal and Lucille Kettell, Douglas Daniels, Betty Bright, Stella Religa, Donna Brown and Joe Madera. It should be mentioned that during the whole two-year Teaching Mission time above-mentioned, Betty Bright, was also a faithful Transmitter/Receiver. She relieved Douglas of his transmitting duties when his work or personal commitments kept him away. It should also be mentioned here that there were other individuals who had attended some teaching mission sessions who were not there on this day. Henry Zeringue was one of these.

All of us; individually and collectively, were encouraged to begin to develop 'projects' of a spiritual nature with which we could feel comfortable. As a group project, the Arcadia Teaching Mission coordinated the Spirit Fest III gathering in June of 1996, which was at the El Chorro Conference Center in Los Osos, California (near San Luis Obispo). This was the third year that the Spirit Fest gathering of all the Teaching Mission groups in California had been held at that site.

Time passed quickly and some members of this original group began their own projects. Donna Brown began a bi-monthly study group in her own home in Temple City which lasted for a year. She also wrote more poems which she has shared at some of the UB conferences. Henry Zeringue began hearing more and more from his personal teachers and shared printed transcripts with us of all their teachings to him, as well as messages he believes were directly from his Adjuster. Of course, Stella Religa had maintained a study group in her own home during this entire time, which is current even today. And Hal and Lucille continued their weekly Monday night study groups consistently, with or without the Teaching Mission being active.

Then, in November of 1996, word was sent to the Bakersfield group that JarEl was back and would like to meet again with the group in Arcadia. By this time Henry Zeringue had developed his abilities as a Transmitter/Receiver and was able to receive JarEl's messages for the group. The group has continued from that time, on a monthly basis, Sunday afternoons, starting at 1:00 with a potluck lunch, followed by the message from JarEl in the living room of the Kettell's very lovely and hospitable home in Arcadia. Although Betty Bright moved to Ohio and Douglas Daniels now lives farther away in California, the Teaching Mission group has still grown to the point that two dining room tables are now needed in two different rooms to accommodate the people. Average attendance is from 17 - 22 members.

This author, Donna Brown, has been a regular attendee and can affirm that the food, the fellowship, the love, the camaraderie, to say nothing of the teaching from JarEl and the stimulating conversations and questions and answers are wonderful beyond compare. There is no place I would rather be on a Sunday afternoon.

And we are all living ... happily ever after. Come and visit us sometime. Love and God Bless.

More From Larry Whelan:

After reading the copy of the Light and Life Journal, I immediately called Paula Thompson at the Jesusonian Foundation and asked about the books on the Teaching Mission that she was selling at IC-99. She told me that they had them in stock and if I wanted to order them she would be glad to send them out in the mail. Of course I ordered all three of them and received them in the mail the following week.

After reading all three books, (*Fruits of the Spirit* from Teacher Tomas, *The Center Within* edited by Fred Harris and Byron Belitsos, and *Correcting Time* written by Fred Harris) I was convinced that the Celestials were communicating with different individuals. It was indicated in *Correcting Time* that there was a Celestial Teacher available for anyone who desired one. Learning about Stillness from Teacher Will in "The Center Within," I begin to practice the Stillness for ten minutes twice a day.

In our family room in our home we had two blue lazy-boy recliners, one for my wife Diana and one for me. Each day, twice a day, I would recline in my lazy-boy, taking several deep breaths, close my eyes and relax. I would first talk to God, praying prayers of gratitude, thanksgiving, forgiveness, healing and peace. I asked the Father and Michael to send me a Celestial Teacher if it was their Will to do so. And then I would go into the Stillness. "Be still and know that I AM GOD." Admittedly, many times my Stillness sessions would end in a short nap.

After many weeks of Stillness practice, it was on Thanksgiving Day 1999 that my wife and I were in our lazy-boys. As I reclined to a more restful position, I told my wife that I was going into the Stillness. At which Diana said Stillness was my excuse for taking a nap. To which I protested and told her that while it may end in a nap, I did my Stillness before I took a nap. After saying my prayers and asking God and Michael for a Celestial Teacher if it was their will, I went into a deep, relaxing Stillness. And on that day, November 25, 1999, at 9:00 pm, in my home in Ventura, California, I heard:

"I am Andrew; I will be your teacher. God LOVES you."

When I heard the words, "God LOVES you" I became a little angry; I didn't need a Celestial Teacher to tell me what I already knew. But wait a minute, did I just hear the words "I am Andrew, I will be your teacher. God LOVES you"? I wasn't sure, but if I did not hear the words, I felt the words throughout my whole being. I would not again hear from Andrew until May 14, 2000.

Duane Faw told me that he believed that the Teachers were celestials communicating with us. He gave me the telephone number of a person in Malibu who was involved with a Teaching Mission Group. I talked to a lady on the phone who said that they were not having Teaching Mission Meetings any more but that I would be welcome to come down for their Urantia Book Study Group. I went to her house. She and her husband were very friendly and we had a good time reading a paper from *The Urantia Book* and discussing it. However, neither of them would talk about their experiences with the Teaching Mission. The following week I went one more time to their Urantia Book Study Group, and this time I took a copy of my book, "Jesus - The Words of Jesus." We read and discussed another Paper, but they still would not discuss anything about the Teaching Mission.

I had been on the Internet reading many of the transmissions from the different teachers and loved most of what I was reading and the truths that I saw. I think it was at about this time that I got on TML (Teaching Mission List) where you could get different lessons from different Teachers and there was also a discussion group. It was on this list that Fred Harris invited people to come to Celestial Nights in Florida in February 2000. Having trouble finding any Teaching Missions Groups in Southern California, I signed up for Celestial Nights.

Then in December, after telling Saskia Raevouri of the problems that I was having in finding a Teaching Mission Group, she told me about the Arcadia Teaching Mission Group which met in the home of Hal and Lucille Kettell in Arcadia, California. Saskia gave me their phone number and said that I would be most welcome there. Arcadia is a city about 70 miles South of Ventura and about 11 miles East of downtown Los Angeles. I called and talked to Lucille Kettell who immediately invited me to their next meeting which would not be until after the Christmas Holidays, on the first Monday in January.

On the first Monday of January 2000, at about 7 pm, I parked my car at the curb in front of the Kettell's home in Arcadia, California. It had taken about 2 hours to drive the 70 miles from my home in Ventura. The Freeways were very crowded due to everyone commuting home from work. I was warmly welcomed by Lucille and Hal Kettell and introduced to everyone there, 10 people were present. I had met Lucille and Hal before when they came up to Ventura for Jesus' Birthday Celebration the previous August. Stella Religa and Norman Ingram were also there, whom I had known from other Southern California Urantia activities. There were many Urantia Book readers that I met for the first time, including Donna Brown who impressed me as being a very pretty and intelligent lady.

The first night, being shy, I sat in the corner by the entrance into the front room where the meeting was held. I was kind of nervous meeting new people and not knowing what to expect during the meeting and the transmitting/receiving from their teacher JarEl. Someone said an opening prayer and then we all went into the Stillness. After a few minutes JarEl, Arcadia's Celestial Teacher, began to speak through the transmitter/receiver, Henry

Zeringue. At the meeting I was not impressed one way or another. It was not until later when I read the transmission from TML that the truth spoke to me.

After the meeting and before going home, everyone came over to thank me for coming and gave me a hug, including Donna Brown. They invited me back for the next meeting in two weeks.

Two weeks later on January 17, 2000, I was again parking my car at the curve in front of the Kettell's home in Arcadia, California. When I went in I was greeted and hugged by everyone, including Donna Brown. I sat in the corner again and listened as JarEl gave his lesson and did questions and answers. Donna had asked a question which was so intelligent, and her voice was like music to my ears. I noticed that she sat on the couch where she had sat two weeks prior. I had brought copies of my second book, "Jesus - The Revelation of Jesus" and gave everyone a copy after the meeting. After signing each copy and hugging everyone, including Ms. Donna Brown, I left for home feeling very happy that I had discovered the Teaching Mission and made many new friends.

During my third meeting to hear JarEl, I got to the Kettell's home a little early and greeted everyone with a hug as they came in. Before Donna had a chance to sit down, instead of sitting in the corner as I had during the previous two meetings, I went over and sat on the couch next to the spot where Donna usually sat. Sure enough, when she came into the living room she sat down next to me in her usual spot. Over the next few months Donna and I became good friends. From that point on, that is where we both sat – and sit even to this day.

In February I flew to Florida for the second annual Celestial Nights Gathering. There were over 50 Teaching Mission, Urantia Book Readers and non-Urantia Book Readers in attendance. Fred Harris picked me up at the Airport in Panama City, Florida. Fred owned a summer home on the west coast of Florida on Cape San Blas. His beach house was in a colony of thirty to fifty homes on a west facing beach. Most of the houses were three stories high with 3 to 4 bedrooms and their own bathrooms. A lot of the homes were owned by people who lived in Tallahassee, about two to three hours inland. During the winter months these homes could be rented. Fred, along with the Tallahassee Urantia Book and Teaching Mission Study Group, organized the Celestial Nights Gathering for four days and four nights, including food, for only $200.00 per person.

The weather was perfect, in the 70's and 80's. The food was prepared by Judy Langston, a wonderful gourmet cook, with help from the Tallahassee Study Group. Judy owned her own restaurant in Tallahassee and she cooked many Southern dishes which I had never eaten before; the food was delicious. Celestial Nights was a wonderful experience, we hugged and shared stories of how we each found *The Urantia Book* and the Teaching Mission. We hugged and danced; we hugged and took walks on the beach; we hugged and sat around a bonfire on the beach; we hugged and ate southern food prepared lovingly by Judy Langston and her Tallahassee friends. About the only thing that didn't happen was a communication from our

Celestial Friends, which was the main reason I had come to Celestial Nights. However, I had a most wonderful time. I met and made many new life-time friends.

Back home in California I would travel from Ventura to Arcadia every two weeks to hear JarEl's teachings. And, of course, I would sit next to Donna Brown on the couch as we listened to the transmissions. In May of 2000, JarEl gave us a lesson on Transmitting/ Receiving. And so, on May 14, 2000, 4:12 PM at my home in Ventura I sat down at my computer and typed out a message from Andrew. This was my first communication from Andrew since Thanksgiving, 1999:

May 14, 2000, 4:12 PM
Ventura, California

I am Andrew, your teacher. I love you, as the Father loves you. So as the Father loves you, allow the Father's love to flow through you to your loved ones; your wife Diana, and your children Tim, Dan and Shari. Allow the Father's love to flow through you to all that you meet each and every day. As has been said before, love is the currency of the Universe. Be patient with your wife and give her lots of hugs and the reassurance of your love. Show patience and love towards your son Dan and allow the Father's love to shine on him. Love, love, love is the answer to the problems in relationships. Thank you for your effort this afternoon. Keep up your routine of the Stillness. God loves you. This is Andrew, until next time.

This was the beginning of my TR'ing with Andrew over the next 7 months. A few times I also received messages from Michael. I would eventually receive 102 pages of transmissions from my Teachers. Some of which I will include in this story but not all. I called my 102 pages: "Conversations with my Brother Andrew and Our Elder Brother Michael" by Laurence Whelan, Andrew, and Michael/Jesus.

At the end of June 2000 there was to be a National Teaching Mission Conference in Oklahoma. The day before leaving for the conference I received this transmission from Andrew:

Wednesday, June 21, 2000, 10:35 PM
Ventura, California

Larry: Good evening Andrew.

ANDREW: Good evening Larry. I am always happy when you contact me. I love to have our conversations. I love praying together. We are certainly blessed. I see you are ready for your trip. I will be in Oklahoma also. Larry, you shall enjoy your time together with your spiritual brothers and sisters from the Teaching Mission. It is of great joy when we can all get together in the Father's Love.

Larry: Yes, Andrew, I am looking forward to the Teaching Mission Conference. I will be on a panel and I will talk about self-publishing and printing on demand. Xlibris.com has a new service where they will publish your book for free. I believe that this will be good for the Teaching Mission to put many of the lessons in book form.

ANDREW: Yes, Larry, you are right. This would be of great benefit to the Teaching Mission. Just as you have shown so much interest in the lessons, there are a lot of truth- hungry souls who would like to read such books. Now with no cost, the Father surely has blessed us once again. What an opportunity you are presenting to Teaching Mission members. Have a good trip, Larry. I will be with you in this adventure.

Father, bless Larry and be with him on his trip.
Father, bless Larry as he takes your LOVE and gives it to his spiritual brothers and sisters.
Father, bless Larry as he gives his presentation at the Teaching Mission Conference with your LOVE in his heart and mind flowing out to those present to hear him talk.
Father, bless Larry for he loves you and all of his spiritual brothers and sisters, your sons and daughters of the Family of God.
Father, bless Larry your son and my brother.
The Father loves you, Larry.
I love you, Larry.
Amen.

The next day I flew to Oklahoma and met Bob Devine, his wife and daughter at the airport and we drove several hours to Eufaula, Oklahoma, the site of the Conference. Many people attending the conference I had met before at Celestial Nights in Florida the previous February. However, there were many new people to meet and enjoy as we got to know each other. After arriving at the Eufaula Conference Center and while registering, I met Chet Olson and we decided to share a room to save on the expense of the hotel. Chet had done the same thing in his search for truth, he had written a book about the life and teachings of Jesus, just as I had done. So, of course, we traded copies of our books with each other. After checking into our room I found out later that in the room next to ours were three ladies who had traveled from California together on a road trip. Their names were: Gerry Baker, Sue Allbritton and Donna Brown.

Since I had gained a few pounds more than I wanted to weigh, I decided to diet while I was at the conference. However, meal times were the best times to get to know people. So, I would still go to each meal and have a cup of coffee or a cold drink. Most of the time I would sit at a table with Donna Brown in the group, since by now we were friends.

Donna and I attended many of the same breakout sessions together. We usually ate our meals together (she'd eat and I'd drink something). In the evening, with her friend Sue, Donna and I would meet downstairs in the lounge for a cold drink and Donna and Sue would sometimes sing karaoke together. When Sue sang by herself I would ask Donna to dance and when others sang I would ask Sue to dance. At one point when Donna and I were sitting there enjoying Sue sing a song, I told Donna what a pretty and nice lady Sue was. Donna immediately told me that Sue was in a committed relationship.

One afternoon Donna and I took a walk outside. It was very warm and humid and cicada bugs there were making a loud noise. We walked down towards the lake, the ground slippery with bugs. I took Donna's hand so she would not slip and fall. During our walk I told Donna about my Teacher Andrew, from whom I had transmitted about 20 pages so far. Donna said she would like to read them. So later, as we sat at a picnic table, she read them. She could see many mistakes in the grammar and spelling of words and offered to edit my work. Of course, I accepted her offer of assistance. I had previously asked my wife, Diana, to proofread my transmissions, but being a Jehovah's Witness and considering *The Urantia Book* a book of the devil and the Teachers as evil demons, there was no way she would do it.

Back home in Ventura I continued to go to the Arcadia Teaching Mission Group and sometimes to the Arcadia Urantia Book Study Group. On Monday afternoons before the Arcadia Meetings, Donna was also attending a study group reading and studying "The Center Within," so I started to attend that group with Donna. It was during this time that my feelings for her started to grow.

Before self-publishing "Jesus, The Words of Jesus" I had paid a lady to edit my book for spelling and grammar, so I offered to pay Donna for editing my Andrew Transmissions but she refused to accept any money. I then offered to take her out to dinner between the meetings for "The Center Within" and the Arcadia Meeting, which she accepted. A few times I would stop and pick up flowers to give her to show her my appreciation for the help she was giving me.

Towards the end of summer there was going to be a Regional Teaching Mission Conference in Northern California at a Buddhist Retreat Center. I really wanted to go because I knew that Donna would be in attendance. However, Diana and I were making a motor-home trip through California to Oregon to visit friends and relatives. I wanted to stop at the Buddhist Retreat Center on the way home to attend the Conference and I asked Diana to go with me. She elected to stay with friends above Sacramento to help with their daughter's wedding preparations. I went to the Conference by myself and returned to the wedding at the end of the week.

It was at this conference that I realized the depth of my love and feelings toward Donna. During the conference Donna and I sat under the starlit sky and discussed our situation. With me being married there was no way that our relationship could continue. When I left the Buddhist Retreat Center to return to the wedding, I was heartbroken, thinking this was probably the last time I was going to see Donna. As I drove I also cried for a good hour or so.

After returning home, I received an e-mail from Donna telling about some work she had just had done on her patio and suggested that I come down and see this new design in the middle of her patio of the three concentric circles. This was in August of 2000. So we continued going to "The Center Within" Study Group, dinner, and the Arcadia Urantia Book or Arcadia Teaching Mission Study Groups. Each time I saw Donna, my love for her grew. It was in the middle of August when my wife Diana asked me if I had a girlfriend, which I denied. At that moment, I now see that my marriage had become one big lie which lasted until March 9th of 2001.

In reality I was like an ostrich with my head in the sand about my marriage to Diana and the developing situation with Donna. Donna, being a Marriage and Family Counselor, could see the dilemma that I was in and suggested that I get some professional help and seek counseling. My employer Ventura County offered counseling sessions, so in September of 2000 I started seeing a counselor. Of course, we talked about my ostrich-type behavior in regards to my marriage to Diana and the situation with Donna, but we also talked about my transmitting/receiving with Andrew.

After a few sessions with the Counselor I told my wife about the other woman and Diana asked me to move out. For the next two weeks I lived with my daughter. I also went to see Donna and we had a long talk about our love for each other and my guilty feeling in treating Diana so poorly after 38 years of marriage. Donna suggested that because of my feeling so guilty, I should go home and see if I could salvage my marriage. During the two weeks apart, Diana saw a lawyer about getting a divorce. After two weeks with encouragement from our children and counseling from two of the Jehovah's Witness Brothers, I moved back home. We agreed that Diana needed to see a counselor by herself and that we would both go to a Marriage and Family Counselor together. I agreed not to go to the Arcadia Study Groups. During the fall and winter months I went into a deep depression, having a broken heart, because I could not see Donna anymore.

During this period my daughter broke her leg and had to move back home while she healed. One day I took her dog for a run and a pit bull attacked and killed it during our run - which saved me from any injury. On another day I was working an extra shift at the Fire Department and as I drove home I became very short of breath with a sharp pain in my chest. It went away, but after telling my wife and daughter about what had happened, they both insisted that I go to the hospital and have it checked out. After staying overnight in the hospital and having several tests done, it was determined that there was no problem with my heart and that this was probably due to stress. Of course, I knew immediately that it was due to the stress of my deep depression and my ostrich head stuck in the sand about my failing marriage and not being able to communicate with Donna.

During the winter months I saw Donna at the L.A. Urantia Readers Meeting every two months. And we worked the Urantia Booth together at the Whole Life Expo. Donna and I both attended Celestial Nights in Florida in February of 2001.

Then it happened. In the first week of March my wife Diana asked me if I had e-mailed Donna. And not wanting to continue the lie which had become my life, I said yes. To which Diana replied, "Get out. I never want to see you again." So on March 9, 2001, I moved out of my home and on the following Monday I received the divorce papers.

Donna and I lived together for a year until the divorce was complete. On February 14th 2002, Valentine's Day, we were married at Celestial Night's with 50 of our Urantia and

Teaching Mission friends in a circle around us on the beach in Florida at sunset. And then again on March 9th we were married in Arcadia in Lucille Kettell's backyard with Urantia and Teaching Mission friends and family members in a circle around us.

After seven years of being married to Donna, I can say that these have been some of the most joyous years of my life. I am so thankful that Diana set me free. If it was not for her courage, we would probably both still be in a marriage where we had grown apart. I will always be thankful for thirty-five good years of marriage. We had three wonderful children together and we have been blessed with four wonderful grandsons. I retired a month later after the separation. It took a year for the divorce to be completed. We split all of our assets. Diana got the house and 50% of my retirement and I agreed to pay for her medical insurance for five years until she qualified for Medicare at age 65.

In marrying Donna I gained another son and daughter and two granddaughters and a grandson. Donna and I have had a wonderful 8 years together. We have attended Urantia and Teaching Mission Conferences. We have traveled, taken up square dancing and joined the Unity Church, where we both teach Sunday School once a month. We also conduct a Urantia Book Study Group each Sunday afternoon at the church.

This Saturday and Sunday Donna and I will head up *The Urantia Book* booth at the Body, Mind & Spirit Expo in Pasadena. We hand out Spiritual Vitamins, which are little rolled up scrolls with quotes on them from *The Urantia Book*. After a person reads it we tell them that the quote is from *The Urantia Book* and tell them a little something about it. We also give them a copy of the table of contents with the Web sites: www.UrantiaBook.org and www.TruthBook.com and tell them that it is in most libraries, can be purchased in most bookstores or read, listened to or downloaded free.

After reading *The Hidden Messages in Water* by Masaru Emoto we came up with the idea of Blessed Living Waters. Each label has the following prayer on the inside of it:

Father bless this water with your love, light, energy, truth, beauty and goodness.
This living water shall become in me a well of refreshment springing up to eternal life.
I am so grateful and love you Father for all the blessings you have bestowed upon me.
Out of me shall flow rivers of living waters. Thank you for the many blessings given me.
Help me to be a good steward of these gifts. I love you Father. Your will be done, amen.

On the outside of the label it reads:
BLESSED LIVING WATERS
A quote from *The Urantia Book*: "God is the source of truth." *The Urantia Book*, Page 23 (1:2.1)

And:

God is LOVE.
God created you in LOVE.

God LOVES you.
Be the LOVE that you are.
Live in our Father's LOVE.
Discover
"*The Urantia Book*"
Read the Revelation!
www.UrantiaBook.org

We still attend Urantia Book and Teaching Mission Meetings at Lucille Kettell's home each Monday. We have gained many new friends through all of these activities. I have joined the Pasadena Crown City Men's Chorus, which has 47 men. We have a cat named Chesley and live in the nice home where Donna raised her children. Our love continues to grow for each other, day by day.

Our Experiences in the Teaching Mission
The Painter Brothers

From David Painter:

Early in 1992 I was introduced to the Teaching Mission by a friend. I was given lessons from two teachers, Will and Ham. The lessons were beautiful and I sensed something very real about the delivery method. Having been a reader of the UB since 1972, I was open to alternative sources of information.

As the group in Indianapolis continued to read and discuss the lessons from these two teachers, we decided to request a Teacher to deliver lessons to our group. One of our members asked another Teaching Mission group if that would be possible. The answer was simple, "Yes, you can." Once we received the answer, we began to discuss who would be the T/R. Everyone seemed hesitant at first. And since no one really took the initiative, I volunteered. My attitude was to challenge the reality of the Teachers (same as I did with *the Urantia Book* when I first started reading). My goal was to remain as objective as I could.

Soon after I agreed to be the T/R, we were advised that the name of our teacher was Welmek. I was given instructions to go into Stillness, listen, be patient, and once contact was made, follow his directions. Three weeks after attempting to make contact, nothing happened. I was beginning to think nothing would. Then one morning, at 6:00, I sat straight up in bed from a dead sleep, wide awake. I had this strong urge to get into Stillness and wait. Thinking this was my own desire to have a Teacher for our group, I promptly disregarded the inclination and went back to sleep thinking that nothing was to come of this mission for Indy.

The next morning, promptly at 6:00, the same thing happened. This time I said OK, let's get this on. I wasn't sure if this is what it claimed to be but I was tired of wondering! I got out of bed, went downstairs, started my Stillness session and waited. And I waited and waited until I thought nothing was going to happen. As I was about to end my Stillness, I "heard a voice" inside my head saying, "This is Welmek, your teacher and your friend".

At first I denied this "voice" thinking it was my own wishful thought. As I sat in meditation, I began to feel something, a warm and calming sensation. I heard the "voice" again. This time I started to ask questions, still unclear if this was my own thoughts or the 'real thing'. I was asked to have the members of our group submit written questions about which I was not to know the content. Once the questions were ready, I was to get into my Stillness, have a question read, and allow Welmek to provide the answer while the entire process was being tape recorded.

The questions came in and it was time to start the process. I was very nervous but still willing, unsure of what was about to happen. I started having thoughts of men in white jackets coming to the door. Suddenly, my left leg started to shake involuntarily. At this point I'm really getting thoughts of why did I volunteer for this assignment. But I remembered my instructions and became quiet again. The next thing I remember, Machiventa introduced himself. From that point on, there was no break in the conversation.

Each question was asked and answered. Although I was awake, I knew I had to keep my mind quiet. I remember talking but could not remember much of what was discussed. After the session I listened to the answers. I then called a couple of the members and shared the answer to their questions. They were quite impressed.

The next message I received was a few days later asking that I get the Indy group together so Welmek could be introduced. I did what I was asked to do. Finally it was time to start the meeting. Sitting in front of the group made me a nervous wreck. All the fears and doubts came to the surface of my mind. But I remembered what I was told earlier that day: "I'll do the talking; you be still of mind".

The meeting went very well. Everyone seemed to enjoy the entire process. Each person received something important, some special idea or encouragement. From this point on, the meetings grew in attendance. At times there were as many as 45 people gathered in my house. If you would have told me just a year before that I would be doing this, I would have told you "You're crazy." But there I was. These meetings have continued, on and off, since then. It's interesting to me how most people would come to a meeting, take what they needed, and never come back. It reminds me in a way of the so-called miracles Jesus performed. Once the crowd had their fill of wine and food, off they went, content for the moment, not really reflective of what just happened.

During the years of my T/R experience, what I have enjoyed the most were the private sessions between the teacher and the student. From the first private session to now, I have done over 100 private meetings. The questions asked and the lessons shared are truly remarkable. So much comfort and thanksgiving has been realized by many.

There are many who have become T/Rs. Most, I believe, truly feel they are part of something beyond mystical representations. I must admit that some of the lessons I have read or heard about seem more reflective of human desire than teacher inspired. If someone were to ask me today if I thought this is a human mind function versus teacher personality expression, I would answer this way:

I could argue both points of view. What matters the most is not the method of delivery, but the MESSAGE.

From Michael A. Painter:

It was the summer of 1992 when my brother David called me to tell me he believed he had been contacted by a Teacher. I had heard of the alleged messages from non-human sources coming to humans in New Zealand and Utah, but I hadn't paid much attention because my previous experience with similar transmissions had not been positive. They had been associated with "end of the world" scenarios, chosen people delusions, or mentally unstable people. However, it was my brother! I knew him well; we had shared much of our spiritual journey, and I considered him quite normal.

Within a couple of days, I was sitting in his house, and he said the "teacher" wanted us to ask questions. So I and the few others present did. What I observed was that the personality coming through my brother was different from my brother's as well as the manner of speaking. The responses were clear, reasonable, and friendly if not loving. Still doubtful after a few sessions, I was asked by the teacher through David if I would consent to a private session. What have I got to lose? In the course of that session, I gave the teacher my permission to "scan my mind". The teacher went on to address some very personal issues I had been struggling with, ones I had not shared with David. Needless to say I was impressed.

A couple of weeks later, I was sitting at a picnic table having lunch in a downtown park near where I was working. A voice came clearly into my mind. The voice asked me if I would consider being a transmitter for a teacher. The tone was very gentle, and there was no coercion of any kind. I was told there would be no consequences of any kind if I refused and that I should simply look at it as a way of being of service to others. After asking me to consider it for awhile, the voice left. Wow! Actually, I didn't think it was crazy because I'd had a previous occurrence in Viet Nam when I heard a clear and distinct voice tell me to avoid a certain situation. Had I not followed that voice's instruction, I wouldn't be writing this now.

Thus, David and I both became transmitters. At first the curious came and there were as many as 30 people at our meetings. However, when it became clear these teachers were more interested in helping us with our spiritual progress than answering questions about UFOs and other paranormal activities, the size of the crowd dwindled. Our Indianapolis group was assigned a specific teacher by the name of "Welmek". Welmek was gentle but direct. He claimed he was a former mortal from a more advanced planet. He and other teachers had volunteered to come to this planet to help raise the spiritual consciousness. He said there were four practices that would help us grow spiritually and that he would give us instruction and mentor us as we struggled to incorporate these practices into our lives.

The first and most important was "Stillness." This was his term as well as the other teachers' term. Stillness practice seemed to me to be the dominant and most consistent theme of the "teacher mission." It essentially meant we needed to spend time in personal communion with God each day. From this we would come to actually experience and feel the love of God versus intellectually assenting to it.

Moreover, building this personal relationship with God would enhance our lives in many ways. He claimed this practice was a part of the daily routine of all universe ascenders. The other three elements of his teaching were to learn to pray more effectively, to look for opportunities for service in our daily life, and to learn to see the presence of God in others.

The meetings continued on a weekly basis most of the time. A few others in the group also became transmitters. Sometimes I would travel to Bloomington or Cincinnati and transmit for their groups. Over the years there have been conferences where I transmitted, and I did private sessions occasionally.

At first the message came as if someone were typing words across a blank mental screen and I simply tried to read them accurately. Over time, the process became more fluid and I simply began to speak the words coming into my mind. At first I had little to no remembrance of what was said, but over the years I began to be more conscious of the messages.

There were always doubts about the reality of what I experienced, but for me the "proof" was how these teachings were changing the lives of those who participated for the better. They were becoming more loving, patient, less prone to anger, and more forgiving.

A sort of crisis came when several transmitters claimed that a Melchizedek would materialize at an upcoming conference in Naperville, Illinois. The materialization didn't happen and some people terminated their association with the teacher mission. I decided I would take a six-month hiatus and see if there would be any desire left after that.

Finding myself still drawn to the profound spiritual message of the teachers, I began transmitting again with the agreement with Welmek that there would only be spiritual material. I didn't want the responsibility of leading people down a false path regarding earthly decisions. Still today I tune out whenever "end of the world" predictions, magisterial missions, stock investment advice or any other message about the material world is transmitted. "What does any of that have to do with our spiritual growth?" I ask, and the answer is always "Nothing." I haven't transmitted for several years, and I leave the question of whether I will again as open-ended.

As I reflect upon my experiences over the years and having detached myself from it for several years, I still find myself with mostly positive attitudes toward the teacher mission. There are many transmissions I have listened to over the years that I do not believe are genuinely coming from the teachers, but there are also many messages that I do believe are genuine. I see the issue as being similar to belief in a sacred book, the Bible, *the Urantia Book*, etc. There is no "proof" that any are genuine and we won't empirically know until after physical death. Yet, there is this overwhelming sense within me that spiritual reality does exist and that I can trust this inner spiritual guidance to help me discern what is true.

I cannot say if Welmek is real, though I believe he is, but I can say some of his messages ring true to me in the deepest part of my soul. Whatever the reality of the teacher mission turns out to be, I am thankful I was allowed to be part of it.

Experiences in the Indianapolis Group
Linda Buselli

It took the teachers several attempts to get the Indianapolis study group interested in asking for a teacher. As Area Urantia Book Coordinators for Indiana, Bob and I had received a letter from a New Zealand group in 1989, but had filed it away as 'flaky.' Then we were contacted by a member of the Fellowship General Council early in 1992. This individual had witnessed Machiventa's address to the Council in Los Angeles, but hadn't taken any new truth from it.

In February of 1992, Bill Bryan's brother, Chuck, who was a member of our study group, started bringing us the tapes Bill was sending him. By April, we were fascinated enough to ask for our own teacher, particularly as we discovered the Fellowship did not seem interested in further investigation of the phenomenon.

Within a week the group in Woods Cross, Utah, told us our teacher's name was Welmek, and we later found out that he had been assigned to Indianapolis since January, which indicated, shall we say, a determination on the part of the teachers.

We asked the entire group to meditate, but didn't reveal the name of te teacher until a woman in the group kept getting "Wilma, Wilma" when she meditated on the subject. We thought that was close enough, and then revealed Welmek's name. David Painter came on line in July, and we officially began our group teacher meetings the first week of August.

Meanwhile, we had been receiving the Ham and Will transcripts and passing them around in our group. Everyone had become so enthusiastic that we had around three dozen attendees right away. Mike Painter and I began transmitting shortly thereafter, followed by several others, and we were moving right along.

We never mentioned the TM meetings in our regular study group. Some of the people in the group were antagonistic to the mission, and it was thought best to separate the two meetings completely.

As part of the mission we occasionally held 'healing' meetings following a short transmission from the teachers. On one memorable occasion, a visiting teacher answered questions on healing for over an hour.

Meetings ran about two hours each week, and I typed the transcripts (approximately 27 pages each time) and mailed them to anyone who asked. Ron Besser was kind enough to prepare an index of topics of the various sessions for us.

Following Machiventa's non-appearance in Naperville in April of 1993, we lost three-quarters of our attendees, and the ones who stayed were original members of *the Urantia Book* study group. We continued to meet fairly regularly with different TRs, but eventually we stopped the meetings for varying lengths of time until people showed an interest again. In recent years, we've begun taking recess periods of several months between a series of regular sessions.

In defense of the Teaching Mission, I wrote the following letter to a critic in which I shared my opinions on the phenomenon.

"I want to thank you for your reply to my letter. I can certainly understand your concerns regarding this form of communication, and I agree that there are dangers associated with it. However, I don't know of any problems with members of the teaching mission that are not common to Urantia Book readers as a whole. They seem no more and no less stable psychologically.

"For myself, I have Bob to act as my canary in the coal mine. Apparently after 13 years with the mission I am no more peculiar than I ever was. (He is not in the teaching mission.) Let me say now, that everything in this missive is my own personal opinion. I can't possibly speak for anyone else, only about what I have observed.

"I totally agree with your statement regarding your growing beliefs about the locus of spirituality being in the domain of interpersonal relationships. Not long ago I asked the members of our group what it is about the teaching mission that is the most important to them. The answers were all the same. It's the personal relationship with the teacher that matters most.

"This is something the Urantia movement lacks. We can love the book, but a book doesn't love us back. And there is a feeling of love and caring that comes forth in these sessions. Whether that arises in an actual relationship with a celestial being or in the personality of the T/R, I can't say. I do know that mission members know that not every transmission is 'real', that is, one hundred percent the teacher. We poke fun at ourselves over this all the time.

"But something happens that inspires the participants, and that is what matters. The teaching mission made *the Urantia Book* go from black-and-white to color for me. The information wasn't new, but putting it into the experiential context of personal relationships increased insight.

"Your assertion that the 'process of receiving messages and sharing them with a community of believers lays the foundation for a religious hierarchy and a priesthood' is historically valid, which makes it especially significant to me that the Teaching Mission has never created a real organization. It remains wide open to all comers, and there is no indication thus far that any hierarchy or priesthood is even being considered. A few individuals organize the conferences, but they are not given any special status that I know about. All comers are invited to learn to T/R for themselves, and I think that is much healthier.

"Your concern for the moral issues involved in T/Ring is important. I would like to stress that the T/Rs I know are quite concerned about these very questions. I have known several who have 'retired' because they made an error in a transmission. The teachers made it clear from the beginning that this is not a perfect process. The T/R is aware of what is being said and has the control to halt the transmission if they desire. The teacher does not 'take over' the personality. The personality cooperates knowingly and has the ultimate control of the transmission.

"I do have some comments about your statements regarding prayer and meditation. I don't see them as a shutting down of the operation of the adjutants, but rather as a relaxation of the conscious mind. I once inquired of a teacher the reason for taking time to do this and he replied that the Adjuster acts instantaneously, but it is the mortal that needs the time to let this contact work its way from the superconscious into the conscious mind. As I recall he said, 'The Father doesn't need the time, you do!'

"There are many different definitions of the word "meditation" currently in use which cause confusion, but *The Urantia Book* says on page 1777 [160:3.1] 'Meditation makes the contact of mind with spirit; relaxation determines the capacity for spiritual receptivity.'

"I think this is what the mission is teaching, although it is often misinterpreted by those for whom 'meditation' has another definition.

"In regard to your comments on the ego, I was told not to lose my ego but to 'enfold your ego in Michael's purpose.' I think the confusion arises because the Buddhist ideas of losing the identity in nirvana have become part of the mindset of many people, including some Urantia Book devotees. Course in Miracles fans are especially entranced with this idea.

I've had to make it clear in study groups many times, that that concept is not in accord with the Urantia teachings, that we retain our identity in eternity. As far as I know, the teachers emphasize this, not the loss of ego or the identity. A woman recently told me 'One is a quality as well as a quantity.' and I intend to use that concept when this subject comes up in future.

"I am still curious as to what you mean when you indicate that the mission's cosmology does not agree with the cosmology of *The Urantia Book*. I don't know of any mission statement regarding cosmology, and I would like to know the reference you're using so that I can read it. If you are referring to the Magisterial Mission, I found this reference on page 642 [56:7.5]

'Each new evolutionary attainment within a sector of creation, as well as every new invasion of space by divinity manifestations, is attended by simultaneous expansions of Deity functional-revelation within the then existing and previously organized units of all creation. This new invasion of the administrative work of the universes and their component units may not always appear to be executed exactly in accordance with the technique herewith outlined because <u>it is the practice to send forth advance groups of administrators to prepare the way for the subsequent and successive eras of new administrative overcontrol</u>. Even God the Ultimate foreshadows his transcendental overcontrol of the universes during the later stages of a local universe settled in light and life.' (My emphasis underlined.)*

"This statement puts the idea of "advance groups of administrators" into the realm of possibilities for Urantia, and doesn't seem to preclude personal contact with mortals. I hesitate to circumscribe the activities of celestial administrators or limit their possibilities, or probabilities, for that matter.

"In addition, I have thought for some time that revelation in the form of a book is not ideal. Since this is an unusual approach, I gather that some other means of revelation is usually preferred. Is it possible that mind-to-mind contact is more common in universe missions? Even if it isn't, an unusual method has already been used here once, and may be again.

"I understand that for you as an intellectual, and one who has had a bad experience with "channeling," the teaching mission presents problems; and I respect that. I think that the mission members are not anti-intellectual; but they enjoy a more emotionally satisfying approach. The book reminds us that *"..you cannot imprison truth in formulas, codes, creeds, or intellectual patterns of human conduct."* [180:5.2] (P. 1949) and:

'Jesus taught the appeal to the emotions as the technique of arresting and focusing the intellectual attention. He designated the mind thus aroused and quickened as the gateway to the soul, where there resides that spiritual nature of man which must recognize truth and respond to the spiritual appeal of the gospel in order to afford the permanent results of true character transformation.' [152:6.4] (P. 1705)

"In short, we all seek the method of spiritual growth that best suits us. Some years ago, a man in our group asked the teacher why they allowed TV evangelists to operate as they do, taking people's money for so-called religious activities, etc.

"I remember the teacher saying something about no one, including them, being able to judge what would open someone's mind and heart to the presence of God, or something like that. But his final statement burned itself into my brain. He said quite crisply 'I am not asking you to accept the cause, but to respect the effect!' I've tried never to forget to discern the value of the effect regardless of the cause.

Namaste Now!
Manu Puri

Imagine a fine, misty and unending drizzle; a refreshing drizzle that blankets the entire blue planet. This soft rain falls on everyone and everything, gently soaking everything it touches. Now imagine the golden morning Sun as it makes its way higher into the sky, surely and certainly bathing all in its path with the goodness that only light and warmth can bring. The fine drizzle and the golden warming Sun only begin to represent the all-encompassing love, the love of God the Father, that's always present, which surrounds us and soaks us, if we only let it. This love of God and his constant guidance can become a reality for you just like it has slowly become an essential reality for me. Allow me to share this journey with you! Even though this journey began with my birth and ran many courses leading to the present, I share with you the transforming recent years; ones during which I made experientially real, a lot of my bookish spiritual knowledge.

It was a dark, dreary and wet day in January 2002. Our family of four had been in the great Pacific Northwest less than 2 years and 9/11 was still weighing heavily on everyone's mind. On this particular day I felt a certain dread and lack of meaning in my life. I started praying for guidance from the Father. A decade prior to that, I had prayed a similar prayer, one in which I had asked sincerely that the 'truth' be revealed to me. That prayer soon enough led me to *the Urantia Book* [1], but it's only fair to say that God had been active in my life for many years prior to that.

For instance, when I went for my Basic Training with the US Army in 1985, I felt particularly lonely. I asked God for comfort. On my first day at the US Army barracks I found a book in the trash not far from my bunk bed. It was a beautiful copy of the Bhagavad Gita, the holy book of the Hindus! I had been reading the Gita for many years and it was a big source of comfort for me. Imagine finding the holy Hindu book, in a US Army barrack, in a land that's primarily Christian! I was certain then as I am now that God is ever near at hand.

But that day in 2002 I asked for solace and peace. I had known for a while that inner peace just wasn't possible without regular practice of Meditation. Many times I would resolve to start meditating but was never able to make it a habit. I made a determination that day, a determination that came from a certain assurance from that same God that resides inside my heart, and that was a pledge to myself that I would start to meditate regularly from that day on. It was something I had always wanted to do but had never quite accomplished regularly. This time it didn't take much effort at all. I sat down and meditated that day. To my daily readings of *the Urantia Book* I added some quiet time twice daily. And so has it been since then. The daily stillness practice slowly and steadily brought me closer to the divine presence within.

TeaM (and attempts to find a teacher)

There was one more factor, a major one, that got me to commit to my spiritual growth via meditation and self-transformation, and that was 'The Teaching Mission.' The TeaM, as it is also called, grew out Urantia Book readers who became conscious of either the leading of their inner-self ('mystery monitor' as per *the Urantia Book*) or other spiritual entities designated as 'Teachers.' These 'Teachers' made it quite clear that the road to transforming the planet and its people must begin with the individual. The individual must first find their divinity, inside them, connect regularly with it via 'Stillness', slowly transform and then spread the message of *the Urantia Book*; which is that God is our parent, we are God's children. We were to allow God's love to flow through us as we go about serving our brothers and sisters in small and big ways. That's it, plain and simple!

The 'teachers' provided regular lessons via the various groups across the United States and beyond. T/Rs or Transmitters/Receivers were folks who would allow their minds to receive messages via their thoughts. These transcripts appeared regularly, many on a weekly basis and I was thrilled to read and internalize them. I grew keen to have my very own teacher! That was the obvious promise made by all teachers speaking through these transcripts. Apparently anyone could request to have a personal teacher.

I tried. And tried some more; but to no avail. I followed the advice given, however no teacher would appear to make contact through my mind. All other TeaM members were extremely kind and supportive. One such member was Bob Devine(!). Bob had contact with his celestial teacher and suggested that some of us get together regularly, over the phone, to make contact and request guidance. We did just that. Over time this effort grew into the weekly calls now labeled LightLine. Each week a T/R (Transmitter/Receiver) volunteers to transmit a teacher or divine being; many come together, all via the phone!

My efforts to contact my own teacher continued through all this.

The Mystery Monitor

The Urantia Book defines the resident divine presence of God within us as a Thought Adjuster or Mystery Monitor. This godly presence seeks to unite with the personality that we are. It imparts to us the meaning of life and the way forward to perfection in the form of continuous guidance. This guidance is detectable in the form of our thoughts that are of a high spiritual nature. The Mystery Monitor coordinates perfectly with other spiritual influences on our daily lives. The Destiny Guardians (our angelic guides) are such an influence. In my experience, once you decide to do the Father's will and show through intent and action that you mean business, then the spiritual world conspires to affect your life very closely! Life becomes more interesting and challenging then.

What's the purpose of life anyway? That's a question we all ask ourselves in one form or another. One purpose of life is to be conduits of God in our daily lives. We co-create life with God. Such co-creativity is possible due to the influence of the Mystery Monitor. When thoughts or events start to guide us to be more loving and serving to others, then that's proof that God is actively involved in our lives! That's exactly what started occurring in my life. I discovered over these years that God is ever present and active in my personal life. This became even more evident when I would sit and journal my thoughts on my computer. Lovely thoughts and guidance would emerge when I sat and just typed away. Here was the teacher that I had always sought! My teacher was my very own Mystery Monitor slowly making its presence known via lovely thoughts that found expression via my daily journaling. My own personal teacher, coming to me from the deepest recesses of my very being, the very place inside me that God calls his own too. The thoughts thus expressed were filled with love and appreciation for me and with guidance to me to love and serve all I chanced upon. I had prayed earnestly for my personal teacher, and now one was at hand!

Coaching & Namaste Now

Meanwhile, at work, I was fortunate to come upon a new role that involved people management and professional development. Self-improvement and growth had always been a passion and I soon discovered that helping others do the same was an exciting undertaking! I stumbled upon the 'Coaching' profession. As with most other things in my life, this idea had popped into my head several times before but I hadn't paid attention. Well, this time, because even my job called for it, I accepted this idea and promptly started training for, and eventually got certified as a Life/Transformational Coach.

What a delight! I could now (on the job and outside it) help individuals find that which they truly sought. That was my quest too of course. Over the course of two years, I discovered through my journaling, action, and the clues provided by universal forces that my quest, my life purpose, was twofold, both related to each other:

1. Enable people to discover the peace that's inside them. This lead to www.namastenow.com.
2. Enable accomplished yet confused professionals to find their Life Purpose. This lead to my coaching practice (www.thelifepurposecoach.com) and to another blog devoted to individuals who want to be more effective in all walks of life (www.effectiveyou.com).

Through a serendipitous set of circumstances, I came upon Tim Kelley's book 'True Purpose,' which did two amazing things for me. I became even more regular with my 'free journaling' that allowed me to contact my Mystery Monitor, also referred to as a 'Trusted Source' in Tim's book. This is what I had sought all along in wanting my own teacher! Our teacher inside us ever awaits contact from us. Everything we do in life prepares us for the next step in our growth and so it was this time as well. I now became much more familiar with the purpose of my life.

My eternal journey to discover myself via co-creation with God continues, as does my personal discovery of God, step by step, moment by moment. I now strive to live in the present moment called Now, trying when I can to be a conduit of God's love to all others.

Namaste, translated roughly, means "*I bow to the God within you*", or "*The Spirit within me salutes the Spirit in you*" – this sentiment acknowledges that we are all made from the same One Divine Consciousness.

Now refers to the only consciousness of time one can have; we remember the past and can anticipate (or worry about) the future, but we can only live in the *Eternal Now*.

Combine the two, Namaste + Now equals Daily Heightened Spiritual Living, simple and sweet. This is the essence of the message that I have received which I now share with you.

The Urantia Book

The Urantia Book provided for me an almost endless source of answers to questions that had plagued me as I grew up; regarding the nature of Reality and God. It became a constant companion, one which I read through page by page until I had devoured its 2097 pages spread over 196 what are called 'Papers'. Because of the vastness of topics and depth it covers I kept going back to find solace, truth and guidance in the amazing 'blue' book!

The book is divided into four parts. Here's a short description:

Part I: The story of God, the First Source and Center of all that is. God is love and love is the reason everything exists. Love is also the only guide we need to live our daily life fully.
Part II: The story of the vast Universe. This part delves into the structure, the organization and the beings that make up the vast organized parts of the Universe as presently inhabited. We are not alone!
Part III: Is all about our beloved planet, Earth, known to the rest of the Universe as Urantia (yoo-ran-sha). This part describes how our solar system and planet came into physical existence. How life came about on our planet. How spiritual darkness affected life on Urantia at varying intervals; and how it directly impacted life on our planet today. It includes the story of Adam and Eve, as well as how our essential traditions and belief structures came about. This is our own story.
Part IV: Is the true, detail filled and deeply satisfying story of Jesus. His real nature, mission, work on the planet and the future glory of his message are revealed in this part of the tome. His message is simple: We are God's Children; accept that through faith and live life serving our brethren, in love.

Crossroads in My Life
Patije

This is the story of my spiritual history, participation in the UB teachings and the TEACHING MISSION of the Correcting Time. The facts of the T/R would not be complete without the journey of "getting there."

Living in a farming community in southeastern Colorado, I was 13 and, along with celebrating my 13th birthday, there was a BIG decision to make. Unable to make the decision, I had a very unique experience. I learned that all "methods of religion" taught pretty much the same thing but used different words for the manmade interpretations and consequences of not "obeying" them. Here is how it happened:

When I was 5, a playmate invited me to Sunday School with her, and over the years I attended that little Presbyterian church's Sunday School and summer "Bible school." I earned my personal Bible with its beautiful leather cover and my name in gold by memorizing the names of the books of the Old and New Testaments, the Ten Commandments, the Beatitudes, most of the Psalms, the Lord's Prayer, the Golden Rule, most of the Proverbs, and many other verses throughout the Old and New Testaments. I'd actually memorized much of the Bible!

By 7th grade, I was invited to play piano accompaniments for songs, help with crafts, and read Bible stories for the K-4th-grade classes. For my 13th birthday, my paternal aunt gave me a petition for membership in Rainbow for Girls, an organization for the daughters and granddaughters of Masons. At the same time, my maternal aunt was determined that I was going to learn about my mother's religion, Roman Catholicism. So there I was at 13, helping to teach Presbyterian Sunday School and Bible School, attending Catholic catechism classes, and learning the secret "biblical" work for Rainbow!

For some reason (perhaps it was a Sunday School assignment?), I felt I must make a covenant with God at that time. For years I carried this in my billfold: *"It is my will to learn and DO the WILL of our Heavenly FATHER. I'm not here to prove which way is right, only to follow where God leads me. Make me and mold me after THY WILL, O Lord."*

I had married my high school sweetheart and was tripping among the stars in love with life. I was 20 years old, had a good paying job and a wonderful social life! My husband was going to college and everything seemed to be "coming up roses" for us. Then I got pregnant. I was so happy...but my immature husband wasn't ready for a family. My pregnancy was difficult and I was sick every time I ate—for nine months! But I was able to keep my job and keep the income coming in.

At first the new baby didn't change our life style too much. Babysitters were cheap and plentiful and willing to keep my baby day and night. So we continued going out dancing every night and working all day and playing at life. But something in me yearned for more time with my baby and I had to make a decision: baby or husband. Baby won. Husband continued playing and going out every night, while I stayed home with the baby. This lasted until she was three, and then I began to nag like a fishwife for him to stay home with us. He didn't like it and up and left us high and dry, taking the car we jointly owned with him—leaving me and the baby without transportation. About three months later I heard on the radio news that the car we owned had been in a car wreck and the occupants, including me

function

function.

functions

(too badly burned to ID and assumptions made by ownership of the license tag), had been killed in the fiery crash in Kansas.

In my grieving anger, I "heard" the voice in the silence telling me, *"You have built your bridge of faith to take you across the angry waters of your experiences...all is Good and your Good is coming to you."* And I whispered back, "It is my will to learn to do the Will of our Heavenly Father. I am not here to ask why this happened, but what will this experience make of me. Make me and mold me after Thy Will, O Lord."

When I finally began to date again, my sister was engaged to a fellow in the Army who brought friends to meet me. Five years later, I found myself married to a second-generation Polish-Hungarian American and living in a Pennsylvania city where the culture was different from where I had lived in Colorado. I kept more than busy with 20 hours of work at the 200-year-old uptown Presbyterian Church, along with my 44-hour-a-week career, while taking care of my husband and raising my daughter and baby son. I was President of the Women's Association and a participant in its Couples Activities; taught high-school Sunday School; sponsored and chaperoned teenage social, spiritual, and service activities; and edited the weekly church newsletter. In addition, I was participating in interdenominational service activities. I was torn between my career—hitting the glass ceiling working towards management in a national insurance company's headquarters—and my love of church activities. Then tragedy struck. My employer found out I had been diagnosed with an incurable disease and "put me out to pasture" on disability. Multiple Sclerosis. End of career.

Although all looked hopeless, there was a sort of excitement within me as I heard the quiet voice in the Stillness tell me to rely on the bridge of faith I had built through prayer and reliance upon God. I was expecting something GOOD to come from this experience.

At first, I didn't know what to do with myself, having so much time on my hands and missing my 44-hour-a-week job. The intercessory activities turned into an interdenominational Bible study; prayer group; Koinania fellowship group; attending city-wide, state-wide, national and international conferences as representative for our church or the interdenominational group of churches. I went through a few years of yo-yo activity— saying yes to anything someone needed help with at church and suffering an MS exacerbation, leaving me helpless until recovery and then overdoing it again and getting sick again. I was in and out of the hospital a dozen times over the next four years.

I began to research many methods of religion, finding a sort of solace in the hobby of studying religion. I turned to reading Christian Science, seeking a healing from the Multiple Sclerosis. In the meantime, the Koinania group sought Baptism of the Spirit, and its nine or ten members began "speaking in tongues." I was pressured into submitting to the prayer of Baptism in the Spirit, saying, *"Okay, but I don't want to babble words I don't understand, even if it is supposed to be 'my spirit talking directly to God and the Devil can't understand.' What good is it if I can't understand either?!? I'll accept any of the other fruits of the spirit—teaching, healing, discernment, etc., but no babbling!"*

I was prayed for in the method of receiving the Baptism of the Spirit. I kept my mouth shut for the next week, because every time I opened it funny noises came out!

I re-wrote my 1972 Covenant with GOD to do His will.

A few weeks later, I landed in the hospital again, totally paralyzed unable to walk. My "born again in the spirit" friends came to my hospital room and asked, *"What did you do that you are being so severely punished by God? Was it the study of Christian Science, was it refusing the Speaking in Tongues? What was it?"*

I sat there in that hospital bed and searched my soul. To me God was Love. Love was GOOD. God was my Father. Jesus called him Abba, Daddy. A Daddy wouldn't wish a child to be crippled no matter what the offense. I was a mother with two children. No matter what either of those children EVER did, I could not look at them and wish them to be crippled or "punished" in such a severe way. How could God do such a thing? He couldn't. I was certain of that. So I had to walk away from my friends and my spiritual support group.

I remember sitting in my wheelchair at home one day and looking out the dining-room window. By then, we lived on three acres in the farmland of Berks County, Pennsylvania, and it was spring. The dandelions were starting to bloom and none had turned to seed yet. The flocks of birds were returning and often would stop on our acreage. I wished so vehemently: *"Oh, God, I want to run barefoot in the grass again!"* and I heard a voice say: *"Well, make up your mind. Are you going to sit there and feel sorry for yourself as you give up, or are you going to hope and work to get out of that chair?"*

I decided I would get out of the chair. The first time, I fell to the floor and couldn't get back up by myself. The next time, I held on to the back of the sofa and walked holding on to pieces of furniture across the room and back. One day, I managed to walk as far as the end of the garage and back to the living room floor—where I slept for hours until I could pick myself up again. One day, I walked to the end of the driveway (about four car lengths) and back. Then several days later, I was able to walk to the mailbox and back...another four or five car lengths. Day after day I walked as far as I thought I could and still return to the house without having to call for help.

Then one day, I told my kids before they left for school that I was going to try to walk through Alleghenyville and back (one mile down and around the church and cemetery and up the hill back to our house again). If I wasn't home when they got home from school, I wanted them to come find me and bring my wheelchair to help me home. With their assurance that they would, I stepped out in faith with God. I stuffed my pockets with an apple and a few cookies and took off. Much to my surprise, 45 minutes later, I was back in my living room!!! Tired, but successful!

273

I'm not sure what "broke the camel's back" so to speak with my marriage. It had been difficult for years, and many times I could only repeat, *"He that is in me is stronger than he that is in the world"* and *"I can do all things through Him who comforts me"* and *"All things work together for them who love the Lord."* After 13 years of marriage, I was unable to hold a job and support myself and my children; unable to depend on my "loving friends" for spiritual support; unable to count on my estranged husband who had been mentally, emotionally, and physically abusive to me and my children.

He was an elected official in the community where we lived, an elder in our church, and a beloved member of the church. How was I to overcome that, when the few times I attempted to share what happened in the privacy of our home, I was told: *"You must be imagining that,"* *"Surely that is an exaggeration,"* etc.? I often heard the voice in the Stillness reminding me that my "bridge of Faith was strong and would be reliable" to step out on. Always, I felt I was not alone, and when I had the faith to do something about it, my life would change.

I filed for divorce and moved with my son Bill to Florida. My daughter was in college on a scholarship by then. I had friends in Clearwater, but was advised to take my son to Sarasota for the advanced school system. I knew no one. I was turned off by religion/churches. I didn't trust anyone who displayed a cross, dove, fish, or other religious symbol. I felt all alone, with no one but GOD to depend upon.

Once I made the decision to step out "in faith that God would provide for us," everything just fell into place! Pennsylvania had just passed a law giving husband AND wife half of the assets in case of divorce so, although I received no alimony or child support, with that "cushion," I could survive on my disability benefits. I packed up my things and drove to Florida.

The first realtor I consulted knew the laws had just been changed to help single women with families purchase homes, etc., and showed me a house with an assumable mortgage, which was within walking distance of a junior high, high school, advanced schools, a post office, and a shopping mall with a supermarket. Doctors Hospital and physician offices were just a block away, and I soon had a family doctor for us. Once we moved in, registered for school, signed up for utilities, and took care of all those other nuisance things you do when you relocate, I became mildly agoraphobic, seldom leaving the house or yard, and then *only* with my son or neighbor.

I spent HOURS with God every day. I began to go through the Bible from beginning to end, keeping a notebook with my thoughts, inspirational revelations, and questions—all those questions I'd asked over the years (of ministers, priests, and those who should know, whose answers were usually *"Just accept it on blind faith."*) I never was able to" accept it on blind faith" and prayed for answers to my questions. Now they began to be answered. These were questions like:

How come the writers of the Bible who told about Abraham taking Isaac to the mountain to sacrifice didn't record how Sarah must have felt and that she must have begged her husband not to do it? Why don't ministers mention Jesus' brothers? (And I didn't accept that they were "brothers in the spirit," as in "brotherhood.") How could Noah get two of each animal on board one small boat and not have them fight and kill and eat one another? Why did Jesus come to this planet and not some other planet? Surely there is life on other planets. Why did Jesus change water into wine as his first miracle? Was it just to show off or was there a reason for this "petty" (at least in my eyes) demonstration of his power?

I had filled six or seven spiral notebooks full of my self "talk," when I began to realize I would be reading some inspirational passage and then drift into a meditative "listening to the quiet," where I didn't really ask anything, just "soaked up" the wonderful "knowing" God! Sometimes it seemed as if I was transported to a place surrounded by angels, and many times I felt as if they were talking to me, supporting my search for more. I began to call this "entity that seemed to be impressing thoughts upon my mind," this "knowing that I know," by the name of "Buki."

I wanted more and yet I didn't want to leave my home or neighborhood. I was thirsty for God-knowing and brotherhood service, but unwilling to stray too far from home. Then I began to pray for "meat and potatoes" for my spiritual life. I didn't want to go to "those hypocritical churches" where there was more attention given to "beating Satan" than worshiping God. And I wasn't sure I wanted social friends among critical churchgoers. But I craved more spiritual growth and didn't know where to turn.

Of course, life went on. Bill made friends and brought them home. I met my neighbors and was sometimes invited places. Bill and I went to a Silva Life Method workshop, and I began to use the teaching in my life. But Buki was still there, impressing thoughts on my mind.

One neighbor invited me to a "Parents Without Partners" meeting and, for some reason, I went—almost as if my body moved against my druthers. I enjoyed it, joined, and went to the meetings and "family activities" where I could take my son along. But I didn't go to the social activities or "mid-week outing," which was usually held in a restaurant, bar, or nightclub.

One Wednesday night, I'd just settled down with a book when the phone rang. It was one of the ladies from the PWP group, telling me they were having a great time and I should come join them. I declined and went back to reading. Soon the phone rang again and another friend from PWP was calling me to urge me to come join them in a nightclub. I said no and hung up. The phone rang again and this time it was a group calling and claiming I was missing out on fun and someone who needed to talk to me. I explained that I was reluctant to go out at night and would never walk into a nightclub alone. So...the next thing I knew, three of them were at my door, insisting I go with them.

I reluctantly walked into the nightclub with them and saw that the PWP members were all clustered around a long table together. There was only one seat left, so I took it. I quickly learned that the lady next to me was sad and confused because her sister had just been diagnosed with Multiple Sclerosis. A light bulb went off in my brain! Ah! God sent me to talk to her about "life after diagnosis." I can do that! And I did so for more than an hour.

I was getting ready to find a way home when a strange man came over and asked me to dance! I declined and those who had heard, knowing how hard it was to get me to do anything for fun, teased me into accepting. He led me to the dance floor and we had danced about ten steps when he said, *"You are into spiritual growth and yearning for more!"* Surprised I gasped, *"Yes, how did..."*

He continued: *"I want to take you to a Urantia meeting tomorrow night."* The music stopped and someone came up to talk to him, so I wandered back to my table and sat down. I figured he'd come over to talk to me again, but he never did. After I got home and was ready for bed, I spent some time with God. During my "little talk," I mentioned the incident and said, *"I don't remember what he said it was, but if it is YOUR WILL, then please let him find me and tell me more about it."*

The next night, I'd just finished doing the supper dishes and "discussing" with Bill how much TV he could watch after he did his homework, when the doorbell rang. I went to the door and this stranger from the night before was standing there saying, *"You are ready to go."* I found myself saying, *"Yes, let me tell my son I am leaving,"* and picked up my purse and went out the door with a strange man!!! Me, agoraphobic me! All I remember about that night was that we were at this meeting with about half a dozen or more readers of *the Urantia Book* and I was in awe!

This "stranger" (I never learned his name and we hadn't really exchanged any information) introduced each one of them to me, telling how they got the book, how they found each other, and how it changed their lives. He introduced me to them—telling them about my experience in Pennsylvania and the prayers for more spiritual meat and potatoes, which did not seem at all strange—even though I'd never told him about them. Apparently it didn't seem strange to the others in the group that he knew so much about them either.

We were in front of my house when he asked me, "Well, what did you think?" I said, "Oh! I have to have that book, but I don't know how I can ever find the money to buy a $30 book!"

He said to me, *"IF you are ready for it and are to have it, you will have one."* He said goodnight and left. I checked on my son, got ready for bed, got out my budget and bills, and tried for over an hour to figure out how I could buy that book! I finally gave up and said, *"Father, I want the book. Please find a way for Bill's shoes to last a little longer, the electric bill to be a little lower, or something so I can find the money to buy it!"* And I went to bed, leaving it in God's hands.

I overslept the next morning and ran to Bill's room to wake him and nudge him into hurrying so he wouldn't be late for school. As I ran through the dining room to the kitchen to start breakfast, I saw a brand new Urantia Book lying on the table! I went back and asked Bill, "Did you answer the door last night and have somebody give you this book?" *"No, Mom." "How did this book get here?" "I don't know. Perhaps you put it there when you came home last night."*

Well.... I forgot being agoraphobic and I took off by myself for the PWP midweek social at the nightclub the next Wednesday! I wanted to find this guy and find out how that book got there! I asked each person if they knew the guy who danced with me and each person thought he was someone else. John thought it was Steve's friend, Steve thought it was Jim's neighbor, Jim thought it was Judy's brother, Judy thought it was Linda's boyfriend, Linda thought he was the guy from Sue's bookstore...and so on and so on. Nobody knew him and everyone thought they did! I drove myself to *the Urantia Book* meeting Thursday night and the same thing happened. Jane thought it was Barbara's neighbor, Barb thought it was David's friend, David thought it was somebody else...and so on and so on. No one knew him and everyone thought they did! No one as far as I know has ever seen him since.

I'd like to say I picked up the book and never stopped reading it until I got to the end, but it wasn't that way for me. I'd read some and it would seem to be over my head, and I'd put it down and not pick it up for days at a time. Then I'd be nudged by that little voice that reminded me of how I got the book and I'd pick it up and read it again for awhile and lay it down again. It went that way until one day I decided to skip to the back of the book and read the Jesus papers. Then it came alive! Answered my questions! Opened up things I'd never before noticed in the Bible....

In 1979, I added to my covenant with God, thanking Him for *the Urantia Book*.

My daughter Tere came home from college and wanted to try to find her "Kenny daddy." We had gone to Colorado for my 20th class reunion and discovered her father, my first husband, was alive and living somewhere in Florida. Our car (the one in the fiery crash where the driver and companion were killed) had been repossessed and was being driven back to Colorado by someone else. He wasn't in it. (When his mother found out he was alive, I was already in Pennsylvania and married again. She had moved and cut off all correspondence with Tere and me. Both she and Kenny felt it was his punishment to be denied contact with his daughter since he had deserted us so many years before.)

Tere contacted her paternal grandmother and found him without too much trouble. She had me go with her to meet him for the first time since she was three years old, and told us that she "knew instantly that she had been conceived in love" when she saw us look at each other for the first time in 15 years! Well, to make a very long story short, she found him living in Bradenton, next door to Sarasota. It SEEMED like God had brought us back together, high-school sweethearts, now mature enough to make a marriage, so we remarried.

Tere was back in college when we told her of our plans to get married, and I was told by a dorm mate that she went through her dorm shouting to her friends, "My mom and dad are getting married!!!" (I'd have liked to have seen that!) She came home for the wedding and the three kids stood up with us to say our vows. His daughter, Keni, was two years older than my son and five years younger than our daughter. We made a typical family until Tere went back to college, but we found out it is not easy making a new family out of old families with different traditions and expectations.

A few years into the second marriage to my childhood sweetheart things were falling apart. Having suffered an MS exacerbation which left me blind, deaf, and unable to walk, Kenny turned to drinking and staying away from home. My stepdaughter became unmanageable, as she blamed me for her father not coming home and leaving her, too. I was relying on my son, who had a learner's permit, to take on the grocery shopping and driving me to the doctor and doing laundry and preparing our meals. I told him, *"You can only drive legally with a licensed adult driver in the car with your learner's permit, so be careful. If you have an accident, they'll find out I'm blind and put us both in jail!"* And trusted God to keep us safe. God did. We made it through the crises. I gradually got my eyesight and hearing back, and eventually could walk again.

Ken decided to go on a fishing trip to Canada with the guys and visit our daughter in Pennsylvania. He was gone about three weeks and no one in Pennsylvania heard from him. When he returned, he informed me that he wanted a divorce, packed up, and left that day.

By this time, many things had moved me from my "comfort zone" to a new adventure. I'd discovered the Unity Church through reading *the Urantia Book* with a Unity minister's son. When I said, *"I wish there was a church like this on the planet,"* he asked me if I'd ever heard of Unity. I ended up not only a member of a Unity Church, but a licensed Unity teacher, so I could teach the UB with "authority" to students of both Unity and the UB. Getting my license entailed going to the Unity School of Christianity in the suburbs of Kansas City. Classes could be taken in two-week or four-week increments three times in one year or over a period of several years to accumulate enough credits to graduate with a license. I accomplished it by 1989.

During the mid-'70s, throughout the '80s, and into the '90s, I went to every statewide, area, and national Urantia Book conference and retreat I had the opportunity to attend. I became a charter member of the Florida Students of *the Urantia Book* and also published the FSUB newsletter for about ten years!

During that time, I also had up to nine study groups a week, most in my home. It started because the people in my original study group asked me how to introduce the book to their friends and family members. So...a friend had me introduce the UB on tape and put music behind it, which I reproduced on cassette tapes.

I put together a packet with the cassette and several pamphlets: "Jesus and the UB," "Why I believe the UB," "The Origin of the UB," and a list of study groups and an invitation to join one of them. OR, if they had at least three people, I would come to them for six weeks and they could learn a little and then join an on-going study group.

Then I gave these packets to the members of the study group, people I met in church or at MS meetings, or even sometimes strangers in a store or at a school activity. I always asked them to return the packets to the person who had given them to them. I left some in the church bookstore, along with several UB books to sell.

What I found out is that the small study groups formed a bond and didn't want to join a bigger group. So I ended up having a group any morning, afternoon or evening I could get a group together. I also found that a small group of five to eight was best for beginners. And it was wonderful for me. As I had each group in a different part of the book, it enabled me to grasp a fuller view of the teachings and coordinate passages from each PART with the others! I suspect even then the Teachers were working through me.

If someone asked a question, without hesitation, almost automatically, the answer came through me—unless I was in the way! (Recently, when I asked one friend from one of those nine study groups if she had any special memories from that time 16-17 years, ago all she could think of while on the phone was *"You made the Urantia Book come alive for all of us and the Teacher's messages were so dear to my heart."* Of course, I know and reminded her that *"It didn't come from me but THROUGH me from the Spirit. I could not have done any of that by myself!"*)

I must insert a comment here that I was, indeed, blessed with help from the Teachers, my Thought Adjustor, the Angels, and other spirit Helpers, for I, alone, could not have done a smidgen of what was accomplished during those years. One of my favorite memories of a friend who recently passed through the curtain of death is what she once said to a group of UB readers at a conference: *"I knew Patijé before the UB and she was a wallflower, seldom speaking unless asked a direct question. Now look at her! The UB really changed her life and I can vouch for that!"*

I unfolded the Covenant with God I'd written as a teenager, the one I'd written in 1972, and what I had added in 1979, and wrote in 1989 that I would ask for God's guidance at each step along the way.

At one conference I attended in Oklahoma, I was reminded of something I'd learned way back in my "born-again days," when I attended a workshop and we practiced the "hot pen." But this time it was the "Letter to God" and "Letter from God." After I returned home, I began to use this method as a daily "getting my thoughts together" and *listening to the quiet.* Concerned that my friends and Loved Ones would think I was crazy or weird or something, I never shared this with anybody – it was between me and God until a few months after we learned of the Teaching Mission in 1992.

The earliest "letters to/from God were lost in a computer hard drive failure, but here are two from 1991.

Monday, May 13, 1991

Dear Father, Guide me today. My emotions have been out of balance because of this financial challenge. Help. Since the anger and frustration left, I feel drained. Tired. Oh, so tired! All I want to do is go to bed. Yet I have so many projects to finish, some to get started and things I want to do. Help me. My will is for Your Will to guide my life experiences.

Dear Daughter, You are so quick to become aware when you do not FEEL you are in Divine Flow... But what you are overlooking is that, while you are humanly out of balance, I am still with and protecting you. I cannot adjust your thinking while the out-of-balance emotion is present, nor when your perceptions are narrow and unbending. However, by the time you are aware that you are emotionally out of balance, your thinking is already being adjusted. It is being gently guided out of the self-destructive habit of self-pity and victimization...and is pointed towards a possible solution to the challenge which upset you to begin with. Just wait. Don't act when you are thus engaged in emotional battles. You really are unenlightened of the tremendous spiritual growth you have made over the preceding few years! Wake up! See the Truth! You can have no doubts if you review the confirmations and manifestations that your faith has demonstrated in your own life experience.

Let go of the ego failures. You could not do more in that situation. Know that you did the very best you could do and let go. It does not matter if you fail or succeed in your attempted activities. What is important is that you attempted them, you made the decision to undertake the activity or challenge. You chose to follow Me. When you can see no progress, give it to me. The very action of planting the seed in the consciousness is a job well done. When the time is right, the seed will germinate and grow. You may never see the fruits of your work, but there will be fruits cast to all parts of the globe on which you live! Doubt not! I have others who will pick up and carry the fruit, or nourish the seed, or shelter the small plant. Your job is to plant it.

You will not always be alone. A companion is being prepared for you. You have much work ahead to be ready for your companion when it is time. Work, and play, and study, and use this computer which I have manifested for you. You will see how I work in your life. Trust. Wait. Love. Be gentle with yourself. Rest when your body asks for rest. Work when your spirit is ambitious. Day and night make little difference. Let go the guilt of being caught in bed midmorning. Let go of the need to justify and rationalize. You and I have work to do together and we cannot go forward if you are chained to past programming. Your best time for work is night time. Stay up and work. Your best time to sleep is mornings. Sleep then. Don't apologize. All things work together for good when you love and trust ME and My guidance.
Love Me. Worship Me. Wait on Me. I Am! I am here for you. I love you. Your loving Father

Wednesday, May 22, 1991:

Dearest helper...Thought Adjuster, Father, Take my prayers where they are to go.... I'm not sure where this is happening...in my own mind with the help of the adjuster...or actually from the Father through the TA???

I believe something is happening. I get too confused when I try to find a logical answer. Just know my faith is such that I will listen. It is my will to do the will of the Father...to live my life in service and in love... I strive to discover my potential and to unfold within my personality until fusion with the Thought Adjuster becomes a reality. I am willing Lord, use me. I am willing Lord, send me. I await.

Your loyal and loving daughter in spirit and in mind...

My loyal and loving daughter,
You are, indeed, mine in spirit and mind. I will not forsake you. Lean on Me. Trust Me. Believe in Me. You have done as I asked. There is more. You have diligently sought more in the Urantia Book *than I requested. That is good. You will find your answer. When you know what you seek, come to me and I will affirm or adjust... Do not trouble yourself. All things work together for good...and I am drawing you to Me.*

Your study group this morning was special. Did you take heed? You let it get "off course" and without structure, I was able to move more freely. The personal sharing was a necessary outlet for those who shared. It is good you ended the session in prayer. And it is, indeed, true that you have agreed to allow yourself to have free emotions, and to know your intentions are to do good, wish good, and learn from your experiences.

You are making great steps in freedom. Do you now feel affirmed that Love and Trust do work miracles? Can you now leave the emotions of failure behind and know that you are my expression and good seeds have been planted in the lives and consciousnesses of those who seem to mistreat and ignore you? Remember, I will lead you beside still waters...I will refresh your soul. Yea, though you walk through the valley of the shadow of evil and discord, I am with you. You are safe.

Do not be over-concerned with your task for the days ahead. All is well. I love you, Child. I am with you in all things. Go forward with courage and know that you will not be forsaken. I have great work for you to do. In worldly terms, it is not of great consequence, but in my terms it is good. You have earned this assignment. Do it well.

Your Heavenly Father through Thought Adjuster.

One Monday night in February 1992, at a regular INSCENDERS UB study group meeting in my home, a "Snowbird" member from Canada mentioned he'd just been part of a UB group in Kansas City and had heard about the Teaching Mission in Utah and Los Angeles! Just that morning, I'd gotten a phone call from a friend who told me a group in Tallahassee was getting communication from teachers supposedly from Edentia, but she wasn't supposed to tell anyone. She had transcripts of some of the communications, but she couldn't share them with anyone.

With excitement, all individuals of the study group agreed that Hugh should call the friends in Kansas City and have them play the "invitation from Ham" for all to hear! Hugh called the friend in Kansas and she enthusiastically told us what was happening and played a recording from Utah stating that Teachers were here!

After everyone left, I called UTAH...having a name and number. It was 10 PM here, but I figured it was only 8 or 9 PM there and still early enough to call. At first, I asked only that they ask a question to the teacher for me: "IF I was willing, and I was, would I be included in this mission?"

When I awoke the next morning, the prayer of knowing more about these teachers was still on my mind. The phone rang and the person who had called the day before said, "I'm not going to argue with the powers that be. You can read the transcripts I have if you want to come over." I shot out of here so fast I forgot to finish dressing!

Then I got a call from Tampa from someone who had been to Utah and experienced it all, with an invitation to come to his house that night so he could share what he knew with us. So a group of five or six of us climbed into the car and drove to Tampa that evening. We listened and wondered at the newness of what was happening, and I didn't realize it at the time, but everyone in the small group had somehow gotten the idea it was ME that was going to be the transmitter! I had not yet revealed my secret daily "Letter to God, Letter from God" exercise in the privacy of my home. (I probably did finally share this about the time I realized it felt so strange trying to transmit orally for the group, and so easy when I was alone with God.)

During the evening together, we made plans to bring the entire study group up the next week! On the way home, someone asked, *"Why are we taking eight or ten people to Tampa when those two could more easily come to Sarasota?"* So we decided to have a meeting at my house.

For that first meeting, word spread far and wide! I invited the members of each of the nine study groups and Avis invited her study group. Lee called a few people, because I think Fred Harris was there from Tallahassee. If I remember right, 28 people crowded into my 13' x 13' living room that first night! I had invited a friend that I knew received channeling and she introduced those of us who were insecure to what channeling was all about. Then my friend turned the meeting over to "the teachers" and turned to me.

I was too aware of myself that night, afraid I'd "mess up," and managed to transmit only a short time. Aflana introduced herself and left a message for Lee, which I didn't transmit but told him afterwards. Everyone exclaimed, *"But you can't do that! You have to speak it as you receive it!"* So...I promised in future I would do that IF any Teacher transmitted through me again. It was decided that we'd meet again the next week and try again.

After everyone left, I sat down at my computer with a new page on my Word Perfect software, closed my eyes and wrote to God, and then I received a message:

Thursday, Feb. 20, 1992 (after group meeting):

Dear Father, why do I feel so "down" about what happened tonight in our first Teaching meeting? Why am I feeling so like I let you down? Why can't I believe this is my "job" now? Help me, Father, I am willing. I believe, help my unbelief! Teach me. I love you. I am willing. I want to be your servant in love and peace!

My Child, You are a wonder to behold! You keep thinking your ego is getting in the way and, in reality, your ego is not here at all or you would see that you can do this for me. Your teacher is ready. Your teacher was here tonight. Do not doubt. I can do only so much to reassure you. Did I not tell you I have work for you to do? Have I not adequately prepared you for many months? Just relax and believe Me. It will happen when you no longer try to either make it happen or try to make it not happen. Listen! Listen to your heart. You know in your heart that you are to do this for me. There is no doubt in your heart. Why then, do you hesitate? Because you want it to be true and not just a mind trip. Trust me. Trust yourself. Trust. Be what you are made to be.

[Interrupted by a phone call of excited affirmation from an almost non-believer who was there that night....]

Continue: *Affirmation? Can I give you any more? Even _____ said you were to do it. Do you not see that she has not risen to the higher level? Do you not see why I did not allow the energy of Elayne to "channel" last spring? You have been given a gift of high importance. There is no gimmick to your gift. There are no right energies, no arrangement of energies, no need to sit in a chair with no metal. No need to be barefoot, no need to center everyone's energies around a certain point. Don't you see? I can do all things. I don't need these props. If it is of God, none are needed. I will lead you beside the water of life and you need have no fear of where I take you. I will not forsake you. I will guide and direct you where I would have you go. Are you ready for your teacher? When you are ready your teacher will appear. The name will be revealed as soon as you can transmit. Experiment, practice, do what helps you to relax, find out how to transmit. Do not listen to others as an authority. They know only for themselves. Go to your bed and trust me. You can do what I ask you. Do not fear. Do not hold back your wholehearted enthusiastic service to my purpose. My plan is in need of you. I look to you to join me in this endeavor. We will adjust and make your vessel ready for what it is to transmit. Do not fear. Love. Trust. BE what you are to be. Wait on me. Your Father through your Thought Adjuster*

I continued doing this every single day until the next meeting of the group. Even after oral transmission became common, I felt more comfortable with getting the transmissions when alone in the "silence."

The next time we gathered in my living room, we had about as many people, but some were different. I think a few were curiosity seekers, some were genuinely afraid, and others were CERTAIN this was going to be our gift from God! After a few minutes of sharing and all, I suggested we have a few minutes of meditation and prayer, asking God to be with us, to allow me to transmit accurately and to guide us in this attempt to hear what HE had for us. After a few minutes, Aflana came through with a prayer—one I'd heard at Unity—and she gave us a brief message.

Over the following weeks, our sessions were always started with prayer and meditation, and then Aflana's prayer. Then one night, I "lost the transmission" and another member of the group began right where I ended! How exciting! When a few other members of the group began to think they might be being contacted, those who thought so began meeting in my home one afternoon a week "to practice." It was interesting how Aflana would always begin with me and then tell us she was going to go around the group and each was to speak the thought that came into their minds. Soon many of us were participating in the phenomenon of transmitting the Teachers.

Over the weeks and months, many visiting teachers came and greeted us; out-of-town UB readers began to call and visit and experience with us! I'd get phone calls day and night of someone sharing what happened to them and asking if it was a true contact! I often described my experiences in email and, in December 1993, collected these into a "booklet" to share with those new to the phenomenon. Usually, I'd be contacted by some out-of-town person before they got to town stating they wanted to come "see for themselves" this "thing" that was happening in our group. But sometimes, without warning, out-of-town UB readers would call me from a mile away, wanting to meet and talk to me.

I had people trying to get me to give them personal "readings" and tell their futures. I absolutely refused to do that. I was told in no uncertain terms that I was not to channel "readings." One time I agreed to sit in with Chris as she tried to find out for someone in the group who was going through a crisis, and it failed. All I heard was *"No! Let him be about his business."* Later when the crisis was worsened, I was blamed for telling her to do nothing...when that was a total misunderstanding of what the teacher had transmitted through me. I had learned another painful lesson.

I never totally relaxed when transmitting and occasionally felt a virtual "hot rod" being inserted in my spine when I "froze up" when someone asked a question of the Teacher about something of which I had no knowledge or didn't understand the terms. But IF I could "get out of myself" and allow the transmission to continue, it usually was a beautiful or educational answer for the whole group. If there was any discord or anger or sometimes even doubt voiced BEFORE the prayer and meditation, I'd find myself unable to transmit easily. I had to work at it, therefore making me doubt myself.

One of the Teachers eventually told me that I was so sensitive to energy that when anger or frustration was introduced in my vicinity, they had to work hard to reestablish correcting energy for the transmissions to come through to me. We had been told early on that this house had special energy around it—possibly for protection?—and many who would visit here would be contacted by the Teachers. We often "saw" beings moving throughout the rooms and there was "no one" (no human) there.

There was a night of a regular study group when we all stopped looking at the books and turned to the doorway to see who had joined us. Drew got up and went through the house calling, "Hello? Hello? Come join us." But no human appeared.

There was a visitor to a study group meeting one night who claimed she could sense "two very old beings around me and she couldn't get through them to me." She had been invited by another member who believed in fortune telling, etc., and wanted this person to tell her if what I was doing—transmitting—was real or not. I remember on several occasions when I was tired, nearly "burned out," and trying to get some transcribing done or the house picked up or laundry put away before the group got here for a meeting, and, though all alone in the house, I'd feel a hand on my shoulder and words whispered in my ear reassuring me to just keep going.

One day, I was feeling bad and was sitting in my living room with my head in my hands, my elbows resting on my knees, and I became aware, out of the corner of my eye, that a being had come in from the kitchen and taken the same position on a chair across from me. It felt comforting, but when I looked directly at the chair, there was no one there!

Aflana had told us she was an emergency teacher because our group had come into existence more quickly than it was thought we would! Eventually, LorEl arrived to address our group. She had spent years being trained and had just arrived on Urantia when she came to us. I guess you could say that we were quite fascinated and excited about being included in this historical happening on our planet!

During those few months many teachers and spiritual entities contacted and addressed our group. It became pretty clear that we were an experimental group where various teaching methods were tried and various directions were given for us to learn to be more cooperative and loving towards one another. However, there were some members of a study group who collaborated on a group letter telling me I should NOT be involved in this "movement" and quoted many places in the UB for their position. When I shared this with the group who did accept, they found just as many places in the UB that DID support the possibility of Teachers from Edentia. So...I continued.

Some thought LorEl was my personal teacher, but I never thought that. I still talked to "Buki," as I had most of my life. Many teachers came through to me, telling me their names, where they were from, things they hadn't told their own groups, and this scared me very much! How could I get this information when their own assigned groups weren't getting it first? When a Teacher contacted me, they were usually accompanied by Aflana or LorEL, which eased my conscience a little. In asking once, I received this answer:

You see, My Lovely One, you are well sensitized to the flavors of "teachers" and "spiritual influences" around you. You might think of the chameleon, which changes its colors with its environment. If you were sitting with a transmitter of "Ham," you would also receive impressions from "Ham." If you were near a transmitter of Linnel, you would receive impressions from Linnel. If you were in the presence of Welmek, you would receive impressions from Welmek. If you were tuned to Nebadonia, you would receive impressions from Nebadonia. Your impressions would transmit through your memory banks and would consequently appear in different terms from the other transmitter of the same "Teacher," but they would be from the same Source.

One lady in Venice called me several times a month, telling me about what was happening to her and asking if it could possibly be real. I kept assuring her that it was happening all over the nation, all over Urantia, and to keep writing the messages she was getting. She told me she never got a name ... just the incredible information about things she knew nothing about. I kept telling her to keep doing it.

Meanwhile, in the group there was some disagreement, impatience, and dominating opinions developing, and when the teachers tried to show us "how" to be a dynamic community in Light and Life, it must have been too soon. There were some hard feelings, many misunderstandings, some accusations, and lots of disillusionment among the 20-30 people in the group. The expense of transcribing the transmissions, which were recorded, the printing, mailing copies to exchange with other teaching groups, etc., was great. Having agreed to do this, I felt it was my mission to continue and I ran up a few thousand dollars in credit cards buying paper, ink, and equipment.

My ego began to feel I was beginning to be taken for granted and abused, having to transmit, record, transcribe, print, copy, distribute, and have everything at my house. Although little was said, someone aware and sympathetic with what I was doing had suggested everyone attending leave a dollar to help cover expenses. But a few said, "Absolutely not! There is to be no money involved," so it was voted down. Distrust and wanting things to be different began to overcome the group. People seemed to lose touch with what the Teachers were sharing and were turned away by their own misunderstandings.

I was suffering from MS symptoms and not telling anyone because I didn't want to alarm anyone, but I guess in trying to force myself to "be normal," others judged me to be "passive aggressive," or so I was told. I was pushing myself and probably seemed to be pushing others. I asked someone else to field the complaints that came in week after week. One person would spontaneously bring some homemade cookies and, while most were grateful, one had to complain to me later to ask her to bring sugarless cookies next time "'cause she couldn't eat sugar!" Another was very excited about the spiritual growth she was experiencing and shared a lot with the group, but a few others called me during the week and asked me to ask her to keep quiet because they didn't always want to hear about her experiences.

There were two or three in the group who were always at the meetings, listened carefully, and practiced what was taught, but they were shy and did not participate in discussions. I got phone calls from others telling me to tell them to participate because when they were just sitting there it intimidated others. All kinds of complaints. If we served coffee, we shouldn't have; if we didn't, we should have. I was THE PERSON who got all the complaints, the main transmitter, the host of the out-of-town houseguests, while still trying to find time to transcribe and print and copy, with no time for a personal life or much rest, and the bills were piling up and I was single, living on disability income.

A man had recently come into my life through a Urantia study group and I was falling in love, but had no time for him either! I felt like I was being pulled apart. Yet I kept saying to God, *"Father, I can do all things with your strength and guidance. Help me, I'm floundering here...."* The few who knew the toll it was taking on me told me to stop doing it all, but I just couldn't let go. I had been selected for this privilege and, just because the task was getting harder, that didn't mean I should give up. But the antagonism grew with each meeting and my inability to please everyone, I guess. I finally told them how I was feeling and asked for help. The solution was quite surprising—and not at all what I expected!

We divided into three transmission groups and, before the year was out, everyone in the three groups had moved away from Sarasota, dealt with a death or major illness for themselves or in their family, or something else occurred to cause the group to disintegrate. All of us were scattered around the USA. I was burned out and suffering an MS exacerbation, causing me to go on medicine.

During that time I was told by Aflana and LorEL *not* to try to transmit, as the messages could possibly be confused going through a mind that was on unnatural substances, whatever that meant, some kind of chemistry imbalance, I guess. However, I continued to "talk to"Buki" off and on throughout this "phase" of my life.

At one point a few years after the scattering of the Sarasota Teaching groups, I experienced this prayer and affirmation:

ME: May I ask why Aflana and LorEL gave few impressions to me after the upheaval of our Sarasota Teaching Group? Some thought LorEl was my personal teacher, but I never really believed that. When I called on them, any of the teachers always appeared, but I was no longer awakened nor found myself called to write down impressions from them after the "scattering" of our Sarasota Teaching Group. I felt like such a failure. Felt "deserted" at times, felt unworthy of being a transmitter, even felt "left out" when I read transmissions from other teachers.

REPLY: *My Child, we knew of your heartache. You filled the requirements of your task well and earned a deserved rest. Aflana and LorEl went on to other endeavors. The Sarasota Teaching Group was a tremendous experience in contact and response between the humans tuned to us and the awareness of the Teachers from Edentia. It served its purpose. There was no failure on your part. Your isolation gave us an opportunity to bring you into focus with the companion who benefited from your support and encouragement throughout the past dozen years. Do not waste any time regretting the scattering of the Sarasota Teaching Group. All things work for good in My Time, and the experience of the Sarasota Teaching Group planted seeds of triumph all over Urantia and all the way to Edentia. We are well pleased with the success of the Sarasota Group. The fruits of the experience have been spread far and wide. You need not feel embarrassed or regret the lack of cohesiveness on the part of the participants in that gathering of seeking souls. All received something of great importance, even those who think they did not. When a human participates in the Will of God, all things work together for many consequences and purposes never seen by the ones who were chosen to sow the seeds. You did well, My Child. Go in Peace.*

Since the experience of the Teaching Mission in my home, I've found a serenity in sharing the teaching of *the Urantia Book*. I don't "quote," citing part, section, and paragraph from the UB anymore. I share the teaching of the UB without citing where the Truth comes from. I share it naturally "as I pass by" in email, on the phone, in person, with friends, family, new acquaintances and strangers in the airport or on the bus, in waiting lines— anywhere the opportunity in the conversation comes up. What I'm trying to say is it is all a part of my life and it naturally rises to the surface when opportunity presents itself, without trying to "sell" or "convert" anyone.

Back THEN, I tried to utilize the teachings whenever I could, steer conversations around so that I could mention them, but NOW I live them without thinking about it. The Teachings of the UB have become so much a part of me, my conversation, that I no longer think about who, what, and where I am when I share.

My hobby of genealogy has put me in touch with over six hundred (3rd, 4th, 5th) cousins, and some of us have become regular email "buddies" and I often find myself sharing the "teachings" in my email. So far, several dozen have actually asked me to "tell them more," so I can only hope I'm sowing seeds even where I cannot see them!

My early "transmissions"—and those after the dissolution of the Sarasota Teaching Group —have been more a "conversation" with my spiritual helpers than just receiving "lessons," as most TRs are experiencing. I have become very relaxed and it is a "way of life" for me to converse with these spiritual helpers. I have had some interesting experiences involving healing and finding lost items. I will refrain from giving many examples here of so-called miracles and healing experiences at this time.

I was still receiving transmissions on the computer, but I felt so bad about the failure of keeping the Sarasota transmission group together. Sometimes I felt betrayed and angry, but most of the time it was grief over a feeling of failure. LorEl and Aflana contacted me less and less often. I was specifically told that I had been prepared and everything was in place and I was to rest for awhile before my work would begin again. I had no idea it would be a decade or more before I would be pulled into a new group of believers.

In the meantime, I remarried and had some new goals in my life, among them paying off the tremendous debt (tremendous for me, because I had only my disability income) I had accumulated trying to be "chief enabler" among our Sarasota 'Teaching Group" and all. I continued encouraging by phone and, after a couple of years, began meeting in person with the individual in Venice who was getting transmission messages. The hours spent with her and her messages became the Spiritual highlight of my week.

My son had grown up and had joined the U.S. Army. He decided to make it his career and has been all over the world and deployed in places like Haiti, Korea, Kuwait, Egypt, and in 2006, with only three years to go to retirement, he was given orders for Iraq. He would be running the convoys from Baghdad Airport out to the troops in the field. Every day his life would be in danger.

Although I had built my bridge of faith very strong, I had misgivings about sending "my baby" off to war. I received these transmissions in June 2006, just before my son's deployment to Iraq with the Army:

My Child,

Your prayers and human worries are heard, and comfort will be forthcoming. When one is confronted with the potential for personal human loss or the potential for the loss of a child to death, the "mother bond" responds emotionally.

The mother bond of love and nurturing continues for a lifetime, but maturity brings an ability to release the loved one to the freedom of their choices. The grief of release is natural for the human ego, especially when challenged by a belief in negative results of those choices. Know, Little One, there is a time to protect and nourish and a time to release to the unknown consequences of independent thinking and decision-making. Mistakes are made, but the experience adds maturity to the fledgling personality becoming spiritual.

You, My Child, have taught loyalty to eternal value, intellectual meaning in contemplating possible consequences or results with a great emphasis on finding peace to mental, spiritual, and emotional forces within. You have taught what a mother does to enable your child to be the best human he can be. Your encouragement to be of service and minister where he can as he passes through life and to smile through the clouds of distrust, hate, resentment, discouragement, frustrations and other evils of emotion will fortify him for a full eternal life.

A child's choice to join the military was his to make. His choice to perform the duties of the military is his choice to make. His eager participation in bringing civil liberty in the midst of conflict and chaos in this time of war will add to the success of the great mission to give freedom to a people long suffering under misconception of faith and power-hungry dictators. The "cause" is good and an answer to many prayers of a desperate people. No good thing is ever lost in eternity and nothing good is ever diminished in eternal value.

When your son survives his service in Iraq, he will be a better achiever and his experience will help him make great strides is his eternal development. Perhaps his physical form will be extinguished or compromised, but his life will continue and the choices he made will have eternal value. Allow him to go unhampered by protective emotional fears and support his choice with your heart, mind, and knowingness! What he is prepared to do is good!

It is a mother's heart which clings to a protective fear for the life of a child. This can damage not only the child's ability to make free choices but the mother's ability to progress through the experiences. If one dwells on a loss, one cripples spiritual growth. When one expresses resentment, anger, bad feelings toward any who are considered the perpetrators of that loss, one does severe damage to one's spiritual program and enlightenment. There is a season for all things, a season to mourn and a season to let go. But LOVE blooms in all seasons—whether by choice or natural bonds. LOVE, Little One, is not emotional. Emotional feelings of affection are consequences, not things of themselves.

These experiences are all in a day's work, a day "in eternal school," and can be done well! Go, My Child, and do it well. You are strong with the power of your faith. You are resolute with the ability to see the big picture, and you are steadfast in your loyalty to Truth, Beauty, and Goodness. Love is your bridge and your faith has built a strong bridge!
Rest in the green pastures of knowing each has the gifts of God. Decision-making is only the expression of those gifts.

I love you and bless you. Buki

And I will close with this message:

My BELOVED CHILD,

Some are too busy to grow above religious concepts implanted in their childish (and adult) minds and are therefore in grave danger of spiritual fixation. Ignorance and prejudice are the basic inhibitors of finding new growth in old or repeated circumstances.

Upon Urantia, there are schools for education. Progress had been made as evolution has pierced through rote memorization to the greater access to books and tools of learning. However, passing through a regime of established educational routine does not mean intellectual progress nor spiritual growth. Enlargement of facts and vocabulary does not a character develop. Real education, whether material or spiritual, is predicated upon an enhancement of ideals, increased appreciation of the values of those ideals, new value meaning, and loyalty to supreme values.

The "soil" for true education and religious growth is multiple: an exercise of curiosity, enjoyment and wonder lure of adventure, coordination of natural propensities, experiences and feelings of satisfaction, stimulus of attention and awareness, but also a consciousness of smallness and humility as that which you see when you stand on the mountain and are filled with awe as you gaze at the valley below or the stars above and recognize how tiny your flesh tabernacle is in the vastness of God's Creation!

A time of contemplation and loving devotion to others in this great mountainous environment has renewed your childlike awe and wonder in which physical creation is. Know, Little One, that the inward and upward creation you both are making in your Spiritual Awakening is truly awe inspiring and full of wonder for those of us watching and waiting for you! You both have periodically laid aside the cares of your material world and found the value in the adventure of spiritual Quiet Time and transmission of the communication from the Silence. It is truly a joy for those of us in the higher realms to see this upon Urantia during the Correcting Time.

Remember, Little One, from Urantia the view of the vast universe, all appears as material. But from the view from the highest of the higher realms, this same universe you view in materiality is, for us, spiritual.

When one clarifies one's understanding of "Spiritual," one can also get a glimpse of the spiritual universe through the haze of time and space.

I love you and bless you.

My Experiences with the TEACHING MISSION
Gerald "Jerry" Dalton

For me, the Teaching Mission has always been a very good and reasonable method used by the Celestial Administrators to provide guides and mentors to those truth seekers on our planet that desire further assistance in their life journey. When one considers the plight of the inhabitants of this planet after two major defaults by its assigned leaders to bring about progressive evolution on this experimental sphere, it is no wonder that a special corps of "spiritual teachers" was enlisted to provide guidance. When the call went out in our universe for volunteers for this rescue mission I suspect that the response was overwhelming!

What more glorious opportunity for advanced individuals that had lived their mortal lives on differing planets of the universe, and that sought ways and means to further their spiritual progress throughout life eternal, than to go as a teacher to the very world that had been chosen for the mortal life bestowal of the Creator Son of their very own universe. This world had experienced the betrayal of its Planetary Prince, who led us into rebellion, as well as the default of its Material Son and Daughter/Adam and Eve, who failed to fully carry out their assignment of advancing life on this planet toward its destiny. What a unique opportunity to be part of this mercy mission and provide spiritual guidance and counsel to those mortals willing to participate, receive the training and then go on to assist in achieving the divine purpose for this planet.

It has always surprised me that some question the how and why and means of accomplishing this mission and seemingly think they know a better way - particularly those students of *the Urantia Book* (UB) who have gained great insight into so many facets of life here on this planet and its relative position in the universe, as well as the true nature of Jesus as our Creator Son. One would think that those with more understanding would welcome this mission with open arms, but preconceived ideas and beliefs get in the way of many seeking truth along the mortal sojourn. My experience with sincere truth seekers that are not students of the UB is that when given an understanding of the purpose and nature of the Teaching Mission, they respond with genuine interest and sincere desire to learn more.

Now, on to my personal experience with the Teaching Mission, and how I was introduced to this wonderful opportunity and to the Teachers. In 1992 I was asked by Wally Ziglar, the man who first introduced me to the UB in the mid-80s and my fraternity brother from college, if I would like to participate with him and a group of people meeting at his home in Orange County to receive training from a "spiritual teacher." He explained that while I was in Chile on business earlier that year a few of this group had attended a meeting held during a Urantia Conference in February of that year at a hotel near the LA airport.

At this meeting an unseen "Teacher" identified as Ham was introduced through a person who was hearing his words and transmitting them to those in attendance - this person was identified as the "transmitter/receiver" (T/R) for the teacher. Ham announced through the T/R that a Correcting Time was upon us and that a Teaching Mission had been launched and that he had begun teaching a group that formed in a suburb of Salt Lake City named Woods Cross. In fact, it was members of this group that had caused the meeting to take place in Los Angeles for the purpose of providing those attending the conference the opportunity to "hear" from Ham and learn of the purpose and method of this Teaching Mission.

My friend Wally then went on to explain the procedure used for receiving and transmitting what the Teachers assigned to their group were imparting through their T/R, John Roper, a member of the group, because the Teachers are not seen or heard directly by any of the TeaM groups as they are invisible beings! Wally also explained how he and John and a few others had met in his home after the announcement meeting in February to follow the method given at that time for establishing contact with a "Teacher." They had done this on a few occasions when finally John perceived that someone was communicating to him mentally and thus began the meetings of the Orange County Teaching Mission Group.

A unique feature of this group versus others that formed is that there were two teachers who identified themselves through John as Bertrand and Signa, male and female, whereas all other groups were assigned one teacher, some male and others female, although often several visiting Teachers will communicate during a TeaM meeting.

I enthusiastically agreed to join the group but had to be interviewed by another member of the group and be approved by the Teachers before attending. Wally made arrangements for the interview and to my surprise the man that accompanied him to interview me, Will Fesler, had been my architect on an industrial real estate development project a few years earlier. I had no idea he had been a UB student. The interview went well, I was approved, and I began meeting with the group every week thereafter.

There were usually about 20 of us in attendance and the lessons would run from 30-45 minutes and then the Q & A period would run another 30-45 minutes. These entire meetings were recorded and then transcripts were prepared for each recorded meeting. As a result there is a complete record of what was said by the teachers as well as the questions and answers that developed after each lesson period. It is truly enlightening to read these transcripts. There is a wealth of valuable information recorded. This same pattern has been followed by all of the groups that have begun around the entire country. As a result, there now exists an archive of the lessons and Q & A sessions of numerous TeaM groups beginning in the early 90s and continuing to the present day.

During the initial two-year period, we were relatively passive and simply received instruction from our two teachers who took turns providing the lessons and would both be available for the questions. After about two years, they announced to us that the time had come for us to graduate from phase one of the mission and that henceforth we would be expected to take the information imparted and determine how we would put it to good use, collectively and/ or individually, in our daily lives.

At this time we also transferred our meetings to the home of Will and Susan Fesler with John Roper continuing to be our T/R for approximately another two years until he was transferred to Chicago in his work with Mazda. At the time John and his wife, Jane, moved from our midst we continued to meet as a study group, reading the UB and discussing what we had read as it applied to the Teaching Mission, since we no longer had someone able to act as T/R. We also shared with each other what we each were doing in regard to the assignment given to apply the lessons from the Teachers in our daily lives.

The Teachers are constantly encouraging each of us to practice "stillness" and seek to make contact with individual Teachers that are assigned to each participant. Not all of us were able to make contact but our T/R, John, would assist and act as intermediary between the individual Teachers and the members of the group, such that each learned the name of their teacher and could focus in their stillness on making contact with their Teacher. John also conveyed to each of us the Spiritual Name that was given to each of us by the Teachers. (However, later the practice of using our Spiritual Name was discontinued because it became a distraction.)

It was in one of these private sessions with the Teachers and John acting as intermediary that I learned of the identity and background of my personal teacher. In this manner I also learned of the Teacher assigned to the area of Chile in South America where I was conducting business and meeting with UB study groups in Santiago.

On my business trips to Chile I would meet with the study groups in the Santiago metropolitan area and when the book was first translated to Spanish in the mid-90's I was able to bring them the first copies of the UB in Spanish. It was truly gratifying to be with them when they first received the book in their own language. For many years they had been studying the UB in English one paragraph at a time. A bilingual member of the group would read in English and then translate and explain what each paragraph stated.

Their love and appreciation for the teachings of the book were evident and when they could finally read it for themselves it brought tears to all our eyes as we shared such great joy. They would treat me as an emissary coming from "on high" each time I met with the groups and I prayed privately before each visit that I would be able to properly answer their questions and help inspire their quest for truth.

When I learned of the Teacher assigned to that area of the Spanish speaking world I made it known to those UB students that showed interest in the Teaching Mission and met with them in stillness as they pursued contact with the Teacher that would lead them. Finally, contact was made and they did begin a Teaching Mission group of sincere truth seekers in Santiago. My business trips ceased about that time so I was not able to continue following up with their progress but the seeds were planted and I'm confident the Teaching Mission in that part of the world has grown and benefits countless numbers of sincere truth seekers.

As word spread of the teachings emanating from TeaM groups in various parts of the USA, others in Southern California expressed interest in having a Teacher assigned and starting a group convenient to them. As a result, John Roper and others of our group traveled to meet with those interested and two groups began as a direct result of this effort, in Arcadia and Bakersfield. TR's surfaced in those groups and they continued on in the pattern of two years of lessons from the assigned Teacher and then the assignment to go forth and practice what had been taught with the Teachers available for instruction periodically, but not on the same intense weekly basis as before. This pattern reminds me of the experience of the apostles who were taught by Jesus during his short ministry and then given the assignment to go forth and teach and share what they had learned from Jesus, to love and serve one another following His example.

During the 90's there were several TeaM groups that began to meet in various parts of California and the rest of the Country such that conferences where all could meet together were organized. In California we organized what were called Spirit Fests, and the first of these was held in 1994 at a facility near San Luis Obispo. We continued these for several years. Similar regional conferences were organized in other parts of the country and all participants of the Teaching Mission around the country were encouraged to attend. Our Orange County group cooperated with the Arcadia group to organize the Spirit Fest of 1996 and many of us attended several of the other regional and national conferences.

One fond memory that stands out in my mind from the conference our group helped to sponsor was the "Song Book" that I put together to facilitate group singing. I assembled copies of numerous religious music arrangements with the lyrics so all could participate. Deborah Goaldman, a lady with a lovely voice from the Bakersfield TeaM, assisted me; I played the piano accompaniment as she led the group in singing these religious hymns.

As a former professional musician and vocalist, music has always been an important part of my worship activity and I was missing the singing during our meetings and conferences. It seems that not everyone finds group singing to be an important part of the worship experience so it is not often a part of these meetings and conferences, and I miss it. In any event, the Song Book is available for any who may want to take advantage of it.

Toward the end of the 90's, the Orange County TeaM was no longer meeting. I moved from Orange County at that time and began to attend the TeaM meetings in Arcadia at the home of Harold and Lucille Kettell that sprang from our Orange County group. Hal passed away just a few years ago but Lucille continues as a gracious hostess, though quite elderly and frail and is now assisted by Donna and Larry Whelan.

The Teaching Mission

This group began in 1993 and finished the lesson phase of the mission a couple of years later and subsequently did not meet regularly for a few years but their Teacher, JarEl, let it be known through another group that he visited he would like to reinstitute their meetings. At that time Henry Zeringue had begun making contact with his Teacher and volunteered to be the T/R for the group. They began anew to meet as the Arcadia TeaM and continue to meet at present as the only active TeaM in Southern California.

After the Arcadia TeaM began anew, we were visited by George Barnard from Australia. He explained to us that for many years he had been working in collaboration with several Midwayers. They instructed him to write about his experiences so he had finished five manuscripts of his experiences with them when he first encountered *the Urantia Book* in about 2001. Shortly after that he learned of the Teaching Mission and came to the USA to visit the various groups and see if he could get assistance in having his manuscripts published. Eventually Byron Belitsos, a publisher and longtime UB student and TeaM member, agreed to help him and then I was enlisted to assist also. As a result I had numerous meetings with George, as well as with Byron, and we were able to get his first book published, *The Search for 11:11,* in 2003. George returned to Australia and the following year published his second book, *"In The Service of 11:11."*

One of his manuscripts is suitable for adaptation to a screenplay/movie so I introduced George to a screenplay writer friend, Marsha Kennedy, and we worked towards that end, but when George had to return to Australia due to Visa problems, before we could get the draft of the screenplay written, the project stalled and still sits on the back burner. George sponsors a website from Australia that encourages anyone from around the world that has "spiritual encounters or messages" (particularly those that are related to "digital reminders" such as 1111 appearing frequently in their daily experience) to let him know so he can post their experiences and received messages on his website. He also sends out a weekly email broadcast of the lessons and messages that emanate from several of the Midwayers and other spiritual personalities.

Anyone interested can subscribe on his websites: www.spiritguardians.com or www.1111publishers.com. He is a colorful and most remarkable man who is one of the most dedicated individuals to the cause of our "unseen helpers, The Midwayers" as well as the Teaching Mission as anyone I know.

Many years ago I earnestly initiated a quest for answers to religious and spiritual questions and read much and investigated most of the religious and spiritual paths that exist on earth. Eventually, I decided to narrow my search to all I could locate that purports to be from non-human origin, regardless of how it came into existence. Raised as a Mormon and having been a missionary for that church, I learned to believe that modern day revelation is a reality, so this narrowly focused pursuit was consistent with beliefs I already held to be true. However, I had developed serious doubts about some Mormon doctrine so I began to search beyond my early indoctrination.

The Teaching Mission

When I finally encountered the UB in the mid-80's I had read all the published material that came through Jane Roberts, known as the Seth Material, as well as other writings that purported to be received from non-mortal sources. I had seriously studied and practiced the teachings of A Course in Miracles, which I considered to be quite authentic. As I began my study of the UB I was overcome with the feeling that I had finally found a source for the answers I was seeking and the link to all the other "truths" I was learning.

Later, when news of the Teaching Mission reached me and I began to participate, it felt like The Workbook that is one of the three parts of *A Course in Miracles* – the "how to" part of the course. Likewise I find the Teaching Mission to be the "how to" extension of the UB . . . the Fifth Epochal Revelation.

Often I have been asked why I am not communicating directly with my personal teacher and/or acting as T/R for a TeaM group after all these years of reading, investigating and personal experience. The simple answer is that I am not sure why, although I do question myself at times.

Over the years I have tried all the techniques and methods that are taught and suggested and that have been successful for others, in addition to following the admonitions of the Teachers on how to go about making contact. I have also pursued different methods of inducing altered states of consciousness and even was in partnership briefly with Don Estes, a long time student of the UB who invented technology for this very purpose - synchronized strobing or flashing lights, musical or digital sound and varying vibrations. One can learn more about this at his website: www.vibrasound.com.

We incorporated equipment Don developed in a relaxation center within a SPA located in Beverly Hills for a period of time but the location was destroyed in a fire. Fortunately, we had closed the center just before the fire and thus saved the equipment. This process works wells to bring about deep relaxation and bring the brain waves to their lowest level, but did not help me to communicate with any spiritual being, which had been my primary objective in pursuing the business relationship.

Regardless of my seeming inability to perceive input from non-mortal sources that I can recognize and convey to others, I have and do perceive and recognize inspiration and promptings that validate for me and lead me along my truth-seeking path. I have come to realize that we are not alone in our quest for "All There Is." We have been provided many guides and tools in the form of a personal Thought Adjuster, a personal Spiritual Teacher, a Guardian Angel, Midwayers - who often intercede, The Spirit of Truth - to help us discern truth as we find it, and now the ascending mortal Teachers of the TeaM that have come from around the universe to teach us ways and means of progressing spiritually and putting into practice what our beloved Urantia Book teaches.

May we take heed and be diligent in our never-ending efforts to follow the teachings and admonitions of our Creator Son, Michael of Nebadon, also known on our planet as Jesus of Nazareth, to love and serve one another.

For Better or Worse
Mark Rogers

Dear Fellow Seekers,

If you are reading these words then I know you are a seeker – one who follows the calling to seek and to find what life would bring you. I know you are engaged in the process of stretching your spiritual wings to allow the ascending currents of spirit to lift you up so you can soar. I'll bet you have a certain resolve to search for truth, beauty and goodness and to follow where these things lead you, else you would not be here, looking and seeking.

Yeah, I know. Me too.

I don't know exactly when or how or even why but for some reason I have been absolutely driven to pursue an exploration of spirit. You know: that third part of being a human along with a mind and a body.

Well, now that I think about it, that's not exactly true. I guess I do know some of the 'why' that created the 'when' and the 'how' of my launching out on this journey of personal discovery to explore that dimension of self so apparently undefined in this mortal life.

I was in college, studying philosophy and religion, in "seeking mode" for a purpose to life, and it seems the more I searched, the more random and undefined the meaning of life and our purpose in it became. There seemed to be no overall plan, no consensus on the broader truths, let alone the meanings and values those truths were supposed to convey. We were threatened with nuclear planetary extinction and it seemed as though maybe there was no real purpose or meaning to our lives at all . . . just some sort of cosmic coincidence.

Then everything changed.

A rock-climbing accident, in 1979, resulted in a fall that took my life, or so it appeared, at least briefly anyway, and provided me with what is now commonly referred to as a "near-death experience" that changed my life forever. Let me tell you that this was a "real death experience," albeit one that did not last, but this experience of transition brought me immediately and directly into the realm of spirit where I was in the presence of . . . I did not know what.

A spiritual being of incredible light was there. I thought it must be God because it was so brilliant I did not feel worthy to be in its presence. The sensation of purity and bright light was profound and I felt naked, ashamed, and certainly unworthy to be in such a place with such a being of apparent divinity. Imagine my surprise when I learned that this being (I later discovered was my guardian angel) was there to minister to me.

Then there was this communication – or a communing, really, where descriptive words were not necessary to my real understanding, by means of a "direct transfer" of knowing and the resulting awareness. (Remember the mind melds Spock did on Star Trek?")

My body, my vehicle, had become damaged as a result of my reckless behavior, and now a decision had to be made as to whether to resume my mortal life in the current vehicle and undergo the material and mortal healing process which I was told would be painful and the price I would pay for such a choice, or whether the damage was too extensive to allow for a return.

It turned out that in this case it could go either way and I was given the choice to return and resume my earthly life where I had left off or to simply move on through the transition to the next phase of existence. "Next phase?" I thought. "What do you mean 'next phase'?" I expressed, and my spiritual guide honored my request to know and I was shown a glimpse of the great undertaking, the gigantic plan in place which included me and everyone else involved in this undertaking of growing our souls, our culture, our planet and even our universe.

I was shown my vehicle . . . damaged on the ground . . . and it was then I realized that I was not there—that the part of me which endures through the traumas of life was now looking down on just a body, just a vehicle with no driver. I was alive in spirit even though my body may not be if I did not choose to pick it up again. This realization was so profound and the spiritual realm was so incredibly peaceful and loving that I was sorely tempted to "move on" into my "next phase," to stay with spirit, as spirit.

I was assured that whatever choice I made, either way would make little difference in an eternal career that was slated for me. "Eternal career?" I thought? Just knowing this brought me such peace of mind . . . knowing there was a grand plan, an eternal career, a grand undertaking of which I was a part . . . all meant that my life did have a purpose, that nothing was truly random, and there was great meaning and value in all we experienced if we only could "see it."

I thought of my family and my obligations back "down there" on earth. My brother, who was climbing with me, was still clinging to the rock face, having watched me fall to my apparent death. And now I had finally found what I was looking for in all the seeking I was doing. Seeing what I had just seen had changed everything, and now I wanted to go back and live life knowing what I now knew. I chose to return and my choice was honored, and the next thing I knew I was in tremendous physical pain – the price I was told I would pay for such a choice – but it didn't seem to matter as much because now I knew this was all a temporary experience anyway and therefore my outlook on life had shifted totally.

Nothing was the same for me after that. I had made a commitment, a vow really, to bring the spiritual dimension more fully into my material realm if I could only have the chance to return and try again. I had a burning desire after that to get back to where I had been. I just had to get back to such a place – such a space as I had been in when I was "out there" somewhere in such a place of spirit, such a place of reality that it made everything else seem like a shadow of the real substance I had glimpsed. I knew it was a rare privilege to have this perspective to condition my experience and I was motivated to not waste this opportunity.

And so I set out and became a seeker. And the universe did not take long before I was presented with the greatest written resource on the planet today, in my opinion – *The Urantia Book*. This book provided me with the concepts for a foundation or basis for making sense and coming to a greater understanding of broader spiritual principles that resonated with my truth bells.

A lifetime could be devoted to dissecting the layered truth contained in this epochal revelation to great advantage and in fact we were lucky enough to come together with others in the early 80's who were led to explore this material and we formed the North Idaho Urantia Book study group. This group has been on-going since that time and has shifted to include new "revelatory material" as we have been led to do so.

Then in1992 we heard of a phenomenon that was being experienced by another study group where there was this process of transmitting/receiving (referred to as T/R'ing) in which a celestial personality was delivering lessons through a human counterpart, kind of like channeling except the human liaison was much more a part of the process and was used to "transmit" the thought patterns to be received by a spirit personality and then to be used to "receive" the communication back to be translated and delivered into the material realm.

A few of us in our group made the pilgrimage to Salt Lake City to see for ourselves what was up and to sit in on a "session" with the celestials. When I was there in the group of participants hearing the "teacher" Daniel's message, I felt it again. I recognized the flush of spirit contact I had been looking to connect with and I knew I had to follow this path to where I was certain it was leading.

We formally requested to be assigned a teacher at that time and we were told our group would be issued one and that we should all prepare by engaging in a practice called Stillness – a kind of meditation to quiet the self, to make a conducive environment where we could allow such contact. We tried for some time to do we knew not what, but I had faith . . . if I had nothing else . . . as a result of my previous encounters with spirit. I knew it was out there. I was just uncertain exactly how to access it.

Our group teacher Elyon did arrive to our group as promised and proceeded to provide us with spiritual insights and lessons about whatever we are involved in as we live our lives. His steadfast devotion to our group has meant so much to us all and I believe we can genuinely say he has become more than just a teacher or mentor or guide but a real friend – just as real as any human friend we may have.

Finally, through trial and adjustment, one day at a Michael's Bestowal Celebration, I felt the presence of a spirit personality. I thought I did anyway . . . or more felt than thought. Then

I had to struggle to overcome the resident obstacles of fear and doubt that can so thoroughly paralyze any efforts. I was excited and scared of the unknown but my previous encounter with the realm of spirit gave me the confidence to step out in faith, step off the sure footing of material life into the abyss of an uncertain dimension. And you know what? It was fine. No, it was great! One of the best moments of my life! I just did it – forsook my fears and doubts and just did it.

I have been actively engaged as a worker in the fields of what has become known as "the Teaching Mission" ever since.

I can try to describe what the sessions were like but that would only be a second-hand interpretation from a biased observer of what it really was, so I would invite you to sample some of the transcripts available online. These transcripts may be accessed at www.tmarchives.com.

Remember, these sessions were live meetings where we would get together and often have a group Stillness or centering and then simply allow our celestial friends to contact us, and the T/R would simply speak straight out the words. We would record them onto cassette tapes and then transcribe them into the format you see here as they happened.

Since coming "online" our group has heard from a number of spirit personalities, such as Elyon, Machiventa, Evanson, Stephen, Lantarnek, Lester, Nebadonia, Light, Michael and Monjoronson, as well as the occasional visiting personality.

We knew from the start that these messages and lessons were of enhanced spiritual content so from the earliest communications an effort was made to record and transcribe these lessons for the benefit of all.

We continue to do very much the same thing today. We still meet one, two, or even three times a week and hold meetings, question-and-answer sessions, and even hold live conference call-in sessions to hear from our friends on the other side of the veil and to act as conduits or liaisons for the downloading and transfer of spiritual realities to our world.

The arrival of a new teacher on the scene several years ago, Monjoronson, heralded another shift in development, and many of us have been led to help with what we call the "Magisterial Mission." The service project that was inspired to promote this mission is now known as www.monjoronson.com where we provide a format for questions and answers directly to the participants.

Then a few years ago there was another sudden and significant development in my own spiritual growth when I made the leap from being comfortable with hearing from other personalities in the spiritual dimension to allowing that I could also hear from what I call my "Voice Within" – that divine spark or fragment of the Creator that is within each of us – the one we are really looking to connect with. In fact, this whole earthly life is designed to foster the development of this connection between the creature and the Creator. Truly, this represents the greatest discovery a mortal can make and the whole while it is present within us, it is on-board and simply waiting to be acknowledged. If you go and visit either of the above websites you can see transcripts of what have been named the "Voice Series" (which will be a book of its own one day) in which we provide a platform for the exploration of this connection.

There is a divine spark in each of us that leads us to be seekers and it is in need of expression in an attempt to find meaning and purpose in life. If your seeking has led you here, if any of this has struck the chords of truth within you and led you to check out the Teaching Mission, you will find me there – still involved with the mission and the teachers and the work of bringing spirit to people and people to spirit. For me, this whole experience of working with the teachers and the individuals in our group has been a portal into the spiritual dimension that has been life-changing, uplifting and inspiring. The resulting spiritual growth has forever altered, colored and infused my life with meanings and values I never knew were there.

So I guess I am doing what I was trying to do those many years ago. I'm going out in pursuit of spirit and making it my mission to bring it back to share with others.

Just as I am exercising my mind in writing this narrative, and you are exercising yours to read and interpret it and in so doing we experience the flexing of this part of ourselves . . . or similarly, when we experience a serious illness or childbirth we exercise the part of us that is the body and we are confronted with our animal nature . . . likewise this exercising of the part of us that is spirit enables us to encounter and feel that aspect of our being.

Maybe someone hearing my story will be inspired to take a similar leap of faith and step out into the unfamiliar domain of spirit with confidence, knowing that if it happened to me, it can happen to them.

This has been my calling.
This has been my experience.
This has been my privilege to be involved in.

I have stated the why, the how, the when, and the mechanics of what has been my life's greatest spiritual influence. So who am I to offer this contribution to your process of spiritual growth and evolution?

I am nobody special, just like you.
I am everybody, as we are all one, just like you.
I am a child of God with all the privileges of such a family, just like you.
I am a member of the family of man, just like you.
I am a mind, a body and a spirit, just like you.
I am a seeker, just like you.

I pray my efforts are pleasing in the sight of my divine parents.

I feel privileged to know that they are.
I will remain forever grateful for this gift of grace.

Thank you!
Sincerely,
Mark Rogers
Of the North Idaho TeaM

A Woman in Recovery
Gerdean O'Dell

My name is Gerdean and I am a woman in recovery. I am in recovery from the Lucifer
Rebellion and the Adamic Default and I am in recovery from the effects of those two
primary causes: "self-will run riot," which may or may not include social, mental, and
emotional retardation; genetic disease; spiritual bankruptcy; co-dependence; alcoholism; drug
addiction; defiance; dysfunction; sexual aberrations; the seven deadly sins; and all manner of
behaviors to which human flesh is heir. I am not going to tell my 12-step story here. This is
my Teaching Mission [TeaM] story, but they are remarkably similar. Both are about the
effects of growing up on this dysfunctional planet, they both depend on the grace of God;
they both require humility and animal training; and, alas, both TeaM and AA still carry an
unfortunate social stigma.

I will preface my experience with the TeaM with a true story. In 1968 my neighbor Alan
Smith and I were introduced to each other and to *The Urantia Book* [UB] by a mutual friend.
Alan was a contact personality; he served as the mouthpiece for secondary midwayer 0802-
AB who called himself "Jack." Jack became the focal point of our marriage from 1971
through 1981, nurturing our spiritual path, cultivating our deep mind, and introducing us to
myriad celestial personalities that came to visit with us and teach us over the years. Jack
impressed upon us that Urantia was soon to undergo a new cosmic development, but he was
not at liberty to tell us what that development was, only that we would know it when it came.

After Alan and I divorced, I missed the companionship of these celestials and I found solace
in lesser spirits. Ten years later, in the summer of 1991, at age 46, I had been a student of
The Urantia Book for 23 years; I hosted a weekly UB study group. I had a great job that I
loved and was buying an adorable little adobe house on 1/4 of an acre in the south valley of
Albuquerque, but my life felt superficial and I was very lonely. I had God in my life, a
personal religion, and Jesus was my best friend, but something was missing. Alcohol
dependency was not helping, so I began attending the 12-step program of Alcoholics
Anonymous [AA].

That summer Dr. John Wormeck ("Jeremiah"), a physicist who had been studying with the
Woods Cross UB group near Salt Lake City, was transferred to Albuquerque by his employer;

he joined the small Urantia Book reading group at my home. It wasn't long before I learned that besides attending our UB group, Jeremiah drove a distance of 1250 miles, requiring 24 hours, to Utah and back *every weekend* to attend the Woods Cross group. When he finally confided to me that he drove all that way to hear a celestial teacher address the group, I knew that Jack's prophesy was coming true.

In February 1992, I attended the Urantia Fellowship's Triennial conference in Los Angeles to witness Teacher Ham announce the beginning of the Correcting Time. In my first year of sobriety I was rocketed into a fourth dimension of existence of which I had not even dreamed. The spiritual awakening for me included the realization that a battalion of celestials would henceforth work not only with me in a program of recovery, but with and for the entire planet. How exciting it was to learn that *the planet itself was entering into recovery!* I welcomed our heavenly helpers and rejoiced at the end of isolation.

The Teaching Mission arrived in the "pink cloud" phase of my sobriety. Through the Teacher Corps, the God of my understanding expanded and re-awakened the spirit of discovery I had found 23 years earlier. When I first read the Urantia Papers, I read with a voracious appetite, feeding my mind with its cosmology and history, devouring the many facts and concepts that poured into me, stimulating my spirit, comforting my soul and giving me intellectual peace. Now Urantia Book concepts and AA principles conspired to breathe into me a new life, and commenced to help me learn to live life on life's terms.

No longer was I a lonely, frightened child of nature, dependent on lesser spirits; I was becoming a dignified, noble child of God, "happy, joyous and free," surrounded by and communicating with myriad cousins and elders who were here to oversee The Correcting Time, a global recovery program. Thus was my 12-step program of recovery married to the Teaching Mission's Correcting Time from the outset, and they will be forevermore interwoven in my mind. AA and UB are the warp and woof of my sobriety, and they met in the TeaM.

After the 1992 Jesus Birthday Celebration with the Woods Cross group, in Pocatello, Idaho, I began practicing Stillness, and in February of 1993 I was able to make contact with Teacher Tomas, who, along with my personal guides Trieste and Adrian, taught me how to be a transmitter/receiver [T/R]. They worked with me on issues of personal correction, polishing my lump of coal until finally a diamond was seen to emerge. There's a notation in the AA big book that says that we cannot transmit what we haven't got. How fortunate for me that I had a laundry list of life experiences to draw from! Ready to make amends to God, for what seemed like a grand waste of time that could have been better spent, I committed my services to the Teacher Corps, to give back what I had received. Here is what Teacher Tomas told me during our first year together:

TOMAS: *"Greetings. I am Tomas. I am your Teacher and companion. Our discussion this evening relates to recovery, which is an analogy to Correcting Time, as the intents, motives, ambitions, goals, purpose, are the same. It is not an accident that hundreds of thousands of individuals are seeking enlightenment without drugs, alcohol, or other emotional or mind-altering substances. It is becoming clear to a faction of society that spirit reality is important for peace of mind and a happy, productive life-style. Recovery of the individual is the beginning of the recovery of the race.*

"Correcting Time is overseeing, over-controlling recovery, which is human, and therein the brotherhood of man is being called into play. Communications are encouraged. Seeking camaraderie and divine guidance through the individuals embarked on a spiritual path of recovery fosters spiritual discourse, reinforces worth, value, meanings. Even the dreaded term 'character defects' is useful in that individuals are called upon to determine where they fall short in their goal of God-likeness.

"Recovery is a human counterpart of Correcting Time. The movement toward spiritual awakening and spiritual living will carry mankind into this new age. When the concept of recovery so permeates civilization as to effect ethics and value of existing and future institutions, primitive societies will catch the wave, bridging economic, social and cultural differences to the further realization of the brotherhood of man worldwide. This is the method whereby political systems are forged.

"It has been said that might is not always right but it is what prevails. When recovered individuals - those who seek God first, those who seek / attempt to maintain a fraternal relationship with their fellowman - prevail, might will also be right. In this long process, which already has accelerated greatly, behold the growth of one individual - one seemingly hopeless and helpless individual - rise to self-respect and service. Growth in those who are willing is swift and sure."

As a farmer might shake the apple tree until all the ripe fruit breaks loose and comes tumbling down, the Teacher Corps shook me to my foundations. After my branches were pruned of the shackles and chains of dead wood, I was uprooted from my little adobe house in the valley and led away from my job with the government. Through their patient mentoring, I learned how to live clean and sober . . . not only happy, joyous and free, but useful to God and my fellows! I relocated to the SE Idaho TeaM where my newfound skill as a T/R was challenged and expanded during Teacher Tomas's two-year internship with Teacher Daniel in the Pocatello TeaM, before Tomas was assigned his own teacher base in Pittsburgh PA, near Butler PA, my hometown.

As an example of what I experienced on this faith walk, before I set out from Idaho for the Pittsburgh assignment, I was led through a guided visualization in which I was able to "see" where I would be living: on a main street, over a store, with a stationary shop, a frame shop and a sandwich shop in view; the rent would be: $225. Six weeks later, on a snowy day in December 1995, I was in Butler and was led, through remembering the visualization, to a three-story building that had been constructed in 1863 during the Civil War, whose overhead windows above a flower and gift shop remarkably like those in the visualization. On Main Street, it looked out to all the requisite shops. Upon investigation, it was found to be suitable for habitation and available for $225 - the *precise* amount of money that had been revealed in the aforementioned vision. I moved in, January 1, 1996.

That was my best era. I had come down off my pink cloud and had worked through my most glaring character defects. I had resolved many of my issues through personal Correcting Time efforts, worked off a lot of my messianic zeal and, with the help of the

Teachers, had learned to be a child of faith with my feet on the ground with my eye on the prize. Allowing God to lead me, I enjoyed the most amazing life experiences. I learned that when we set out to work for God, *all* of our needs are provided.

I took the course in The Artist's Way, which woke up my creative nature, which gave rise to a series of lucid dreams, which empowered me to start my own business - a used, rare and out-of-print book store. "Serendipity! Books and Other Wonders" was a vortex of spiritual reality in an otherwise bleak outpost. In the course of the first year, the book store business was launched on the first floor, the abandoned third floor was refurbished as a private suite, and the second and main floor was developed to be used for reading groups, writing groups, recovery meetings, UB and TeaM sessions, a painting studio, a copy shop, typing and editing services, a printing press and a social hub.

In 1998, seven years clean and sober, I was my own person and my own boss. Poor but independent, I ran my own business and enjoyed the enthusiastic society of an array of friends and neighbors both human and divine. Also that year, one of Tomas' students bought me a computer, so at last I was able to sign onto the Teaching Mission List [TML] and hobnob with TeaM peers on-line. There I met Angus, the man who would become my second husband. At the same time, I was corresponding with my former spouse, Alan, arranging for him to fly into Pittsburgh to stay with me for a few weeks while he had some medical matters tended to. It was a divinely orchestrated event when these two men, my past and future husbands, became simultaneous houseguests in the architectural sphere that had been provided by the Supernals, all of us having *the Urantia Book* and the heavenly helpers as a common frame of reference.

Angus and I met among our TeaM peers on TML, fell in love amid our TeaM peers in Pittsburgh and Butler, spent our honeymoon with our TeaM peers at Celestial Nights in Florida, and our marriage at IC-09 in Vancouver, Canada, was witnessed and celebrated by UB/Teaching Mission peers. No matter where we went or what we were doing, we were "at home" in the universe with God doing for us what we could not do for ourselves. We were living life on life's terms with our feet on the ground and our eyes on the pearl of great price. Thus the Teaching Mission became for me not simply a program of recovery, it became a means to an end and a way of life – my culture, even my church.

However, in conjoining with Angus, the energies changed. We became involved in the publishing ventures of Jim Cleveland's Light & Life dot com enterprises and founded the Harp of God publishing venture, which led to publishing Tomas' "Fruits of the Spirit." Midwayer Gorman came to help us and to teach us about "The Father's Business" and we received personal council from a cherubim-sanobim pair about "Intelligent Wedlock." At length, and with their blessing, the bookstore was dismantled. We closed out that phase, Tomas detached himself from his students in Pittsburgh and Butler, and proceeded to the Pacific Northwest where we were to sojourn for a season with our TeaM peers there.

The Church Within provided us transition housing while Tomas co-taught with Teacher Elyon of the Coeur d'Alene TeaM until we found our way into Spokane, where we took up housekeeping and re-opened the Spokane Teacher Base where Teacher Aaron had prevailed years before. There we were visited by George Barnard, facilitator of the 11:11 Progress Group. In all of these places, all of the people we encountered were made real and meaningful through the TeaM Spirit. Such a living love made for a very fine life.

After an 8-year walkabout with Teacher Tomas & Co., when Angus and I returned to the Great Southwest in February 2002, the Rio Rancho TeaM was ready to commence. It was augmented for two years by the dynamic duo of Teacher Anatolia co-teaching with Tomas; and, when Tomas took a sabbatical to visit with the Andover, Michigan TeaM, Teacher Merium arrived to companion us; then, Most High Andromadeus spent a year talking to us about planetary government. A mature group, the Rio Rancho TeaM began to subside and finally phased out. We remain close in spirit, but we have gone our own ways in personal ministry, all of us having benefited from this unforgettable experience.

Sometimes it makes me sad to see the end of an era, or a lull in cosmic consciousness, or abatement in social interaction, but I know the Spirit is alive and well in each of us, individually. The mission of Michael shall not fail. And the epochal angels of each generation have their own method of getting truth across. I have lived long enough to know that things ebb and flow, they rise and fall, even as time and spiritual evolution march on. Sadder still is the reaction I have when I encounter people who seem to go out of their way to vilify Teaching Mission proponents, in an attempt to destroy our faith and our zeal. It is always sad to encounter people who seem driven to destroy that which they cannot understand or that which does not conform to their own ideals and standards.

I'd like to say something here about the process of T/Ring and the effect it can have on the T/R. As I mentioned, my first husband Alan believed himself to be a contact personality for a secondary midwayer well before the Teaching Mission came into vogue and coined the term "T/R." He often thought he was going crazy, and would sometimes refuse access to our invisible friends, insisting that if "they" wanted a message to get through, "they" could jolly well type it up themselves. I never could understand this conflict of his. I always thought it was such a wonderful thing he did, such a service he provided, such a comfort the process offered, because to me it was always so uplifting, thought-provoking and inspiring, not to mention entertaining! But having become a mouthpiece for the Teacher Corps, I now know exactly what he meant.

It is bizarre to derive such soul satisfaction from an activity that cannot be identified, and absurd to continue an activity that brings on such pain from detractors who cannot or will not comprehend your motives for doing such a thing. It is unsettling to not be able to explain what happens in your own mind. Sometimes I want to say to those who jeer: "Yes! I know! It's crazy!" But it is NOT crazy; and I am not crazy. I don't "hear voices." I can't explain it. As I listen to other T/Rs, most of the time I am rewarded to hear Spirit speak to my soul, but it is also true that often the message is a subconscious uprising or a political platform for the T/R, especially those with an agenda. A little tolerance and a little discernment goes a long way in listening, but at its base I believe there is something to this process we call Transmitting/Receiving that won't go away but that is a natural and normal part of our planetary spiritual awakening.

It's not that I have that much faith in me or in other T/Rs, for we are human and we are fallible, but I have faith in what this process does. It helps us lift up and make contact with the superconscious levels of our mind. Just as it is wonderful to see people find AA and get sober, it is wonderful to see people discover the Teachers. Minds are opened; lives are touched; spirits are enlivened; souls are awakened. Students sometimes weep for joy at the opportunity to feel so close to the Spirit that dwells within them. Many times, as a T/R, observing the interaction between a Teacher and a Student, hearing the Student give voice to a new insight that reduces his fear, enlarges his consciousness, and illuminates his soul, I am humbled to see the Mystery Monitor at work. It is a wonderful ministry. It is fertile with possibilities.

Some folks think that I am splitting hairs when I insist I am not a "channeler," and they could be right except for one point worth noting: the gift of free will is one of the most precious gifts given to mortals by Deity, since it is through our free will that we make those decisions that either advance or retard our spiritual development. Thus, for us to relinquish our free will in order to allow any other entity to take over our mind could be considered an abnegation of personal responsibility. In transmitting/receiving, we are conscious of what goes on in our physical and mental environment. We are not in a trance, but are able to observe and judge every thought and word that comes along. We are thus able to reject any word, any concept if it is not in keeping with our free will. We are thus accountable for our every utterance, as I believe we should be for we learn by our mistakes. But it is still difficult to endure the criticisms of those who think we are charlatans and/or self-deluded minions and toadies of the devil himself.

The AA big book tells us that when we make a decision to turn our life over to the care of God as we understand God, we get "rocketed into a fourth dimension of existence of which we had not even dreamed." Similarly, the UB tells us, and the Teachers teach us, that as we relinquish our tenacious hold on the material dimension with which we are familiar and in which we are comfortable, to allow for the influence of God's celestial agencies and heavenly helpers, we are shown a way of life that far transcends the dog-eat-dog ways and means of modern-day materialism. As we relinquish our stranglehold on the finite perspective, we make inroads into refined regions of spirit consciousness.

As we engage in prayer and meditation through the practice of Stillness, we engage in a practice not unlike what religionists have enjoyed for centuries in the contemplation of the inner life we share with God. It is enduring trust and faith in that which we cannot see, but which affects us and how we perceive life, that makes this transmitting/receiving process worth investigating, and that makes this Teaching Mission movement worthwhile.

My Journey with the Teaching Mission
Eric Johnson

My guess is that it was the spring of 1988 when I was first introduced to the teachers. I was attending Mainely Men (yes, it happens in Maine), and one of the workshops being offered was on channeling. So I went to check it out and find out just what channeling was. When I got there, the chairs were set up in a circle and the fellow leading the workshop was standing near the middle of the circle. He asked us to relax and then started to describe what his experiences had been with regard to channeling and the sessions he had attended at an organization in Portland Maine called <u>Project: World Enlightenment</u>. He took some questions and then offered to begin the process. We all gave our assent and it began.

He proceeded to "channel," or transmit, Vywamus, who basically took control over of his body and began to interact with the participants. It quickly turned into one of the most intense, effective therapy sessions I had ever witnessed. Vywamus would ask for volunteers to talk to and then would start asking a few very pointed questions of them. Depending on their answers he would either ask additional questions to get more information or make statements to the participant which hit the nail on the head of whatever the deepest issue was. It was very impressive and I wanted more.

That fall there was another gathering of Mainely Men and as luck would have it there was another channeling workshop offered. I jumped at the opportunity to attend, and it was just as wonderful as the first one I went to. The fellow leading it later gave me the name of someone at <u>Project: World Enlightenment,</u> and contact information, and I was quick to pick up on that lead. I was delighted to discover that they were coming down to Lexington, MA, on a weekly basis to have sessions at someone's house, and I began attending those as I was living near there in Newton, MA at the time.

One session in particular lead me to an epiphany when Vywamus was working with a fellow who was projecting his feelings onto the rest of us. Just as I became aware of the fact that I was feeling his feelings, via a knot in my belly, Vywamus cut him short and told him not to put his feelings off onto the rest of us. The knot instantly disappeared. Wow! I was immediately able to realize that I routinely was put in that position in my first marriage.

She was someone who had a lot of baggage locked away in her emotional dungeon and refused to go in after it to clean it out. Consequently her feelings attempted to find expression in more round-about ways, as in putting them off on others to feel. Sadly for me, I was in a period of my life where I was exploring all emotions and hers happily piggy-backed onto mine. Anyway, back to the story.)

My next move was to start attending workshops up in Portland on <u>Developing Your Sixth Sense</u>, again channeled. We learned how to tap into our intuition and discover that we could learn things about others simply by focusing on them, which we did in short five minute sessions. In addition to that several weeks-long workshop on Wednesday nights (yes it was a long drive from Newton – a suburb of Boston, up to Portland - but worth it), there was a channeling-intensive workshop given. I went to that with my friend Ed and we were treated to an experience I'm still to this day puzzling through. We were told that we had all been alive on Atlantis just before its destruction and that each of us had played a role, as either a priest or a scientist, in bringing about its destruction.

I'm not much on past lives but something about this rang true for me. I do have the feeling that in some past life I had seriously abused my power and that before coming into this one I had shut off my access to this power until such a time as I could be trusted to use it wisely.

I also am of the opinion that Atlantis and the First Garden of Eden were the same islandish piece of land south of Cyprus. . . and that many of the offspring of Adam and Eve re-settled there after Adam and Eve passed away, and that they had a thriving superior civilization for a long time. . . the kind of civilization to rival and surpass Camelot. But then a great tragedy happened when a mighty earthquake caused the Rock of Gibraltar to separate from Africa and allowed the Mediterranean basin to be flooded by the waters from the Atlantic Ocean. It was the mighty flood, of biblical proportions. All human settlements around the perimeter of the Mediterranean were wiped out, as was Atlantis.

The suggestion at this workshop was that I, and the others there, had somehow had a hand in bringing this about. Did we somehow cause this "earth quake?" Did we think Africa was our toy, to do with as we pleased? Curiously, civilization again borders on the brink of similarly catastrophic proportions if a nuclear war were to break out. How could we have learned from our mistakes if those who made them were wiped out by them? And could that happen again? We all hope and pray that the answer to that is 'no.'

From 1989 to 1992 I was preoccupied with the dissolution of my marriage to my first wife, unemployment, and a couple of relocations back into Boston. But soon I was in a new Urantia Book Study Group with a friend named Steven Hecht. At one of our Study Group meetings a couple of fellows from New York came to visit. They introduced us to the Teaching Mission (otherwise known as TeaM). They came with copies of transcripts and stories to tell. I found it fascinating. And given my prior experiences with folks from Maine, I was predisposed to embrace the teachers with open arms.

Several months later Steven and I went to Naperville, Illinois, to hopefully witness the materialization of Machiventa Melchizedek. It was right after one of my men's gatherings, just when WACO was becoming a household word from the tragic battle between federal marshals and religious cultists in Waco, Texas.

At a Holiday Inn in Naperville, a bunch of us from around the country had gathered, I suppose as a kind of test being given by the teachers, on the pretext of something wonderful. Sadly, it didn't happen. We were told that in light of the country's attitudes for and against cults, it had been decided that the Big Mac, as we called him, would remain invisible to human eyes. Those who had arrived skeptical, like Steven, remained skeptical, and those who were already having transmission experiences of their own, became even more steadfast in their belief, given the transmitting that went on there.

One of the key elements to the Teaching Mission was that everyone could have a teacher; they had but to ask for one. So I did. As fate would have it, at one of my energy work sessions with my friend Michael Young, (who had studied under a spiritual teacher named Barbara Brennan), he informed me that there was someone else there in the room. Having just asked for a teacher days before, I immediately hoped that this was it. He told me that his name was Belazar, which he spelled out for me, and proceeded to tell me a little bit about him. . . great leader, etc. etc. Given that Michael knew nothing about the Teaching Mission, I took this as one of the best forms of confirmation one would ever be able to come by regarding the reality of the Teaching Mission. So Belazar was my new teacher. . . He also predicted that I would meet my soul mate in two years time.

The summer of 1993 saw my life in turmoil. My ex-wife, Sara, and daughter, Emily, left Massachusetts for Denver, Colorado, where Sara had secured a new job. I likewise found work not in Boston, but in Philadelphia, PA. At the Naperville event I got to know a bunch of people from various parts of the country. One of them was Jim Cleveland, (for whom I'm writing this chapter), and another was a young woman from Cincinnati, Ohio. Having become recently single and interested in the woman from Cincinnati), I "moved" down there to be with her. "Moved" is in quotes as I was only there on weekends, driving back and forth from Philadelphia on Fridays and Sundays. But as the Teaching Mission group in the area met on the weekends, of which Jim was a part, I got to be in my first TeaM group.

My previous introduction into energy work from Michael, and another Brennan student Anamica, had somehow prepared me to be receptive to the energies I felt from the teachers and angels present at the TeaM meetings. It was like the air was electric when the teachers would start to come through one of the T/R's (short for transmitter/receiver). And the energies would change with each new teacher who would come through. The lessons were superb, and the group was an interesting mix of personalities.

My contract in Philadelphia was short-lived due to a confluence of factors, lasting only about a month. The International Triennial Conference of Urantia Book readers was coming up in Quebec, where I was scheduled to rendezvous with my daughter to spend time with her as well as be at the conference.

My work at Core States Bank in Philly was going painfully slow as their mainframe computer was struggling under the weight of normal processing coupled with the weight of the development efforts we were engaged in. The report I was writing required a series of tests that involved submitting a job, and waiting for it to finish so I could inspect the results, make corrections and resubmit. In a normal shop I would have been able to do several of those each day. But at Core States it took a whole day just to run one job. This was seriously delaying the completion of my work in a timely manner.

As the date of the conference drew near, I arranged with co-workers to finish running my tests. The manager however, being rather dim where Information Technology development was concerned, didn't want to let me leave until my program was finished. If I left to go to a conference, which I had been looking forward to for half a year, and miss seeing my daughter, whom I'd been apart from for more than a month for the first time in her life, I would not be allowed to return to Core States. Jobs are nice, but daughters (and conferences) are far nicer.

At the conference I roomed not with my daughter, but with the woman from Cincinnati (who has changed her name so many times now I'm not sure what to call her). My daughter roomed with her friend Cristina, who had lived in her house in Newton while going to the Berkeley School of Music.

It was a fabulous conference with wonderful workshops, fabulous performances and schmoozing with lots of old and new friends. And even though the TeaM was not exactly in favor with the organizers, we were none-the-less able to secure rooms in which to hold our T/R sessions. At one of those I remember meeting Fred Harris (perhaps for the second time) and had the awareness that he was somehow going to be important in my life in a way I knew not how.

But fate has a strange way of happening when one least expects it. The woman from Cincinnati was not, to use a term I learned later, "reality material." She was/is a free spirit, who belongs to no man. She in fact had made some effort to convey that fact to me early on – citing her two divorces, but my infatuation with her kept me from taking her words to heart. At that conference her affections left me for another man. I was heartbroken.

As my stay in Cincinnati no longer made sense, and my desire to be near my daughter again was strong, I concluded that it would be best if I moved back to Colorado, from whence I am a native, and be near her as well as be near my parents for their final years. As I had not fully moved out of my room in Brighton, Massachusetts, I returned there, rented a moving truck, packed my things, and drove to Cincinnati to get the carload of things I had there. The breakup there was strange in so far as neither of us disliked the other, just that she liked some else better (who I in fact also liked).

The drive to Colorado was emotionally devastating, but as I had made the trip several times before, it was uneventful. Upon returning "home" to where I was born and had grown up, I stayed with my parents for four months – well, on weekends anyway.

I was quickly back out on the road, working on a contract in Richardson, Texas (a suburb of Dallas). There I participated in my second TeaM group, with many of the same sensations as I had experienced in Cincinnati. More wonderful transmissions, more friendships made, and still a sense of loss clouded my mood. Then one meeting one of the T/R's, Joyce, came up to me all excited and told me that Anastasia (one of the teachers) had told her that I was going to get to have the relationship I wanted. As I was certain that I had just lost that woman, I foolishly discounted that juicy tidbit of information. It later became part of the bedrock of my belief, faith and trust in what the teachers had to say. (Ah, how easy is it to say these things in hindsight!)

That contract lasted only a couple months, but the client wanted me to go to one of their other clients in Pennsylvania, this time in Pittsburgh, where I spent the next three months. TeaM group number three for me was at Bea Mouganis' house (to whom I dedicate this piece), and we had the most wonderful T/R imaginable. Beryl not only gave us lessons from the teachers, but she would also sing songs in other languages and recite poetry from them. And the group was absolutely filled with Love. It was there that I had my first lessons on how to T/R myself. I still miss that group to this day.

At the meeting on New Years Day of 1994 Beryl handed out these little boxes with ribbons around them, like little Christmas presents, and gave one to each of us. One of the teachers had given her what each of our spiritual names was and she had typed them up on strips of paper and folded them into each box. Mine read, "Sirrus-Adam – Transformation of habituated patterns and delivery of designated emissions of energy." Oh what a gift that was!

Somewhere in this time frame, Leah suggested we drive over to Cincinnati for another one of their TeaM meetings as there was someone we both knew, Darlene, who was coming in from Indiana to give a presentation. The meeting was going to be held at *her* house (the heartbreak hotel). My initial reaction was to stay away. But, practicing psychology on myself as I often did, I asked myself if I would have gone had it been meeting anywhere else, and I had to admit that I would.

So, was I going to let my lingering feelings for this woman interfere with my greater interest and devotion to divine work? Heck No (or some other words to that effect). But I none-the-less wanted to do it with style. So, in preparation, I decided what better time to practice T/ R'ing than in the moment? I invited my teacher, Belazar, to enter into communication with me via a transmission, and what followed next was quite amazing.

I began to ask Belazar a series of questions. I wanted to know if I should try to block Darlene's presentation and was told 'no, I was to support her.' What? 'Besides that, she really doesn't know exactly what she was proposing.' I was concerned for what I perceived as a fragility in the group, and was concerned that this group was too fragmented to be led off in yet another direction. I also wondered why it was in that fragile state. I was told that I already knew the answer, at which point my mind was drawn to the two leaders, who were in that role not because they'd been elected to it, but rather it was just that they were the patriarchs of the group. And there were one or two other items we discussed as well.

Upon arriving at the meeting, we were greeted cordially and all drama was avoided. But the amazing thing was that the first words out of the Darlene's mouth were "I really don't know where I want to go with this. . . " just like in my session. And when it came time to discuss what they were going to do with the information, one of the sort-of leaders turned to the other and asked for his opinion, not that of the group, no vote, just between the two of them; also as I had foreseen. Damn I was glad I went!

Philadelphia in January is one cold place. The Tuesday of my last week there was 20 degrees below zero Fahrenheit. Brrrrrrrh! Even though the walk from the hotel to the bank was just a few blocks, it was serious frostbite weather. I said my good-byes to that wonderful group and returned to Colorado that Friday. On Saturday, in Boulder Colorado there was an event put on by a group calling themselves Educaré. They called the event Revive! That day was a gorgeous, 60 degree day (that's 60 degrees above zero!) and Revive went on for 14 hours. Two of the key organizers were Errol and Rochelle Striker, and did they ever put on the most wonderful performances for us all. Out of that event was formed The Gathering, which met on Sunday mornings in Boulder. I was home at last!

As my parents' lifestyle at that point was more sedate than my own, my mother gently nudged me out of the nest for a second time. Within a few hours of looking, I had secured my own apartment. Before long I found a job in Denver and my being on the road came to an end. I no longer needed to fly back to Denver every other weekend to be with my daughter. I was already there.

Now there was the question of getting Urantians in Denver and Boulder to come to terms with the Teaching Mission. Boulder was and is a hotbed for Urantian activities and three of the ones from the Boulder group decided to put out a publication called the Invisible Fellowship which slammed the Teaching Mission. The suggestion that the transmissions coming through the Teaching Mission were somehow akin to the means by which *the Urantia Book* came into being was simply abhorrent to the more fundamental thinkers there. (And even TeaM folk distinguish T/R'ing from channeling.)

As I was very familiar with how the "traditionalist" in this very untraditional movement thought, as well as now being well-versed in what the TeaM was and was not, I decided to write my own letter to the editor. I reviewed each side's point of view and attempted to point out where possible fallacies were on either side. My response to the editors, as one of the editors put it, was unique (implying that all the other responses had been either in favor of their position or totally against it).

Meanwhile down in Denver, we started to have TeaM meetings at the Knots' house. One fellow in particular was intent on bringing TeaM to Boulder. That was Daniel Raphael. The two of us began collaborating on how to make inroads into the Boulder group.

As I was living in Boulder when I first started reading the U Book, I adopted the attitude that I belonged there. Having become friends with Mo Siegel at a conference at Lake Eufaula Oklahoma in the late 1970's knew I was among friends. But the two pronged approach by Daniel and myself proved in the end to be quite successful. At one of his initial attempts to introduce it in the "Experimental Group" he was severely interrupted and shut down by Carol Hay. I on the other hand took a more quiet approach. From one discussion to another, I just made it clear that to me the Teaching Mission, whatever it was, was of value and worthwhile.

A few years later however, it was Carol who was offering to do something on the Teaching Mission in the experimental group. Daniel and I were perplexed. What was she planning to do? Many of the dual members (study grouper and TeaM folk) were in attendance that night, and to our astonishment, Carol proceeded to describe where she had been coming from that night she gave Daniel such a hard time, and to basically apologize for her behavior. It was all we could do to keep from letting our jaws hit the floor! Wow! What a night.

Along came August of 1995. In Urantian circles it is widely accepted that August 21⁻ is the Master's birthday anniversary, and that he was actually born in the year 6 BC. That meant that we were now at the 2000ᵗʰ Anniversary of Jesus' birth (given the strange feature of the Gregorian calendar which has no year zero due to a Roman Numeral System limitation). A camping trip was planned in the mountains for a bunch of us to celebrate this occasion. The plan was to stay up until after 2 a.m. so as to coincide with noontime in Bethlehem on the other side of the world, the purported hour of Jesus' birth.

Before going, I received a message from the Master that he wanted me to speak for him at that event. I was humbled by his request, as well as uncertain how to proceed, given that there would be a fair number of my brothers and sisters there who were opposed to the TeaM. Admittedly my faith in the Master left something to be desired. I was also aware of the fact that my ability to T/R accurately was tenuous at best. But here he was saying he would give me the words – and I freaked.

The night of the 2 a.m. vigil arrived and I started to hear his words, a greeting of love and compassion. . . and I froze. I couldn't bring myself to do it – a failing I have been regretting ever since. Days later a friend of mine who had been in a somewhat similar situation in her past who had made the opposite choice, assured me that it would have not gone well if I had transmitted. Still, I was not convinced.

There was however something of a silver lining to that event in that one of the editors of the Invisible Fellowship publication that had slammed the Teaching Mission expressed his opinion that we should put our differences behind us and that he had basically dropped his opposition to our efforts. Hot Damn! Our efforts, Daniel's and mine, were paying off.

As this was now in the two-year time frame of Michael Young's prediction, I tried asking the teachers for the name of my soulmate. I got what I thought was a G and an L. So I deduced that I should be on the lookout for a Gloria. But the only Gloria I met was definitely not soulmate material.

This was also the time when the Internet was starting to really take off. E-mail, Service Providers, browsers, all became household words. It was time to join the electronic information age. I did it in part because I had heard about this discussion group on-line that used a list-server. The name of the group was "Urantial." It was new; it was exciting. . . it was impersonal. But the opinions expressed were something else. I quickly joined the fray. Naturally the division between traditional Urantians and TeaM folk existed here as well. On top of that, there was also a division between those who supported the copyright to the U Book and those who found the copyright too restrictive, and thought that the book and the three concentric circles used as a trade mark, belonged to all of us. But there was one person on this group who stood out above all others.

Her name is JoiLin. The spelling alone caught my attention. And her posts were so filled with love and compassion that I was drawn to her like a moth to a flame. In addition to our posts to the group, we exchanged a bunch of emails individually, and even had a few phone calls. There was just one minor detail. She lived in Florida. Well, okay, two minor details. She was also married.

In December 1995 I started a contract working on the Electronic Federal Tax Payment System. I was the team leader for the Payment Scheduling part of it. It was an intensive development effort that soon required working 50 and 60 hours a week in order to meet an IRS deadline in April of the following year. Suddenly I didn't have any time left over for email at home. Within a few months my inbox was too full to receive any more email, which was okay because I didn't have the time to read any of them either. Thus I made a quiet exit from Urantial. No good-byes, no nothing. But I did have an email from JoiLin wherein she expressed the hope that I would find my soul-mate.

In that vein, my good and long time friend Radine instructed me to create a list of everything I was looking for in a soulmate. She told me to be as specific as possible. I was supposed to have finished by the end of January 1996. I didn't start it until February. I called it my Mate Manifestation Program. It was in Notepad. Every day or two I'd think of something else I wanted to add to the list. By May it was more or less complete.

That summer, another Triennial Conference of Urantia Book readers was coming up, and it was going to be held in Flagstaff, Arizona. It was perhaps my last best chance for finding my soul-mate before I gave up looking altogether. The trouble was, I had developed a cynical streak where romance was concerned and I was seriously in danger of becoming a confirmed bachelor. Of course there would be TeaM meetings at the conference and I knew I would have a good time among friends, but I was so certain that my list was too restrictive that no one would be able to qualify. So I went, misgivings and all.

All week long at the conference a battle raged within my mind over whether I would extend that olive branch of hope, or give into the hopelessness that so dogged my heels. Finally, on the last day of the conference, I decided to give hope a chance. Somewhere in the late afternoon I met a woman whose nametag indicated that she was from the same city as JoiLin was from and I asked her if she would convey a message to JoiLin for me. To my surprise, she said that 'Joi was there at the conference and would I like to meet her'? (Silly question.) 'Of course' I replied. So Helen led me through the dining hall where everyone was having dinner and took me over to Joi's table and introduced us. Ah, a face at last, I thought.

I told her how I was sorry that I hadn't said any good-byes when I dropped off the Urantia list, and she said that it was all right, people come and go all the time. Then she excused herself as she had a meeting to go to and said that it was nice meeting me.

Well, it just so happened that I was going to the same meeting, a TeaM meeting, where she was one of the T/R's. At the end of it, she and a friend were giving folks Reiki and as I had a bit of kink in my neck, I asked for some, too. By then the room was emptying out with just a few folks left doing a little last minute T/R'ing. We started to talk, and talk, then walk, and talk some more. It turned out that she had a list, too. What a coincidence! Then we compared items on our respective lists and lo and behold she had just about everything on my list and I on hers. In the wee hours of the morning we finally went our separate ways.

The following morning, people were leaving the conference to return home or go on to somewhere else. As I had my own car, I decided to take a little trip down to Sedona and check out the Airport Vortex I had heard James Redfield (author of *The Celestine Prophecy*) talk about. So I was sitting there for a short while, grooving on the energy of it (or magnetism), when along comes JoiLin with a group of friends. I somewhat facetiously said "Well, it's about time you got here!" (as I really did want to see her again), and she explained how it came to be that she was there. We talked some more and, to make a long story short, we got married the following summer and returned to Sedona for our honeymoon. And it was Fred Harris who both facilitated her divorce from the husband she'd already given her notice to a year before, and helped preside at our wedding.

Many TeaM events followed for the two of us, including the next Triennial in Vancouver Canada. And one of the traits I've admired the most in Joi was the fact that she didn't seek out ego-boosting opportunities to T/R as she always maintains a healthy degree of skepticism around the whole process. This in my mind was what helped her to be so good at it. In keeping with her doubts, our friend Mary would ask Joi to give her sessions where Mary would ask silent questions of the teachers and have Joi transmit the answers. They were always spot on.

When the bottom fell out of the IT industry, Mary would ask the teachers for information about our prospects for recovery. With each new challenge we faced, she was always there seeking more information for us and about us. We were told time and again that there would be bumps in the road but that I would make it through. But by 2002 a long-standing health issue of mine came home to roost. By the fall, my irregular heartbeat developed into congestive heart failure. After checking into the hospital on December 20ᵗʰ Mary asked these questions again. By now I had experienced the teachers being right so many times in my life that I took those words to the bank. It also kept Joi sane. I never feared for a second that I might die. I found out a year and a half later that I had come within days of doing so.

One heart transplant and a hemicolectomy later I found myself lying on a bed in Intensive Care. The primary goal of the Teaching Mission is to bring all of us into a relationship with our indwelling spirit fragment of God. I had heard and read many times about how much

God loves us. I basically believed it, but I also suffered from earlier teachings about the wrath and judgment of God from my Christian upbringing.

With that background, I was lying there reviewing in my mind all the things that God had just given me, right when I needed it. Just getting a new heart within 24 hours of being put on the list should have done it for me, but no, there were a good half dozen events or so that, when strung together, indicated to me in no uncertain terms that God Really Loved me! Moments after concluding that this must be so, I felt God's Love overwhelm me! I felt it so strong, so completely, that I sobbed uncontrollably from the mixture of how wonderful it felt to how foolish my Christian upbringing notions were – which I could now let go of completely. I also knew from then on that God Loves each and every one of us dearly, and with a Love so strong that it's immeasurable.

After I was on the mend from these operations, some of the women in Boulder threw Joi a party to honor her efforts on my behalf. It was held at the home of one of the trustees to the Urantia Foundation, and what should transpire there but for them to have her T/R for them. That to me was the icing on the cake. TeaM was no longer a dirty word among the "traditionalists." The year was 2003.

THE TEACHING MISSION – My Beginning
Joilin Johnson

I was raised as a Methodist and each summer I went to Methodist Youth Camp in Leesburg, FL. The summer I turned fourteen, for some unknown reason I wanted to know about meditation. I don't even know where I might have heard of it, as my mother didn't meditate nor had she ever mentioned it to me.

While I was at camp, I was always, for the most part, a social kid, always preferring to do things with my cabin-mates rather than alone. However, one day I happened to notice a sign that said. "Meditation Trail this Way," and I thought to myself I'd like to go and take a look, maybe I could learn something, however, I didn't invite any of my friends; I decided to go alone.

It was sometime in the early evening, before the vespers bell would ring calling us all in for dinner that I took that walk. I began walking down the pathway, and suddenly came to a bend in the path. As I turned the corner, everything I looked at changed. . . .everything was lit up from the inside with the most incredible light and colors I had ever seen! Everything, from the individual grains of sand on the pathway, to each blade of grass and the leaves on the trees! I had no idea what I was looking at, it was so beautiful! I'm sure I stood there with my mouth open. All of a sudden it felt as if someone was pressing their hand down on the top of my head, and at the same time I was wrapped and filled with the most incredible love I had ever known!

I wanted to stay there, forever wrapped in that love. I don't know if it was a minute that seemed like and hour or an hour that seemed like a minute, as time was not– time had stood still for me. However, suddenly it was as if someone began to turn a dimmer switch and all those beautiful colors began to wane until everything was back to normal. I was heartbroken! I wanted to go with it, whatever IT was!

I remember there was a bench along the side of the path and I fell onto it sobbing my heart out! I stayed until I heard the vespers bell ring calling us in for our evening meal. I never told anyone what happened, not my cabin mates, nor my best friend back home, nor even my mother; I figured no one would believe me, so why tell them?

Something happened to me during that encounter; from that point forward, I went through every door that presented itself to try and discover what had happened to me and how I might experience it again. I became an avid reader, reading six and seven books at a time.

The years passed and one evening in 1983 I was going to be initiated as a Transcendental Meditator; the meeting was being held at the home of one of the students. As I came in the house I saw that she was reading a big blue book and I immediately asked her what she was reading. She covered the book up with her arm and said, "Oh, it's just a book." That was like waving a red flag in front of a bull, so I asked her again, telling her I was really interested and inhaled books of all kinds. Well, she gave a big sigh, and said, "Oh, alright, if you must know. It's a book about the hierarchy of God, our universe, our planet, and the final part is about Jesus' life as he lived, all of it, no missing years."

Hmm, I thought, this sounds like the kind of book I want to read! I asked her if I could borrow it. She gave another huge sigh and said, "I suppose I could let you have it for a day." A day? Wow, I thought to myself, (the book was huge!), this must be some book if she can't be without it for more than one day!

After the meeting, I took the book home and began to look through it. I looked at the Foreword; yikes! Too complex, and intellectual for me! I moved on to just leafing through the book and came on words like Thought Adjuster . . . wow, I don't want anything adjusting MY thoughts! It seemed as if the more I read, the more I felt like it was just too much for me. I brought it back the next day as promised and she asked me what I thought. I told her I thought it was the most way out Sci-fi I'd ever looked at and I'd read a lot! Well, she looked at me and said, "I did you a grave injustice yesterday, I should have told you that you probably wouldn't understand a lot of what it said, but that it was important to just read the words and let your God within do the deep level processing that needed to be done; in time you would understand it."

I thought that was really weird. Last night she didn't even want to tell me the name of the book, and now she's telling me I need to read it! Her words stayed inside me, however. One day as I was doing some shopping in Tallahassee, where I lived at the time, I noticed a new bookstore that was kind of out of the way, at the top of a hill, a place I wouldn't ordinarily go. Suddenly it seemed as if someone was grabbing me by the front of my shirt and pulling me up the hill! Okay! I thought, I'll just go in and see if they have a copy. Well, they did . . . one. And I bought it. It was thirty dollars back then, a lot more than I generally paid for a book, but buy it I did.

I took it home and put it on my bookshelf, where it remained for a few years. When I finally decided to read it, it took me a year and a half to get through it, when books usually took me somewhere between a few days to no more than a week and a half. The funny thing was that every time I began reading it, after about fifteen to twenty minutes I'd fall fast asleep! I now know that was my God within doing that deep level processing she had talked about!

I eventually wrote to the Foundation, those in charge of publication of the book, to see if there were study groups, as I knew I needed help in understanding it. They wrote back giving me two names that I put on my kitchen bulletin board. About a year and a half later, I was reading the book and got up (I thought to get a cup of coffee), when my hand shot out grabbing that slip of paper and I began dialing the number listed, for the first name. I had to leave a message and back then I never did that; I would just hang up. But leave it I did, telling them my name and what I was calling for.

I got a call back after a while from a gentleman asking me if I knew what had been happening in the Urantia community during the last two years. I told him I hadn't, as I hadn't understood there was a 'community.' He asked me if I might meet him at the local IHOP. He said he'd be the tall man with the big black three-ring-binder under his arm. I told him I'd be there shortly.

Over coffee he began telling me about how a group of spiritual seekers in New Zealand had a member in their group who was in touch with a teacher, and that the teacher was in spiritual form! He told me the story of how the Tallahassee reader group wound up with their very own teacher, named Will! The more he talked the more drawn I was to what he was telling me. It seemed to me that I was being given the answer to my prayers, as for years they had been "Father, I know when the student is ready the teacher will appear, and I know I am ready. Please send me my teacher!"

After we talked, he asked me if I wanted to borrow the notebook and read Will's transcripts. I was thrilled! At that point it was around 9:00 PM and I stayed up most of the night reading the pages until I was finished. Around 10:00 the next morning he called me again, asking me how things were going. I told him I had read all night and asked if there were anymore. He said he'd be right over and trade out the notebooks. By the time I was finished, I KNEW my prayer had indeed been answered! The next time he called, to pick up the notebook, he invited me to the meeting where the local "Teacher" came through one on the members.

That was the day my life changed in ways I'd only dreamed about before then!

I never missed a meeting. I lived for them! I was in awe of the person who was able to bring Will's words to us and wanted more than anything to be able to do it too! They told me to practice sitting in the Stillness (that silent space within our mind), and listen for her words.

Within about three months I began to 'see' words that came in from the right side, sliding into a slot or channel, in ticker-tape fashion, as soon as I verbalized the words they moved off toward the left and new words would come in to fill the slot. If I were ever in doubt, wondering if I had understood certain words, they would back-up and reappear so I could see and verbalize them again. In addition, whenever I sat with the teachers, my entire body was alive with an electric sensation, and my closed eyes would flutter as if I were in the REM state and dreaming.

Over the next months I worked with first Will and Machiventa, and then with many different teachers, as I had agreed to allow teachers who were awaiting contact with their own students the opportunity to experience the transmission process.

At one point, when working with Machiventa, he began giving me lessons, including homework designed to help me heal and remove the 'hidden' areas of childhood trauma. I remember one time that Michael himself brought me back in time to a memory that I was not even aware of, showing me the scene and helping me to -see- it for what it really was. I was able to see that my mother was frustrated and hurt by my grandmother's beautiful gifts to me, when she was not able to afford even a small gift for my birthday! I was able to let go of a deep pain/anger toward my mother I had never been aware of and yet one that had colored my relationship with her all of my life! Wow! What an incredible gift, and from a celestial I couldn't even see!

Over time, I no longer saw the words but simply heard them; all that remained was the fluttering eyes. It was at that time that I began to doubt my own ability; however, I learned that many, if not most transmitters doubted themselves.

Eventually I was given my own teacher, by the name of Ambrose, or at least that's what I called him, and eventually, I received another teacher I knew as AhmaNiden.

Back then, in the mid 90's, being a part of the group in Tallahassee was pure magic to me! When I first began transmitting for the group, I discovered that many of the members had tried to hear Will, but no matter what they did, they were unable to make the connection. One day, while working with a Melchizedek named Mantoube; he asked me if I would be willing to bring into the group a request of his? I said I would be happy to, so he asked me to let them know that he would like to work with all of them and help them come on-line with their own personal teachers.

When I told the group what he wanted to do for them, they eventually agreed to allow him to help them and a 'practice' group was formed. Within a very short time Mantoube had all of them connected. That was when the magic came to life for me! Each week Will's lesson would come through several different transmitters and it was like seeing a gem being slowly turned in the light, with different aspects of her lesson coming through the different members! I lived for those meetings!

One day just before Christmas in 1994, I had gone to the mall to buy several Christmas presents. I was in a small boutique, and had finished paying for my purchase. As I was leaving, my arm reached out and took down a CD from a display. It was not anything I would have bought. For one thing, it didn't even seem to belong on that particular display, as the display had CD's on it that all had nature sounds in their background, e.g., birdsong, waterfalls, rain, and the like. This CD however, had none of that, it was by an Italian pianist/composer, and one I'd never even heard of. For -some- reason that I couldn't understand, I went back in line and stood for another forty minutes in order to purchase that CD. When I got home, I just laid it on top of my rack system and basically forgot about it.

That is, until the evening that I came home from a teaching mission meeting where I had transmitted our Universe Mother Spirit. Whenever she came through it was always very emotional, and her energy stayed with me for several hours afterward. So, on this particular night, I went into the music room where we had a baby grand, with the intention of playing (something that always seemed to calm me down). However, my eye caught sight of the CD and I thought to see what it was like, so I put it on the carousel. As soon as the first strands of music filled the air, everything around me changed. The air became filled with an undulating, blue light/mist. I became aware of hearing words and at the same time I understood that I was to take them down. I fell into my meditation chair, picked up the pen and tablet that lay on the side table and took down these words. Every day for the next several weeks, whenever I played that particular piece of music I had a very heightened spiritual experience, not the same as the initial one, but heightened nonetheless. Following are the words that were written, given during the second week of January, 1995:

MY GIFTS TO YOU BELOVED

"This music, to touch your heart, like none other has. In this music is the reverberation of my love Made manifest in you. You have asked to feel my love for you. So I have given an expression of my love to you, blessed child. Know always that I will give to you what you seek, in my name. Nothing is impossible unto me. And to see my love reflected in your light, gives me great joy! You have promised to walk wherever I lead. So come, blessed daughter of light, the dance has begun. I will lead you to waters never tested, and show you wonders no man has ever conceived. Come beloved, be not afraid. I am here. I hold your hand. Come, let us begin."

WHAT GIFTS WILL YOU BRING TO ME, BELOVED?

And I replied: "My open heart. My loyalty and faith in you. The music of my soul - the note that is yours alone. The love I have for you, unbounded by time or space. My joy in all your creation. My selfless love for others. My deep desire to help mankind and my planet. My trust that your hand will always lead me where I need to go. The knowledge at long last, of your love for me!"

AND NOW, COUNT ALL THESE AMONG MY GIFTS FOR YOU

"Music that moves within your heart - it is I! The colors of a dawn sky or dusk - it is an expression of both hope and rebirth I give to you. The glorious sight of a rainbow to rekindle anew, my promise to you. Your senses, which you are just now receiving. The experience of life and the knowledge that both before and after the door - I am. The knowledge that you are my beloved child, unique, Like no other, irreplaceable in my heart. Wind chimes, birdsong, the sun on your face, The smell of lilacs, a summer shower, newly fallen snow, The crash of thunder, a waterfall, a baby's sweet breathe. The love of a friend, a mother's faith, a child's trust, The first flower of spring, and autumn's splendor, Physical expressions of love, Your ability to pray, and your ability to communicate with me, All the gifts manifested through nature, Your ability to think, to envision, to be. All these gifts, to you my beloved child. Think on what new gifts your eyes will see, your ears will hear, your heart will feel, as we begin this journey into yesterday's dreams! Listen, my beloved, as I call your name. Your name that is both joy and light!

"My child, you were given a pattern - the unique wonder that you are - at birth. I would have you uncover this perfect pattern and begin the journey of discovery, of recognition, of all that you are, of all that you can be. Your life's journey thus far has caused my gift to become hidden. Look within my child; look with both your mind and your heart. Seek to recognize the false patterns, those put down by your ego self, and those pressed upon you by others.

"Look as well for those you put upon yourself, in defense, of your original pattern. Do not think this will be an easy task, for it will not. It will take a degree of honesty you may yet need to nurture, and much soul searching. What I can give you, is my unending love and support along the way, and the promise that the journey, while it may not be easy, nor without obstacles, will engender much growth and joy.

"And at the end my beloved child, you will be free to begin your Life as I intended you to, before your world was torn asunder by Rebellion and darkness."

LOVE IS CREATION

"Open your hearts, my dear children, to the love that is within. I am the life and the resurrection, I am here, I walk beside you! Look to my light. And trust in your connection to me. Where you walk, I am. Where you dare to explore I will be! Open your hearts, my dear children, for you are the Light of this world. In me you have your being; in me you have your strength. Follow me into the light of this new dawn. Follow me and watch a New Age begin. From me through you. Love is creation. From me . . . through you."

WHEN THE CIRCLE CLOSES

"I am filled with such love for you, my Father, it seems I cannot bear it! My old life is passing away, and I am reborn! The world and all I look on, has filled with your Light. You have become my sustenance, my strength, my very life! I know you now, like I never thought to, yet I want to experience more. My love for you knows no bounds. No limits. I yearn to be held forever in your embrace! And I know -that- gift too, will one day be mine, as I seek ever more to know you, the circles will begin to close, and we'll meet heart to heart, will to will, light to light. You are me, and I am you together in eternity!"

BELIEVE AND RECEIVE

"You are my brother, you are my sister, and I love you with such compassion! I would give you the gift of love, if you would but let me. I have come to help open doors, to show you your heart holds the key. Look within to the Father, for He is there. And look without, for He is there as well. Open your hearts and receive his gifts: Seek and ye shall find. Ask and ye shall receive. Was not said to deceive. The gifts are yours, and freely given. So open your hearts, and receive!"

I AM HERE

"I live within the citadel of your heart. I am here! I live within you, my beloved children. Look to me. I am the way. I am the door. I am the pattern of life everlasting! You stand at the door. Do not be afraid. Take my hand. I will lead you through. The gift I would give will fill all your needs; the gift I would give you is love. Drink deeply, my children, from the well that's within. For I am the water of life! How long have I yearned to show you the way, to remove the darkness brought on by the rift! We walk, you and I, hand in hand through the mist, as we watch the New World unfold. Our time is now, our hour has come. I am Here! Feel my love, experience my tears of joy. As you open your hearts, and connect. From me . . . through you . . . to all! This world is beginning to be bathed in the light, the love from the heavens above. So too, will my voice that was once so obscure, Begin to be more fully heard! A New Day is dawning, the age where enlightenment reigns. Where hearts will all open and let go of their pain. No more will I cry out in vain!"

HOW MY HEART SINGS!

"Oh, my Father, how blessed is my life! Why did it take me so long? To recognize that your touch, your hand, has always been there, and it was I that was too blind to see? How my heart sings, as I begin each new day, to know I will spend it with you! You are my life, and all that I want, Is to pattern myself after you! Please help me dear Father, as an act of my will, to make of myself a reflection, as I know all I am, or ever will be, is directly related to you. Help me to walk through each day of my life, accepting each day as a gift. To be used as a channel for extending your love, to my brothers and sisters, from you."

I AM NOT SPECIAL

"Oh, my soul! How wondrous is this adventure we begin! I stand in awe of how it is that I have been chosen to participate in this wonder, this gift to our planet! I am not special. There is nothing about me that would help me to understand why I've been given such joy, such incredible joy! Have I done something of which I am not aware? I do not believe that I have. I have looked, and cannot find such a treasure. Why, then, I ask my soul, why? The exquisite joy and wonder of it is almost unbearable. What have I ever done, my Father, that you would choose me, above others, much more worthy than I?"

"Why have I chosen you my child? The wonder of it, Beloved daughter, is that it was not I, that chose, but you! And the heavens rejoiced on that day, while your song, the unique note that is you, reverberated across the sky!

"Look to the patterns that flow through your life to understand your part in the universal melody of eternity. This is the song of the spheres, the music that ties us together. The dance of life is the dance of love, as it weaves us together through you. You are the pattern that becomes ever clearer as we seek our connection with you."

BETWEEN ME AND THEE

"Oh, my Father! I am so blessed! How did I ever come to believe that I was happy before you came into my life? To even try to compare the two feelings seems ludicrous to me! There simply is no comparison. Nor the words to describe to another, the joy, with which you have filled my entire life! It begins within as an up flowing of what seems to me, the most joyous, tender, understanding love, I have ever known, and then you move out and beyond this body to fill every space within my environment. You are everywhere I look. The feeling of being totally cherished, and understood beyond all measure, is so incredible to me.

"I feel this moment as if I am a newly created butterfly, just emerging from my chrysalis wings still folded, and shimmering with the dampness of birth and as your music, this love, within which I am held, permeates my being I begin to move my wings to stretch to begin to feel such an exuberance for life for love for giving myself in your service, in how ever many ways, you will make known to me! I pray Father that I may never move from this space this place of gentle nourishment within my soul!"

I know that I am a very different person as a result of working with these lovely celestial personalities. So many of the questions I sought answers for, were answered by them. One question that had plagued me for years was the idea that I had to let go of my devotion to the Blessed Mother. You see, after that incident at the age of fourteen, I became a Catholic and developed a very close relationship with Mary. It was Ambrose who opened the connection with Nebadonia, our Mother Spirit, who then told me that all of the prayers, love and devotion I had heaped at the feet of Mary had always been received by her! That in fact, I didn't have to let go of anything save the name I knew her by! In the late 90's it was through working with Ambrose and AhmaNiden that I was able to connect with my indwelling fragment of God!

I will always hold close to my heart my memories of my loving teachers, and look forward to working with them, perhaps even on the Mansion Worlds.

How We Found the Teaching Mission
Virginia Kelly

My husband Bill was introduced to *the Urantia Book* in 1986 by a science teacher. He wasn't really interested in it, but when he promptly got a coffee stain on the cover, he felt obligated to look it over rather than returning it damaged and unread. As he read, paper by paper, he would comment at various times: "If this is a fraud it is certainly a consistent fraud;" "It fills in so many things that the Bible omits;" or "How can any one human being imagine, write and share these ideas and not want the credit?" Soon thereafter we joined a small study group and our path was determined. Bill became a "true believer" and gave away more than a case of the books to friends and family.

In 1991 one of our study members brought a transcript from New Zealand that was supposedly a recent contact with the same beings that gave us *the Urantia Book*. Again, Bill was not interested but our friend Debbie and I said we were! During that same time period Martha, a member of the Woods Cross Urantia Book reading group, moved to Pocatello to be next to her sister because of family tragedies. She shared with us what was happening in Utah, but Bill was not interested and told her so. However, she brought recordings of the sessions, to which and Bill was surprisingly open. He told Martha he would listen to the tapes. Not only did he listen, he spent his Christmas school vacation transcribing every one of them. Once again he spoke of consistency . . . not only within the tapes but also as they related to *the Urantia Book*, which he now claimed as a divine road map for human beings.

As a result of Martha, the Pocatello group was invited to Woods Cross for one of their meetings. I am unsure of the exact date that Debbie went down, but I believe it was January 6th, 1992. She came back from there and spent the next week in meditation and contemplation about the Teaching Mission, asking if she was going to be able to transmit and what was the name of her teacher, and who the Pocatello teacher might be. During this week she shared very little with me, and certainly not the name she received in her mind's eye, as she wanted some confirmation that her "hearing" had been correct.

On Monday, January 13th, 1992 several people from the Pocatello, Idaho, area drove to Woods Cross, Utah, to meet with Teacher Ham. We were all anxious to know if Debbie had heard the name correctly and if a teacher would be coming to Pocatello. When Rebecca began transmitting and introduced our teacher with the name of Daniel all our heads turned to look at Debbie. Her face reflected elation, confidence and gratitude. She thanked Daniel for the week she had spent with him trying to know what was reality. Debbie had been a friend of mine for many years and thus, to have her be the transmitter was helpful to me. Questions were asked that night which led the Pocatello group to begin meeting at Debbie's house on Sunday mornings. Our quest of continual spiritual growth was given a new path to follow.

On Sunday morning, January 19th we had our first meeting with Daniel. That first lesson was an encouragement to follow change and growth. In the first lesson he also said "My teachings are important in furthering your understanding of the book". We accepted the Teaching Mission as a "workbook" of the Urantia text. Bill accepted the role of transcriber and he did that for at least 15 years, spending five or more hours every week, even when working full time.

He was truly dedicated to the possibility of spiritual growth. If an individual had no e-mail he sent copies in snail mail throughout the United States. We have received hundreds of lessons through many people and many celestial helpers: Daniel, Tomas, Iruka, Lorenzo, Linda, Klarixiska, Minearsia, Ham, Abraham and others. Very early in this experience he started practicing T/R'ing during his lunch hour with a friend. This eventually led him to be the primary transmitter when Debbie died and situations of other members changed.

I began keeping a journal but was reluctant to share this for many months, partially because what I was hearing was basically encouragement for my positive attitude toward life and to continue to grow. I had not experienced such continuous accolades. Usually I was and am beating myself up. Certainly what I was putting in my journal was not the voice I was used to hearing in my mind. Meditation is still the requirement.

There have been negative and positive situations within our Teaching Mission experiences but I would close with this:
"Train your memory to hold in sacred trust the strength-giving and worthwhile episodes of life...."
The Urantia Book, (160.4.6)

The group now has almost twenty years of transcripts that repeat over and over again that the purpose of the contact now available with our unseen friends is to follow a path on a spiritual journey that will eventually lead us to our Father, the Father of all. As long as I keep focused on these original lessons I had heard and continue to hear, my attempt to grow by balancing mind, body and spirit lead to truth, beauty and goodness, which should be the end result.

Daily meditation for me continues to be the requirement.

Our Teaching Mission Experience
Leoma Sparer

Serena first made herself known to us during a Teaching Mission gathering in Boise, Idaho, in 2004. She and three others of her order revealed their ministry with me through our new friend, Donna D'Ingillo. Serena, Helena, Leslie and Margo have been with me ever since. Later, in our Andover, MN, TeaM (Teaching Mission) meetings with the teachers, we learned Serena is of an unrevealed (up until that time) order of Descending Daughters. Now we are told that she is Chief of Staff for the Magisterial Mission.

What can I tell you of this dear teacher and friend whom I have never seen with physical eyes? She has a lovely countenance, a gently strong, soothing presence. Serena is gracious but persistent enough to tell other mortals she wants to talk with me when I am not listening! Recently, at the end of a conference prayer call with Donna, which I signed off of early, one of the other callers reported to Donna that Serena wanted me to work with her. She won my attention! I now invite her ministry with me each morning in meditation time.

Serena and her sisters often work with mortals without any announcement, message or words (though of course, never without some type of invitation or permission). Many times we have felt their presences like weaving of light strands around and between members of the group who were in stillness with us, especially when we are helping to introduce others to their personal unseen teachers. We are sure that they minister to us when we are completely unaware, but feeling the subtle movement of healing energies they bring is beautiful. More recently for me, this healing has been carried along vortical strands of light, spiraling gently around my body, releasing old patterns energetically stored in my cells while simultaneously replacing them with new patterns for upliftment.

Compassion and a deep generosity of spirit characterize Serena as well. Back in 2006, my mother lay dying several hundred miles away and I myself had been sick, so I could not travel to be by her side as I had long desired. Serena gave me an incredible gift I will never forget.

Our Andover Teaching Mission was meeting. Since my mother seemed to be lingering on unnecessarily, as part of our session of effective prayers that evening we visualized my mother surrounded with light and embraced by Mother Nebadonia's love to help her pass. Even before this prayer or the subject of my mother came up, Serena had blessed me with an unusual exercise. She led the group, through my husband, in imagining my body suspended as pure energy in the middle of our merkaba energy construct and then passing the Father's loving energy, light, to my energetic body with their intent. This was heavenly, but there was more to come.

Later, after my prayer, my husband said Serena was with my mother, and that I could connect to her through Serena. Indeed, I felt a stronger connection with her than had I been physically present. I said, "Serena, tell my mother that I just want her to be released into Mother's wonderful arms and to know the absolute love that awaits her." Serena reminded me that "you maintain this web of connectivity with all that know and love you. . . I can facilitate such connections for you, but have faith that you can do this yourself." [Session #17, Feb. 2, 2006] So I communed with my mother and told her not to wait for me to get there. She died peacefully in her sleep three hours later. My gratitude cannot be expressed in words, but Serena knows. . . .

The following week in our group session, the Most Highs came forward with this message:

The Most Highs: We are in part upholding and uplifting your efforts at communication with another some distance from you [], in Chicago]. The light connection with the TR's mother is also going on as we speak. This is what the T/R is feeling. . . a direct connection with her mother. It is feeding both ways. This open connection, feeding light from the merkaba with your intention in the group, is facilitating the recipient's entry into the morontial journey. It also clears the way for the clearing of grief and regret. This allows the pure joy of the former physical life association that took place between mother and daughter. The feeling of that relationship will never change into all eternity. The realization of the nature of the gift will expand over time with personal spiritual growth. As this interchange of positive and healing energies continues, both are receiving benefits to help them on their journeys. Both are being connected on a level not experienced before.

This kind of energetic connection is what the lesson is about, not just tonight's lesson but the lesson for all of your life. Perceiving your mindal and energy connections, not only with others you have been in direct relationship with on the physical plane, but also to realize that deep connection with the Paradise Father and all of His creation. It is ongoing. It is broken only from your perception and the way you experience things in your life. It continues even when you have no perception or awareness of it.

The effectiveness of the connection of your entrance into the circuits is determined by the condition of your body and mind, your awareness and willingness to be connected. It is all up to you. The exercises in which you partake, the toning, connecting with the light anchor, establishing the merkaba, taking care of your bodies, working to release negative energies, all of these things contribute to your welfare, your well being, and your growth into the spiritual realm. Your daily living is enhanced by these practices. We encourage the continuation and the eventual expansion of these practices until you reach the point where they are continuous, moment to moment throughout your life. [Session #18, Feb. 9, 2006]

The Andover TeaM

Now that I have introduced you to Serena, let me tell you a bit about ourselves. My husband and I met in Kansas and were married in 1989. He is a scientist, and I have been a food service manager, church secretary, and stay-at-home Mom and Grandma.

We moved to Minnesota in 1995. Soon after, my husband found *the Urantia Book* online, and that led him to discover information about the Teaching Mission. He absorbed information from stacks of lessons from many of the Teaching Mission groups in Colorado, Idaho, New Mexico, California and Florida. I also read many of the lessons he recommended. When we learned of a Urantia Book International Conference in 2002 at our favorite vacation place, the YMCA camp near Estes Park, Colorado, it was a "no brainer" – we were going!

Our hopes to connect with members of the Teaching Mission there were fulfilled. The people we met were so welcoming and encouraging, that after having not transmitted for 18 years, I was excited to have the privilege of being the vessel for the Most Highs one evening.
  It was the beginning of new relationships with seen and "unseen friends" that continue to grow. We have been on an "excellent adventure" ever since, one that just keeps getting more amazing as we travel this path together.

It was our dream to form a Teaching Mission group of our own in Minnesota, so we sent out prayers, contacted people, and waited. At first we were a group of Urantia Book readers. Finally, early in 2004, our little group posted its first transcript on TM Archives. We posted about 60 teacher lessons in the four years that we met. In that time, my husband also learned to T/R. He received lessons on toning, "shining the pearls" and other techniques of raising our frequencies to reach the teachers, from energy teachers especially assigned to him for that purpose.

Lessons were forthcoming from the ever-talkative and wise-yet-amusing Tomas, who eventually announced to our surprise that he was being assigned to our group after 25 years following the T/R that is now in the Albuquerque area. He gave us information on forms of energy (light, life force, love energy), intuition, divine mind, DNA changes and Earth changes taking place.

We also were visited many times by Christ Michael, Nebadonia, the Most Highs, Machiventa Melchizidek, Monjoronson, Serena, WAVE and Nathaniel. Other named and unnamed personalities brought their energies and lessons as well, and many times we felt surrounded by the presence of angels or other celestials, filling the room with their love and support.

Building upon the scaffolding of the lessons of other TeaM groups we had studied, the teachers launched us into sessions that were experiential, what we call "energy lessons". The usual format after initial preparations and prayer included a message of encouragement and instruction on a topic, often responding to conversation before we began, perhaps on a section of *the Urantia Book* we had just read, or continuing with the next step from a previous lesson.   Then an energy lesson was presented, after which questions were addressed.

The power of group energy, and the potential existent within a group of like mind, intention and sincerity is the basis from which our group functioned. Tomas delivered lessons pertaining specifically to the importance of intention and how to focus it in a group.

"Focusing intent is important in all spiritual matters. When you focus your intent together in a group the end product is far greater than the summation of the individual parts. You would be amazed if you would be able to foresee what you can actually accomplish by focusing a pure God-aligned intent. You can accomplish so much beyond what you can now imagine. This is one of the great lessons that we wish to bring to you. That working in a group can be so powerful, and yet before you can be truly effective you must realize your own individual potential." [Session #3, June 14, 2005]

All subsequent lessons were founded on this principle.

Over time, our group developed a few ways to help us connect energetically with each other and with Spirit.   Group meetings always began with stillness.   Then perhaps some toning with the piano or ringing a Tibetan singing bowl, connecting with the pillar of light anchored in our midst. We learned how to create a merkaba, or energy construct, which remained in the space where we met to harmonize our energies.   Then with a prayer of gratitude to focus the group's intent for the evening, inviting the teachers to minister to us, we waited expectantly. Effective prayer for others or sending light to a troubled spot in the world was often incorporated into the evening, sometimes even led by our unseen friends.   We were always aware that they joined us in doing this work, adding their energies. Indeed, we were taught to ask for celestials' assistance in all service work.

Light Anchor

Aside from the lessons the Andover TeaM received, we learned much from people in other groups.   Someone we met during a Teaching Mission gathering at Stella Niagara Retreat Center in New York, later came to visit us in our home. She showed us how to establish a light anchor in our living room where we conduct our TeaM meetings. Since that time, the pillar of light has in fact operated as an "anchor" for all our sessions and energy work, including our personal stillness time.

The Most Highs had this to say about light anchors:

"We are most pleased that you have shown the interest and have asked for help in establishing the light anchor here. We need more willing souls who invite this into their homes and lives. The more there are around the planet, the greater the light pouring into the planet, which upsteps the whole correcting time process. We welcome and applaud the effort at creating the light anchor here and encourage you to use it as much as possible. As you do, it will strengthen and grow. Indeed, it can be used for any spiritual purpose."
[Session #3, June 14, 2005]

We perceive the light anchor as a cord or pillar of light that originates with the Paradise Father, through Divinington and our Michael Son, to Urantia. To establish such a pillar that is "anchored" in place and remains is not difficult. Once a person is feeling "in the spirit," or spiritually connected, then one can visualize the light coming from on high, through Michael and down into the core of the earth. With prayer and celestial assistance, the light is now established as a permanent fixture. Think of it as a "superhighway of energy." It remains unless circumstances cause it to be diminished, or it is intentionally removed. When we were taught how to build a merkaba, the light anchor acted as the axis for the merkaba construct, described here.

Building the Merkaba

Others in the Teaching Mission first taught us how to build a merkaba. My husband gave this description to begin one of our TeaM meetings:

R: "Now remember how we connect to the merkaba. See the shaft of light that is running through your spine that connects your chakras. Take the top part of that, coming out of the crown chakra, and connect it above us to the light anchor that runs through this living room. And then take the part that comes out of your root chakra and connect it with the lower part of the light anchor. When this happens, a sphere of energy forms, a globe of energy that we call a merkaba. There are energy lines of longitude and latitude that make up this spherical energy construct.

"The longitudinal lines are our heart lines. You may see these lines as pink or red. They run from the earth center, up through the light anchor / lower line, up through your right leg, through your heart center, back down through your left leg, down the lower line, and then up the line to the next person on your left and so on around the circle.

"The mind lines are the lines of latitude around the sphere. You may see these as blue and at a higher frequency. Instead of going clockwise around the circle, they go to the right. Imagine the energy line going from your left temple, through your head and out your right temple, into the left temple of the person on your right, until it connects all in the circle."

Groups like this that are linked with a common mindal intent and common heartfelt feelings are empowered when they use the merkaba. The energies that come through them multiply geometrically, approximating an output equal to the square of the number of participants. . . much more than the simple arithmetic sum of the participants.

We ask the celestials who are with us to please help with the energy connections, and aid and participate with us. [Session # 20, Feb. 19, 2006]

Once we got the hang of creating, maintaining and connecting with the merkaba in our living room, teachers gave us lessons and experiences in using the energy construct effectively. The following lesson takes us on a little excursion.

"Expanding the merkaba to benefit others with light"

Tomas: *"With this we have an energy construct.* [Referring to the merkaba.] *It is a reality, yet it is a reality only because you have imagined it. You have intended it into creation; otherwise it would not exist. You would simply be sitting in a room together, sharing space. But now in a very real sense you are sharing energies together. They are not just your own but those that come from the First Source and Center and the Planetary Supreme, Urantia... all one continuum of energy that is reality. You have done well in this group to connect your imagination with this reality and to realize that it is creative in nature, meaning what you can imagine you can indeed create as a reality. You do this every day in your lives, even in the smallest of details, without realizing it. But here with your common intent, your stated purposes, you have shared your energies and created something far greater than your individual parts could have done on their own. You are one body.*

"As you know, the celestials here present join in. They add their energy as well upon your invitation. The energies are thus constructed with intent and purpose to do good not only for yourselves, but in the world. By creating this, if you do nothing more with it, you have already helped the world. You have created a place in time filled with light and peace. . . in a world that has carried a lot of shadows. This is an important step in and of itself, to create a place of light.

"As I have been speaking, the energies have been building and moving, raising your bodies' vibrations. Sense within your body, if you can, the movement of the energies. Allow your imagination to step to the forefront to sense the energies. Refrain from allowing your rational mind to talk your imagination out of it. Allow your rational mind to step aside for a few moments. Allow your imagination to run free. [Pause]

"You may see colors. You may feel tingling. You may simply feel peace and centeredness. These are all real. These are all part of experiencing the merkaba. Not everyone experiences all of these effects. Even if you feel or sense none of what was described, please be assured that you are in the merkaba. You are receiving the benefits and you are contributing your energies. Be assured, you are contributing simply by your intent. [Pause]

"Now we will use these energies to expand the merkaba. Allow your imagination to make the merkaba larger in all dimensions so that it is filling the room. . . now filling the entire house. . . now expanding outward into the neighborhood. [Pause; deep breathing]

"What we are doing is expanding the goodness, beauty and truth of this light . . . extending it out toward others so that those not in this circle sitting here tonight may benefit from your gathering. This is how light expands. In this way the shadows, the dark places in the world, are dispelled by the light. Where there is disharmony, discord, disillusionment, there may now enter in harmony, peace and truth. For those ready to accept a higher truth, for those ready to accept more light into their lives, know that this benefits all those in this expanding merkaba. The effects do not diminish as the merkaba expands. Celestials are helping with this effort.

Light Energy

The main themes for our group were spiritual energies, love and light: receiving, raising, and using such for the highest good. Light energy was one of the topics of our early lessons.

Tomas: *"I wish to speak with you tonight further about light energy. I remind you that the light of which I speak is not as you imagine in conjunction with your ideas of electricity and the light produced by electricity. This is a light far beyond that vibration. This is a light originating from the First Source and Center. The way that it comes to you, as we have spoken, is through the coordinations through Divinington. A portion of this light process is circular since it returns back to its Source. The portion of which we wish to speak tonight are your bodies as receptors of this light.*

"It is true that your bodies can receive more of this light as your vibration frequencies rise. Another important aspect to receive the light within your cellular being is to be cleansed and cleared of the effects of the Lucifer rebellion and the other occurrences that have added to the "sludge" of which we have spoken before. The darkness that weighs upon your soul, none of this belongs to you my friends. Yet, the effort must be made for each individual to be cleansed of these effects in order to be able to receive the light of which we speak.

"Closer to your world as a conductor of this light, is Christ Michael. You have often spoken of putting people in the 'light of Christ'. You have practiced this in your prayers. This is a very real and effective activity. You may think that it is only your imagination when you envision someone in the light of Christ . . . someone who is far from you. Yet if you could see light as we do you could see that the effect is real. Whether the receiver of the light is aware of it or not, that person will receive the light sent to the degree to which their body can receive it. The very being of Christ Michael is as a conduit of this light. Christ Michael is such a clear conduit that he is not aware of what is happening. It is a constant for him. It is a fact for his existence that this light passes through him to others. It is available for anyone to use with their intent to send to another or to allow themselves to be surrounded and be filled with this light.

"There are many between Divinington and Michael who coordinate this energy. That will not be the subject for our lesson tonight . . . perhaps for the future. For now we wish for you to focus on Christ Michael as the conduit for this light for he is close to you. You have a clear concept for who Christ Michael is, as one who walked among you and yet is the son of God.

"In your desire to serve the world, to help heal mother earth, and to uplift others around you, all of this can be served by using the light which Michael conducts to you. There is no effort that needs to be made other than on your individual receptivity. It is our desire for you to learn ways to use and direct his energy. It is

not difficult, my friends. It does not take much time. It only takes remembering and the effort of focusing your intent to use this light.

"There are many ways this light can be shared. . . in your circle passing it around from person to person until it flows and then can be focused for a certain purpose [editor's note: using our light anchor and the merkaba group energy structure to amplify the energy; we send light in prayer to others.

"Be assured that distance is not a factor in effectiveness in the use of sending light. This light with your focused intent can be sent anywhere without losing any of its effectiveness. Remember that when you have this intent and are working in the name of Christ Michael, you have so much unseen help sending this light. They are just waiting for the opportunity. There are energy controllers and boosters who will help carry this light so your thought of it being deleted or diminished as it travels long distances need not be a reality. You need not be aware or knowledgeable of this assistance. It simply is there. This is part of what is meant by the saying that where two or more are gathered in the name of Christ, he is there also. There are many more to assist along with Michael's presence.

"As you sit in your quietude, we wish to infuse more of this light of which we speak into your bodies. Allow this light to penetrate deeply. Visualize it entering every organ in your bodies, every energy system, every cell... enlivening every molecule of your physical body. [pause]

"This is the life force with which you were created. It is this life force that sustains you. It is the same life force that is in your food. The food that you eat, to the degree that it still contains the original life force, can harmonize with your body. It is beneficial to eat food that has, as much as possible, been grown near to where you live. . . without chemicals. . . without artificial light... as much as possible with nourishing rain and healthy soil, with the microorganisms and the crawling things that were intended to be there. This kind of food harmonizes with the frequencies of your bodies. Feel the truth of this within you. Some of the foods you eat are not called junk food for nothing." [Session #7, Aug. 23, 2005]

Making a Heart Connection

In this simple exercise within the merkaba, Serena demonstrates how connections between people, and sharing love via those connections can be effected intentionally. This lesson dovetails nicely with Monjoronson's message on harmonizing group energy.

Serena: *"I would like you to attempt to connect with each other across the circle, to those of you facing one another, at your heart chakra level. Imagine a direct line of light between your heart centers. Do this for a few moments. [Pause] Once this is established, next I would like you to do the same with your third eye chakra. Allow them to be connected if only in your imagination by a line of light directly connecting your third eye to the one across from you in the circle. Allow this for a few moments, while also keeping the heart connection.* [Pause]

"Now I would ask you to soften these lines of connection. Set aside your rational thought, your observing mind which wants to grab onto what is happening and understand it; relax that idea. Allow your connections to soften and just allow them to be, without any expectation. [Pause]

"Do you begin to perceive, my friends, that in this way you observe and feel that the two of you are very much alike, yet quite individual? You have similar desires for your life. You have the same God connection that is recognizable. It is familiar. It makes you all one. This is a beginning exercise in showing you how Jesus connected with those whom he met during his physical life on this planet. It is how he had compassion for each individual, and this is how he knew what was in their thoughts and in their lives, what was important to them and what they needed from him.

"Now that you have heard these words, concentrate again on your connection, on these two connections with the chakras, allowing those connections to be soft and easy. [Pause]

"Do you perceive, my friends, that with the heart chakra connected, you feel a two-way flow of love? You are receiving and you are giving. In this connection, there is great compassion for one another. This is the type of energy exchange which Michael was very familiar with all other mortals. Within this exchange you may feel the actuality of God's presence, the energy of our Creator being exchanged between you in a finite manner, yet supplied by the Infinite." [Session #37, July 27, 2006]

The value in sharing these lessons with you is that they can be re-created, re-experienced at any time. Often the teachers assured us that merely reading these words can have an effect, as they carry the energy and intent of the experience that can resonate in the reader's being.

Managing Changes

Earth changes, political and economic concerns, worries about life as we know it changing for the worse, and even our own personal "spiritual growing pains" can throw us off balance, set us off course. Contained within many of the lessons we received from the teachers are instructions which contribute to a foundation of stability to assist people in all situations of life, including changes that could be catastrophic.

Messages given could be summarized as: 1) remain present in the NOW, which is the only place wherein creative action can occur, 2) continue with inner personal growth, especially daily stillness, and 3) maintain a personal center of stillness and peace as the best preparation and antidote for potentially stressful changes.

The following excerpts from lessons delivered by Serena on balance and Nathaniel on stillness, discernment and staying centered, provide a basis for living life in general, as well as being prepared for crises or stressful situations. In Monjoronson's message, he asks and encourages us to be the hands and feet, eyes and ears of the Correcting Time. Then he leads us in effective prayer and sending light.

Point of Balance

Serena: "You may perceive myself and those of my order with me tonight as movement around your circle, presently in a clockwise direction. We are moving among you, exchanging energy with each one of you, and would ask that you simply allow this for a few moments in silence, without analyzing or wondering why. Simply allow. [Pause]

"Perhaps as this exercise was taking place, you perceived the movement around the circle, the energy increasing to a very high rate of vibration and high speed of movement to your perception around the circle. Then a band of energy connecting your hearts centered you there more solidly. Now you should be feeling very well relaxed and centered at that supreme point of balance. We have done this to aid you in remaining well balanced in your heart center, so that whatever vicissitudes come your way, you will not so easily be shaken. If you are, you will more quickly remember and be able to return to the balance point.

"Whether you fully are aware of this or not, you are learning to remain in this balance point, and to return to it more easily when something throws you off. It is coming to you that it does not feel right to be any other way. So when something upsets you during your day, or seems to be throwing you off this center, pause for a moment, take a deep breath, and with your thought-intent, return to this feeling. Think of this moment you are sharing now, of solid balance, unshakable balance. It belongs to you. Each time you practice this and return to it, it becomes even more solid a foundation for you to be one with." [Session #43, Nov. 16, 2006]

Nathaniel: Centeredness, Stillness, and Discernment

R: "I would like to understand more about those things that are important for us as we manage our lives through this Correcting Time and the changes that it brings us."

Nathaniel: *"That is a good angle on the question. It is first and foremost my place to tell you to stay the course, as it were – to remain in your current habits of spiritual attainment, those activities that you have found aid you in your process of spiritual growth. This is a basic response of providing yourself with a solid base from which to work in response to any outside stimuli that comes your way that may without your grounding serve to knock you off balance. So remain steadfast in your earnestness to grow this solid foundation, to be centered, to be striving to communicate with your Thought Adjuster and allow your will to mesh with that of the Creator Father. Then it need not be your concern what vicissitudes, what difficulties may come your way or not, for to you it will not really matter. You are standing steadfast and ready for service should the need arise.*

"Secondly, you will want to shift your ability for discernment into a higher gear. The information you will be receiving and have been receiving through your usual channels of the media and educational channels will be quite confusing on the face, at first glance, on the surface. So you must dig a little deeper, gather information from other channels such as your own intuition and feelings, your own personal guidance, your own Thought Adjuster. Remain in your place of centeredness as much as possible as you sift through confusing bits of information, all the while not allowing the disturbing portions of the information to throw you off that balance, even though you may believe that you would be quite directly affected by certain events or changes or situations. In this way you will be able to more intelligently discern a course of action if one is needed, and your emotions will not carry you away. You will more easily be able to react in any given situation with calmness and peace. You will be of much greater help to yourself and others.

"Thirdly, I would recommend that you practice stillness if possible more than once a day. Make it your goal to be increasingly connected with your perception of stillness throughout the day, throughout your activities. This may seem difficult at first, but without your realizing it, the stillness is permeating more of your daily

life. Allow this to percolate and infiltrate every activity of your waking hours." [Excerpt, Session #44, Nov. 23, 2006]

Be the Hands and Feet

Monjoronson: *"This is just the beginning, the mere advent of a new age, of a new dispensation as the old one passes slowly away. There is much turmoil, tragedy, and strife on your world. Many specific things are on your minds at this time: disasters, failures of your government and your leaders to be truthful and honest with you. There are many things that will be changed almost overnight, things that will be revealed that will turn things, as you might say, upside-down. You will need to hang on to your celestial help, to your faith, to the knowledge that you are not alone and that you are not left to your own devices.*

"Those of you that understand the energies that are entering and changing this planet during the correcting time will be called upon. You will be needed increasingly now to calm the fears, to minister to those around you. You have been taught and strengthened. You have the resources within you. You have the close association of the indwelling Father Fragment. You can call upon all of these resources and those of us who have been over-lighting your world for a very long time and are here to assist.

"We are ready to do all that we can do. Yet you are the hands and feet. You are the mouths and the listening ears. You are the eyes that see where help is needed. You are the ones that carry out Michael's ministries among your peers. We call upon you to fulfill this plan of correction which now is coming into your neighborhoods, into your very homes, where ministry will need to take place, person to person, group to group.

"The outcry is growing in intensity, as is the spiritual growth expanding to be able to meet these growing needs. You CAN carry out this mission. You CAN handle these problems. They are opportunities for you to reach out and to be the light of Christ to others. You are the ones who will reach out and allow the Christ light to flow through you to others so that they may see the truth. so that they may receive the love of the Father which comes continuously, unceasingly, without limit, without end.

"It is good, my friends. It is good that you are here to listen and that you have asked how you may serve. Having asked and received direction, you have taken the bold steps forward to do that which you believe is necessary. Each individual has their own mission to carry out. It is for that individual to discern, using their own particular gifts and interests. Yet individuals need not work alone. They may join hands with others in other groups of like-minded service to work together, remembering to call upon their unseen friends for help in their endeavors. With this kind of union of effort and focusing of intent, there can be no failure.

"The plans for healing and for changing this world for the better are progressing and will continue to progress at a rate greater than we had anticipated. As we step forward to bring in this new dispensation, the upward movement, the expansion of the light of the knowledge of truth, of the love from the Mother Spirit is growing ever-more powerful each day, each hour."

Effective Prayer

Monjoronson continues: *"I wish for you to know, my friends, the most powerful tool you can use right now in this world is effective prayer, prayer such as you have used to send light to the troubled regions. Time and distance are of no matter when it comes to prayer. Prayer enters the realm beyond the space - time continuum and is not limited by those. Your prayers, heartfelt, sincere, focused with your intent, particularly in a group, are boosted and helped along with many of your unseen friends. Invite them to join you in this effort; the effectiveness grows even more. You will learn in the coming days that such prayer, such union with all those unseen around you, working together, can truly move mountains, can truly heal the environment, and can truly do what you think of as the impossible. Use these tools we have given you and you will begin to see miracles. The greatest miracle being that you have learned to communicate and to be in union with us.*

Rather abruptly, our little Andover group which had met so regularly couldn't seem to get together any more, and simply dissolved. Apparently, it was time to shift into a different phase of our journey. Since then, my husband and I have "not been inert", as Tomas once put it after an absence. We continue with the stillness practice, and realize that our ability to "connect" with Spirit gradually improves over time. Lessons continue to come, tailor-made for our individual growth and learning. Through the Center for Christ Consciousness, we have received immeasurable benefits from continuing sessions of Transformation with Donna D'Ingillo.

We find ourselves establishing light anchors wherever we travel, most recently on the island of Maui. There we were led by Monjoronson to anchor pillars of light at several points on the island, which became a network or grid of light energy encompassing all of Maui. It is so easy and gratifying to do; we believe it makes a great difference. It can just as easily be done remotely, from any distance.

It is our firm conviction that participating with others in effective prayer for the troubled spots in our world is perhaps the most important work any of us could be doing right now. Sending light, love, or concentrating on forgiveness and mercy for peoples of the world, no matter how remote, has an effect far beyond our abilities to observe or comprehend. The teachers have demonstrated and affirmed for us over and over again how vital this work is, and how completely possible, indeed necessary, that we ourselves change the world in this way. This paves the way for Light and Life to come to Urantia. Individuals may add to this, of course; yet groups working together with the same intention and love in their hearts are exponentially more potent.

To imagine our lives without the beautiful, aware and intelligent friends we have made within the Teaching Mission is impossible. Even though some have crossed our path only once or twice, their love and influence are indelibly written on our hearts, woven eternally into the fabric of our journey, past, present and future.

This applies also to our many unseen friends. It has taken some practice, but the invisible teachers are as immediately "real" as those we can see. Messages and lessons are always in sync with our interests and abilities, yet stretch us to take the next steps, building upon what we have previously acquired. Our struggles are always met with grace-filled encouragement, our questions answered with aplomb and even humor. Their love and deep compassion for all Urantians is unquestionable. They have our trust, yet they would be the first to remind us to use our own discernment in all matters. Always we are reminded to seek the stillness, to spend time in the embrace of the Paradise Father, Mother Spirit and Michael.

This adventure is taking us beyond anything we could ever design for ourselves. We know there is much more to come, and have confidence that our guides and teachers will make sure we are prepared! Mere words cannot contain our deep gratitude and love for what the teachers and Spirit have opened to us, giving us hope of fulfilling some measure of the potential and purpose for our lives at this time, on this planet. Let the adventure continue!

Spirit Fest Memories
Karen Roberts

The Teaching Mission has been an opportunity for making new friends and renewing old friendships. I heard about it when I went to Urantia reader gatherings. My friends who were attending the Teaching Mission meetings seemed to have been positively uplifted by the experience. They were exhibiting the fruits of the spirit and love, as I would imagine Jesus would love us.

Early in the Teaching Mission, Spirit Fest started. I loved going there. It was an annual gathering of the Teaching Mission in central California. We have been fortunate to have such a diverse and dedicated group of people interested in actively working with the Teachers.

Preparation for the conference started early in the year. Sometimes we would transmit the Teachers and Christ Michael during these meetings. They have a way of gently and kindly opening us up to new ideas and possibilities. The Teachers would give us the kind of information that would stimulate our imagination, not giving us specific instructions on what to do.

Carpooling to Spirit Fest was part of the fun. There was always lively conversation, getting us into the spirit of spiritual celebration. It seemed like the Teachers were with us, sharing love and joy as we rode along. There was a lightness of being that I associate with the Teaching Mission meetings that started as soon as we all got in the car. This lasted all weekend and through the ride home.

Spirit Fest, being an annual conference, we quickly got to know each other. When I would arrive, I would keep my eyes open for newcomers and welcome them. We met at a rustic, affordable camp, great for families. Spirit Fest 1997 I was in charge of the children's program. I brought toys from home and my friends organized activities for the children's program, including hiking, tie-dye, reading stories. There was a mandala activity for both children and adults. The mandalas were displayed, decorating the main meeting room.

During the evening session, we set up a line of chairs for volunteer transmitters to sit and wait their turn. We would start with some stillness to facilitate the connection. The transmitters would be moved in the spirit to share messages from their group Teachers and other celestials. I was part of the East Bay Group with Althena as our Teacher. I felt at ease transmitting Althena, as she brought forth messages with graceful elegance. The Teachers seem to have planning meetings of their own. As their lessons come forth, they seem to speak to the theme of the conference. The lessons complement each other with some repetition and variety, a sign of good teaching style.

As the weekend progresses, I feel like *the Urantia book* comes alive. Many of us are long time Urantia book readers. We have read about various types of celestials in the universe and suddenly they are speaking to us through these transmitters. We hear from Christ Michael, Nebadonia, Melchizedek, Adam and Eve. Through these transmissions we get to know them more personally. Going back to *the Urantia Book* and rereading the sections about these celestials, confirms and expands my knowledge, understanding and appreciation.

Saturday afternoon we break into small groups. Sometimes it is as simple as a transmitter, tape recorder and a willing audience. Sometimes a group leader leads a discussion. I go down to the creek with the children and some adults. We pick up instruments and share our voice and song, allowing our hearts to be moved in the spirit and share joyful noise. As the afternoon wears on, we reach into our hearts for a deeper connection with God, and peace settles upon us and harmony shines forth. Improvisation can be a way of bringing music into your heart and soul and sharing on a deeply spiritual level, with a variety of musical experimenters. With my childlike musical abilities, Lester and I create this song:

Keep on moving
Keep on dancing
Keep on sharing
From the bottom of your heart

Keep on clapping
Keep on snapping
Keep on loving
From the bottom of your heart

Keep on playing
Keep on saying
That I love you
From the bottom of my heart

Rayson seems to have carefully studied our difficult situation in this world, recognizing through his experience what we could do to overcome obstacles in daily life that keep us from enjoying our Heavenly Father's love. I personally took time to get to know Rayson when I found out he had been a physician as a mortal and I didn't have health insurance. He helped me with my health issues and I made a concerted effort to transmit his hopes for the transformation of our society.

In 1998, in an afternoon session, I transmitted Rayson. We struggled with questions and possibilities as we talked about the problems in our society. It was a sad time for us, as the problems seemed overwhelming. There seemed to be few of us to encourage others to powerfully transform expectations, hopes and longings and allow Father's love to support and guide us.

Sunday morning we have a remembrance supper with prayer, worship, music, grape juice and bread. Sometimes we read out of *the Urantia Book* about the Last Supper. Always we know that Christ Michael is personally there. Christ Michael persists in reaching out to all of us. He regularly brings messages and good tidings through the transmitters. He is adept at answering our questions and focusing us on God the Father. At times he can be powerful, majestic and magnificent. Other times he is very kind and gentle, personally helping us take important baby steps.

Our closing meeting could be very heartfelt and touching. Hopefully somebody volunteers to organize for next year. Feedback is shared while we are together, working as a group year after year. It is heartwarming for me to hear people sharing their deep concerns, sharp criticism and extravagant hopes. Our time together has strengthened us, so we really listen to each other, yet take time to discern what is best for the group as a whole.

There are pleas for a more comfortable conference center, but price wins out, so families and whole groups can afford to show up next year. I listen sadly as people complain about the children interrupting the adult sessions. As the kids grow up, they prefer the children's activities, as opposed to sitting in their mother's laps with the adults and the problem is resolved!

Northern Colorado TeaM History
Roxanne Andrews

My husband Jim and I began reading *The Urantia Book* in early 1974 after a particularly rocky time in our marriage. The teachings of the book provided exactly what we needed to repair and enliven our marriage, and were of great assistance in raising our three children. We hosted a weekly study group in our home that continued for about 25 years. As we approached our retirement years, Jim was diagnosed with leukemia and, due to chemotherapy, was no longer able to work, so he retired, and I figured that I would have to work at least another 5 years until I could join him in a "life of leisure." We dreamed of where we would like to spend those years, and vowed that we would both like to spend much more time working on our spiritual growth and being of service.

Imagine my surprise when one day, Jim called me at work and said, "Turn in your resignation! I don't know why, but I felt this 'urge' to put pencil to paper and decided that you could retire now, if we are willing to be frugal." We both wanted to leave the congested Metropolitan area of Denver for a smaller town and we continued to be "drawn" to Loveland, Colorado, although we were not sure why, since we knew no one that lived there. Later we learned why this sequence of events occurred, and several other events as well, and it was all due to our "intention to work on our spiritual growth and serve our Father." Father took us up on our offer and had something specific in mind for us to do.

Shortly after getting settled in Loveland, I was browsing the Internet, looking for books that would further our spiritual growth. I "happened" to come across Fred Harris' book, The Center Within. After we both read it and had a profoundly spiritual bond with it, we looked for more books by Fred, and ordered The Correcting Time. Again, we wanted more of this "spiritual feast," and started an Internet search, whereupon we found Jim Cleveland's web site, "Light and Life.com." I made contact with Jim Cleveland and he told us of a Teaching Mission Conference in Utah that was only two weeks away, so we packed our bags and went.

On the steep road up to the Snowbird Lodge in July 2001, our car began to give us a warning light and the engine was misbehaving. We had the car towed to a garage in Salt Lake City, and hitch-hiked up to the Conference. We had a wonderful time and loved the people we met! When it was nearly time to go, the garage said they could find nothing wrong with the car, and we could pick it up. As Jim drove up the hill again to get our luggage, the same problem with the car presented itself, but at least he was able to reach the Lodge this time. Feeling concerned about whether we could make it home safely or not, we asked if anyone else would be going in our direction, and could we travel by caravan, in case our car died? Joan and Jerry Evans and Daniel Raphael agreed to follow us back to Colorado.

We stopped along the way for a meal and I mentioned that we would love to start a Teaching Mission group if we could find someone to T/R. Daniel, with a sly grin on his face said, "I can T/R." We set a date for Christ Michael's birthday, Aug. 21, 2001, and the Northern Colorado TeaM had their first session. Christ Michael welcomed our group's beginning. Our group was assigned Rayson for our celestial teacher, and he stayed with us as our main teacher for about five years, until Monjoronson began to work with us on a regular basis. We also had other teachers along the way—Sondjah, Machiventa, Mantutia, Andronason, Gabriel, and of course, Christ Michael and Mother Spirit, among others.

When my husband Jim was learning to T/R, we had a set time nearly every evening when Rayson would transmit through Jim and answer my questions. It was during these times when we learned that Rayson had been watching us for many years, as we conducted study groups, and was "involved" in getting us to move to Loveland, as there was a need for a Teaching Mission group and a merkaba anchor in this region. I suspect that the Midwayers were involved in our car troubles at the conference, as a ruse to get us to meet with Daniel, Joan and Jerry, and to start a group, as the car was just fine after we returned home. It turned out to be nothing more than a "slightly wrong gap" on one of the spark plugs, and we were never in any danger because of it. I imagine our Guardian Angels, Rayson and the Midwayers were snickering all the way home at how well their plan was turning out.

In December of 2001, Rayson gave our group a series of lessons on the Universe Energy Circuits, how to join our heart and mind energy circuits, and how energy can be manipulated by mind. He then taught us how to form a merkaba, and with the help of Machiventa, Sharrah, Michael, Nebadonia and Rayson, it was permanently anchored and dedicated. It took me awhile to fully understand what the merkaba was all about, as I was not very sensitive to such subtle energies at the time, but eventually I began to appreciate its power for healing and creating goodness in our world. For example, our T/R, Daniel, fell from a ladder and tore a large chunk of muscle out of his upper arm. It was a serious injury, and because he didn't have medical insurance at the time, he did not see a doctor. Instead, several times a day, Jim and I would link with the merkaba and send healing energy to Daniel. I was thoroughly amazed at how quickly he healed from a wound that could have easily become badly infected and possibly even life-threatening.

Another example of the power of the merkaba, we discovered when Jim and I traveled to Almaty, Kazakhstan, to visit our oldest son, who was posted there with the American Embassy. Jim would frequently wake up at 3:00 AM, and go outside to sit on the porch and converse with Rayson. Together they would link with the merkaba anchor at our home in Loveland, Colorado, and send love energy to those in the city who believed in God. (Almaty was about 70% Muslim.) Jim could watch the sparkles of blue light that would form over the city and then softly fall down to scattered individual houses.

As an added bit of interest, our son had taken 40 Russian Urantia Books to Kazakhstan to donate, and other than the two books he had given to his housekeeper/nanny and her sister, he had been unable to distribute the rest of the books, because the government frowned on proselytizing. The last week he was there, he and his wife prepared a "thank you dinner" for their household staff and their immediate families. At the dinner, the sister started asking my son questions about *The Urantia Book*, and he found out that she had been photocopying papers out of it for about 15 of her friends. Because the book was so precious to her, she would not lend it out to anyone for fear that something would happen to it. Needless to say, the remaining books in Russian went home with her that evening, with instructions to give each of her friends a book of their own, and to give out the others to future students. Perhaps many of those books went to the God-loving peoples of Almaty, who received the blue sparkles of love energy in the middle of the nights, of many months before.

Readers of Teacher Rayson's transcripts are often very curious about him. On March 10, 2002, Rayson responded to a question about himself:

Guest: "I guess I would just like to know more about you, where you are from, a little bit of your background, if you would, please."

RAYSON: *"Yes, we covered some of that last week and you missed a rather exciting session. It was a private experience for several people, who wanted to visualize my home planet. So I was their Tour Guide.*

But to let you know, I have completed approximately half of the Mansion Schools. I have been in the morontial state for several thousand years. Age is not a factor, to us; it does pass in the morontial state, but is not really relevant. Development is more important than timeliness. My planet is approximately across the Local Universe, closer to the center than your sun. When I had the opportunity to participate in the Correcting Time, I volunteered immediately. As you know, I have been a teacher for a number of groups around the United States and elsewhere. Others know me by other names, but you in the English language know me as Rayson.

"I seem to have a propensity for, and talents for, aiding new groups to coalesce, come into existence and to begin functioning. I am very pleased to do this for a number of reasons, one of which is that it is a measurable outcome and I like measurable outcomes. Also, I can measure too, but [it] is less defined, the 'awakening' that occurs in the individuals who participate in this activity, to see their lights become brighter, to see individuals gain hope in a cynical world, that too frequently settles for mediocrity; to see people strive for excellence in their spiritual growth and in their relationships with others.

"I participate with a group in Edentia, my associates. We confer regarding these efforts; we have what you would call, a 'working team' to work on initiating new groups. That is not our 'function' but that is what we do. We assist each other too, to help fine-tune each other. We have retreats where we go to the 'hills', (I guess you would call them hills,) to natural settings where we confer about problems and difficulties and sincerely examine each other to see whether there are impediments within ourselves that prevent us from being more effective. And if there are areas that need developing, seek out training and counsel and assistance to gain that. We have a very evolved relationship between ourselves; we are not competitive, we are not egoistically driven to compare ourselves with each other. We strive to aid the best efforts of each and to reveal those areas that need growth, and willingly open ourselves to others to reveal that. You would call this 'intimacy,' being vulnerable, opening yourselves to others, revealing yourselves and then trusting others to aid you, rather than to hurt you.

"Do I like this work? Oh, I like it very much! I know that when my work is through and I have 're-upped' on an indefinite basis, that I will come away with an experience far surpassing those individuals from my planet in contemporary times, who did not have this experience. I do not say that to demean them or to cast any aspersions towards them, but to know that my resume, my history will be very much more developed. I am exposing myself to error, the possibility of becoming 'God like' if I wanted to, in this group, but I don't. It would be far less than the Father's will, or with Michael's delight for me to do that. That would be the way of error. I don't have any plans, what I will do after this mission and this job is completed, I rather expect it will take many centuries of your time to do that. I look forward to the development of events that will occur on your planet, and experience them for myself. I know that this experience will be mightily handy for me in the future of my ascendant career, and whatever comes in the seventh state that develops, of which we know not much now. Is that sufficient?"

Our loyal band of Northern Colorado Teaching Mission students is made up of people who have been dedicated readers of *The Urantia Book* for many years, and we felt extremely fortunate to have Rayson as our Teacher. Rayson had worked with many other individuals and groups before ours, and is considered a Senior Teacher because of his experience and exceptional abilities. Coupled with Daniel Raphael as an experienced and capable transmitter/receiver, Rayson asked us at one point, if we were willing to allow him to teach our group a series of lessons that he "had been sitting on" for a long time, and he wanted them to be made a part of the record for Internet distribution. Thus, he gave us a series of lessons on building "Self-sustaining Intentional Communities." These began on May 19, and lasted through August, 2002.

At the time, our group didn't know of future events that are starting to be in play now, but these lessons will be very valuable as we start to rebuild our cities, towns and governments. Rayson began to prepare us for cataclysms in December of 2002, and in January of 2003 he discussed the turmoil and "global warming" in this manner:

Student: "And since we're moving in this direction, do you have an overview of the Correcting Time that you would be allowed to share?"

RAYSON: *"Yes, most gladly. I am authorized to say far more than I think you were prepared for. The Correcting Time is going quite well. It is a developmental scheme as we have said many times. It is only developmental; it does not operate on a temporal mode; it does not have a time line, but a developmental scheme or schedule. (And I am reluctant to say even "schedule" because there is the great interplay of all elements.) Your world is now in much disarray. Almost in every nation throughout your world there is something going on that is unsettling, and some of it—a lot of it—is very good. There can never be change in a staid environment, an environment that is static. This world of yours is now in great agitation—this is good. It causes much thought provoking examination by individuals, and of course, you know that individuals are truly responsible for the conduct of their nations, whether they participate or not. These changes, this Correcting Time, has created an opportunity for much greater participation by citizens in their own governments. This is just one facet.*

"You are seeing your world in much turmoil also due to climate changes. Your concerns are almost at a point of neuroses; but you need not be neurotic about realities of your weather, for the weather of your world has been far more extreme in the past than you are aware of. The droughts that you experience now of three or four or five years are really miniscule compared with the centuries-long droughts that have occurred in some parts of the world.

"Likewise, when glaciers recede or glaciers grow, they cause tremendous change in the environment. This, too, is much different now than in the past. You must recall, or remember, or think that your world now is coming off of the last glacial era. Your world has not gotten to the point of being between glacial eras. Let that sink in a bit. It means that your world is warming; it means that this has been going on for many hundreds if not thousands of years, and it will continue on for centuries into the future. Your world may see that there is an interim period between eras of glaciations that could be a hundred thousand years long. Anyone who lives during that era would think that their world has always been that way. So, too, you think of your world as always being this way, of having glaciers that once ran many hundreds of miles out to sea, and now they are only tens-of-miles long.

"How does this connect with the Correcting Time? This is a wonderful opportunity for your technologies to learn how to conserve water, how to live stingily on the resources that you have, whether it is water or petrol or any of the other limited products. It is this particular time in your world that the Correcting Time has

occurred, the most opportune time for great change, with a great number of souls on your planet. This is a very productive time for soul growth for individuals and for the planet.

"The Correcting Time is doing very well; it is now invested in almost all spheres of human activity on your planet, in all nations. There is almost no human activity that is not involved, is not impregnated with these Correcting Time changes. You can anticipate more agitation and difficulties in areas of human activity and endeavor before they begin to settle. Yet some areas are already beginning to show promise of settling. We will not disclose what those are at this time, but let you wonder what they are and hope for them to increase in all areas of human activity."

On January 26, 2003, with the American Teaching Mission about 12 years old, Machiventa expressed what is expected of us students:

MACHIVENTA: *"And though you, my dear people, have been with the Teaching Mission and Correcting Time for oh, so many years, this will require you to be very thoughtful, to think clearly, to become real thinkers and real feelers, real believers and 'knowers' of those higher truths that have always existed. To apply your teachings of the wisdom to the individual's relationship with the Creator will require you to reinterpret the old, traditional relationship in new terms. It will require you to grow so you can help traditional believers grow.*

"You have been faithful to this cause; now we ask you to step out a bit from this comfortable edge and begin to explore how you would apply this to your existent religions that inhabit this planet, occupying many billions of people's minds. For those of you who are familiar with religions that do not incorporate a Creator God, you will find the language to do that and to help those individuals. And this is not a condescending approach to those individuals you go to, or to those religions—not at all, for your own expertise is marginal at this point—you must do so with eminent humility, that as you approach these individuals you are exploring the edges, the forward edges of your own beliefs and capability to explore your new religion with these individuals.

"And what is the primary criterion for this development? That is to become ever aware of the God/Goddess, the Divine Fragment that resides in each one of you, and to have a loving relationship with that being and to know this, and to express it through your lives. It is this relationship that will carry forward with you into your infinite journey to Paradise and the final embrace with the Creator. This is the steadfast, sure, relationship that exists past all time. Begin to learn it now and to share it with others. You need not develop a cajoling, argumentative, confrontational approach, but use the simple, loving, reasoning logic that is consistent with the inner Divine guidance that each individual has, consistent with the teaching style of Jesus. This will be sufficient to show the way. Your teachings will be such that the answers are eminently approachable, reasonable, and easily understood. There will be no need to argue against past beliefs, but of course you must understand them too, how they came into existence, and how they are not reasonable, not logical, not divinely developed.

"This is not a Diaspora where you are broken and shattered and sent into the hinterlands—far from it. This is merely a seeding in new fields; a seeding that will challenge you to grow. You have worked this last decade to believe this process that you are experiencing this afternoon is real, to know that it is existent, to know that it is true and that it does not lead you astray or deceive you. You know this already. So now,

345

what do you do with it? Do you just continue doing what you do every two weeks for the rest of your lives and years ahead, a redundancy, a re-habituation? No, now it is time to sow these wisdoms, this thought, this encouragement to humanity into new fields where your friends live, whether they are neighbors or people far away.

"Speak the new truth, the new light, and always see in each individual that light in each one of them begin to glow brighter. Before you go out into the fields, send your thoughts, your wisdom and your Celestial Teachers ahead of you, to share the word and wisdom, grace, and loving understanding. You do not need to make this happen as an executive decision, but to let it happen. Begin to do your work with yourself, with these re-interpretations; do this by yourself, do this in small groups; approach this in a developmental manner. How would you take on this new chore as an individual and as working groups? Yes, this is a new venture with us, and there is an experiential learning curve involved that we too will use to our advantage.

"Your question must be—one of many questions—must be, 'Is this the way?' And as you have read in the scriptures, Jesus said, 'I am the way. Follow me.' And so you will know the right way; you will not go down blind alleys. There are always avenues that will take you further along. I wish you could see as I see—the whole planet and all the marshaled teachers, angels, and assistants all ready to help wherever they are called upon to help. You are truly surrounded by all the support and light and wisdom and love that you need to do this, and you will not do it alone, for this is a co-creative effort. You have volunteered to participate, you have asked what more you can do, and now you know. And as we have said so many times in the past, the healing of your planet could occur in a twinkling of an eye through our Father in Heaven's influence. But that is not the way to achieve great soul growth, personal growth, and inner development of surviving souls who go onward to become those wonderful Finaliters, those agondonter Finaliters, which you will become. The healing of your planet will occur co-creatively, with your active participation; it will not occur without it."

On May 5, 2002, Machiventa Melchizedek spoke to the Northern Colorado (NOCO) Teaching Mission group, announcing that a Magisterial Son would be coming to Urantia, as part of the Correcting Time Plan of Christ Michael. He asked that the members of the group and those that read the transcripts, begin purposely preparing themselves for this event by applying the lessons taught throughout *The Urantia Book* and the Teaching Mission, to heal our lives, hearts, fears and egos, so that we can better serve to heal our planet, with the guidance of the Magisterial Son. Rayson and Machiventa continued to give lessons on how to achieve this healing so that we could apply the lessons to a wider public.

On August 24, 2003, Rayson continued to weave together the concepts that are contained in the overall plan of the Correcting Time, individual spiritual growth, planetary corrections of our failing institutions and governments, excessive population growth and other concerns of a global nature.

Student: "Is there a connection between all the lessons of 'community' and the arrival of the Magisterial Son?"

RAYSON: "Yes, most definitely! Your Magisterial Son, who is coming, must be able to arrive in a situation or an environment that is cooperative. The teaching of community is more than political, it is spiritual, it is in essence the ethos of humanity, living together in peace. Community developments will not work well until your political agendas are set aside. The arrival of a Magisterial Son would be premature without the acceptance by organizations, communities, much as a family member who has gone afar and comes back, decades later—the family "waits" for that individual; so too, there must be family and community "waiting" for the Magisterial Son. More is needed than preparations of temples and rituals and ceremonies; and that is the openness to receive one who has been anticipated."

New Student: "I have a question. You mentioned before that to be ready for a Magisterial Son, that humanity would need to take some steps forward in community and willingness to welcome this Son, and my question is, how can we effect that, how can we uplift humanity to be ready for that? What can we do to help with that?"

RAYSON: *"You have already done a great deal yourself, in your life's work, in your efforts to assist the union of religions, those commonalities. You are seeking a commonality with others, as we do. You are open to a larger consciousness. It is important that this community of like-minded individuals be capable—not only capable, but active—in discerning false prophets from those who are not. Times as these bring forth many individuals, who through their ego, or through their psychic development, feel that they are the "chosen one." What can you do? Be discerning. We ask that you discern, we ask that you cooperate with others who are of a like mind, without being over zealous. Yes, every one, every nation, even those godless countries, seek a "savior," someone they can rely on, to foist their problem upon, yet this one who comes, will be here to teach, to aid you, to guide you, to advise you. He will not take your problems from you, but he will show you the way, socially, politically, and in community and through your families, how to make your lives more productive and peaceful.*

How can you aid these ends? Seek those ends already that you are working on; the ends of community are to aid the growth and development of individual souls, so that they do this on their own, through moral and ethical decisions, through their service to others. How can you do this? By living your life in larger community as you have already sought to do. You have much to share with others about this; you are already seeking a larger community to find like-minded believers without antagonizing others. So too, will the Magisterial Son, seek through this same process. Only those who are in agreement will arise to the occasion."

"You see many things in your communities that do not work; yet you easily see those that do. Support those that do, adapt those practices that Michael has advised you through your papers, in your daily lives and your family lives. To prepare the way, simply prepare yourself. The way is not outside with the Magisterial Son, though that is a means of aiding the Correcting Time and the days of light and life to appear; the way is through the individual, and the individual must not look outside or outward for solutions, but to look inward for the solutions, and you become a living part of the solutions.

"I know that is difficult for you, as your groups tend to look outside. It is a very difficult balancing project that you have before you, to grow inwardly, yet anticipate in the arrival. That is why the means and the time will not be revealed. This too is a winnowing process of those who can support this, sincerely, humbly, without seeking aggrandizement on their part.

"Jesus did the winnowing, as you know; you have read these passages and know what he did. You have seen this occur also through the Teaching Mission, as many were called, and many fell away. So too, as this free

entry period exists, there will be many who will be attracted, and many will fall away. This is a process of the Master teaching the students before his arrival; it is a process by which you grow. We do not support non-growth, or non-discovery, and non-discernment, but growth, discernment and education that lead to fulfillment on your soul level."

On September 21, 2003, our Magisterial Son, Monjoronson, met with our NOCO group for the first time. He presented his role to uplift our world and answered several questions. A few of his comments in this transcript were:

MONJORONSON: *"Good afternoon, this is Monjoronson. (Welcome!) You no doubt had hope for the arrival of one of the Descending Sons, upon the first time of your reading* The Urantia Book, *that section. [The Urantia Book, Paper #20, The Paradise Sons of God.] Many of you have earnestly prayed for some approach of a being whose capacity could help amend the immense difficulties and learning deficits that are so apparent to any insightful mortal on this planet. And long before the Correcting Time was evident on this planet, millions upon millions of earnest believers in traditional faiths of the west and other religions, which are God centered, prayed earnestly for peace, for well-being, for prosperity, only praying for eras that would be such, never anticipating that peace, prosperity, contentment might be perennial. Now that is an option.*

"And just because a Descended Son is here, does not mean that your well-being will be uplifted immediately. There are still many preparations involved and needed before the arrival is made apparent to the multitudes. It is not a matter of time but of the development of good order, good preparation for that arrival. And it will not become apparent to the multitudes simultaneously or instantaneously, much as the arrival of the Spirit of Truth was evident to believers. You should imagine great rollers on the ocean, as waves of awakening; and even on the shores of consciousness of developed individuals being close at hand, that wave must strike that shore many times before it is acknowledged, let alone accepted."

. . . "we anticipate that you will participate positively, constructively, and supportively with these changes.

"Viewing your culture, here in this nation, you think in terms of personalities of movie stars, presidents, senators, representatives, Supreme Court judges—people of political power and position. Do not anticipate that these bastions will be amended rapidly or soon, for the true changes, developments—positive, constructive, evolutionary changes—that occur in a society and on a planet, as a whole, are slow and must be infused in the individual and expressed in their enthusiasm for change, for positive change. Your representative governments will remain; your democracies will remain; they will evolve, as will other government, political systems evolve, but only through the participation and urging of the individual, that person with a new state of consciousness, who will use a new reality to amend their world.

"You can then see through this that this truly will be co-creative, will be re-educated, but of your own volition. You will have a new community, which you will build. You will raise your own children in a different manner, with help. None of the chores of humanity will be abandoned. And as your societies are amended, you must see that the elements of peace grow, and the elements of destruction diminish. Surely there will continue to be a need for service to the governance of your world, your nation, your states, your counties and cities, and it may even be obligatory, but will become service in the name of peace and social growth and development. If you wish to see a parallel, then view the parallel of the Great Depression that affected your

world in the 1930's and 40's, and the infusion of assistance of your governments in positive, constructive, civil work—this is a very similar parallel to the Correcting Time.

"Michael is investing immense resources heretofore unknown in the millions of years—billions of years—of Nebadon's existence. Never before has a world been reconstructed through co-creative participation of the mortals who live there."

. . . *"You who are here today and those who read this transcript, take this to heart—listen, see, and ask for insights and guidance —not only pray for your own upliftment and healing, but for insights on how to apply yourself, your time, your lives, and your co-creative participation with Michael and this wonderful corps of beings who are on this planet to assist him."*

"You may wonder where my place in all this is —for me it is one of the grandest adventures a Descending Son could ever possibly participate in —I am not going to a planet that is on the edges of Light and Life but on the edge of chaos and planetary destruction. However, I see potential spiritual growth of each of you and all of you, and the whole planet. In coming events you will see effective participation on my part in your world around you long before I appear.

"And neither do I usurp the authority of Machiventa, the Planetary Prince. He has plenty of work himself to do. You see, there are many agendas at work in concert for your planet. Think of the largest, possible human endeavor that has ever taken place on your planet, whether it is the building of a huge hydroelectric dam, the interstate highway system, moving cities, developing a complete infrastructure for a nation, building an immense sky-scraper, then multiply that by a thousand, or a million times, and you have an inkling of the magnitude of the effort Michael's individual, personal effort, to help heal your planet."

Rayson continued to teach the NOCO group on a variety of topics related to the Magisterial Son's Mission—additional material to be added to the archive of Teaching Mission transcripts, the need for worldwide access to the transcripts via the Internet—Melchizedek Schools, Retreat Centers, the Second Revelatory Commission, morontial education—to name just a few topics that were covered in 2004.

In March of 2004, Andronason, a Melchizedek assigned to the staff of Monjoronson, nearly created an "earthquake, tsunami and typhoon combined," within the larger group of Teaching Mission students, when he presented a lesson about the coming earth changes that will be of natural occurrence to our geologically active planet, concurrent with the beginning ages of the Magisterial Mission. Periodically, other teachers gave additional information on the earth changing events: Mantutia Melchizedek in September of 2004, Machiventa and Christ Michael in September of 2005. In addition, the announcement that Urantia was to have an Avonal Son, called Monjoronson, created another "hurricane of immense magnitude" to some of the students in the Teaching Mission, who found it difficult to believe at this time in the earth's history:

September 24, 2005 -

MICHAEL: *"My brother, Monjoronson, as you call him, gives up a great deal to become a mortal among you. I understand this well. He will give up powers and degrees of consciousness, which you will never aspire to for many, many of your lifetimes in the universe. His adjustment will be immense. It is one thing for a descending Son to come upon a planet with some semblance of social order, to see the filaments of belief and faith enacted in institutions that are supported by governments and organizations of a global nature. It is quite another to come upon a planet as yours that is so distraught, in such disarray.*

"The challenges for him are not so much administrative, as it will be to adjust to you, to your ways of mortality, the beliefs that you have. This is not what you would call "culture shock," but something that one must enter into a coma and then wake slowly to become acquainted with. Now multiply that by over a thousand times, by all the cultures—what you might call "data sets"—sets of data for each culture, for each belief system, for each nation, for each heritage, for each history, for each ethnic group, and you will begin to appreciate the grandeur of his intelligence, the breadth of his consciousness, and the depth of his compassion. I am very pleased that Monjoronson is among you. I am so very pleased that his emissary, his pro-tem Chief of Staff is here, to aid in the organization of his permanent staff, the organization unbeknownst and unseen to you, of members of your ranks who are preparing to step forward into columns and rows, and the ranks and profiles of those who serve most directly.

"My friends, my children, during this era of great physical difficulty on your planet, it is more than hope that I want you to have; it is more than faith that I want you to have; more than belief—I want you to have trust, I want you to reach for knowing that you are loved, cared for, and that your way is made clear to you."

October 9, 2005 –

Student: "I'd like to ask about some of the things that are happening here on earth with the storms that seem to be building up, and the earthquakes. Is this a pattern that is becoming more severe, or just appears that way? And is there anything we can do about it?"

ZARATH: *"As mentioned earlier, this is an evolutionary planet, with a core of great energy. The energy effects of the core are cyclical in nature, and this is what is being experienced at this point in time on your planet. The intensity, however, has been exacerbated by your neglect of environmental concerns, and the population currently existing, creating even more problems for the atmospherics and the oceans. So, this will not run its course in just a few years, but will present even more and more problems to be faced by the current inhabitants.*

"There will then come a decrease [in intensity], consistent with the increase in morally corrected and spiritually corrected human approaches, within the various countries and cultures. It is in preparation for this that we advise you to look with faith to the future, accepting the difficulties that come and providing growth for you at the same time in your opportunities to help those around you, as well as yourself. One should be prudent, but without fear, for all of these are opportunities for advancing Christ Michael and Monjoronson's efforts, to bring you through to the start of Light and Life. Be of good cheer."

The year of 2006 contained in-depth lessons by Monjoronson, Rayson, and Zarath in preparation for the mission ahead, where Celestials and mortals will work side-by-side, co-creatively, to solve problems. Again and again, Monjoronson or other teachers discuss the wisdom behind waiting for the proper time and circumstances for the physical appearance of Monjoronson on our world:

June 11, 2006 –

MONJORONSON: *"As I approach materiality, more and more of this Magisterial Mission becomes "locked in" to the temporal pace of your planet. We are not ready to lock in place this mission yet, for there is so much work to do. I will lose my flexibility when that occurs. In many ways I will be a captive of this planet, though I will have the same capacity to lay down my body and travel elsewhere, as I am needed, or as is required, there upon returning to my body, taking it up, and traversing as a captive on the planet again.*

"So many of you are waiting. So many of you are prepared. So many of you will be gone before I appear. Those of you who are prepared and waiting, you are much like those so many years ago, who waited for the "return," who waited for the healing of your planet, healing and completion, patiently waiting for years, decades—perhaps centuries. I do not and will not reveal to you when the mission will become corporeal in full, and operational at a level that you can participate in. It would be foolhardy to do so. You are agondonters. I envision that one day, a decade or two after the mission is in its corporeal form, that someone will write a novel or a true story of the last agondonters as a chronicle to those who waited. Those of you who believe, have faith, trust and know that I will be here in material form, that Christ Michael will then follow me in the time after that in the distant future."

Another topic that created a great deal of commotion within the Teaching Mission community, concerned population density:

Student: "I have a question. It says in *The Urantia Book* that the man to land ratio is key to the well being of the human race. Is our population in line with the man to land ratio? They predict that there will be nine billion people by 2050. Are you able to speak on that, or how do we keep our population within limits?"

MONJORONSON: *"This is not a function that is governable by individuals, or even by societies or nations, except that individuals may responsibly raise a reasonable number of children, so that they are cared for, educated and prepared for their future. The population of your world is grossly out of balance. It will be at that time, which you state, approximately three times larger than it should be. There is truly an equation for the number of people that can successfully, productively, rationally, spiritually, occupy land in relationship to the square mileage or land mass.*

"Your other question obviously must be, "How will this be aligned?" We will not institute any global program of eugenics. This situation of over-population of your planet will be self-rectifying. It is unavoidable; it is now in preparation, we are aware that there are forces in your world, which will change the population level dramatically in a very brief period of time. We work with all individuals; we work with all souls. We wish that the production of healthy, whole, heavy souls occur on every planet, and that every soul that leaves this planet be weighty with wisdom, experience, understanding, insight, and personal reverence.

You make them by moral and ethical decisions; you make heavy souls with the addition of service—not required, obligatory service, but joyful service, generous service, gleeful service, service that is done from the heart.

"Look about you in your world. How many people serve easily, generously, passionately? How many people are making good moral, ethical decisions, given that they are presented to them every day? Many souls leave your planet light as a feather, with very little survival capacity. Yet, many of you leave this planet as heavy souls, having made many weighty, consistent, good, ethical, and moral decisions and have provided wonderful service to your fellow brothers and sisters.

"The opportunity for decision-making is before everyone. The opportunity for service is before everyone. The awakening of the Thought Adjuster, the awakening of the individual and the connection with the Thought Adjuster, the Father fragment, is essential to the growth of the soul. You here are heavy souls; you are weighty with good decisions and wonderful service. You will survive, if you wish to. This, too, is a decision; this too is part of an intention for living. These are decisions that you must make, consciously—not flippantly or errantly, but consciously with good intention. What I am saying in answer to your question is that we appreciate the number of souls that are on your planet, yet we know clearly that many will leave here deciding not to continue the journey. Many will leave here having no idea of what their life was about, and many will be leaving here who have great value.

"This scythe that will cut across the populations of your world, is no respecter of status, power, authority, monies, or spiritual development—it will strike evenly to everyone. And it will reduce the population of your planet—it is unavoidable; it is inevitable; it will occur. And when you do cross, whether before or after this occurs, we are there, we are so close to you. We will help you make this transition more easily. Thank you for your question."

From June 11, 2006 to January 1, 2007, Monjoronson presented a series of lessons on sustainability, which Daniel Raphael has turned into an e-book, called *Global Sustainability and Planetary Management: The Revealed Future of Humanity As Seen Through Celestial Eyes.* (This e-book is in PDF format at the web site below, and can be read or downloaded in its entirety.)
In addition, the topics presented to the NOCO group by Rayson and Zarath during this period, also focused on "sustainability" in all areas of life on Urantia.

In May of 2007, Monjoronson turned our group over to Sondjah Melchizedek for a new series of lessons on leadership and working in teams.

The Northern Colorado TeaM group was inactive from August 2007, until December 2008, while Daniel worked on other projects in service to Christ Michael and Monjoronson. It was at Monjoronson's request that the NOCO group started meeting again about once per month. The "economic collapse" of 2008 was one of the events that was foreseen by our celestial friends, and although they "hinted" that the financial empires were not sustainable, they were not allowed to give us details before hand on the actual collapse. Once the collapse had occurred, Monjoronson wanted to use it as an example for how to build a sustainable economy, in a co-creative process. In this case, the Most Highs are working through liaison personalities to offer them a broad spectrum of opportunities and creative solutions to the current crisis.

The lessons now in 2009 are largely about current global events and the interactions of mortals with spirit to create solutions, rather than just solving problems. The pace is quickening as the stage is set for great social upheavals in all areas, but solving complex problems will take time to resolve. One thing is certain: Christ Michael has given us all the celestial help we can possibly use to advise us of better ways of doing things. Now, if we can only supply enough steadfast mortals to serve on the other half of the co-creative teams, this planet will one fine day in the future, reach the stage of light and life! Michael can count on the NOCO TeaM to give our all to this worthy endeavor.

Transcripts mentioned are at: www.tmarchives.com. A discussion group on Monjoronson and the Magisterial Mission is at: www.monjoronson.com

(Roxanne Andrews, longtime reader and home host for Urantia Book study, has been a member of the Teaching Mission since 2001, and a transcriber of the lessons. She is a board member of Starbridge Communications, Inc., as well as secretary, associate treasurer, special projects manager and website assistant. She retired from 19 years as a water quality analyst for Coors Brewery, and as an analyst in research biochemistry.)

My Experiences with Celestial Teachers
Daniel Raphael, Ph.D.

My first personal exposure to my celestial teacher, Mor-gan, was in the early spring of 1994. And a few months later with contact with my Guardian Angel, Leah. It was a halting experience to begin, but gradually over the months of using the keyboard to T/R, I could hold a slow but continuing dialogue with either of them. As I was new to Colorado and socially isolated by living on a ranch, I benefitted greatly from the discussions I had with Leah.

I can remember on one occasion I asked Leah what I should do for a particular problem. No answer! So, I asked her what options I had regarding this problem. She quickly delineated not one but ten options for this particular situation! The decision(s) were mine to make, and action to take, with my responsibility for the decision decidedly mine . . . but! she had told me the options. I was pretty impressed, and even today, I continue to ask my teacher, Mor-gan, and Leah for options concerning some difficult situation that faces me.

I continued to use the keyboard . . . well I have to confess that I bought some nice little glass beads at the hobby store, cleaned my keyboard keys with alcohol, and then super-glued one each to the "d, k, @, -, and delete" keys. Then I could close my eyes and still type and make some of sense of it all rather than looking like a cat on catnip had danced on my keyboard! Eventually in late '90s I became a clairaudient T/R for others in group settings.

My public T/R-ing was at first plodding and slow, but once I took the plunge to just let what was coming through flow out of my mouth, rather than storing it away bit by bit to then paraphrase to the listeners, it has become much smoother. Since then, it has become fluent and "unconscious" to me as I listen to the T/R session just like someone in the audience.

You may be wondering if T/R-ing has assisted in my own spiritual growth, as much as the audience. As a T/R, you cannot help but be highly influenced by the Celestial Teachers, Christ Michael, Nebadonia, numerous Melchizedeks, and assorted other personalities when their wisdom comes ringing through your mind, out your mouth, and then back again into your ears. These multiple impressions on the TR's mind have an indelible effect upon his/her personality, mind development, and soul fulfillment. I have found the overall effect as aiding the TR's approach to the lower morontial levels of awareness and learning. But, I still don't understand Morontia Mota very well!

One long held prayer I have stated hundreds of times has been, "It is my will for my life to make some contribution to Christ Michael's efforts to advance the arrival of the era of light and life to this planet, if by only by one second. And if my life could contribute to the arrival of that era sooner, then guide me, show me, instruct me, challenge me to explore that venue of service to accomplish that meager end — all in accordance with God's will for my life, for the highest and greatest good of all concerned." Essentially, this is a request to be of service to our world and its advancement.

Fortunately, I was invited to attend the TM Conference at Snow Bird, Utah Ski Resort in 2001. This initiated the development of a program of service in my life that continues today. Well, I have to tell you that having met Roxanne and Jim Andrews at Snow Bird was the beginning of an ever-broadening river of exploration of service. We formed the Northern Colorado (NOCO) TM Group, which has continued to produce transcripts periodically since.

Whether one is a T/R or not, becoming of service begins first by working through our own maze of personal personality immaturity issues. When disappointments do not have the sting then once had, when the unreasonable expectations for life that were held so tightly in younger years have evaporated, and when the deepening relationship with the TA becomes more sure, then comes service. Then comes service: SERVICE!

My path of service has evolved and developed. And I can count myself very, very fortunate to be able to dialogue with my Celestial Teacher, Mor-gan, or with Christ Michael about anything at all. I still have to make the choices of the options available, and explore the way forward. And that path offered the option of the 2007 Workshop at Snow Bird, Utah, where we explored the fundamentals of the Co-Creative Design Team, and the 2007-2008 exploration of an experimental Co-Creative Design Team in Evergreen, Colorado, guided by Sondjah Melchizedek.

That experimental platform proved that the CCDT Process was viable with ordinary individuals, and that meaningful results could be quickly attained. Then in 2008 I was given an opportunity to facilitate a bi-lingual Co-Creative Design Team Workshop in San Miguel de Allende, Mexico. These three CCD Team experiences provided an evolutionary progression, but one pivotal element was missing from the instructional manual – the spiritual development of the individuals who would participate in working CCD Teams.

Working with the Teachers is sometimes a trying experience. For myself they provide a trail of "bread crumbs" of opportunities that lead me into a productive future, and when the bread crumbs stop, I know I need to reassess my position, ask them numerous questions and then pick up the trail of opportunities and proceed again. Right now, I am working on a very strong trail of opportunities that have led me to develop a holistic curriculum for the Melchizedek School and for the Melchizedek University. This series of classes was designed to aid the spiritual development of the individual student, which supports their becoming a productive member of a working CCD Team. In this way, students, too, can grow in their spiritual maturity, and then advance to a team environment working with a consulting Melchizedek to the team, where they can be of service to their families, communities, and the world.

It is no mistake that the Teaching Mission begins with teaching individuals the essentials of moral, ethical, and a socially conscious life through the lessons given by the Celestial Teachers. What often follows is an era of personal development and experiential exercises in real life living out the challenges of those lessons. And when those lessons are learned, then the adventure of service begins. I cannot think of a better way to learn the lesson and experience of service than under the tutelage of the Spiritual Consulting Melchizedek in an operational Co-Creative Design Team. You see, once we learn how to live in harmony with ourselves, then it is time to learn how to live in harmony with others, socially. And then it is time to design our societies so that they contribute to the social evolution of individuals.

My adventure began with a question to Christ Michael after the third time I had experienced a Celestial Teacher (Abigail) in Salem, Oregon in 1992-3, "Christ Michael, do you think it would be useful for me to become a T/R? And if so, would you teach me how to become of service to this world?"

I invite you to join me in service to our world to bring the era of light and life to our world sooner by our efforts.

My Teaching Mission Experiences
Marty Risacher

I am honored to recount the story of how I became involved in the Teaching Mission and its profound effects on my life. Without doubt, the relationships that I have developed over the years with the many celestials with which I have had the opportunity to interact have been the source of great encouragement, wisdom and understanding. However, the greatest gift I have received from these relationships is the incredible outpouring of unconditional love from these Beings. And foremost among all of these relationships is the very precious and special relationship that I have with my beloved Welmek, the very best friend I have ever had. I so look forward to the time when we embrace on the first mansion world.

Background

I was born in 1947 in rural, southern Indiana as the first born of five children to a father returned from WW II and a woman who was called upon to raise a second family, the first being the family in which she was born where she took over a parental role when her mother died at an early age. My mother was harsh and angry. My first memory of her was being beaten when I was in diapers. This continued until adolescence when I stopped the physical abuse. The mental abuse continued until her death in 1975.

This experience had significant effects at all areas of my development although I was largely unconscious of the full extent of its impact until much later in adulthood. I mention it here because of its relevance to the impact that Teaching Mission has had and continues to have on me.

On the other hand, my father was a kind and loving man. He took me off to work with him at the family dairy when I was but 8 year old. I suspect now this was his attempt to protect me from my mother.

I developed a strong love for God at a very early age. I remember adults remarking on this and suggesting that "he must be going to be a priest". I remember talking to Jesus a lot when I was very young and how much comfort that brought to me.

All of that changed when I entered into Catholic school and encountered nuns wearing black habits that often matched their moods. I was a cut up at school and received many beatings from the nuns.

I recall being taught from an early age that God expected me to live without sinning and that if I died as a sinner, He would send me to an everlasting Hell where I would literally burn in fires that perpetually would torture my being. I was taught that I suffered from original sin and that it was obligation to behave always without violating any of the Ten Commandments.

Specifically, I was consistently taught that not only was it a sin to engage in any type of sexual activity outside of marriage, it was a mortal sin that would send me to heel to even have an impure thought. Needless to say, this idea caused great anxiety, fear and worry for me when I began puberty. These ideas were drilled into me day in and day out all through the 12 years of Catholic grade and high school. It is hardly a surprising that the heavy use of alcohol was the most common strategy used by me and my peers at that time in my life to cope with these intense feelings. Interestingly, the priests and nuns virtually ignored the subject of alcohol use.

I went to college in 1965 and utterly failed at being able to generate sufficient self-discipline to even go to class. When I flunked out of college 1966, I got drafted into the Army expecting to go to Viet Nam. I completed OCS and was commissioned a 2d Lt and instead was sent to Germany where I drank a lot, drove sports cars and enjoyed as much sex as I could possibly get. Eventually, I concluded that I no longer believed what I was taught about God and really did not pay much attention to the subject as I was totally immersed in the pleasures of material life.

After release from the service, I began college again. My age and maturity gave me a great advantage over those coming from high school. I became a straight A student.

It was at this time that I began the process of a total metamorphosis. I began using psychedelic drugs on a daily basis. I became a student radical. I also decided that I would begin to decide for myself and from my own experience exactly who I was and what was my purpose.

For several years, I engaged in the intense study of Hinduism, Buddhism, Taoism, Confucianism, Shintoism, American Indian traditions, Sufism, and a variety of New Age philosophies and thought. Nothing was too far out or weird for me to look into and study. During this time of intense searching truth I had an experience which changed my perspective considerably.

When during a time of quiet introspection, I recall making a sincere request for some guidance or sign from God of His existence. Immediately, I felt a presence that transported me to a state of being that was beyond time and space where I felt energized but totally at peace and a sense that I was connected to everything that was. After this experience concluded, I decided that I would spend whatever time that was necessary to have this happen again. It took quite a while.

Introduction to the Urantia Book

I married a wonderful woman in my senior year in college. She like me had been wounded by her experience growing up Catholic but unlike me had rejected any interest in finding God some other way. However, it was her sister that introduced me to *the Urantia Book* in 1972 when I was a first year student in law school living in Bloomington, Indiana. This occurred "by coincidence.

I found this Book absolutely fascinating. Initially, I could not put this Book down even though I was working 3 jobs, trying to keep a difficult marriage afloat and getting through law school. I was on one hand afraid of the UB for some reason but also inexplicably drawn to it.

I gave it to fellow seeker friend of mine who became even more obsessed by the UB than I. We read it while getting high and discussed it constantly. We finally decided to find out who was behind this and learned of the UB Foundation and Fellowship in Chicago.

We began attending seminars in the Midwest of UB readers. We met many interesting and engaging people. We also met many people who seemed to think that an important measure of spirituality was how many times that one had read the book and how familiar one was with the minutia contained within. I felt inferior to these people who knew the book so much better than I did.

I often thought to myself that there must something more to spirituality that just the UB because I did not feel like I was getting all that I needed from it. There seemed to remain a void within me no matter how much I read the Book and enjoyed the insights it gave me. I finally came to believe that the Book was what it said it was but I was not fully satisfied from just reading it and discussing it with others. Something seemed to be missing.

In 1975, I graduated from law school and was immediately appointed a trial court judge in rural, southern Indiana where I grew up. My friend and fellow UB reader coincidentally had moved to that region to live simply off the land. I appointed him my bailiff and probation officer. We decided that we would try to run the court in accordance with the spiritual principles that we found in the UB.

We later introduced the UB to a mental health counselor and his girlfriend. This became our study group. The counselor soon joined the court staff too.

Needless to say, the people in this rural county did not know quite what to make of us. Surprisingly, we did seem to fit into the social fabric more than would have been expected. This was a time of great economic insecurity generally. I and my friends devoted great effort to becoming self sufficient by building homes, raising our own food and essentially trying to separate ourselves from the rest of society which we viewed as bad and corrupt and destined to fail.

Consistent with our understandings from the UB, we did become active in developing a number of community organizations to help those who were unfortunate and troubled due to alcohol and drug addiction or abuse within the family. We started a Boys Group Home, a Girl's Group Home, a Community Services Program and a comprehensive Alcohol and Drug Treatment Program that became a model for the rest of the state. I was invited to become a faculty member at the National Judicial College in Reno, Nevada where I taught and encouraged judges from around the world to establish drug and alcohol treatment programs as an alternative to incarceration those efforts bore great fruit as these types of programs exist at every level of court now in this country and others.

Of course, I had no way of knowing at that time that one day I too would be entering a drug treatment program due to a severe cocaine addiction. It is funny how ironic life is!

In 1986, I suffered an election defeat that caused me, my spouse and my four year old daughter to move from our 40 Acre home in the Hoosier National Forest to a suburb of where I landed a position in a highly respected law firm.

I also joined a very active Urantia Book study group typically hosted by Bob and Linda Buselli or Mike Painter. This study group was comprised of a number of long time UB readers who were very serious about the Book as was I and much more knowledgeable. .

Over the next decade, I became a well recognized litigator in my law firm where I made lots of money, had lots of status and increased the influence of an ego full of pride and arrogance. Interestingly, my reading of the UB actually reinforced the delusion of how very special and superior that I was. But "pride goeth before the fall" as they say. .

Consistent with my deep love for my daughter, coupled with my understanding from the UB as to the importance of child rearing, I did my very best to be a good father but by this time in my life, my alcohol abuse has progressed to the point where this was not all that possible. I ignored this fact and continued on my path of self delusion...

Introduction To The Teaching Mission

In 1992, an event occurred that changed my entire perspective on who I thought that I was and why I exist. It began with a telephone call from Bob Busellis in July of 1992 where Bob asked me if I would meet with him for lunch to discuss something of importance. Bob was a bit mysterious about the subject at the time but I thought it might be something personal. At that point in time, it was not that unusual for Bob and I and sometimes Mike Painter to have lunch together on occasion.

Anyway, Bob and I met for lunch soon thereafter where he advised me that approximately a year earlier he had received a letter from an individual from New Zealand that he threw away because he thought it came from a nut. According to Bob, this individual indicated that he belonged to group of people who met regularly to meditate as a group. The letter went on to relate that during meditation on one occasion one of the members of the group began speaking aloud and said something to the effect that:" I am Abraham and have come to announce the final adjudication of the Lucifer Rebellion." According to Bob, the letter went to say that there was an effort underway to bring all of the worlds in isolation back into the spiritual circuits including this one. The letter further indicated that part of this effort involved sending celestial Teachers to UB study groups to assist them in advancing their own spiritual development. The author of the letter went on to say that Abraham instructed this individual to send this letter to known UB study group on the planet.

Bob then told me that apparently not all those in the United States threw their letters away like he did. Bob advised that there was a group in Idaho and one in Florida that took the letter seriously and apparently made requests for the assignment of Teachers to their respective groups. According to Bob, the Teachers were giving their lessons by a process of speaking through a human transmitter. Bob looked at me kind of funny and asked me what I thought of it.

I immediately responded that it was one of two things: either it is a grand hoax or it is the most important thing to happen in our lifetimes. At the time I said this, I felt a very discernable sensation of excitement arise from my being. At some level I already knew that something very important was about to occur for me.

Bob asked what I thought about our group asking for a Teacher. I told him that I was all for it. I told Bob that either it doesn't happen and we will all have a good laugh or it does happen and our lives are going to change forever.

Bob then gave me some transcripts of some of the transmissions made by the two groups that were operating already to read. I read the transcripts voraciously. While much of the material seemed a bit trite with questions about flying saucers and spiritual names and the like, there was a certain air of elegance in the teachings of Ham and Will. I especially liked Will's style for some reason.

I was quite intrigued by the possibility of something wonderful happening when I arrived at the Buselli home on a Saturday afternoon in July of 1992. The front room and adjoining room was full of people, a good number of which I did not know. Apparently, Bob and Linda had been busy in contacting people. I recall being quite nervous and apprehensive about what might happen. In fact, nothing happened.

We decided that we would all try the stillness as suggested by the transcripts of the transmissions from the other two groups. Because I already had some experience with meditation based upon my many inquiries into eastern religions, I was generally familiar with this process. Well, we meditated and meditated and nothing happened.

After several hours of nothing happening, we discussed as a group what we should do. I recall speaking up and suggesting that we should come back one more time to try and that if nothing happened, we could quit trying. We decided to schedule a meeting for that next weekend. I do recall being quite disappointed that no fantastic thing happened and thought it was probably another spiritual hoax that like so many that seemed to be around in those days.

Anyway, I was surprised to receive a telephone call from David Painter a few days later who told me that he had been contacted a teacher who called himself, Welmek. I recall saying something like I can't believe that it would be you, David that would be the contact. I considered David just a regular guy not as involved with the UB and its organizations like his brother, Mike Painter or the Busellis.

This of course was at a time when I suffered from the misunderstanding that spiritual advancement could be measured from the achievement of some position of power and influence in a spiritual organization. I have since come to understand that often the opposite is true.

Anyway, I would never have considered David the top choice in our group for this so-called exalted position. The fact that I considered a T/R an exalted position is further evidence of my inability at that time in my life to separate the messenger from the message and the principle from the personality. It is a matter of great interest how pervasive this misunderstanding still is even by those who believe themselves to be spirit guided. But this was at a time when my human ego was very active and involved in constantly engaging the process of evaluating how I measured up and compared to the accomplishments and status of others. But at that point in time I was largely unconscious of what ego is, how it operated and how it controlled very aspect of my life. .

In this telephone call, David invited me to a meeting held at his house to be held a few days where we would hear from a Teacher. I was so excited by this news. I could not wait for the day of the meeting and it finally came. After hearing from David, I called my friends who still lived in southern Indiana and told them of the news.

I recall that when I arrived, there were around 20 or so people who I knew and several that I did not. My friends from southern Indiana eventually arrived too.

I can distinctly recall the excitement when I heard David begin the session by the words: Greetings, I am your friend and Teacher, Welmek". I have since heard this literally thousands of times.

I do not remember much at that meeting except being somewhat intimidated and a bit overwhelmed. I was confused by it all but was not yet prepared to either accept or reject its validity. But I kept coming back week after week after week. The crowds became bigger and bigger each week until they filled David's house and even his porches outside the house.

In the early days, I recall much attention in the meetings to issues having to do with whether or not the transmissions were true and accurate or the figment of David's imagination. There also seemed too much interest by individuals in learning their spiritual names, the names of their angels so on and so forth. Often, we would receive transmissions from other Teachers such as Rayson, Tomas, Phyllis and a crowd favorite, Machiventa, who we called affectionately, "Big Mac".

I do recall that the Teachers uniformly and consistently suggested that we each begin the daily practice of stillness. I did as suggested and have continued to do so since that time except for an approximately 2 year period of time when I was in full blown active addiction to crack cocaine. There will be more about that later.

In the early days, the Teacher would typically begin the lesson by giving a presentation on some topic like prayer, worship, stillness, tolerance, patience, anger or the like and then fielding questions from the attendees on the subject or on other subjects. The meetings typically lasted 1 ½ to 2 hours each. The meetings were taped and the tapes transcribed by Linda Buselli and sometimes others.

After awhile, I and most of those in attendance, started to accept the sessions as real as crazy as it seemed. We all talked about issues of keeping this to ourselves for fear that our friends, fellow workers and neighbors would think that something was wrong with us and shun us. All that seems somewhat humorous today but back then I and others it seemed were very interested in protecting some image that we projected to others. Today, I understand that this was yet another example of how thoroughly I was subject to the complete domination by human ego.

Even after months of weekly meetings crowded with people, issues of proof of the truth of what was happening persisted. Welmek continually pressed us on this issue of how to decide what is real and what is not. Welmek advised that the true test of what is real comes from within through the inspiration of the Spirit of Truth and no objective event would ultimately suffice. He directed us to the miracle of the loaves and fishes remarking that of the five thousand of those who personally witnessed such an astounding event, only five hundred remained as followers within a few days.

I don't recall specifically how it occurred today but I do remember that others and I included told Welmek that we would be totally convinced of the reality of the Teaching Mission if he or some other celestial personality would become material and be seen. This happened on several occasions that materialization seemed to be a common desire of those present to confirm their belief in the existence of what was happening.

Today, I cannot remember when exactly it happened but I remember that during the course of a lesson from Welmek, it was stated that Machiventa would in fact materialize in the very new future as part of an event representing a change or alteration in the planetary administration. I recall now that we were all excited and thrilled by this news.

Soon thereafter, other groups began reporting confirmation of this from their own Teachers. It seemed that this topic began taking up the attention of the group each meeting notwithstanding Welmek's attempt to get the group to focus on issues of spiritual development.

Naperville

While I cannot remember today the details, I recall that at some point in time that it was announced that Machiventa would materialize in a suburb of Chicago, Naperville, Illinois in April of 1993. We began to make our plans to go there and were excited about it.

I do recall very distinctly today that something puzzling began happening at the last few meetings before the scheduled materialization. During the course of one of my opportunities to interact with him, Welmek asked me if I intended to go to Naperville. I told him that I would not miss it. He asked me then what I expected to see there. When I answered him as to my vague expectations, he asked what I would do if the materialization did not occur. I was puzzled by the question but indicated my firm belief that it would happen and recall asking if he had some different understanding. I do not remember today what Welmek said but it seemed puzzling to me at the time.

I also remember talking with David at the time when we were making arrangements to go when David said he was not going. I was somewhat shocked at this and asked him why. David said he could not afford it and furthermore did not think anything was going to happen. I offered to pay David's way but he would not relent. However, at the time I thought that David was just being stubborn. I never thought to even question my belief that this event would occur as indicated and as Welmek told us.

The trip from Indianapolis to Naperville was a lot of fun. By this time, many of us in the group had achieved some skill and experience as TR's. Several of those who were T/R-ing their own personal Teachers conducted a rather lively session on the way to Naperville where enroute several Teachers spoke to us. The mood was light and festive although again I recalled after the fact some questions by the Teachers about how we might react if nothing happened. It went right by us or at least it did me.

When we arrived in Naperville, I met up with my sister, Jody, who had traveled there separately with a group from Cincinnati. We went into a large conference room where hundreds of people from all over the country were present. I recall that someone from Arizona seemed to be in charge of what was happening and spoke with a microphone. Behind him was a group of people dressed in white, flowing robes that began singing or chanting. It was at this point that something resonated within me that this does not feel right. But my intellect told me that I had no business evaluating what is necessary for the materialization of a celestial Being and that I should be ashamed of my lack of belief.

Well, the chanting went on for a long time and nothing happened. I recall the lights were dimmed and nothing happened. I heard a murmur from the crowd at some point but I did not see anything happen. Eventually, all the chanting and dancing stopped and there was an announcement of some kind about why Machiventa did not materialize that I considered totally bogus.

I felt incredibly disappointed and duped. I was somewhat angry but mostly angry at myself. My sister and I shared the moment. I felt ashamed that I had brought her into this and felt responsible for her decisions to get involved with the Teaching Mission at Cincinnati and coming to Naperville. To her credit, she said that she gained a lot from the lessons from Tarkus and it was her own decision to decide to come to Naperville. We did share our disappointment and finally went our separate ways.

It was a quiet ride home. No one felt like transmitting and I don't think that I would have given anything said any credence whatsoever. It was some weeks later that I decided that I would give this another chance. I really did miss the meetings and felt like they had changed my life positively whether or not Machiventa materialized.

The Lesson of Naperville For Me

After the disappointment of Naperville, I still continued to do stillness on a daily basis as I had already been convinced of its value to me. I suppose the fact that stillness had worked so well for me caused me not to reject the value of the Teaching Mission as well. I truly did miss Welmek and the lessons he provided to us. In looking back I was not prepared to close the door on what seemed to have great value to me.

It is my recollection that at some point I called David to see if he would resume the meetings. David indicated a lack of interest in resuming transmitting. I recall also talking with Linda Buselli too who said she would come if we resumed the sessions but that she doubted that Bob would. It is also my recollection that I also spoke to Mike and Donna (now Donna D'Ingilo) too. It could be that one of them called me as it was apparent at that point in time that some of us were not prepared to throw the baby out with the bath water.

Mike said that he would be willing to transmit but we all had to promise that our lessons would be devoted strictly to personal spiritual development and no longer focused on the fantastic and the speculative. I agreed and was so thankful that the lessons would continue.

I do remember that we did discuss Naperville among us but I don't know that we ever arrived at any decision as to what did or did not happen there. I remember that there was one train of thought that the whole thing arose from David's mind and that the Teachers decided to let it run its course. Another explanation was that the transmissions were real and accurate but for reasons that are unclear the materialization did not take place either for a problem with the process itself or because it was thought wiser not to do so. I don't know that it was that important for us to reach a consensus about it at the time or even now about what happened. I do recall seeing a transcript at the time that attempted to explain what happened which I reviewed again before writing this but I cannot say that I find it compelling one way or the other.

But to me, Naperville served to separate those who were interested in miracles and the sensational from those who truly were interested in doing the hard work of self transformation. I distinctly remember a lesson from Machiventa during that time period where he recounted his experience while on the planet in the flesh. Machiventa stated to the effect that back in his days as a mortal that often crowds would gather around the fire for the "meat and the stories" but when the food was gone and the lessons began, they would drift away. He said that he did not view the humans of today any differently in that regard from those of the past.

For me, Naperville was an important crossroads for many who came to meetings because they were intrigued by the speculations of future glory but had little interest in engaging in the personal changes necessary for this to occur. Consistently, the Teachers would tell us that it was up to us to change our own world. They were here to help us but no one was going to come down from the heavens and make everything better overnight.

To me, the most important lesson of Naperville is just this. It is up to me to do the hard work necessary to bring spirit into my life. No one else can do this for me no matter what their status may be. While the universe is populated with scores of beings who want nothing more than to assist me in developing spiritually, they exist to encourage, teach and provide a model but they simply cannot do it for me. I must find the God within me and make the choices on a daily basis that makes it easier for me to accept His guidance. In other words, I make my own reality.

Post Naperville

For the next 7 to 8 years or so, a small core of us met. Our group had essentially shrunk from 50 to 5 after Naperville. Instead of lessons engaged in speculations about sensational futures of personal exaltation, we tried to become increasingly serious about dealing with personal issues that posed obstacles for personal growth. I recall having a number of private sessions during this period of time but lacked the courage then to genuinely face up to the very core issues of my dysfunction nor to honestly discuss my alcohol abuse and sexual promiscuity both of which were becoming more prevalent in my life with the disintegration of my marriage. I recall an occasion when Welmek told me in effect that I would likely have to experience some times that would try my soul but that he was confident that I would come out on the other side because he saw a solid spiritual foundation in me. I had no idea what he was talking about then but sure do now.

I also recall that within a few years of the resumption of our meetings, Mike Painter, Donna Painter, Jim Cleveland, Susie Roweland and I formed The Stillness Foundation, Inc., and a non-profit corporation that we used to try to disseminate to others the value of practice of stillness. We advertised in newspapers and hosted seminars but not much happened with this. Mike did record a cassette that outlined the practice as Welmek had taught it to us which eventually was made into a CD and still disseminated today. In fact, it is much more popular today than ever.

As a result of these efforts, we did get a few more individuals to join our group and who still come even today. During those days over a decade ago, Welmek tried several different approaches with us. Based upon his suggestion that we would all at some point be called upon to teach these principles to others, we would have session after session where each of us would be called upon to teach some hypothetical person who came to us and asked us a question about a life problem. Welmek explained that three would come a time when we would be given the opportunity to join a project of planetary significance that would be the beginning of an effort to bring this planet into a new phase of spiritual enlightenment. Welmek said that some of us would be teachers; some would need as administrators and some as healers. All would be needed and that the Teachers would provide us with whatever instruction seemed appropriate based upon what it is that we chose to do.

In those days, Linda Buselli, Donna Painter, Sandy Porter, Mark Hall, myself and of course, Mike Painter comprised the regular group. Occasionally, we would have others attend one or two sessions but not come back. Sandy lives now in Florida as do I during the wintertime. Mark and Linda still live in Indianapolis and continue to attend the meetings that we continue to have.

I remember distinctly that in those days in the 1990's that Donna Painter was enthusiastic in her resolve to be a healer. I recall that she spent virtually all of her free time engaged in instruction from a host of celestials about healing. In fact, in the late 1990's, Donna split up with Mike and moved to California on the strength of her calling from Michael in this regard. I remember well this decision and how agonizing it was for her given that she was living a good job and going somewhere that she had never lived before and knew only a few people much less a job. But she did do so and has been an inspiration to me ever since about conquering fear by completely surrendering to faith.

I also remember attending some Teaching Mission seminars in the 1990's at various locales. I even have a hazy memory of being involved with a presentation of some sort that may have also involved Donna, Mike, Jim Cleveland and perhaps others. I also recall that there seemed to be a general dying out of the enthusiasm and energy in the Teaching Mission over this time. Certainly, this occurred in the Indianapolis group

Sometime in the early 2000's after Donna and Mike split up, the group lessons began to become more sporadic for reasons that were unclear to me now. I do recall that I was increasingly feeling much more ambivalence about attending myself.

Of course, I was aware that there continued to be personal behaviors of mine that were inconsistent with what I knew to be proper. In other words, I knew that I was no longer even trying to follow God's will. Even though I was still doing daily stillness, I did not often speak with the Father or ask for guidance for fear that this would cause me to confront that which I could not face at that time. To my mind, what I could not face was the fact I was not happy in my marriage. At the time, I assessed a large portion of the blame on my wife who disapproved of my spiritual practices and criticized them. However, I came to understand some years later that my problem was me and not her.

Anyway, there came a time when Mike became involved a romantic relationship with a woman from a strong fundamentalist background and he stopped transmitting for the group. It was never clear to me exactly what his reasons were but I assumed that he had decided that his relationship would suffer if he continued on with his active involvement with the Teaching Mission. As I recall, Linda and I were able to convince David to become back involved. While both Linda and I had the ability to T/R, we both felt more comfortable listening to David than transmitting ourselves.

2004 to August, 2010

The time period of 2000 to 2004 is very hazy for me to recall. I do recall being heavily invested in making money and trying to be a good father. I was pretty good at the former but not so good at the latter. I was also still pretty good at drinking heavy and chasing loose women outside of marriage which was at this point long devoid of any affection whatsoever. But I was hell bent on staying in the marriage until my daughter was out of school notwithstanding the damage it was clearly having on her.

I recall some attendance at Teacher meetings during this period of time and engaging in daily stillness but my interest was focused on how to deal with the very serious problems that my daughter was encountering in adolescence rather than my own behavior. I avoided all discussions of my role in anything at this time in sessions and hoped that Welmek would not raise this issue in a session. He never did even though he was certainly aware of exactly how much I was avoiding the truth of my life.

Among many things that I respect and love about the Teachers is the consistently tolerant attitude always expressed towards us. I have never been in any meeting and I have attended thousands where a Teacher called out anyone even on occasions when the human was insulting to a Teacher. There was never an occasion when Welmek stated anything that could be construed as disapproval of my behavior although I fully expected it. I am certain that he knew that I was headed towards a disaster and knows that if it were up to him, he would want me to avoid it. But he always respected my choice no matter how much it caused me pain and suffering. This for me is a great lesson and one which I treasure greatly now: respect, tolerance and understanding for each and every one no matter what level of their development.

Nonetheless, the early 2000's were a very unhappy time for me. My relationship with my wife was barely tolerable. My daughter became more and more embarrassed by me. She began to suffer serious dysfunctions of her own. All of this added to my guilt and anxiety.

I recall learning sometime around 2004 that a Being named Monjoronson had become prominent in transmissions. I further remember that Monjoronson may have even addressed our group but from TR's other than David. Based upon what I heard in transmissions and what I read in our transcripts of his lessons, I developed the belief that Monjoronson was who he said he was, that at some point in time he might live on this planet in human form and that this might even occur in my lifetime. This was an exciting possibility for me and I was hopeful that I would have the chance to serve in such a mission. However, I was also becoming aware that my personal problems were becoming more significant and I concluded that I really was not spiritually fit to be of much service in that regarded.

It was at this point in time that I made a decision to separate from my wife and live on my own. When I made this decision, I knew in my heart of hearts that I would either immerse myself back into spiritual development or go in the opposite direction of pursuit of material pleasure. I chose the latter.

The next few years were a blur of emotional pain and spiritual isolation. As some point in time one of my female companions provided me the opportunity to try crack cocaine and I did so even though a voice in my head told me that it was a terrible mistake. This began a 2 year descent into agony and despair.

I stopped doing daily stillness the day I first used this drug. Slowly but steadily, my life fell apart in all areas. Most of all, I lost a good part of the relationship I had with my daughter.

Eventually and inevitably, I ended up at a point in time where I no longer wanted to live but was afraid to die. I called out for the Father and He was there for me instantly, filling me with love and telling me that He had been waiting for me. I knew at that point that I had to decide to continue on to total self destruction or to completely and without reservation, consecrate my will to that of the Father's. I obviously chose the latter or this story would not have been written.

Immediately after making this decision, I met with Linda Buselli and asked her to transmit Welmek for me. Welmek told me that he had never doubted that I would come to my senses and that he would be there for me at all times during the difficult times that immediately lay ahead in rehab. He then told me that someone else wanted to speak with me. I then heard from Machiventa who also shared his love and compassion for me. Machiventa told me that he had ordered that I be attended at all times henceforth by several beings and that every spiritual resource that I required would be immediately available to me as began the process of recovery.

I spent 53 days in rehab. I resumed daily stillness and often spent 3-4 hours a day in intense stillness. During stillness and often during the day, I was in conscious contact with Welmek and other beings who became my companions and teachers. During rehab, I began sharing on stillness in groups and conducted sessions after hours where I introduced a number of individuals to stillness. I told a number of individuals about the Teachers and later learned from Welmek that a number of these individuals made requests for their own personal Teachers in stillness.

When I left treatment and began my life anew, I became more and more devoted to following the Father's Will. I received many private lessons on the nature of the mind and ego. I came to understand at the most personal and intimate level how seriously I had been affected by the child abuse I experienced as a child. I learned that I experienced a sense of not only unworthiness but self loathing at my deepest level.

It was this core that spawned the development of an ego that strived to create an image for me that I was willing to uphold at any cost. It was the source of the constant judging of others and either feeling superior or subordinate. It was the source of the tendency to criticize myself and others. Because my ego lived solely in time, it caused me to focus on the past resentments and guilt or generated fear and anxiety based on projections into the future. In short, I leaned that I had been for all of my life a prisoner of my own mind and that my actions were largely totally conditioned by my experiences.

Through the help of Welmek, other Teachers and Michael, I learned how to first forgive myself and then to forgive others. Just this year, an event occurred during the course of a private session that effectively removed the last obstacle to the uninhibited receipt of the Father's love in an unparalleled way for me. I have been requested not to provide the details of this event but it was in the form of an unusual and special gift of grace directly from the Father for which I am truly eternally grateful. After this event, I have experienced such an influx of love, inspiration and spiritual energy that it is hard to even know to describe it.

Suffice it to say, I now know what it is to live totally and completely without fear, anxiety or worry. To live in the present with no doubt that whatever lies ahead will be good for me is state of mind that generates joy, peace and serenity beyond anything I had ever imagined.

In the last few years, I have had the privilege of interacting with beings from all over the universe including a wonderful Being who characterized himself as a First Stage Spirit who hails from the Superuniverse Headquarters. He told me that we would meet again and advised exactly at what stage of my universe career that this would occur. He had a significant impart on my awareness of what it means to have an eternal career.

I have also been honored to interact with beings who reside on neighboring planets on other worlds in isolation. During a private lesion, I agreed to answer questions from these beings. This was an incredibly interesting experience.

However, perhaps the event that caused the greatest conscious impact for me was a lesson by a non-fused being currently on the mansion world. While I was used to talking with a host of beings of high status and accomplishment, it was this being not far removed from my own level that provided an inspiration that was most meaningful to me.

At the time that I was interacting with this ascendant mortal, I was feeling pretty good about myself. I had become more and more peaceful in nature and more and more comfortable living in faith. My mind was not only clear but I was becoming proficient at employing it to do those tasks that I assigned rather than being a slave to its impulses. I was dong stillness hours at a time. In short, I had become to feel pretty good about myself.

But this being put me directly in my place. After he introduced himself to me, this being asked me if I would permit his speaking frankly and directly to me. I told him to go ahead. He then said to me: "It is time for you to get off your mountain top and begin to serve your brothers and sisters in earnest."

I was somewhat shocked and a bit insulted at first. But today, I understand and am so grateful for what happened. This lesson caused me to indeed get off my pedestal and begin the wonderful and rewarding work of personal ministry to others.

Since that day approximately a year ago, I have been blessed that not a day goes by that I do not have an opportunity to become engaged with someone that I can serve. This time period has been a series of events that involve one coincidence after another. Without question, it has brought me to an entirely new level of understanding and awareness. I would never have thought that my life would ever be this good.

Today, I enjoy excellent health, have economic security that permits me to do whatever I want, have the greatest relationship that I have ever had with my daughter and most importantly, a close and intimate relationship with my inner spirit that provides me with the guidance that I need. Today, I have involved with a least a dozen or so individuals who look to me as their spiritual advisor, I am involved in a half a dozen social ministries and several spiritual projects. I truly love my life today notwithstanding its many varied challenges. This is the life that Welmek promised me many years ago would be mine if I followed his suggestions. He was right in every respect.

In closing, I want to express my deepest gratitude to the Teaching Mission itself. Without exposure to the wonderful, loving beings that have come to this planet to minister to us, I hesitate to think how dark my life would be today. I will forever never forget the loving service so consistently provided to me in my most desperate hours of need.

I thank our loving Creator, Michael and his consort Nebadonia for all that they have given me and what they give me each day. I am honored to serve Michael's Plan any way that I can. Finally, I thank our Heavenly Father for giving me all that I have and all that I could ever want. His love and affection for me is truly beyond any comparison. I am honored to give my commitment without reservation to always and everywhere consecrate my will to that of His as I journey every closer to Him.

And, I thank my good friend, Jim Cleveland, for his unqualified effort and persistence in putting this marvelous book together that will stand as a permanent testament to very personal value the Teaching Mission has had to these mortals whose stories will live on in these pages. Thank you, Jim, for your gift of love to us all.

August 4, 2010

Celestial Contact . . . the beginning years
Mark Austin

I was told that my great grandmother founded the first Pentecostal Church in Lubbock, TX, where I was born. As a young boy, I was initially amazed and fearful of some of the older people's behavior, spending many nights watching them as they spoke in tongues while the rest of the people waved their hands in worship and the band played from the pulpit. Sometimes, as kids, we would be taken outside for the rest of the service. While still fearful, an adult would try to explain, to ease our ruffled feathers.

At seven, I was baptized at the 25th Street Baptist Church in Lubbock. I remember dad saying that I didn't know what I was doing, (getting baptized). My mom, of course, was felt sorry for by some family members since her beliefs followed a different path than Pentecostal. Finally, after talks with the Avon lady, my mom decided to teach us about God until she found a church that believed more of what she believed. She used to gather us in her bed on Sundays and read bible stories. My dad would read the paper, barely out of sight, but within listening distance. What a wonderful picture of life.

My family moved to Dallas the day before school started my senior year. I had plenty of distraction for several years, having moved from a country town setting. I started dabbling in music and was afforded an opportunity to express feelings I didn't know I had, therefore leaving room for new feelings and thoughts I was also unsuspecting of. I began to take up my search for God again. I started in the bible, right where I left off as a kid.

As time went on, I was hungry for answers and frustrated with "a house divided." I felt that we all must be worshiping the same God, so I wanted to know all perceptions of God, for surely he is beyond what we can imagine. I read a book about the Dead Sea scrolls, then eastern philosophy and Edgar Cacey, among others. I started to build on a personal relationship with God again, and experience feelings of purpose and individual attention.

My wife (girlfriend at the time) found *The Urantia Book* about the time an international Urantia conference was going on, about July 1989. I was completely awestruck by this two-thousand page book. My prayers for clear-cut information about this universe had been answered. I had been waiting for this information all my life, in particular, since the end of '84 when I vowed to the Father to write my music with him in mind. (By the way, I'm a professional musical artist, musician and songwriter.)

I spent about 25 hours a week in this new and wonderful book for the first six months or so, and continue to re-read it. My wife, being the very resourceful person that she is, immediately contacted a study group in the Dallas area and we began to attend weekly. This went on for a few years, except for a month here and there when we became distracted.

Finally in my life, an affirmation of the feelings I had felt! My connection with creativity was affirmed. The channels of creativity were made clear and reassuring. My purpose as an artist made perfect sense as I had suspected. The revelations were astonishing, and life became "animated" in my experience of watching it work out. This book contained everything I'd been looking for and so much more that I didn't even suspect.

The Urantia Book integrated science, religion, and philosophy, helping to expand my personal relationship with the Father in ways that I couldn't even imagine before. It helped me to understand more about the design of the universe, and let go of much superstition. This caused a more responsive knowingness in my heart for truth. It allowed me to better use the keys of sincerity, in understanding myself and my relation to the environment. It gave me a clear knowledge of facts to apply to the ruthlessly practical demands of everyday life. It helped me to see order, and unify my experience.

The 776-page account of the life of Jesus left me in tears many nights as I began to view Him with a greater depth, reverence, and understanding of his teachings, while observing the almost day-to-day record of his life. My faith, as well as intellect grew daily. Inspiration became even more readily available. Life began to make sense. Truly, I became more attuned to the reality of the Father's love. What could ever improve on this?

Upon returning to the study group following a short absence, I heard someone speak of a celestial teacher named Welmek. I was later told that a few people in the group were meeting on another night of the week to study transcripts from these supposedly "unseen teachers." I discarded this in my mind and went about my business.

The Teaching Mission

After a while, I was given audio tapes of these "celestial teachers," one in which a celestial artisan conducted an exercise using music in preparation of stillness. Being a professional musician, I knew of this experience and the effect of this exercise because I had been experiencing it for years. The bells of truth begin to ring. I listened to the rest of the tapes and spent a lot of time asking for the Father's assistance. I could no longer deny the attention given to me in this responsive universe of love and wonderment.

Upon acquiring all the transcripts I could, and attending the "Teaching Mission" meetings and UB study group meetings, I began to read and study. (Incidentally, most all of the regular UB study group members were now in attendance at the TM meetings.) We had put in a request, although did not have audible group teacher contact at this time. So we studied the transcripts we had, mostly two teachers named Welmek and Will among others.

The group became, in my eyes, more personable and loving; less judgmental. After three or four months, we gained teacher contact. The feeling was real but the content was sometimes not what I'd expected, particularly compared to other transcripts I'd read. I had private sessions with the only T/R in the group, probably one of the most courageous people I know, and still was not satisfied with the content completely. I must have had some degree of contact myself because I knew somehow the teachers were real. I then began to develop contact on my own.

Never before had I practiced the "stillness" to the extent that I was now achieving. Soon we were told that we all were getting personal teachers. The group dynamics were exciting and often tense, forcing us to confront issues and learn the hard way how to work out whatever was discouraging progress.

Then we heard of an upcoming Naperville, Illinois, event, encompassing all involved in the teaching mission. Rhonda and I did not have the money for the journey, but it seemed to materialize out of nowhere thanks to a kind and responsive heart who footed the bill. So ten of us traveled on a train to this suburb of Chicago.

Arriving, we were greeted with love, and made our way to the hotel. We had left the previous day about 4 p.m. Being a day sleeper, I had not had any sleep. It was about 5:30 p.m. I caught a nap and attended the opening speech, given by a California psychologist named Bob Slagle. It was wonderful.

The next morning we set the alarm clock for 7:30 a.m. That was not too much later than the time I would normally go to bed. I woke up rather grumpy, still drowsy from the sleeping pills I'd taken the night before. While Rhonda was in the shower, I decided to meditate. I barely got my eyes closed when I got this rush of energy. It was amazing. I was bouncing off the walls when Rhonda reminded me that our teachers suggested that we stay calm.

After breakfast, I took a seat near the piano in the lobby to smoke a cigarette. I thought about playing the piano and decided I was too nervous and excited. So I went up to the room to meditate and again was blown away with the energy I felt. I had the thought to play

373

the piano. And again, I discarded it. The lady I rode down the elevator with said she had hardly slept, being sensitive to the energy. As soon as I walked around the corner from the elevator, one of our group members asked me if I would play the piano.

It was as if a little light went off over my head, and then I became aware I was being urged to play by celestial friends. I began to play with an ease I had only felt alone. I am, by profession, a bassist and had only used the piano to write with. Never before had I played the piano for such a large group of people. I felt very much appreciated and was later complimented.

After playing a half an hour or so, someone came up to me who happened to be waiting in the hotel with friends. He was from a production company or something apart from the TM group. He said he was a musician and wanted to know what turnarounds I was playing. He said that it had affected him in the most soothing way and that he could not pass up the opportunity to ask. And then, almost in mid-sentence, he said he felt he had been lead here to speak to me and he didn't know why.

It was more than just the music. This was a familiar circumstance with me as it has happened countless times over the past few years. I told him I understood his feeling and gave him information about *the Urantia Book*. He was excited to have this new information. He took my name and number.

Soon it was time for the main event. The entire ballroom was full of people. We were asked to manipulate energy in specific directions. Again I was blown away. I could actually hear energy. It sounded like a cross between a train and the wind. The feeling of it was intense, moving literally around the room. I was told it was designed to raise our vibrational level and that a new spirit was also poured down upon us; a spirit of liberation. It was quite moving.

Later that night Rhonda and I went out to a Chicago blues club with two other couples. I've never in my life been around so many unconditionally loving people. The bond was telepathic, it seemed. It was the largest, most beautiful group of people I've ever experienced.

Before continuing, I feel it necessary to clarify designations assigned to certain word symbols and/or phrases already used and/or to be used. The unseen teachers I speak of are mostly ascendant mortals from other worlds, sent here to teach and learn. Michael (Jesus) is our creator. Existing within us is a pre-personal fragment of Deity (The Thought Adjuster). T/R means transmitter/receiver, the person receiving messages from the celestials and transmitting verbally the communication.

We had been told on the train ride to Chicago that each of us had already been assigned a personal teacher. On the way back, I asked a very gifted transmitter from Norman, Oklahoma, to transmit my personal teacher in a private session. She graciously agreed. This was an event that changed my life. My wife, myself, the T/R – and one other person from Norman – crowded in a train bunk. We went into silence and then the T/R said a prayer.

As soon as she started transmitting, it became apparent to me that this wonderful unseen teacher had complete access to my thought patterns as well as memory.

I could ask a question in my mind without verbally sounding anything, and the T/R could transmit the teacher's loving answer. It was as if there was some sort of mind-meld happening. I could physically feel the output of the teacher's signal resonating through me. In fact, it was a familiar feeling. Now I knew what it was. During the session – you know when someone talks to you, saying something profound, and you start thinking about something they said and developing your own train of thought, while the other person continues to speak? – When I would start a train of thought about something the teacher said, he would pause until I finished my train of thought before continuing to speak.

This wonderful teacher knew me better than I knew myself. He knew I wanted firm, matter of fact answers, and he could give them in such a way that only emitted love. He was so completely non-judgmental and loving. Knowing my life the way he did, he could easily explain some things to me concerning previous experiences I'd had. It brought me clarity and affirmation. Most of all – finally in my life – I felt someone truly understood me. I couldn't have dreamed anything this beautiful. The clear fact that this was real was overwhelming.

When guiding me in understanding our relationship, he spoke metaphorically and with an almost poetic quality. Listen to this: "So that I may better reach into your thought processes, I bring to you a flower. Hold and balance this flower in the palm of your extended hand. It shimmers and rises with the heat of your loving nature, which is projected to the universe. We perceive a very direct contact with this loving energy which you exude and wish to comfort you in the knowledge of our perception of this. The flower which I have picked, if you will, resonates with your love. It is met by your love, it blossoms by the same energy. It is a flower of your personal choice. You decide on its color, its beauty, its size."

At one point, I was being hard on myself. In my mind I was thinking I shouldn't do this or that. I was basically criticizing myself, when he responded, *"When one participates in life at an operational level, there is much calculating that may occur. And I am predisposed to inform you of the specific example which may help facilitate change. When once I was in a similar predicament, I chose at that time to pursue God's faith in me. I followed the path which led me to find the truth of God's spirit within and further chose to believe in the Father's ultimate acceptance for me as a creation of his universe. Until this occurred, however, I followed a path which created for me many obstacles. I perceive you creating a similar path. I cannot choose for you; however, I may enlighten you to the choices which you have before you. Release, for a moment, the concerns which you hold in your thoughts."*

"Now I request that you join with me in a simple, prayerful moment in which we pray together, asking for Michael's (Jesus') assistance in this matter. I lead you in prayer at this time."

"Michael, in Heaven and on Earth, we pray together for your assistance in leading my fellow loved one in order that he may discover his true path to enlightenment. He requests your help for he truly believes in your

power and encourages faith in himself and in others. I join in prayer with this loved one so that his path may be eased in order that he may find joy and love in your holy presence. Amen."

I was so blown away again, I couldn't even think of questions to ask. Rhonda then reminded me to ask about music. He replied, *"When one explores the fortitudes incorporated in the production of musical insight, we all belong to a similar belief. The production of such beauty is incomprehensible, and we find joyous revelation in your ability to produce such extraordinary sounds for our ears to behold."*

"When, in the production of such heartfelt music, you feel some timidity around the expressional aspects, you may find resolution by searching inwardly, deeply, into your own spirit-led self to discover a true vision of what it is you believe is potentially available for you. If this is not clear, may I paint a picture for you?" I replied, yes.

John: *"Imagine, if you will, how it feels for you to be at the most heightened level of musical expression you may have experienced. Take this precious moment – this music, spirit, love-filled inspirational moment – and hold it in your memory while I speak to you of the creation of God's love in particular. Know in your heart what is truly possible is coming."*

After an interruption from the train conductor, John guided me again, saying: *"Proceed now to a similar vision. However, this time, I wish for you to image a golden ray of light which emanates from a cloudburst that exists far up in the heavens, far away, yet the golden burst of light shines directly into your being. You are worthy of this light, my son. Open yourself readily, open yourself fully in this moment. Precisely feel the connection."* During this, I had feelings far too deep for words.

"Harmonious in nature, it is absolute, 100 percent perfection. It lifts you off the ground so that you are weightless in its light. You are resonating with a frequency which reminds you of the most extraordinary tone, a tone which resonates with your inner most, spirit-filled being."

"This resonating tone then is expressed in a myriad of violent displays of light. It radiates out through your consciousness and reaches into your groundedness. Reflecting from the spirit, it increases in vibrational intensity and use of color expands as it emanates from your source. These bands of color resonate in various melodies that create in tonal (or internal? fusion that creates ecstasy for all ears to listen and turns their attention to the glory-filled mirror which brings to them great pleasure and peace, so that as they perceive the messages which are being sent from your spirit-led self, they continue to open and search for God's love within themselves as well, which thus creates a resonating pattern within themselves and so on as they pass on the gifts of your spirit-filled music."

"You are continually filled by the extraordinary beam of light which flows from the heavens. Enlighten yourself to this possibility, for it is created within yourself. Enlighten yourself to the possibility of God's glory, for it is within your potential. You are a perfect creation of God's universe, and rest well in your intentions to provide for the Father a most perfect creation.
Hold this image as you may in your heart. Follow my intent that you may see for your own best interests this potential. I am pleased to be in partnership with such great potential, happy to be with you."

I was so humble, happy and excited after that session there were only two things important in life; communion with the Father and service to my fellow man. I was so up, there was no way I could sleep the rest of the train ride even though there was another 14 hours or so to go. I told everyone from the group who chanced to wake, of my experience.

For about three weeks after that experience I had constant contact with John. Life was completely new and exciting with my newfound celestial contact. My meditation was now about an hour and a half long each day, usually twice. I begin to transmit my teacher, our group teachers, Machiventa Melchizedek, and later on, even Michael. These sessions were a profound experience for me and others in the group. I also did some private sessions for a couple of people.

The teachers could basically share my conciousness and input thought patterns in my mind for me to then say out loud. It was a very trying, and at the same time, healing experience to transmit. It caused me to search deep in my heart for the honest truth. There was nowhere to hide now, only open-ness and truth. Through effort and out of confusion came clarity, at least for a while. As time went on I began to fall back into old thought patterns and loose the sharpness of contact that I had felt before.
Soon we decided to go to Norman, Oklahoma, to visit our new friends that we had met on the train. One of these friends had transmitted John, my teacher, on the train ride back from Chicago.

Five of us from the Dallas group made it to Norman late one night. I felt a kindred love and a new connection anticipating another session with this admired T/R– to be able to hear John clearly again. I remember going out in the front yard that night and looking to the stars and thanking the Father.

I believe it was the next morning we all decided to meditate together. In the middle of meditation, suddenly my friend started to transmit. She had never transmitted before, but she did a wonderful job. The teachers thanked us for following their urgings to come to Norman. This was news to us, we thought it had been our idea.

Eventually, that afternoon I got the chance to have another session. When we started, I said casually, "You know what's going on in my life and I'm sure you know what to share." He addressed every concern and problem with complete tact and love. Here are some highlights:

"I enlighten your burdens and ask that you receive me without doubt of comprehension. Now, whether to the left or to the right makes no difference, for your path has truly been chosen by you. Now you see the twinkling of the stars and know that truth lies within your very own heart.

"Dearest one, indeed, the pleasures you have discovered in the stillness incorporate the usage of channels that facilitate the agreement between your mind reception and the output of my signal towards your center. When you discover that you are off your center, it is difficult but not impossible to regain contact. Wavering slightly is admissible, for you have just begun and soon you may discover that contact can be reached in ordinary ways

such as driving or walking down the street, watching TV or through listening to music, talking on the telephone. Then contact may be purposeful and continuous without need for deliberate sitting in the stillness practice. However, I will say to you as well that stillness is vital to reception on an ongoing basis, so do not tire of this method. It is foundation work required to facilitate the ongoing communication in your everyday, eventful life."

The "angels" can and do input thought patterns in our mind. We all have available to us the mind of our Creator, should we see through the illusion we think is reality and trade our mind for His. I think ultimately, to channel our Creator is our natural state. For we are truly all one in the Father. We may not be who our conscious mind believes we are. Being one with our Creator is knowingness beyond perception. The conscious mind is an arena of perception. We must reach toward superconsciousness.

The unseen teachers have been called "cosmic psychologists" by Dr. Slagle. They're masters at not fostering co-dependency. I've learned that decision-making, and adding to the equation — based on our intentions — is a means of ascension throughout the universe. They will not make our decisions for us. They will, however, enlighten our choices and guide our growth. All the knowledge that we need is held safely within. In the stillness we discover the potential that awaits. There is truly order and personal attention given, should we desire this love.

Life has become truly "animated" in its outworkings. Evidence of God's love, and celestial guidance, is manifesting on all levels and in all contexts. I had experienced many events in my life for years that I felt was orchestrated and that now makes sense. It is true, spiritual forces can be measured in our own experience. I could not begin to list the orchestrations in my life because they have been so frequent. After a while, this "animation" of life presents such beauty and love. It's as if I'm a child in a toy store.

Since receiving this wake-up call in my inner-life, I often take time to communicate inside about the events of the day, to review my reactions to life, especially when that day involves many interactions with other people. I think how to better facilitate the outworkings of the Father's plan in my life.

This does not mean that I do not have problems. It means that I am finding, with at least a measurable degree of success, a functional way of dealing with problems, in sharing them with the Father, and therefore, sharing all of my life with the Father. At this point, for me, life tends to be learning experiences. There is definitely more to life than anyone realizes.

Sometimes, when I've found myself in times of distress, Michael has made his presence known, to comfort me, literally resonating through my body, making me feel loved, easing my disarray and calming me. These experiences, I will never forget. I had felt this experience to some extent even before we went to Chicago. At the time, I did not know of the source.

I've discovered that whatever way I direct my conciousness, the best is made of it. Pretend you have Jesus to walk with all the way, every step in life — consciously. All I have to do is desire to know the Father's will. Every serious direction of thought made is orchestrated and animated in life – as though to let me learn by giving the chance to live the truth I desire – thereby experiencing truth. Truth is an experience of the soul.

I feel I've tapped into the universe by applying meanings and values to my life. And because of this effort, a variety of rewards in life experience have evolved. Questions of life bring experiences in life. Reason seems to create probability which faith may then transform into a moral certainty, even a spiritual experience. Truth, beauty, and goodness are, it seems, a constant theme. I'm learning so many things that I had knowledge of in my mind, but had not experienced in my soul until now.

Stillness or meditation seems to connect me with the energy and love I need to more successfully serve my fellow man as well as sustain my center. It seems as though my life has been carefully guided, helping me to better understand myself and others through carefully orchestrated studies, prayer, meditation, thought, and experience in relationships – both human and divine. I can better love someone and meet their needs when I truly desire to understand them instead of desiring to be understood first. Having contact with these "unseen teachers" has helped to secure the need to be understood.

I'm seeing the universe as a vast system of energy, and we humans being capable of securing and extending energy. Hence there is need for prayer and meditation as the only healthy way to secure this energy. Without that, I've found that most people secure energy from other people they come in contact with, usually someone they control in some way. I think that's why a lot of relationships end up in power struggles. If I am centered and keep conscious of this, I can give energy without being controlled or depleting myself of energy. Then, it seems to flow through. The Source of this energy is the place to go.

I think that's one reason why Jesus was always off by himself at night in communion with the Father. Truly, the Father lives in us, loves us and has a beautiful individually wrapped package plan for each and every one of us. Having a personal relationship with the Father, and knowing it's available to everyone. What a life!

(Editor's Note: Since these writings, Mark Austin's spirit quest has continued to flourish and he recounts many of his newer experiences and views at: www.markaustinband.com. Mark is a hard-working bass guitarist, singer, composer, and music producer. Son Jared is a gifted young violinist with the Dallas Junior Symphony.)

An Instant of Breakthrough. . . Continuing Discovery: Learning to Take Dictation from the Celestial Teachers

Jim Cleveland

How many years will comprise your life, how many days, how many hours and seconds? Will there be a special moment, even a second, that will dramatically alter your course, open a path to your greatest triumphs in life? Can everything change in an instant?

One can only endure those horrifying seconds of violence that we may encounter that forever scar our minds – tragic accidents, being witness to murder, a terrorist explosion. One might look up and see an airliner crash into the World Trade Center. Such incidents cause challenging traumas in the hearts and minds of all fellow souls on their sojourn.

A positive moment or second to some can be their introduction to their true love in life, or a spiritual guru who will have a profound influence on their outlook. They will never forget the moment they looked into their lover's eyes, or shook hands with a person of renown. But many times, these are infatuations that don't last.

In considering my own years, I can see that special instant as the time that words rolled from my lips without my speaking them.

It was within a simple moment, a restful hour, on my bed. I was relishing in worship, feeling the eternal love, wanting to give loving service to everyone, sincerely trying to empty my mind of analysis or agenda, wanting to hear some simple celestial message in order to make the connection. I had learned not to 'try' and was simply open to release.

At that instant, my mind only saw the gray canvas at the back of my eyelids and there was nothing there to think about. I was an objective journalist, now resting in Stillness. My deep breathing had allowed any and all uncontrolled energy to waft away.

My lips blurted the words and I don't even know what they were. It felt awesome that this could be given to me. I just spoke the words without knowing what was coming next. They came of their own volition as sound wave vibrations. I could hear them a little as they came, but my mind was disengaged. I only wanted the flow to continue so I left it alone.

At this time, 1993, I had voraciously read hundreds of pages of transcripts, and other individuals within the Teaching Mission were transmitting entire evenings of lessons from celestial teachers. I soon served in this capacity in Cincinnati for several years, and also at gatherings, but at this moment, I had barely made a connection

Even so, being a professional writer, I found it reasonable to apply the transmitting process to writing on the keyboard. To my amazement, I could type a question, relax into stillness of body and mind, and begin to take dictation.

The Teaching Mission

On December 1, 1993, I asked about finding the truth, the meaning of life.

"It is not the knowing of the truth that is important, but the searching for it. There can never be a realization of complete truth in this life; but only the quest. This is what the Heavenly Father desires of us, and what we truly must do in order to be fulfilled.

"There is this inner fire, this nugget of spirit, this fragment of the Father inside us which seeks to show us the way. To the extent that we are open to its leadings and attuned to an appreciation of the truth, beauty and goodness that it represents, then we will reap the harvest of this faith and trust.

"There are those who are afraid of their inner selves, seek not to find it for fear of awakening a beast inside. I tell you that the beast has been evicted and sent to oblivion. There is no more devil to blame our troubles and our evils upon. There is only ourselves, as there always was, now just a little freer, a little more imbued with the spiritual energy that reverberates throughout the universe outside of our troubled sphere. Channels are being opened for us; we have but to step inside and communicate with those who would guide us lovingly in the path of the Father, and always pledging to allow your free will to be supreme, as the Father intended it.

On another day, I asked for more of their agenda.

"There is a oneness that we are seeking to achieve with each of you, that you may be fully attuned to the leading of the spirit throughout your lives. In this demeanor and disposition, you will find happiness, the true happiness that eludes so many of you in the noisy, daily battles against themselves and their environment. Ask of yourselves each day whether you are contributors or users, producers of wealth or among those who would drain it without making adequate redress with your own production.

"As you attune your mind, so also will your heart, your emotional spirit, begin to open itself more to those whom you might have disdained before, the diseased, the dirty, the vile. You will begin to see them with the empathy that our master showed. Although he was not able to help everyone, he nevertheless was always loving and charitable with the knowledge that the misled would eventually find the true way and correct the errors of their misfortune. For he came to give opportunity, to reveal the true nature of the Father as a loving, compassionate creator, to live as a human, suffer and die, in order that his final act of supreme forgiveness could be fulfilled.

"And what a rallying point for mankind. In the suffering, death and loving forgiveness of the master, we see the path of true righteousness that we can never hope to approximate as rising mortals, but can achieve in the fulfillment of our long universe ascension career. It is this suffering, and the realization of the master's gift, that has unified Christians for centuries. Though the churches be besmirched with all manner of corruption, forsake them not, for they continue to offer the best hope for mankind's collective spiritual advancement.

"In his suffering we were revealed his strength and beauty. In his noble bearing we see the certain faith that he could suffer no harm, that he would rise above all adversity in spiritual glory, forgiving and offering salvation for all of those who plotted against him and scourged him. This ultimate triumph over mortal death is the way he shows us all, for we all will be resurrected as well if we honor the Father who created us. This powerful act of blanket forgiveness is what he asks us to practice in our daily lives, reaching out to our

brothers and sisters, without malice, to share in this world of time and space that the Father has created for us.

Indeed, Michael/Jesus, our creator, our earthly brother, made his incarnation on Urantia one of the most profound experiences ever known or felt in the universe. And all eyes still remain on this world."

I asked: Am I to be given the name of my collaborator?

"You are the creator. We are the inspiration. What is any writer without inspiration? So indeed you shouldn't feel badly for availing yourself of it. We are One with you. We will work with you as the fullness of the Teaching Mission unfolds. You will be valuable in helping us maintain and expand our following.

"Get yourself centered. Diet. Exercise. Meditation. Prayer. Worship. Reading. Thinking. Interacting. The balance is there; you must simply find it. You are progressing well; continue."

I asked about the pace of personal spiritual growth.

"The energy that comes to you is being measured, appropriately to your stage of development and in keeping with your needs at the time. As a hole in the dike, as this portal widens, you are able to let in ever more spiritual energy. Things do and will get better and better for you if you remain steadfast in the path.
"Do not fear diversions for they will be constant, but you can always re-center yourself in the Father's light, and receive guidance and the inspiration you need to carryon. Your thoughts are essentially true, for they are influenced by your willingness and desire to hear our revelations of truth to you. Attune and you receive. This is the simple lesson that you must tell all others about the stillness, the sincere upreach. In their personal experience, not yours, they will."

While I considered this to be wise advice for anyone, and still do, there has now been some 20 years of time that the Teaching Mission has made an impact on the planet. And even now, the Urantia movement remains fractured over its validity and value, notably because of that infamous Fatherhood of God conflict of 1983. The purported Midwayer messages to one charismatic Urantia leader of that time, now disgraced by the winners of the ensuing political struggle, were hauled up into the 1990s to refute the growing influence of the Teaching Mission among Urantia Book study groups. Some strong judgments were made against 'channeling.'

For most of these years, I have been more concerned with nurturing the connections, with the teachers, Christ Michael, the Melchizedeks and Celestial Artisans, than to delve into the particulars of that unity shattering incident of many years ago. There were, after all, more pressing conflicts in those years, with the Urantia Foundation divorcing itself from its outreach organization, the Urantia Brotherhood, in a loud global spat. The disgust among readers at these divisions seemed more important at the time than trying to understand the movement's bizarre controversy of 1983-4.

382

The Teaching Mission

My journalistic mind can now continue to see a growing body of sound spiritual lessons from an array of teachers. I have gradually, steadily become blessed with higher levels of truth as I could absorb them. I have become tolerant of all sincere, baggage-laden struggles of humans for spiritual growth. I remain intolerant of self-serving phonies, a trait I developed in the 1950's.

I reflect now, once again, on the instant of celestial connection that can change a life forever. Having read the Urantia papers, I had a sound background for spiritual inquiry. Given the plan of our first group teacher, Tarkas, I could apply worship, prayer, forgiveness and love into the Stillness time, energizing the experience far beyond meditation and contemplation into a viral and mind-opening conversation with a new wave of celestial teachers.

The words came on their own.

I didn't know or care in that moment that naysayers would refute our connections and our lessons for years to come, even as the transmissions grew into thousands of pages, then tens of thousand and more.

We began to understand that the Teaching Mission is interplanetary and includes all of the worlds of the Lucifer Rebellion and many of the altruistic Oneness in God movements across our planet. Urantia readers are only a part of it, and the Internet has freed this previously guarded revelation to virtually anyone on the planet.

We also learned that the mission is a continuation of the Fifth Epochal Revelation, teachers for the tome. *The Urantia Book* provides the basic foundation of the personal religion so extolled by *the Urantia Book*, a direct connection to the Universal Father and the plethora of divine ministry that he sends to us.

Over the years, I have been blessed with mentorship and inspiration from a number of celestial helpers, including the Midwayers. I came to speak conversationally with a primary teacher, Mantoube Melchizedek, who accepted me as a student over 10 years ago.

To a question I asked about current controversies of society, he said:

"Some humans are highly confident in the falsehoods they believe. Some are motivated to preach and share them. They should remember to stay on the learning plane forever, and try to learn more from God each day. Wisdom is shared daily for those who go into a stillness time with God. Yet too many humans are advised to pray and demonstrate righteousness and fear of "the Lord," and too few are advised and motivated to follow this with pure listening and contemplation. Combined, this listening for God's voice while the mind is engaged to contemplate what it hears is a miraculous and wonderful connection of which you should take maximum advantage. Do it daily and you can absorb the wisdom in manageable bites."

Q. Most people still don't trust their minds enough to get inner guidance, much less type up responses, don't you think?

"I don't know about what you call 'most.' I am certain that in recent years this number has become 'less.' Receiving inner guidance is a concept of growing strength and efficacy. People are recognizing it as the truest guidance and are more willing to take responsibility for some spiritual growth on their own.

"We hardly know what goes on in the minds and hearts of individuals, but be assured the indwelling spirit of God is there, present, and knows it well. If you continually remind people that this guidance is there, in the stillness and silence, and in their faith step to build this relationship with their Universal Father, then more and more people will believe it and actually begin to do it."

Now in 2010, I can reason to myself that my instant of celestial connection opened a threshold of luminosity of all things. It was a life-changing event for me and, therefore, can also be considered the most important knowledge that a human desiring spiritual growth can obtain.

Yes, you can.

There are many spiritual teachers out there willing and anxious to work with you in your personal growth, to help you understand and practice worship, prayer, forgiveness, love and the other basics of spiritual advancement, the growth of the soul. They will inspire and propel you to use your talents and your intentions to be a valuable part of this ongoing spiritual renaissance of the planet.

Many individuals are hungry for personal spiritual guidance; it comes from within. Tune out the cacophony of the world and seek God in the Stillness. You don't have to fight the dogmas of the world; you can develop your own personal dogma built around truth, beauty and goodness.

Of course, I wondered if transmitting or channeling is truly a panacea, every word being holy writ. There are still detractors who say the teachers get between us and our indwelling 'thought adjuster,' our indwelling 'God fragment' or 'indwelling spirit' where we should address our concerns. They also believe that mankind can rarely if ever make that connection at this time in our evolution.

Mantoube addressed these concerns:

"Channeling is by no means a foolproof exercise. Just as a pastor can misunderstand scripture and preach it that way, so too can persons remain engaged with their thinking mind while trying to transmit, and can send forth messages that are inaccurately weighted and can cause misunderstandings. To make a pure and fortuitous connection, you will do well to still your mind surely, open it into a wide and open plain of peace, and be fully separated from the voice that comes through. Submit unthinkingly, unwittingly, allowing your voice to blurt what it will.

"It is not as much a task of trying as one of release, finding the center of worship, connect to it, and be an open page to what the celestials present with no analysis on your part at all. It is a flow, and coming from elsewhere than you, truly above and beyond.

"Yet you can find truth from preachers or even people on the street if you are open to it. Each person has a unique vision of the world and their own solutions to its woes.

"In all those unique, free will visions that you find today, there is already a deep inherent knowledge that spirituality and religion are personal, that God is personal to us, and that the churches either do the best they can, or they don't. It's not the critical thing. What is critical is how we live our lives, the growth of our soul into something of value, worth salvaging, worth saving, worth forgiving, worth supporting as we try to do better and the best we can. It's all personal. True religion is your personal relationship with God."

Do you have concerns? Make the connection and they will address them as well.

The Teaching Mission - A Newcomer
Blanche Irene Berland

When I was a child, I was considered to be disruptive and unruly. This was told to my parents and grandparents by the head Rabbi at our Orthodox Temple. They also were told I was no longer welcome there.

My grandfather was, to say the least, angry, so he started a new Conservative Temple.

As I got older I questioned everything about Judaism. I started visiting other churches. No matter which church it was, my questions were answered the same way. The words were different but the dogma was the same. I always came away disappointed. My belief in God was not shaken, but any belief in institutional religion I may have had was gone.

During February 2004 I met David L. Hubbard. We became good friends from the start. David has great intuition about people. He has been a Urantia Book reader and scholar for a long time.

Within a week of our meeting he started talking about a special book, a book he believed held the answers to all my questions. At first he just started to reading from this 2100 page book. Every question I asked he found the answer right in the book. I was amazed.

By the following week I started reading the book myself. Within a month David took me to a UB study group. More amazement. Everyone I met was welcoming, warm and not judgmental.

Later that year David decided to start a study group mostly for new readers. We met on Sunday afternoon. Sometimes there were only three of us. Other times as many as twelve or fourteen readers would find their way to our group. This was the start of great changes in my life.

It was on a Monday morning that I woke up early, finding my bedroom filled with a bright light. I heard a voice saying to me, God is good and Jesus loves me. This happened every morning for the next six days. On Sunday I told the study group about this and to my surprise they didn't think I was nuts.

David started telling me all about the International Urantia Conference which was to be held in July of 2005. He told me about all the extraordinary people I would meet and how much I would benefit from the conference. I decided to go.

As the months rolled by, I became more and more excited about the conference. Then, on June 30, I lost my job. At first I, thought maybe it was not the best time to be going on a trip, but I was paid in full so why not. Just to go anyway. Three days before departure I had a panic attack. Maybe I should cancel. Maybe I would not fit in. There were a dozen maybes in my head.

I called my friend Alison to talk it out. She told me to stop questioning myself. Just go and have a great time. So off I went, doubts and all.

The conference was everything David told me it would be and much more. There were approximately 615 people attending, coming from many states and countries. There were people from the worlds of science, philosophy, law, medicine, music, education and many more. Everyone was there to listen, study and learn. Newcomers like myself and those who have been readers for many years all came together to share the book.

During the second evening I met Jim Cleveland. I did not know it at the time, but once again life was really going to change. Jim and I spent the evening together talking and learning quite a bit about each other. We spent every night of the conference together. Five years later we are still together.

I am once more a newcomer, this time to the Teaching Mission. I am learning about the Stillness. I am reading many of the wonderful lessons and I am amazed.

And It Came to Pass Even More
Barry Bartlett

In the early 2000s the next shift occurred, the loss of a job, a wife and eventually the house created a massive shift and moved me to start searching again. I found a meeting to go to, walked in and there were a couple from the Abraham class, part of our 'family'.

At this first meeting I attended I also met up with another medium/teacher and I was guided to have a reading with her. She wanted to know why I was attracted to England and what was Stansted? At the time I was contemplating attending my High school reunion in England and all I knew was that Stansted was an airport north of London. I phoned my daughter because I had a feeling her mother, my first wife, who is also a medium, knew about Stansted.

It turns out that Stansted is the home of the Arthur Findlay College, the world famous Spiritual College. I obtained a prospectus and found a course that fitted in with my plans. Sorry, that course is full! Almost every day of the year there will be up to five different courses running at the same time and in different languages so the prospectus is a reasonable sized book. Inserted in the book was a single sheet for an additional course 'Introduction to Spirit' but a week after I was due to return. I extended my stay so that I could attend.

Prior to my trip I attended some lessons with this other teacher in New Zealand. One night during meditation we went to meet our guides. Up the staircase I went, "Hello Michael," "NO", "who are you then?" "I AM Ishmael!" I took note of the name, it seemed familiar but I was not sure from where. Of course when I investigated, Ishmael is Abraham's son.

While I was in England I was staying on my own in my brother's flat while they were on a world trip. After the school reunion, a long way for a three hour get together, I was alone meditating and was told to go and buy more tapes for my video camera, I had used a lot when I was in Egypt. Off I went to town and bought some more tapes.

Back at the flat I resumed meditating but with the camera running, as I was told to do. That was my introduction to channeling. Ishmael came through. This was all preparation for my upcoming visit to Stansted because when we did the class on 'deep trance meditation' I was able to channel and knew what the feeling was like.

I know I was guided to the 'Introduction to Spirit' course because it covered everything. Platform mediumship, meditation, sound healing, color healing, psychic art, dousing, wax art, psychometry and of course 'deep trance meditation.' All these would be useful for me years later when I got the shop so that I would be aware of what was being discussed and offer advice.

We practiced channeling in our class in New Zealand and I brought through a Native American, White Wolf. Every time he came through in my visualization we would be standing by a lake with a range of mountains across the lake. One night/early morning I was moved to get up and paint this view and I had the picture for a couple of years.

In 2004 after the Boise conference I was driving across country back to San Francisco before flying home and I was moved to turn off the highway to a camping ground and trout hatchery on Salmon Falls Creek, Nevada. I looked around the hatchery and then walked through the trees to look at the reservoir. There it was! Apart from one slight deviation in the skyline this was the place I had drawn those years before. Just then a Native American canoe came around the headland and completed the picture. The photograph now sits in the corner of the frame of the picture.

While on this trip I was looking for a piece of turquoise. We had been using the phoenix in our class to symbolize our changes. Again I was guided to pull off the highway for a break into the small town of Battle Mountain, Nevada. I drove through town to the railway line, looked down the road and there was a sandwich board on the curb that said 'Antiques.' So I thought I would stretch my legs in there.

When I asked her if she had any turquoise she produced trays of it! "I bought these 20 years ago when the mine closed down," she said. There it was! A ready-made cabochon with an inclusion that looked like a rising bird or spirit guide. After some negotiation it became mine and I now wear it regularly. I had missed the turn off to the Hickison Petroglyphs. If I had found it I would never have gone through Battle Mountain!

After meeting up with some of the old Abraham family, we re-established contact. As it turned out they, and their daughter, who was also part of the Abraham class, had, in 1993, been involved in a horrific car crash to such an extent their daughter had passed away but was revived. It was at that time she had full realization of why she was here and what she was to do, teach.

While still in hospital she kept talking about speaking with Jesus but everyone put this down to the drugs. Apparently because she did not want to come back again and have to go though birth, schooling and puberty again she successfully argued the case that as this life was being cut short now the next time she came back she would be back at the beginning so why not let her continue this time.

Despite a broken back and multiple other injuries she remained on this plane. She started to use self-healing techniques on herself as the doctors suggested she would not walk again. Being a black belt in Karate this was not a thing she would accept. Then other people suggested if she could heal herself perhaps she could do it for others. She was very spiritually aware from a young age and because of the understanding from our 1987 classes it was no surprise when in May 1999 she started to channel.

So I started back at class. This was different from our old classes; here were numerous teachers all teaching in their own style and their own subject, maybe more than one at each class and definitely a different one every week. They are referred to as 'The Team'.

Having seen quite a bit of channeling, this is completely different. Not the eyes shut sitting on a chair channel. This is eyes open, walking about, drawing on the white board channeling. It is amazing how the different teachers affect every thing of our channel. Due to her accident she still has trouble walking but when the Team are there she is very near normal as they use her body to teach us. The most noticeable affect is on writing as well as speech of course. The writing reflects closely the teacher who is there; robotic teachers use a cuneiform type of lettering. We still have to help out with language as some teachers have difficulty with English and the nuances of different words.

It was during this period I was introduced to the American Teaching Mission and established contact through the wonders of the Internet. I read with interest the teachings and the ebb and flow of comments until I was moved to attend the Boise conference to meet up with all these bodiless voices I could read on my computer. Once I made the decision to attend, work flowed in to ensure I had enough money for the trip.

Then I was invited to speak. I had concerns as to what was being said on the net and the theme of the talk evolved. Our class suggested I practice on them, so one night I gave the brief outline of what I was going to say. Abraham arrived and said "Do not alienate your audience; I am aware of how that is". I changed tack after that. When I got to Boise I heard the story of someone who channeled Abraham at a Urantia Book conference and was virtually thrown out. What a small world this is!

Back in New Zealand my radio show has continued every week, pre-recorded when I travel, without fail for the last 6 years. A myriad of local and international guests have shared their stories with me. World famous and not so famous authors, mediums, channels, musicians, healers, astrologers, gurus, scientists along with readings from channeled messages all interspersed with up lifting music from all around the world. As I travel my selection of inspirational music grows.

Our channel held classes twice a week, a public one and a private one for us that have been together for years. After ten years she dropped it back to a weekly private one, by invitation only, and a monthly public one. We needed to ensure that those who were very well versed in the teachings could progress without having to listen to all the same questions when a new seeker arrived to learn the basics.

As my divorce was being finalized the land we had been trying to sell for years suddenly sold. Oops another 'nudge'. Weeks later the lady who ran the books and crystal shop that was sponsoring my radio show said she was selling out and moving away. How fortunate that the money was put in place for me to take it over.

Two years later I finally found the venue I was looking for. We moved from our little shop to our bigger premises where we are able to seat up to 50 people. We now run seminars, talks, workshops, films, classes and have six or seven regular practitioners doing readings, healings, massage and classes every week. So far we have had people from America, Japan, India, Australia, South Africa and England all using our premises. It is a safe haven for those that are seeking, worried or plain scared of things they don't know about or understand. During this same period I was given the opportunity to take over a nationwide spiritual magazine, unfortunately with the change of habits and more Internet, this has now closed.

More and more people are drawn to us. We now have people who channel all sorts of different teachers. The most impressive was a young couple who came in searching for answers, and were guided to us. Ostracized by their strictly religious family they needed direction. Now some months later the wife is currently channeling master teachers and guides and with our help over the last six months is slowly being helped along her path to teach many. Because we have the experience it is not unusual for us but to her it is so strange and daunting. She has just started her public classes after lots of practice with her husband, friends and us at the shop but is still very nervous but at soul level she now knows what she is here to do.

Our classes continue every week with regular weekend seminars, all designed to help us move to enlightenment and peace on earth. Many who have attended the classes over the years have gone on to become healers, clairvoyants and channels. Since the beginning of this year, 2010, there seems to be a noticeable shift in energies so consequentially there has an increase in people who are searching or are being made more aware. More and more channels are appearing around the world, all with their own style and followers but with a common message of love and hope for all, all part of the Big Plan.

Abraham: 17ᵗʰ December 1986:

"There are those who are fearful of love, in that they do not have recognition of the truth of themselves, of others or God. There is fear to recognize the God within themselves or others. They close the door of their soul memory and have a complete physical life, wherein their light does not burn. It may be possible to open the door of their soul memory by showing the light of the God within yourself"

Abraham: 21ˢᵗ January 1987:

Tread your path in Light.
Tread your path in Truth.
Tread your path in Love.
This path leads to God and you shall become a 'Luminary'

I AM Filip/Barry

Part Four

Teaching Mission Gatherings 1994-2009

In 1994, participants in the new, so-called Teaching Mission gathered on the Eastern Washington University campus in Cheney for the first of what would be many gatherings over the years.

The program's planners took the novel approach of assembling the scores of people on hand and drafting a three-day program on the spot. Who would like to speak, and on what subject? We filled a blackboard and had a fine conference, making a new network of friends that spanned the country and beyond.

Like so many other things in the Teaching Mission, a few people just came together and made it happen. There has never been a board or a slate of officers in this non-organization. The fact is, the organization happens on the spirit side. The Correcting Time on the planets that rebelled against God is administered by celestial personalities. The Teaching Mission is more of a process of teaching and learning, not a movement to champion.

Over the years people have always responded to the mission's immediate needs as we have explored this phenomena together. We have developed friendships with both humans and the supernal personalities whom we engage; we regard these personalities as friends with a lot more universe experience.

In memory of these gatherings over the years, here are just a few of the transmissions that have signposted our journey and inspired us onward.

Excerpts are from:

1995-Fayetteville, Arkansas
1997-Snow Mountain, Colorado
1997-Loveland, Ohio
1998-Nashville, Tennessee
2000-Tallequah, Oklahoma
2001-Park City, Utah
2002-Estes Park, Colorado, after hours meetings at Urantia Book conference
2003-Niagara Falls, NY

2004-Boise, Idaho
2005-Albuquerque, NM
2006-Albuquerque, NM
2006-Santa Barbara, CA

Network of the Heart Teaching Mission Conference
Fayetteville, Arkansas, 1995

LANAFORGE: *"Good evening, this is Lanaforge, system sovereign. You have been prepared for your work, for your lives. You have chosen this path, this destiny, which you could have deferred, yet you have not, you have been drawn to this Mission, this work. You have been prepared by some of the best teachers in all of Nebadon. Millions of [former] mortals, from millions of planets volunteered to be a part of this. Many thousands upon thousands have been selected and there are more than enough to fill the ranks, one by one, beside you.*

"This Mission began so long ago, long before any of you were born, and we see in your courage and the rapidity of your growth, your earnestness, your dedication, and the joy that you feel from your fulfillment now, that we have chosen well. You have chosen well. Your growth has prepared you now to begin outside yourselves.

"On behalf of the Most High Fathers, I am pleased to announce that the wider expansion of the Teaching Mission has begun. The way has been prepared for you as you go forward. As you go forward in peace and love, rather than the old ways of your human race. Millions upon millions of angels have been assigned to this planet, to assist the forward motion of your work with us. Do not doubt or falter upon this path that you have chosen, for we have many beside you, behind you, before you, going to assist you, where you go.

"Know dear ones, that the progress has gone forward, there is no going back. The crack in the door of darkness is beginning to shine light. We are working with you to open that door. You push, we pull. We are drawing you into a wonderful path of soul growth, at the same time that you are healing your planet, and healing your own lives. We will be successful and by we, I mean mortals and we on this side, for we are together in this effort.

"I wish I could share with you the kind of joy that we feel, that your personal overcomings, your personal conquerings of your difficulties and the joy that we feel at your coming together and sharing your accomplishments here, the accomplishments that you have achieved in your personal lives and in your world. Michael's light is powerful, His presence is ever with you. He is mighty, to overcome all darkness. His patience and mercy have been long enduring. His wisdom in exercising His authority has been guarded.

"In guarding this wisdom, in guarding His decisions, He has granted you the opportunity of great growth, though you often see this as great difficulty. In the words of your contemporary society, no pain, no gain. You have gained much; you have gained so much.

"One day, when you can reflect in peace about these days, about this life, you will look back and reflect upon it with great admiration and feeling. You will look at your lapel, so to speak and see all the ribbons of your campaigns of soul growth, and you will have a story for each one. You will be as grandfathers and grandmothers on the frontier telling their children in modern times about their difficulties of overcoming physical hurdles, of living in the wilderness.

"You live in a moral and spiritual wilderness, yet know that the support for taming that wilderness even, within your own being, exists as close as the Father within. It is through stalwart, courageous individuals, as yourselves, that this planet will be tamed completely. As you go forward to where you work, where you play, where you associate, bring this gentle Mission, this powerfully gentle Mission of love and empowerment to everyone."

Love in Action Teaching Mission Conference
Snow Mountain, Colorado August 20-24, 1997

MARGUL (T/R: Rick Giles): *"I have willfully accepted this task to bring this report. I am of the Daynal Order. I have completed a survey, as my associates have likewise completed a survey of the sister planets in this Correcting Mission.*

"It has been accessed that progress is being made according to plans. However, the decimal worlds are lagging, not surprising considering the conditions left from the rebellion.

"I am directly associated with the Melchizedek Teaching Mission only insofar as inaugurating Light and Life. The Avonal Sons here on this world have assessed the many dimensions of human life activity and have announced that you are making acceptable economic progress. Pockets on your world are making higher strides in cultural and social values. Your military is becoming an antique. The peaks of progress are very small, but the small surfaced areas are touched by the luminosity of the spirit. Many valleys of deficit exist.

"As you have heard, Michael has decreed the acceleration of plans on this planet. Many in my field of vision are quite busy. In making this report I add caution to relate to you that you will not see the acceleration for those committed to this upliftment have pledged to never fall the way of the Lucifer effort – in circumventing the natural process of growth.

"Our timetable can be hastened. You must continue to assimilate according to your digestive abilities. Much time has been devoted to your increased appreciation of sonship in Michael's family. During this interval wherein you have been called to this planetary effort, you are here charged to increase your capacities for citizenship involvement.

"There are two basic perspectives for you to maintain in all aspects of your life. First and foremost is your re-personalization of Michael's approach to kingdom living, entailing even communion with God. And two, improve standards in your life whereby your relationship with Him becomes obvious to your fellows.

"The other primary focus is for you who have been called to the service of the Master Seraphim to hone your skills and career that contribute to the outworking of procedures currently underway on your planet for the next epoch.

"Far is the distance to traverse. This must encourage you, for without the efforts of the initial surge of ministry on your part, subsequent advancements will not be made. I am speaking to you as conscious citizens of the universe.

"One of the factors for volunteering for planetary uplifment is that your life gets complicated. All on this world are free to live the life as Michael has called you to live. But you who choose to participate in planetary growth have taken on extra-curricular activities.

"If you are a social worker, continue to improve your abilities. If you are a politician, demand of yourself the standards you hold ideal, and forcefully promote them in your arena of influence. All occupations are needed for uplifment. Love does go a long way to encourage the human condition. When it comes to the planet, love must be accompanied by an army of skill, talents and dedication.

"Rest not upon your attainments in the soothing sense of sonship. Rather, charge yourself with the sense of responsibility to be about, not only the business of the Father, but the business of Michael, and Lanaforge, and of Machiventa. This does complicate things, doesn't it?

"I will be off this planet for some time, but I will observe the processes and procedures that have been inaugurated here, and will continue to tally the data and make suggestions to your resident staff that will help in the effort of steady progress toward a perfect world and a supreme universe. I, Margul, will take my leave."

Heart of the Message Conference
Loveland, Ohio 1997

TARKAS: *"You ... are the Heart of the Message. You have the hands and hearts here on Urantia. Our hearts have been mortal hearts as well, and we now are part of the heart of the universe. We remember well the challenges you face, though not to the great degree of suffering we see here on Urantia, for we are sometimes overwhelmed at the magnitude.*

"You are the heart of the message that this must end. And indeed it will end through faith. It will only end through our cooperative, collaborative, correlative coalescing, through all of us working together.

"You have seen many nuggets of shining opportunity spread before you at this gathering. You have seen diamonds. Do you recognize them? But what is a nugget, what is a diamond, what is a spark, what is a light?

"Those things are you. They become you, shining examples, shining streams of evolutionary growth, when you make choices. There is no escape on Urantia. There is only life. And life is what we make it. You are the heart of this message."

ELISHA: "Make no mistake. We are individuals with personalities, with styles, with our perceptions of what is true and what is beautiful and what is good. They are our perceptions. We would only share them with you. We would not compel them to you. We would be your friends. We are another rung or two up the ladder. We work here with you, in spirit, I think. From just a rung or two up, we can reach you with our hands and help you step up the ladder. We have not reached the top.

"We do not know absolute truth. You can find the closest thing to absolute truth in your text, which we have followed by some years. The simple message is: You have personal spiritual guidance. And with incremental openings of energies projecting and expanding truth and beauty and goodness comes your own incremental openings of your treasure chests of nuggets and diamonds. There is more truth than you can perceive! Bringing a smile of delight ... a little more feeling of goodness inside.

". . . [K]now as well that we will be with you. Always. By this I mean that our friendship will never be broken on this other side. If the skeptics and cynics are able to inject in you these poisons of distrust, not to have faith in yourself, in your mind, in your ability to discern what is real ... if they would question you ... If you would fall into despair, you may break this friendship, but we would never do so. There are no doubts on this side. We know that we want you to be our closest friend and we think that you will continue in this friendship, not only through your mortal lives here but through transition. We will be friends from now on."

ANDREW: "Sure, we know that many humans cheapen the very idea of faith and sense of humor. Humans have a tendency to cheapen, even vulgarize things which are, in truth, great gifts. Great gifts! In your relationships with others, to touch, to hold, to hug, to embrace. Sexual liaisons can be, oh, so much more!

"These are adventures in the senses and the cause of many problems. You have not been able to open yourselves fully to these tools of growth. There will come a time but, too late for some of you. Transition will come and you will be over here working with me, perhaps, to continue exploring a sense of humor on Urantia.

"Sense of humor. It is a sensual experience. And did you ever recall the tickles that brought tears and laughter and you could not control it. It was just so ecstatically humorous. Well, this is sensual, my friends. Humor! There are nuggets, there are diamonds here. Cultivate those! And don't dig in the cold depths. Cultivate the highest humor. Self-effacing, maybe. Never angry. Never destructive. If so, go out to that person and hug them; don't be afraid to touch them! Don't be afraid to hold them! Don't be afraid to look — look at people's eyes. Therein you will see much that now is escaping your attention.

"But can you do that? People look in your eyes and you look in their eyes. Is there a sense of humor between you? Can you smile? Can you joke? Are you tuned in to the human race? Do you love these people?

"You are love. Living in love is the most glorious adventure you could imagine, and you will get there. You will get there."

EL TANERE: *"This is El Tanere. The love of God uplifts you. The light of God surrounds you. The power of God protects you and the presence of God is with you always.*

"Do you not know that with the elimination of fear, you will have no more terrorism? Your cancer will be eliminated. Many, many diseases will no longer be. It is the fear emotion that you earth entities express which is the food that allows this to take place.

"We recognize where your fear came from, where it originated, in the very beginning of time, in the beginning of evolution, the fear of survival and the unknown.

"You who are fortunate enough, with open minds, to have received and welcomed and understood the teachings in the Urantia Papers no longer need to be concerned about either survival or the unknown, for it is truly truth that you all know.

"Teach this. Practice it. Every time a little teeny tiny fear enters into your mind, emotional self, put a red circle around it with a red slash through it – cancel it. And immediately replace it with love, for love is God and God is love. Love is all, that's all there is. And it is true that you mortals on the earth plane think of love as you find it in relationships or in parenthood, or something that you just like. You love it! You love your home. You love your job.

"But love is an energy.

"Become aware that love is an energy, powerful! And know this – you have been given this. Use it! Always, always, for the highest and best choice that you can make. Become aware, aware of everything that you think, say and do.

"Therefore, that is the trinity within you. First the thought, then the expression, and then the action. Become aware of the results and the outcome on yourself and the world, on everything that you think, say and do.

"Be honest! Totally and completely honest. In every endeavor. In everything that you think, say and do. To thine own self be good. To thine own self be true.

"It was as the Master said, follow the golden rule and apply it. Responsibility. Be responsible for what you think, say and do. It is not necessary to blame anyone or anything. Take the responsibility for your own thoughts, your own expressions and your own actions, for, you see, it all begins with you."

A Teaching Mission Gathering
Nashville, Tennessee - July 15, 1998

NEBADONIA (T/R: Rebecca): *"Dear Ones. I am your true motherly source, your true motherly anchor. I watch you with the closeness and the love of an anxious mother only I have no anxiety. I have no doubts. I know your hearts. You belong to me. When you are tired, think of your mother bringing you refreshment and rest. When you are unhappy, think of your mother giving you encouragement. When you go out in the world and see some of the sufferings of your brethren, remember, their mother goes with them, also. Their mother is there.*

"And children, open your hearts to receive my ministry. Open your hearts to receive the seraphic ministry that is constantly surrounding you. Open your hearts to receive the motherly love that is as strong and as pure as Fatherly love. When you reach for Michael's hand with one hand, reach for mine with the other. I am like a gentle breeze blowing through your souls. I am like a soft rain reviving the thirsty soil. I am like a green leaf, tender and supple and growing. I am like the sunshine, soothing and life giving. Come to me. I do hear you. I do hear your prayers. Come to me. And allow my love to soothe your aching hearts and to wash away your tears. Always remember and think of my love for when you do, I am there. I am with you.

NERO on The Few and the Mighty (T/R: Jim Cleveland): *"I am Nero, a teacher in this mission. And in this beautiful farewell evening, I would like to address you for a moment, you, the few and the mighty. For sometimes I know you consider yourselves small in number and you wonder with some worry of your significance in such an awesome challenge as planetary change.*

"Perhaps I can add some calm and peaceful insight to this intermittently nagging consideration. Had you been an apostle of our Master, you would hardly know that you, an ordinary man, is helping to bring forth upon the world a brand new religion. For you may consider yourself a fisherman, a man of modest means, a working man, a family man. And would you have the time to help create a new and expanded religion?

"And you yourselves daily face all the challenges of a mortal life, and seek to find these times between in which you can contribute great work can be accomplished by the few who are spiritually connected to the energy. And who have learned to bring ideas, visions, hopes and dreams to fruition with bold actions. The few can be the mighty. The motivated charged electrified with the energy of the spirits.

"How many people does it require to seed the Urantia Book in every country of the world? Surprisingly few. The worldwide web at work has been inspired and co-created with you for the purpose of bringing this arena into potentially powerful and quickening exhilarating interaction. The speed of change will be greatly accelerated in years ahead. You are the threshold of a beginning. And though you are few, I want you to understand in your hearts that no matter the burgeoning publishing of spiritual ideas, inspirations, and motivations, you have a message, it could be called a marketing niche by the secularists, which no one else has in its pure and simple form.

"You have a unique message that many will find to be the kernel, the nucleus, that will unify and center their spiritual growth. These people will range form the mainstream of organized churches to the bold adventurers of the so-called New Age, which often resembles the ancient age revisited. All of these proliferating

movements, in fact, mean that you are not the few; you are a unique band with a special heartening nuclea-ized message that cuts to the heart as no other movement seems to be doing, this incisive and liberating message of God presence inside. You are attuned to strong and powerful truths through your cosmology text, which provides over-encircling foundation, and a newly dramatized teaching of these concepts, which have been ruminating within your minds these many years.

"It is time for action. You are taking these actions; you are revealing God inside. You are revealing the art of listening, hearing, and interconnecting with celestials of many personalities and many missions who are flooding, flooding, flooding to this sector of the universe for purification. You are part of this purification, beginning, as all other great movements begin inside, inside the hearts, the minds, the souls of each of you. All great movements emanate from within. Therefore, one goes within to begin personal growth and purification, after which time, you will be sponsored and accompanied, side by side, with your celestial friends who move forth in living service.

"There is some impatience that things move too slowly, but I ask you to consider with truthful heart if your own purification has been manifested. And if there are not other lessons to learn individually personally that will make this precious limited mortal time more appropriate. And in this purification comes the preparatory skills and personality balance resembling to the degree of possibility the supreme balance of Christ Michael as Jesus the son of Man.

"You may be few, but you can bring yourself, your personality, into a state of balance that you take greater satisfaction in knowing that you at least resemble and emulate the precious Jesus. While you may not find this perfection in every day of your mortal life, you will find a balance that helps you to glide and not take hard steps, that smoothes your day by day transition into a feeling of blended, encircled peace and energy intertwined that will carry you through each day. And you will know restful sleep that truly nurtures and refreshes and invigorates.

"You as individuals can reach this level of purification that you may go forth as apostles, working in twos, and doing great work. Do not be impatient. Look in hindsight, as a tool, to see how far you have come. And you have come far. For your relatively few numbers, we consider you the most dynamic, the most heartfelt, and the most contributing segment of this textual revelation. You were chosen many years ago, most truly as children, because you asked for higher spiritual understanding, and you have been led to learn this cosmology as a curriculum to inspire you to teach universal truths in your daily lives. Many skills, many talents come into the fore, and many great works are done by individuals in very small groups, working together.

"Do not despair of the media. The media is also changing. And the media will change even more. And do not feel because you are one or because you are few that you must carry this great load of planetary evolvement upon your shoulders. For truly the energies are emanating from each heart of atheist and agnostic becoming increasingly restless, disillusioned with what they have found to be not true, hungry for a deeper depth of understanding. And on every point of light on Urantia, from the monasteries, to the churches, to the synagogues, we work with individuals, bringing forth from within, the indwelling spirit, those concepts and inspirations that are needed.

"This is a massive planetary awakening. And the mission is even more massive to your points of view when considered form a local universe context. For Nebadon virtually vibrates with excitement of epochal *purification of planets, of worlds, and this work is so incredibly exciting that I wish you could see it from our perspective.*

"However, your perspectives are what you must refine now. This is your opportunity for life in the flesh and experiential learning as has been said. It could not be obtained in any other way. Patience, of course, is required. Patience, patience. For this time of unfoldment is not only an exercise in developing your individual purities, your individual strength of will that will make you as an individual a forceful warrior for love and peace. It is also an exercise in cooperation, for while the individual must realize self-potential, and a level of self-reliance within the context of grace, you must learn to work with others who have differing often frustrating views as you have learned in the trials of your various groups.

"It is all about learning and growing and that is what is going on. It is all about evolution and that is what is going on. And so as you learn the strength of the one, the strength of the small groups, the strength of the many, you must also learn that cooperation in enterprises of this magnitude require even more, they require intergenerational cooperation, ordinarily not done by the father and mothers of today, but the continuation and completion of this great purification and reclamation must be done by your children and your grandchildren. And we encourage you to take yet another responsibility in training them well. Training them to carry on, through the generations, an amazing story will unfold on this very special planet.

"And always know and always understand that the doomsayers, apocalyptic prophets my friends, from my perspective as a teacher in this mission, I say to you that these catastrophes will not bring this world to ruin. As you grow in spirit, you will realize how preposterous this idea is. I do not believe the Father is inclined to destroy a perfectly good planet, or to allow his hungry crying suffering children, whose pleas for help have touched the Father and touched all in Nebadon and many beyond Nebadon, these cries of suffering are validation that you have paid heavy dues, you have suffered already.

"You are working for spiritual peace, you are asking, you will receive, indeed are receiving incremental openings of energy which allow incremental openings of your perception of truth, appreciation of beauty, desire to live in goodness. These energy openings can cause disruptive and nonsensical actions which you would consider marks of insanity. Indeed, if you look around, while you also have trained yourselves to look at the positive examples of the Correcting Time, you will see many weird aberrations of people who seem to, as you say, have become very "weirded out." I say to you, you will be called upon to help many of these people regain their balance, regain their center, for they are floundering without the nucleus that holds the power structure together.

"Without this anchoring heart of goodness, without the realization of the one God inside, many will fall to the various vices and self-indulgences and frustrations that lead to violence and conflict. These are your brothers and sisters. Help them to find this center within. This center within is the nucleus from which all grows. It is the flowering blossom of beauty. Nature encompasses lessons in every being, in every action, in every changing season. Much can be learned from an acorn. From a seed. From a cat. Much can be learned from the earth, and the earth itself combined with the stillness can become a powerfully energizing influence. Find these pockets of energy in the stillness. Keep your tank filled because you never know what tomorrow may bring.

"What opportunity to be of service. And if you have been a slackard in energizing your spiritual self, you will often not be prepared to confront the one in suffering, the one who attacks you, the pitiful beggar in the street, the one whose eyes ask you for compassion and help as you walk on by. It is the stillness that energizes, this is the place to go for powerful illuminating energies, incremental additional elements of truth and beauty and goodness to fill and permeate your soul. And as you are filled to overflowing, as your purification reaches levels for which you can feel a peaceful satisfaction, then you will be called upon for service, which relates directly to your talents and skills.

"I know this is perhaps a compilation of much you have heard before. But in the rearranging of information and the various combinings, I pray that my lesson and my insights and perspectives have been helpful to you, and that you will take them for your consideration into your moral and spiritual fabric, and I will be pleased and gratified if you make this part of you.

"Thank you for listening. I am overjoyed to have the opportunity to work with the courageous mortals of Urantia, a special place, for which I volunteered and was genuinely excited upon receiving this assignment. For of all places in Nebadon, this is the where we would want to be. And we would hope that you are happy to be here too. Peace to all of you and good night."

Oklahoma Teaching Mission Conference
Closing Message from Michael - June 25, 2000

"Greetings. I am with you and I would like to speak a few personal words, my children. I am MICHAEL, your Brother/Father/Friend and Spirit-mover. As long as I have known you I have loved you and become more alive through you. I would give to you my gratitude for your persistence in carrying out this Mission project.

"As you leave this gathering there will be decisions to make. There will be life transformations. There will be questions you must answer. Our Mission must be based on the firm foundation of reality, reality not as you know now, but reality that is always in a state of becoming. Whom do you serve? As you go about your daily living could your fellows see the answer to that question in you?

"I also have lived in two worlds at once, the mortal and the spiritual. I also had decisions to make, life transformations and goals to complete. As a boy I had the faith of a boy. As I grew I attained the faith of a man. Through experience I came to realize the reality of the divinity within me. The experience brought me to that reality, good or bad experience. It was the path.

"And while I was a child, I hesitated to drink the Father's cup, but as an adult, I was committed to whatever cup Father put before me. As an adult I had to release childish thinking, for my divine intake was making me grow and I could not go back to the old ways of childish thinking.

"My children, this Mission has caused you to grow, and your thinking is maturing, of course. You cannot return to those ways of thinking as a child just beginning. As you abide within this Mission you are

committed to growing come what may. There needs to be that dedication to drinking whatever cup Father puts before you.

"You will all experience growing pains and this is to be expected. Through commitment to staying the course, our Mission foundation is strengthened. Let each child realize the small purpose they have within the Mission. Let each group across the land realize its responsibility to the overall Mission purpose. While you may face difficulties with personality differences within the Mission, know that each child is loved for who they are now and allowed to grow into who they are becoming.

"Whom do you serve? How can you live a divine life in the flesh? How can you stay committed to the Brotherhood even when you feel separated, or somehow left out, or ridiculed, or not accepted? Each of you has personality characteristics which brings balance and stability to this Mission. It was meant to be that way.

"Do not think you are not known, for I have loved you upon knowledge of your existence. I have been among you as water among the rocks in the river. I have found it a complete joy to carry you when you would allow me to. I would have you know my dedication and strength is one with yours. I am so that you may be made more.

"Make those decisions, children. Whom will you serve? As you return to your everyday living, make a decision as to which life you will live. Is the spiritual life only practiced at conference time or weekly group meetings? I have mastered the mortal life so that you can do the same. I would have you know I am among you whether you are together or not. I would oversee that the foundation we make today is strong enough for future generations. We must embrace spiritual reality with practical arms.

"I thank you for your invitation to bring me here to your gathering and to your individual personal lives. Know that with each year, month, week, day, hour, minute, I am with you. I grow every moment more in love with you. Children, carry on."

2002 Urantia Fellowship International Conference
Estes Park, CO, June 30-July 6, 2002

Teaching Mission Gathering, July 1, 2002
Teacher: **ABRAHAM** (T/R: Nina):

"I am Abraham. Greetings. What an honor to be a branch on this family tree. I realize that to many there seems to be various divisions within the Urantia community. There are some who are perhaps feeling excluded or too different to be included as a part of the whole.

"I, representing my associate Teachers, would express to you our joy at our perspective of this overall family community. Where one group may be representative of ideas, the Correcting Time participants are the action of those ideas. Where one group may be the thought of good intentions, the Teaching Mission is living those good intentions. Where one group is intellectually expressive, the Teaching Mission is about everyday living practice, knowing full well the pitfalls of the mortal struggle.

"The Urantia Community is like the body of Christ, every group having a function and purpose, every group attempting to put forth their highest ideals. The body, however, would suffer disease if the parts would become a stumbling block to other parts. It is our prayer that the parts of the body would work to make it easy for the other parts to function. One part helps the other. No part is any more significant than another.

"Michael said, 'I am the vine and you are my branches.' Together the tree is healthy and growing. Should one branch attempt to overtake the tree, then most definitely would there be an upset of the whole. If the Urantian community cannot find a way to work as functional parts of the whole, then I say, what other community can?

"You are our hope. You are our voice for the changing world. You are the action for our thought. You are the way-showers to a new and better world. The differences between you each matters not. The trust you have in Father to do His bidding definitely matters. What will last will last, and what doesn't, will not. It is all a matter of trusting in the Supreme Overseers. The universe will support those things that are true, beautiful and good, and no man will stop that.

"Your most productive focus would be to love one another with a Fatherly affection. Father loves the child in spite of his actions. You may not always agree with your brothers and sisters, but you can save energy by focusing on loving one another, instead of trying to cast out what you believe is non-reality. Trust in Father to make those things that are 'real' lasting. That is most definitely not our place to choose what is real and what is not.

"The measure in which you feel welcome here at this function will be the measure of love you receive. If you feel not welcome, this becomes real in your own mind. You are all children of the living God, all cosmic citizens, all brothers and sisters. You are welcome. You are supposed to be here. You are loved. You are the way-showers of the future.

"Have faith in Father, and one another, that while there is a sea of endless possibilities, know that you are trusted to follow your Indwelling Fragment to do what you feel is right. Know that we are here. We are here for you. We are with you and determined to see Urantia enter into that age of Light and Life. I leave you to another. Shalom."

Teacher: **WELMEK** (T/R – Michael Painter):

"I am your friend and Teacher, Welmek. This evening I would like to take you on a journey. Our journey will be to climb a mountain; it seems appropriate, given the setting that you are in. We all start at the base of the mountain. As you look up, you cannot see the top; it is so far away. You begin to climb and there are many with you-there are parents, families, relatives, friends-and the journey is not too hard, for when you are not sure where to step, they tell you, they give you guidance.

"As you continue on your journey, you find that each person begins to find a unique path, a unique trail that will lead them up the mountain. The goal for everyone is to reach the top of the mountain, but the path will be different for each person. As you continue to climb and you find that your path seems to separate from others, you begin to grow more fearful. What do you do with this fear? You try to remember all that you have

been taught by your family, your friends, all of your experience, your education, and you trust your intellect to guide you, and you use reason to decide which way to move on your path.

"Sometimes you stumble, but it is not too severe, so you trust your experience and your mind to get you back upon the path. But as you continue, the path becomes more difficult, there are more obstacles, there are more sheer faces of the mountain that you must climb, sometimes not even be able to see where you are going. This creates more fear. As you get stuck and are not sure which way to move, you look around. To your left and right, you can still see others, also climbing, and you call out to them, "Where is a ledge that I might place my foot to be safe?" And they answer you, giving you their best advice. Or perhaps, you see someone, slightly below you on their path, and they can guide you, tell you which direction to move. Or perhaps someone is slightly ahead of you, and they look down and they can tell you which way is the best road to take, the best path to continue your climb.

"And so, you continue, you listen, you follow their advice.

"Sometimes again you stumble, but you continue on your path. But as you continue, you see fewer and fewer of your fellow travelers, there are fewer and fewer to give you advice, there are fewer who can see or understand where you are on your path. There is one who can see all, one who can see from the very base of the mountain, to the very top. You have heard of this person, called "God," but you were never quite sure if this person really existed.

"But as you continue on your path, you find fewer to advise you, you find often that their advice is mistaken. And so you are again filled with fear. What will you do? Your friends, your fellow travelers, cannot always advise you correctly. Your own judgment, your own intellect, has sometimes faltered, and you have fallen. How can you possibly continue on this path to reach the top of your mountain?

"In moments of despair, in moments of great fear, there is sometimes a "still voice" that comes into your mind, "I am the way and I can show you the way." Now you face your greatest decision of all, and this decision is, "Will I trust this voice?" Your intellect struggles, your intellect says, "Trust me, do not let go of me, I have guided you this far, and I can take you the rest of the way."

"But you are not so sure, because your intellect has failed you at times; it has not always guided you in the right way. And so, as you trusted your human parents when you were at the base of the mountain, now you must make a transition, you must make the transition to begin to trust your spiritual parent, this God, this Heavenly Father, who calls to you. Some will not trust, they refuse, they continue to fall. Sometimes they fall so far that they cannot go on in the journey, and they stay broken-hearted wherever they fall and land. And that is where they spend the rest of their time on their journey.

"Others choose to take that leap of faith, choose to take a chance and trust, to trust that inner voice that calls to you. And so, the voice says, "Try this way," and you move that way a small step, but you are safe. This is the beginning of your faith, for what is faith but living trust in this inner voice of our Heavenly Father? You continue to climb; there are times when you cannot see anyone else, when you cannot see even the next step ahead. You are filled with doubt and you are filled with fear, and so you constantly have to decide, "Will I doubt, or will I trust?"

"Sometimes, along the path, your reach a valley, and in the valley, there is a beautiful clear lake and a beautiful clear stream, and beautiful flowers all around. And you know that it is time for you to rest, time for you to relax, to enjoy the beauty of the sunshine, the smell of the flowers, a gentle breeze upon your face, to drink the clear water. There are other fellow travelers who are there; and you meet them and you enjoy their companionship. You share your stories about the climb and you talk about what lies ahead. After a rest, it is time to move on, to continue your journey.

"You start out again with some of your fellow travelers, and as you continue to climb, you will find only a few travelers who share a similar path. As you continue your climb, you decide to not move too far ahead of the others, so that each of you can help each other, and you can climb together. You call this "fellowship." But yet, even though you share the journey with these other fellow travelers, there are still times in your path, when they can hear you, but they cannot guide you. And so, the decisions that you make, are still the same. How much will you trust in your guidance? How much will you rely upon our Father to get you to the top of the mountain?

"As your text tells you, all life comes down to decisions, the decisions of faith against doubt. This is the struggle; this is the climb, the great climb of life. Where are you in your climb, my friends? It is hard to know, but in your climb, you can look around and see others who seem to be on a similar path. There are those that you meet who are ahead, and can sometimes look down and guide you, can sometimes reach down with their hand and pull you up. And then there are those who are beneath you in the climb, and they see you and they call to you, and they say, "I need your help; I need your guidance." Surely, you would not deny them, for as others guided you, surely you would return the favor. You were given service freely; freely must you give your service in return, for this is the way of the climb; this is the only way the climb can be successful.

"As you continue your climb and your trust and faith grows, you find that your fear diminishes. The climb is not necessarily easier, but your ability to climb is easier. It is not so fearful; you are actually beginning to even enjoy the climb. You feel more confident that you are on the right path; you feel more confident that you will reach the top of the mountain. Why is it that you succeed and others do not?

"It is really quite simple, it all comes down to those decisions you made about whether you could trust your inner voice, to let go of the intellect for awhile and learn to follow and trust the inner voice, the voice of our Heavenly Father. This is not to say that your intellect is not of value, for it is a great tool, and your intellect can help you understand and learn much along the path. But there are times when you must trust, trust in your guide, your Heavenly Father, your inner Spirit, your Thought Adjuster, whatever name you choose.

"If you wonder where you are on the path, ask yourself this question, 'Do I trust more now in the Heavenly Father's guidance then I did a year ago, five years ago, ten years ago?' If the answer is 'Yes,' then you are growing, and you are climbing your path in the way that our Father wants you to. There is not 'one right path;' all the paths will lead to the same mountaintop; no path is exactly the same. There are similarities that you can share with each other, but you must climb your own path. And there is only one guide, one person who knows exactly what your path is.

"Share your journey, enjoy it, and give of yourself as others gave to you. But in the moments of darkness, in the moments of not knowing where to put your hand or your foot next in your climb, remember, there will always be the still inner voice telling you, 'This is the way.' Good day, my friends."

Teaching Mission Gathering, July 2, 2002
TARKAS (T/R – Jim Cleveland):

"Good evening my friends, this is Tarkas, a teacher for these blessed ten years or more in this Teaching Mission, and still wondrous every day of the magnificent vicissitudes of this growing, evolving planet learning to live and love during chaos and the horror and joy.

"My colleague, Welmek, speaks of many paths on the Father's majestic mountain. So true, and each of you climb your own, seeking the joy of achievement, and as you come together in meetings like this, eight hundred or more . . . you may go home to the aura of your loved ones, and spread love in so many, many, many, many ways. And, this is the way the Mission works. We don't seek to change the world; we seek to inspire you to change, to become loving creatures, joyous givers of love, joyous seekers of Truth and Beauty and Goodness. And you have found many of these beautiful nuggets of wisdom today.

"I would speak tonight about apocalypse, the lesson beyond apocalypse. Truly, apocalypse is something that frightens the fear-based religions, and so, the end times become powerful dramas of struggle, fear, power, and they're quite inspired by it.

"However, as you know, there are two great motivators - fear and love. There's a place for the love-based religion to eventually become the over-encompassing mighty, joyous, spiritual force on this planet. In the meantime, the fear-based religions get you through this next apocalypse and beyond. For, it is dirty work to make the world safe from the horror, the evil terrorists who kill the masses and spread plenteous destructions. This is work that must be done in the Correcting Times. Best fear-based religions think upon this responsibility, as you are to spread love and bring forth the joy that will replace the great struggle that they call the apocalypse - Armageddon.

"Of course, it has been repeated many times through the centuries as great and beautiful cities and civilizations have been destroyed to rack and ruin, pillaged libraries burned to the ground. And so apocalypse is ever present as good and evil play out. This force breeds a stage upon which you are players.

"And so, what is the onerous apocalypse and why would anyone believe that this beautiful planet would be laid to ruin, when all the evidence points to the opposite? The world of the cross . . . here . . . Michael brought down the Lucifer rebellion – victory! - a great achievement, the magnitude of the Lucifer rebellion taking more than thirty planets down into rebellion against God.

"He triumphed. But, the biggest thing is that He triumphed in the guise of you, as a human. He showed the way. He brought forth the faith in you that He always had in His children, he had lived through life in this incarnation and sent the dark prince falling, screaming in ruin, and in discredit.

"And so, it was not only the victory but also the style in which our magnificent Creator Son set Himself apart. And in like style, He will not only get you through apocalypse to the rebirth of this planet to light and life, and the others as well - all of the others as well - but He will do it with a cleverer and cleverer twist.

405

The Teaching Mission

"It was mentioned last night that Godless power structures are beginning to self-destruct. I think it an appropriate irony that they destroy themselves as we watch . . . But we will build forth a new civilization full of Truth, Beauty and Goodness, and beyond that, the hallmark of our special, and clever, and resourceful, and creative Creator Son.

"So as you read about massive accounting scandals, corporations stewing in their own corruption, evil vying itself out, death and destruction that infuriates and brings forth to higher spiritual service all the good and honest and beautiful people on this planet

"As you see all these things happening before you, do not think of apocalypse, think of new growth. When I first visited Cincinnati ten years ago there was fear of just these things: economic collapse, nuclear destruction - fear, fear, fear. I said then that these kinds of destructions would be seen. Disintegration is always seen before new growth. That is my story and I'm sticking with it.

"And so, we continue to play out this grand scenario on life's stage on this little planet in this local universe - the struggle of good and evil, and there's a purpose for that, which we certainly don't have time to get into.

"Thus, simply reach beyond apocalypse. What do you have to fear? This is Michael's planet. This is Jesus' planet. This is your planet. You are empowered. You are emboldened. You are full of love. Can you see the destruction? Or, can you not see redemption? Redemption. Would Michael fail? I think not. Would this mission fail? No.

"And you have nothing to fear from this Teaching Mission. It is relatively simple. We are Morontia teachers coming back to teach people who supposedly know less than we, although, on occasions we may question that.

"Nevertheless, we stick to our stories, even repeating them endlessly, until you actually do go into the stillness every day. Do you understand?

"We nonetheless maintain our good humor when you do not. It's rough just living in this place. It's rough in so many ways. And you are getting through it, and you are getting through the apocalypse in grand fashion. And you will get through the next apocalypse the same. However, let evil be destroyed, and it can be brought down in our lifetime by evil's own hand, as Jesus wants them to destroy themselves.

"And don't invest your currency, your time, and your efforts to institutions that are corrupt and dishonest. It's time to make a choice and find those strong institutions that can withstand, or new ones that you can build in the glory of a new beginning. It is not an end. It is a new beginning. It's a beautiful story and it's true. I thank you for your time tonight. I love you all.

"This Mission has been joyous for us and we certainly have learned as much as you have, and probably much more, since teachers usually do. We are here for the long haul. We are with you.

"If you want a teacher, you simply ask. You can simply sit down and put words on paper once you encircle yourself in the loving light of the Father, through worship, or prayer, or whatever. When you ring God's telephone, God will answer. How could you go wrong in the circle of love? Transmit your words, write down

your words and then read them back and see what you think of them. Practice makes perfect as you speak through and learn to release yourself. Just release and don't try.

"Speak words without even thinking about what you're speaking. You perform a good secretarial service and that's what they need on occasion. But the key to this Mission is not to go to readings and listen to people like me transmit so much as it is doing this yourself, and, yes, you can.

"You all have indwelling spirits, Thought Adjusters, who are always, always in charge, especially in liaison with morontia teachers. There's nothing to fear. You are so in good hands - the same, loving enfolding arms, the everlasting arms of the Father that lives within you. The teachers are here to help. We are here to help, and I pray that we do. We are certainly enjoying you and we are enjoying this beautiful setting with you. Good night."

Thursday, July 4, 2002
Teacher: **CORELLI** (T/R – Stella Religa):

"Good evening, friends. This is Corelli. I am a long-time acquaintance of Stella, who we were glad to say, agreed to transmit. She is a reluctant transmitter, however, will agree to transmit. We greet you at this wonderful place at Colorado; there are thousands of us here. We all volunteered from various planets, now that the circuits are being opened. This was under the direction of Christ Michael and Prince Machiventa.

"The ideas for these transmissions took place many hundreds of years ago, after Jesus' death on the cross. The idea was that this world needed much spiritual upliftment. There were many attempts during the past thousands of years, ranging from the Prince Caligastia One Hundred, who arrived on the Persian Gulf, to Adam and Eve, Melchizedek, and even our Lord Jesus. These were successful to a certain extent. However, we felt that possibly the best way would be to reach people on a personal level.

"We are happy to report that the success of the Teaching Mission has gone even beyond our expectations. We now have contacts, not only in the United States, but also in Canada, Mexico and it is happening in the Orient and in Europe. Many of these people are astounded, as you were, when they are contacted. Some refuse to go along with what they call this "strange phenomena," but some do agree, and we are so happy to welcome them. There are thousands of transmissions, all with the aim of spiritually enlightening the human race.

Your country includes many of various religious faiths; all of them are good to a certain extent. However, many of them still preach the doctrine of "blood atonement," that God is a "wrathful master" and is eager to seize on any wrongdoing. We hope that with these individual contacts, that these erroneous ideas are laid to rest. This may take many, many years because many people are very reluctant to leave their old traditions. Much of this is due to fear that if they question God or the holy writ with which they have been brought up, that somehow God will be displeased and will punish them in some degree or another. These punishments, they think, take the form of the death or loss of someone, of a loss of jobs, a lack of money, lack of education. But these are not the results of God's wrath; rather they are the results of human greed, or not caring enough for their fellow man.

"God gave you a beautiful world. It will be up to each and every one of you to bring about a better world of love and kindness to one another, to participate in your government so that you have a government responsive to your needs. There is no need for this great suffering, this hunger, disease, lack of homes, corruption in business and in government. You must all be vigilant. God cannot do this; He can work through you, He can suggest paths of endeavor, but it is strictly up to you.

"As you know, many people still blame Satan for the wrongdoing that they do. In reality, these actions that may be evil or corrupt, stem from their own innate reasoning or acting. So we beg of you, go out into your communities, be loving to all those who are in need; help them as much as you can in your circle of friends and in your communities, but also look at the larger picture. This larger picture is influenced by your actions on an individual level. What you do, what you bring to your community, radiates out of your particular area, and people will recognize that what you are doing is for the good.

"One of the greatest teachings on your planet is doing the 'greatest good for the greatest many.' As you start in your own way, this will radiate out to others and eventually, it will encompass the world. Many of you are still afraid that the world will end with Armageddon, End of Time, that some Anti-Christ is out there-none of this is true! God and Jesus never taught such erroneous ideas. The God that sent Jesus is a loving God, and it is a 'just' Universe. You may feel you are suffering greatly, and many of you are, but with the help of fellow man, this can be eradicated. But never, ever believe that God was the instrument of this ugliness that exists in many parts of the world and in your own country.

"We are reassured that there is a growing awareness that we are responsible for our brother's keep, and for our sister's keep, and for our children. And we must all work together to create this better world, which is the first step in ushering in the Age of Light and Life. Our Lord Michael, sends greetings to you all. You are loved, more than you can believe. And do not be afraid, any one of you, that somehow your little missteps will jeopardize your Eternal Life. All that is negative will fall away from you. And if you but choose Eternal Life, your rewards will be great, you will have an opportunity to do that, which you failed to do in this life, or were unable to do because of circumstances beyond your control. But know one thing – you are loved!

"This is a just Universe; Christ Michael will never allow the world, the planet of His birth and death to be destroyed. Man is too puny, too small in the cosmos to destroy something that was created by Christ Michael. Certainly, there is much you can do; your air, your water, your land, your forests-they must all be preserved. And we can see people who are very concerned, and they are working to preserve a world that future generations can enjoy.

"We thank you for the privilege of being here. There are many, many watching in this room today. They love you, they are so eager to contact you. So do not be afraid, if by chance, you should hear a little voice some day, say, 'This is So-and so. I would like to contact you.' So please do it. We love you and we send you our love. Good night.

The Teaching Mission

Niagara Falls Teaching Mission Gathering
Opening evening, Thursday, 7-10-2003

BAKIM, a celestial artisan: *"It is my joy to work in cohesion with many beautiful artists who come to grace your blighted and troubled, but very inspirational planet. Here we see the genuine article; here we see the front lines of spiritual conflict; here we see grand and glorious stories of soulful redemption as you grow and blossom fragrantly in the empowering and growing light, the light that you reflect so grandly, and the faith that has brought you across many geographical expanses to this holy and beautiful place where you flow, living waters together, of love, of faith, of courage, compassion, mercy and joy, of ultimate joy, the joy your Creator Son brings to you and each of us, servants, artisans, teachers, guides, and angels who flock here to be part of this glorious time of redemption and spiritual growth that extends across the universe and indeed across the universe of universes, for your Creator Son manifested one of the greatest glories of the time and space worlds right here.*

"And, of course, this world is protected as you are protected. You are a greenhouse of growing spirits and souls, luxuriously green and blossoming into your individual and highly motivated and spiritualized missions to bring love. You do this so well.

"It is not your quest to sit and think about stillness or to think about finding connection, or to think about becoming a spiritually connected person. As you think, as you try, as you strive, you fail — for truly this is a matter of celestial release. As you sit in the stillness, bring it forth to affirmative purpose from head to toe. Your head must be in balance, both sides of your mind in pure balance. And you can bring forth, through the worshipful experience, as this balance occurs within your head and mind, the lightness in your mind can bring forth an imaginary wafting away of all cares and concerns.

"In this lightness you are opened and you bring forth the energies that permeate your being to your feet, anchored and rooted to the earth. I ask you to visualize, intuit, and feel these connections, for mind is the controlling factor that brings forth this connectivity. As the strength of your roots, as the strength of your upreach grows in intensity, then your whole body begins to vibrate, and in not trying comes the successful connectivity that makes you an electric lightning magnetic conduit." (T/R: Jim Cleveland)

Morning Keynote, Friday, 7/11/2003

TARKAS: "I am so honored to keynote in representation of my beautiful brothers and sisters on this side as we gather ourselves in this beautiful and holy place to worship with you, to rejoice in the presence of the All, and the All One.

"We have seen years of progress in this mission and we have seen evolvement and blossoming to understand that it is not a small thing. It is vast, and encompasses not only your world but also the worlds of rebellion and, in fact, all of Nebadon, which follows closely the world of the cross.

"You are much blessed to be here, to be on the path which is longer. The longer the path, the more consummate are the great spiritual joys that await you at the end of this living rainbow of living water. You are living water! Not drops, but a rushing torrent of brothers and sisters throughout the planet, in tributaries

like blood vessels that permeate the world and bring life to all corners. These tributaries flowing into an ever-greater ocean, which is the realization of God, and this loving ocean, grows as each of you grow from within. The Correcting Time begins within the hearts and souls of each of you.

"The Center of Renewal – upon your sheets, upon your pillowcases, you see C.O.R. It is a Center of Renewal. It is a core (COR), a place where you can get in touch with the core of your goodness and begin to bring it forth as we change this world and bring it to light and life.

"From this core come changes that affect the universe. From this core of which the Holy Father had so much faith that he imbued a spark of His life within yours, so that no longer do you have to feel desperate for Father, or hungry for Father, or long for Father because Father's love lives within each of you." (T/R: Jim Cleveland)

Afternoon Session, Friday, 7/11/03

PARAMAHANSA YOGANANDA: *"Greetings dear ones, friends, children of God. I am Paramahansa Yogananda, a good friend to all of you, for I, too, am a child of God. I, too, lived the life that you have lived on this planet in the material body, yet yearning always to know God and to be like him. I, too, have trod the many steps that you have trod in order to arrive at the place that is our destiny. Our destiny is to become more like him every day. We all have that yearning desire, that burning desire, to know him, to love him.*

"I wish to share with you today a little message, a message of hope and inspiration and perhaps a touch of guidance for you. Keep at it, my friends. Never give up. Each day you arise, thank your Father for the day you have before you. Each day, whenever you take a step in which you feel you may stumble, thank your Father for giving you the opportunity to take the step.

"In this manner you are building the soul, you are building your connections to God. You are asking him to be a part of each little act that you take in your daily life. This is how the soul is built, not by the leaps and the bounds and the triumphs, but rather the small everyday steps that you take to love your fellow man, your sisters, your brothers, those who perhaps may have a station in life greater than yours or a station in life that may be perceived as less than yours. Your life in the eyes of God is as important as any other life. It takes each one of you to build his kingdom.

"So I ask you humbly and with my heartfelt prayer for you, to take your steps slowly and carefully, with purpose and design, always with the thought that you are becoming as God in your daily lives. As each year goes by, you will become more like Him. Never give up, and always approach each day with joy, purpose, and ask your Father to share every moment with you.

This is my thought, my message I wish to leave with you today. I am Paramahansa Yogananda, your friend and fellow traveler. Namaste." (T/R: Eugenia Bryan)

Friday Evening, 7/11/03

Q. I have a question about potential and finding your highest potential, or the manifestation of one's highest potential. I would be interested in hearing what you have to say about this. Thanks.

AARON: *"Simply the willingness to do the Father's will, will manifest your highest potential. The method to gain that knowledge is the stillness, in worship time, seeking directly to the Father in communion. There are no requirements that we could put forth to guide one in manifesting the particulars, but this process of consistent connection with your Indweller will begin to open you up inside to recognize who you are, where you can achieve, where you may perceive weaknesses that may need adjustment. By taking these issues into your stillness and placing them there at the foot of the Almighty, you allow the cleansing process, the slow and gradual healing and the turning of your intent toward the highest source.*

"The healing that flows from that connection will begin to manifest and you will begin to notice the higher possibilities of achievement for yourself. You will begin to become a bigger risk taker, so to speak, someone who will try new things, who will test the waters to find if a particular path has some meaning or merit or worth for you. It no longer is a fear of being wrong in life, but instead, a willingness to be wrong in the knowledge that what you are seeking is right. By doing this, you will open into the universal possibilities and potential."

TOMAS: *"My friends, again, it is important in our lives together, in these expanding circumstances, to learn to follow the direction set in motion by following the leading of God, for He began an eternity of sharing a limitless love with everyone He meets, and such love is compelling. The invitation, over time, is to help magnify this love in each of you, in all matters, in your own efforts, and within limitations, such as are found in the material creatures of His creation.*

"This Teaching Mission is not a crusade. Yet it is a campaign. It is a campaign to win every heart and every mind. Not only to win every living being throughout this sector of Nebadon, but all who have suffered, as you have suffered, this hole in your heart, wondering where this missing piece is. Missing not by any choice of yours, but by the circumstances of time, for which all conspire to elevate the amplitude of these waves of affection. And so we ask you to pay attention to lessons of divinity attainment in most infinitesimal beings over time and space which Our Father gives us to gather you and your fellows into His arms and into the arms of each other. Love is the greatest reality in all the universe

"It is not a cause won by the use of swords or even words, so quickly are they exchanged one for the other — all to do battle, rather than to make peace. Your thoughts, your words, your actions spring from the choice. All flow in the presence of I Am / We Are. It is Our Father's will for you. Here again all of this, where we are in the end of our striving, is in this very peaceful place. Throughout your journeys, your adventures On High, this constancy of magnifying the joy, the love we will share together, you will so spawn. How might we use the sounds, the circuits at this moment? Would they distract you? These are opportunities to receive a greater range of affection. Can you dwell in this place at all? This eternal moment? Realize the Stillness and yet walk on the earth? Showering your fellows with love you have felt poured upon you?"

"Your challenge is not to build physical structures, though these have their place. Your challenge is not to produce manuscripts to allow your lives to be translated. Your lives compose the archives of Nebadon. It is from these we draw our lessons. This soul we share in company, this soul of supremacy. Our friend, our Father/our Brother Michael, shows all, all this, to the Supreme as a Sovereign Creator Son.

"Each of you has your own sovereignties to attain. Every day of your lives, as by each of his life incarnations, you are earning your soul. We assist you, as we are part of you. And how happy we are to share this love! In this moment of history, we are making the effort. The records of your world may not reflect this change for some time. But you see it. You feel it. You know it. In the depth of your being. Share it like this. In any heart that seems suited. Invite us to participate with your struggles. Share with us."

MALVANTRA MELCHIZEDEK: *"Valiant travelers on your ascension scheme, being washed by the vibrations of your creative musical endeavors, feeling the pleasure as your internal being vibrates with the joys of your brethren's song, so too does your divine essence titillate with the exquisite divine vibrations emanating through the Source Center of your central Being. You are connected in the most luxurious fashion with the endless Source of all creative energy. You rest in the heartland of the majestic Trinity who outpours in the most unified fashion waves of eternal love. When you gather for worship, your concerted and social grouping exemplifies the purpose of sharing in unison the beautiful unfolding of your gratitude in a welcoming fashion for the gifts bestowed instantly, constantly, forever.*

"The bridge of size is but a passage through the gateway of the immortal portal and entrance into a dimension that will fill you with awe, captivate your imagination and sustain and nurture with divine nutrients: the essence of all being, the ambrosia of living existence, the soma of infinite life. Your song vibrates as a reward for the honor that's due your grouping as a result of the loyalty and your fidelity to your Sovereign who recognizes and acknowledges his children of light.

"Let the rule of Michael commanding your mission be remembered through the age of the Supreme beyond the confines of your universe with a purposeful reputation as agondonters to impress and forever shatter a reputation that the Urantians are a weak race. Let the blood run strong and let your faith be fired and sparkle as you galvanize and proceed with your precious mission." (T/R: Stephen Mark)

Saturday Night Session, 7/12/03

MANTOUBE MELCHIZEDEK: *"Greetings fellow servants in this mission. I am Mantoube, a Melchizedek. I am assigned to this sphere to enhance the work of the Correcting Time. In cohesion with many of my colleagues I sometimes am aligned with this willing vessel in order to bring his enterprises to fuller fruition and as such, commingle with you, his many associations, to expand this work to each of you. I simply come to pledge to you that your Melchizedek Teachers, now many in number, are determined to rebuild and reestablish spiritually viable educational institutions and systems in the correcting worlds, yours among them, numbering three score and more depending upon your measurement of relative reality. It is certain that your beleaguered world is in this number.*

"We are pleased with what we see to be rapid progress made possible by the quickening spiritual energies being brought forth by many in cohesion: life carriers, energy directors, administrators of many kinds, and personalities working together along with neighbors from other parts of this grand local universe. It is a

privilege to be here. We will work with you co-creatively to manifest light and life upon all of these troubled worlds, each having somewhat complex and individual problems of its own.

"Each sphere is populated by unique personalities at various stages of rebellion disruption. This greatly magnifies the undertaking of this Correcting Time, which is not your world alone as you see. All of these planets are receiving the watch care and ministry of all of us on the celestial side and all those countless mortals who join with us on all these spheres. Once again, you must broaden your thinking to universe realities. You are doing so nicely.

"My second reason for speaking is to tell you how enormously impressed we are at the enlightened rapport and camaraderie that we have seen emanate so brightly from this gathering, for most gatherings of mortals upon Urantia spawns a cacophony of resentments, phoniness, role playings, desperate agendas, cries of, "I am someone, listen to me."

"The many celestials gathered here find your behavior toward one another to be exhilarating. We see in this our own success and it brings us great joy to see you interacting in the spirit, sharing the joys of the spirit with a bare minimum of personality discord. We applaud you. You are our good friends.

"As we influence you to the light we take great pride in this service, and I assure you the pride is felt by the highest personages of this Correcting Time all the way to those who are, shall we say, in the trenches working with individuals each day as individual teachers, our beautiful morontian children who have seen the light and come back to share it, as many of you will do one day, reaching back to help those along the path.

"We applaud you because you are the ones who have taken our very fine inspirations, I must say, and made them happen. You are the hearts, the minds, the hands, the feet, the souls on Urantia. We are not the citizens of your world. We are not the guardians. We are not the protectors. We are not here to save you. You will save yourself. We will work together and this will be our triumph together.

"This is the cooperative way of the universe. Droplets are weak. Living water is strong and flows surely into the ocean of the universal Father's bound-less infinite and unparalleled love for each of you, who so loved you that you are indwelt with this glorious spark of light that shines ever brightly.

"As the years roll forward you will see profound things. You will be part of profound things. And we will make a profound and glorious future for Urantia and for these other worlds of the rebellion. So far, so good. On behalf of the Melchizedeks, thank you. Goodnight." (T/R: Jim Cleveland)

Association for Light and Life Gathering
Boise, Idaho - August, 2004

LANTARNEK, a Melchizedek: *"I have accepted assignment upon this planet with the purpose of instilling morontia methods of progress. It is my desire to foster your pre-morontia unfoldment by overlaying patterns that are used in the training you will undergo subsequent to this human life. Primary in all* *attainment in personality ascension, in soul growth, is the acquirement for the ability to love. Love is the primary receptor. It is the opening to greater experience. It is the method whereby all learning takes place.*

"You are aware of the distinction between knowledge in the mind and experience in the soul. One learns in the mind and can do so without love. Soul learning requires love as its partner. Coupled with love and learning is the true test of your morontia training and that is living, living your experience ever adjusting and refining your understanding, ever deepening your ability to receive and express love.

"This wonderful world of Michael is spectacularly beautiful. Were you able to draw far in miles from this little orb, you would be profoundly attracted to its vitality. Life crawls all over this rock, a cosmic ecology. You who identify with one or more expressions of spiritual ministry are part of the balance required to reveal the Father more fully. Existential absolute is impossible of description. Father presence is freely reveal-able, but Father is not simply one spark within one. Father turns in all directions through each one of you, my friends.

"While you seek ever more deeply the divine presence, and while you investigate further cosmic understanding of deity, remind yourself when you feel yourself inadequate as a representative of God, that you are his unique directional manifestation, and your neighbor is a complementary manifestation of a slightly different character. Assembled together you are as like a giant meadow of wildflowers.

"Behold one in its beauty, behold all in its' beauty. To you I give the salute from my order of beings for your dedication to the outworking of the plans for light and life upon your world. The work is great. Your patience will be required, coupled with your perseverance. My friends do not wait, work. Thank you for allowing me into your consciousness this day. Thank you for reflecting upon my message. Love Michael, love his associate, Spirit Mother. Learn from one another, live for God, live for your fellow man. Thank you, I take my leave."

A Teaching Mission Retreat
Canossian Center, New Mexico, February 2006

TOMAS: *"I ask you to see beyond the limitations of this process to the truth of the process, which is bridging the gap between the finite and the infinite, opening the door between the material world and the spiritual realm, and developing a working relationship between this paradigm and the next — indeed, allowing them to merge, so that there is not such an abrupt change between here and the next level, but a natural process of growth."* (TR:Gerdean)

MICHAEL: *"Seeing with new eyes. My beloved brothers and sisters, I am Michael. I will speak to you tonight about a heart cry of many of you. When will I be ready? When will I be ready to step forward into the place that I have been called? When? When will you send those that you wish me to serve and minister to? I would say that you have long been ready, and I have sent many to you. There is one in your own home who cries for understanding and they are just engarbed of needlessness, and so you look past them, but you yourself have closed yourself in this closet to appear not to be needed, so you should understand this false attire and because of this, you walk past the ministry. You have read in books, "when you are ready, I will send them to you." Oh, I have sent so many that you did not see.*

"I call you, brothers and sisters, to see with new eyes, to see the Beloved in your own home, in your own workplace. I have said to many of you, the value of a smile to one who so needs a smile and a hug to the one that you may think must remain hopeless, "Take into your day me, as you, for from this one who speaks to you now I have said these very words: I am the hands and the feet and voice of God. And she adds to this prayer daily, I am his smile. And I would say to you all, my beloveds, put on this garb each day. There is no time. There is no when for ministry that comes. Your ministry is now." (T/R: JOYce)

Association for Light and Life
Santa Barbara, CA, July 2006

MICHAEL: *"Long have we awaited this time of development on Urantia when the circuits that were disconnected at the time of the Lucifer Rebellion were reinstated and the infusion of spiritual energy to pour upon the planet to stimulate the minds and hearts of every inhabitant therein. Each of you has been prepared. The hand of your Mother has been active within you, bringing you into deeper and more fuller realizations of who you really are and the glorious unfolding of the light of truth and love on Urantia."*

JESUS: *"My brethren, this is your elder brother. This is Jesus. While you have known me as your Father Michael, I ask you now to draw upon your love for me in my human identity as Joshua ben Joseph of Nazareth. Feel me in your hearts. Allow my presence to commingle with yours. I am here and I wish to share the experiences that you are now undertaking as ministers of mine and your Mother.*

"The power of Michael is growing within you. It is also my desire that you carry this particular energy signature of that which I experienced in my human life as your brother Jesus. I lived this life that you live. I know the joys, the sorrows, the heartaches, the triumphs, the loneliness, the connectivity, the isolation and the ecstasy. All of you have the capacity to feel these ranges of emotion. They are all good. They are all part of the plan.

"When you are in times of sorrow, you only have to call upon me to ask me to share that experience with you. I will lead you from sorrow to joy! I will lead you from fear to faith. Have I not said, 'I am the way? That all who come in search of this shall receive?' In your hearts, my brethren, is where I long to be anchored. Hand in hand, going forth with each one of you, combining our love in service to our brethren— the hungry, starving, abandoned, sick.

"You all have such healing powers and potential. When you call upon me in the purity of your desire to serve, can I then blend in what is my heart's desire to achieve, for my love for this world has never ceased. My participation in the human events unfolding here has never languished.

"You who have stepped up to partake in the ministry of healing, receive me now. Healing hearts, healing minds, healing bodies—all of this is part of the plan. Doubt not your capacities to do this. When someone is presented before you, you only have to turn inside and to ask me to commingle with you so that my love for this child, this precious, precious child can be carried through you into that individual to nourish them at a deep level, the level they need. If this is something you desire, my beloveds, drink deeply of me now.

415

"Those of you who have awaiting my return in the flesh or in a morontia vision will receive this energy signature in their beings. They will receive what they long for, a deeper impression of me, and my love for them.

"So remember, my faithful brothers and sisters, to come to me as your elder brother and to ask to be a minister of our Father's love and know that you shall receive all and even more to share with your beloveds, and our family shall grow. You will have sublime satisfaction in knowing the joys of service.

"So I will take my leave of you in this manner, still residing in your hearts. As you breathe deeply into the energy of your heart, I will remain ever present, my heart in yours, your heart in mine, creating the unshakable, unstoppable bond of love from which all good things shall pour forth. Good day, my beloved brothers and sisters."

Images numbers relate to image chart on next page.

1. JoiLin Johnson 2. Susan Rowland 3. Gerdean O'Dell and Angus Bowen
4. Marty Risacher 5. Gerald Dalton 6. Donna D'Ingillo
7. Jim Cleveland 8. John Creger 9. Manu Puri
10. Mark and Mary Rogers 11. Donna and Larry Whelan 12. Deborah Goaldman
13. Mary Livingston 14. Daniel Raphael 15. Karen Roberts
16. Blanche Irene Berland 17. David and Susan Butterfield 18. Oliver Deux

A Gallery of Photos

16 17 18

Mark Farley and the late Thea Hardy, a loving couple of spiritual seekers in Oregon. She was a valuable networker and graphic designer for the Teaching Mission and transmitted many lessons from Christ Michael, LinEl, Serena and other teachers.

Bill and Virginia Kelly. Bill transmitted a wonderful archive of lessons from celestial teacher Daniel and others before passing. Virginia and others continue to meet in Pocatello, Idaho.

Norman Ingram and Stella Religa. He has been instrumental in sowing *the Urantia Book* into libraries worldwide. She is a longtime transmitter and author of *The Last Revelation*, which relates the Urantia Book teachings to the Book of Revelations.

Three transmitters with spiritual names in Idaho from the 1990s: 'Pamella' – Nancy Kelly; 'Gerdean' O'Dell; 'Rutha' – the late Debbie Roberts.

'Father Bob' Schuer, late of Columbus, Ohio, facilitated Urantia Book study groups and participated in the Teaching Mission in Cincinnati and Columbus during his long and active years as a 'retired' Catholic priest. He presented a Urantia Book to the Pope for his library.

The Teaching Mission

The Hunt Family of Urantia Book readers, and students of a celestial Bright and Morning Star named Astara transmitted by mother Bonnie. Father Bob Hunt, a professor of mathematics, is joined here by his late wife, Bonnie (far right), and most of their children and grandchildren in 1977.

With Idaho mountains as a backdrop, Judy Langston of the Tallahassee, Florida, group; Barry Bartlett from Hamilton, New Zealand, and Mark Austin from Dallas, Texas.

Fred Harris and Mary Livingston at one of the Celestial Nights gatherings in Cape San Blas, FL, hosted by the Tallahasee Urantia-TM group.

Jim Cleveland, with the late Bea Mouganis of Pittsburgh, while visiting as a guest transmitter for the Pittsburgh Pumpkins group.

Michael Goodwin, a fine artist, and the late Susan Kimsey at the first Teaching Mission gathering in Cheney, WA, in 1994. Susan was a pioneer transmitter with the mission, with a lengthy body of work from Oflana, Tarkas and others out of Half Moon Bay, CA.

(lesft) Rick and Barbara Giles of the Coeur d"Alene, ID Teaching Mission Group

(right) New Zealand Teaching Mission Group

Part 5

Paths of Truth; Corridors of Credulity:
Unraveling Urantia's Conflict with Celestial Contact
Jim Cleveland

How could the Teaching Mission hope to take root and grow within a movement that quickly gave a resounding and stinging rebuke to our sessions with the celestial teachers? We were branded as 'nefarious channelers' in an official publication devoted to students of *The Urantia Book* and disdained from ever holding a Urantia Foundation affiliation.

Even though the teachers extolled the Urantia text as the highest collection of spiritual wisdom on the planet, we were seen as coat-tailing onto that proclaimed epochal revelation with 'sordid spiritualism.' Channeling was distracting, unreliable, and had no business within official book study groups.

I decided to do some research into Urantian history. It would be a detective story, to find and define this schism between what I considered a published celestial revelation and the celestial teachers who come now to support it.

As a benchmark, I knew that the Urantia Foundation's highly-touted papers were, in some measure, the unknowing vocalizations of a mysterious altered state 'sleeping subject' who spoke it like rote, without conscious involvement or even interest in what was being dictated to him. Urantia lore also includes actual 'materializations' of printed words inside a bank vault. The phenomenon was adamantly stated to not be related to the channeling séance sessions which were more prevalent in the early years of the 20th century.

During that time, a collective of Chicago area scholars was formed under the leadership of Dr. William Sadler, a medical doctor, an academician, author, former Seventh Day Adventist, and an active debunker of spiritist scams. The group was called the Contact Commission and they were allegedly in touch with "midwayers," Urantia-related personalities who bridge the spirit world, in forging the final printed book. They deemed it an epochal spiritual revelation and the midwayers formed a Revelatory Commission to work with the humans.

The name of the conduit human remains purposefully anonymous so that the text can be considered as itself, and without the distracting involvement of some "special" human personality.

The Commission, now the Urantia Foundation, finally published the text in 1955, after several decades of preparation. As a publishing enterprise in an era before computers or even fax machines, it was quite an undertaking.

The publishers expected the 2,097 page tome to be well-received by thoughtful world leaders. It was sent to a list of luminaries. Such was not the case.

Since that time, it's been a struggle for the Urantia papers to get beyond the occult world and into the mainstream of science, religion and philosophy discussion, where I think it should be. It synthesizes them well. But there seems to be no room in those fields for a purportedly dictated revelation from spirit world personalities.

To the custodians of the 196 papers, this was a one-time rare and bonafide communication with celestials. Civilization was just not ready to understand and accept it, especially in its conflicts with existing religious scripture. Over the movement's history it soon appeared that anything else purporting to be received from celestials would always fall short of the pristine perfect English quality of their text.

Ironically, Urantia readers had largely debunked the Judeo-Christian Bible as heavily flawed. In turn, their tome had been largely rejected by Christians. And now both camps would likely debunk our celestial teachers today.

The Urantia Book was accepted, to the word, as infallible scripture by its movements. Their primary objective was to protect it, keep it inviolate. Unreliable and uncontrolled channeling could bring forth many falsehoods and aberrational fantasies that influential Urantia leaders saw as rampant in the so-called 'new age' arena.

Our Teaching Mission concept that individuals in worshipful silence and in communion with others can actually contact and learn from celestial teachers was a concept to be battled, a re-emergence of the spiritist séance factions that Dr. Sadler and the Urantia founders so disdained last century.

It didn't seem logical to brand us with this. We weren't bringing back dead relatives to chat and the ability to receive and transmit, a new process, was available to anyone who put forth the effort. Make your own connection; get your own individual lessons. Read these 'fruits of the spirit' we transcribe and make up your own mind.

It seemed to me a battle over the reality of a new wave of spiritual guidance and the validity of Stillness time of worship, prayer and up-reach to actually make these connections. The book's official custodians condemned these efforts as unreliable given the inadequacies and trickeries of the human mind. Some even believed that opening oneself in stillness would open the door for the Luciferian demons of their lore to come in and control us.

On the other hand, after all these years, I knew that my free will had always been respected by the teachers, and they are kind, gracious, and very knowledgeable on the ways of the universe and the role of ascending mortals in God's plan.

If this spiritual consciousness threshold is indeed available, as we have experienced, then why don't the custodians of an epochal revelation want to open themselves to this reality too? What fears are involved and are they valid in any respect? We are natural extensions of the text; we now have teachers for the text. Or so it seemed to me. Was it true?

INTERPLANETARY IMPLICATIONS

Within all these streams of thoughts finally came a realization that impressed itself upon me insistently, as the teachers can be.

The Teaching Mission is interplanetary and includes all the worlds of the Lucifer Rebellion.

Yes. And so the Urantia movement is actually part of the Teaching Mission on the planet, along with everything else. The Urantia movement presumes erroneously that we would be part of them, just because they are custodians of the text. And yet the book and the teachers are for everyone, every living soul, and on more planets than this one. Organizations of readers should not impede the continuing revelation or the broadness of its application.

Where was the fault line that separates book students who work to spread a textual revelation on the planet and those of us who interact with celestial teachers to help us realize more truth, beauty and goodness in our lives, and bring the text to dramatic life? Who drew the fault line and why?

There is a time factor. Just as the book's believers consider it to be the planet's highest revelation of truth, many think that, in its complexity, it will suffice as revelation for the planet for a long time to come, over many generations. They cite mandates pointing to the need for vast numbers of book study groups in the world and more generations of evolutionary struggle toward an era of planetary enlightenment. They believe in patience and slow word-of-mouth growth, no media to criticize them. World thinking is just not ready for some of the truths within Urantia's pages, but future generations will be.

While the book says that Urantia is "quivering on the brink" of massive change, many devotees seem most inclined to consider a very long view.

So, in 1992, when the First Urantia Society in Los Angeles heard the official announcement of the Teaching Mission and an interplanetary "Time of Correction" following the recent adjudication of the Lucifer Rebellion against God, many did not believe it and they have pursued a determined course of opposition. They also distrust and disdain the process of 'channeling' as they define it.

Numerous narratives from the Urantia Papers do show that the universe is teeming with teachers and universities, from the mortal level all the way through the human ascension plan, including seven teaching spheres dedicated wholly to the education of ascending mortals. None of these pages have appeased the doubters.

A CLOSET OF DISCONTENT

It was the Vern Grimsley/Family of God debacle, of course. That was the schism, the breaking point, where Urantia officials drew a line in the sand against celestial messages. It seemed that channeled voice predictions of World War III did not happen, simple as that, and so purported messages from those celestials who gave humanity the Urantia papers can't be trusted any more.

The tumultuous political struggle that developed over the authenticity of the messages had resulted in Grimsley's retirement from Urantia involvement and the ascension to power of former friends, now critics, who would cement their hold over the Urantia Foundation and fortify an indelible disdain for a lot of things they considered "New Age."

The Foundation took the stance that the midwayers had left humans on their own here many years ago, and that adherence to the revelation meant using it as the one and only source of spiritual enlightenment, the one sure thing. They equated the book with a new religion of authentic Jesus teachings, not on the false atonement doctrine of Christianity influenced by Paul, which had constructed a religion 'about' Jesus which was not true to his teachings about God as a loving parent.

Grimsley seemed to be doing that at the Family of God Foundation in California, but in time, he had been charged with having "audio hallucinations" about war. This evaporated Urantia support, and the Foundation collapsed.

This prevailing blanket opposition to celestial messaging, then, had seemingly aligned the Foundation only with itself and its own self-declared higher truths going forward. This made it fundamentalist, judgmental, and unwilling to meet any of the other numerous spiritual paths on the planet on any terms except from its own critical judgments. This was like another church, which many Urantia readers said they didn't want to be.

This judgmental attitude is hardly espousing the new religion of Jesus that the book mandates, I thought. This kind of spiritual elitism cements a "holy scripture" view of the book, rather than accept it for what it is: a transitional guidepost for all of humanity, every individual child of God, to learn and shape their spiritual destiny by loving and working with one another. Religious belief systems are generally beside the point. Loving one another and learning to work together is the point.

AUTOCRACY AND CONTROL

As the Urantia Foundation established its autocratic rule in the 1970s, I discovered, it had led to an era of stringent licensing demands, and debilitating and divisive protectionist lawsuits against many loyal readers. This seems to have also destroyed the best and brightest hope for some meaningful evangelism for the book, especially with the Family of God conflict. There, the movement had a charismatic minister with strong Urantia knowledge and a worldwide radio audience for his Urantian message of all one people under God.

But I knew there could be a big difference in what seems to be and the facts. My ideas could be wrong. I asked myself what really happened with the WWIII scare at the Family of God since new information had revealed just how perilously close we actually were to an attack by the Soviets in those pivotal autumn days of 1983.

Urantia's midwayer personalities are also residents of our planet, invisible to our material eyes, living in a dimension between the physical and the spiritual. So says the Urantia revelation. They would be greatly concerned about nuclear war, as most people in the U.S. and the Soviet Union were.

But our Teaching Mission today had only a peripheral relationship with the midwayer personalities. We were working in a prescribed personal growth curriculum with ascending teachers who were previously mortals, and their Melchizedek mentors. Authority of the mission rested with Christ Michael, who was incarnated as Jesus on the planet, and was now here again to redeem it with the anticipated 'Second Coming.'

Compared to our mission, midwayer doomsday warnings would seem to be another matter entirely. Our teachers' messages are not warnings designed to save lives and carry forward the epochal revelation. They are lessons for personal spiritual growth. So was there any actual relationship with what happened at the Family of God Foundation and our teachers today?

Fortuitously, some information began to fall in place, as if that was the celestial plan. Eventually, I would find that the simplistic summations and hearsay history of the Family of God war scare contained deeper and different layers of reality.

First, however, came a research narrative that made me finally convinced that the Teaching Mission is a natural extension of the Urantia Revelation.

FAITH OVER APOCALYPSE

In the summer 2010 issue of the Fellowship Herald magazine, published by the Urantia Fellowship, I came upon a feature story by two longtime Urantian leaders. The purpose of the article was to refute the plethora of doomsday stories in the media. It pointed out on page after page that the Urantia revelation shows a much greater destiny for the planet and in many ways.

I was absolutely stunned to see that every quote and supposition pointed directly to the advent of the Teaching Mission and described it well. Beyond that, the article moved directly into the Magisterial Son Mission that is destined for the planet, and I came to realize that the large archive of lessons now being produced by Magisterial Son Monjoronson are also linked directly to what *the Urantia Book* says is coming to this "quickening" planet.

No longer did I have to be concerned with any disunity in the book and the teachers. There is none. And the authors had excellent credentials. Carolyn Kendall has been a reader since before publication; and along with her parents, brother, and late husband, was a founding member of the First Urantia Society of Chicago. She and her husband Tom served in various leadership roles. Co-author Barbara Newsom had studied *the Urantia Book* since 1965 and also served in leadership roles. Their presentation came at an April 11, 2010 meeting in Schaumberg, Illinois, and was printed in the Fellowship Herald in the summer issue.

The authors state an optimistic view of the future: *"In contrast to these fearful forecasts, the Urantia Revelation promises that the world does have a future! It is our contention that the Book projects in considerable detail an increasingly spiritualized planet. Not only will Urantia continue to circle the sun, it is evolving toward an inspiring and radiant future."*

"Urantia is now quivering on the very brink of one of its most amazing and enthralling epochs of social readjustment, moral quickening, and spiritual enlightenment." [195:9.2] (P. 2082)

The authors stated early-on that *the Urantia Book* itself was not the whole story: "This revelation is a unique phenomenon in the local universe: it is in written form. The book is probably not a finished revelation — an end in itself; but rather a precursor — the first stage of an on-going revelatory process that will continue to unfold in future years."

The authors effectively opened the door here for continuing revelation and living truth, the stuff of planetary evolution. I could never believe the revelators gave us a scripture and then left us on our own to absorb its complexities.

Following a review of planetary history to date, the Fellowship Herald authors begin to touch upon the most divisive issue between readers. Has the Lucifer Rebellion really been adjudicated, as a number of Teaching Mission personalities report? The authors, neither of them Teaching Mission participants, open a crack in another door:

"And now, 2,000 years after the bestowal of Michael, and 200,000 years after the Lucifer Rebellion, there are subtle indications that the case against the perpetrators is moving toward adjudication, and that our isolation may be coming to an end in the not too distant future. The Urantia Book reveals the following intriguing details:

"The first hearing in the case of Gabriel vs. Lucifer occurred on Uversa, the capitol of the superuniverse, 'during the time of effecting this revelation.' [54:4.8] (P. 616) Why is this significant? We are told that immediately after Lucifer and his associates are annihilated, the circuits of communication between our world

The Teaching Mission

and the headquarters worlds of the system, constellation, and local universe will be reinstated. Worlds not in isolation ordinarily receive broadcasts of events transpiring in the universe."

In the Teaching Mission, we are advised that Gabriel won the case, the energy circuits are being opened incrementally, some rebels chose rehabilitation and others, including Lucifer, chose annihilation, and this has cleared the way to send a vast amount of help to the planet. With the adjudication effected in the local universe, some of us believe that we see it well underway on the planet as well, as the forces of darkness and light come into much clearer view and each one of us will make decisions on where we will stand. I can see 'times of correction' everywhere, though I realize that many others see only the continued greed and drudgery.

The Urantian authors continue to speculate on precursors to a coming planetary adjudication, noting that Lucifer's accomplice, Satan, had been detained during the 20th Century presentation of the Urantia papers, and that an archangel divisional headquarters had been established on the planet in "more recent times." They note that the archangels are major participants in planetary dispensations, which are the mass resurrections of mortal souls, so-called "sleeping survivors" of the ages. The last recorded dispensation on the planet had followed the incarnation and resurrection of Jesus, whose triumphant life as a mortal finally destroyed the Lucifer Rebellion and bankrupted Lucifer's philosophies.

Teachers in the Mission have stated that a dispensation occurred at or near the same time the Gabriel vs. Lucifer case was adjudicated, but say that the events were not related. They state that the residual effects of evil that remain after the adjudication of Lucifer and company are a considerable challenge for all of humanity, and for them.

The authors quote the Urantia text: *"Archangels are also the advance guard and right-hand associates of Paradise Avonal Sons during magisterial missions to the inhabited planets of time. Think about this enigmatic passage: 'Do you grasp the significance of the fact that your lowly and confused planet has become a divisional headquarters for the universe administration and direction of certain archangel activities having to do with the Paradise ascension scheme? This undoubtedly presages the future concentration of other ascendant activities on the bestowal world of Michael and lends a tremendous and solemn import to the Master's personal promise, I will come again.'"* [37:3.4] (P. 409)

The authors speculate on the "concentration of other ascendant activities" with these passages.

"It would not only refer to the mass resurrection of our own sleeping survivors of the current dispensation, but it may also be a subtle way of telling us that survivors from other isolated worlds will be brought to our world to be trained after their resurrection on the mansion worlds. If this is true, it could be planned to happen in conjunction with Michael's promise to return. If that seems like wild speculation, recall that after Jesus was resurrected, the surviving morontia mortals and their associated directors from the seven mansion worlds were brought to Urantia to go through the morontia experience with the risen Jesus here on earth. The

427

planet upon which the Creator Son completed his bestowal career will be an important field trip for a new class of morontia beings."

Correct. The teachers often refer to how much they are learning from humans and events on this rebellion-retarded planet. Truly, Michael has returned with a great wave of morontian (graduate school?) teachers, as well as Melchizedeks and other spiritual personalities. It is a reclamation and redemption mission to all of the worlds of the Lucifer Rebellion. With the dispensation and adjudication of the cosmic court case, Urantia and the other rebellion planets are receiving the mercy, compassion and forgiveness that are the hallmarks of Christ Michael, and others in his local universe are getting great, even unprecedented, opportunities for education and service on these troubled worlds.

I looked up the passages from the Urantia papers in this particular time frame of Jesus' appearances after his resurrection: "The next day, Monday, was spent wholly with the morontia creatures then present on Urantia. As participants in the Master's morontia-transition experience there had come to Urantia more than one million morontia directors and associates, coming together with transition mortals of various orders from the seven mansion worlds of Satania. The morontia Jesus sojourned with these splendid intelligences for forty days. He instructed them and learned from their directors the life of morontia transition as it is traversed by the mortals of the inhabited worlds or Satania, as they pass through the system morontia spheres."

All is education, at all levels short of God.

Kendall and Newsom delve more into Archangels: "The Urantia Book *notes that Archangels are "dedicated to the work of creature survival and to the furtherance of the ascending needs of his realms. A Master Son may at will vary the order of the spiritual adjudication and evolutionary adjustment of the inhabited planets. And such Sons do make and carry out the plans of their own choosing in all matters of special planetary needs, in particular regarding the worlds of their creature sojourn and still more concerning the realm of terminal bestowal, the planet of incarnation in the likeness of mortal flesh."*

I thought upon reading: *"The rebellion planet of Michael's bestowal as Jesus seems a fitting place for the Archangel headquarters, and their role appears to be key to the recent dispensation and to the personal survival of these millions of souls caught up in the Lucifer rebellion adjudication and rehabilitations."*

In the Teaching Mission, we believe in the deep involvement of Christ Michael himself in nurturing we humans who would represent him. He has spoken personally to many modest gatherings, that in itself provoking criticism that he would not have time for such visits. They underestimate his powers, which go well beyond time and space, and they underestimate the deep empathy and caring that he is capable of showing to every mortal child on the planet, every sheep in his flock.

Besides, we have taken a big step of faith to go into the Stillness and seek contact. That and other steps of faith seem to always open new possibilities and realities. Those who seek

God, it is said, can be assured that God has already found them. I believed each individual step of faith is rewarded in incremental expansions of truth, beauty and goodness.

AN EXPERIMENTAL PLANET

The Herald article then picks up the Urantia notation that our planet is among the 1-in-10 designated for experimental expansion of the standard planetary life forms. It is also said to be unique in actually having a printed planetary history. The authors conclude that this makes *the Urantia book* an experimental book on an experimental planet. Surely, much can indeed happen on such a planet whose leaders revolted against God himself, where the incarnated Creator Son was executed, and where evil forces of greed have now put the planet's resources and well-being in great jeopardy.

But what is the solution? The authors quote *The Urantia Book* to note: *"Michael cannot bestow himself a second time in human form, but he could be manifested in some other manner. Add his not-so-veiled promise to return to the mix: 'When this gospel of the kingdom shall have been proclaimed to all the world for the salvation of all peoples, and when the fullness of the age has come to pass, the Father will send you another dispensational bestowal, or else the Son of Man will return to adjudge the age . . . ."* [176:2.5] (P. 1915)

So, while Michael is not personally incarnated now, there are legions of Correcting Time personalities and resources dedicated to the task of cleaning up after the rebellion and making the way for his promised return.

More clues come to the authors' minds that lead to the reality of spiritual activity now, right now, on the planet.

"The supervisor of Nebadon's decimal (life experimental) planets is Tabamantia, who visited our world on a periodic inspection 38,000 years ago. Within one hundred years of that visit, Adam and Eve arrived. We know from subsequent information that his latest visit occurred just a few months before the first Urantia papers were transmitted. Might we look forward to the arrival of a divine visitor within one hundred years of Tabamantia's last inspection?"

In a word, yes. Not counting Christ Michael's Teaching Mission, we have the recent messages of Magisterial Son Monjoronson. With my research interest whetted in this purported divine adjudicator, I went to read his transcripts, including 101 Q&A sessions with human transmitters I knew, under auspice of www.monjoronson.com. I found that the transcripts add admirably to a collected body of transmissions at several related websites without any alarming red flags. Is this a logical flow, I asked, from the book to the celestial teachers to the Magisterial Mission?

The authors added more possible substantiation. They note that we are not so different from a neighboring planet described in The Urantia Book, *one with a single progressive and advanced continent and others that were much more primitive. The article quotes* The Urantia Book: *"If a Magisterial Son should soon come to [the most] advanced nation, great things could quickly happen on this world." [72:12.2] (P. 820)*

The writers respond: *"The inference that an Avonal (Magisterial) Son would come to a world where only one nation or continent has risen to a requisite level of civilization is both intriguing and reassuring. Apparently, an entire world is not required to reach readiness for revelation as the criteria for a super-mortal visitation."*

Indeed it isn't. It could be argued that planets in greater need would get the help, worlds that were thrown into disarray not altogether by the failings of its citizens, but by the principal failures of Lucifer and of Adam and Eve who also defaulted their biological uplifting responsibilities. It might be believed that worlds suffering from such deleterious activities of our assigned celestials would qualify for some very special, extraordinary help.

Authors Kendall and Newsom speculate further: "Another perplexing passage: *'Only a bestowal Son can re-establish interplanetary lines of communication on such a spiritually isolated world.'* [35:9.9] (P. 394) We've already had our one allotted bestowal Son. Since only a 'bestowal Son' can re-open the circuits, and a Magisterial Son cannot come on a "bestowal mission" then who will re-establish the circuits? They tease us with this: 'ordinarily only once will a bestowal Son serve on the sphere.' [20:5.4] (P. 228) So, which Son will end our isolation? Will a Magisterial Son be sent on another bestowal mission to terminate the dispensation and reestablish the circuits when the Lucifer Rebellion is settled? Or will our bestowal Son Michael return specifically to 'reestablish interplanetary lines of communication?'"

ENERGIES, OPPORTUNITIES RISING

Relating this to the Teaching Mission, we hear that the energy circuits are being incrementally re-established, not all at once. We see Michael's overall leadership of the Correcting Time in the rebellion worlds, with Machiventa Melchizedek in direct charge and specifically headquartered on this planet. After some 20 years in the Teaching Mission, we have seen a melding into the Magisterial Mission of Monjoronson, and his transmitter/ receivers are saying that eventually he will be incarnated here in the flesh.

It might be noted here that Teaching Mission participants have, through the years, questioned the authenticity of some transmissions and even transmitters. We have not been uniformly accepting of all messages, seeking validations, maintaining healthy doubts, and even quarreling on internet discussion lists. Some, at this date, are not fully accepting of Monjoronson's presence or his messages.

This, of course, does not invalidate 20 years of exceptionally good spiritual advice from these teachers that are highly compatible with Urantia, considering that some things have changed since its 1955 publication, such as the continuation and quickening of evolution. Inaccurate so-called transmissions can be expected on this bizarre, rebellion-scarred world, where many would-be individual 'transmitters' might well prove to be unreliable.

The Teaching Mission

An important tenet of the Teaching Mission is Stillness, wherein participants center themselves in worship and prayer and love, creating this aura and making it much more than a metaphysical exercise of curiosity and wonder. We are knocking on God's door, our creator Michael's door, with every good intention. Who will answer?

Upon its publication in 1955, *the Urantia Book* stated that the planet "is a full dispensation and more behind the average planetary schedule."

To Teaching Mission believers, there was a reported dispensation of some kind, apparently in 1984 or 1985 by our calendar. This would presumably be with our assigned Magisterial Son's participation. The task at hand is now to clear the residual aftermath of the Lucifer rebellion. Though Lucifer may be dematerialized, becoming as if he never were, I believe that his philosophies endure and the "dog eat dog" world is at least a reflection of that, and our natural animalistic evolution from mammals is now spirit imbued but is a long way from being perfected.

The Urantia Book, as quoted by Kendall and Newsom, speaks a lot about Monjoronson's identity: *"Magisterial Sons are the high magistrates of the realms, the adjudicators of the successive dispensations.... They preside over the awakening of the sleeping survivors . . . [and] reassign the space creatures of planetary ministry to the tasks of the new dispensation ... His presence constitutes a judgment of the realm."* [20:3.1&4] (P. 226) *"When Paradise Avonals come on magisterial missions, at least the initial one, they are always incarnated."* [52:4.4] (P. 594) appearing *"as an adult of the realm by a technique not involving mortal birth"* [20:2.6] (P. 225) and are in *"physical contact with the mortal creatures of his day and generation."* [20:4.1] (P. 226)

As teachers, Magisterial Sons bring spiritual enlightenment to the mortal races, as with the recorded lessons of Monjoronson to date. Will we be alive if and when Monjoronson makes a physical incarnation on the planet to bring us into fruitful, cooperative service? We wait and see together.

Given that the Teaching Mission critics don't believe any of this, while still believing in the pristine perfection of their text, is a strong indication that these people will never be able to accept any continuance of their print-bound pages into real life. This could change with the dramatic appearance of a charismatic leader personality or the inevitable contact with extraterrestrial visitors. But there again, these people might well allow their fears and see devils and the anti-Christ in anything of this nature and battle against it.

BEYOND IDEOLOGICAL STRUGGLE

Authors Kendall and Newsom go well beyond The Urantia Book's publication in 1955 to help unconsciously validate the advent of teachers. They relate a reading from the midwayer revelators to assembled Urantians right after permission was given to publish the book. It is recorded that the midwayers said:

The Teaching Mission

"We regard The Urantia Book *as a feature of the progressive evolution of human society. It is not germane to the spectacular episodes of epochal revolution, even though it may apparently be timed to appear in the wake of one such revolution in human society. The book belongs to the era immediately to follow the conclusion of the present ideological struggle. That will be the day when men will be willing to seek truth and righteousness. When the chaos of the present confusion has passed, it will be more readily possible to formulate the cosmos of a new and improved era of human relationships. And it is for this better order of affairs on earth that the Book has been made ready.*

"But the publication of the book has not been postponed to that (possibly) somewhat remote date. An early publication of the book has been provided so that it may be in hand for the training of leaders and teachers. Its presence is also required to engage the attention of persons of means who may be thus led to provide funds for translations into other languages."

"You must learn to possess your souls in patience. You are in association with a revelation of truth which is a part of the natural evolution of religion on this world. Over-rapid growth would be suicidal. The book is being given to those who are ready for it long before the day of its world-wide mission. Thousands of study groups must be brought into existence and the book must be translated into many tongues. Thus will the book be in readiness when the battle for man's liberty is finally won and the world is once more made safe for the religion of Jesus and the freedom of mankind."

The midwayers note twice that the book is a part of normal evolution on the planet, though the planet has been abnormal in many ways. They separate it from "spectacular episodes of epochal revolution," such as, presumably, World War II.

But they also discuss "the present ideological struggle" and the "chaos of the present confusion." Do they mean the ideological struggle with Communism, this being in the volatile times of the Cold War with the Soviet Union? A Contact Commission member had once stated in a newsletter that the midwayers had declared war on godless Communism and were determined to prevail no matter how many years it might require.

The United Midwayers of Urantia are said to be a proud and determined group, with a motto stating that whatever they undertake, they accomplish. While humans could not see the end of Communism in the 1950s, the midwayers reportedly could foresee victory confidently, and so they gave permission to go ahead with publication of the book.

Is this accurate? Were they so confident in their creed and in conditions on the ground, since the world was in for more horrendous Cold War chapters, including arms build-ups, confrontational facedowns, terrorist attacks, all with nuclear holocaust just a button push away, and with hostile, angry and frustrated men poised over them. I noted to myself that the Family of God episode was still decades away.

RUSSIAN AND COSMIC REALITIES

History will indeed reveal that the facade of Soviet strength was even then beginning to unravel as the empire began to slow down and stagnate from societal malaise, low living standards, inefficiencies, corruption, and outmoded technology. It was a system that just didn't work, lacked resources and was spread too thin trying to maintain so many satellite territories and a massive military readiness.

The decline would come into sharp focus in the country's soul-searching and self-examination during the later ascension of Mikhail Gorbachev, leading to dissolution of the union and perhaps the victory the midwayers proclaimed.

Early-on, the midwayers might have been able to see the foundational rot that would lead to ruin. They have been living here during the life of the planet, after all, and have seen passing generations of transient humans, who are in an ascension plan that they, themselves, will follow once the planet is settled into an era of Light and Life. Achieving that path is their long-enduring mission on Urantia, and they have seen many generations of humans come and go.

But perhaps they didn't refer to Communism at all, I now thought. We humans often have a narrow and limited view. With an expanded perspective, we see a much greater struggle–the adjudication of the Lucifer Rebellion and full restoration of the validity of the Universal Father/First Source and Center and his myriad time and space ascension worlds plan. These concepts were directly challenged by Lucifer and he brought 37 worlds into his ideological rebellion. The court case of <u>Gabriel vs. Lucifer</u> had begun in 1935 and was well underway.

Or perhaps the midwayers referred to both. Perhaps Communism on our planet has close kinship with Lucifer's ideas and they represent the same parallel threat to humanity, and to God, on different levels. Could that be possible? Two great struggles mirroring one another? God versus atheism on both cosmic and mortal fronts?

One has to remember, of course, that the expressed ideals of Communism did not survive in the reality of the oppressive Soviet state, which did not live up to them in any respect. In like measure, our expressed American ideals when the Constitution was written, did not jibe with the reality of slavery and generational streams of inequalities and corruptions. Stating ideals is one thing; reality is another. The midwayers would not go to war with idealisms of equality but with the Soviet's perversions, and most vitally, the state's atheistic doctrine.

MOBILIZING HUMANS

As the Herald article continued, I was further enlightened on the logical relationship between the Urantia papers and the teachers of today. In 1967, a Contact Commissioner reportedly ended her speech with an excerpt from Revelatory Commission (midwayer) instructions, and the article quotes:

"I have heretofore reminded you that the celestial supervisors of Urantia are mobilizing small groups of spirit-led men and women throughout the world—among all nations—and these truth battalions, these selectmen, are concerned today with scores of vital enterprises which have to do with the rehabilitation of the world following the ending of the present distressing conflicts." (She uses the plural, "conflicts.")

"And of all the emergency corps of mortal selectmen on Urantia, none is charged with a more solemn obligation than our group. We have been called to the great work of taking the first step of offering to mortal man a new light, a new revelation, of the love of God. The easy jog-trot religion of former days no longer suffices to meet the challenges of today. Following Jesus' way of life calls for an act of complete commitment, a dedicated intention, a resolute purpose, a trumpet call to a life that will not compromise."

So if dedicated souls are being assembled on Urantia for service, then the Urantia readers who are among the 'selectmen' must surely be some of our Teaching Mission folks and all of the various service projects they have spawned, supported and nurtured over the years. Our teachers tell us essentially what this contact commissioner said so many years ago in the first lessons. It's time to take on the Father's business: learn the basics of personal religion and go out in service, spreading goodness, love, and random acts of kindness.

It seemed to me that much of the point of the Urantia revelation was getting beyond dogma and developing that self-same relationship with the Universal Father. This can only lead to a service venue.

But I also reminded myself that the celestial Correcting Time is interplanetary and includes all of the worlds of the rebellion. As Urantia readers are urged to do in the text, we need to have 'universe awareness' and 'cosmic consciousness.' And this dictates that we expand our mind even more.

Creator Son Michael (who incarnated here as Jesus) is credited with creating this entire local universe of planets. The after-effects and the adjudication of the Lucifer Rebellion provide a valuable, even essential, learning experience for all the worlds. It is said in the book that the positive results of the Lucifer Rebellion, ironically, have now far outweighed the damages done by it. It has been a massive teaching tool that continues on. And with the adjudication, celestials themselves can now come and lend a hand in one of the greatest service opportunities of all time, learning themselves all the while.

TEXT AND TEACHERS TOGETHER

In concluding their Fellowship Herald article, the authors state their assumption again, that *The Urantia Book* is the first phase of a two-stage epochal revelation.

Our mission, then, would be a logical blending of teachers to text, just like a material university. We have administrators, professors and instructors. We have a curriculum and texts. And with the Urantia Papers midwayer project, we have a printed history for our planet. So our teachers are also using the best collected wisdom on the planet, and with mortal participants going out to seed the teachings once more.

The Teaching Mission

Urantia insiders will recall that much of *The Urantia Book* is gleaned from human writings, confirmed by years of source research. The revelators were straightforward in noting that they used the best spiritual knowledge available on the planet at the time, while embellishing it with revelation, and while still avoiding the revelation of information that could be considered unearned – information that we can preferably discover ourselves in keeping with the evolutionary world mandates.

Disdaining the 'dark projections of our media and literature,' the Herald authors state that we must be ready for the advent of a Magisterial Son and the possibility of a return visit by Michael: "Although we are advised not to attach Michael's return to any particular era, as he or others could come at any time, they WILL come; of that there can be no doubt!"

Earlier in the piece, the authors had noted that Michael's return would/could not be in human form. So with the Teaching Mission it would appear that he has sent waves of teachers and Correcting Time administrators in preparation for his personal return at a later time, maybe soon, maybe later.

The authors can see the future from the prophecies of the Urantia papers:

"Our eternal lives will be played out on the architectural worlds of space, but our immediate planetary futures are linked with orders of beings who are managing our world behind the scenes. The purpose of The Urantia Book *is 'to endeavor to expand cosmic consciousness and enhance spiritual perception.'"* [F:0.1] (P.1) *"The quickest way to realize the brotherhood of man on Urantia is to effect the spiritual transformation of present-day humanity. The only technique for accelerating the natural trend of social evolution is that of applying spiritual pressure from above..."* [52:6.7] (P. 598) *"Religious revelation is essential to the realization of brotherhood on Urantia,"* the authors state.

Yes, and I expect it to be continuing.

The authors' summation and quotes were further instructive. The Teaching Mission can be considered that gentle pressure from above, urging us to spiritize our minds, and this must come in comprehensible increments. The teachers themselves pay tribute to the midwayers, who live between the material and spiritual planes and reportedly provide vital conduits to contact.

Quoting the Urantia papers again: *"What a transcendent service if, through this revelation, the Son of Man should be recovered from the tomb of traditional theology and be presented as the living Jesus to the church that bears his name, and to all other religions!"* [196:1.2] (P. 2090)

I believe that. And let's employ our cosmic consciousness and universe awareness as best we can. I don't believe that the Teaching Mission or *the Urantia Book* initiatives are nearly all of the Correcting Time on Planet Urantia. A spiritual renaissance is underway, an adjudication, and of course, it encompasses all of the worlds that rebelled, and it also includes the remainder of the local universe of Nebadon where the rebellion is a powerful teaching tool.

435

Even beyond the local universe of well over 600 inhabited planets, one would think that the adjudication of a 37-planet rebellion against God would warrant broadcast news.

I turned to the Urantia papers themselves for a summary of the magazine piece, and on page 1025 it poured out some perceptions that fused much of my understanding on how our mission experiences dating back to New Zealand link into the Urantia papers.

"Recent rulings handed down from the Most Highs of Edentia, and later confirmed by the Ancients of Days of Uversa, strongly suggest that this bestowal Melchizedek is destined to take the place of the fallen planetary prince, Caligastia. If our conjectures in this respect are correct, it is altogether possible that Machiventa Melchizedek may again appear in person on Urantia and in some modified manner resume the role of the dethroned Planetary Prince, or else appear on earth to function as vicegerent Planetary Prince representing Christ Michael, who now actually holds the title of Planetary Prince of Urantia."

The paper also states: *"And all these speculations associated with the certainty of future appearances of both Magisterial and Trinity Teacher Sons, in conjunction with the explicit promise of the Creator Son to return sometime, make Urantia a planet of future uncertainty and render it one of the most interesting and intriguing spheres in all the universe of Nebadon. It is altogether possible that, in some future age when Urantia is approaching the era of Light and Life, after the affairs of the Lucifer rebellion and the Caligastia secession have been finally adjudicated, we may witness the presence on Urantia, simultaneously, of Machiventa, Adam, Eve, and Christ Michael, as well as either a Magisterial Son or even Trinity Teacher Sons."*

A BROKEN LINK TO CELESTIALS

There was still more research to do. As I was more convinced than ever that Michael and the Teaching Mission are an authentic extension of the Fifth Epochal Revelation to Urantia, I had even more incentive to explore the broken link that had defamed and eliminated the Urantia movement's evangelical wings, created a bastion of defense against any celestial messages from anywhere, and forged what seemed to be an elitist attitude that spanned from the traditional churches all the way to the new age mystics. It seemed that they believed one should only use the new religion of Jesus in the Urantia papers, and nothing else. I believed such an attitude would lead immediately to religious bigotry based on immature human judgments.

But I knew the Urantia Foundation and Urantia Brotherhood, which had united to take firm anti-Grimsley control and power over the book in 1984 had itself fallen apart disastrously in the early 1990's. As an enthusiastic new reader in 1991, I was barraged with a blizzard of paper, legal and personal accusations, defenses and counter-charges.

I was quite impressed with the text of the book, and unimpressed with what seemed a broadside of personality spats.

Who were these battling personalities? It turns out that the main players in Urantian discord over the years were five fraternity brothers from the University of Kansas, all of whom would become leaders in the movement. They were Martin Myers, Vern Grimsley, Richard Keeler, David Gray and Hoite Caston.

I learned that the conflict over messages and who is receiving them had roots much deeper than 1983. The biggest issue shaped up as some Urantia gossipists had talked about from time to time: Who is the anointed heir to Urantia, the one who represents a new generation of leadership, the one who might be contacted by celestials, the real and genuine member of the "Reserve Corps of Destiny," a designation of honor that seemed to be so relevant to Urantians, and a point of contention.

A TRADITION OF DISCORD

I recalled at this point the much-respected "Christy," the late Emma Christensen, who had survived Dr. Sadler's death in 1969 and had passed in 1982. In her final words to the movement, she urged leaders to rise above the current acrimony, divisiveness and regional rivalries and "make spirituality a priority" in the days ahead. So discord was happening then, in 1982.

I recalled more history: Martin Myers, a lawyer, had taken residence in Chicago in 1968 to help manage the Urantia Revelation and look after Dr. and Mrs. Lena Sadler. They reportedly had longed for 'some young man' to come and help with the revelatory work. Christy was a prolific transcriber and administrator from the beginning, in those long ago days of manual typewriters and carbon paper. She was also aging, and the batons had to be passed.

I thought,... if I were to write a movie treatment about Urantia history today, I might pattern it after the Facebook epic, The Social Network, and call it The Urantia Network: Five fraternity brothers from Kansas vie for control of a sacred book, an epochal spiritual revelation.

Where were the first signs of conflict over celestial messages? It surfaced in a book by Larry Mullins, A History of the Urantia Papers, written with Rev. Meredith Springer.

Remarkably, I discovered that critics such as Mullins and Hoite Caston had painted Christy with the very same brush as they would paint Grimsley many years later.

Mullins' book noted that Christy was becoming increasingly irritated by Myers' take-charge attitudes and actions in the Chicago headquarters in the 1970's. I recalled that she urged an end to personal, competitive strife before she died, and to establish "spiritual priorities" and work together.

Myers moved strongly toward protecting the Urantia Papers and the trademark blue circles by copyright. Christy agreed with the copyright mandate. He ordered the original printing plates for *the Urantia Book* destroyed in 1971, the same year that he and Grimsley, in California, were named as Special Agents for the Urantia organizations.

Urantia Foundation trustees are appointed by themselves, not elected. Myers joined the board in 1973. He would be deposed in 1992 after an acrimonious era of divisive legal battles with book study organizations. He sued to get back on the board and failed.

Mullins' main point of contention with Christy was her using alleged midwayer contact in matters of Urantia Book editing, including the correction of grammatical errors in the first edition of 1955. He demeans her alleged "unique" status with the published pages, and the reality of her contact. He states that there has been and will not be any future contact with midwayers since the book's publication. He quotes the aging Dr. Sadler, before his death, noting that the midwayers had told humans that we are 'on our own' and that they had left 'without even a goodbye.' Rev. Meredith Sprunger, who assisted Mullins with his book, had made this point of the midwayers leaving as an absolute truth as well.

When the midwayers stated that we are "on our own," then I can only assume that Mullins and others took it to mean for all time to come, eternity. How could they believe that when such a proclamation for eternity could never be made in the spiritual realms? How could they not surmise that the comment had to do with the actual publishing of the book, the job at hand, which humans themselves had to do? Why do the two men want to close the door to midwayer or celestial contact in the certainty that it isn't possible? They unabashedly speak for the celestials in this matter, when they seem not to be able to speak objectively themselves.

Their reasoning for Christy and later for Grimsley, is that emotional stresses were just too much, her bearing the full weight of the revelation and Dr. Sadler now 92; and that Grimsley, in 1983 was also in a "serious emotional state" after Christy's death and in the midst of purchasing a 25-acre property in Clayton, CA, for his Family of God Foundation's Spiritual Renaissance Institute. There must be some logical reason for hearing 'voices,' and Mullins and Sprunger grapple with any other reality except the reality of such celestial guidance.

CHRISTY AND VERN

The reality of a close relationship between Vern and Christy is evidenced in a letter from the period. It also expresses their vision of bringing forward the biblical Jesus of Nazareth into his greater reality as Christ Michael of Urantia's Jesus papers. This would wed the 4th and 5th epochal revelations.

It seems there were already forces that didn't agree with their ideas, their plans or their methods. Grimsley wrote:

Miss Emma Christensen
533 Diversey Parkway
Chicago, Illinois 60614

The Teaching Mission

Dear Christy,

Your recent, delightful letter – in which you shared with us your joy over our new URANTIA Society and our global radio broadcasting – was a pleasure to us all.

Moreover, the enthusiastic words in your letter regarding our worldwide Family of God broadcast – "This is a real inspiration. Just wish Poppy Sadler were here to know about it" – started me thinking about those earlier days which Nancy and I shared with you and Dr. Sadler in the planning of our mission. I too wish he were here to rejoice with us in our subsequent growth. Thus, in a mood of nostalgia, I took out some of my personal files (consisting of hundreds of letters from Urantia friends) and reviewed our many past correspondences and my notes from countless telephone conversations with 533 Diversey through the years, clear back to the middle and late 1950s.

One letter from Dr. Sadler particularly caught my eye. It was his immediate response to our Family of God Foundation Prospectus, in which we formally outlined our project of U.S. radio coverage by the end of 1975, global broadcasting by 1980, the training of teachers and leaders and serving as a "John the Baptist" movement to prepare the way for the eventual worldwide acceptance of *the URANTIA Book* on the planet. I am enclosing a Xeroxed copy of that particular letter from Dr. Sadler, and his reaction to the idea of the Family of God Foundation; it brings back to my mind many memories of conversations with him both before and after he wrote that letter, and the numerous excellent bits of advice and counsel which he provided us in founding and developing the Family of God Foundation.

It also brought me a fleeting moment of pain as I reflected upon the unfortunate misunderstandings on the parts of two or three newer members of the movement who have not been fully aware of this long history of the development of the Family of God Foundation in complete <u>cooperation</u> with the URANTIA Foundation and the URANTIA Brotherhood, and the well-thought reasons for which, during all these years, the Family of God Foundation has been carefully fostered. In reviewing our years of correspondence with Chicago this morning, I became mightily moved by the conviction that nothing must be permitted to drive the slightest wedge of suspicion or distrust between the work of the Family of God Foundation and the headquarters of the URANTIA movement in Chicago.

Here in Berkeley, we require that all Family of God Foundation coworkers must FIRST become members of the URANTIA Brotherhood; this has always been our policy. Our loyalties to Chicago are clear and unwavering. The Family of God Foundation has become both a helpful spiritual ministry within the URANTIA movement (see the Oregon letter for example) and a growing spiritual ministry to the entirety of the world.

439

The Teaching Mission

We have long enjoyed strong support from old forum members, Brotherhood Executive Committeemen and URANTIA Foundation trustees. There are good reasons for this support: These long-term students of *the URANTIA Book* are more aware of the history, development and purposes of the Family of God Foundation. They are more vividly cognizant of such quotes in the book as these:

A Melchizedek of Nebabon writes on page 1041, "All Urantia is waiting for the proclamation of the ennobling message of Michael, unencumbered by the accumulated doctrines and dogmas of nineteenth centuries of contact with the religions of evolutionary origin. The hour is striking for presenting to Buddhism, to Christianity, to Hinduism, even to the peoples of all faiths, not the gospel about Jesus, but the living, spiritual reality of the gospel of Jesus." And the Master himself declares on page 1930: "The persistent preaching of this gospel of the kingdom will some day bring to all nations a new and unbelievable liberation, intellectual freedom, and religious liberty."

Thus – as you so well know – *the URANTIA Book* clearly and repeatedly calls for the preaching of this spiritual message in our day. This the Family of God Foundation is doing. And it was a moving experience for all of us last summer when we heard longtime URANTIA leader Anna Rawson at the General Conference in Evanston declare before the full assembly of hundreds of Brotherhood members that in her opinion the work of the Family of God Foundation is comparable in scope and planetary importance to the work of the apostle Paul, and that we are carrying the URANTIA message to mankind "with such enthusiasm and newness and freshness" that we are destined to "revive" the world.

Your support has meant so much to us too. For instance, in one of your letters to me back in March of 1966, you not only gave us some superb advice, you succinctly expressed the essential purpose of the Family of God Foundation. It has been this sort of advice which has been so valuable to us through the years, and which we have been attempting to follow. You wrote:

"I agree heartily with you in your thinking regarding the mention of *The Urantia Book* in your lectures and on the radio. Of course this should not be done. In other words, Vern, what we want to do is to try to get across to the public some of the truths contained in *the Urantia Book*; in short to lay some fuses for its eventual wide distribution, but that time has not yet come. I am glad you are bootlegging some of the materials in your sermons. The book is of course secondary to the revelation. We must teach the soul-stirring message of the book. Jesus carried no book under his arm as 'he went about doing good' and teaching about his heavenly Father. I depend upon your judgment and know you will be wise in what you say."

This very idea – that the Family of God Foundation is laying fuses for the eventual wide distribution of *the URANTIA Book* – is the fundamental concept underlying both our lifework and the Family of God Foundation itself. It is this which you and Dr. Sadler and numerous other leaders of the URANTIA movement have for years encouraged us to do. And now we are doing it. Your counsel has been of tremendous assistance.

As you well know, the Family of God Foundation was no causal accident. It did not just "happen." It came into existence as the result of many years of prayer and seeking of the Father's will, and what we are doing is based on two decades of study of the teachings of *the URANTIA Book*. The URANTIA movement, rightly, does not engage in publicity campaigns. "The hour has not come" for proclaiming the book to the world. BUT – "The hour IS striking" (direct quote from 104) for proclaiming the newly-revealed religion of Jesus to the world ... in order to prepare the way for the ultimate planetary acceptance of the fifth epochal revelation. The Family of God Foundation is engaged in precisely that task. And we are presently reaching over 100 million people internationally yearly with "the greatest truths that mortal man can ever hear – the living gospel of the fatherhood of God and the brotherhood of man. (2086)

The reason we at the Family of God Foundation established this work of spiritual teaching as a legal entity – a nonprofit foundation – was in order to facilitate our function in a world of myriad legalities. Example: lawyers long ago advised us that it was better to sign our broadcasting contracts with radio stations as a corporate foundation rather than as private individuals. (It even enables us to acquire a 15% reduction in broadcasting costs). Needless to say, our foundation was not established in competition with the URANTIA movement, but in service of the URANTIA movement.

The Family of God Foundation has brought into existence within the URANTIA movement for good and important reasons – many of which are so far-reaching that none of us will live to witness their full consummation. Just one example among many: the first known URANTIA study group in all of Asia came into existence in Yeditha, India, in 1975 through the broadcasting outreach of the Family of God Foundation. And such events as these are but the first intimations of thrilling things to come.

You, Christy, have personally helped, inspired and encouraged us immensely in our work through all these years. I am writing on behalf of all of us here at the Family of God Foundation to express our profound gratitude to you. You have in every way assisted and backed us – and the result is now a worldwide work of spiritual teaching which is preparing the planet for the fifth epochal revelation. The Father's hand is in this rapidly and attained such impact globally in such a short span of time without tremendous help from on high. And we thank the Father for the tremendous privilege of engaging in such a joyous task.

Bless you, Christy, for all your assistance to us!

And much love to you from a fellow coworker in the URANTIA movement!

Affectionately,
Vern
VBG/vbg

So, in 1976, one can see cracks beginning to appear in the relationship with Chicago leadership. Myers has already begun his litigation-riddled reign and there would be struggles ahead for prominence, control, and monetary support.

Where Grimsley saw a ministry for the 'entirety' of the world's people, Myers saw a 'sin-seared' and rebellion-scarred planet where the sacred book must be protected by law. Where Grimsley wanted to bring a spiritually hungry world gently into the Urantia teachings through the common bond of Jesus, critics talked of his 'bootlegging' the book without giving credit.

In summing up the years before 1983, I could see discord from the beginning about the validity of Christy's messages after Dr. Sadler's assertion that the midwayers had left.

Christy's death may have aborted any further criticisms of her alleged contact, but in 1982 the mantle of leadership seemed to have been passed on to the charismatic Grimsley, an exceptional orator and philosophy scholar, the colorful presence who had become the centerpiece of the Urantia movement. He was not a Trustee, as was Myers and remained a Urantia 'special agent.'

He would become a big target, especially since Christy had noted frequently that he was indeed a member of Urantia's Corps of Destiny. The book says: "The twelve groups of Urantia destiny reservists are composed of mortal inhabitants of the sphere who have been rehearsed for numerous critical positions on earth and are in readiness to act in possible planetary emergencies."

This became a matter of prestige, personalities and politics. The Family of God profile continued to grow and bring in more money, some of it no doubt diverted from contributions that might have been directed to the Urantia Brotherhood in Chicago.

Then came the pivotal year of 1983. Grimsley began getting messages from the midwayers. He was told to be prepared for a nuclear attack that would 'touch American soil.' There was the strong backlash from the Urantia movement. The Reagan administration and the Soviet regime went to the very brink of nuclear war. It was a fascinating three-way timeline, all leading to the weekend of November 18-20.

FIRST STRIKE AS STRATEGY

First, I plowed into former Central Intelligence Agency analyst Peter Pry's well-documented book, War Scare, and the website, both providing historical information on exactly how close we came to all-out nuclear war in September-November, 1983, and especially near the dates when the Family of God was seriously worried about it. The sources reveal a situation much more perilous than U.S. intelligence thought at the time, leading them to greatly underestimate the impact that the Reagan administration's words and policies were having inside the Soviet Union.

In fact, Reagan's confrontational rhetoric and the huge U.S. arms build-up were substantiating a long-held view in the Soviet military that the U.S. was maneuvering toward a first strike, and that, indeed, a first strike was the best possible option and likely the only option that they themselves had to win such a war. Soviet textbooks from the 70s and 80s now confirm the prevalence of both views, as have former Soviet military officers.

In 1981, the Soviets were already fearful and frustrated that their defenses weren't adequate, having been revealed so by U.S. spy plane probes which happened with impunity. Premier Leonid Brezhnev announced to a reportedly amazed audience that the U.S. was planning a first strike once it achieved military superiority.

He also announced the advent of Operation VRYAN, which mobilized every worldwide Russian resource to glean every possible bit of information about the intentions of the U.S. and the North Atlantic Treaty Organization. The partnership of two jealous and bickering agencies, the GRU and the KGB, was surprising enough. The massive devotion of manpower to this mission was unprecedented. At that time, War Scare author Peter Pry notes that the KGB alone "dwarfed both the CIA and FBI" in its size.

So, seemingly unknown to U.S. intelligence, the Soviets expected to be attacked at some point. Reagan, as late as 1983, expressed disbelief that they would think such a thing. There has been revealed by subsequent history a serious disconnect between our intelligence understandings at the time and cold reality.

Tensions, arms build-ups, missile placements, and nasty rhetoric were all part of the Cold War scene. The military machines rolled in both countries, and when Brezhnev passed on in 1982, his successor was Yuri Andropov. He is described by Pry as the architect of VRYAN, which is a Russian acronym for 'surprise first nuclear strike.' So a man implicated in massive oppressions and millions of deaths in Poland succeeded as premier.

In September, 1983, a KAL Korean airliner was shot down by a Soviet jet, ushering in a dangerous game of inflammatory accusations and condemnations. Reagan called the USSR an 'evil empire' in a speech to evangelical Christians and it surprisingly hit global headlines.

The facts now show that U.S. military submarines and jets had been repeatedly violating Soviet territory for months before the airliner shootdown. More than 20 U-2 spy planes had actually been shot down over the years, dating back to the days of President Dwight Eisenhower. The U.S. was consistently testing Soviet defenses, finding gaps that embarrassed the Russians, raising their fear level and promoting an indelible idea in Russia that the U.S. had gained superiority and they were lagging dangerously behind.

As Reagan escalated the conflict, fears grew of a U.S. first strike, with that related idea that only a Soviet first strike could win a war. Conversely, the attitude that seemed to be prevalent in the U.S. was that we were trying to catch up to the Soviets or so went the political rhetoric to get military build-up funds through Congress.

In either and both cases, it led to huge expenditures of money and manpower in the production of bombs, missiles, tanks, planes, nuclear subs, and all the other trappings of war. It fueled the war industries and heightened tensions constantly. It was all keeping up with the Joneses in a highly volatile way.

The Korean airliner had reportedly entered Soviet airspace along its parallel route from New York to Seoul. This presumed navigation error scrambled Soviet defenses. When it reportedly crossed into Soviet airspace a second time, a Russian jet pilot chose to shoot it down, with two missiles.

A key to pilot Gennadi Osipovich's motivation may be seen in the fact that he was paid for the kill and complained that it should have been more. In an interview 13 years later, the dedicated communist, said he had seen that it was a passenger plane but knew they could be easily fitted for a spy mission. He took some pride in his kill and reasoned that it should have been worth more than 200 rubles.

At any rate, the Soviets maintained it was indeed a spy plane and that the provocation had been created by the Americans to discredit the Soviets, condemn them to the world for the senseless loss of life, and pave the way for the subsequent congressional bills that greatly expanded the U.S. war machine in its quest for superiority.

BATTLES AT THE BRINK

Highly advanced Pershing II missiles were also set to be deployed in Europe to face Russia and counter their many missiles already facing the NATO countries. The Soviet knew that these placements would disastrously reduce their possible time for reaction to a first strike, to about six minutes. This heightened fear of an anticipated U.S. first strike fueled the strategy of making a first strike as the best and only way to win.

The deployment had not yet begun, but some Soviets believed that it would create a decisive element of surprise for the U.S. to attack well before the deployment. And the combined American-British war game in November would then be an even better cover.

This would be the largest WWIII simulation war exercise in history, ABLE ARCHER-83, November 2-12, 1983. It would be a full-scale alert and a full round of simulated reactions. The Soviet Operation VRYAN was on full alert to tip off any signs of a NATO strike.

At the time, the Reagan administration was also financing insurgencies in Angola and Nicaragua, and had actually invaded the island of Grenada on October 26 to overthrow an aborted reign by Cuban revolutionaries. Battle lines were drawn. The Soviets expected a possible invasion of Nicaragua. The U.S. was concerned about possible missile placements there.

Reagan's announcement of the Strategic Defense Initiative, bringing outer space into the Cold War equation, prompted loud denunciations from the Soviet, which called it aggression and a provocation to war.

British complaints about the Grenada invasion greatly increased communications between Margaret Thatcher's government and the Reagan administration. Grenada was part of the British Commonwealth and the British were left out of the mix, which infuriated Prime Minister Thatcher. The Soviets reportedly mistook this spike as war planning for that strategic first strike against them.

Meanwhile, Reagan and advisors appeared oblivious to the seriousness of the situation, seeming to believe that the strong protestations in Russia were only political rhetoric, generated for the Russian people. I wondered: Did he think the Soviet rhetoric mirrored the kind of political posturing he himself was taking to get military funding for the Pentagon and its war industries?

I recalled President Eisenhower warning the American people of this self-same war industry that could suck up our wealth and literally leave hungry children in its wake. Prime Minister Thatcher eventually visited Reagan personally in early 1984, advising him to tone down his evil empire provocations because the Russians were taking it more seriously than he was.

Thus, in November 1983 fear of nuclear war was commonplace in the U.S. and there was a 'better safe than sorry' run to build shelters and locate the nearest civil defense haven. If the midwayers had an ideal place to safeguard *the Urantia Book* and some knowledgeable, spiritual-minded survivors, then the Family of God's new center might be it, a safer location than Chicago. But critics still note today that Clayton was within range of some likely military targets.

Pry's book notes that ABLE ARCHER 83 that November did not trigger WWIII because the situation cooled because of the last minute revelations of two embedded Soviet spies.

CALLING ON MIDWAYERS

I decided I should go next to the midwayers themselves, and so to their alleged point of contact on the planet, George Barnard, and the 11.11 platoon of midwayers and teachers. I had corresponded with George years ago. He was still in Northern Australia, and now had a global network of channelers and spiritual activists who are attuned to the 11.11 prompts and transmit lessons from a variety of spiritual personalities. They seemed to exist in parallel service to the Correcting Time but I couldn't begin to fathom the various roles of the myriad of universe personalities who were involved on the planet in these eventful years.

Even though the midwayers had worked with the *The Urantia Book* commission and Dr. Sadler's forum for years, I didn't know about a connection today, after their alleged departure from the project, and the alleged and contested connections that followed. I wondered if connections were forever severed today between the midwayers and the custodians of the book.

Barnard himself has no Urantia roots. He only came to realize in the 1990's that the supposed 'dead spirits' he had been seeing since childhood, around the family dinner table, were those self-same 1,111 planetary secondary midwayers and co-residents of the planet described in *the Urantia book*. Once this discovery was made, George visited some of the Teaching Mission groups in the U.S. He maintains friendships and continues to market an Akashic Construct for meditation that came from his hypnotism therapy work. In his books, he relates how midwayers have long been sending him troubled patients for healing.

When I approached him for midwayer input, George already was aware of an incident in September, 1983, that colored his thinking. For some years, people have been equating this earlier incident with the episode in November, but the dates don't match with Grimsley's messages. Midwayers, however, may well have been involved.

In September, with alerts heightened after the Korean airliner went down, the Soviets had launched a brand new eye-in-the-sky surveillance system called OKO. It was very new, and when it indicated on September 26, shortly after midnight, that the U.S. had fired its intercontinental Minuteman missiles and a nuclear attack was underway (as expected), it posed a frightening dilemma for Lt. Col. Stainslav Petrov, the duty officer in charge of the surveillance satellite.

Petrov waited for several agonizing minutes without signaling the alarm, painfully waiting for radar confirmation. It did not confirm, and the duty officer decided on his own that the new system had malfunctioned and given a false warning. Those few minutes of nuclear nightmare ended Petrov's military career with a nervous breakdown. He reportedly received a small retirement home outside Moscow and did not have to wait his turn to get a telephone.

The Soviets were likely distressed again, over the failure of their new advanced warning system. ABLE ARCHER 83 was only five weeks away.

On October 10, 2010, George Barnard replied to my inquiry with a transmission that truly lifted my question of their involvement up to a level that relates to their long experience on the planet. The words came from Bzutu, a midwayer Chief:

"There are circumstances under which a simple 'yes or no' to your earnest questions will hardly suffice, and this is one of those circumstances. However, this lecture is not to be a 'poor, poor me' on either your part or mine, because misunderstandings will continue to plague us for centuries to come, as we try to bring the only partially-adept-to-receive into line with those of more regular worlds.

"Consider now the claim of Nostradamus that 'the god stands nearby.' Hardly! His Thought Adjuster had business to attend elsewhere, and the fully appraised DEF-5 was certainly no god, nor has she attained that elevated status by this present time.

"Your dear friend ... and mine ... Dante Alighieri was allowed to catch but a fleeting glimpse of the smartly attired Beatrice (ABC-3), neither knowing her to be a permanent resident of the planet, nor ever understanding just how many celestials shared in his writings.

"And, my brother, your Joan of Arc was equally fooled by her own mind in believing she was under instructions from Saints Michael, Margaret and Catharine. Michael, yes! Once again, here we find a project succeeding well, yet misunderstandings galore.

"How we battled for so many years to make you hear, understand, catch on, to what we wanted you to know and act upon, when you battled to understand, yet excelled in seeing us before you, each time we attempted to converse. Not in our world's past nor future will we find many that are ideal on both scores — the visual and the audible. We carry on with our tasks, never give up, and only in retrospect will those of your kin who assisted us find recognition on Mansonia and beyond, as will the one (Vern Grimsley) about whom you inquire.

'We, on our part, may well be advised about circumstances that may become a close call in potentially dooming all life on this planet, and we may be ordered to go into action. We are rarely, if ever apprised in advance of the outcome of our efforts to thwart human free will, as was the case in which you viewed the Russian technician."

Along with the transmission, George offered the idea that the midwayers have nothing more to say on the matter.

I noticed a quotation on the bottom of George's e-mail: *"You lit a Flame, and it will become a Raging Fire."* –ABC-22.

Was this the midwayer personality who worked with Dr. William Sadler and his group in bringing forth the Urantia text? In a memorial service to Emma Christensen, I had heard Grimsley on an audiotape asking the departed matriarch to 'say hello to ABC and the others.' Barnard later told me that it was not the same midwayer personality.

I wondered if the roles of Grimsley and Barnard might be related, both being humans working with midwayers, both helping them deal with emergency situations on the planet. Again the Urantia papers provided perspective on humans who are pressed into service.

On page 1257, the book notes that these mortals benefit from spiritual influences that the midwayers are important in facilitating, as they were in the appearance of the Urantia papers in the last century. "Such potential contact mortals of the evolutionary worlds are mobilized in the numerous reserve corps, and it is, to a certain extent, through these small groups of forward-looking personalities that spiritual civilization is advanced and the Most Highs are able to rule in the kingdoms of men." The book notes that "these reservists of destiny have seldom been emblazoned on the pages of human history."

The teachers have told us in recent years that the ranks of this Corps of Destiny have been greatly expanded with the ongoing Correcting Time on the worlds of the rebellion.

I wondered if ABC-22 of today could actually be persuaded to provide more information, something less philosophical and more direct. Perhaps I should produce that timeline sequence of Cold War events and Family of God messages.

MESSAGES PROMPT TIRADE

To capture the political element in the drama, a new document came into hand that appeared to show the very crux of the determined attack that eventually brought Grimsley's organization down. It includes the transcript of a meeting between Grimsley and 26 Urantia movement leaders in California on November 1, 1983. Grimsley had been receiving audio messages at odd times, and the latest one: *"Prepare for World War III"* had caused a stir.

The revealing document was a lengthy report to the Urantia Foundation and Brotherhood published on June 17, 1984, copyrighted by the author, Hoite Caston, and called "Vern Grimsley Message Evaluation." It is replete with warnings that quoting is not permissible and it is intended only for people in the Urantia movement. As I had been an active reader for over 30 years, and also a journalist doing historical research, I read it.

It was caustic and deeply personal. His condemnations of Grimsley's messages were strong, and apparently influential in the demise of FOG and Grimsley's retirement from the Urantia movement. A full reading would share much additional perspective and provide a strong sense of the Urantia community discussions centering around the messages, especially Caston's November 1, 1983, tape-recorded session featuring Grimsley and those members of the California Urantia communities.

Caston showed up ready to do battle, following up the meeting with a long list of his concerns and using the tape recording in his subsequent evaluation reports. As he faced off against the strong physical and rhetorical presence of Grimsley in that room, it now seems to have been the first battle in a war for control of this little known epochal revelation that Caston felt had been upstaged by either hallucinations or by manipulation. He was adamant that the Revelation could positively not be held hostage to someone who hears mysterious, disembodied, and alleged messages and uses them to control the movement.

How did this major personal confrontation come to pass? I decided to do the three-way timeline, linking the world war that did not happen, the war within Urantia that did happen, and find some vital pieces of the puzzle to understand all of this in a proper context.

I was betting that some essential points had been missed, as always. This might be in like manner to the Fellowship Herald article that proclaimed the reality of the Teaching Mission and the Magisterial Mission without knowing it, and looked into the possible future without observing the realities of the present, and the past 20 years.

TIMELINE 1982-84

November 1982. Leonid Brezhnev dies and hard-core mass murderer Yuri Andropov, called the 'Butcher of Poland', takes over as premier. Hatred and distrust in the Cold War ratchets up. U.S. President Ronald Reagan is staunchly anti-communist.

December 16, 1982. Vern Grimsley surveys a property near Clayton, California, for the growth of the Family of God Foundation and the new Spiritual Renaissance Institute, now at about 40 staff members. He receives what he called a 'contact' while standing under a large oak tree. The voice says: *"This is it."* He calls Martin Myers about it, for one.

At the November 1 meeting, Grimsley had already told the story a number of times. He spoke again:

"I was instructed by a contact, not just a mental guidance, but a very different, and for me the first time, a very different phenomenon, which I'm not going to discuss in detail. Dr. Sadler used to say, 'If I told you everything I knew about the exact details of how *The Urantia Book* came through, you'd still be just as confused as ever, and just as confused as I am.' And so, therefore, I am not going to be talking about the mechanics of it, but it was very different from the sort of praying and getting a sense of some inner guidance ... but an actual contact. And I did, as you know, purchase that place, St. Anthony's College, in Northern California."

January 7, 1983. Grimsley reports a "voice" telling him that he and members of the Family of God should be especially diligent for their safety, since they are an important team.

January 21. Grimsley reports the message: *"The hour has not come to publicize the book."* He relates on November 1 that he was not aware at the time of a movement by wealthy and dedicated reader Harry McMullen, a former FOG member, to launch a national magazine advertising campaign for *the Urantia Book*, due to hit in March. When he finds out via a phone call from Carolyn Kendall, he states that he subsequently shared the message with the Urantia Foundation and Brotherhood.

Critics would later note that Grimsley had said *"the hour has not come"* to promote the book for some years, nothing new except the claim of spiritual imposition. They note that McMullen had previous disagreements with Grimsley.

On November 1, Grimsley professes not to know the reason for the "hour has not come" message. He mentions a "mustard seed project" in Houston, Texas, Urantia circles, but didn't think that would be worth "this very sort of stern, loving but stern, wording" from the midwayers.

February. Premier Yuri Andropov, architect of the worldwide Operation VRYAN, is an advocate of the strike-first nuclear strategy—to find any inkling of an anticipated U.S. first strike, and then preempt it. His kidneys fail sometime this month. As a suffering near-invalid facing death, his mental state could be questioned.

February 26, 1983. Grimsley's meeting with the executive committee leads to an official statement by the Foundation, the Brotherhood, the General Council and the Trustees of the Foundation that there will be no media advertising and publicity about the book. Caston states later that this is but a reiteration of Grimsley's long-standing position and that his influence on the authorities was over-stated at the November 1 gathering. He makes note that the advertising campaign would have been very modest, only with reader ads in the back of magazines such as Psychology Today.

March 1983. Reagan announces the Strategic Defense Initiative. Moscow sees it as an act of aggression, to implement secret space weapons against the USSR.

September 1. Soviets shoot down the Korean airliner, killing all aboard, and leading to an escalation of fear and tension. The official Soviet newspaper, Tass, summed up their position: "The plan was to carry out without a hitch the intelligence operation, but if it was stymied, to turn all this into a political provocation against the Soviet Union... the entire responsibility for this tragedy rests wholly and fully with the leaders of the United States of America."

September 16. Grimsley gets the message: *"Don't split up the book."* It initiated a ten-minute session with the celestials who clarified that it should not be published in multiple volumes because the whole book is needed to understand the parts. They referred to such a division with the French translation that had led to uneven sales, and applauded the newer decision to print it in one volume.

Again, Grimsley appears unaware of another idea by McMullen. He relates on November 1: "Well, it turns out there was something of a movement afoot to ... want to put out maybe a paperback ... copies of *the Urantia Book* in multiple volumes. And some people are talking about just printing The Life and Teachings of Jesus as a kind of 'come on' ..."

Critic Hoite Caston later would note that McMullen was one of the first five members of the Family of God, had left the movement for family business reasons, but had been involved in several policy arguments with Grimsley over the years. He speculates in his report that this could have been a factor in the messages, which he nevertheless claims were only reiterations of Grimsley's long-held opinions about publishing the book.

The Caston report is filled with suppositions, speculations, hearsay, and rhetorical questions. It includes quotes from McMullen saying that the movement shouldn't be influenced by people who 'get messages in their bathtub,' as was the claim, and that the war scare messages could bring a torrent of damaging doomsday cult media coverage and discredit the Revelation.

September 1983. Andropov's health worsens. A kidney is removed. He moves into a special VIP hospital suite. He tries to continue running the country through associates, including Politburo protégé Mikhail Gorbachev.

September 26. The Soviet duty officer overrides a new surveillance system's warning that the U.S. had fired missiles. Had he heeded the message and not suspected a malfunction, the Soviets would have moved to full battle alert.

October 6. Grimsley receives an afternoon message: *"Prepare for the third world war. Be not anxious. Fear not. But be prepared."* He later noted that they put strong emphasis on the last two sentences. *When the messengers were questioned they added "Actively prepare ...."* And Grimsley was also told: *"Tell people you don't know when because we don't know when."* And also: *"Get maps of escape routes. Store food and water. Know where fallout shelters are, or build them as needed. This one will touch American soil."*

Grimsley related later that he had received some inkling that this kind of message would be coming forth. He and the voices had initiated a protocol he insisted upon, "almost a ritualistic series of checking and rechecking before I pass any of this along to anybody else, because this is a very difficult subject."

October 7. The next message to Grimsley is *"Confirmed. Proceed."*

October 10. Urantia Foundation and Brotherhood leaders gather in Chicago to hear Brotherhood President John Hales report on the events in California, from where he had just returned.

October 11. Grimsley gets a call from Hales. By telephone he writes down eight questions pertaining to the messages and the role of the Urantia organizations. He sips on some more coffee and opens a session with the "Voice."

On November 1, he relates that the answers came in two different sessions. In the first, the midwayers had been brief and guarded in their responses, but after a break to obtain additional permission, they returned and were more forthcoming.

To the first question of whether he had any doubts of the messages, Grimsley said he had none, and noted that about 50 people at the Family of God shared his belief in the contact.

Is World War III inevitable? The answer was: *"Yes, unless we send an emergency son on an emergency mission. This is under active discussion. This is our view as of Tuesday morning, October 11, 1983."*

Is nuclear holocaust inevitable? The answer was a curt: *"No."* Grimsley noted that this didn't change from the first and second session.

Should the Urantia Brotherhood take any official action? The answer: *"Only what you have agreed and discussed. You have been well led in your deliberations."* Grimsley acknowledged that this was the beginning of some "kind of fuzzy answers" since he and Urantia officials had talked about so many things and not always agreed.

In the second session, the message was amplified. *"The institute in Clayton is projected to be in the top ten percent of functional/protectable locations given current data."* Conversely, the Chicago Urantia headquarters was in the top ten functional but the bottom ten percent in protectable. The 'voice' advised keeping open the mailing address but be prepared for a possible evacuation to Clayton as an emergency headquarters.

How much advance notice will we get? *"Maybe none. Study the news daily. Rely on radio over TV. Keep fresh batteries in cold storage and tube radios tuned to all news stations."*

Truly, in a push-button nuclear war, missiles were only minutes away from any major target on the globe. With Cold War confrontations happening constantly, one can imagine the collective concerns of a group of spiritual people in the influence of a persuasive minister who laid out the messages in a caring and sharing way. If Grimsley was using all this to control people, however, it was certainly subtle. He himself expressed wonder himself and presided over a scenario of joint exploration.

The second session with the midwayers was "a lot more laid back," said Grimsley. "It's like they were kicking their feet up on the desk and saying: 'Okay, well, we'll talk about it'." They shared these messages:

"Concerning timing, as difficult as this may be to mortal comprehension, there is much that we don't know... There is much that we don't know. Concerning many of these matters, we can only speculate. So we therefore repeat: You may not know because we may not know. Be not anxious. Fear not, but be prepared. And we love you, all of you. Proceed as if this were your final instruction."

Grimsley noted that this touch of finality was a relief to him personally. "Otherwise," he said, "it's like waiting for the other shoe to drop all the time."

At the November 1 gathering in Los Angeles, Grimsley added a layer of his understanding regarding "Prepare for World War III," noting: "I checked the definition of a world war. It

452

means one in which all the major powers of the world are involved. That's the usual definition."

As I mulled over this, I was reminded of the status of midwayers on the planet, certainly co-residents but, like us, not knowledgeable about what future events may come. Midwayer Chief Bzutu had said that they simply go into action, not knowing the outcome for sure. And here seemed a case like others Bzutu had mentioned, in which human understanding is askew and the results undetermined. Neither humans nor midwayers have the proverbial crystal ball, both of us being just children of the universe.

October 16. The Family of God mails letters to 100 Urantia leaders around the world, especially new contacts in Paris and Asia, advising of the war warnings and the sanctuary efforts at the Clayton institute, which is nestled on three sides by mountain peaks but actually not deemed by experts to be a completely safe haven from nuclear fallout.

The mailing was not on behalf of the Urantia Foundation and Brotherhood though Grimsley had been a "special agent" for some ten years. It would become a point of contention that the mailing was not authorized and that it deleteriously linked the Urantia organizations to the alleged messages, guilt by association, as Grimsley was a well-known champion of the book.

His supposed "messages" were apparently appearing to some as manipulation, using proxy votes from unseen messengers on high to effect policy for the organizations. I recalled that the two projects to divide the book and promote it in the media had been undermined by these special orders. But Grimsley, of course, had admitted little or no concrete knowledge of McMullen's ideas at the November 1 meeting.

It crossed my mind that his reports of a celestial message might also be added inducement to get the financing to buy St. Anthony's in the first place. It seems that motives are always questioned, everybody's and all the time. Both Caston's motives and Grimsley's could be questioned; my motives could be questioned for doing this research and writing something from it. If I'm criticized, the motives of my critics can be questioned.

I also recalled that Grimsley advised the Urantia questioners that the midwayers said they should take no official actions on the matter. The mailing, then, was naturally from the Family of God, which was committed to the messages where the Urantia organizations were definitely not. Grimsley once said he would be the "lightning rod" for the messages if they proved to be false.

Later, Caston would liken this and other of Grimsley's actions as working to effect a Urantia power transfer to his Clayton Institute and to pre-empt the democratic workings of the organizations. He sarcastically noted, in what was perhaps the biggest crisis to threaten the movement, if not the whole world, that the democratic Urantia organizations were being asked not to lead.

The Teaching Mission

I was thinking again, at this point, that money would either be flowing to the Urantia organizations or to the Family of God and the new Spiritual Renaissance Institute. The question at the time could have been whether the Revelation itself is being serviced with funding, or Grimsley's institutions, which were taking a much broader position, to represent every child of God on the planet.

October 23. Jim Mills writes a letter to Martin Myers, later posted on the Urantia Fellowship archive. He notes his work at Florida State University in studying psychic phenomenon.

Mills quotes some notes from Dr. Sadler regarding the reception of the Urantia papers in the 1920's. Sadler notes that there are "some unusual activities of the marginal consciousness." Says Mills: "These included writing, talking, hearing, which he called 'clairaudience,' seeing, thinking, remembering, acting, personalization, and combined and associated psychic."

Mills quotes Dr. Sadler dramatically: "The technique of the reception of *The Urantia Book* in no way parallels or impinges upon any of the above phenomena of the marginal consciousness." In his twisted reasoning, he comments on Grimsley's messages: "This removes it from claims of consideration for any events related to the Urantia Revelation."

Here it was. The research was striking gold. Mills can only see that methods used by celestials to produce a printed 2,100 page book on the planet, are not the same methods by which spiritual forces have been communicating with humans for generations. To Mills, this one method of communication, which mysteriously produced a singular book on the planet is okay since it involves his perfect English Urantia Book. But in his mind he separates this particular form and incident of communications from any other, and expresses doubt about anyone, any movement, any other kind communications technique, or any kind of message at all. I truly believe that the celestials can use any number of communications methods to reach humans and they have told us so.

Mills dismisses all other forms of alleged communications with spiritual messengers because they don't have *the Urantia book* to prove them. Seemingly under the influence of academic strictures of proof and lab experiments, Mills writes a narrative that gives the Foundation all the rationale they need to ban the concept of getting spiritual advice from spiritual teachers for the foreseeable future. The policy is based on the false rationale that none of the other methods other than the mysterious, still hazy book creation project are reliable for guidance of any kind, personal or group.

Mills notes that all of the "'clairaudience' techniques are 'products of the subconscious mind,' although he fails to quote Dr. Sadler in saying so. He comes down hard: The people at the Family of God getting these messages 'need diagnosis rather than responsibility. I would be fearful of placing my future in the hands of such people. I would strongly recommend that they be impeached for conduct unbecoming their offices.'"

He goes on into another blistering paragraph: "Now, this is the kind of conduct common to esoteric cults and the occult-oriented groups. If word gets out, where is the dignity of the Urantia Brotherhood and Foundation? It is lost for at least a generation. It would be better for us to close shop right now and reopen in about 25 years. If we don't stop this nonsense immediately, we better join the rest and rent a mountain top where we can establish a colony to await the end of the world or 'the second coming.' This will be the image these people are sponsoring And, once established, we may never be able to get rid of it. I cannot criticize and deplore enough the conduct of people who are fostering this image whether acting in good faith or not. The same people who are writing with so much dubious erudition on 'advertising' are the very ones whose activities question whether they can be trusted with anything more intellectually demanding that [sic] using an electric pencil sharpener."

"Let's forget about all this 'love' for a moment," says Mills, "and take a look at the second paragraph from the bottom of page 1222 in *the Urantia Book*. This is the way we have to react in a real world. We have been overly sentimental in the conduct of our business for far too long. Now it's a deeply-ingrained habit, difficult to eliminate"

That paragraph reads: *"The expansion of material knowledge permits a greater intellectual appreciation of the meanings of ideas and the values of ideals. A human being can find truth in his inner experience, but he needs a clear knowledge of facts to apply his personal discovery of truth to the ruthlessly practical demands of everyday life."*

Mills' condemnations were even nastier than Caston's. And unfortunately, Mills had philosophically, psychologically, emotionally and vindictively deemed any kind of celestial communications as "subconscious mind" figments. *The Urantia Book* is unique and it is the one and only truly reliable spiritual revelation on the planet, according to him, and the Foundation.

October 26. The Reagan administration invades and "liberates" Grenada from the rule of communists aligned with Cuba. Operation VRYAN gets very suspicious of the heightened amount of ciphered communications between Reagan and Thatcher, not linking it to Britain's anger at having a commonwealth country invaded. The Soviets reportedly considered it part of the ongoing planning of the two 'war parties' of the West that would lead to an invasion of Nicaragua and the veiled and disguised actual attack that would come during the November 2-12 war games.

October 26. Caston hears the WWIII messages straight from Grimsley at the new Spiritual Renaissance Institute in Clayton. He later stated that he was in shock, not wanting to believe the messages. He reports talking to Grimsley by phone later, and being urged to talk to Martin Myers about accepting the messages. If he didn't, it could lead to trouble in the movement.

October 27. At a meeting in Boulder, Colorado, Morris (Mo) Siegel, founder of Celestial Seasonings teas and longtime Urantia leader, speaks about the messages and preparations for war. On November 1, Grimsley had recalled a chat with Siegel in which they calmly and without fear decided on the better-safe-than-sorry approach. Grimsley quoted Siegel as saying they should err on the side of caution. If they didn't, he didn't want to face having his 'butt kicked' all over the heavens for failing to take action. Could they have imagined at the time that just by taking precautions, and even with a sense of humor, they would eventually wind up on the backside of a political broadside?

Siegel noted that there were enough shelters for all of Boulder's population of 120,000. He said the reports on fallout severity are overblown, and that people can survive. He talks with them on being prepared whatever the case and being more safe than sorry.

The Boulder (Urantia) School had been abuzz about the messages for some weeks. Those running the meeting demanded that the night's lesson on "Forgiveness" be delivered, and that the buzz must not interfere with the book study as it had previous evenings. Clyde Bedell, who produced a concordex to *the Urantia Book*, came to the meeting with a written narrative "To Be (Upset) Or Not To Be."

After the formal meeting, Siegel presented what Bedell would derisively call a "scare talk." Bedell was not coming from a political stance but rather speaking for his faith in God. In the course of colorful, wide-ranging remarks, he stated:

"This is a time for Urantia-inspired love to embrace us all, of whatever opinions. Let this affair not divide us, but lead us to embrace our guidon more warmly than ever. Whatever is your brother's or sister's conviction regarding possible catastrophe, he or she will be strengthened by words of sympathy rather than criticism in this so-distressing time for some readers. Our Overseeing friends are resourceful. They surely will see that an all-out nuclear war is avoided if that is at all possible. All things are possible with God. You may be quite sure that NO CIVILIZATION DESTROYING holocaust will occur."

To me, and with my faith, this made perfect sense. I don't know if I had that amount of faith in 1983, but I don't see today that God/Spirit and the celestials would allow our infantile and bellicose condition here and stupid free will decisions, to destroy millions of innocent people and set back the evolution plan so badly. Some will disagree and say that God doesn't micro-manage and we are left to our fates, even if it is planetary destruction. Faith in God is likely involved here, and certainly faith in humankind.

October 29. Caston calls Martin Myers with his concerns and is told that the messages are not reliable. Both Grimsley and Myers, in Caston's reporting, had concerns about Myers being jealous that Grimsley was chosen as a receiver of celestial messages. Myers denied the charge and Caston reports that he laughed uproariously at the idea.

October 30. Caston and wife fly to San Diego to meet with Mr. and Mrs. Richard Keeler. He reports that after several hours of questioning and speculation, and then after re-reading *The Urantia Book* on subjects relating to mysticism, leadings, and spiritual communications, he began to develop in his mind a disturbing scenario of what could be happening with Grimsley. Later, he would complete the defamatory evaluation report which he defined as mostly "a study of Vern's credibility, based on his past and present actions, and an evaluation of the origin and content of the 'messages.'" He would later give credit to Keeler for his "tough editorial eye" that greatly strengthened his document.

Importantly, Keeler was a financial supporter of the Family of God. Over the years he had contributed heavily to the organization, and had reportedly earned the organization a lot of money with his investments. His will contained a large gift to the Family of God. Mullins' book says it is his entire estate.

October 30. Trustees of the Urantia Foundation and Brotherhood vote to revoke Grimsley's "Special Representative" status. Caston reports that Grimsley again asks him to talk to Myers, persuading him not to do anything "rash" that would cause problems in the movement.

October 31. Caston flies to Chicago, compiling notes during the flight, and has an evening visit with Martin Myers and Diane Elder regarding the FOG messages. He reports that he was impressed with their "sane reasoning" and loving attitudes, and left convinced that the Grimsley messages represented a "major crisis" for the Urantia movement. He committed himself to a presentation at the Los Angeles meeting, which he said he did not know Grimsley would attend.

November 1. The first Pershing II missiles were scheduled to arrive in Europe, but the project is behind schedule. They were nonetheless included in the ten-day war game for the first time. Operation VRYAN is on high alert, and Moscow presses all agents worldwide for information, especially anomalies in normal operational procedures.

November 1. Grimsley meets with 26 concerned Urantia Book leaders in Los Angeles, including Caston, who arrives late and later states that he didn't hear the early request not to tape the proceedings. He said he placed his recorder on a table in plain sight and did so. Not realizing that Grimsley himself would be at the meeting, he decided to use his limited tape to record Grimsley's presentation rather than save the tape for his own, as he had intended.

Caston's verbal confrontation with Grimsley that closed the evening was not recorded. Caston subsequently included a transcript of the recording in his message evaluation report, which was mostly Grimsley's discussion of the messages.

Ironically, as Grimsley had viewed Caston as a mediator with Myers, Caston turns out to be the one who directly confronts him. He had in hand a list of 23 questions and observations that he had intended to air, and when he was called upon in the question-answer portion of the meeting, Grimsley's presence didn't deter his presentation. Caston notes later that confronting Grimsley on any matter was a formidable task and he states that he must have gone into "fight or flight" mode.

During the subsequent exchange of views, Grimsley admonished Caston for not bringing his questions and concerns to Clayton as he and others had been invited to do, before unloading them at the meeting. Caston felt vindicated based on his busy schedule of conferring with Myers, Keeler and perhaps others in his travels from Seattle down to San Diego during the past week. So let's deal with them now.

One attendant noted that it was Caston who seemed frantic and quarrelsome, and not Grimsley, who was, after all, an extraordinary preacher, remaining calm and reasoning. If that were indeed the sense of the meeting, it might help explain why Caston, embarrassed, might take the issue on as a vendetta to validate himself. At any rate, he left the confrontation undeterred and began a systematic campaign to get feedback, corrections to his presumptions, and any information that would refute his charges against Grimsley. He would confront the Grimsleys directly.

His premise is stated as number six in a list of possible scenarios that would explain and characterize the "Grimsley incident." This is the one Caston said he believes, whereupon he launches into a lengthy document of suppositions and assumptions to prove it.

He states his belief that the messages are false, but actually believed by the receiver as part of his "marginal consciousness." He states that the messages are "auditory hallucinations" and that they spring from "the seeds of mental fatigue, emotional stress, self-delusion, or some form of ego-based, self-fulfilling desire, all planted in the fertile seed of a religious cult."

And so, I thought, it was all going back to the time-tested homily that if he's hearing voices, he's psychotic. Well, then, was the mysterious so-called "sleeping subject" who anchored the incoming Urantia revelation psychotic too? Ironically, some people who had received arguably the most comprehensive and admirable piece of channeled material on the planet seemed to be fighting the whole concept that they lived under.

Or was it just Grimsley, personally, who was unconsciously manipulating everything with invalid and unreliable imaginings with his self-anointed special status? Midwayers may exist, but they're not talking to Vern. Celestial contact is real, but not this time. Mystery rages on when we are always questioning people's motivations.

Caston is highly critical of Grimsley's claim that Christy had confirmed him as a member of the Reserve Corps of Destiny. While Grimsley did not call himself a member of the Reserve Corps, Caston disdainfully notes that he had, more than once, relayed the statement by Christy, using it manipulatively.

November 2. ABLE ARCHER-83 begins, six days after the U.S. crushes the upstart communist regime in Grenada. Andropov condemns the U.S. as warmongers in very strong terms. KGB operatives worldwide get the message that the situation is critical, and to expect a surprise U.S. missile attack. Originally, it was planned that Reagan and Vice President George H.W. Bush would themselves participate in the exercise. For unclear reasons, it was decided that they would not, perhaps in deference to Soviet concerns.

November 6. At the height of ABLE ARCHER-83, the U.S. Navy and a Soviet submarine are playing cat-and-mouse games in the deep Atlantic, 470 miles off the U.S. coast east of Charleston, South Carolina. This was standard procedure to train personnel and protect U.S. ships. The Victor III Russian sub was equipped and designed to kill U.S. subs before they could launch their intercontinental missiles. The U.S. part of the scenario was to destroy the Victor first.

Victor III becomes disabled and floats to the surface, becoming a major embarrassment to the Soviets as it floats helplessly toward a haven in Cuba each day, with U.S. planes buzzing overhead. Author Peter Pry thinks the presence of the Russian sub near Charleston was not likely a coincidence to ABLE ARCHER-83.

November 6. With the Victor III drama playing out, Soviet VRYAN reports that ABLE ARCHER-83 is like an acronym-laden actual countdown to a U.S. first strike. Intelligence estimates went worldwide, that it would likely take 7-10 days to put everything together to launch a nuclear attack. Dating from November 6, then, they could expect a U.S. strike in 3-6 days, from November 9-12.

November 8 or 9. When allied forces simulate the highest alert DEFCON-1 status, the Russians mistake it as real and put their own forces on a highest alert status, including nuclear capable planes in East Germany and Poland. They are celebrating a Communist Revolution holiday and some believe that the U.S. might think them distracted. U.S. intelligence services remain oblivious, according to Pry, who believes the Russians made a too-literal interpretation of work processes.

November 10. A letter from Church of Christ Minister Meredith Sprunger, an ardent student of the Revelation, disdains Grimsley's messages and their supposed political manipulation of the Urantia movement. He speaks strongly on behalf of Democratic rule.

November 11. ABLE ARCHER-83 ends. In War Scare, author and former CIA analyst Peter Pry thinks that even another 24-hour cycle might have led to a nuclear holocaust. In these critical days and hours, for whatever reasons, no missiles were launched. Much credit can apparently be given to two embedded Soviet spies, Oleg Gordievsky in London and code name 'Topaz' in NATO, who both assured the Soviets near the end that NATO was definitely not involved with any war action and had turned out the lights and gone home.

It seems that two well-placed Soviet spies gave the all-clear then that eased the precipitous pressure being felt in the Soviet and finally ended the war threat.

November 16. Grimsley converts foundation assets to gold, explains that gold should have a higher real value after a nuclear war. It amounts to about $1,300,000.

November 16. On that day, Caston mails the first version of his message evaluation report to Grimsley, with a separate copy to wife Nancy Grimsley, and other officials of FOG. He asks for correction of any errors. At the same time, he says that he mailed it to other FOG officials and the executive board of the Urantia Brotherhood. He knew they would be meeting the following weekend and wanted to give them "another perspective." Later in his report, he notes that he also sent the report to eight Urantia Book students, unidentified, for their evaluation.

Caston said he also had a two-hour conversation with Grimsley about the package, during which he admonished Caston for not talking to him personally before distributing the report, and for strongly implying that Grimsley knew his "special representative" status had already been revoked at the time of the November 1 meeting. Grimsley denied knowing it.

November 18. Concerns at the Family of God are reportedly high and Caston says that people are coming to the Clayton shelter, fearing events of the weekend.

A telephone conversation with Delores Nice, a former Family member, takes issue that the gathering that weekend was a war scare. She noted that members were simply working on an upcoming anniversary celebration in December. She also notes that there was no bomb shelter in Clayton, that it was more like a storage area. Importantly, she refutes rumors that members were storing arms to protect themselves after an apocalypse. She adds that Caston's report was rift with errors.

In that very report, Grimsley denies that he had celestial messages about the weekend, only some premonitions in his own head. He has a speaking engagement in Oregon for Saturday evening, and comments that the location should be a safe one in case of a nuclear attack. He was said to have speculated, "Maybe that's not a coincidence."

By this time, other FOG members had reportedly been encouraged to engage their "marginal consciousness." One person's reported vision of the future was of Grimsley signing papers for the St. Anthony's property purchase, and he made reference to it in his meeting under the oak tree. Encouraging such mysticism, engaging in 'marginal consciousness' in others was another of Caston's numerous indictments of Grimsley's leadership.

In his report, Caston also relates that a member of the Family of God, name unrevealed, had served on a Grand Jury during the fall, and a spy case involving nuclear strikes had provided inside information that was truly disturbing to the individual. No doubt these sharings would have raised the anxiety level within the Family.

November 19. Grimsley receives a message that says simply: "We've won." He reportedly sends the message to the Urantia Brotherhood, which was scheduled to discuss the matter that very day. What could it mean? He goes to his Oregon speaking engagement.

In his criticisms, Caston decries the brevity of the message and its lack of meaning, asking whether the messengers would really give us such short shrift. But at the same time, he notes that Grimsley has been subjected to growing criticism and was increasingly reluctant to share any more messages.

Caston says speculators look at three scenarios. First, that FOG has enough executive committee votes to prevent a strong stand against the messages; second, that sufficient numbers of people in Urantia would be supporting the revelations; and third, that an emergency son would indeed be sent to avert a nuclear war.

Amazingly, there seems no speculation that takes the midwayers into consideration, only a human and political interpretation. Perhaps they were saying that the dangers of a Soviet first strike are over for now, as of the ending of ABLE ARCHER-83, and World War III won't happen. That would be a 'win' and that was truly the most important battle going on.

November 19. John Hales chairs a meeting of the executive council of the Urantia Brotherhood to discuss the events in California. A letter was to be drafted, separating the war messages from any relationship to the Brotherhood.

November 20. Keeler resigns from FOG, announces that he has taken the organization out of his will because of his disagreements with the war preparations.

In the matter of complete accuracy, I recalled that the midwayers had assuredly not predicted World War III but urged that we prepare calmly for the worst scenario. American citizens were being encouraged into that very action by Civil Defense authorities. They urged people not to be fearful but to be prepared, just like the civil defense authorities. Grimsley did understand them to say that it would "touch American soil."

The midwayers apparently offered no advice on how to deal with a political "kill-the-prophet" fallout that would seriously fracture the movement all the way to the present time.

November 24. Andropov announces that the USSR would implement an "analogous response" to the Pershing II deployments. Soviet mobile nuclear missiles would be moved closer to Western Europe and nuclear-armed submarines would move closer to the United States. The old guard Soviets still feared a U.S. first strike and considered their own preemptive strike the best strategy.

November 28: Post Office returns Caston's express mail package to Grimsley. His phone number is handwritten on the envelope. It is marked "Unclaimed." Caston reports the conversation with Grimsley, and says he is told by Keeler that Grimsley considers the report to be "vindictive, libelous and slanderous" and with "a reckless disregard for the truth."

December 15. The Urantia Brotherhood sends the official statement to the full membership. Signed by Hales, the letter never mentions Grimsley or the Family of God by name. It adheres to the Caston-Keeler-Myers position. "Urantia Brotherhood must conduct its affairs through the insights acquired from evolutionary experiential wisdom, epochal revelation, and the personal guidance of its members as all of these resources find group expression in the democratic process." Hales pleads for unity whether or not one believes the messages.

The statement said, in effect, that Grimsley's messages or guidance is a personal thing, not for the Urantia Brotherhood to condone or refute. Such guidance should be personal and separate from the decision-making processes of the board. I thought here that Grimsley might agree and recalled he had always employed more of a democratic than autocratic position in revealing the messages and openly discussing their authenticity and meaning.

December 31, 1983. Tom Kendall, President of the Urantia Foundation, is deposed. His had been the lone dissenting vote for the December 15 Brotherhood letter to Grimsley. In Mullins' book, he reports that Tom and wife Carolyn Kendall had gone from Chicago to visit the Grimsley's in December, even as Myers demanded that he not go officially representing the Foundation. By the time he returns, he has been removed from power by Myers and the rest of the board.

Kendell is quoted by author Mullins as saying: "I began to realize that Martin believed that he, not I, should be president of the Board of Trustees.... I suspected that he was waiting for a plausible excuse to have himself installed as president. The Vern Grimsley controversy presented the opportunity."

Myers' document charged Kendall with being "subject to the influence of psychic phenomena" and that such as this "were in degradation of the teaching of *The Urantia Book* in that the book urges the function of evolutionary wisdom and rational judgment as amplified by one's own spiritual experience in solving problems and challenges."

I knew from having read the voluminous Urantia Book for many years that, like scripture and even more so, its massive weight of science, philosophy and religion is not easily understood in its entirety and dangerous to pull out of context. Yes, we are to rely on ourselves in this mortal adventure and, yes, there will also be continuing revelation and constant, unspecified spiritual assistance.

I noted to myself that the ouster of Kendall at the end of 1983 climaxed a good year for Myers. He had taken over as board president and discredited Grimsley, ultimately leading to the destruction of the Family of God. This would thereby bring a lot of money back to the Chicago power structure and not into Vern's charismatic grip. The Family would no longer take the spotlight or the money.

January 16, 1984. The influential minister, Meredith Sprunger, delivered another blow to the Family of God with a condescending call for members to renounce their erroneous path and come back into the Urantia mainstream as repentant and subservient. In this letter, after revisiting his earlier call for more democracy and a competitive slate for every election, he delved into what he called the "Clayton incident."

Sprunger wrote: "There are many who feel it would be unwise to ask Vern or the Family of God to fill leadership or speaker roles at the General Conference in August. I, personally, love Vern and the Family of God people and believe they have some of the finest talents in the URANTIA movement. I think our objective in our relationships with them should be to help restore their credibility and lay the foundations for their renewed service in the Brotherhood."

Sprunger thus takes on the mantle of the anti-FOG forces that there was no WWIII threat and it was all a misguided fantasy. Now, given the facts of history, I knew the threat was real and so did the highest powers in the U.S. and in the Soviet. But Grimsley's critics would allow him no slack.

Sprunger continues by suggesting that Family of God people serve in "non-leadership positions for a couple of years and through fellowship allow confidence to rebuild by this quiet person to person relationship."

"I would hope," said the Church of Christ minister, that Vern would not continue to publicize his 'special' position of 'special' messages. I pray that this 'contact personality' phase of his experience will go into quiescence or may function as a quiet personal religious experience and that he will be able to serve with humility in the democratic processes of the Brotherhood. If this does not happen the service of his great talents will be largely lost to the Brotherhood."

Having FOG members play prominent roles in the upcoming conference, Sprunger reasoned, would "only deepen the divisiveness within the Brotherhood and lessen their future service potential." Members of FOG should be accepted and loved, he said, and other Urantian authorities should be "helping them regain the confidence they once enjoyed in the Brotherhood."

The letter was too much "repent and do penance" for me given that the nuclear attack could have been imminent. Since it didn't happen, and we were saved by whatever means, doesn't mean that legitimate fears and warnings from FOG should be cause for punishment, ejection from meaningful Urantian service and banishment to a subservient acquiescence to the doubters and cynics.

But the FOG attacks were persistent and the Urantia support went away. While Caston noted that Grimsley was pretending to "get back to normal" in Clayton in the early part of 1984, he still prodded hard to know if Grimsley was still hearing voices to the detriment of the movement, or was ready to renounce the war warnings. The pressure stayed on.

Grimsley persistently stood by his messages, I had been told, until his death in 2010. Since his passing, many in the Urantia movement have expressed appreciation for his life's work, and resurrected some of his radio broadcasts. They precisely voice the very same new religion of Jesus that the Urantia papers say is most needed in the world. The Family of God was doing it. In Jesus' incarnation on the planet, he also gave people exactly what they needed, I reasoned, and he was killed for it.

February 27, 1984. Caston writes Nancy Grimsley and sends her three copies of his report. While he asks for any factual corrections, it's a loaded offer, specifying that he would correct any errors of logic or interpretation if he could actually be convinced of the inaccuracies. This would open a long and contentious debate not in the best interests of FOG or the Urantia movement, he was told, first by Mrs. Grimsley, then by attorney Bob Blackstock on FOG stationary.

Both urge Caston not to publish the report because of numerous inaccuracies and distortions and because it amounts to legal malice. He is undeterred; he is dealing with a crisis that was threatening democratic processes. Blackstock contends there are over 300 errors in the first 105 pages; Caston continues to demand that even one be pointed out. Correspondence continues, with Caston imposing two deadlines for the Grimsleys' responses, both being ignored.

Caston manages to talk to Mrs. Grimsley by phone. She reportedly explains that her husband believed the messages and believed that they should be shared, and that proving the validity of them "would be like proving the existence of God." Failing to get any FOG feedback, Caston subsequently makes widespread distribution of his report within Urantia circles.

March 9, 1984. Andropov dies.

June 17, 1984. Caston publishes the report, 238 pages plus appendix. He puts everyone in the Urantia movement into a difficult position. Either you vote for democratic rule, or Grimsley or any other such instigator could try to manipulate and control the movement on celestial authority. In its August 1984 annual Council meeting, the Urantia Brotherhood voted to support democratic standards, though falling short of any criticism of Grimsley or the Family of God Foundation. I would look for the minutes.

In his conclusions, Caston stated displeasure at what he called a weak Brotherhood statement. He openly advocates that any human at all who professed to receive celestial messages in relation to this "aberrant episode" in Urantia history be forbidden to hold any leadership status at all in the movement.

This seemed, in effect, to disdain any kind of spiritual guidance that Urantian leaders might feel, as it could be unreliable, and could therefore interfere with the democratic principles that should govern the movement. If you are on the Council, for example, and you feel spiritually guided to a position, then keep it to yourself, don't ask and don't tell, and don't admit that you seek and receive spiritual guidance in all matters. It's assumed that you do, but don't speak of any "messages."

Today, Teaching Mission participants are constantly urged to seek direct spiritual guidance on all of our issues in our Stillness time, and with attunement to one's own indwelling spirit, can continually be guided by spirit and live in the spirit. But such persons would have to be truly open to celestial guidance, and not fearful of it, and not be fearful of one's own mind.

I could see, at this point, that the possible midwayer effort to preserve the Urantia revelation in case of nuclear attack had not been proven or disproven in the report. As hard as Caston tries, he can't disprove them. He dissects Grimsley's every word and action to question his motives and speculate the very worst, all to his own discredit, and he still doesn't make a reasonable case.

He makes note of possibly 3-4 million dollars going to FOG because of Grimsley, funds that he says could have supported more book translations. I recalled at this point that Caston remained on Facebook today speaking unofficially for the current Urantia Foundation, extolling the outstanding book translation and dissemination work that they have done over the years, with more needed.

The conclusion of his 1984 report also smacked of resentments against the way Grimsley operated FOG. On the one hand, the report criticized him for "bootlegging" the Urantia teachings by not giving proper credit to the book as their source. On the other hand, he is critical that Grimsley uses the support of the Urantia organizations to bolster his own credibility.

The contradictory logic continues. Caston is obliquely grateful that Grimsley is a bootlegger and doesn't mention *the Urantia Book* directly, given the WWIII "doomsday cult" pronouncements and its guilt by association. He worries loudly that people will link him to the official Urantia movement, besmirching its reputation as a sane and stable organization. He even takes issue with a FOG newsletter note that its contents are not copyrighted and can be disseminated freely. Somehow, this violated his sense that the newsletter should be for Urantia people only. Somehow, he doesn't seem to understand that the Family of God Foundation was not subservient, and confined to communicating with only Urantia readers, and that being a "special agent" shouldn't necessarily tie Grimsley's hands or oversee FOG operations in some way.

I decided at that point to apply Caston's original summed-up charges against Grimsley to himself, given that he had traversed the country, devoted many days of contentious battle and later moved into an official Trustee position in Urantia politics because of his relentless drive. Here are the reversed charges with only slight change of wording, as noted:

"Caston's charges are false, but they are sincerely believed by their deliverer. The 'voices' of his thoughts are a product of his 'marginal consciousness.' They are hallucinations springing from the seeds of mental fatigue, emotional stress, self-delusion, or some form of ego-based, self-fulfilling desire, all planted in the fertile soil of a religious cult."

Yes, I decided. This all seemed to apply to Mr. Caston, according to his own document anyway. And from his heated rhetoric on Facebook, I could believe that he and Myers were cut from the same bolt of yarn. A staff member once described Myers as subject to paranoid rages in the 1970's and 80's, stomping about the room and railing about those who would ruin "my revelation."

Live by the law, die by it, I thought. The midwayers and the celestials both likely wanted the Urantia text to be shared with the world in the 21st century, and they may have actually helped remove it from the hands of the Urantia Foundation, which espoused a go-slow, one person at a time sharing philosophy and one source, themselves, for books that had become cost prohibitive for the common man. At any rate, the midwayers would not likely support legal controls over a book they freely presented to humans, hoping for widespread sharing, without the shackles of shortsighted control battles.

It was interesting that Myers was deposed as the 1990s got underway, at about the same time that celestial teachers started arriving on the planet to implement the continuing Fifth Epochal Revelation. The copyright control was lifted as an unnecessary barrier to revelation.

A NEW TIMELINE TO DISASTER

But while Urantia officials made their split with the Family of God over Grimsley's 1983 messages, the drama was far from over. The Family and its new Spiritual Renaissance Institute in Clayton was seriously damaged by a declining membership and the breach with the Urantia Foundation but it was plodding along and may have survived.

Then came a flurry of new war messages, revealed in a new timeline provided by a loyal FOG staff member. It led me to more published documents that traced the complete destruction of the organization when a precise and very wrong prediction of a nuclear attack came for 3-5 a.m. on the morning on March 24, 1985.

Given the consequences of the 1983 messages and the institute's much-criticized preparations for survival, I wondered how this could possibly happen. Much was revealed, as we follow the action based on a timeline report provided by a FOG staff member who wishes to remain anonymous.

October 12, 1983. Urantia organizations are much astir about Grimsley's war messages, not wanting to appear as a doomsday cult, and striving to elevate themselves from perceived occult status and into meaningful recognition by society's institutions.

The Family of God meets that day in its Berkeley, CA, headquarters to discuss how broadly Grimsley's messages should be disseminated. Staff member Tery McCade is reported to be alone in voting against any dissemination. The timeline also notes that FOG members were asked on that date to sign a secrecy pledge and not to divulge the war warnings.

November 1983. Even as Grimsley's messages are becoming controversial within Urantia circles, he and the Family of God staff are moving to the new Clayton property in eastern California, some 200 miles from San Francisco. Food stores would include such items as wheat, beans, sugar, flour, and canned goods, all carefully packed in plastic containers with dry ice and stored in 55-gallon drums. Sandbags were filled, as possible barriers to radiation contamination. In case of war and social breakdown, the institute planned to have food for themselves and survivors in the surrounding area.

Critics within Urantia would later relate that the new institute, with its submerged Urantian ties, would be part of a power grab from Chicago. It was cemented by the war messages, with the assertion that vital Urantian documents might be much safer in Clayton. That would seemingly draw the new power base to California, and with all the attendant opportunities to bring in money.

I thought here: There are human minds which seem to be eternally political, and focused on power, money and control, territorialism in the animal world. It seemed altogether possible, on the other hand, that Grimsley was trying to be a good Apostle, a vanguard for the Urantian enlargement of Jesus, and was not concerned with Urantian politics at all. He had preached unity and friendship with the Urantian powers until his passing.

November 20, 1983. Richard Keeler tells the Family of God that his resignation as treasurer has nothing to do with Grimsley's request that all liquid assets be turned to gold. He disagrees with the war preparation activities.

January, 1984. Nancy Grimsley leaves full-time employment at the University of California at Berkeley to work full-time for the institute.

February 8, 1984. Grimsley volunteers for a "psychiatric consultive examination" with Dr. F.C. Newsom, a longtime psychologist practicing in Wichita, KS. The diagnosis: No mental disorder.

January-June, 1984. Institute work included the building of a recording studio, landscaping and drilling of a water well, which proved difficult and required three holes. A short landing strip was leveled for a Cessna 180 aircraft that had been leased by FOG. Bob Blackstock was the pilot. One insider said he doubted that Grimsley ever rode in the plane.

Early 1984. Though controversial and criticized, Grimsley is reported determined to fill his speaking engagements. It would be his last tour.

He returned to FOG and was producing one to two new radio broadcasts every week. They were heard first by the FOG crew and voted up or down. There was apparently a democracy at work. David Kantor, a dedicated Urantia scholar, had designed the recording studio at FOG, and had become a salaried staff person.

Weekly meetings included a discussion of the ongoing messages conflict, responses to mail, and hearing Grimsley's new broadcasts. There was a designated person to report on world news. When Kantor took over the role, he reportedly brings touches of humor. He notes on one occasion that news stories can be twisted in a particular direction by reporting all of the facts accurately except for one, and then twisting that single fact into another direction – the art of deception.

June, 1984. Caston's report is read to FOG members and considered to be "filled with half-truths, innuendos and flawed conclusions." He is advised not to publish it, but does so anyway.

July, 1984. The Family is still publishing a newsletter, and I was favorably impressed with the words of Editor Rebecca Marshall. I was further enlightened about the Family's vision, and how it extended far beyond Urantia's politics.

"The Family of God Foundation, Inc. is one small part of a growing global effort to bring about a spiritual awakening on our troubled planet. Individuals and groups participating in this worldwide ministry can be found on every continent and in every race and religion. These thousands of people may not know one another but we do share one thing in common – wholehearted dedication to the proclamation of a new and uplifting planetary perspective, one which views all men, women and children as brothers and sisters in God's universal family.

"Every person who participates in this great adventure is a pioneer; the ways in which these seeds of hope are being planted are as unique as the individuals and groups who are planting them. The work is challenging, even difficult, sometimes even misunderstood, but the joys of introducing our brothers and sisters to the good place of their place in the Father's family are equaled only by the enthralling experiences of one's own personal relationship with God.

"We are grateful for the words of love and support which have been sent our way during these past few months. Every letter has truly made a difference, and we thank all of you who have continued to inspire us with your encouragement as we press onward toward our goal – a spiritual renaissance predicated on the global realization of the Fatherhood of God and the brotherhood of all mankind."

I found more telling words in the July 1984 newsletter from Nancy Grimsley herself in the Family of God Diary.

"Growth doesn't occur without turbulence, and I doubt any living thing on this planet, be it an individual or an organization, survives two decades without difficulty. In fact, we can jolly well count on it. If human beings are involved in any project we can figure there will be humor, frustration, happiness, distress, and probably a goodly dose of misunderstanding. But there is inherent joy in struggling through it all, and keeping on keeping on with the varied perspectives that make up life. It is my experience that there is a lot of goodness in life and in people, if you keep looking for it.

"Look for our big twentieth anniversary issue in the fall." – Nancy

Grimsley himself was also taking a candid look at himself, his situation and what he would later in life refer to as "my prophecies."

November 4, 1984. A letter turned up in Urantia's historical online archives – from Grimsley to John Hales on this date. The letterhead is: VERN BENNOM GRIMSLEY, International Broadcaster, headquartered in Berkeley, California. He wishes Hales well with the Boulder, CO, Urantia School, then operational, and refers him to a letter he wrote to Clyde Bedell on

November 1 of '84. Since it was his first written response to the events of the past year, he wanted to share a copy.

I noted the November 1 date–exactly a year from the night when Grimsley and Caston went head-to-head at the Urantia gathering in 1983, breeding the defaming diatribe and the eventual historical disruptions. From Grimsley:

> Dear Clyde,
>
> I just received your letter today and feel that I must address a serious, though certainly sincerely held, misunderstanding you appear to have about me.
>
> You requested that I 'desist from your present self-casting as an inerrant Creator Son, and become Vern Grimsley, human being, capable of possible error.'
>
> The fact that I have continued to stand unwaveringly by what I have said regarding the need to prepare for a war is in no way, shape or form equivalent to casting myself as 'an inerrant Creator Son!" Such an accusation deeply wounds me, Clyde, and I think it only could have emerged in the midst of the storms of distortion, rumor, hearsay and untruths which have swirled across our movement over the past year. I have never made such claims, nor do I now. I have never had such delusions of grandeur, nor do I now.
>
> I, and all the other people who have ever known me or have ever worked with me, know full well that I am an unquestionably less-than-perfect specimen of Homo Urantius. I am subject to the same sorts of human faults and failings as anybody else – from errors of judgment and misunderstandings to taking on more projects than I should. But since I have never made any such claim as you assert, there is no way I can retract it.
>
> I am a man born and reared in the farming and ranching flatlands of western Kansas. I was so painfully shy as a boy that I took up the hobbies of doing magic tricks and ventriloquism to help me overcome it. My shyness has oftentimes been misinterpreted as aloofness (a shortcoming I am working to overcome.) But, for as long as I can remember, I have thirsted in my soul to know spiritual truth. Imagine my joy back in the mid-fifties when Dr. Sprunger introduced me to *the URANTIA book*! I was overcome with feelings of gratitude which are undiminished to this day.
>
> Among the greatest privileges of my life were knowing Dr. Sadler and Christy. When she, the last of the contact commissioners, asked that I preach her memorial sermon, it was one of the highest honors I have ever had bestowed on me.
>
> But – for reasons now only known to her – before she died, Christy chose to tell not only me but a number of other leaders in the URANTIA movement in Europe, Canada and the U.S. that I am a member of the Reserve Corps of Destiny.

She told none of us that it was a secret. She gave no admonition that it shouldn't be discussed. Indeed, having told as many people as we know she did, she virtually guaranteed that eventually it would be discussed. At the Green Lake Conference this summer, several leaders told me that, messages or no messages, in their opinions it was only a matter of time before I became very politically controversial in the URANTIA movement because Christy had told a number of people I was a reservist before she died. Maybe they're right. I don't know. There's a lot I don't know. Anyway, I'm certain Christy had some good reason for doing it. Literally, all I know is that Christy told me that, and that I have had some very unusual experiences the past couple of years. Period. Add it up any way you want to, Clyde – that's all I know about it.

Believe it or not, I have done the best I could through all of this. The twistings and distortions of my life and our ministry have sometimes been extreme. There are hundreds of distortions and errors in the 'report' to which you alluded. If you're willing to believe that thing, I've got some swampland in Georgia you might be interested in.

Here is an excerpt from a letter a URANTIA Book student in New Mexico wrote to me.

"You are probably very familiar with this Abraham Lincoln pronouncement but I want to share it with you anyway: 'If I were to try to read, much less answer, all the attacks made on me, this shop might as well be closed for any other business. I do the very best I know how – the very best I can, and I mean to keep doing so until the end. If the end brings me out all right, what is said against me won't amount to anything. If the end brings me out wrong, 10 angels swearing I was right would make no difference.' It is the most difficult test of the very fibers that make up our beings, when the attacks come from the very people who should be, if not supportive, at least tolerant. Unkindness, intolerance, harshness, condemnation and all other unlovely behaviors have no place in the program and daily will of our Father for us. We can only pray for those who are still clinging to those unlovely characteristics in their lives in the name of whatever they elect to set up as right. We all have so much to learn and it may take some really tough school days in order for us to learn it. I often chafe against the process but I do desire the final outcome."

That pretty much sums up why I haven't been publishing rebuttals or scheduling public debates on all this during the past year.

And since you also asked about my 'mental stability,' I am enclosing a copy of my psychiatric diagnosis.

I was saddened to read in your letter, "I still would like to see you redeem yourself with most of the active leadership of our Movement, and I, of course, do not refer to the inactive and negative leadership (?) at 533." [Editor's note: Urantia Foundation headquarters was at 533 Diversey Parkway in Chicago] Clyde, I continue to support both the URANTIA Brotherhood and URANTIA Foundation with vigor. The people at 533 are wonderful folks who are doing the best they can amid difficult circumstances. I was saddened too, to read what appeared to be a spiritually judgmental attack on Martin Myers. It is not for us to make such judgments, I know Martin, and know his dedication and sincerity to be wholehearted.

I love you lots, my dear man, but I will ask you kindly to cease and desist from telling people that this highly imperfect, grey-templed, cigar-smoking, bar-b-q loving, joke telling, post-nasal dripping back-aching, arthritic Kansas cowboy and amateur evangelist has convinced himself he's 'an inerrant Creator Son."

Your brother in our Father's family,

(s) Vern
Vern Bennom Grimsley
VBG/rm

Grimsley's self-effacing graciousness here mirrored his open sharings of the messages a year earlier, in 1983, hoping in vain to share the phenomenon of continued midwayer contact with the Urantia community in an open-minded exploration of... wherever it might lead.

His personality seemed consistent here, with tolerance for Myers' sincerity and a desire for Urantia unity. It would be another seven years or so until Myers would be forced out, but Bedell's letter already showed dissatisfaction with the Chicago power structure, which had been growing since 1970.

I also noted that he had enclosed a psychologist's report in his letter to Bedell, likely the one from Dr. Newsom in Wichita. This apparently was in reply to Caston's heavy-handed indictment of psychosis due to overwork and mental strain and his solicitation of his own psychologist to make an analysis. It was a matter of dueling psychiatrists.

I thought at this point that the character who had suffered the most mental strain was Caston himself, with his political machinations, the exhaustive hatchet job of a report, his harassment of the Grimsleys to start a debate, and all of the blowhard rhetoric he had put on internet discussion groups over the years even into 2012, and even with veiled threats of more exposures about the Family of God. His Facebook condemnations of the Teaching Mission had been particularly nasty.

I was pleased to detect no mental strain with Grimsley here, only a wise and graceful response which verified some of my previous determinations and added some new details.

August 11, 1984. On this date the General Council of the Urantia Brotherhood held its annual meeting in Green Lake, Wisconsin, with 35 voting members on hand. The minutes are a masterful presentation of understatements regarding the lengthy discussions about the FOG messages. Those on hand included familiar players Nancy Grimsley, Carolyn Kendall, Thomas Kendall, Harry McMullen III, FOG officer David Gray, Martin W. Myers, Mo Siegel and Rev. Meredith J. Sprunger.

The minutes report: "The Chairman (John Hales) reported the history of events as concerns the actions taken by the Urantia Brotherhood in response to activities of the Family of God Foundation in Clayton, California, concerning preparations for war. An individual was claiming to be receiving messages from unidentified sources directing this activity. In response to the concern and confusion created among readers of *the Urantia Book*, the Brotherhood sent a letter, December 15, 1983, to the entire mailing list stating its disassociation with such phenomena. A lengthy discussion followed."

There were three petitions to the Council from individual members, Caston's included. They were read to the Council by Duane Faw, who had introduced Grimsley at the November 1 meeting when Caston made his confrontation. Faw is notable to Teaching Mission members as a retired U.S. Army general who became an advocate of the teachers and hosted the transmissions of celestial teacher Rayson in his Malibu home about a decade later.

The Council battled over an official statement until the following afternoon and finally approved this one: "We support the policies and positions of Urantia Foundation and the Executive Committee of Urantia Brotherhood which reject and disregard unidentified voice communications to an individual as a basis for official action."

The statement seemed reasonable, but my impression was that Grimsley himself would have voted to approve it. I recalled that he never presented the messages as dogma but rather as a phenomenon. He had indeed passed on these messages to movement leaders, but he would deny that they were a manipulative tool to get his way. He would also deny that the midwayers predicted nuclear holocaust and were only prescient in seeing and logically preparing for the dangers posed by those incredibly critical days in November.

There was one final refutation of Grimsley and the Family at that August 1984 Council meeting. He had to be nominated from the floor to compete with Ronald S. Law to chair the committee on fraternal relations. This was simply a committee post and Grimsley lost the vote 27-8.

Tom Kendall, also a FOG member and supporter of Grimsley who was purged in December, was also nominated from the floor to compete with Philip A. Rolnick as judicial committee chair. He lost 20-15.

During this time the FOG timeline reports that the membership was feeling isolated and under siege. With no new messages, 'we just kept trudging along.' The financial condition was deteriorating as interest and membership declined.

At the Wisconsin conference, Grimsley kept a low profile and members reportedly felt ostracized, a reality that showed itself in the board minutes. "Vern was subject to a great deal of criticism and he was an easy target," said one friend. "His reaction to this was to somewhat isolate himself. No one enjoyed being constantly attacked."

Fall, 1984. Grimsley continues his broadcasts. The FOG crew is reported to be increasingly critical. Internal dissension about the merits of Caston's report and what is called the 'current controversy' further divides the membership, which is plummeting.

December 1984. The Family celebrates 20 years of radio broadcasting. Gathering is estimated at 50-100 people.

January, 1985. Sara Blackstock says she has been contacted and is receiving messages, and she reads them to the crew. Tery McCade walks out, stating his disbelief. For several weeks, she maintains her contact which is again centered around World War III preparations. The timeline says the remaining FOG members were somewhat reinvigorated.

"Vern is silent and appears to be in a conundrum," an anonymous insider reports. "He can't take the position that only he can receive messages, and he doesn't really validate Sara's messages. So he is silent. He is losing control of the Family of God."

Late January, 1985. David Kantor announces with certainty that he has been contacted, just after taking a shower. He describes the experience. His wife, Sue, asks if the group wants to hear her opinion. After assent, she states that she doesn't believe any of the messages. While the group is reportedly taken aback, there is also faith in Kantor, a FOG mainstay with much internal responsibility, including a near open checkbook for the war budget.

Kantor begins to control FOG with his hand-written celestial messages, usually 1-2 pages, and in the form of questions and answers. The new messages become the central point of weekly meetings. As they start coming, a budget is established and a pre-emptive strike from the Soviet Union is expected.

A request is made to gather the lessons of Blackstock, Kantor and Grimsley so that they could be studied together and without the human commentaries. This didn't come about.

Late February, 1985. Kantor receives the specific message – a nuclear strike between 3-5 a.m. on March 25, 1985. It is stated that many Americans will never recover.

Within this time frame, Grimsley wants to provide a disclaimer for anyone calling the institute, to the effect that messages are being received that can't be validated. This was reported to either have been voted down or ignored.

One member asked that Kantor ask the midwayers how many socks were in his top drawer as a validation. The test was not done.

Doubts began to rise when Kantor's messages said more phone lines should be installed for heavy traffic a week before the March 25 nuclear strike. In fact, there were few phone calls during the week, raising suspicions that all wasn't well.

March 24-25, 1985. Some 20-25 FOG members spend overnight in the institute's shop. Grimsley spends the night in his second floor area. Sue Kantor stays home. The couple was destined for a divorce.

By 7 a.m. the group was disillusioned with the false prophecy and most went home to deal with it. A smaller group stayed at the institute to discuss what had happened, with Kantor absent and gone. McCade reportedly heard him say, 'it's all gibberish' when he left the building. Kantor also reportedly approached Nancy Grimsley in a laughing manner and said he had just telephoned Keeler.

It was a somber meeting, but when a FOG member showed up with coffee and donuts, one staff member thought it humorous, and saw it as one of the best comments that could be made given the circumstances.

Early 1985. In the Soviet Union at this time, there were the enduring tensions that the U.S. was striving for military superiority. Andropov had died in 1984 but Soviet generals remained fixated on a possible first strike scenario. They believed that the U.S. space shuttle might well be a secret 'space bomber' for that purpose. In February, 1984, the KGB stated: "With the aid of this system (SDI), the Americans expect to be able to ensure that United States territory is completely invulnerable to Soviet intercontinental ballistic missiles, which would enable the United States to count on mounting a nuclear attack on the Soviet Union with impunity."

March-early April, 1985. The war date debacle had been devastatingly embarrassing. FOG members drafted an apology letter for the Urantia movement that 19 members signed. It was not signed by a few members, including Grimsley, McCade and Ms. Kantor. Perhaps this trio felt they had no apology to make.

Grimsley is also reported to have written a letter attempting to explain the more recent messages, but the group rejected the letter. The letter hasn't been seen, and neither have the 1985 messages that dealt the institute its lethal blow.

Spring-Summer, 1985. Grimsley goes into the community to replenish defections, leading him to spend more time on his talents as a guitarist and singer. More music is heard in the institute, and he plays other engagements with friends. On one of these, on a rainy night, he is seriously shocked by a microphone and is rushed to emergency care. He later recalls a remarkable near-death experience, saying that he had crossed over and returned.

At that time, FOG had already laid plans to file a suit against the Catholic order from which they had purchased the Clayton property, citing discrepancies in selling prices and disclosures. With Grimsley disabled for a time, much of this work fell upon Nancy.

During the litigation process, Kantor is accused of communicating with the Catholic order and criticized for it. In one last meeting at FOG, Kantor reportedly urges the group to vacate the premises so that the church order could move in. He is still on salary at FOG at the time, but McCade demands the return of his keys.

March 25, 1986. The institute is lost to foreclosure and on this date, exactly a year after Kantor's war watch episode, it is repossessed by eviction. The sheriff and the attorney for the Catholic order showed up to serve the papers. A small group was there.

Grimsley reportedly walked out of the glass front doors and showed the attorney the plaque that he had made for the institute. It read: "This studio is dedicated to Jesus of Nazareth and the continuation of his mission and message – the Spiritual Renaissance Institute, Clayton, California."

He carried it with him and continued to make radio broadcasts from a new home he called "The Ranch." He and Nancy lived on the western slopes of the Sierra Mountains near Yosemite National Park.

Through the years, he moved on and continued his ministry, never disavowing his midwayer messages and staying away from Urantia politics.

THE AFTERMATH: Voices of Explanation

Two central players in FOG and the 1985 incident, however, were more vocal as the years went by. I still couldn't connect for certain midwayer warnings of decades earlier with Urantia's sour view of our teachers today, but I would continue trying by seeing what people thought in the aftermath. Was there a prevailing Urantia mindset now that precluded any celestial contact? Did the March 25 debacle irrevocably end the possibility of the Teaching Mission being accepted within the book's organizations?

Mr. Kantor spoke candidly in 1993-4 on the new internet e-mail discussion group called UrantiaL, a forum managed by Michael Million. It was rich in Teaching Mission validity debate in 1993-94 and hundreds of pages are chronicled at www.tmarchives.com on its history pages. When the forum developed more traffic than Million could manage, he turned it over to the Urantia Foundation in 1995.

Ms. Blackstock made a Urantia presentation of the follies of FOG as well, and also challenged a message from an alleged midwayer trying to comfort her. Both personalities remain prominent speakers and leaders in the Urantia family and speak well to the events within the Family to help us understand the workings of their minds.

The Teaching Mission

On January 30, 1993, Kantor addressed a San Francisco forum to study revelatory processes.

"The last time I addressed a group of readers of *The Urantia Book* was the occasion of a dinner which The Family of God Foundation put on to celebrate 25 years of radio broadcasting. My objective on that occasion was the articulation of arguments which would convince the listeners that we at The Family of God Foundation were working with the Planetary Spiritual Government and were involved in a special project which was a critical component of the fifth epochal revelation – the protection of the revelation during a period of global chaos and the training of teachers to be involved in the subsequent rebuilding of the world.

"In the course of pursuing those delusions an estimated $3,000,000 in resources was consumed. In addition, we destroyed a twenty-five year effort to create a service organization which was beginning to establish international operations. Numerous individuals experienced substantial personal suffering in the destruction of ideals, hopes, marriages, careers and life savings.

"An even greater loss was the destruction of Urantia Brotherhood by Urantia Foundation and the millions of dollars consumed by the latter organization on legal matters of dubious value.

"We must wake up and recognize that at the source of each of these tragedies lies the claim that someone is acting as a special agent of the source of the fifth epochal revelation. Until we come to terms with this reality, we will continue to flounder as a movement and will continue to consume the resources of the group dealing with the repercussions of failing to wisely manage ourselves."

PITFALLS IN THE MIND; DANGERS WITHIN THE STILLNESS

On March 8, 1993, Kantor authored a post for UrantiaL called 'Fog reflections in TM twilight' in response to fervent debater Leo Elliott. With the emergence of the Teaching Mission, he goes back to FOG history to issue a strong labyrinth of warnings and admonitions. While this was all posted as one paragraph, I've sub-divided it to enhance readability.

Hello Logondonters;

It's a pleasure to participate in this exchange and I again thank Michael Million for making this possible. Leo (where do you get time to write all that stuff?) and others have been prodding me for a story about the FOG affair and I find it very difficult to even know where to begin.

While I cannot claim to have any particular purchase on objective reality, I can make some comments about how the process of functioning as a conscious entity

476

in this strange enchanted world appears to me; my comments here are strictly subjective observations.

There is a problem with adequately describing my experience. This is not due to any repressed emotional reactions to the topic, but rather to the nature of the experience and the virtual impossibility of adequately describing it. This problem stems from the fact that symbolic communication presupposes a description of a logical sequence of events or facts, or an analogy in which the known is compared with the unknown so that its nature may be communicated. Because our experience became increasingly non- rational as time went on, it does not lend itself well to communication with symbols which require a rationally structured linguistic foundation as a presupposition to their use.

My experience at FOG (and I have to restrict myself to my own experience – there are as many stories as people involved) was such that with receiving messages and changing our lives so that we were increasingly living relative to their content, we gradually, almost unconsciously, over a period of many months, slowly left the domain of rational access to our thoughts and actions. There seems to be a holistic quality to consciousness in that patterns of cognition and responses to stimuli which occur under certain circumstances begin to affect one's cognition and responses in all circumstances. There cannot (in a healthy mind) be radically different modes of conscious response from one set of stimuli to another. The primary task of the ego is to maintain integration within the psyche. Rationality is a human artifact brought to the system – the ego could care less about it. So when we make a conscious choice to suspend rational judgement in one domain of our conscious functioning, and that particular domain comes to have a powerful attraction for us, the ego will slowly begin to take these new patterns of associative activity and apply them to other domains of our conscious activity.

The reception of our messages required the complete suspension of critical judgement and evaluation. In order to receive them, it was necessary to enter into a stillness and let them enter, uninhibited by any humanly-created factors in our consciousness. This was difficult at first, but became easier with practice. It was made easier by the emotional rush of thinking that we were actually in contact with the planetary administration, and by the social closeness which was felt with other individuals who were experiencing the same thing. What had formerly been critical consciousness wherein ideas and experiences were evaluated by more normative criteria of rationality and relatedness to other known phenomena gave way to a hyper-critical consciousness which evaluated every experience and idea for confirmatory reinforcement that what we believed to be happening was actually so.

This is somewhat akin to putting out to sea in a sailboat and then deciding that the mast and sail are blocking the view and proceeding to destroy them. This makes for a great unobstructed view and one has some time to enjoy the uncluttered view of the horizon and the full dome of stars at night. But sooner or later, a storm is going to come up. Good Luck. I hope you enjoyed your unobstructed view because now the only thing of any concern is going to be survival. You no longer have any means of negotiating the sea because of your impulsive foolishness. The elements are unleashing a fury unlike anything you ever imagined. If you survive the storm, you will be fortunate. Once the storm is over you will still have the problem of getting back to land to repair your ship and make it seaworthy once more. And if you were foolish enough to take all your friends with you in your boat, there won't even be anyone back on shore to help you make your way back in.

In a situation such as prevailed at FOG, we had been into it for so long that all our closest friends were involved. When the moment of truth came and reality shattered, we could no longer turn to each other for advice and support because we realized how we had all led each other into this blind alley – no one could be trusted to render a clear picture of our situation. It was very lonely and psychologically scary – we had the unpleasant experience of peering into the abyss of total insanity and comprehending its nature. I cannot overstate the danger, neither do I have confidence in my ability to communicate the nature of this danger. It is beyond rational articulation.

At any rate, we slowly, willingly abdicated rationality to the point that when things started getting really strange, we were unable to evaluate or act in any way other than trying to get more messages to clarify our situation. The stranger things got, the stranger the messages became as we found ourselves in an undocumented region of collective consciousness which resembled a multi-dimensional hall of mirrors. Our whole orientation to reality had become conditioned by our messages and our personal identities had become wholly tied up in being persons who received such messages.

I think the situation is made even more difficult at the present time because of the contemporary influence of traditional eastern mysticism on Christian religious culture. The problem lies in the divergent objectives of the two. Eastern mysticism concerns itself with providing the disciple with the means of attaining a specific state of consciousness – with using techniques of consciousness to bring about a particular neurological state which can then be experienced by that consciousness. Christian culture is far more concerned with gaining access to information and with the processes by which that information can be used to bring about a spiritual transformation of human culture.

Christianity is a communal religion. I think it is a particularly illusive undertaking which attempts to utilize the techniques originating in eastern mysticism to attempt to achievement of the purposes embodied in Christian culture. Consider the issues of the Lucifer Rebellion. The primary issue was that Lucifer felt the culture which the Creator Sons brought to the planets in their local universes was imported for purposes of political control and maintained by conspiratorial consensus amongst the Creator Sons and their staffs. Lucifer proclaimed the doctrine of individual liberty and rejected the conceptual foundations which our Creator Son was attempting to utilize as a basis for evolving spiritual life from biological antecedents in these domains which we now inhabit. These issues need to be more fully understood by our community of readers.

I would be foolish to say that contact with superhuman intelligences was impossible or should be completely ruled out. Our problem here is one of epistemology and predates our old testament heritage. This problem of "discerning of spirits" has a long history and has posed serious difficulties for the best spiritual minds on this planet for over 2,000 years. *The Urantia Book* simply gives a more detailed conceptual foundation upon which the same issues are being recast.

For me, this heritage of Christian thought is a gold mine of diaries and journals of fellow travelers. I find much succor here. It's as if I lived in the mid 19th century on the east coast of the US and wanted to load up my stuff in a wagon and head out west. Would I be wise to trust my rugged independence and personal judgement, and simply point my team and wagon towards the sunset? It might be fine as I made my way across Iowa and Kansas but when I hit the canyonlands of southern Utah or the Rocky Mountains, I might begin to wish I had spent a little time in the saloons in St. Louis, talking with people who had made the journey before and knew the way through what would otherwise be insurmountable obstacles.

But then this is an adventure, right? A quest on the part of each individual, and each one of us must chart our courses and be loyal to whatever we most deeply believe to be the truth. We are all lost in a labyrinth and can only follow the Master's advice about knowing the truth and the truth making us free. Wherever we happen to exist in that labyrinth, we can be certain that the honest pursuit of truth will get us out. We will take odd routes, get stuck in cul-de-sacs, take long detours when we could have taken a shortcut, but it's important that we are on our journey, that we are actively involved in it and that we are sincerely pursuing truth and utilizing all available resources in that pursuit.

Take care, friends; I greet you through the soft hail of electrons upon which this message is modulated....

Kantor had framed the stillness experience as an invitation to profound errors, a dangerous course to follow. I reminded myself that the Stillness we advocated required the mind to be turned off so that it wouldn't play tricks on us. It seems to have done so with Kantor, or at least he blames it.

But he also seemed to believe that turning off the mind would open one to dangerous influences as well, seemingly the loss of rational judgment. He himself could not seem to turn off the judgments in subsequent posts which became more candid.

JUDGMENTS AND THEIR SUSPENSION

On March 10, 1993, Kantor explores on the list his mindset upon first joining the Family:

"You are very perceptive in your comments about isolation having set in with the FOG crew prior to any messages. Not only this, but the beginnings of suspension of rational judgement had also set in long before the messages.

"When I first visited FOG, I was really turned off by their approach to dealing with the 5th and I thought that Vern was a bit marginal. The only reason I went over there was because in the late 60's, I had spent several days in Chicago visiting with Emma (Christy) Christensen discussing the possibilities open to a young person fairly committed to same 5th. She had spoken highly of Vern's work and suggested that I consider working with him.

"So when I visited Berkeley and observed my reactions, I chided myself for being so judgmental and critical – after all, weren't they getting the teachings of Jesus out over the airwaves? (airwaves – now there's an interesting term!) So I thought I needed to suspend my own prejudices in order to participate in a group effort, x and I think I was correct in my assumption that I could accomplish far more as part of a group than as an individual.

"I'm not rationalizing here, simply recounting the beginnings. I really got into it and appreciated the opportunity to produce and publish the multi-media programs which were performed over the years. I felt some really good work got done. Incidentally, this issue remains a problem – doesn't one always have to sacrifice some personal freedom and independence in order to participate in a group effort? And where does one cross the line separating social accommodation from a loss of personal integrity?

"So I made my compromises with my ideals (having read in the UB that one's highest ideals are not necessarily synonymous with the will of God) and proceeded on my path. This turns out to have been the experience of many of us with FOG, so you can see the developing nature of the self-selected sample which later crashed and burned when these compromises continued to develop to their logical conclusion."

Kantor says nothing about a new religion of Jesus and more about trying to suspend his prejudices.

Immediately, Kantor was questioned on UrantiaL by Byron Belitsos, an author and publisher with strong Urantian roots and a Teaching Mission explorer. He makes an effort to gain access to the 1985 messages for the good of the movement. Belitsos writes:

The Teaching Mission

"Ex-Foggers aside from Vern himself believe that the messages received by Vern, and by Dave Kantor and Sara Blackstock (whose transmissions in early 1985 further embellished Vern's original WWIII messages), were of origin in their own subconscious – yarns of the mind at mischief. It would be a true service to the community if the actual content of these messages, and the inside story of the FOG experience, were fully disclosed. Eight years is enough time for healing and reflection. This event profoundly affected us all; therefore, it now belongs to the whole community. These 'channeled' texts belong to the public domain. It is part of our lore, yarns or not. I for one call upon Sara and Dave – and even Vern – to disclose the details of their contacts. Does anyone out there join me? The two made a good start at this disclosure during the Forum."

Kantor replied on March 10:

"I appreciate your call for more information about our experience at FOG. I think there are important lessons there for all of us to learn, but I am not sure how to access or present the relevant information. My talk at the forum was a start. I have been critical of the failure of the readership to assimilate these lessons but I have been unable to contribute information which might facilitate this process and remain uncertain about how to do so. I am leaning toward the opinion that such disclosure can only be relevant when it is a part of an interaction with other individuals, which is why I am participating in this electronic forum – perhaps a way will be made clear.

"I was somewhat surprised by your statement that "eight years is enough time for healing and reflection." Upon what do you base this? How do you come up with a time period after which an individual should have "recovered" from an experience whose nature, by your own statements, you do not understand? We didn't fall down and scrape a knee.

"In many ways your call for us to disclose our experiences is a request to do something which is humanly impossible. This is due to the unique nature of the experience and not to any residual feelings about it. I feel a sense of responsibility to try to share our experiences more broadly, particularly in light of the present enchantment with the TM, but I remain mystified as to how to adequately do so. Any factual description of our experience would fall far short of communicating its essence.

"Your call is similar to a request to publicly describe my experience of the death of my child after a long illness. Such a description would be humanly impossible to render – not because of its emotional nature but because its depth far exceeds the conceptual capacity of linguistic symbols. (I have not had such an experience but use it as an example). Such experiences can at best be communicated through metaphor or poetry but certainly not in a factual disclosure.

"If you aggressively try to probe into these matters I can guarantee you that you will destroy a process which has taken eight years to begin. There are many individuals who were involved who will probably not recover during the course of their mortal lives.

"The best I can offer at this point is to try to be in sincere dialog regarding the issues. I am willing to share my ideas but have no interest in attempting to dissuade anyone from pursuing whatever experiences they wish to pursue. Neither do I have any interest in mounting a defense of my position.

"While I feel that my position is well-grounded and based on the best I know as well as being under continuous scrutiny and processing, I could well be wrong – it's happened before. In addition, I have a great deal of personal respect for the privacy of my fellows who shared in the experience.

"No amount of factual disclosure could reveal truth. A collection of facts would only provide a basis for individuals who did not share the experience to project their own meanings on the facts and I think the present situation with the TMers indicates massive, uncontrolled psychological projective processes are in full operation within the readership. The meanings of facts cannot be ascertained apart from the values of the individual attempting to assimilate the facts.

"The real bottom line is that I am not really very interested in the topic – I am involved in a number of things at the present time which I find to be far more stimulating, productive and relevant.

"It's been a matter of interest to see that those individuals who experienced the FOG episode who are involved today with the TM scene, are almost without exception, individuals who telephoned me within a few weeks of the FOG collapse to tell me that they didn't think we made a mistake, that somehow the situation had changed and that it was the external situation and not our messages that was the problem. I couldn't believe my ears when I heard this happening and I see these same people today, eagerly embracing the TM movement. They appear to me as individuals who were unable to assimilate essential lessons the first time around and I suspect they will have to repeat the class until they do.

"You have called for me to disclose details of my contacts but I have repeatedly stated that there were no contacts. In addition, I have attempted to articulate some of the factors which I think led us to believe that we had contacts. If you have questions about the FOG situation which are relevant to your own on-going quest for truth please contact me here, publicly or privately. If you seek information for any other purpose, please look elsewhere. I don't believe that anyone's personal experience, under any circumstances, is public property.

"I encourage you to utilize your critical consciousness which I have seen you effectively bring to bear on many situations in the past."

Kantor is correct that FOG didn't just scrape a toe. Purported messages into untrustworthy minds did bring down the organization. Grimsley still stood by his 1983 contacts, even as Kantor was painting him with the same brush he was painting himself and others such as

Blackstock, who professed being deluded. He spoke out again on March 12, and revealed a stronger judgment of Grimsley.

"You state that we had "the rest of the UB movement to turn to ..." which from an external view would seem true, but from my viewpoint was not possible because I had destroyed my connection with that larger community. The fact that that larger community may have been available was of no help until I could change enough to reach out for it. You are absolutely right that we "REFUSED deliberately and knowingly to turn outwards for critical evaluation" and that "many opportunities were given..." I can remember Vern consigning letters which had been written by concerned UB students to the trash without even reading them. I did not want to even hear from anyone who didn't believe our messages because my own hold on them was so tenuous and I relied on that hold for my entire social identity and psychological well-being.

"I know this must sound stupid and incredulous, but I must report my best recollection of the experience for better or for worse – this is not a forum for my articulation of my good judgement. And, while I must assume responsibility for my own attitudes and participation, I will say that Vern fostered a sense of superiority in the group which we all bought into. He (as well as Christy, when she was alive) would constantly tell us about our special mission, how we were chosen to bring a special message to a benighted world, how we each had very experienced thought adjusters, how we had all been brought together by divine guidance, etc., etc., etc., ad nauseam. – And I and others bought into it. Because our entire sense of self was thus built up over a long period of time, many of us were ready to defend this source of reality-definition to the death because we had become it and it had become who we thought we were.

"This is precisely the type of closed, subjective isolation of self which I see beginning to develop in the TM movement. The danger of the illusion is that it creates within the individual the perception that he/she is becoming more in contact with the universal while in reality he/she is becoming increasingly isolated in a subjectivity which is increasingly reinforced by other individuals experiencing the same thing. As events continued at FOG and got worse and worse, the psychological stress was such that we simply could not entertain the cognitive dissonance which would result from a serious consideration of an alternative viewpoint. Rather than honestly confront the critical assessments of our actions, we chose to categorize the individuals who were providing the criticism as ignorant of the true reality of what we were about; therefore their criticism was seen as irrelevant and ill-informed.

"I suspect that Vern purposely isolated his organization from you folks on the other side of the bay because he recognized that your critical assessment of his activities would reveal him to be like the wizard of oz, hiding behind his screen manipulating the images of himself which were seen by the public. I sincerely apologize for my participation in this unfair and un-Christlike isolation of one group of believers from another."

Kantor soon says more on the list, relating the Teaching Mission to the violent confrontation between federal agents and well-armed religious zealots in Waco, TX.

"How close was FOG to the kind of situation which developed in Waco? Good question. It is fortunate that the UB does not present the image of a violent God as is portrayed in much of the Bible. Compare the images of violence and wrath and apocalyptic presented in the Bible with those presented in the UB. Not much in the UB, is there? So even when UB readers go non-linear and become overpowered by their archetypes, those archetypes are not likely to contain images of violence, so I think it would take a particularly misled group to stray so far from the images contained in the UB that they would take such drastic action.
As an aside, it is interesting to see how easy it is for individuals and groups to accumulate substantial arsenals of weapons and ammunition in our culture. We never were able to locate a 50-caliber machine gun though; I have to hand it to those folks in Waco–they do know how to run a serious show and there's little doubt that they fully believe in what they're doing...they would probably tell you about the kind, sincere, loving guidance that David Koresh has provided for the group and how wonderful the group was....

"Let's describe the situation that developed at FOG as "potentially" volatile. We did manage to extricate ourselves before things really got out of hand, but the potential for disaster was within reach. In light of the fact that we had substantial supplies as well as $1.5 million in gold stashed at the institute, Vern had told me to do whatever I thought was necessary to provide for security, including purchase of weapons and seeing to it that people were trained in their use, and had given me access to virtually unlimited amounts of money with which to do so, although he told me that he didn't want to know anything about it so that if anyone asked him about it he could legitimately deny knowledge.

"Now I'm not a person particularly prone to violence and the individuals in our group pretty much abhorred the idea of guns even existing on the premises – it was a matter of no small controversy within the group. We did not develop this potential beyond the purchasing of a few rifles and handguns, not much more than would be used by a security force on a college campus, but had Vern given such free reign to someone whose underlying social pathology was a little more developed than mine, the results could have been substantially different.

"To me, one of the most curious remaining questions from the FOG episode has to do with the nature of social psychology. If you posit a group level of the collective unconscious as is posited in Jung's work, and if you give this group level of consciousness some pre-volitional attributes, a very interesting model of what happened at FOG emerges. My interpretation (based on only a superficial understanding of Jung's work–I have not studied it in detail) of Jung's ideas would lead me to believe that, just as the ego strives to maintain integration of the various components of the individual psyche, there are similar forces at work on various associative levels of the collective unconscious as well. I think this idea is fairly well substantiated with studies on family psychology and tribal psycho-social systems.

"In other words, these social systems have their own innate psychological dynamics which work to maintain the unity and integrity of the group. Here is what is so interesting to me about what happened at FOG: I think that by the early 80's there was a general recognition by the group that Vern's–let's call it "style"–was not very conducive to the kind of growth and development of our organization which we all could sense needed to take place. Vern was having an increasingly difficult time managing his organization, his marriage was plagued with violence, and he was developing an alcohol dependency (although these latter two elements were well concealed from most of the group.)

"His claim to be getting messages "immediately" brought the organization back under his full control. Once the organization was fully back in his grip, his own paranoid tendencies began to dominate his messages. As time went by, he stopped getting messages and his power within the group again began to weaken, but he attempted to maintain power and control by taking an unyielding stance and attempting to assert authoritative power. How could the group possibly rescue itself and maintain its integrity when it's [sic] objectives had become so dominated by this man's delusions and shaped by his unresolved psychological conflicts?

"Here's how: The group seized full power by beginning to get its own messages independent of Vern; he became confused and organizationally impotent. These messages even pointed out defects in Vern's personality as reasons why he was no longer competent to get messages, isolating him even farther from the center of group power.

"In addition, we were able to set a date by which Vern's original messages would be either proven to be true or disproven–the collective unconscious of the group engineered and executed a very effective solution.

"Once we rescued ourselves from the psychological hole we had gotten into, I personally (for better or worse) got involved in some specific legal actions which would do as much as possible to prevent Vern from being able to do the same thing again with another group of individuals anytime in the near future and perhaps for the remainder of his life, and this last statement is really all I want to say on the legal issues, as all the relevant documents have been sealed by the courts and are inaccessible.

"Please bear in mind that the above psychological story is only one model, only one way of looking at what happened, but I find it an interesting speculation on the dynamics which were in operation within the group; it provides an explanation of the dynamics involved which is accepted by many who were a part of the group."

ENDING OF A THREAD

At this point, I had heard quite enough from Kantor. In this narrative, he appears to outline how the organization was wrested from Grimsley's control in 1984, after Urantia's crippling withdrawal, with members establishing independence from his outdated style, and setting up the March 25 event to finally prove the idiocy of channeled messages. In all of his very informative rhetoric, I heard nothing related to spirituality coming from him at all. I could only recall that he had to submerge his prejudices when he joined FOG in the first place, and now he seemed to be Grimsley's biggest critic.

And once a person gets into marital discords and personal attack on an internet forum, it's altogether more than I wanted to research. I only knew that the Kantors divorced and he was subsequently married to FOG staff member Rebecca Marshall. There was hearsay that he and Vern were not on good terms.

But my basic research question was why the Urantia movement is suspicious to disdainful of channeled messages from their advocates. There seemed no relationship between the Teaching Mission's spiritual lessons and Urantia's controversial midwayer message board which contained no semblance of spiritual information. And with Kantor's constant and voluminous confessional warnings, into which he inappropriately pulls Grimsley, it's no wonder that Urantia is consistently fearful of the process.

They are fearful of the trickery of their own minds. They should learn to control them.

And they are fearful of turning off their minds and releasing to spirit. It perhaps had not occurred to many that when one goes into stillness to know and experience the Universal Father, with worship, prayer and the desire to grow, then that will surely happen. But TM people seemed to have a faith not present in the analytical and fearful Urantia circles. If you weren't constantly thinking and judging, you could slip into a danger zone and be deleteriously influenced by your lower self.

The teachers have constantly reminded us that we are all either motivated by fear or love, and we can make the choice.

Kantor's motivations over the succeeding years have been to charge various personalities with manipulating the Fifth Epochal Revelation to their own ends, including Grimsley, Myers, McMullen and Christy. Later, there would be vehement criticism of the Urantia Foundation's policies. There was a falling-out with Keeler, the first person he called after his March 25 debacle. He accused Keeler of making a death threat when he reportedly said he would like to see Kantor experience "a slow and painful death." Much of this dirty laundry and more played out on internet discussions.

I had been warned in the beginning not to get embroiled in Urantian politics. I could see why. To equate all of this with the Teaching Mission purposes, the curriculum, and twenty years of foundational spiritual wisdom was an impossible stretch, but Urantia readers were making it routinely.

THE AFTERMATH: The Blackstock Papers

But what of Ms. Blackstock, known as a loving and caring person with plenty of intellect. She made some confessions in a paper called "Pitfalls of Spiritual Community," delivered at a gathering in Illinois. She is not kind to herself.

"The little vignette I am going to share with you came literally at the very end of this experiment with spiritual community. You may not remember that day about seven years ago in March of 1985 when about 40 of us almost literally disappeared into our own fog – down into a shelter which we had spent more than a year preparing based on 'channeled' messages which predicted a nuclear war."

As I read the paper, I saw the power of human psychology once more, as the author turned her rationalizations in that direction. I recalled that she was married to lawyer Bob Blackstock, who had represented FOG and Nancy Grimsley in communications with Caston over his infamous evaluation report. I recalled that Caston had enlisted a psychologist, Dr. Paul Knott, who agreed with his perceptions about the Grimsley messages. Dr. Knott, the psychologist and a Urantia Book reader, noted that people in stress can indeed hear a perceptible voice, like the reassuring words of a loving parent.

"The difficult decision is thus made for him," said Dr. Knott, "his anxiety is relieved, and the purchase (of the Clayton property) is subsequently made." This explained everything for Caston, about both Christy and Grimsley.

Blackstock admits to an "all in" commitment that WWIII would hit on that March 25 date. She and her husband loaded survival goods onto a rented trailer and uprooted their whole life to get to the shelter by midnight. They brought aged "Grandma Lou" with her potty chair and privacy screen. Her son had been allowed to get camouflage clothes and a dirt bike so that he could be a messenger boy after the apocalypse. For days after March 25, she admits to breaking down in tears over the experience, even while stating that all of her experiences in the Family of God contributed to her spiritual growth.

She outlines several pitfalls associated with a spiritual community in general, as well as antidotes for each.

First pitfall was an evaluation that "the group was following an ideal as a 'shell' because many did not have the foundation within their own lives." She notes that some had even skipped the "essential experience" of family in their own lives, including the Grimsleys. Others had skipped scholastic opportunities or family callings to pursue the work of the Family. Blackstock thinks people should pay primary attention to building "foundational ideas in their own lives" first. She says people in spiritual communities should "get their priorities straight" and "It is NOT to first go out and tell the world about God; it is to first live it in one's own personal life."

With pitfall one, Blackstock clearly describes herself since that is what she knows. It isn't clear if her judgments do indeed pertain to others who didn't get their priorities straight and devoted too much time to FOG service and too little to other things that she considers priorities. It seemed reasonable to me that all people must make decisions between building their own spiritual lives and living lives of service to others. One is also free to raise a family or not on the planet without having their decisions questioned. First-hand parenting experience didn't seem mandatory before building a Jesus ministry or a fellowship of altruistic believers.

Pitfall two for Blackstock was a vacuum of knowledge within FOG of cult and channeling phenomena and "psychological processes accompanying social and spiritual development." She mentions textbook definitions of falsely predicted catastrophes and influential preachers who hold people in their sway. She points to a book on channeling published by Arthur Hastings in 1990 and a workshop on Urantia and the psychology of Carl Jung, sponsored by the Golden Gate (Urantia) Society of the San Francisco Bay area.

With psychologists continually trumpeting how the mind can be untrustworthy, I wondered how you could persuade people to go into stillness and trust any messages at all. Psychologists seem to feed the fearful with what they fear.

Conversely, the teachers say that if you can't trust your mind when you open to God, then you should learn to do that first. It's your first consideration.

It seemed rather perverse that the custodians of the most complete cosmology of the universe and the true story of Jesus' incarnation should spend so much time battling the concept of celestial connection, and letting psychologists rationalize it as unreal. After all, I believed that most academic and practicing psychologists on the planet today would throw huge doubts at the revelatory claims of their beloved Urantia papers. Urantia advocates want respect from academia, but the academy doesn't respect spiritual revelation. Urantia advocates often try to distance themselves from the so-called 'new age' paths, and it only retards sharing and acceptance of their book in those active circles.

Pitfall number three for Blackstock was a "chosen people" attitude that she saw developing among the Family members. This again was her speculative judgment of others. It seemed to me that people who are doing significant spiritual work likely do believe themselves to be imbued with spirit and doing special service. I didn't see a clear relationship in her argument, but her key antidote is to "live a normal, ordinary life, and to establish the kingdom by such methods." She makes a clear, free will choice that many have made when public service gets to be too much – get back to spiritual basics in my own life.

Pitfall four for Ms. Blackstock is that FOG members lacked the ability to be self-critical as an organization. That seemed to me a problem with any kind of organization and, in reflection, her other pitfall-antidote mixes could be applied to other spiritual and secular organizations of all kinds.

So did pitfall five, in which she thinks they gave over too much personal decision-making to other people. She states: "This is probably one of the more elusive and difficult ones to analyze because each one of us thought that we were asking the Father what His will was, and each of us thought that we were following that will to one degree or another. We really felt that we were willing to go anywhere, do anything to serve God. It did appear that we participated in making our own decisions within the context of the group. I don't think at the time we felt we were being controlled by our own unconscious desires to be great and do great things, or that we were responding to archetypes of leadership or importance."

She concludes that people didn't realize "we were being controlled by our own unconscious desires to be great and do great things." Is she saying this is a bad thing? Isn't it a good thing to be inspired to do great work and at least attempt it?

This language of 'unconscious desire" seemed again to smack of a psychiatrist's couch or the thick theories of an academic paper. If there was really communication with midwayers, it must supercede earthbound academic explanations. They can no more explain it than Blackstock can. They can no more refute the messages or confirm them than anyone else can.

Blackstock's antidote on decision-making comes appropriately from the Urantia Papers: "Sometimes the planting of a seed necessitates its death, the death of your fondest hopes, before it can be reborn to bear the fruits of new life and new opportunity. And from them (the ministering reserve seraphim) you will learn to suffer less through sorrow and disappointment, first, by making fewer personal plans concerning other personalities, and then, by accepting your lot when you have faithfully performed your duty."   (p.555) [Blackstock's parenthetic]

She also quotes the perceived wisdom of Grandma Lou, who said she got one of the best nights of sleep in a long time in the shelter. She later said she knew there would be no war, and also commented about the people involved: "And they all looked so normal."

In her report, Blackstock never mentions receiving any messages from midwayers, nor anyone else.

A MIDWAYER RESPONSE

In February, 1993, as the Teaching Mission was getting underway, Lamphere, identifying himself as a primary midwayer, transmitted a message intended for Ms. Blackstock through a young and uncertain new transmitter in Sarasota, Florida, with the spirit name, Patije. After some equivocation, doubt and delay, the transmitter passed on the message.

Patijie had met her at a Urantia conference and admired her, but didn't know her very well and was hesitant to pass the message on. As it turns out, this was an important dialogue to understand the Urantia reader mindset.

While intended to be private to her, Blackstock made a public reply to Lamphere's message and the transmitter on UrantiaL, in February of 1993. This was a Urantia-based internet discussion group, whose postings can be read at www.teamarchives.com in the history section.

The Teaching Mission

After reading the message and the reply, I could see more of the enormous differences in the way midwayers and humans think. They have lived here through many generations of humans, while each of us starts as an innocent, unknowing babe with a finite future. Think of the differences in perception regarding God's universal plan.

Lamphere, the midwayer, made these statements to the transmitter (Patijie) after she was awakened from sleep and made a commitment at that moment to do the Father's will.

"I am Lamphere, primary midwayer, faithful and true without default. My partner and I have worked for many of your planetary centuries of time measurement. It has been our responsibility to warn those who had the revelation . . . textbook during crises times upon your planet.

"Several years ago, there was a crisis building in which all of our efforts seemed not to come to fruition until the very last moments of human free will choice. During this time we were advised by Christ Michael to appear to selected mortals to begin a counter-effort for preservation of the epochal revelation and those mortals who were prepared to execute preparations for the Reserve Corps of Destiny, which had not yet been activated but would soon be so.

"It is unfortunate that humans have the unforeseeable make-up of debilitating doubt or extreme intensity about carrying forth what they know that they know. Much progress has been made for the celestial contact upon Urantia in this Correcting Time. I want you to know me. My integrity is without blemish. There is one who suffers great alarm at any suggestion of possible contact by a midwayer. I desire to relieve her suffering. However, not understanding the dire circumstances and being devastated by disappointment, my efforts to illuminate have been thoroughly and unequivocally rebuffed from explanation.

"Inform that dear one, Sara Blackstock, to wrap herself in God's light of protection and ask to have an explanation which will be for her ears and knowingness alone. None other will understand the devastation and betrayal that dear one has known. She alone will know the truth of what is to be said. Her loyalty and steadfast faith was sorely tried and the sensitivity of knowing not from where the message originates nor why she responds within while rejecting from the strength of her mind – which is great! –causes bewilderment and confusion to her.

"We would say to her: Put aside fear and embrace the Father's will. You will not be forsaken nor betrayed for your faith in truth, beauty and goodness. We are here. We are real. This is contact. This is not evil. You know us by your experience and you never got to know the fruits of your labor, only the consequences of the negative side of the action which did not materialize. Only moments intervened to enable us to enjoy in our success to divert the disaster for which you were prepared.

"With regrets we honor your free will choice and stand by allowing the pain and disillusionment to soften and disappear. We are only a short ways from you, dear sorrowful one. You can call upon us with but a whispered word. We await your call.

"My assurance not to compromise nor interdict (?) your unquestioned free will accompanies this message. We will not overstay our welcome if you bid us passage(?). It will remain your choice – always. [Question notations concern whether this is the correct word that is being transmitted.]

"I, Lamphere, draw close to the end of my message. It is true even we are limited by the free will choice of the individuals to which we are drawn. We stand by helplessly wishing to relieve discomfort and promote healing and can do nothing until it is asked for in prayer and accepted in knowing from the knowing point within one – the spirit of truth speaks softly."

In response, Ms. Blackstock utilized the list to explain how she had dealt with the episode.

"It was indeed a short-term devastating experience, but as I began to realize how egocentric it was of me to feel 'devastated,' about NO WAR, and I began to understand some of the causes for the downfall of FOG, and I got more integrated into REAL LIFE, and I felt the love and support of all around me, grieving occurred and over a period of time I feel that I have been not only healed but liberated from that experience.

"It is no secret that I do not believe that the channeling phenomenon is what it says it is – messages and teachings from superhuman or 'others.' There are several views on this subject, perhaps with a little of each making up the Truth. I tend to embrace the psychological explanation, maybe because I understand it reasonably well, living with my husband who has read Carl Jung for years. He and I have had hundreds of hours of conversations about basic concepts in psychology, such as the personal unconscious, the collective unconscious, collective consciousness, projection, compensation, archetypes, and the alter-ego and wish-fulfillment concepts. I also gained a deeper understanding of what *the Urantia Book* means when it says that "Mind does not well stand conflict." These psychological understandings helped me to express my grief, going through a very intense and real grieving experience over the loss of a commitment and an ideal, and then to understand, at least partially, how it happened that I ended up getting messages from 'others.'

"Because of my own experiential understandings and my progressing education about psychological concepts and an increasing, although still limited understanding of the workings of the material mind, at least my own, it appears to me that every student of *the Urantia Book* ought to be educated in at least the basic concepts of psychology in order to evaluate his/her experiences with the powerful realities which are presented to us in *the Urantia Book*. If we do not educate ourselves we will continue to fall prey to our own fantasies, needs and confusion over the archetypes which have been developing in our collective unconscious since the times of Dalamatia.

"I do believe that everyone I have talked to who are TR's, or are involved in the channeling phenomenon are very sincere people, dedicated to God and doing his will, and are truly searching for truth, and thinking they have found truth in the 'Teaching Mission.' I have even seen some 'fruits' in the sense that people have been told to read *the Urantia Book* more, to pray more. I believe that their own soul and consciousness is telling them to do what they should have been doing from the time of realizing that God was real. But it is good that they are doing more of this now. And probably very few of us are overdoing worship!

"I am very disturbed, however, that you and many others think that this phenomena is REAL. We are all CHANNELS. We all have true spirit guides living within us and interacting on a constant basis with us – the highest guides in the universe – a spark of divinity, the Spirit of Truth, the Universe Mother Spirit, and all of the agencies that work with her, and our own angels. If we 'listen' to these perfect guides and do what the deepest and truest part of ourselves tells us, we do not have to have any other 'guides' who make gross errors which seem to be easily rationalized away. If the universe teachers were as disorganized as they seem from the transcripts I have read, the predictions which have not panned out, and some major errors, then it would indeed be a universe unworthy of our hard work to progress."

It seemed clear that Jungian theory worked for Ms. Blackstone. She could rationalize the Urantia revelation as being true, but seemed to believe that further efforts to reach into the spirit world would likely send you into the world of psychosis, perhaps onto a psychiatrist's couch, and you would be talking to variations of yourself and your unreliable mind. There seemed no notice that one can transmit volumes of well-founded personal spiritual advice as seen in our archives. There seemed instead an obsession with the process of transmitting itself when the focus should be on the fruits of the spirit. And our mode of conveyance and communications with the teachers seemed personal, unobtrusive and gracious, especially after our groups center themselves in spirit with worship, prayer and dedication to service.

Ms. Blackstock correctly asserted the truest guidance as being God's indwelling spirit, the Spirit of Truth, and the Universe Mother Spirit, but then so do the Teaching Mission Melchizedeks and morontia teachers, all together, part of the plan and not competitors. Morontian teachers, I knew, filled an intermediary role, like university instructors, learning, teaching and ascending themselves all the while. Some Urantia readers disdained these intermediary connections as unnecessary, distracting and fraught with the opportunity for error.

Ms. Blackstock continued her internet post by directly challenging the voice known as Lamphere, especially his analysis of her mental state.

She is apparently stung by Lamphere's statement: "I desire to relieve her suffering" and despite her earlier pitfalls paper, in which she said she could only cry and look at the walls, she counterattacks now: "I lead a wonderful and joyous life, richer and more challenging than ever, with love being experienced everywhere I turn. I would hope that our midwayers have more to do than to 'comfort' one who does not need it. If I do need comfort I go directly to God, and then to my husband and my friends."

I thought, at this point, that the midwayers really don't have anything better to do than to look after the welfare of spiritually dedicated humans such as Ms. Blackstock. This is what they sought to do in the Grimsley affair, and in its aftermath where they sought to comfort and advise her but were disdained in favor of psychological explanations.

Ms. Blackstock seemed unable to separate that Lamphere's remarks were for her suffering 'then' and not related to her life 'now.' Neither is the connection made (and exemplified through Lamphere's empathy) that the celestial realms have subsequently blessed her and are surely active in promoting her current well-being. She is loved for who she is and her life of service is both blessed and facilitated.

But at the time of this writing, she is ready to take issue with another Lamphere term, "dear sorrowful one." She again answers from the perspective of her present life.

> "I feel myself to be filled with joy most of the time. I do sorrow but it is no longer about FOG, but over the tragedies which my loved ones bring upon themselves, the distortion and distraction in the Urantia movement over the 'teaching mission', the lack of laborers who really are willing to get their hands dirty and serve where it counts instead of sitting around muttering phrases filled with errors."

I only thought here of the dedicated workers and service projects that have been inspired by Teaching Mission believers and hoped that the extensive list published here would be complete.

Lamphere had also noted that "... you never got to know the fruits of your labor, only the consequences of the negative side of the action which did not materialize...."

Ms. Blackstock interjected: "This is just not true! This may be the way Patije looks at me, but any midwayer would know that my personal experience was quite different. I did indeed get to know the fruits of the 'messages.' I saw most of my friends and longtime coworkers freed from an imploding phenomena of egocentric importance regarding the position of FOG and the revelation. Many of us climbed up out of that shelter which we had built to protect ourselves from the ravages of a nuclear war, very desirous of leading a normal, average life. I climbed up out of the physical, mental, psychological and spiritual 'shelter' with a deep conviction to attempt to live the rest of my life as did Jesus."

She quotes *the Urantia Book*: "The secret of his unparalleled religious life was this consciousness of the presence of God; and he attained it by intelligent prayer and sincere worship – unbroken communion with God – and not by leadings, voices, visions or extraordinary religious practices."

"I decided," said Ms. Blackstock, that if this was good enough for the Master, then whatever meager attempts I may make toward this way of living would be more than good enough for me."

The Urantia quote reminded me that the lessons of worship, prayer and developing a deep personal relationship with God is indeed the central tenet of the Teaching Mission and the goal is unbroken communion with the Universal Father. This communion was central to Jesus in his incarnation; it is central to our incarnations in flesh and blood as well.

As Christ Michael, he has now followed the Lucifer adjudication by sending waves of teachers to our planet. It was a pity that some see an either/or situation with Michael's Teaching Mission, but I was sure she would be no less blessed, and she has been, as a prominent personality in the Urantian community, and a frequent speaker.

But I believed in this case that her adamant stand about having seen the fruits of her labors was misapplied to her personal life. I thought that Lamphere was referring to the dissolution of the Family of God, arguably a much greater loss than what any of the humans might have individually suffered. It was the evangelical arm of the Urantia Revelation.

FEAR OF THE SEDUCTIVE

On the UrantiaL list Ms. Blackstock responded authoritatively to more prodding from publisher Belitsos regarding the Teaching Mission:

"Let us discourse on this. My experience with this stuff from the very first seconds of the "contact" I experienced 8 years ago in the middle of the night that said: "We are here," and continued on for the next 3 months on a daily basis re FOG preparation for WW III has continually been one of opening to such and then pulling back with increased discriminatory thinking processes as I became and become clearer about at least my experiences.

"I felt somewhat open to Rebecca's message from "Ham" in L.A. in Jan. '92 but as I continued to read the transcripts which I had been able to write verbatim because the communication was so slow, I was very disappointed in the quality of the answers to the questions and the outright evasion of some of the questions. There is a seductivity about these which is troublesome.

"I have experienced this at other times too as I have opened myself to the possibility of the reality of them. Bob Slagle told me his TM got the message that the WW III was averted and I played an important role in this. For one second, or one minute I felt elated to think that I could have helped the spiritual government in this way. And then I left that feeling and began thinking. That's where the problem with this stuff happens - on the logical level of thinking.

"I really appreciated Marvin Gawryn's question to Rebecca in L.A. - what is it that you need out of this experience? This made a lot of sense to me based on looking at my own experiences with FOG era messages. I needed some things from those messages which my subconscious created:

1. "I was in conflict and you know what the UB says about that. My conflict was several fold – I had dedicated the rest of my life to working for FOG; I had raised my sons– 12 years – with Vern as a model for him; I was watching my friends leave FOG as the preparations for nuclear war went on; and my husband was having more and more doubts about the situation and Vern's messages which had come about a year prior to mine which I began to receive in early Jan. 1985. This is a lot of conflict when you consider that my belief and devotion was "consciously" unshaken and grew stronger with each passing carrot which was stuck in the sand and sand bag which was filled.

2. "For my 15 or so years of working with FOG I worked mostly with the children - I loved doing this and felt that it was important, but I was far from the INNER CIRCLE of people. I realize now that on a subconscious level I really wanted to offer something more to the group than taking care of the kids. I believe that my subconscious found a way to do this.

3. "Although Vern was always kind toward me through all of those years, I certainly was not one who he would ask any advice of and I felt that he thought all I could talk about was kids. I realize now that I wanted to feel important and recognized by Vern for something else other that working with kids. There are others aspects that I could talk about, but this is enough to give you a good idea of things that I became aware of after the fact.

"If I had had some basic education in basic principles of psychology, perhaps I could have recognized my neediness and conflict and would not have elevated what was "alter ego" type of thinking to the realms of being "messages" from others. Obviously at several levels of unconscious activity my mind was trying to work out these obvious and strong conflicts and needs (not obvious at the time). As you know from some of your past experiences our minds can be very creative in rationalizing our assumptions and belief systems. Hence people come up with 25 past lives with great detail and ingenuity; hence people come up with superhuman beings who talk to them.

"I do feel repelled by the seductiveness of Lamphere's message: "We are only a short ways from you, dear sorrowful one. You can call upon us with but a whispered word. We wait for your call." It is my understanding that this is not even what primary midwayers do and why they want to comfort me when there are people in great need dying for great causes all over this planet who really need to be comforted is to me a dead giveaway as to the psychological nature of this stuff, not the spiritual reality of it.

"I would hope that Patije is mature enough to recognize that we must develop the ability to express ourselves with the integrity of our own thinking and experience in a clear, concise, and logical way with ideas and opinions about which we may have strong disagreement while feeling kind, compassionate and loving about the person with whom we are discoursing. I work with over 100 school age children and a staff of 12 as we attempt to do this every day as we live together in the day care center.

"If anyone on this network missed the "message" from Lamphere - a primary midwayer - via of Patije Mills and my response which Bryon calls a vehement rejection, let me know and I will download it again. I believe that it was sent out via David Kantor last Thursday. It is too bad Patije heard about her letter being out there before she got it. This is a very fast way of communicating compared to mail and perhaps it would have been more diplomatic to have been sure she received her letter first. Sorry, Patije.

"Life calls - must go be a "boss" and hang out with 100 kids and laugh with my staff, etc. I look forward to further discourse. I believe that I may have told Byron that after 8 years of processing the FOG thing that I thought I was 99.9 % clear about my interpretation of my experiences, I feel it would be presumptuous of me to assume 100 % certainty - this leaves a little window for me to look at each and every thing that comes my way, and I have read many transcripts and heard tapes and talked, talked to many who think this is REAL, and continue to be greatly disappointed. I am not sure if it is dangerous or not - I am still analyzing it. One thing for sure a lot of people are going to learn something, one way or another!"

"As I tell the kids - the first person who does a put down - negates another - is the one who first throws the weapon with desire to hurt. We see this as being much different than saying - "I do not agree with you and here's why; or I do not like what you are doing; or what you are doing makes me angry or hurts me." Amongst 300 school age children there is hardly ever a "put down" and if there is I often hear about it. But kids are talking all the time about their problems and their differences. I would I hope that we can do as well here."

There was much to appreciate in Blackstock's overall analysis. She clearly is an example that we should take to heart. A person can apparently trick themselves into thinking that what 'comes to them' in their mind is actually a spirit voice, a higher being with guidance. And in the Family of God, no doubt you could tend to put yourself in a special place because of your record of dedicated service.

I was also reminded that the teachers advised us not to 'try' so hard to make connection, that we would fail. In trying to force a connection, there is mind activity. One does better to simply release to spirit without calculated effort.

Could these failures at the Family of God have assisted in designing Michael's teaching curriculum today, with ways to avoid the pitfalls when humans encounter the doubts and fears of spiritual communication. In history, it seems that celestial messengers always appear with the same words: Fear Not. Fear of channeling, however, seemed rampant in the Urantia communities.

So came the first instructions to us – get your minds out of the way. Still your busy mind and open to the Father. I hoped that twenty years of Teaching Mission transcripts might assuage some of the fears and show the value of the insights being shared with us. I hoped that Urantia's analytical scholars might see that they are basic lessons for everyman and not intended to compete with their epochal tome from the Spiritual Hierarchy.

The Teaching Mission

There is no special person involved in the Teaching Mission who would seek to control Urantia politics, although Caston and other critics do accuse us of assuming a 'chosen persons' role. This truly does not exist, when all are invited into the stillness for contact. All are invited to receive. All are encouraged to seek that quiet, still voice inside.

If we would influence or guide the Urantia movement, it would be to encourage persons into regular stillness practice to develop the personal relationship with God that supersedes human dogma and represents the highest possible kind of religion, according to the book. And, yes, if a person hears messages from spirit, he should listen, consider, and use the experience in his decision-making within any framework. I had read no evidence anywhere that this is not wise and workable.

Beyond politics and psychology, the Teaching Mission is more concerned with its honest explorations of the phenomenon and its continuing evolution than with continuing the conflicts that have long sullied the Urantia movement. We never intended to cause yet another political battle; we only wanted to learn the stillness and work with our celestial teachers, not thinking it would cause an uproar of 'nefarious channelers' accusations. I remembered that Abraham had told us early on: "God is simple, mankind complicates."

I concluded that it was several years of personal spiritual contact that convinced me of the mission's reality. I couldn't confirm that Grimsley received any messages, or that he didn't, and neither could anyone else. But we were truly on the brink of a nuclear attack when his came. Kantor said his own alleged messages were trash and I tend to agree since that's his appraisal.

The same statement is true for the Teaching Mission today. One can say we are talking to ourselves; one could say prayer is talking to oneself too. One could say that the celestials would not be communicating with us like this and there is no evidence that the rebellion is adjudicated. One could also say that this is the best and less obtrusive way to communicate with free-willed individuals on the planet, and that they should believe the messages about adjudication, and observe it happening all around us.

So many people, even Urantia readers, could not seem to see realities on a planet that the book says is 'quivering on the brink' of massive changes.

THE AFTERMATH: Soviet Stagnations

Looking at the nuclear war situation today, it was instructive to see how things have worked out since the tumultuous events of November 1983.

In the Soviet Union, Andropov's incapacitation in 1983 and eventual death in March, 1984, made the situation all the more dangerous, thinks author Peter Pry. After all, the dying premier was involved in the death of some 20 million people over his long career in the Soviet military and KGB, including the oppressions of Stalin and the genocide inflicted in

Poland. In his condition, he might be all the more willing to carry out a first strike for the USSR, especially when he thought the U.S. was planning to launch one.

His death was the beginning of the end for the old guard in Russia, as aging personalities died and a new wave of leadership came on. Tired of a succession of decrepit fossils, the Soviets in 1985 named Gorbachev as president. He was only 60, the first Soviet leader who hadn't served in World War II.

With prescience, he could see that the Soviets were hopelessly lagging in technology and many agencies were shells of inefficiency and corruption. The old guard still seemed to believe that war was imminent and inevitable, and a first strike, more than ever, would now would be the only way the beleaguered Soviet system could win. Calmer heads made more sense, in that nuclear war victory is no victory at all.

The tense situation with the U.S. would continue for a while, but Gorbachev came into power with a mission of pulling the world back from the nuclear brink. He was, in fact, a well educated and dedicated Communist. He believed that corruption and inefficiencies had betrayed the ideals of Communism and led to the country's problems.

If the midwayers had truly declared war on Communism, then the dissolution of the USSR and easing of the hair-trigger war scare status has to be counted for a victory. Today, we see Communism in China and no doubt more adventure for mankind ahead.

With an idealist like Gorbachev in power, it seems that the battle was against corruption all the time. Perhaps the conflict is always with those who disdain and corrupt good and great ideas. The true stated ideals of Communism rival our own Constitution in its promises for our individual and mutual welfare. Corruption destroys ideals.

As for the 1983 war scare, it has been validated again by declassified documents and by extensive published notes from still-classified documents, that nuclear war could have been minutes away. The Center for Public Integrity collected documents for a file report, which adds detail to the history, and frames the top secret Able Archer-83 simulated war exercise as part of a larger Soviet face-off program called "Autumn Forge," initiated in the summer of '83.

Sources in the report believe the '83 initiatives were intentionally provocative and amounted to 'sabre-rattling' to intimidate the Soviets and impress them with superior American power.

In the United States, governments have come and gone. The provocative Reagan era did not produce nuclear holocaust in the end, but the immediate dangers are now more fully appreciated. And intelligence reports to Reagan at the time have been discredited.

Pry references a national intelligence estimate that went to President Reagan in early 1984. It stated: "Soviet talk about the increased likelihood of nuclear war ... has been deliberately manipulated to rationalize military efforts with domestic audiences and to influence Western political elites. Some Soviet military activities have also been designed to have an alarming or intimidating effect."

It was seven years later that the intelligence community recanted the report and deemed it "a major intelligence failure" in a 1990 classified report by the President's Foreign Intelligence Advisory Board.

An unclassified 1996 study by the CIA's Center for Historical Intelligence noted that many Western observers discounted the '83 war scare because its worst case scenario, a surprise nuclear attack, was "too out of touch with reality" to be credible. The report notes that Americans just didn't see things like they did in the Soviet.

Today, Republican partisans credit Reagan with winning the Cold War. His administration did build a near invincible military machine with huge outlays of money. Was our strength the reason that the Soviets never implemented their first strike strategy? Or was it the reluctances that anyone would have in initiating global holocaust so that the surviving government could declare 'victory' at a horrible price? Even Andropov, who had already killed millions, did not do it. Did celestial forces have a hand? They never seem to leave a trace.

THE AFTERMATH: Urantia in Recovery

In the Urantia movement, there are signs that the massive split between the Urantia Foundation and the Brotherhood, which is now called The Fellowship, are healing. At the Fellowship's 2008 international conference in Los Angeles, it was reported that people were talking who earlier 'couldn't stand to be in the same room with one another.' Such is a modicum of progress, even as conference attendance has dropped considerably since the debilitating animosity of the big split, continuing its slide in 2011 in Salt Lake City.

The Foundation maintains a strong policy position against any form of channeling. It competes with Fellowship study groups with its own network of groups. The Fellowship has attempted to straddle the fence, not wanting to anger the Foundation and its monetary supporters, but not wanting to pass unspiritual judgments and restrictions upon the good people in the Teaching Mission and the service groups it has fostered, not to mention other free-thinking and loving souls who don't want to be restricted by an arbitrary five unelected Foundation trustees who are accountable to no one.

New age pollution was the enemy under Myers. And there were some interesting episodes to come as Myers invoked licensing controls, and brought copyright and trademark protection lawsuits against various Urantia societies and even a conceptual artist.

In time, Myers would alienate large numbers of people. In 1981, he sued Arizona homemaker Kristen Maaherra for sending out an electronic study guide to the book, which did not exist at the time, and then sued companion Eric Schaveland for using the concentric circles logo on a website. Some critical battle lines formed and his days were numbered.

The couple received numerous Urantia reader donations for their legal expenses, and the near decade long court battle sapped Keeler and the Foundation of much of the war chest they had used to sue readers. Myers was forced off the board by Keeler and associates in 1992 and went out kicking and screaming with yet another lawsuit, this time against the trustees.

While the Foundation eventually won the Maaherra lawsuit on appeal, and caused untold personal stress and damage to their victims, some of the factors which arose led to a second suit in Arizona which brought down the copyright for good, after pulling more valuable dollars out of the movement for legal fees. The Foundation was reduced to characterizing the book as a "work for hire" because humans did some cosmetic roles such as organizing the papers. The federal courts did not agree.

At this writing, the Foundation continues to hold onto the trademark registration of the three blue concentric circles. *The Urantia Book* says that this is the banner of the Trinity Sons of God. Nothing in the text indicates that humans should trademark the symbol and license it for use. But they maintain it is a seal of approval that theirs is the authentic, inviolate text. The same text, of course, is now available from various sources across the world, including the Fellowship's published book and also downloadable electronic files of all 196 Papers. There is also a burgeoning library of secondary study materials.

I think the midwayers won this battle too. Worldwide interest in the Urantia papers is growing, and there is a groundswell of interest in higher spiritual values, personal guidance and the Family of God's "all one people" theology.

THE AFTERMATH: Ragings blow hard

Do these conflicts continue today? Yes, they do. Caston continues to rail against any kind of celestial communications that "threaten the credibility" of *the Urantia Book*, represented in recent years by the Teaching Mission. He wishes for acceptance of the Revelation within the academic community, at long last, but association with the occult is damaging to its credibility.

Caston avers that Grimsley would have nothing to do with the Teaching Mission today because he loves the book too much "to be associated with a group that poses so much danger to the Revelation." He could be wrong, since I've been told by several Teaching Mission adherents that they've enjoyed a personal visit with the Grimsleys in their home.

Caston notes that Grimsley's reputation is "irretrievably tarnished by his association with dubious, 'channeled' messages." It seemed to me, however, that Caston was a ringleader in tarnishing Vern's reputation with the incessant vendetta which continued months after the episode, and that same insulting, protectionist rhetoric persists to this day. It is not comforting to know that this voice of a former trustee is considered to speak for the Urantia revelation.

Says Caston on Facebook in May of 2011: "For the sake of Vern's peace of mind and the good memories that remain of his tattered reputation, I would advise you not to risk getting to the darker allegations that were left hidden in the behind-the-scenes shadows of the cult-like operations of his former Family of God Foundation."

So, even 28 years after the FOG crisis, here was Caston ad nauseum, still poised to deliver character attacks of some sort to support his "audio hallucinations" theory. I personally could not imagine that the midwayers would refuse to work with appropriate humans in regard to the war danger, no matter the details of their mortal lives.

It appeared when I read this that Caston was still standing ready to stir up more discord than the Grimsleys would ever want to endure today. But I could spin the situation. If the Grimsleys were indeed rid of the people that took over the Urantia Foundation, then they came out of all this best of all. Rid of Myers, rid of Keeler and Caston and Kantor. Good! And I can see good reasons why the Grimsleys would have no need for Urantian politics, ever again.

Then, in late 2011, Vern Grimsley passed on. Caston reportedly went to his side during his final hours. Mrs. Caston lauded him in a Facebook post. Yet Caston himself attacked the Teaching Mission with another lengthy broadside only days later.

He called the mission "group hysteria" and noted: "It is a Urantia Book induced 'channeling' phenomenon that was triggered by the death of Emma 'Christy' Christenson, the last remaining contact commissioner and the only person who could have spoken with authority on the legitimacy of such purported 'messages' from sources alleged to have a direct relation to the Fifth Epochal Revelation."

Since Caston had issues with Christy transmitting messages herself, it seems strange that he notes her as a name-dropped authority here, one who could sanction these messages or not. It is my view that Christy would continue her strong support for the Family of God were she living today. And while Caston could be considered irrelevant today, his writings reach a lot of people on Urantia lists, and he unfortunately provides a face and voice for the Fifth Epochal Revelation in his rantings.

THE AFTERMATH: Sprunger takes another stand

As this text was being written, Rev. Meredith Sprunger, respected patriarch of the Urantia family, whom we visited on earlier pages, also passed on and into the higher education spheres of the Mansion Worlds.

Once more upon the revelatory internet, I discovered another letter from the Reverend which summed up his ideas following a second disillusionment – first Grimsley, then Myers. It was written in May of 1991, as Myers' reign was being ended. The recipient name is blank. As Dr. Sprunger is considered one of the finest scholars of Urantia, then it demanded study.

Sprunger relates his history as friends of the Sadlers and a reader of the first edition. He maintained that the Urantia Foundation and Urantia Brotherhood were designed to be "separate and independent organizations with synchronized and supporting relationships." He relates how "legal minds" devised a way to control the entire movement with its stringent copyright and licensing regulations. He notes the resignations of three Urantia Foundation Trustees in 1989 in objection to Myers' "autocratic domination."

Sprunger says that Urantia societies and members can follow this "power oriented leadership" if they choose. "I'm confident," he said, "that the spiritual purposes of the Fifth Epochal Revelation will overcome any roadblocks placed in its way. The potentials of the Urantia movement have never been better. We have escaped attempts at charismatic captivity and legalistic-autocratic control. The freedom of the spirit working through the dynamics of participatory democracy will lead us into creative ministry. Let us have the courage and stamina to turn from those who would waste our energies in controversies and dedicate ourselves to the joy of spirit-guided service."

So the Reverend saw a charismatic threat from the Family of God and a legalistic threat on another end of the spectrum. He took the Family's dissolution as a victory just as he did Myers' discredited reign. How ironic that these opposites be lumped together by him as being threats to the Fifth Epochal Revelations – - too much mysticism and altruism on the one side, too many court suits on the other. And he was a Church of Christ minister serving with what he had in-between.

It was a greater irony that the Teaching Mission personalities have unanimously brought its students along a path to "the joy of spirit-guided service" that the Reverend visualized. Even the basic tenant of the Urantia papers is celebrated by the teachers, a personal religion built upon a "Be Still and Know That I Am God" mandate, a Urantia text ascension plan built around God's "Be Ye Perfect" evolutionary design, and a clear example of what can be done on the planet and how to do it by studying the life of Jesus.

It seems today that the basic, elemental, foundational lessons of truth from the Teaching Mission personalities are just too unfettered and simple for people with complicated minds and political agendas. It's personal. It's not another clash of belief systems.

The Teaching Mission is entry level spirituality for most souls on our Urantia/Earth, and that is just what is needed. The teachers are here to teach its true values, not laden by dogmatic baggage. They show the way to spiritual comprehensions and clarities in your own individual and unique life, your own personal guided path to answers that reside within.

I raised a voice on a Urantia Facebook discussion in an effort to correct falsehoods and provide a more clear picture of the Teaching Mission.

Hello – my brother, and others,

The Teaching Mission

Your post gives me a great deal more clarity on the roots of the hanging tree built by our Teaching Mission critics. I do appreciate your thoughtful analysis and willingness to keystroke your arguments to the list. Many of your points are well taken, but are flung in other directions than the Teaching Mission I've experienced for some 20 years.

You are simply looking for the wrong teachers in the wrong locations at the wrong times, and I expect you're misreading the curriculum as well.

We are working with Melchizedeks and many Morontian teachers, who are serving in their ascension plan, not angels, midwayers or your dead uncle. Urantia speaks at length on our constant and continuing education in our ascension careers, including within the Celestial Overseers section. Seeking our authenticity within Urantia, we ourselves have large collections of quotes that support us from the Revelation itself. The whole universe is a school.

We're not talking with midwayers in the Teaching Mission and, to my knowledge, no one has ever heard an 'audio hallucination' message by a 'chosen person' in all these years. Midwayers have many roles other than teaching us a curriculum of basic spiritual values. Such as helping mightily to save our butts from a near nuclear war. But that story has a lot more to do with Urantia politics than it has to do with personal spiritual growth with teachers sent by Christ Michael, following the adjudication of the Lucifer Rebellion in the early 80s.

The right location to find the Teaching Mission is within yourselves. It's not about going to meetings and hearing a fellow spirit who is bold enough and gracious enough to be a group transmitter. This is social growth. The real growth is in one's willingness to go into Stillness time and throw yourself in front of God. Dump the world, clear your mind. Worship God and develop that real, personal relationship with the Universal Father that the Revelation extolls. Stillness is deeper than meditation and requires the complete release to Spirit in faith and in dedication to being perfect in the plan. If you have fear of this, your own mind, then this is your first problem to overcome.

Guidance from spirit can only lead to a service venue. Knowing and feeling the spirit inside, Teaching Mission folks are serving well in many places. The place they went to begin the journey was into the Stillness, to consciously take a step of faith, to embrace the Thought Adjuster, embrace the Mother Spirit, embrace the Spirit of Truth, embrace the Guardian and Service Angels, embrace the teachers, artisans and spirits of your own Melchizedek University, a Church Inside.

Critics may also be looking at the wrong time to identify the Teaching Mission. We have group sharing sessions but the real connection is made between you and your Thought Adjuster, and the teachers that are assigned to you, for your specific needs to grow in spirit. This is a connection that every free will individual can make, and no one else can make for you. This can eventually lead to making the time of connection anytime that you walk the earth, in the balance of character that Jesus himself represented as a mortal day after day, as he passed by.

A wrong reason to seek the Teaching Mission is to get prophecies of doom or resurrection, of planetary cleansing or evacuation, or renaissance. Our Morontian teachers would like to reach every soul on the planet first of all with basic foundations for personal spiritual growth, not changing the world but changing ourselves, so that we will go out and do it, the Father's Business, our contributions on a quickening planet quivering on the brink of great changes. After 20 years absorbing thousands of pages of spiritual growth lessons, along with *the Urantia Book*'s prior foundation, I am like so many others, motivated to service in a world where needs are critical everywhere you look.

Once connected to Spirit, you can more satisfyingly enjoy little moments throughout your day, mini-stillnesses because you are open to spirit, open to giving a kindness, open to hearing bursts of insight through your vitalized and energized Thought Adjuster, who is now more radiantly alive because you made the connection and became more greatly aware of this Inner Light. Some of our more experienced transmitters have learned to bring forth inspirations from their own Adjusters that are well worth the reading and consideration, and that's all they ask. Teachers help facilitate Thought Adjuster contact, and Midwayers help facilitate many things which have to be downstepped to mortal comprehension.

What do the teachers do then, and why do you need them beyond the Urantia text? To bring your inner spirit alive and to recognize and embrace Christ Michael, the Melchizedeks and a wave of loving Morontian teachers. If a critic wishes to remain logical, he may now read tens of thousands of pages of teacher lessons in libraries and archives. If a critic wishes to actually have personal spiritual guidance, he must merely ask God about it and RELEASE oneself to the messages by turning off the analytical buzzbomb in your head.

This is what Faith is all about. Christians, too, may equate it with going to meetings at God's house. They spend a lot of time building them, often for modest use.

But you are God's house. You are his child. God has not just built a house inside you; He has built a Home, a family that can grow together.

Be Still, and know that I AM God.

This is the opportunity of the Teaching Mission.

Do it otherwise if you wish.

And it is pointless to criticize us, the humans who are participating in the spiritual phenomenon. We only know what we've learned by hearing and experiencing the Teachers. As with *the Urantia Book*, we are students. There are no human experts on either. We have been guided well, plain to see, and we still love the Revelation.

One of our most prolific teachers, Rayson, once noted that the behavior of humans in going to other humans for spiritual guidance is "baffling."

In time, I think we will all learn this truth.

SOME AUTHOR CONCLUSIONS

Why, then, do many Urantia readers disdain the Teaching Mission? They don't know what it is. They misidentify it based on their own tumultuous politics and personality spats, and it has nothing to do with either. They compare the quality of our teachers transmitting basic entry-level spiritual lessons in our living rooms with a 2,100 page spiritual revelation. Our critics resent the teachers' support of the Urantia text in their disbelief of the teachers, but if it is the highest collection of wisdom on the planet, why wouldn't they recommend it?

The altruistic message of the Family of God and the Spiritual Renaissance Institute is in many places today though the organization is gone. Urantia's Fellowship and Foundation are still trying to mend their differences and still not integrated into the science, philosophy and religion mainstream.

It's just sad that while the entire nation was on edge for a possible nuclear attack in those tense Cold War days, the Urantia personalities who shattered the Family of God and usurped the movement somehow found the logic to demonize the greatest evangelist and global networker they had because his organization was simply prepared as best they could be.

It seemingly didn't matter to the Urantia coup members that the cold war had escalated into a precarious day-by-day situation given the Korean airliner shootdown, the Grenada invasion, missiles build-ups and a dangerous, dying mass murderer at the helm in the Soviet Union. It didn't matter that every city in the country had civil defense plans and shelters and that Able Archer 83 had greatly aggravated the tension.

What mattered was their struggle to configure and control their copyright, knowing its spiritual and market value, and to get rid of Vern Grimsley and his family of mankind philosophy. Myers and Caston saw a global threat to the Revelation from new age spiritualists and channelers. They saw a troubled world racked with rebellion, replete with Lucifer and his kind on the ready to dupe us and compromise or even destroy their epochal revelation. Opening one's stilled mind to such possible intrusions was unadvisable to unthinkable.

The mainstream world simply didn't know about the Lucifer Rebellion and its dark curse on the planet. The mainstream needed the inviolate, copyright-protected Revelation. The Myers regime ran on for two decades and drew many battle lines to fight in court.

Today, there is no church or fellowship devoted to a Jesus of Urantia ministry, even as the text says it will someday come. But there is indeed fear – yes, more fear – of trying to start one. We don't need yet another church, some assert, apparently not acknowledging that it doesn't have to be flawed in the ways that they see other religions. It could represent what the Urantia papers say. It is an opportunity to transcend.

But their collective thinking is really miniscule in the context of personal child of God realities. What matters is the "entirety of the planet" that Grimsley noted. What matters is every soul on the planet finding and embracing God's grace and will in their lives. What matters is going into the stillness and working on your spiritual growth with the Universal Father/God/First Source and Center. This opportunity is what all humans should know, what the Teaching Mission is about, and what this book should help affirm.

What matters is not the conflicts and struggles among the myriad array of rebellion-scarred people on this planet, but to muster up that "universe awareness" and "cosmic consciousness" and know and live the reality of the fact and the opportunity.

In the end, the protagonists given voice on these pages were all thinking and doing what they believed to be the right thing at the time, what they had to do or needed to do. It's not my job to judge them; it's their responsibility to evaluate themselves, and be of greater, more enlightened service going forward. Listening in the stillness will bring insights that help along the way. It will bring the broadened realization that.... The Teaching Mission is interplanetary and includes all of the worlds of the Lucifer rebellion.

The Urantia Revelation movement for this planet needs to expand to include every soul in this world and respect their sincere paths. With that purpose, I have proposed a new Universal Urantia Family which adheres to the principles of ONEness among all people and disdains bigotry and spiritual judgments. Here are our eight principles:

Urantia Universal

1. We believe the Urantia Revelation is compatible and should be desirable by all faith movements to whom we can introduce it and we are not fearful of stepping forward with it. We who share it should show non-judgmental respect and good will toward others on their particular spiritual paths, whether it be ancient or new. We can find common truths and still care for one another through diversities. We believe in pursuing the Oneness of all humanity and the Oneness of spirit which resides within each of us.

2. We believe in receiving spiritual guidance through concerted practice of the Stillness, and, as our spirits develop, in minute-by-minute interaction with our Indwelling Spirit and other spiritual presences, in living a fruitful life of service.

3. We will counter any forms of bigotry within our Urantia family. We are dedicated to an exploration of how the Urantia Revelation relates to the world, to science, philosophy, religion and the everyday challenges of life. We have long studied the book; we want to understand how we can relate it to our societies and use its principles to unify people and build communities around the "Love One Another" concept.

4. We encourage those who would serve the revelation of truth-beauty-and-goodness to hear each other's views and concerns, and to work proactively and creatively to foster meaningful relationships with proponents of the emerging new spiritual movements. There is a place for the foundational spiritual truths of Urantia everywhere. Our greatest task is learning to work together in harmony and progress.

5. We know from two decades of experience and our huge archive of spiritual lessons that both the celestial teachers and Christ Michael's mission to reclaim Urantia and the rebellion worlds are real. As co-signers we stand on this truth without apology and encourage others to make this contact. We reject the idea that the Urantia Papers refute these realities in any way. We believe that much in the Revelation supports our experiences with teachers and spiritual influences. We also believe that much has happened to change conditions on our planet and in the spiritual worlds since the Papers were published in 1955 and we don't hold the Papers to be the end of all reliable truth.

6. We believe that a person achieving spiritual contact in the Stillness would be one of his life's greatest achievements. It is the threshold to the development of Personal Religion, the only religion that the Urantia text considers to be real.

7. We believe that we are all one people on Urantia. We love the Father, and the Father tells us to love each other. We love Michael and the incarnated Jesus, and they tell us to love one another. Within Urantia our first mission is clear then. And if we practice it, we will be less judgmental about things we don't understand. And the more we truly know our fellows, the more we will come to love them.

8. We believe any and all leaders in Urantia should work actively toward establishing the new Religion of Jesus that the text mandates. We see no reason to wait. We see a lot of hesitating and a lot of non-cooperation and non-support of various Urantia-based initiatives. We need to support inspired secondary works which explain, clarify and promote our central text.

These are the keys to the Urantian revelation taking strong root and growing on the planet. It is now a time to build bridges, not fences . . . a time to find common spiritual ground and stand up on it together.

CELESTIAL CONCLUSIONS

While mine seemed a fitting set of conclusions about the Teaching Mission, I subsequently found that the most revealing and illuminating commentaries on these matters would come, not from the human side, but from the celestial side. Several transmissions put much more in perspective for me than I had been able to glean on my own.

As far as receiving personal guidance in the Stillness, the midwayers of today offer a greatly simplified reality that we should know, from transmitted lessons published by the 11.11 Progress Group in February, 2013.

Allowing This Cultivation

Mentor: *"Thank you for lending me your ear. Please type what you hear and when you fall behind in your typing and lose track of what is being said, do not abort the project as I am about to convey things that need to be said.*

"I may at times sound somewhat stern, but that is for a reason. You mortals spend too little time listening to the Still Voice within from where all insights come. You mortals are more prone to be obsessed by the outward clamor and noises of the world around you, hardly giving yourselves time to come to your senses. You are heir to many pitfalls in your world, due to your lack of quality thinking, and you also indulge in negative thinking, which only makes your life more difficult and somber.

"Think about how the Guiding Light, that Spark from God, is there within you to help guide you in the right and positive way of life. When will you learn to walk on the sunny side of the street? Oh yes, there will be shadows but that is merely what they are. Darkness and light are always in balance to help shape you, and for you to become more aware of how all things work together for good.

"There are many people who have lost the ability to think for themselves, so they need a guru, or some other guide to help them sort things out, and they will go to great lengths to spend great sums of money so others can spoon-feed them. Do you not know or remember that the greatest Guide lives within you, and all you need to do is go into the stillness of your hearts and allow this Guide, this personal Spark from the Creator God, an opportunity to speak?

"Please, train and allow yourselves the development of your inner listening skills by giving yourselves permission and allowing yourselves some daily time to acquire this most important habit. It will be the best time you will ever spend on yourselves. In doing so, you will overcome many maladies in your mental-emotional realm. It will also reflect on your physical well-being as you learn to better cope with the vicissitudes of life.

"There simply is no better way than for you to develop the ultimate trust in the highest Power possible. Life can be so simple, so why do you persist in making it so difficult? All you need to do is get into the habit and allow yourself the time to develop your inner listening skills. It will be your best habit ever to cultivate and it will give you an indescribable and untold deep inner joy and feeling of belonging to God's great family to eventually meet your other kin from other worlds, who are likewise cultivating their souls to perfection.

The Teaching Mission

"It is the Eternal Creator's greatest pleasure to create mortals with the capacity to think for their selves and return to Paradise as perfected beings. This after they have enjoyed their ages-long exhilarating ascension adventure to refine their character, polish and cultivate their personality and shape themselves increasingly towards perfection, all through an ongoing choice and decision making process.

"This is the true allowing and cultivating yourselves to become what you are capable of becoming."

Celestial Receptivity

Thought Adjuster: *"In a regular world, communication with Celestials is a common occurrence, almost a routine affair. The vast majority of various populations enjoys this experience, and is more spiritually receptive than you are. This is also subject to the kinds of brains the mortals on certain planets have. The ones with three brains are the most receptive, followed by the kind with two brains – as are the mortals of Urantia. Least receptive are those with one brain.*

"In this world it is particularly difficult to develop faith in what cannot be seen or heard. Even whilst you are of the two-brained kind, your spiritual receptivity is almost nil. Few among you have managed to gather enough faith to 'listen' and believe they have heard. Since this phenomenon is rather rare those who listen are considered strange. The experience of listening is something that cannot be taught, because it is an individual and private experience; something that has to be tried and succeeded with in order to be comprehended.

"Now your sphere is being re-routed onto the normal path of evolutionary worlds. The number of humans who listen grows each day, and your children are being born with a greater ability to receive. In a very short time – compared to general world time lines – those who listen will be the majority and the phenomenon of communication with the Father and His 'agents' will no longer be a mystery, or a fantastic occurrence. The increase in the number of those who desire to know God on a personal level will be the impulse this world needs to establish the age of light and life.

"Those who have learned to listen in these times of doubt and confusion are the pioneers – the agondonters – whose faith is beyond normal. [In Urantia terminology, this is a person who can believe in God through faith and without physical evidence.] It is a great accomplishment for your future to have done this by your own means of overcoming your limitations. What you are doing will not even come close to what future generations will be able to achieve in this area of celestial communication. However, you can do plenty with your fragile faith and your desire to know more – your love for things spiritual.

"You can be sure your Father understands and knows of your struggles. He sees the doubts in your heart and doesn't judge you because of this, since he knows well how hard it is for a mortal creature in a world such as this to free his or her mind of external influences, and to learn to think freely and independently. This is always a personal choice of a few courageous souls that jump into the adventure, onto the roads that have seldom been traveled by their peers of the past. This is being a true pioneer, and a true agondonter.

"Let my words serve as an encouragement and provide the impulse to help you move forward. You have achieved much but it is just a drop in the ocean to what is still unknown to you. Continue exploring, continue searching and ask for what you need, because this is the way you open your mind and your consciousness to receive. It is up to you to identify the gifts of the Father and take advantage of them to do His Will."

509

THE MAGISTERIAL MISSION ... IF YOU'RE READY

On May 10, 2013, the Northern Colorado Teaching Mission group, held its 75th "Conversations with Monjoronson" series. Transmitter was Daniel Raphael. He answered several direct questions with perspectives on both the Family of God crisis and human involvement in the Correcting Time.

He was asked if he had a comment on humans being part of it.

MONJORONSON: "One moment. Yes, briefly. That is that the Correcting Time being a co-creative development has two partners: that of spirit, which is personal and which is planetary and local universe in dimension, and our mortal companions. There is a true need for your conscious participation with us to bring this Correcting Time into development and fruition. This cannot be done without you, and I am here to tell you that we will not do it without you!

"We ask you to be open and receptive to those opportunities which come to you, and if you ask, we will make them so forthright, so obvious that in order to ignore this opportunity you would have to be quite spiritually and energetically blind.

"We are not talking about intuitively aware, but to be obviously aware in the dimensions of your world around you, to be aware and cognizant of opportunities, something that presents itself which does not look like the past, something which is developmentally new—familiar, but new—something that you could participate with and contribute to. This is what we ask of you, to do this.

"You see, the events and developments that are occurring on your world right now will continue on, and though you live here securely in one of the states of this nation and other nations around the world that live in peace—relative peace—you are seeing events in the world which are powerfully changing the future, destructively. Your conscious participation is needed to change that destructive future to a constructive one.

"It is a process. It is not done by instantaneous miracle. Just as you see the fragmentation and disintegration of civil life in the Middle East, you also see this as a gradual development.

"Your participation helps to change the development of events into the positive and constructive. You may not see that, and it may not be obvious to you, but you are needed to assist us. Even if you do not have hands-on contributions to what we are doing, you can have conscious minded hands-on participation with us. This is definitely needed.

"It is not that we are dithering and do not have a clue about how to proceed—quite the contrary—we are very definitely aware of what is needed and the probable outcomes. We need to assist you to guide those positive constructive probable outcomes.

"I hope you understand that at any given moment, there are multiple, probable lines of development that can occur from that moment. They can vary from the most destructive to the most constructive. Your consciousness, your conscious participation with us can tip the scale in the direction of positive outcomes. You are needed. You are useful. And though you are one of billions, you are powerful to affect the course of those billions. You simply have to believe so and consciously direct your minded energy to positive outcomes—even if it is solely to the extent of asking us to participate in a positive outcome for some development.

"If you ask us to do that, you might also want to ask, "Are you in agreement with that? Would you support that?" and almost all of you will hear our response. If it is "No," that will be very clear; if it is "Yes," that will be very clear. And if it is "yes," then we ask you to urge us on to do the work.

"It is like asking your partner or one of your children, or a friend to come over and assist you to plant the garden: "Would you help me to open the packages and plant the seeds in the furrow to help me do this?" "Would you be willing to do this?" and they say, "Yes." "Then please come on over in a half hour and we will begin."

"So, our relationship with you is just as pragmatic as it is with your friends, neighbors and family; it is an agreement. Many of you ask us to do something, but you assume that we are sent to do so. When it is for the obvious good of something, you can assume that we will. However, when it calls for co-creative enterprises and activities, then it is best to check with us to see if we will.

"Oftentimes, mortals ask us to do something and we do not do it, simply because it would work against the ultimate good of the individual or someone else or your environment. This conscious relationship helps you know where you are with us, and you can know what we support or do not support. This is a learning activity. Do you see that you are in a learning situation?

"Many social action scientists have described these two situations as: Learning situation #1, and learning situation #2. What you want for a learning situation #2 is feedback whether you are on course or not. And when you understand you are on course, then of course, obviously you would want to always amend your statements of empowerment to us, to align yourselves with God's Will through us, so that your will and our will and God's Will are in alignment.

"This is where you want to be in this lifetime, all of your morontial lifetimes, and all of your spiritual lifetimes and your eternal exercise in the Corps of Finality."

Later came a question that led to this explanation of the Grimsley controversy.

MONJORONSON: " . . . Mr. Grimsley did rightly perceive and receive the messages that support the pronouncement he made at the convention in Los Angeles. The world was on the brink of nuclear war.

"As you recall, the situation that developed, which the celestials foretold Mr. Grimsley about, developed from the NATO exercises in the North Sea near Russia. The United States and NATO forces were conducting their training exercises using live ammunition and so on. It was a very hostile and threatening situation to Russia and it was done with the intention on the part of NATO members to actually threaten Russia with the power of its might.

"Of course, given Russia's background of disempowerment to most individuals, the culture that gave rise to serfdom and its permanence in the genetic code of those people, it raised their arrogance, their anger and their hostilities to the point where they too had activated their nuclear defense systems and were in preparation to make pre-emptory strikes at the NATO forces, and then at the capitols and major cities of NATO members around the world.

"It was only through the open-mindedness of individuals—several individuals, but particularly one who came to the courageous position to call and ask the Russian Commander what the situation was. Your celestial friends had been an influence to the minds of all involved in making those ultimate decisions, giving them options for probable outcomes. Individuals chose to stand down, backup and to neutralize their systems—put them in the inactive mode—and prevent a nuclear war.

"It was a period of far less than a minute in which those ultimate decisions were deferred. Now, listeners, I wish you to see the power that we co-creatively have with you, to give you and others options for decision-making. This is co-creative participation. Mr. Grimsley did the right thing for the right reasons, with the right intentions to develop the right outcomes. Now, if you were a Planetary Manager, what would you say? That was the wrong outcome? Peace? Standing down from nuclear war? It was the right outcome.

"Now, what was the outcome for Mr. Grimsley? We knew beforehand the probable outcomes of his personal life and his professional demise, yet in the management of a planet, this is a hugely important and necessary sacrifice. Mr. Grimsley's recovery from that has been a wonderful process to see. Had he committed suicide that would have ended his possibility of recovery in this terrible personal and professional cataclysm. He was strong to remain among you.

"Those who stood by him also suffered tremendously. In the saving of your planet and your civilization, 25 years ago—or longer—this was a necessary sacrifice that even the process of revelation from the Father to each individual, would be in denial by the fundamentalists of the Urantia Book movement.

"These things can be recovered in time, though this situation has persevered for so long with such tremendous negative impact upon the spiritual growth of your planet, it nonetheless will recover in time, as will the understanding of every individual once they cross into the morontial realm.

"The most destructive outcome of all from this, besides the collapse of marriages, professional lives and the loss of personal resources, is that personal revelation has been denigrated because of the beliefs of these few people.

"Why is it, do you think, that the Urantia Book movement is still held as a cult movement in the world? It is because it has not come around to accept personal revelation that occurs new to each generation. God speaks to you. God speaks to you through himself as your Thought Adjuster; God speaks to you through his delegates, his hierarchy of light. These are directly in alignment with his authority and his personhood.

"Christ Michael speaks to you personally, as personal revelation of the Father. What is needed for The Urantia Book and its membership to come into the light of this world is to reunite with the acceptance of revelation. This is immensely important.

"If you look at the success or the growth of the Urantia movement in relationship to your world population, it has failed every year. The percentage of believers of the Urantia Book movement has decreased percentage-wise every year since its beginning, particularly more so as the world population grows. These are hard words for me to deliver to you, but there is a somber message for each of you, that God loves you, God speaks to you, your angel speaks to you, your celestial teacher speaks to you and has words of wisdom for you to accept. All we ask is that you be personally discerning in your wisdom quotient to understand whether these statements by celestial beings are in agreement with God and God's Will.

"Though the miscreants of the rebellion are gone, yet the remnants of negativity and disincarnate beings still remain. Some of these are benign; some are totally neutralized; others actively affect those people who are naïve and who are untrained.

"The Teaching Mission came here to do several things, one of which was to tell you that you are sons of God, that God is with you, that you need to learn the moral, ethical socially conscious ways of living to grow spiritually, to know what revelation is again, to identify and discern what is of the Father and what is not. And in this discerning, you discern also what is from the Father through your fellow brothers and sisters.

"Many of them are religious, but they are not spiritual, and in their religiosity, they are even egotistical. You must discern what is of God and what is not of God.

"We are not anti-religion, as you know; we thoroughly support religion of the worship of the Father. We also support the revelation of God through his speaking in your mind; his speaking through myself; through Christ Michael—as he did through his Son, Jesus Christ.

513

"Revelation continues; be open to it; discern it; learn it; and learn how to work in co-creative participation with us. This is what is needed to heal your world, to bring it into the days of light and life, co-creatively with us. If you are unable to learn those things, your world will continue as it is—that would be most unfortunate.

"Later, you will be able to see clearly in your monorail review time, where you failed to take advantage of those opportunities that were so blatantly obvious in front of you.

"You see, although it is not a sin not to take advantage of these opportunities, it is an act of omission. We ask you to act in commission, co-creatively to heal your world and to literally save it from centuries of darkness."

With all of these perspectives in hand, from both humans and celestials, it is finally left to the reader to evaluate, discern, judge and continue to exercise free will to influence the planet. I believe these same spiritual insights were in the heart and mind of Vern Grimsley. He spoke eloquently to them.

All humankind are one vast family
This world our home.
We sleep beneath one roof
The starry sky.
We warm ourselves before one hearth
The blazing sun.
From one floor of soil we stand
And breathe one air
And drink one water
And walk the night
Beneath one luminescent moon.
The children of one God we are
And brothers of one blood
And members in one worldwide
Family of God.

Part Six

The Future

The teachers have mostly refrained from prophecies, noting that the future is being made by many free will beings of the continuing generations and, in large measure, it is for us to decide. But they have been forthright in talking about the future with advice on how we should look to it. They make us aware of serious and impending global challenges, environmental breaking points, a pivotal time of reckoning and awakening in a turmoil of conflicting sides.

Here is a timeline series of lessons, most in response to questions, starting with a 1996 statement to a pioneer T/R group which published a book of their lessons with celestial teacher Will, *The Center Within*.

MANUTIA, a Melchizedek, in Tallahassee, Florida, 3-10-1996

"The administrators, those on high, within whose care the guidance of world affairs has been given, has begun a program, under Michael's guidance which will culminate in sweeping changes upon this world. You who are committed to walking with Him will be the first to be given an awareness of those who walk among you. Indeed there are already those who have been sent as the vanguard.

"Your faith has kept you true to this path and for this many praises have been sung in your name. For unto you has been given the task of opening the way to a broader acceptance of celestial intervention. We give no timetable for already have you understood that due to human nature and human free will, this is not possible.

"Yet I say unto you this evening, keep your eyes open, your ears as well, and open to the guidance you receive from your own inner spirits. Accept the possibility that indeed within your lifetime this will come to pass.

"A Magisterial Son has been mandated for this world in the near future. Praise be to the Father on high! For now you begin the long struggle from the dark into the fullness of day. Blessings on you children, for your faith, your perseverance, indeed for your open and loving hearts. I leave you now with my blessings and the sure knowledge that the love of the Father is indeed upon each of you. Shalom."

TARKAS, Cincinnati, OH, 11-22-1996

"There were things said earlier concerning difficult times coming to your sphere. Indeed, we have spoken of these things in the past and you may expect an accelerated period of learning and growth, for this opportunity has been opened to you from the adjudication and the incremental openings. This circuitry must be opened to bring Urantia into glorious reunion with the universe. As these energies are activated, there is the great need for individual and group meditative worship and prayer. The energies that you can release through these activities activate, in essence, the power of the Father's unfoldment as well.

"As we have talked about, love given leads to love received. Steps of faith lead to rewards. So too will your conscious attuning to energies and sincere, loving up-reach activate more energies to heal. We still will say to you that while there will be many difficulties, great catastrophes can be avoided, but only with the attunement of the faith and love of each, and many, many of you need to bring forth these energies and help in this planetary transformation.

"Traveling to love and light, to Light and Life, is not an easy journey, for an easy journey provides no adversity, challenging and growing experiences that will make you strong, that will make you a fine, spiritual warrior for the Father, perhaps, in even building new lives. Gain your strength while here on Urantia. Make each moment of material life be impactful for positive spiritual change, for the record you are making moment-by-moment builds your place in eternity.

"There will be the need in coming years for each of you to act with calm and inspired spiritual deliberation, for people will come to you in anguish and suffering and misunderstanding. They will be confused as even to appear nonsensical, for many factors contribute to annoying thought lines that cut through logic, that cut through common sense, and begin to take on a perverted unreality of their own. These things to an enlightened, spiritual mind can be seen in newspapers, in the evening news, in which you will ask yourself, "How can these things happen? How would someone act or think this way? Why would they take these actions?"

"As you continue, you will come to spiritual truths, you will continue to gratefully lose that linkage with the madness that seems to run through society, and I believe, as do my fellow teachers, that this madness will grow, the frustration and violence, and, as you have already seen, that the controlled energies of fusion within the earth will also react to these circuitry openings with some strange and unpredictable and sometimes destructive weather.

"But I say to you that working together we are confident we can bring about the great healing of Urantia, and we confidently feel that your destruction is not in the Father's plans or in the plans of Christ Michael who remains one of you, who incarnated here to live with you as brothers and sisters.

"We believe, in fact, there is a great time of enlightenment, Light and Life, coming to Urantia, and the challenges between now and then may be laborious and tragic for some, but together we will work together to bring forth a great healing and enlightenment to all.

Q - You speak of things to come and I was wondering, do we need to put things away?

TARKAS: *"We remain confident that through teaching and healing and ministry of all kinds in this, what might be called a "battle against time," we will be fortuitous and victorious, but there are dangers. The planet remains highly unsettled. Environmental excesses have damaged the aura around your planet and they are in many areas . . . much toxic waste, in the water, in the soils. These threats are very real, but at the same time we see many evidences that the wakening is somewhat on schedule.*

"Each day many people who have positions of influence and power become more and more enlightened to higher purpose. In fact, it will become a thriving business, from the capitalistic sense, the environmental clean-up. This can be a growth industry, as you call it, when the right economic parameters are aligned and put in place.

"The circuitry that will bring strange mental connections to people can cause disruptions of unknown kinds, for we are dealing with complements of people here who are widely divergent in resources and mind ability and opportunity of all kinds. Effects of circuitry openings can be a somewhat blanket occurrence, in that each will be affected who live here and each may be affected in different ways as befitting their personalities.

"There is a necessity to turn loose of the appeals of evil and violence and conflict, which many still dote on in your so-called entertainments. In time these will become distasteful and many will savor instead a more enlightened outlook of stories of challenge, perseverance and triumph. You begin to see this in the media already. You begin to read surprisingly enlightened views of individuals like yourselves in many places, people who surprisingly will bring forth testimonies of love for God and their own feelings of connectedness.

"Watch these enlightenments for they will be sweeping your world, as lights going on, sparkling ever brighter, and as you attune to daily meditation, you take in these energies for you are opening a conduit of this up-reach and these energies manifest in many good ways, in many good feelings.

". . . [I]t would be good precaution to be aware of changing events, stay attuned through meditation and prayer, for there may be some startling and surprising openings in circuitry. We do not, frankly, know. There are higher powers driving this train across your landscape. We are highly observant of what the next unfolding plans are for Urantia as we serve in this mission. We are often surprised at how things can change in short order, how views can change within staid structures that seem impervious to change, and true enlightenment will help to intensify your feelings of beauty."

JarEl, 4-1999 in Arcadia, California

"Awareness is beginning to take effect on the minds of the inhabitants of this world. And this has a tremendous effect in affecting change on a social level, as individuals become profoundly moved to do something about the conditions in their life. They begin to inspire others, and there is at present on this world a birthing experience of awareness. People's eyes are beginning to open, as well as the eyes of the mind. It is the eye of the mind that sees.

"I wish I could say that great and profound social changes are on the brink of transformation this year, but I cannot say that. Though, as individuals begin to change and transform, the potential for more people changing increases each time. Believe it, that when a certain saturation of awareness and clarity begins to indwell the minds of the inhabitants of this planet, it will become easier to make better qualified decisions, to reinforce

517

and to strengthen the faith and belief of the people on your world, much like your president whose speeches attempt to encourage the citizens of this country.

"You must understand that great and profound changes take place not on grand scales, but in very subtle and small moments in individual lives of people. For this really is where the drama takes place, is it not?"

CHRIST MICHAEL, 11-29-2009, Center for Christ Consciousness

"My children, this is your Father Michael. As your world reconnects itself to the heartbeat of the universe, you will notice many things changing in the way you think and feel. The spiritual energies you are now being connected to have a physical consequence in your bodies and on your earth. Uncomfortable as some of these changes are from time to time, they are here to help you transcend the stagnant energies of fear and doubt that have long festered in human consciousness. Welcome this time of "uncomfortableness" as it is moving you from chaos to glory!

"Participate more fully by your agreement and commitment to change — changing your thoughts, changing your habits, and recognizing that the positive direction of peace, love, forgiveness, compassion, and tolerance is always what you want to focus on. You are in control of your minds, as in reality this is the only thing over which you really have control. Your Mother and I have given you many lessons to help you understand this most marvelous vehicle of life you have been given-your consciousness, and now it is time for you to become masters of it. Much help is provided if you continue to strive in this direction.

"Focus your minds as you sit in quiet reflection upon me, my children, and your Mother and I will fertilize your thoughts with peace and security. Learn a little more each and every day what it means and what it feels like to sit with us as we grow you in the loving circuits of life and light. Welcome these changes, beloveds, and know that you are doing your part to transform not only yourselves, but your world!"

NEBADONIA, 2-28-2010, Center for Christ Consciousness.

"The universal mind you share with me entitles you to receive a bounty and wealth of information. This occurs over the network of sensory mechanisms of your body and mind and discloses new ideas and concepts to add to your evolving cosmic frame of reference. Therefore, you can never stop learning and aligning your perspectives to what is available to you in the great universe we all share.

"As your planet undergoes more vital change, you will notice how your perspective shifts—ideas you once never ever considered will seem like second nature. It is that your minds are all being upgraded to capture these new idea-thought sparks that are a part of my being, and to help you understand the workings of reality, far beyond what your planetary culture conceived heretofore.

"Sit in my presence, my beloved children, sit with your Mother, and allow me to expand your consciousness through my Breath of Life. Your abilities to retain more information and to sort through the errors of the past to glean the truth will be easier for you to assimilate when you spend some time each with me. Know that I take great delight in all of my children as they come to me and grow strong and capable as universe citizens. Trust that I will help you find those places within where you need my life sparks to plant the new ideas as

seeds that will bring wonderful new information to your mind and hearts, and speak deeply the words of LOVE into your souls."

Magisterial Son Mission Transmissions

MONJORONSON announces his presence.
2/5/2004 at Celestial Nights gathering, Cape San Blas, Florida

"Greetings, I am one who is known as Monjoronson, and I take this opportunity to communicate with you tonight on the topic of preparation. I do not refer to the preparation for my arrival on your world, but rather to the preparation of your souls for being receptive to the divine leading.

"There are many conjectures as to the import of my presence on your world, and the time of my arrival, but I would ask you to consider where the real importance lies. For my mission is not the mission to make Monjoronson known, but indeed, as your Master Michael's was, my mission is to bring awareness of God's love to a world languishing in spiritual poverty.

"And so I ask you to look at the ways that you can be part of this mission. I do not require that you prepare for me. Instead I would direct you, my friends and dedicated missioneers, to the real mission of increasingly absorbing the reality of the Father's love and subsequently letting that energy flow through you to those whom you know, whom you contact with, whom you communicate with. I am not coming to change the focus of Michael's mission, but rather am I here to bring Michael's message to the world in ways that can be enhanced by my arrival.

"The date of my arrival is not yet set, for there are circumstances on your world which must occur before it is fortuitous that I am present, and those circumstances, in part, are out of your control, for the planetary alignment of different cultures and ideas must occur.

"And yet you do have a role to play, and that is to be the best representative of Michael's revelation that you can be. The mission is what you can do today, here and now, to prepare the souls surrounding you for the arrival of Michael's Spirit of Truth, Mother's unifying love, and the Universal Father's promptings in their lives. Without this focus and without the application toward these principals and endeavors, the mission will stall.

"So tonight I ask you to recommit to preparing your soul for being the broadest manifestation of truth, beauty, and goodness that you can be. Find the community of the Brotherhood of Men, and yes, realize that the male dominance on your world will diminish in times to come such that brotherhood and man are not the dominating aspects of that phrase.

"Institutions will change; cultures will change; governments and politics will change; but that change must come from heavy preparations in your lives and by sharing that truth with those who chance to come in contact with you, whether it be with your group, or with you as an individual.

"Indeed are we blessed to live in these times, to be available to manifest the mission of our Father to bring light and life, not only to your world, but to a universe. Lift yourselves up to the reality of the increasing connections being developed throughout this universe and the enhancement of the circuits, so that your doubts and fears may be strengthened in the realization of this energy broadening and increasing for you."

Question: "I understand that modern scientists say that approximately 96% of the universe is a mystery as opposed to the 4% of ordinary matter of which we are a part. How do the teachings of *the Urantia Book* fit with this piece of knowledge?"

Monjoronson: *"Thank you for this question. Your concern touches upon one of the base concepts in* the Urantia Book, *the concept of ascension, the concept that the universe is one giant educational and functional facility. It is designed to be a mystery because man must traverse each new depth of space in order to claim such an understanding of that space and what lies within space. The universes were created with intelligent personalities to particularly guide the pilgrims of time to a well nigh complete and utter understanding of the greater universes and the potentials of Havona.*

"Science definitely is a perplexed science on Urantia. As one traverses the universe, science becomes part of the understandable mechanisms that is used to operate the universes of time and space inhabited by the . . . spiritual personalities of time and space. The well nigh infinite personalities of the Third Person of Deity, personalities of the Eternal Son, and the co-creational aspects of their children throughout the universe, insures that the children of time will have a thorough and complete experience, knowledge and working understanding of all aspects well nigh of the universes of time and space before one enters the shores of Paradise. This is the perspective that the Urantia Book *offers a believer. An incredible journey awaits the pilgrim of time. Thank you for your concern."*

101 Lessons from Monjoronson: Excerpts

The History of Urantia 12-26-2009

Question: "Is there a plan with your coming to Urantia for humanity to regain more knowledge about its past? Will the midwayers be allowed to share their knowledge with us about this planet during the Magisterial Mission?"

MONJORONSON: *"The full display of the Magisterial Mission on Urantia will not be in herald to the masses. Things that are revealed and what man needs to know will be on a basis that is decided by spirit, not necessarily by mankind. Mankind may want lots of things. It may be determined best to begin to respect and appreciate the few things that man will have left at his disposal. The bio-dynamic program of the earth has already built in its cyclical patterning. The earth already knows how to repair itself.*

"It will be tremendously difficult for mankind during this transition of the world repairing itself and mankind having to rely on what it had been used to. Then a phrase that is in the Urantia Book *will become very important. The phrase is: Uncertainty with security is the essence of the Paradise adventure.*

Even here on Urantia you will get to experience uncertainty with security of knowing that spirit will be attempting to do its best at all times.

Again I will repeat myself: Spirit will not change its functioning and its service to Urantia just because Urantia needs to go through and reform and resuscitate itself. Again, in terms of the question, the information which spirit has that humans desire will be accessed on an individual and need to know basis. It is too early to manifest details about circumstantial things concerning the mission or what will take place once it begins to unfold on a greater level of manifestation on your planet. Much of this you cannot prepare for."

Past Abuse of The Planet Requires Correction, 12-26-2009

MONJORONSON: *"It seems tonight that some of the information being brought in by my representatives is causing people to be somewhat concerned and aware of impending conditions and situations. This evening, I have been trying to explain that it is not spirit that is causing these conditions on your planet. The conditions of your planet are resultant actions and consequences of decisions made long ago and perpetuated and abused and indulged by groups of individuals around the world on your planet.*

"True, the majority of the world must experience the results along with the few but the planet has been brought to a stress level and its default mechanism is to resuscitate itself. It is hard wired within the planet. Whether the poles shift, whether the magnetics are off, whether land masses rise and fall, whether magma is spewed through the cracked mantle of the earth, whether the ice poles and the polar caps melt and flood areas, whether famine, disease, pestilence, corruption begin to rule the world, spirit will not alter its stance to mankind.

"Spirit continues to serve mankind and through these times of foreboding change, all the more will spirit stand steadfast and ready to assist and help mankind.

"Spirit is only able to do so much. The ingenuity within mankind must begin to show itself and mankind must begin to show itself and mankind must have the courage and the wisdom to use its own resources. All too often mankind has been clever in its ability to disguise the truth. The fact is that the metal is beginning to rust out under the car and it's beginning to come through the paint and the veneer of mankind is beginning to erode. The depths of corruption are coming to the surface.

"In the correction time God goes deep within to the base and loosens up that which does not belong and it is breaking up and rising to the surface. It is coming to a head; it is coming to the light of day so that all begin to see.

"Again, in these times it is important to begin to exercise modesty, modesty in thought, modesty in action, modesty in spending, and mankind is moving into an era where he is beginning to experience the pull of the spiritual pressure of the brotherhood of man. It is like a weight that has fallen on all of you to follow, that is, working within the conditions presently to move you into a greater sense of who you are in your response. This is all.

"Spirit desires a tremendously simple life for you. You make it so complicated. This is not the result of spirit. Even if the representation of spirit has been corrupted on the planet, humans still have choice, they still have

wisdom, understanding, counsel, knowledge and courage to come together and to worship God, not worship man or man's achievements.

"Man should be proud of his great achievements and he should be tremendously thankful to God who provides the wherewithal and the ability for man to achieve such. Within your own souls, have you kept your part of the bargain? To those who give, much will be given and to those who take, all will be taken away.

"There is much truth in old sayings on Urantia, for the problems which beset biblical times beset you now. You will learn as a body united, to come together to solve the great condition of life. This is also the way it is designed and good luck on your journey."

The Process of Transmitting and Receiving 2-23-2010

Question: "Judging by some transcripts, at some point the receiver starts to interject their own thinking process into the communicated messages. We aren't sure at what point contact stops and human involvement begins. Can you tell us something about what is happening here?"

MONJORONSON: *"No, not really. I can say that the effort to make contact is an effort that is double ended as the human transmitter attempts to perceive the urging of spirit within their mind capacity to perceive in symbol. It is unfortunate that you would like something greater, but something greater is not possible at this time. When it will become possible to have almost the universal ability to hear, that is when no more transmitters are needed and that each one can perceive the inclinations of spirit for themselves.*

". . . [T]here is a tremendously creative leeway into the thought projections of humans and the inclinations of spirit, for spirit tremendously reinforces the positive. No matter what it is, at some point the positive will transform as it needs be into what it is to become. What is important is that there is an effort made on the part of human resource to contact spirit in an attempt to perceive information. Be not fooled by the eloquence of speech or the patterns of words. Learn to discern the spirit behind the words, and in between the words and the meanings which are not being revealed. I like the parables spoken by your Master as He lived on the planet, parables . . . are stories which necessarily involve multiple capacities for understanding. The language of spirit is . . . perceived on multiple levels of understanding of what the human is able to access through spirit.

"If you perceive that the current dialog is crude, consider that the text of the Urantia Book was brought in by special delivery. There was no human interface to receive the message; it was directly dictated by spirit through spirit so that there would not be any compromise within the human condition.

"It was considered necessary to put [the revelation] into the true words of spirit in a human object-book form. In the day and age in which it has been placed, and up until this time, there is not very much noticeable transformation as is intended by the text within your human society, within the human social organizations, and religious organizations.

"So I am not sure of how to answer your question. For now you will have to be satisfied with what is being presented until at a future time communication abilities improve. This is basically where we are at this time. Thank you for this concern."

Question: "Dr. Sadler wrote a book titled The Mind at Mischief. This questioner believes that even T/R minds can get into mischief and they ask if you would speak to the kind of mischief that minds the teachers work with get into? Could you also discuss and give us an idea of the accuracy of transmissions when the mind is not at mischief?"

MONJORONSON: *"Thank you for the question. It is an understanding that The Mind at Mischief was a title of a work that dealt with the many different activities that the mind is involved in. The text written by Dr. Sadler first mentions a reference to a process, probably the process used to contact Dr. Sadler through a liaison personality, in which spirit was able to speak by using a technique of Adjuster mindedness. Spirit speaking through the human mind is what Dr. Sadler referred to as the 'mind at mischief.'*

"Again, the Urantia Papers did not use a human transmission technique. It used an intrusion of spirit through human consciousness by agreement with the Adjuster mindedness within the individual who was used by spirit to speak through. Again, this was necessary to produce the quality of text that exists as the Urantia Papers. I would say at best, in terms of the transmission of truth, that the majority of what is transmitted contains truth. There is not much misinformation being transmitted.

"When humans attempt to subject spirit to a more specific time and space related event, there may be difficulty in a human perceiving that these events happened when they happen, but as human consciousness is, humans try to define things which are indefinable. This is the quality of mind on the human level.

"The transmission process is not intended to be 100% accurate from either side. Again, what is important is that humans attempt to reach out and discern the quality of spirit, the quality within spirit mind and to discern through spirit what spirit dictates to humans. These are much like the early telephone, tin cans with metal wires strung between them, crude, yet able to discern. This is quite similar to the T/R process, which utilizes faith and trust as the connection and condition to receive information.

"Then again, if you are not getting the information you need through a T/R, well then it is necessary for you to contact spirit yourself and get the information first hand. That way it will not be necessary to criticize a process which is at best tremendously inspiring, faith filled and trusting."

Direct Path to Truth 4-13-2010

Question: "I know there are many paths to the top of the mountain. I have been on a lot of them, some with dead ends and sharp rocks, potholes and brush, and some impassable. There are gurus galore, a plethora of preachers, massive amounts of ministers, tons of teachers. Some call themselves Melchizedeks channeling different teachers with all kinds of conflicting and confusing teachings. Is there any way to avoid so much exercise to provide ourselves the pearl of truth without so much debris around it?"

MONJORONSON: *"I am charmed by your description and find your phraseology delightful. As you have recited that there are many paths to the top of the mountain implying the mountain of truth, I must draw your attention that it is not at the apex that truth is found but found at all times at every point on the mountain. This is why you have the wide range of wisdom.*

"Truth is an encounter; it is not a verbal description of reality, of what is. It is a living interface with reality, a conscious engagement, an energetic entanglement. How you can dispense with all the confusing forms, descriptions, and paths is to simply stand in your own shoes and realize. Of course the pondering philosopher would say, 'I am not interested in my truth; I want all truth,' and begin again the desire to ascend to the apex of the mountain. But all truth contains every single truth. To discard your truth at your present level of unfoldment is to discount a valuable element of all truth.

"The living of all truth is occurring throughout the entire universe; the living of each truth is occurring in each creature. You do not need as a single personality all truth to be truth. Every flame within a forest fire is burning; no one single flame is the entire fire, but each one is nonetheless performing the same function.

"There are those who, if I may use your expressions, ³hang their shingle² and teach a way to truth, and we accept these personalities so inspired to do so. But they are a presentation that is orchestrated and perhaps contrived in the sense that it is organized in its presentation, not in the sense that it is trickery or deception.

"But every one of you are doing the same thing when you comprehend truth, that is, engage in the living experience of truth and then manifest your comprehension of that experience to others. All these sharings are subsequent expressions of an encounter with truth; they are not the truth itself.

"I will use one more image before we proceed to the next question. As your earth rotates the sun takes an appearance of moving around the world. In the segment of this rotation wherein the sun shines its light upon your planet you have daylight. Some individuals are experiencing daylight at dawn, others at noon, and others near dusk. It is still daylight, and that is what the experience of truth is to the personality."

Missions Outside of the Teaching Mission 4-13-2010

Question: "What other efforts aside from the Teaching Mission and the Magisterial Mission are being taken by non-human personalities present on Urantia to bring awakening to large numbers of people? Is Abraham just teaching in the Teaching Mission or is he assisting elsewhere?"

MONJORONSON: *"This question fits well within our discussion this evening, for the celestial ministers attending to this planet are working with the variable cultural contingencies existing upon your world. You are discerning in your questions that there are many avenues wherein these beings are engaged to bring about change upon the planet. Abraham and others are contacting individuals throughout your world through the means most receivable by those human beings.*

"While I regard my mission here as a form of an umbrella mission in that it has a span of outreach that embraces all missions of contact, I regard all these efforts in whatever form that they are encountered to be of equal value, for we are functioning as a unified force. Our goal is not to be recognized by our mission but to

bring each one of you into a new era of refined thinking, of improved relationships, of keen discernment, and a peacefulness in living your life.

"You have many forms of stories in your literature. The episodes, the actions that take place, are variable, but oftentimes the plot has a moral that would be repeated over and over again. That is what these missions of contact are doing, expressing the same moral to the story through all the variations that are comprehensible by human beings."

Question: We are guessing that the Magisterial Mission will become the oversight agency for revelation on Urantia after the mission's appearance here. Will the Magisterial Mission become the sole administration for decisions to provide The Urantia Book to future Urantians? How would you characterize the Magisterial Mission's role in coordinating contemporary episodes of revelation to Urantia?

MONJORONSON: I must first make clear that this Magisterial Mission and any subsequent Magisterial Mission to your world is one to prepare transition to another era of planetary development. So the management we overlay upon the progress of humankind is only that which is preparatory to the transition.

It is not our focus to establish behavioral patterns, organizations, or perspectives. While you as a planetary race make decisions and develop organizations and societies and other groupings, we will work within those structures to foster growth, all with the goal of attaining a status wherein you may transition into a new era.

We will not manage how the Urantia Papers will spread across the world. I may liken it to the waiter who brings a meal to your table. That waiter delivers the dish and walks away. You must do the consuming of the food. This waiter may return and ask how it is. Your response may be likened to either the crystallization of the revelation as dogma, the rejection of it as untrue, or the acceptance of it as truly divine. But this waiter will also return and offer you desserts, or a subsequent phase of your dining experience; that is what I am here to do, to offer you the next course in the meal with the eye that this next course will be complementary to the course in which you are engaged.

Scope of the Fifth Epochal Revelation 3-4-2010

Question: "Does the Correcting Time as Michael's umbrella of policies for the reformation of Urantia contain more than just the Fifth Epochal Revelation to do this?"

MONJORONSON: *"Indeed it does, for Michael's purposes on Urantia entail every phase of planetary development. These epochal revelations are keyed to every epoch. In your text you have been told of the seven basic stages of planetary development. There will be subsequent epochal revelations until Light and Life when the planet itself will stand as a revelation of the goodness of God and the culture will radiate the divine spirit in all ways.*

The Teaching Mission

"While Michael partook of the force in his bestowal, he has been ever watchful of all epochal transitions and the developments within each epoch. I might add that he is doing so upon many worlds. There are also such stages we may liken to epochal eras on a planet on every system and constellation under his guidance. Our Sovereign Son is quite busy and engaged in many facets of growth in Nebadon. His management is broad, but he is also very concerned and lovingly engaged in every stage on every world as it unfolds."

Stillness and Awareness 3-16-2010

Question: "Is the ultimate consequence of stillness and of these processes intended to create a continuous and permanent link to this greater source of awareness?"

MONJORONSON: *"Stillness is a greater source of awareness. The greater source of awareness is not so much in the result; it is in the ability to perform in the process. It's the ability to be able to find and exercise process to control your mental activity to control your thoughts to hone in your ability to focus, to use the extraneous mental capacity that rarely gets used.*

"In accessing this part of the mind and by strengthening its working within your mind, it is intended to balance the neural energies as they are coordinated with activities of thinking and perception of external stimulus such as hearing and seeing something which causes you to overreact or to have the ability to not overreact, to consciously be able to hold the space of consciousness which allows you to access wisdom; to either hold your tongue, control your emotions and therefore make the correct choice in deciding how to deal with these things.

"So stillness does access a greater awareness but again, the importance is in the practice of shutting down the mind chatter, the recurrent tape patterning within the mind, the definition of your boundaries within your mind to expand and use other abilities which the mind possesses, to access the greater part of the unused mind, there are muscles which must be exercised and used.

"So it is intended that this explanation clarify somewhat the process in stillness in terms of the internal out-workings of this effect within the human mind. Thank you for this."

The Planetary Adjudication 3-16-2010

Question: "Can you explain what it means when you call all Urantia to justice and how you will cleanse her of the evil done for so many years?"

MONJORONSON: *"This is a dispensational act involved in the cleansing. It is a way of removing those individuals who have refused to move on. The earth will be cleansed of those who have died and are sleeping and waiting to move on. It will be a time of removing those who have resisted this movement.*

"Your world is deeply in need of cleansing. It has great difficulty in raising the total consciousness at this time without the removal of those presences that carry malevolent energies and dark energies that subdue the brighter energies of your world.

526

"The terms that were used also are carried in the larger long-term program. We do not necessarily mean that this cleansing is instantaneous or occurs over a very brief period of time but is in addition, a thorough going program of upliftment, of cleansing wrong thoughts, wrong consciousness and actions that are not productive."

Tremendous Changes Coming 3-16-2010

MONJORONSON: *"Your world is undergoing tremendous changes from our perspective and in the realms that we deal with. Your world at your level is also undergoing immense changes in most aspects of its social existence, and [the term] social may include agriculture to finance, family politics to global commerce, and so on. You are blessed with this change yet many of you will see it as almost a curse because of the immense obligations and changes and disruption that it will cause on your world.*

"Machiventa and myself are greatly invested in moving this world ahead, not recklessly but carefully and rapidly. The future of this world is now known very well for the next 5 to 15 years. [In that time] we wish to fulfill those plans within a reasonable capacity without overburdening the world population or the energetic friends who have been helping us, such as the midwayers. Everyone here has rolled up his sleeves and is working overtime and the obligations of doing so are felt by everyone at our level of enterprise.

"There are factors which will develop in your world which will be most surprising and will knock most of your populations off balance in the ideas of what they thought should happen, should exist, should occur, and what they had as expectations for tomorrow. We have access to numerous realms of assistance that we will bring to bear upon your world.

"We thank you for this opportunity. We apologize for being nebulous in description, but you will feel these changes in concrete terms in your world very soon, within the next few months and couple of years. I do wish to remain non-specific about these as they tend to cause a great deal of concern, worry and distress in many of your populations which is completely unnecessary.

"I thank you for this opportunity to speak with you and to participate in your lives, as I am able to through these communications. Know that our forces of light and light energy now are surrounding you and bathing you, as you are able to accept our presence and our energy, good day."

ABRAHAM & MARY MAGDALENE
January 23, 2011, Woods Cross Group,
Salt Lake City, UT

"I am ABRAHAM. Greetings. I am with new hope for our new horizons ahead. The Correcting Time as you know it is seemingly slow and quiet, but there are other plans that were laid a long time ago coming into fruition. You have known what it is like to play the game of chess or checkers. You as mortals and we as teachers have made our move so that Michael and His associates are able to now make theirs.

"When we started this Correcting Time in this region of the world there were a great deal of obstacles that we had to overcome. Previous teachers, as well as myself, were instructed to stick to certain topics. While this method of communication may have seemed a novelty at the time, many grew bored with the real work. But the hopes and goals we had set were indeed met. We are still working with other areas in the world to accept the Mission as it is, without fanfare or people belonging to some sort of special society.

"Now our communication with many mortals is commonplace, promoting deep thinking and faith and ability to act upon what you know to be truth, beauty and goodness. We are not so much saying to our fellows 'observe this technique of communication,' no. We are saying 'listen to these words of logic and help for daily living.'"

"I am MARY. Again I am happy to meet with you. I am feeling a job well completed and ready to move forward in Michael's plan. Like the winter's in this region, there is a lull in the minds of men, but soon the Spring will be at hand and the busyness of life will again show itself. I am, myself, a creature of habit and can be hesitant in new endeavors. With the fast training I have received I am now able to see the bigger picture of forward momentum, and for that, I am excited.

"You each have also received a great deal of training to incorporate the bigger picture into your thinking. You have been able to keep up with small tasks knowing that it is another brush-stroke in the universal painting. We are about to begin another phase of our Correcting Time and are waiting on instructions from our Superiors. We will then move forward with lessons to our students.

"At this time I would make time in your daily moments to reflect on what you have learned over our years together. Also, it is a good time to ponder your courage for taking on new endeavors. What would be the benefits you have learned over the years of spiritual studies that have prepared you to take on newness in our Correcting Time?"

CHRIST MICHAEL
March 21, 2011
Mill Valley, CA, in Marin County

"This is the wealth that is being presented now, this variety, this wonderful variety of viewpoint, this burgeoning, expanding marketplace of ideas. With your more modern communications this is what is really opening up the world, just as a previous Renaissance came about when more and more of the world's fundamental religious texts were for the first time being printed, so that the middle class folks could afford a copy of the Bible, or the Koran, or the Upanishads.

"When all these religious texts could be printed they were no longer the exclusive possession of an ecclesiastical cast. This led directly to the Renaissance and, if you are familiar, led to quite a contention like some famous examples of the early scientists conflicting with orthodoxy, and then were either burned at the stake or put under house arrest to be examined by the Inquisition because they were daring to proclaim as fact certainly demonstrable things that went against orthodoxy.

"So this is the essence of a Renaissance, a rebirth, an expansion of shared knowledge, and it can't help but conflict with any kind of orthodoxy that is founded upon a deliberate obscuration of some fundamental facts. As Mother Spirit said, some of the long established religions and political organizations, the nation states of the world, are now having their populations demanding more freedom, freedom of expression so they can communicate directly with each other. And for all the unsettled nature of this conflict we ask you to see the enormous outburst of individual creativity that is coming about, first of all because folks have greater access to each other.

"But then also as some of the pretension of these orthodox positions; some of these pretensions are seen through with an increasing transparency. Another part of the equation of this balance, this shift of power, is that individuals are thrown back upon themselves more and more, especially all the individuals who depended upon a certain kind of blind belief in some system, some political party, some orthodoxy, are suddenly faced with having to decide for themselves what is true and what is not.

"Here again Mother Spirit and I can only advise and encourage you always and in every situation like this when you yourself are confronted with some startling new facts, especially if they are challenging some of your longest held beliefs, always ask yourself: what is true here. You need to acquire the ability to assess things in and of themselves regardless of their origin.

"The origin of some particular fact will always be part of it, certainly, but you can trust your own inner sense of evaluation to examine and evaluate something in and of itself — which is what Mother Spirit and I have suggested you do with our lessons all along. Evaluate what we say with how it rings true within you, whether you feel we or anyone else is encouraging you to go ahead and examine what we say from all different points of view. Compare us to anything else you care to, to all of what you've known before."

Teachers in this Volume:

Aaron
Abraham, of the Bible
A'Cilla
Aflana
AhmaNiden Melchizedek
Alkon
Alphonso
Alana
Althena
Anatolia
Andrea, a Celestial Artisan
Andrew
Andronason Melchizedek
Astara, a Bright and Morning Star
Bakim, a Celestial Artisan
Berca
Bertrand
Buki
Corelli
Daniel
Elisha, a Celestial Artisan
El Tanere
Elyon
Foehn
Ham
Iruka
James
JarEl
Jared
Jessona
Josephine
Klarixiska
Lanaforge, System Sovereign
Lantarnek Melchizedek

Legion
LinEl
Lucio
Lydia
Machiventa Melchizedek
Malvantra Melchizedek
Mantoube Melchizedek
Manotia Melchizedek
Manutia Melchizedek
Margul, the Daynal Order
Michael, our Creator Son
Monjoronson, our Magisterial Son
Monmacion Melchizedek
Nathaniel, an Apostle of Jesus
Nebadonia, the Mother Spirit
Nero
Norson Melchizedek
Paramahansa Yogananda
Olfana
Paulo
Rayson
RondEl
Serena
Tarkas
Themoia
Thomy
Tomaray
Tomas
Verona
Veronica
Welmek
Will

Urantia Book Terminology

The Teaching Mission is not confined to readers and students of the Urantia Papers on this particular planet, of course, but these study groups do possess a superb collection of revelatory knowledge that the teachers highly recommend as a foundation and measuring stick of truth.

Since the Urantia Papers deal with personalities and places of the spiritual hierarchy, there are naturally names for every personality and thing. The teachers naturally use them in their conversations with humans who study the Book. Here are some simple definitions to help with teacher references.

URANTIA is the name of our planet, located in the system of SATANIA, and the local universe of NEBADON, which now has well over 600 inhabited planets. We are a small part of a massive Creation, with a Super Universe that encompasses seven universes, and vast numbers of planets and personalities.

MICHAEL is one of many Creator Sons of God, and the creator of our local universe of Nebadon. He incarnated here in the final of seven incarnations in personalities of his creation. As Jesus, he justified his rule and brought down the LUCIFER REBELLION against God, the Universal Father.

LUCIFER, a brilliant administrator, was joined by our own Planetary Prince CALIGASTIA, in the rebellion, hundreds of thousands of years before the advent of ADAM and EVE. This materialized couple was our assigned Planetary Son and Daughter, here to foster biological and botanical development. The curse of the rebellion even touched the Garden of Eden and caused the default.

The Teaching Mission's leader today is the Christ, Michael of Nebadon, and the teachers of THE TEACHER CORPS herald a CORRECTING TIME to heal our world of the rebellion's pervasive corruption. Active in the mission are MACHIVENTA MELCHIZEDEK, who incarnated here as the biblical Sage of Salem, and his student ABRAHAM, who carried on the truth of the One God concept on the planet. They serve together even today.

Many of the teachers are ascending MORONTIA personalities who have had mortal lives on other planets. In God's 'be ye perfect' ascension plan for mortals, they have advanced beyond human status but are not yet altogether spiritual beings. The universe is one giant complex of universities. Great resources are devoted to education of time and space mortals. MORONTIA is between mortal and spiritual, in the way of thinking and being.

MIDWAYERS, the invisible offspring and descendents of corporeal personalities who came here to serve our ultimately rebellious Planetary Prince, are invisible to material eyes. The Midwayers of today are rebellion-tested, and are active in many capacities to serve the needs of our continuing civilization, all without violating the mandate to never interfere with the human free will.

Inspired Service

From the beginning, our celestial teachers have encouraged us into daily Stillness to develop a vibrant and growing relationship with our Creator.

In this quiet aura of Worship, Prayer, Forgiveness and Love, we are prepared for our ultimate goal on the planet – using the talents that we have honed over the years in service to our siblings

Some among us have developed projects involving ministry and media that we can easily note here. Many others are simply living their lives in love and kindness, helping to light the way for those within their influence. I know light bringers who are nurses, social counselors, hospice workers, musicians, artists, youth guides, teachers, and entrepreneurs in many fields who bring the loving attitude with them each day.

Some of the greatest service to the Teaching Mission itself is provided by those human vessels who allow themselves to be receivers and transmitters of the supernal messages. I have observed them over the years, and they are all gracious and giving host voices for the celestials. They have been chosen wisely. They are able to step outside of themselves and bring the teachers into the room.

They are joined in laudatory service by the diligent transcribers of the messages, many of them flowing across the Internet for many years now, tens of thousands of pages thanks to their diligence and perseverance in the service.

This is an effort to round up some of the service projects and creative work that relates to the contributors in this book. Please go to the links for more information:

The Teaching Mission Network www.teachingmissionnetwork.com
A network of global friends who work together to help individuals make contact with celestial teachers. Chair is Jim Cleveland, Co-Chair is Deborah Goaldman, Webmaster is James Leese., at this 2014 writing. Members have personal introductions on the site, which includes an array of spiritual media. The Network also has a discussion group on Facebook.

The network has published a CD, *The Joys of Stillness: Where Meditation Meets God*, featuring instructional narrations and musical guest artists such as Pato Banton, Antoinette (Rootsdawtah) Hall, Michael DiMattia and Beth & Cinde/Wild Roses.

The Center for Christ Consciousness
www.ctrforchristcon.org   Donna D'Ingillo

The Center nurtures people in their spiritual journey, helping them access their own Indwelling Divine Source, and develop an intimate and healing relationship with our Universe Parents. Transformational tools provided are books and CDs.

Light and Life Publications, *An Exploration of the Spiritual Universe* www.lightandlife.com
Jim Cleveland
10 CDs with MARK AUSTIN at www.cdbaby.com/all/lightandlife and music services.
Jesus of Urantia: In His Own Words, with Stephanie Gjerde
Celestial Fusions: Realities of the Teaching Mission
Grinning through Apocalypse: One Armageddon at a Time (humor)
The *Soul Series* of poetry/music: *Souls Pouring, Souls Blooming, Soul Struggles, Souls Restless, Soul Stories, Souls Rising, and Soul Synthesi.*

9 Books at www.authorhouse.com and at Amazon and other booksellers
Novels: *The Alien Intimacies, Edge of Dark Light, Dark Riders, Lucifer's Gardens*
Poetry & Lyric: Celestial Songbooks 1 and 2
Beyond Cynicism: Liberating Voices from the Spirit Within
Celestials over Cincinnati: Lessons of the Planetary Correcting Time
Sauntering Through Apocalypse: IN-sights, OUT-rages, and ID-iocies

Harp of God Foundation (http://www.harpofgod.org)
Harp exists to broadcast the good news. Its website features an overview of The Urantia Papers as a primary source of inspiration, supported by the many service efforts of The Correcting Time and the Teaching Mission. Harp hosts an on-line e-group, and has published five books: Fruits of the Spirit, Secrets of Promise, and The Zooid Mission by Gerdean O'Dell; The Mind of Christ by JOYce Brenton, and Welmek's Lessons on Prayer T/R'd by Donna D'Ingillo.

www.theteachingmission.com
Lesson collections and commentaries from Gerdean O'Dell and celestial teachers.

Tmarchives.com (http://www.tmarchives.com) is a teaching mission library managed by Ron Besser that stores and displays the lesson transcriptions of celestial teachers who have been teaching on Urantia since 1991 as part of the overarching Correcting Time.

Manu Puri sites
www.EffectiveYou.com
www.TheLifePurposeCoach.com
www.NamasteNow.com

ORIGIN PRESS:
http://www.originpress.com Byron Belitsos
Publishers of: THE CENTER WITHIN: Lessons from the Heart of the Urantia Revelation
Compiled and edited by Fred Harris and Byron Belitsos.

The Teaching Mission

Based on the core lessons of the Teaching Mission, its 130 lessons, transmitted by the teacher named Will, are designed to be a helpful and practical companion to the complex Urantia text, as each instruction is matched with a pertinent quote from *The Urantia Book* itself, allowing the spiritual essence of the Urantia revelation made easily accessible.

THE SECRET REVELATION: Unveiling the Mystery of the Book of Revelation with a Urantia Book perspective.
by Stella Religa.

This book challenges Christians with a hopeful and original interpretation of John's prophecy based on *The Urantia Book*, and with a comprehensive introduction to Christian believers.

THE ADVENTURE OF BEING HUMAN, transmissions from Christ Michael and Mother Spirit Nebadonia by Jerry Lane in Marin County, CA, with editor Byron Belitsos.

The Daynal Institute and The Nordan Symposia
http://www.daynal.org Rob Davis
This is a network of persons from many walks of life that, in the course of exploring the heart of cosmic reality through communion with its Source have discovered Trinity Teacher Sons as the architects of spiritual education administered throughout the Master Universe.
While the forms of instruction vary widely depending upon local circumstances, these are enjoined by beings of every order of intelligence focusing their attention on the lessons of living experience, the master of all Teachers in the art of living.

THE URANTIA BOOK FELLOWSHIP
A global organization of readers, www.ubfellowship.org

THE JESUSONIAN FOUNDATION
A huge collection of Urantia-related media from the Boulder, CO organization. www.truthbook.org

TRUTHSEEKERS www.truthseekersquest.org
This youth organization evolved out of the Tallahassee Teaching Mission group through the leadership of Fred Harris and Tom Choquette. Truthseekers fosters the discovery and living of truth by young people. It is an independent nonprofit educational organization that emphasizes character development through continuously cultivating higher values.

Truthseekers sees higher values as those emphasizing concern for others while lower values are those that are selfish and self-centered. We teach that all persons can find their own individual truth and happiness by caring about others, forgiving others and serving others.

Truthseekers encourages individuals to have an active relationship with their own inner spirit and to use that relationship in the pursuit of their higher values.

THE CHURCH WITHIN
Pastor Daniel Megow – www.churchwithin.org

THE 11:11 PROGRESS GROUP, George Barnard's site based in northern Australia is dedicated to introducing the character and the services of the secondary Midwayers on the planet. They are described in the Urantia papers. www.1111angels.net

Urantia University is online for study of the Urantia papers and training the teachers and leaders of tomorrow.
www.urantiauniversity.com

www.squarecircles.com
Urantia Book Sources and Resources

NOTES AND UPDATES

IN MEMORIAM

In summarizing 20 years, my first thoughts are to the admirable men and women who were pioneers in the mission and have passed on. I think of Gerdean O'Dell Bowen, first of all, who transitioned during book production after providing excellent advice and both editing and networking assistance to get the project completed.

I think of Thern Blackburn and John Wormeck of Salt Lake City, who brought the first teachings from New Zealand.

I think of gracious Debbie Roberts from Idaho, a fine transmitter who visited us in Cincinnati, and Susan Kimsey from Half Moon Bay, California. We both transmitted a teacher named Tarkas and were excited to meet each other in person years ago at a Urantia gathering in Quebec. She was a joyous light in this community for years.

From my own Cincinnati group, Father Robert Schuer was my first Urantia study group contact when I moved there from Urantia-starved Mississippi. Supposedly retired from service as a Catholic priest, 'Father Bob' was a busy and always cheerful servant. He led Urantia and Teaching Mission groups in Columbus and Cincinnati, and once presented a Urantia Book to the Pope's library in the Vatican.

Also from Cincinnati, we lost the ethereal social worker Stephen Mark, a gentle and loving man who became a fine transmitter of the Melchizedek, Malvantra. We also lost Jack and Joyce Burdick, Jack Saunders and Betty Bright, who was a participant in California before moving to Cincinnati. As she lay dying, I will never forget our last gathering with her and our joyful and comforting transmissions from Christ Michael and the teachers.

Also departed is Bill Kelly, a retired Christian minister, an open-hearted and open-minded spiritual seeker, and transmitter for the teacher Daniel and others for years. This group continues to meet with the teachers in Pocatello, Idaho and their collected transmissions would fill a worthwhile book.

The loving soul known as "Roland" has left the planet, and gone is his shiny and open personality that could light up a room. He was the real-life character in Fred Harris' popular book about the Teaching Mission called *The Correcting Time*.

In California, we lost the esteemed Army Gen. Duane Faw, who championed the mission and hosted the lessons of Rayson and others in his Malibu home, with his gracious wife, Lucille.

Thea Hardy of Corvallis, Oregon, was a light in the mission, a gifted graphic designer and networker, and transmitter of Christ Michael, the teachers Serena, LinEl and others.

I fondly remember the gentle and loving Bea Mouganis from Pittsburgh, who hosted many fine spirit-infused gatherings in her home.

I met a gentle man named Peter Quinn in South Florida, a Urantian scholar of note and study group leader. He embraced the teachings with a whole heart and read many transcripts. But soon he was gone to age and illness and now waits to meet again in Mansonia.

I also only knew Jim Andrews for a short while. He and wife Roxanne started up a group in Loveland, Colorado, and it has been of major service in spreading the good news and developing social sustainability projects. Jim and I were surprised to find that we shared the services of a celestial artisan named Elisha. Roxie holds forth as a versatile contributor to spiritual sustainabilities.

The buoyant and ever-positive Bill Bryan of Lawrence, Kansas, has moved on, while his loyal companion, Eugenia, carries on here in her retirement years.

In 2011, Rick Giles passed suddenly in Idaho, an admirable man in all regards: theology scholar, farmer, musician and craftsman, and a gifted transmitter of the teacher Elyon and other celestial personalities over the years. They have a treasure trove of celestial transmissions.

Of course, others have passed on over the years whom I didn't know, adventurous souls who helped establish the Teaching Mission and enjoyed its fruits. I honor them no less.

A FEW UPDATES

THE ADVANCE CORPS

(An addendum from co-editor Gerdean O'Dell) There were many who worked with the celestials prior to the onset of the Correcting Time, independently probing into the phenomenon of contact with invisible beings. They were true reservists, whose names will never be emblazoned on the pages of history, but whose courage forged a path for the celestials to follow in discerning what kind of effect these communications would have on mere mortals. Would they become fanatics? Or would they provide the foundation for the next dispensation? How well would they be received? How would their contribution advance humanity? Alan F. Smith was one such contact personality.

NEW ZEALAND

Members of the original spiritual study group who transmitted Machiventa Melchizedek and Abraham are now part of the "I AM" movement and continue to work with celestial teachers in personal growth programs. The Hamilton Spiritual Centre is rich with seekers exploring their various paths with decidedly open minds.

THE WOODS CROSS GROUP and T/R 'Rebecca'

This small Teaching Mission group continues to meet, and the single transmitter brings forth Abraham and Mary Magdalene. When transmitter Rebecca left the city, the group suffered through some credibility and personality conflicts and now stands as small and staunchly conservative within the TM family, disdaining some transmissions and transmitters as unreliable and generally in doubt of the emerging Magisterial Mission. They are adamant in their stance that the genuine lessons are about personal spiritual growth and do not deviate into human agendas, as they believe some have.

My friend Calvin McKee from this group showed up at the Urantia Fellowship's 2011 conference in Salt Lake City. He made a presentation on *the Urantia Book* as perhaps being a revelatory text expected by the Mormon church. With friend and T/R Nina on hand, we also had a typically word-by-word wrought evening transmission from teacher Ham, which was keystroked by Calvin on the scene and read back to the audience. This is the deliberate manner in which this Woods Cross group continues to work with celestial teachers, which are invariably Abraham and Mary Magdalene. The messages seem to suit the mood, the tempo and the needs of the audience.

REBECCA, TEAM PIONEER

Pioneering T/R 'Rebecca' advises your editor that the social activism causes she now supports with her writings and talents are intended to be separate and distinct from her previous service as transmitter of Ham. This ranges from the initial mission announcement in Los Angeles into her transmitting service with the Woods Cross group and later in Nashville, after her marriage to songwriter and recording artist Hal Bynum.

The lessons of Ham in both groups stand as a worthy groundbreaking collection of good spiritual advice. Rebecca Bynum is a well-known essayist, author, social and spiritual thinker who can be found readily on the Internet.

URANTIA ORGANIZATIONS

The Urantia Foundation remains adamantly opposed to 'channeling' within their circles, and judgmental of the process as a major and unreliable distraction to book study. The Urantia Fellowship, is cautiously tolerant of Teaching Mission people and their "special interest" activities. TM people remain active in various Urantia-related programs in a kind of "don't ask, don't tell" relationship. After all, one's religious or spiritual affiliations other than book study are one's own affair.

After disenfranchising the Urantia Brotherhood, the Urantia Foundation began organizing its own study group network around the world, in competition with the re-organized

Fellowship's groups. They remain a house divided, against themselves, the Teaching Mission and arguably many of the other spiritual paths being walked on the planet today. The Foundation continues to publish new translations. Their official policy states that their book and their activities should stand "unencumbered" by any attachments to new age spirituality or traditional religions.

Those various spiritual and religious organizations, of course, must be seen as "unencumbered" by *the Urantia Book* as well, and it's too bad that they can't just openly and respectfully share what they believe.

Little respect was shown for this history book at the Urantia Fellowship's 2014 international conference in Massachusetts. After staff members initially approved the book for sale in the Jesusonian Foundation's bookstore, a special committee was formed, through which conference chair Angela Thurston and others voted successfully to ban this book and others related to the Teaching Mission.

ONENESS

Meantime, the concepts of Oneness, and all one people in unconditional love, are sweeping the planet through various personal minds, movements and organizations. While Urantia Book readers are urged to have "cosmic consciousness" and "universe awareness" in the text, they haven't yet enjoined with other movements that have compatible theologies.

Efforts are now being made to bring the Fellowship and Foundation into a closer relationship again. At the international Fellowship conference in 2011, Mo Siegel, a Foundation Trustee, said 'the war is over.' They are working together on Internet book study initiatives.

The longtime dissension prompted readers in Quebec to host a "Urantia Family" conference in 2010 in an effort to bring about more cooperation and mutual respect between the two factions. When Teaching Mission participants felt a bit left out of the 'family,' the planners then graciously included our representatives in the mix. We subsequently presented a workshop on Stillness.

The Family of God Foundation strived for many of the same all-one-people values seen now throughout the new age spiritual communities. Mr. Grimsley retired from ministerial service before passing in 2011. Many of his excellent sermons can be accessed at the Jesusonian Foundation's Truth Book website. Its founder, Mr. Siegel, was a friend and admirer of his work, which included global radio broadcasting via the Voice of America and other venues on Jesusonian values.

ONWARD TO SERVICE

On another page, we list the Teaching Mission Network and other organizations that have grown out of the basic teachings and inspirations of the mission. Years of lessons have focused on worship, prayer, forgiveness, love, faith, and the joys of service. They are basic building blocks for spiritual growth, a foundation of personal religion truth that transcends all human dogma and rises up to where your Truth Bells ring.

With this foundation, our participants have reached out in a wide variety of service projects, from music and the arts to ministry, healing, networking, publishing and youth counseling, and the landscape is ever-changing and growing.

INWARD TO DEEPER CONNECTION

The teachers have stated from the beginning that the ultimate and most desirable connection is not with the teachers, but with our Universal Father in the Stillness time, urging us to release in love and faith in a daily program. They are simply teachers, former mortals, who would show us the way. Urantia readers know this inner connection to God as our "thought adjuster" and others may reference it as our indwelling spirit or soul.

At this writing, a few of our experienced and devoted transmitters are now making this connection, calling it the Inner Voice. These deeply felt personal lessons are growing within our archives.

THE MAGISTERIAL MISSION

In these pages, you've read contributors who are active in welcoming Monjoronson, our Magisterial Son, to the planet, to adjudicate the effects of the Lucifer Rebellion. Others have expressed doubt in the veracity of some of these transmissions, and these credibility problems are being worked through along with the other adjudications.

These newer lessons carry warnings of cataclysmic events on the near horizon, reducing our unsustainable population and adjusting to global warming, effecting a necessary release of thermal energy pressures relating to our earth's core and the planet's polarity.

Some have doubted the specificity of some warnings and the reliability of the transmissions. Others take it to heart, and believe that those who remain will be charged to rebuild society in a better way, with built-in sustainability and direct contact with spirit world helpers and their altruistic values.

Also to come will be the materialization of Monjoronson, the Magisterial Son, on the planet, date unknown, and timeline compatibilities unknown. The teachers have said that evolving events do not happen by a calendar timeline but as a natural chain, with specific events having to occur before subsequent ones can come.

As concerns about the validity of these celestial messages continue, so do the disasters themselves, from the Gulf oil spill to Japan's hurricane, tsunami and nuclear crisis, to the deadly tornado swaths, massive brush fires, mass animal and fish die-offs, power hurricanes and storms striking the populous Northeast, melting icecaps, and some dire global warming predictions involving our unstable planet.

THE CORRECTING TIME

This era for the planet is not one in which we are miraculously saved from our evolution and the problems with our evolving. It is an era in which humans and spiritual teachers and guides in the service of Christ Michael/Jesus will learn to work together. They will vitalize and build a new world upon true spiritual values. It has been explained in this volume uniquely but compatibly here by a plethora of celestial personalities. Evolution, one of God's greatest creations, continues.

SUBSEQUENT VOLUMES

We are now working on volume 2 of the Teaching Mission History, which will feature many topical lessons from the Teacher Corps and a complete volume on the practice of Stillness and celestial connection.

CHRIST MICHAEL
a benediction

My children, I come to you from afar, but I yearn for you to share your consciousness with me for a few moments. Feel my love, feel my presence, and bring me forth.

My children, my friends, my colleagues, my brothers and sisters when I was with you in the flesh, there are so many things that we share. Know that your faith is always rewarded. Know that I know each of you intimately. I know your troubles. I know your deepest concerns. I know that you will triumph over them, for as my spirit is joined with yours in an immersion with a beautiful and powerful benevolence of our Universal Father, there is no doubt that great changes will be made upon this troubled world.

I came to you once before and on that evening I felt very close to you as we talked about your individual goals and aspirations. Each of you in this room has felt my presence many times and in many ways, sometimes not defined as such. Each of you has been inspired to press forward, to plow the earth with your gleaming, shining shafts of truth and beauty and goodness, all that you can muster and bring to your mortal children— hearts, and all of this love and all of the things that you do on behalf of my mission, know that I love you, know that I bless you for these acts of kindness, those times that you have represented me so well.

The essence of my ministry was mercy and compassion. My essence remains so and these needs are still very great on Urantia. My mercy and compassion was poured to all of you and I left this gift with you as your inner Spirit of Truth and conviction. My mercy and compassion even extended to the dark prince, that even after he was struck from the sky, leaving himself alone and in disgrace, and still my mercy and my compassion was ever constant, is ever constant, is ever constant.

My children, the times before us will be of sweeping change. Many things will come to the public agenda that you will find nonsensical, wrought of madness, brought of such faulty logic, such twisted thinking that you, my enlightened children, will find them amazingly ludicrous. Know that the twisted minds that come from these expanding energies are temporary things in this planet's evolutionary growth to light and life, for you will carry the lights that will overcome and overwhelm and bring this madness to an eventual end.

For when more and more and more can see the madness, and when egos can be released and new growth can come, new ways of thinking, where molehills do not become mountains, where dirt does not become revered, when illogic does not become truth, but when truth and beauty and goodness can be seen more clearly by looking within and bringing them forth to reflect outward, the world will change one person at a time, one heart at a time, one mind at a time, each of you unchanging personalities that can change the world, constant in the faith, constant in love, willing and able to share all hardship, willing to suffer atrocity from madness, but also willing to realize greater heights of potential individually and in cohesive, cooperative, spirit– driven teams.

All of these exciting times lie before you, times of madness to be overcome with the power of love.

So my children, my friends, my beautiful brothers and sisters, as Jesus I lived here in turbulent times, incarnated to experience many things. You too are incarnated in tumultuous times; you will experience many things, and each of these experiences you will come to know as a nugget of understanding. You are a jewel of truth on a black obstruction to be cast away, discovering good over evil, truth over error, the power and glory of universal, unconditional love.

And this is what I offer again to you this evening. I give to you, I share with you, the mercy and compassion I feel for all in this sphere and all of the other spheres of my creation. I am in each of you; I live within you, and I suffer, at times, at the very little understanding that you seem to have of this. I will share with you, I will experience with you, I will be at your calling. I will always answer you. I am here. I am there. I am everywhere. I am the resurrection and the light and I will show you the way. (Cincinnati, OH / T/R: Jim Cleveland)

CPSIA information can be obtained
at www.ICGtesting.com
Printed in the USA
FFOW02n2058090215
10957FF